The Government ... s o...

D0351871

This book is to be returned on or before

This fifth edition of *The Government and Politics of France* offers a fully revised, updated and comprehensive view of the contemporary French political scene based on the work of the leading specialist on France of his generation. It covers such events as the dramatic presidential election of 2002 and includes a major new chapter on France and European integration, culminating in the historic rejection of the European constitutional treaty by French voters in May 2005.

Although particular attention is paid to the most recent period, the book covers the whole of the Fifth Republic in depth, from its heroic beginnings under de Gaulle to the period of reverses and defeats sustained by successive governments under the Mitterrand and Chirac presidencies. The contemporary period is placed firmly in the context of those long-standing political traditions which have maintained their power to shape French political behaviour to this day.

The long view supplied in this book allows a unique understanding of how the dynamic, confident economic and political power of the early de Gaulle years has become the more hesitant and troubled nation of the early twenty-first century – and of the points of continuity that underlie this development.

The Government and Politics of France is the authoritative guide to French politics and is essential for undergraduates and postgraduates with interests in French politics, European studies and political science.

Andrew Knapp is Professor of French Politics and Contemporary History at the University of Reading. He is author of *Parties and the Party System in France* (2004), *Le Gaullisme après de Gaulle* (1996), and, with Yves Mény, *Government and Politics in Western Europe* (third edition, 1998).

The late **Vincent Wright** was Official Fellow of Nuffield College, Oxford, and one of the world's leading specialists on French and European Government.

The Government and Politics of France

Fifth edition

Andrew Knapp and Vincent Wright

Routledge
Taylor & Francis Group

LONDON AND NEW YORK

First published 2006
by Routledge
2 Park Square, Milton Park, Abingdon, Oxon OX14 4RN

Simultaneously published in the USA and Canada
by Routledge
270 Madison Avenue, New York, NY 10016

Routledge is an imprint of the Taylor and Francis Group, an informa business

© 2006 Andrew Knapp & Vincent Wright

Typeset in Times by
RefineCatch Limited, Bungay, Suffolk
Printed and bound in Great Britain by
TJ International Ltd, Padstow, Cornwall

British Library Cataloguing in Publication Data
A catalogue record for this book is available from the British Library

Library of Congress Cataloging in Publication Data
A catalog record for this title has been requested

ISBN10: 0–415–35733–0 (hbk)
ISBN10: 0–415–35732–2 (pbk)
ISBN10: 0–203–40260–X (ebk)

ISBN13: 978–0–415–35733–3 (hbk)
ISBN13: 978–0–415–35732–6 (pbk)
ISBN13: 978–0–203–40260–3 (ebk)

To the memory of Vincent Wright

Contents

Appendices

Figures and maps

Figures

Maps

Tables

Preface to the fifth edition

Much of the new material in this edition is framed by two polling days: 21 April 2002, when France's voters surprised themselves and the world by putting a candidate of the extreme Right into the second ballot of a presidential election, and 29 May 2005, when they rejected the constitutional treaty signed by twenty-five European leaders the previous year. The former is incorporated chiefly into the chapters on party politics, the latter into an entirely new chapter (Chapter 14) on France and Europe which I had already decided to add to the text, and drafts of which David Goldey and Wilfrid Knapp were again kind enough to read. All other chapters have been revised and updated to varying degrees.

France in 2005 was prey to a bout of (not wholly unfounded) pessimism about its own long-term future, and this will doubtless appear in some of the following pages. But it has not stopped being one of Europe's most enjoyable countries to study; it is to be hoped that the rest of the book reflects this too, as Vincent Wright's earlier editions did so well.

Andrew Knapp
Reading, July 2005

Preface to the fourth edition

'You'll be doing all the work, so don't bother to put my name on the cover. This is the last wish of a dying man – the ultimate form of blackmail!' Thus the injunction delivered, with a rather unsettling laugh, by Vincent Wright as we discussed the revision of his book a few weeks before his death from cancer in July 1999. There was never any chance that I would follow it. This is still, to a great extent, his book. The overall structure is largely his. He wrote significant parts of the first and last chapters, which are new. The other chapters build on the structures and the material of earlier editions. My task of revision was a constant dialogue with a great scholar who left us far too soon and whose work deserves to stand for a very long time.

Yet the revisions, which we planned and I implemented, have been on a large scale. Events determined this. When the third edition was prepared, 'cohabitation' between a president and a prime minister of opposed political camps could still appear as a temporary interruption to a normal pattern of presidential power. The rise of the Front National was still a recent event. Decentralisation had barely taken root. While the economic U-turn of March 1983 had demonstrated the limits to France's economic independence, the manner in which the effects of globalisation and Europeanisation would be diffused through the whole political system, from the executive to interest groups, from parties to regions, from parliament to the administration, was still largely unforeseen. The transformation of relations within the executive necessitated a major restructuring of the relevant chapters, for the prime minister can no longer be treated, as was still possible in the third edition, as the 'other executive', normally a secondary player next to the president. The roles of France's two executives are so closely inter-linked, and in such complex ways, that it seems appropriate to discuss the two in parallel throughout. A similarly large restructuring has transformed Chapter 9, where the interplay between the tendencies to bipolarity and fragmentation within France's party system has been given a more synthetic treatment than would have been possible in the former framework.

Chapter 13, on the rise of judicial power in France, is a particular case. Though new to this book, it appeared in an earlier version, written entirely by Vincent Wright and entitled 'The Fifth Republic: from the *Droit de l'État* to the *État de Droit?*', in *West European Politics*, volume 22, no. 4, October 1999, pp. 92–119. This special issue of *West European Politics*, including the same article, also appeared in book form as Robert Elgie (ed.), *The Changing French Political System* (London, Frank Cass, 2000). Chapter 13 has been revised by me, but contains much material from the earlier article, which is included by the kind permission of Frank Cass Publishers.

Robert Lane Greene gave valuable assistance with bibliographical research. David

Goldey and Wilfrid Knapp read substantial parts of the draft and made invaluable suggestions for improvement, for which my heartfelt thanks. The responsibility for errors lies, of course, with me; they are practically certain to have crept in since the third edition.

Sara and Viveca Knapp, finally, allowed me to shut myself away on the second floor more frequently than they, or I, would have preferred, over two long Auvergnat summers; and sustained me, in an infinite number of ways, when I came downstairs.

Andrew Knapp
Reading, October 2000

1 French political traditions in a changing context

'Our whole history', proclaimed General Charles de Gaulle (1890–1970), leader of the Free French during World War II, head of the Provisional Government from 1944 to 1946, founder of the Fifth Republic in 1958, and its first president from 1959 till 1969, 'is nothing but the alternation between the immense sufferings of a dispersed people and the fruitful grandeur of a nation rallied under the aegis of a strong state.' Modern French history is riven by deep and often murderous political conflict in which Frenchmen killed Frenchmen and régimes were toppled by protest from the street, defeat in war, or both. These events are remembered, and referred to regularly, by contemporary politicians. But French history has also, paradoxically, been marked by the near-continuous presence, under successive régimes, of a strong, activist, often intrusive, state. The traditions of political conflict and of the strong state in France are the subjects of this chapter. It will be argued that many, though not all, of France's traditional political conflicts are now played out; that the state tradition is under threat from transformations in the European and global economies; but that both traditions nevertheless continue to structure the French political landscape.

A legacy of conflict

France invented the terms Left and Right early in the great Revolution of 1789–94 which first limited the powers of, and then overthrew, the Bourbon monarchy. Those noble members of the first National Assembly who wished to limit the powers of the monarch moved to sit with the commoners on the left of the Assembly; those who still supported the absolutism of what was shortly to become known as the *ancien régime* sat on the right, as seen from the chair of the presiding officer. The modern National Assembly has a similar seating plan, with Communist Deputies on the far Left, Socialists next to them, and so on round to the racist Front National, whose very rare Deputies have sat on the extreme Right. In the nineteenth century, Left and Right were convenient shorthand expressions used by parliamentarians and few others. By 1900, however, they had passed into general political discourse. And they can be seen as useful baskets within which to place a series of political conflicts that have divided a nation on broadly bipolar lines. The French readily recognise the expressions and use them themselves. The terms should also, however, be treated with caution, for two reasons. Left and Right have meant different things at different times; and there are some political divisions, chiefly but not exclusively over France's foreign relations, which have never fallen neatly into a Left/Right categorisation.

Table 1.1 presents, schematically, the main issues that divided Left from Right for some two centuries after the Revolution. The long-running ones have been threefold: the nature of the régime, the relationship between Church and state, and the relation between the state, the economy and society.

The régime

For most of the 170 years between the Revolution and the establishment of the Fifth Republic in 1958, France suffered from a lack of consensus about the nature of the

Table 1.1 Left, Right, and the tradition of political division in France

Area of division	Left	Right
Régime (early Revolution)	Submit exercise of royal power to consent of an elected National Assembly	Maintain pre-1789 absolute monarchy
Régime (nineteenth century)	Republicanism, including universal suffrage and civil liberties (press, assembly, association)	Monarchism (divided between support for Bourbon, Orléans, Bonaparte dynasties)
Régime (first half of twentieth century)	Parliamentary republicanism: political power to be vested in a National Assembly, preferably unicameral	Moderate republicanism: power of National Assembly to be tempered by an indirectly elected Senate, and/or a strong executive
Church (nineteenth century)	*Laïcité*: limit the Church's role to matters spiritual; limit its role in education; separate Church from state; anti-clericalism	Maintain Catholicism as official state religion; maintain or reinforce the Church's role in education
Church (twentieth century)	Maintain strict separation of Church and state: no state subsidies to Catholic schools	Reinforce the Church's role in education, notably via state subsidies to Catholic schools
Economy and society (late nineteenth century)	Income tax to finance social reforms: shorter working week; factory legislation	*Laissez-faire* capitalism, plus protection of French agriculture and industry; no income tax or social security
Economy and society (1905–85)	Replacement of the capitalist system by socialism, whether via gradual reform or (for Communists) through more or less violent revolution	Maintenance of capitalism, more or less tempered by social reforms (after 1945) and by protection (at all times)
General temperament	'Party of movement'	'Party of order'

régime under which the country should be ruled. The result, as Table 1.2 shows, was régime instability: a dozen régimes have ruled France since 1789. Most régime transitions involved popular (often Parisian) insurrections and bloodshed. The first Revolution, for example, left 20,000 dead as a result of the Terror of 1793, and as many as a quarter of a million more through the suppression of a Catholic rebellion in the Vendée, to say nothing of the European wars that followed in its wake. The overthrow of the Restoration monarchy in 1830 caused 500 casualties. The 'June days' of 1848, when the Second Republic suppressed its more radical working-class elements, claimed perhaps 3,000 lives. The Third Republic's repression of the radical Paris Commune in 1871 was bloodier still: 20,000 *communards* are estimated to have lost their lives. The Vichy régime enthusiastically collaborated with the German Occupation troops in fighting the Resistance forces (as well as in deporting Jews): 20,000 *résistants* are estimated to have fallen within France, many at the hands of the Vichy *milice*; some 30,000 civilians were shot or massacred. They were avenged, in part, at the Liberation in 1944, when some 10,000 collaborators were summarily executed.

The initial division between Right and Left, concerning the desirability of limiting the king's powers, rapidly gave way to a simpler one, which lasted through the nineteenth century, between monarchists and republicans. To be a republican was automatically to be on the Left and to identify with the heritage of the Revolution, in particular its commitment to popular sovereignty and to the 1789 Declaration of the Rights of Man and the Citizen. But republicanism was long the cause of a minority, failing to take root among large sections of the peasantry who represented some

Table 1.2 France: régimes since 1789

1789–92	Constitutional monarchy: king's powers limited by National Assembly
1792–1804	First Republic: elected National Assembly, but political power resides successively with the Committee of Public Safety (1793–95), the Directorate (1795–99) and the Consulate (1799–1804)
1804–14	First Empire: rule of Napoleon I, legitimised by (rigged) plebiscites
1814–30	Restoration monarchy: Bourbon monarchy of Louis XVIII and Charles X, plus a parliament with limited powers
1830–48	Orleanist monarchy: constitutional monarchy with ministers responsible to a parliament elected by limited suffrage
1848–52	Second Republic: both National Assembly and President directly elected by universal adult male suffrage
1852–70	Second Empire: rule of Napoleon III, legitimised by plebiscites, with concessions to parliamentarianism from 1869
1870–1940	Third Republic: Chamber of Deputies elected by direct universal male suffrage; indirectly elected Senate; weak President and Prime Minister
1940–44	Vichy: personal rule of Marshal Philippe Pétain, constrained chiefly by the German occupation of France
1944–46	Provisional post-war government: single-chamber Constituent Assemblies, elected by direct universal adult suffrage (including women voters)
1946–58	Fourth Republic: broadly comparable to Third, with weaker Senate and women's suffrage
1958–	Fifth Republic: President, Prime Minister and Government, National Assembly, Senate (cf. Chapter 2).

two-thirds of the mid-nineteenth-century population of France: for them, it was too readily identified, thanks to the experiences of the First and Second Republics, with urban power, particularly that of Paris, and with political instability, foreign wars and godlessness. The monarchists, on the other hand, were divided between supporters of the three different houses that had ruled France in the half-century after 1789 (Legitimists, Orleanists and Bonapartists), and weakened by the more or less disastrous record of the monarchs, culminating in the crushing defeat of Napoleon III's imperial forces by Prussia in 1870. When the republicans scored a durable victory (and the Third Republic lasted longer than any régime between 1789 and the present), it was won in part by default, as 'the régime that divides us least'; that expression was coined by Adolphe Thiers, who is remembered both as the butcher of the Commune and, with Léon Gambetta, as one of the Republic's founding fathers.

A peculiarity of the French republican tradition was its intense mistrust, from the later nineteenth century, of a strong executive. This was born of bitter experience: each of the two Napoleons had assumed executive power under a Republic, only to replace the Republic by his own personal rule as emperor. Thus the major constitutional battle of the 1870s was between Thiers's successor as president of the Third Republic, Marshal MacMahon, who sought a return to the monarchy or, failing that, a Republic with a strong executive presidency, and Republican parliamentarians who were determined to make the Chamber of Deputies the centre of political power. The Republicans had won by 1879, though at a price: to reassure rural France, they conceded significant power to an indirectly elected Senate, whose conservatism was in direct proportion to the substantial over-representation of rural areas in its ranks. By 1900 all serious hope of a restoration of the monarchy had disappeared, and the Third Republic commanded broad popular support, or at least acquiescence. When the question of the régime re-emerged, in the 1930s and 1940s, it placed the mainstream republican tradition against both the enemies of democracy who sought some form of authoritarian or Fascist régime (they had their moment of success under Vichy), and more mainstream right-wingers like André Tardieu who stressed the need to reinforce the executive within the Republic. It was de Gaulle who took up this theme in his Bayeux speech two years after the Liberation (and five months after his own resignation as head of the Provisional Government). He was not heeded by the left-wing majority that controlled the National Assembly. The Fourth Republic, with its combination of a strong but undisciplined National Assembly and a weak president and premier, was the last victory of the classical French republican tradition. It was only when it had manifestly failed either to provide stable government or to deal with the challenges facing France (particularly the war of decolonisation being waged in Algeria), that de Gaulle was recalled to power and given his chance. The régime he created, which combined a republican constitution with a strong presidency for the first time in 110 years, won the support of nearly 80 per cent of the voters when submitted to referendum in September 1958. That did not prevent François Mitterrand, who emerged as one of the main leaders of the left-wing opposition, from attacking the Fifth Republic as a 'Permanent Coup d'État'.

The Church

The Catholic Church had been the *ancien régime*'s most important ideological and institutional support. Tithes, and ecclesiastical corruption, had made it deeply unpopular by the time of the Revolution, at least in the less devout parts of France. It is thus not surprising that the Revolution called into question not only the Church's privileges, but its very existence. In the most extreme, Jacobin, phase of the Revolution, Church property was confiscated, abbeys turned into prisons or arsenals, Christian services replaced by Festivals of the Supreme Being, and the Christian calendar abolished. The biggest domestic military challenge to the First Republic, the rebellion in the Catholic Vendée area, was put down with extreme savagery. These events left a legacy of enmity between Catholics and the Republic that was to last well into the twentieth century. 'Le cléricalisme, voilà l'ennemi!' declaimed the Republican politician Léon Gambetta, at the outset of his final confrontation with President MacMahon in 1877 – his argument reinforced by Pope Pius IX's *ex cathedra* condemnation of all forms of republicanism and liberalism as incompatible with the Christian faith. Anti-clericalism (a hostility towards the Church as an institution, though not necessarily to Christianity itself) became as much a badge of the Left as republicanism. The form it took might be instrumental (believing in a secular society) or picturesquely expressive (public orgies of sausage-eating on Fridays). By the late nineteenth century the debate had centred on two main issues: the Church's position as the established religion of France, and its control over the education system. One of the founding acts of the Third Republic after its consolidation was to give France a universal system of state education – 'free, secular, and compulsory'. The separation of Church and state followed in 1905, after the hostility of the Church – or of its most vocal 'defenders' – to the Republic had been confirmed during the Dreyfus Affair. Thereafter, Church–state relations turned essentially on the issue of public subsidies to Catholic schools, an apparently limited policy question which nevertheless aroused fierce passions on both sides for half a century. The Debré Law of 1959 settled the principle of subsidy, and its main mechanisms. It did not prevent the issues of the volume of subsidies, and the degree of state control that should go with them, from mobilising impressive street demonstrations by the partisans of both secularism and of Catholic education, as late as 1994. Indeed, both survey data and electoral geography show that practising Catholics still vote on the (moderate) Right by a proportion of three or four to one – a much better correlation than that offered by class, the other major sociological variable.

The importance of *laïcité* or, roughly, secularism to the identity of the French Left cannot be overstated. At the centre of the French republican model is the belief, fostered by eighteenth-century critics of the *ancien régime*, in the power of human rationality to create a community of free and equal citizens, and to promote human well-being through scientific progress. Crucial to both of those goals is education, which should communicate verifiable truths rather than religious beliefs (or superstitions, as true anti-clericals regarded the teachings of the Catholic Church), and should offer the diligent individual an opportunity for upward social mobility. In short, the republican ideal, as well as the practice of successive Republics, involved the removal of the Church from the leading positions within the state and within the education system to which Catholics believed it had a right. The opposition between the Church and the French republican model allowed one party, the Radicals, to make anti-clericalism its main stock-in-trade throughout the first half of the twentieth century. It also helped limit the impact in France of Christian Democracy. Post-war France, like other European countries such as Italy, Germany and Belgium, did see the emergence of a Christian Democratic party, committed to democracy, reconciliation between the former belligerent powers of Europe through the construction of European institutions, the construction of a welfare state, and industrial co-operation between workers and employers, in the name of Christian social principles. But France's Christian Democratic party, the MRP (Mouvement Républicain Populaire), though electorally successful in 1945 and 1946 because it was the only party with a Resistance pedigree which was not anti-clerical, attracted mostly conservative Catholic voters, many of whom deserted to Gaullism or to the traditional conservative Right as soon as it was possible or respectable to do so. Christian Democracy in France never won the status of permanent party of government that it enjoyed elsewhere in Europe.

The politics of class

The politics of class is the single most common factor dividing Left from Right in West European political systems, with the former seeking social justice through redistributive social and economic intervention by the state, and the latter committed to defending capitalism and private property (and, it would argue, prosperity) against the threats thus posed. But the manner in which class politics is played out in each country depends both on the other social and political cleavages present, and on the national pattern of economic development.

The French Revolution was a source not only of national pride (as the bicentennial celebrations of 1989 showed) but of severe economic dislocation. Some of this was lasting: where France had possessed an economy comparable in size to Britain's in the 1780s, the pattern in the nineteenth century was one of almost uninterrupted relative economic decline. The western half of the country was condemned to a century and a half of underdevelopment, after the prosperity of its Atlantic ports was wrecked by war and blockade. The Revolution gave France a class of independent, and inefficient, small peasant farmers, with little or no incentive to move off the land; it was a class that actually grew in the later nineteenth century, as falling land values enabled tenant farmers to realise their dreams of ownership. Nature had provided France with limited, often poor-quality, reserves of coal and iron. Not surprisingly, then, France's industrial revolution proceeded in fits and starts, notably under the Second Empire and in the first and third decades of the twentieth century; it was only completed after World War II. In 1900 nearly half of the French population still worked on the land (compared to under 10 per cent in industrially advanced Britain). Their woeful productivity is measured by the fact that France, with twice Britain's territory for the same population, was still not agriculturally self-sufficient. Industry, on the other hand, was still dominated by the small family firm and the small workshop, with only a handful of companies, notably in the nascent automobile industry (before Ford, France was briefly the world's biggest exporter of motor cars), escaping the pattern.

For the Left, the major consequence of this pattern of slow growth was the relatively small number of industrial workers, their geographical dispersal, and the resulting weakness of the labour movement: in 1914, the Section Française de l'Internationale Ouvrière (SFIO), founded in 1905, had 75,000 members compared to a million for the German Social Democratic Party (SPD); 16.8 per cent of the vote to the SPD's 34.8. On the Right, meanwhile, there was no very substantial constituency for a classical liberal party, committed to secularism, the extension of civil and political liberties, and free trade. The Radical Party, the pivotal force in every governing coalition for the first four decades of the twentieth century, was the nearest thing France possessed to a liberal party. But it was too rooted in provincial France, the France of the anti-clerical country schoolmaster and the small family firm or farm, to be a zealous advocate of free-market capitalism – or, for that matter, of the urban social reforms undertaken by the British Liberals in the early twentieth century. Napoleon III had briefly committed France to free trade. But tariffs were reimposed in 1871, initially to raise the revenue to pay reparations to Germany after defeat in the Franco-Prussian war, and with the Méline tariff of 1892 France reverted to full-scale protectionism, while the Radicals relapsed into anti-clericalism and abandoned concern for urban social reform. The France of small firms and small farms stayed protected until the European Economic Community (EEC) began to bring the tariff barriers down in the 1960s.

The relatively small number of big firms and of industrial workers did not, however, blunt the edge of class conflict in France. On the contrary: if social reform was slower and later than in Germany or Britain, class confrontation was fierce and often bloody. The French working class acquired a series of its own memories to add to the more general insurrectionary tradition of 1789. The Paris Commune of 1871, hailed rather misleadingly by Karl Marx as the 'harbinger of a new society', was not only, perhaps not even primarily, about class conflict. But the presence of both workers and socialist leaders among the *communards*, and the savagery of the repression by the conservative government forces, turned the Commune into a powerful and enduring legend. The formal right to join a trade union was only conceded in 1884. Its exercise remained fraught with danger: over the next thirty years, troops, and live ammunition, were used against striking workers with depressing regularity. Twentieth-century working-class memories include the Popular Front government of 1936, the wave of spontaneous strikes that greeted its election, and the reforms that followed, notably the 40-hour week and the first paid holidays. A further layer of memory was added by the Resistance (in which left-wing and working-class forces were particularly active) and by the great reforms of the Liberation, in particular nationalisations and the creation of France's social security system.

The numerical weakness of the French socialist movement was matched by its doctrinal division and its habitual political ineffectiveness (except on the occasion of rare victories, as at the Liberation). One of the main failings of the Third Republic was its inability to achieve the political integration of the working class: for neither of the two major traditions that claimed the loyalties of workers, anarcho-syndicalism and Marxism, espoused progressive reform within the capitalist system. Anarcho-syndicalism drew from the disastrous experience of the Commune the lesson that mainstream political activity offered no hope of social improvement and was best avoided altogether. Instead, it focused on militant rather than organised trade union activity, and cultivated the myth of the one great strike that would overthrow capitalism. The insistence by the main trade union confederation, the Confédération Générale du Travail (CGT), on its complete independence from political parties helped to perpetuate the organisational weakness of the French socialist movement compared with its British, Belgian or German counterparts. Marxism, in its most doctrinally rigid form, became the official dogma of the largest single French socialist party of the late nineteenth century, the Parti Ouvrier Français founded by Jules Guesde; it largely superseded earlier French varieties of socialist doctrine. As a revolutionary myth, Marxism was an attractive response to the hardship of the working-class condition, to its political isolation, and to the violence that was regularly visited upon workers by employers, the police or troops. But as a programme for action for a country with a small working class, it was deeply misguided. The socialist revolution being unattainable, at least in the short term, reforms within the existing Republic were the only available means to improve the workers' condition. But the only government that might implement such reforms would be a coalition between socialists and non-socialist forces such as the Radicals. Such a coalition would inevitably water down reforms. Moderate socialist reformism, however, was a force within the French Left that dared not speak its name: the practical moderation of the SFIO was overlaid with a rhetorical commitment to class struggle and the overthrow of capitalism. The contrast between revolutionary rhetoric, on the one hand, and less than revolutionary practice, on the other, and the inevitable accusations of betrayal that result, has been a constant in the history of the French Left ever since.

The most important force sustaining the intellectual hegemony of Marxism (in its Leninist, and then Stalinist, forms) on the Left was the Parti Communiste Français (PCF). The PCF was founded in 1920, at the Congress of Tours, when the SFIO, like other European socialist parties, split on the issue of whether to join Lenin's Communist International. The Leninists actually won a majority at Tours, winning control of the party's assets and its newspaper, *L'Humanité*, for the PCF. For the next fifteen years, the sectarian, Moscow-directed PCF lost ground steadily to the SFIO, though it still supplied enough competition to pull its older rival leftwards. After the mid-1930s it gathered strength first from the anti-Fascist Popular Front alliance with Socialists and Radicals, which allowed it to gain important positions in the trade union movement, and then from the leading role it played in the internal French Resistance after June 1941. The PCF's own wartime record, and the prestige enjoyed by the Soviet Union after the Allied victory in Europe, won it the loyalty of a quarter of French voters. It was the largest party in the 1945 Constituent Assembly, with ministers in France's post-war governments. But the onset of the Cold War led to the ministers' dismissal in May 1947; the Cold War cleavage split the Left durably (with the Socialist leader Guy Mollet saying that the Communists were 'neither on the Left nor the Right, but on the East'), and excluded Communists from national office for over a generation. Indeed, the fact that the PCF remained the dominant force on the French Left for the thirty post-war years helped to keep the Left out of power. The Socialists, without the possibility of a Communist alliance, governed under the Fourth Republic with parties of the Centre, chiefly the Radicals and the MRP, with generally unimpressive results; under the Fifth Republic the Left was out of government altogether for twenty-three years. Despite its political isolation, however, the PCF continued to dominate the doctrinal debate on the Left, ensuring, for example, as a result of its rigid loyalty to Moscow, that the stock of the Soviet Union long stood higher in France than in other Western states. The PCF's ideological force resulted partly from its size: no major project on the Left could be achieved without the largest left-wing party that possessed the most members, the biggest electorate and the toughest organisation. The PCF also benefited from its success in attracting prestigious intellectual and artistic figures like Louis Aragon, Pablo Picasso and Jean-Paul Sartre who, whether as party members or as 'fellow-travellers', helped ensure that Marxism occupied the intellectual high ground during the post-war generation.

Le parti du mouvement et le parti de l'ordre

The Right and the Left, it has often been claimed, are not merely coalitions of dispersed and at times antagonistic interests like the American Republican and Democratic parties. Rather, they are *globally* opposed political families, each with a distinct set of common values, which François Goguel, the doyen of French political science, has characterised as the 'party of movement' (the Left) and the 'party of order' (the Right) – though of course neither Left nor Right has ever managed to unite into a single political party. Left-wing values, according to this broad distinction, include the belief in the power of human reason to achieve progress for the benefit of the human race; secularism or *laïcité*, seen as necessary to remove the impediment to progress represented by the institutional entrenchment of any religion; the belief in the exercise of sovereignty by a nation of free and equal citizens through their elected parliamentary representatives, and thus a mistrust of strong personal political leadership insofar as that distanced the exercise of political power from the nation; and a belief in the use of politics to achieve a measure of social justice to match the political liberties and rights of the Republic. For its critics, the Left was regularly guilty of crass and intolerant anti-clericalism, unrealistic social reformism, doctrinaire Marxism and class hatred. The values of the 'party of order' include a scepticism about the capacity of radical reforms to achieve the human well-being they seek, and a sensitivity to the anti-competitive consequences of reforms affecting the workplace; a belief in the value of the Catholic Church, both in itself and as an instrument of social cohesion; and a belief that a country as prone to social and political divisions as France stands in need of strong political leadership. For the Left, this translates as a selfish and reactionary opposition to long-overdue measures of social justice, a wish to impose the doctrine of the Catholic Church on the population, and a penchant for authoritarianism and repression.

This bipolar vision of the French political landscape has many attractions. Opinion polls show that the French have little difficulty in placing both themselves and leading politicians at a particular point on a Left–Right continuum. Left and Right have been regular terms of French political discourse for over a century (though for long periods, and certainly during the post-war generation, very few politicians would openly admit to being right-wing). But the bipolar vision needs to be qualified, in a number of ways.

- The content of Left and Right has varied over time. To be a republican was to be unambiguously on the Left in the nineteenth century; the two became much less closely associated in the twentieth.
- The divisions within the two families have at times been as important as the divisions between them. On the Left, the Radicals tempered their love for the republican ideals of the Revolution (in which anti-clericalism was often salient) with a cautious conservatism on most economic issues; the Socialists combined Marxist rhetoric with reformist practice; the Communists' claims to be the revolutionary workers' vanguard were long a façade for a more or less slavish obedience to Moscow's dictates of the moment. Political alliances between these three parties, as occurred, for example, during the Popular Front period of the mid-1930s, were hard to achieve, inherently unstable, and susceptible to accusations of betrayal on all sides. The Right, too, has always included distinct currents. René Rémond distinguishes three: a reactionary element, deeply hostile to the ideals of the 1789 Revolution; a moderate conservative grouping, committed to balanced government and a measure of economic liberalism; and a nationalist current, standing for strong leadership at home, with close links, through plebiscites, referendums or direct election, between the leader and the people, and national self-assertion abroad. To these might be added, especially during the post-war generation, the

Christian Democratic current represented by the MRP and, later, by the various parties identified with the Centre, more liberal in politics, less *laissez-faire* in economics. The Left's mistrust of strong political leadership, it might be added, was shared by most of the moderate Right, at least by the post-war period; while the supposed (and, at times, real) authoritarianism of the Right was at least equalled by the internal practice and external ambitions of the PCF.

• For many decades, the practical realities of French politics coincided hardly at all with the bipolar vision. For much of the Third and Fourth Republics, France was governed by coalitions of Centre-Right and Centre-Left that straddled the divide between the two big families. Parties like the Radicals or the MRP made a virtue of their centrist positions, claiming to offer a *juste milieu* between the excesses of Soviet-style collectivism on the one hand and free-market capitalism on the other. Many of the great survivors of twentieth-century French politics were men who knew how to trim their policies and their alliances to circumstance: men like the Radical Édouard Herriot (collector of ministerial offices during the Third Republic, three times prime minister between the wars, president of pre-war and post-war National Assemblies, and mayor of Lyon from 1905 till 1957), Jacques Chaban-Delmas (Gaullist prime minister from 1969 to 1972, and mayor of Bordeaux from 1947 to 1995), or even François Mitterrand (who first won elective office as a fierce anti-communist in 1946, became the Fifth Republic's first Socialist president in 1981 thanks in part to a rapprochement with the Communists, and proceeded to ditch many of his party's left-wing economic ideas in the face of hard economic realities).

• Attitudes to certain fundamental political questions, including the character of the nation, France's role in the world, and the role of the state, largely escape categorisation into the families of Left and Right. These issues will be examined in the next two sections.

Nationalisms

Nationalism was at first a left-wing ideal: against the principles of dynastic inheritance and the divine right of kings which underlay absolute monarchy, it opposed the freedom of a sovereign people to choose its own government. For Jacobins, France had a unique mission to spread the values of the Revolution, in particular those enshrined in the Declaration of the Rights of Man, to the whole world. Perhaps the defining event of this type of 'civic' nationalism was the Battle of Valmy in September 1792, when France's citizen army defeated the invading Prussian grenadiers – sent, in the not altogether inaccurate popular view, by a league of European despots to destroy the Revolution: the First Republic was proclaimed two days after the victory. A similar nationalism was displayed by the Left in 1870, when republicanism went hand in hand with a determination to pursue the war against Prussia even after the crushing defeat at Sedan. The Communists, born as a pro-Soviet party opposed to all wars between nations (though not between classes), prospered only when they captured this part of the Jacobin legacy, first through their hostility to Nazism before 1939, and then during the Resistance after 1941. The Jacobin conception of citizenship was a broad one: it stressed both the rights to citizenship of all individuals born in France whatever their parentage (a principle of nationality, the *jus solis*, that predated the Revolution by over two centuries, was abandoned by the Revolutionaries themselves, but reinstated in

1889) and the duty of citizens of non-French origin to integrate into the nation, in effect leaving their non-French origins behind them.

A more ethnic nationalism of the far Right, opposed in almost every way to the Jacobin tradition, also took shape in France during the last fifteen years of the nineteenth century. Its pedigree stretches from Paul Déroulède's Ligue des Patriotes, founded in 1885, to Charles Maurras's Action Française, dating from the turn of the century, to right-wing leagues like the Croix de Feu of the 1930s, to Vichy, to the last-ditch defenders of *Algérie française* in the early 1960s, to the contemporary Front National. Resulting initially from the frustration of the Right at the consolidation of the Third Republic, this brand of nationalism has specialised in the identification of scapegoats to blame for France's real or supposed ills: Protestants, Jews and Freemasons for Maurras, Jews and Freemasons again for Vichy, North African immigrants and Jews for the Front National. This approach was meant to provide the popular support that royalism and then traditional Catholicism could no longer muster from the enemies of the Republic. Because the nationalism of the far Right has sought to separate, on more or less racial lines, the 'true' community of the French from the supposedly corrupting elements within the national territory, it has been variously referred to as a *nationalisme d'exclusion*, a *nationalisme identitaire*, or a *nationalisme de repli*: a nationalism, in other words, that is far more concerned with an inward-looking attempt to defend a supposedly true French national identity than with the more open, expansive Jacobin tradition. Not surprisingly, the nationalism of the far Right rejects the values of the Revolution, preferring hierarchy to equality and a muscular brand of fundamentalist ('*intégriste*') Catholicism to secularism. It also seeks the replacement of the *jus solis* by the *jus sanguinis*, under which parentage rather than place of birth defines citizenship. Initially, the nationalism of the far Right was fiercely anti-German, calling for an early *revanche* for the defeat of 1870. That its only experience of government was acquired thanks to the German Occupation of 1940–44 is one of the more piquant ironies of French history.

The defeat of 1940, and Charles de Gaulle's decision to call on the French to continue the struggle under his leadership, gave a new and forceful expression to a third variety of French nationalism which had been crowded out by the extremists. In many ways Gaullism owes more to the Jacobin tradition than to the extreme Right. Its conception of citizenship is an inclusive one, and its preoccupation is with France's independence and standing in the world, and its unique contribution to human progress, rather than with a narrow conception of the national identity. But de Gaulle's 'certain idea of France' transcended the values of the Revolution to take in the whole of French history: *ancien régime*, Empire and Republics. And, as he stressed in the opening pages of his *War Memoirs*, it was at least as much felt as reasoned. There is more than a touch of mysticism about the images he chooses to express his love of country: a Madonna in medieval frescos, a princess in a fairy tale, or, later, sunset on the cathedral of Notre Dame or flags on the Arc de Triomphe – symbols more redolent of the monarchist Right than of the republican Left.

De Gaulle liked to claim that France (and therefore de Gaulle) were beyond the confines of Left and Right. The French did not, on the whole, agree. Voters both for de Gaulle and for Gaullist parties have come predominantly (though never exclusively) from the Right. In many ways this was logical. De Gaulle's conviction that France needed strong leadership (his own, in the first instance) placed him firmly on the Right in the constitutional debate. A lifelong Catholic, he fully approved the Debré Law fixing permanent subsidies for Church schools. In other ways, though, de Gaulle's claim to transcend has some justification. The war years placed him on the same side as the predominantly left-wing Resistance. As head of a post-Liberation provisional government that included Communists, he nationalised banks and basic industries (as well as Renault) and signed the decree creating France's social security system. That act was perfectly consistent with a nationalism that sought to underpin France's ambitions abroad with political and social measures designed to appease conflicts and build national cohesion at home. Indeed, he worried his more business-minded supporters (not least his own prime minister and successor as president, Georges Pompidou, a former banker) with his long-cherished ambition to 'replace capitalism' with some form of 'third way' between the market and Soviet-style collectivism. This dream, of early twentieth-century social Catholic inspiration, never became a project of substance. But it illustrates the difficulty of positioning de Gaulle as a straightforward conservative. And the Gaullist insistence on France's independence and status in the world has taken its place in the national diplomatic discourse, whether uttered by Gaullists, Socialists, members of the non-Gaullist Right or even Communists.

Gaullism weakened Christian Democracy in France. On internal questions the two had much in common, appealing notably to Catholics with a social conscience. But de Gaulle's intense preoccupation with strong leadership and with national independence, his rejection of American tutelage in the world of the Cold War, and his sceptical, even dismissive, attitude to supranational institutions, all marked him out from the Atlanticist, pro-European Christian Democrats, whom he personally viewed with barely concealed contempt.

The division between Gaullists and Christian Democrats offers one illustration of the difficulty of placing foreign policy issues into the categories of Left and Right. There are plenty of others.

- Jules Ferry, one of the leading statesmen of the early Third Republic, both achieved the impeccably left-wing goal of free, secular and compulsory primary education, and established the French protectorates in Tunisia and Indo-China. His republican successors participated actively in the late nineteenth-century 'scramble for Africa', and exempted from their anti-clericalism those Catholic missionaries who furthered France's imperial designs through their conversion of the heathen. At the outset of the Algerian war in 1954, no major party of Right or Left favoured independence for France's most important, and most densely colonised, North African territory. While groups of the far Left rapidly came to support the independence movement, it was de Gaulle, a right-wing soldier, who finally cut the ties between France and Algeria, as well as granting full independence to France's colonies in sub-Saharan Africa.
- The issue of France's response to the rise of Nazism and Fascism in the 1930s divided Left and Right alike. The Left found it increasingly hard to combine the pacifist sentiments inherited from the aftermath of World War I with its opposition to Fascism; the Right had difficulty maintaining its earlier anti-German stance in the face of régimes that presented themselves as bulwarks against Soviet Communism. A further twist was added by the Communist Party, vigorously anti-Fascist until the signature of the Nazi–Soviet pact in August 1939 obliged them to change policy overnight and abstain from attacks on the Soviet Union's new ally until Hitler's invasion of the Soviet Union on the night of 22 June 1941.

- De Gaulle's wish to demonstrate French independence from the United States, and his sympathetic view of the Franco-Russian alliance of his own formative years, led him into an early policy of *détente* with the Soviet Union, much to the annoyance of the Americans (who did the same thing themselves, but nearly a decade later). In internal politics, this earned de Gaulle guarded praise from the PCF, but criticism from the Atlanticist parties of the Centre-Left and Centre-Right.
- A similar division has regularly pertained over Europe. Under most circumstances, Gaullists and Communists have been the most reticent towards anything smacking of federalism, and most Socialists, all Christian Democrats and the rest of the non-Gaullist Right being favourable to further integration. The referendum of 2005 on the European constitutional treaty, called by a neo-Gaullist president, Jacques Chirac, very broadly confirmed this pattern, although the opposition to further integration was much more skewed than usual to the Left: only 41 per cent of Socialist supporters voted yes to the treaty, compared with 76 per cent of sympathisers of Chirac's party, the Union pour un Mouvement Populaire.

The apogee of France's tradition of intense political division was reached under the Fourth Republic, when the country was typically viewed by observers at home and abroad as an impossibly fragmented and conflictual society, rent by bitter ideological divisions which were reflected in an unstable multiparty system. Its schismatic political culture was contrasted with the integrated, homogeneous and consensual political culture of its neighbour across the Channel. But France was also an oddity in European terms. The parties that formed the basis of stable multiparty systems elsewhere – moderate Social Democrats, Liberals and Christian Democrats – were all singularly weak in France. To this fragmentation and instability should be added the legacy of bitter civil strife. The dates which figured (and continue to figure) most prominently in the French historical consciousness – 1789, 1793, 1830, 1848, 1871, 1936, 1940 and 1944 – all recall periods when French people were at their most bitterly divided. When a British politician invokes history it is normally to buttress an unconvincing appeal to national unity; a French politician (unless he is president) will cite historical examples to illustrate the perfidy of his adversaries (and, at times, his allies as well). The great political battles of the Fourth Republic – over the European Defence Community, Algeria or state aid to Church schools, for instance – were infused with a peculiar venom, as each released the accumulated rancours of generations. A tendency to over-intellectualise problems, so that concrete issues were approached with reference to abstract and intangible principles, plus an all too ready recourse to language that was excessive and emotionally explosive where it was not personally abusive, compounded the defects of a political discourse that apparently left little room for dialogue or bargaining. This type of rhetoric, required to satisfy restive and sceptical activists and voters, was the stock-in-trade of parliamentarians and ministers in a chronically divided Assembly. But behind it, the politicians of the Centre knew that they had to surmount their differences so that France might be governed and the state preserved (and controlled).

A counterpoint to the legacy of conflict, then, is the continuity of the French state. It is a tradition less obvious to the outside observer than conflict (though all too tangible to any foreigner in France who has had to apply for a residence permit, complete a contract of employment as a public servant, send a child to school, or seek reimbursement for medical expenses). Since the Revolution, changes of régime have left the apparatus of the state, as well as a significant body of legislation, largely intact. The law requiring passengers on public transport to make the appropriate connections, for example, dates from the Revolution. The licensing laws governing every French café date from 1942 – that is, from Vichy. More remarkably, all the judges active under Vichy survived the Liberation. One of the greatest compliments a French politician can pay to another is to concede that he possesses *le sens de l'État*. It is to the state tradition, or rather traditions, in French political culture that we now turn.

State traditions

'France', as Georges Pompidou (1908–74), de Gaulle's successor as president, put it succinctly, 'would not exist without a state.' The English have (or had) a Whig tradition that saw the struggle for, and eventual triumph of, freedom from arbitrary rule as the dominant theme of the nation's history. The dominant theme identified by many French historians, usually of a conservative bent, is that of state-building, in which a series of monarchs (Saint Louis, Louis XI, Francis I, Henri IV, Louis XIV) contrived, through a combination of statesmanship, strategic marriage, ruse and military conquest, to weld a geographically and linguistically disparate collection of provinces into a state ruled from Paris, and thence into a nation. The process was far from smooth. The Hundred Years War of the fourteenth and fifteenth centuries, the Wars of Religion of the sixteenth, the Fronde of the seventeenth, all interrupted it, serving to show the need for more or less absolute power at the centre to preserve the state and the nascent nation. From this perspective, the great Revolution of 1789 was merely one further, albeit spectacular and far-reaching, interruption in the state-building process; for the great nineteenth-century political analyst Alexis de Tocqueville and his intellectual heirs, it further consolidated the centralisation of the absolute monarchy, the two Napoleons continuing the process. The state-builders of the late nineteenth and twentieth centuries – Thiers and Gambetta, the two founders of the Third Republic, Georges Clemenceau, who led France to victory in 1918, and de Gaulle himself – could be seen as worthy democratic successors to the *ancien régime* monarchs.

If this broadly conservative view of French history stresses continuity, an alternative view highlights the sharp hiatus represented by the Revolution of 1789. For much of the Left, the Revolution represents the real birth of the French nation, because through it, the French were able to throw off the shackles of absolute monarchy and establish a Republic of free and equal citizens. 'The Revolution', argues the left-wing writer Régis Debray, 'is the touchstone of the (Republican) constitution.' Its principles are set out in the Declaration of the Rights of Man and the Citizen of 26 August 1789, which still forms part of the preamble to the Constitution of the Fifth Republic. As we have seen, the revolutionary tradition associates the Republic with equality between citizens; with unlimited popular sovereignty ('the law is the expression of the General Will', says Article 6 of the Declaration of the Rights of Man); with the eighteenth-century values of rationalism and enlightenment; with secularism; with education; and with progress towards ever greater prosperity and an ever fairer distribution of society's wealth.

The common core

Despite the obvious differences between them, these two views of French history have much in common – besides their tendentiousness. Both insist on the role of the state, not merely as the tool to undertake certain functions for society (at the very least, defence, public order and justice) but as the very creator of the nation – whether through the gradual establishment of the royal writ throughout the land or through the explosion of national self-consciousness embodied in the Revolution and the subsequent wars. These converging views of the primal role of the state in history have also been reflected in comparably convergent views about the state's contemporary role, and its autonomy and primacy in relation both to subnational levels of government and to civil society in general.

- The kings of the *ancien régime* constantly sought to demolish or erode the autonomy of provinces within their realm, and of the nobles who made the provinces their territorial base. The Revolution gave France the uniform scheme of *départements* which remain the second tier of French local administration to this day. Napoleon I gave each *département* a prefect, the symbol for two centuries of an intrusive and arbitrary central authority reaching into the most obscure corners of the furthest provinces.
- Because the medieval corporations and the estates of the *ancien régime* had to be destroyed in order to establish equality before the law and a Republic of citizens, Jacobin mistrust of local autonomy extended to any body or group that appeared to stand between the individual citizen and the state by representing a partial and therefore suspect interest. However, the most notable expression of this mistrust was a partial one: the Le Chapelier law of 1791, which banned trade unions and other workplace associations altogether. The law survived for nearly a century, under all régimes, until its repeal in 1884. Except during the German Occupation, liberty of assocation has been guaranteed since 1901; but Tocqueville's intellectual heirs have claimed that the French are still reluctant to join associations, and tend to refer to the state problems that would be dealt with within civil society in other countries. Others have argued that politicised activists (for example, Catholic and Communist trade unionists) have discouraged the less militant majority from joining anything, and make co-operation between those of similar interests impossible.
- The Church, too, was subordinated to the state not only after but also before the Revolution. The Concordat of Bologna, signed by a reluctant but impotent Pope still reeling from his defeat by Francis I of France at the battle of Marignano in 1516, secured permanent royal control over French Church appointments. Under Francis I's successors, the 'Gallican' Catholic Church became as much of an institutional and spiritual prop for the monarchy as the Anglican Church was in England, but without the trouble of a break with Rome. United in hostility towards the secular Republic, French Catholics, both clergy and laity, divided over the submission of the Gallican Church to an obscurantist Ultramontane Roman Curia. De Gaulle's family were a good example of the Gallican side of the divide: loyal to the Church, but wanting it run from within France.
- The primacy of the state over its own servants is also part of the French state tradition. The judiciary, in particular, was constrained before the Revolution by the king's untrammelled right to make law. After it, ordinary judges were excluded by Napoleon from protecting citizens from the excesses of his administration (though the Conseil d'État, the body entrusted by Napoleon with the handling of disputes concerning the servants of the state, did soon acquire a measure of independence). The hierarchical subordination of magistrates to the justice minister and the political authorities' tight control over appointments and career advancement have been

maintained, in their essentials, ever since. The view of law as something subordinate to the higher interests of the state still has willing contemporary supporters on both Left and Right, whether the Socialist minister André Labarrère who told the right-wing opposition that 'You are legally in the wrong because you are politically in the minority', or the Gaullist Interior Minister Charles Pasqua who delicately argued that 'Democracy ends where *raison d'État* begins'. The doctrine of the separation of powers has also been used to protect the state's servants (and thus their political masters) from the attentions of the judiciary.

- The state, finally, was the agent of French power abroad. For some two centuries, from 1650 to 1850, France possessed the largest and most formidable army in Europe. Whether it was to extend French territory to include pieces of Flanders or Savoy, in the name of frontiers spuriously considered as 'natural' from Louis XIV; or to throw back the forces of the crowned heads of Europe at Valmy; or to embark on the conquest of Europe behind Napoleon; or even, in the last quarter of the nineteenth century, to extend France's 'civilising mission' to Indo-China and Africa, the French state was identified with military prowess – and unsurprisingly, was shaken in the event of defeat, whether in 1815, 1870 or 1940. Not for the French the acquisition of an empire in India by the armies of a private company.

In short, while régimes might come and go with alarming frequency, the culture of the French state, and the powerful reality of its army and bureaucracy, remained. The notion of the state might convey somewhat different meanings to the Right and the Left, but neither seriously questioned its primacy, its autonomy or its power.

Liberty, equality, fraternity

To the common core should be added two more distinctly modern notions of the French state, one built around the republican triptych of liberty, equality and fraternity, the other the set of economic doctrines and relationships known from the mid-twentieth century as *dirigisme*.

The adoption in 1880 by what was to prove France's longest Republic, the Third, of the most obvious Republican symbols – the *Marseillaise* as the national anthem and the 14th July, anniversary of the storming of the Bastille, as the national holiday – was swiftly followed by more concrete steps to realise the ideals of *liberté, égalité, fraternité*.

- In the first place, the Republic was a guarantor of certain liberties, enshrined in law between 1881 and 1885 and not rescinded wholesale since then except under Vichy. They included freedom of assembly, of association (extended and reinforced by the law of 1901), and of the press (in the late 1920s George Orwell was to observe that 'Paris alone has daily papers by the dozen, nationalist, Socialist and Communist, clerical and anti-clerical, militarist and anti-militarist, pro-semitic and anti-semitic'); freedom for all men over 21 to vote (from 1848) and to choose between different candidates (from 1871); the right of municipalities (except Paris) to elect their own councils and mayors.
- Equality between citizens, at least of a formal sort, was guaranteed, in the first instance, by universal male suffrage. Equally universal, for men, was the duty of military service, to which few exceptions were admitted after 1870. Like other nineteenth-century continental powers in an age when military strength depended

substantially on the ability to put large numbers of trained men into the field, France maintained a conscript army, with 736,000 men under arms *before* mobilisation in 1914. Military service, in turn, became a rite of passage for generations: part of the process identified by Eugen Weber by which peasants of far-flung provinces were turned into French citizens. A third manifestation of republican equality was to be found in universal primary schooling: the Ferry Laws offered, in principle, an identical chance to children throughout the territory of France to better themselves through education. The Ferry Laws and the universality they embodied were important not only in themselves but also as a foundation, in three senses. First, they stood as the prototype for a widening range of public services, especially after 1945: supplied by a central state monopoly and accessible to citizens throughout France's territory on an identical basis. Second, they were the basis of an educational cursus that combined equal chances for all (in principle) with increasingly ferocious selection through competitive examinations. Third, competitive examinations also served as the basis for recruitment into the service of the state, embodying the Republican ideal of the 'career open to talent' (as opposed to the noble status and patronage of the *ancien régime*).

- The third element of the Republican triptych, fraternity, is the most elusive. It is perhaps best conceived as the capacity of the Republic to integrate Frenchmen of the most diverse regional origins into a nation: a process which, in the view of Eugen Weber, was not completed until the late nineteenth century, by which time universal education and military service, as well as relatively cheap rail transport, had done their work. Integration, however, extended beyond the ranks of the native-born French to immigrants. By the late nineteenth century, sluggish demography (in 1800 the population of France, at some 27 million, was nearly three times that of Great Britain; a century later each country had about 40 million inhabitants) had made France – most unusually, for a West European country – a land of immigration. The new arrivals, whose numbers peaked in the prosperous 1920s, were mostly other Europeans: Poles, Belgians and Italians in particular. Their children born in France attended French schools and, thanks to the revival of the *jus solis* in 1889, grew up as French citizens, frequently marrying a native French spouse and becoming fully integrated with the French population within one or at most two generations.

The relationship between state, nation and citizens expressed by the Republican triptych differed significantly from those current in the United States or even Britain. Associations were tolerated and enjoyed a legal status, but the state, rather than holding the ring between plethora of competing interests, was placed above them as the expression of the general will. Tasks such as education could not be delegated to local authorities, because the state alone could guarantee the equality of treatment to which each French citizen had a right. At the same time measures to limit substantive inequality, through wealth redistribution and the creation of a welfare state, waited longer in France than in northern European countries. No concessions, finally, were made either to the regional or to the non-French origins of citizens; the only true community was that of the nation. France's state tradition has been identified by Kenneth Dyson as something of an exception in Western Europe. It helped make France especially receptive to the great expansion in the role of the state that occurred throughout the developed capitalist world after 1945.

Dirigisme

A prime example of a state-led consensus between apparently opposed political forces is *dirigisme*, the term coined to characterise the intervention of the state in the post-war economy. *Dirigisme* is worth considering in some detail both because it demonstrates the array of state institutions deployed to manage civil society, and because it will illustrate the difficulties encountered by France in adjusting to a more globalised, liberal world economy.

Like the broader culture of the state, *dirigisme* in France has roots in the *ancien régime*, being especially identified with Louis XIV's minister Colbert. The eighteenth-century French state managed not only clearly strategic activities, such as arsenals, but also those that were less obviously so, such as salt production (for fiscal reasons) or the Gobelins tapestry works (for sumptuary ones). Even in the relatively *laissez-faire* years of the late nineteenth century, the state raised tariff barriers and built railways. But the biggest impulse to *dirigisme* was given in France, as elsewhere, by World War II and its apparent lesson that successful economies were planned economies. Both under the German Occupation and after the Liberation, France's technocrats, and thence the politicians too, rejected the relative economic liberalism of the pre-war years and embraced the new interventionist orthodoxy. That orthodoxy included, as in other post-war West European states, a mix of Keynesian economic policies and social welfarism. It also embraced large-scale industrial interventionism. Herein lay the most specifically French manifestation of the post-war economic consensus. *Dirigisme* in its developed post-war form was a complex phenomenon which may be seen as at least nine different things.

- *An ambition*, an expression of national will by a traditionally active and ambitious state. Provoked by the wounded nationalism of French elites following the defeat of 1940, *dirigisme* was also moulded by a collective awareness of the opportunities of the post-war world, and by an optimistic belief in the capacity of elites to forecast the future, and sustained by self-interested coalitions and a supportive public consensus. The nature of the ambition changed over time: reconstruction after 1945; increasing productivity in the 1950s; the creation of internationally competitive firms in the 1960s and 1970s; a break with capitalism (rather less consensually) in 1981; modernisation and successful insertion into the European open market from the mid-1980s. Each of these ambitions, though, was under-pinned by a common set of 'can-do' assumptions, according to which the state could and should be an active policy initiator in the economy, and wielded the capacity both to plan for the long term, and to impose its will when this was necessary to achieve its policy aims.
- *A shared culture*. The coalition (or unholy alliance) supporting *dirigisme* included modernising technocrats with a taste for economic 'rationality' and 'progress'; Gaullists who viewed the interventionist state as a crucial agent in ensuring France's diplomatic and military status, as well as a stabilising and depoliticising factor in a fractious and overpoliticised country; bureaucrats intent on maximising their budgets; Catholics heedful of the Church's strictures on unrestrained capitalism; the social engineers of social democracy; and Communists whose general penchant for control was reinforced by the awareness of the potential that a big public industrial sector held for them and for their trade-union satellite, the CGT.

Divided in its ideological justifications for *dirigisme*, the coalition still shared a common aversion to what was called *capitalisme sauvage* and indeed to the market in general, and an assumption that heroic state action, for example in financing France's first jet airliner, the Caravelle, in the 1950s, or the high-speed train a generation later, was not merely justified but a positive duty of the state. The tenacity of the *dirigiste* culture can be explained not only by its ability to tap different aspirations, but also by the omnipresence of its proponents, who occupied the senior civil service posts in all ministries, staffed the private offices of politicians of all colours, and the boards of state-run banks and public enterprises, as well as playing a role as opinion-formers through publications and part-time professorships at Sciences Po, the nursery of the political and administrative elite from which they themselves had, in many cases, graduated.

- *An overarching strategy*, defined in the early post-war period by the National Plan – the '*affaire de la nation*' according to its creator Jean Monnet, an 'ardent obligation' for de Gaulle. Starting in 1946 as a broad set of industrial objectives to make good the damages of war, the Plan became increasingly bureaucratic in its elaboration, detailed in its recommendations, and, in an ever more complex environment, inaccurate in its forecasts. By the early 1980s, and despite the election of a Socialist government in 1981, the Plan had suffered the worst of all fates: it was ignored. From the 1970s, the 'overarching strategy' was to be sought more in the industrial policies of successive governments: the identification and strengthening of 'national champion' firms in niche markets under the Giscard d'Estaing presidency (1974–81); the vertical integration of firms through the entire range of activities in a sector under the Socialists after 1981; the promotion of small and medium-sized firms from the late 1980s.

- *A set of state-directed policies*. Through financial aid, ownership, public procurement contracts, research and development assistance, and export drives, the state rationalised large parts of French industry. The state forged alliances between firms, or even mergers (Peugeot-Citröen in automobiles, Rhône-Poulenc in chemicals, Thomson-Brandt-CSF in electronics, Usinor-Sacilor in steel, Péchiney-Ugine-Kuhlman in aluminium), and restructured entire sectors (computers, steel, electronics, electro-nuclear, machine tools, aeronautics). It protected national champions (Bull in computers, Renault in automobiles, Thomson in electronics, CGE in heavy engineering) and nourished lame duck industries (shipyards, textiles, steel, machine tools). Most distinctively, it gave birth to a series of *grands projets* including Concorde (with Britain) in 1965, the Plan Calcul (for the computer industry) in 1966, the more successful Airbus (1969), the Ariane rocket (1973), the Surgénérateur (a French-designed nuclear reactor) in 1974, and the TGV (high-speed train) in 1977.

- *A set of policy instruments*. The French state had a vast range of tools of economic intervention at its disposal. They included one of the largest public sectors in the Western world, created by the Popular Front government of 1936 and the Liberation governments of 1944–47, and extended by the Socialist government of 1981 (as well as through the acquisition and mergers policies of the nationalised industries). By 1982, the state owned thirteen of France's twenty biggest firms and almost the entire French banking sector (a major contrast with Britain). The public sector accounted for 24 per cent of employment, 32 per cent of sales, 30 per cent of exports and, most crucially, 60 per cent of annual investment in the industrial and energy sectors, where private investment had withered in the 1970s. The state held monopolies in gas, electricity and telecommunications. In other sectors, including non-ferrous metals, aerospace, mining, heavy chemicals and petroleum, over half of annual turnover was accounted for by the state. Second, the state controlled the monetary and credit system exercised by the Bank of France, by the Trésor division of the Finance Ministry, and by its satellites such as the Crédit Agricole, the Crédit National, and the Caisse des Dépôts. They fixed interest rates, controlled capital movements, and set credit ceilings to promote modernisation and growth. Initially, much industrial finance emanated directly from the Trésor, but from the 1960s funding tended to come from (state-owned) banks. Bank borrowing soared at low or even negative real interest rates – a situation which was to prove damaging to industry when real interest rates rose sharply from the mid-1970s. By 1981 – *before* the Left won power – 70 per cent of all industrial credit in France was linked in some way to state loans, grants or guarantees – a situation perpetuated by a weak Stock Exchange and under-capitalised firms. The state also possessed the right, by virtue of de Gaulle's *ordonnances* of 1945, to control a vast range of prices; it constantly added to a thicket of regulations covering most branches of economic activity including the labour market (the minimum wage dates from 1950); it used public procurement policies, made possible by the state's role as the country's biggest purchaser of certain goods, to shape the general industrial landscape, control the policies of individual firms, or favour the success of *grands projets*; it deployed a variety of contractual tools, linked to financial inducements, to promote or succour specific sectors or nationalised industries; it wielded an extraordinary array of protectionist devices, whether official or unofficial, open or disguised, to shield French industry and particularly the national champions; it allowed, through inflation in the Fourth Republic and episodically in the Fifth, the burden of state debt which had substituted for the raising of capital to be purged.

• *A dense institutional architecture*. A full description of the institutions involved in French economic policy-making would require a hefty encyclopedia. At the summit, with overall responsibility for macroeconomic, fiscal and monetary policy, were the Presidency (after 1958), the Prime Minister's Office and the Finance Ministry. Microeconomic policy involved the above bodies, but also the Industry Ministry and other ministries such as Defence, Transport or Public Works, as well as the Commissariat Général au Plan. There were also sector-specific bodies such as the Commissariat à l'Énergie Atomique and activity-specific bodies such as ANVAR (Agence Nationale de la Valorisation de la Recherche), as well as the enormous publicly owned banking and industrial sector noted above. This dense variety of institutions was given (some) horizontal co-ordination by an equally dense network of overlapping interministerial committees, with territorial co-ordination being ensured (in principle) by the Délégation à l'Aménagement du Territoire et à l'Action Régionale (DATAR). Within this system, effective internal constraints on state officials were few and weak: autonomous competition authorities were toothless, the Bank of France largely subordinate to the government and generally favourable to investment and growth, and the Cour des Comptes (Court of Accounts) inclined to reveal the misuse of public funds sporadically and late, if at all.

• *A network of interlocking state-based elites*. The power of the senior officials who made *dirigisme* work rested on their common educational origins and the networking that resulted; on the job mobility of key individuals; on their self-proclaimed (but also widely acknowledged) expertise; and on their ubiquity in the decision-making chain. A typical top official is a graduate of one of a small handful of *grandes écoles* and a member of a particular administrative or technical *corps* (such as the Inspection des Finances or the Corps des Mines). Such officials move in the course of a career between mainstream civil service posts in ministries, jobs on ministers' staffs, and positions at the head of public and private firms or of bodies such as the Commissariat au Plan, as well as doing stints as ministers in a few cases. Whereas in Britain experts were supposed to be 'on tap and not on top', in France the same quite small group of individuals, often known to each other, controlled a wide range of public, para-public and even political jobs, and were present at all points in the decision-making process, from initiation to implementation.

- *A rhetorical device.* Successive governments legitimised state intervention in general, and their own interventionist policies in particular, by associating them with vital national ambitions and interests. *Dirigisme* was thus justified in the name of reconstruction (after 1945), industrial competitiveness, especially in the face of the 'American challenge' (in the 1960s and 1970s), the preparation of France for the single European market (from 1986), or social cohesion and regional development (more or less continuously). More specifically, massive aid to France's ailing steel industry was justified in terms of its supposedly strategic place in the national economy, while the Socialists' big nationalisation programme of 1981 was sold to the public in a variety of more or less contradictory ways, each designed to broaden support for the measures by presenting them as a 'national imperative'. The *dirigiste* system had articulate admirers abroad: Andrew Shonfield's influential *Modern Capitalism*, written in 1965, was a brilliant apologia for the French model. At home, where *dirigisme* and the economic success of the post-war generation were linked by most commentators, a cult of heroic founding fathers (Colbert inevitably, but also Jean Monnet, Étienne Hirsch and François Bloch-Lainé, for example) was created and sustained by high priests many of whom held key posts in politics and the administration.

- *A tool of national cohesion.* In a land prone to murderous political divisions, *dirigisme* appeared to be a positive-sum game in which everyone could win: not only the elites who conceived and managed it but also groups that were marginalised from the decision-making processes. The main employers' organisation, the Conseil National du Patronat Français (CNPF), liked the protection and subsidies *dirigisme* offered to the big firms that dominated the body. Trades unions, sidelined from industrial policy-making and often weak on the shop floor, enjoyed substantial side payments in the shape of cash subsidies, privileged positions within the institutions of the French welfare state (particularly the social security system), and an 'inflationary social compromise' that allowed the minimum wage, and thence a broad swathe of industrial wages, to rise at least in line with inflation. More broadly, the *trente glorieuses*, as the French came to describe the three decades of expansion between 1945 and the mid-1970s, saw both the heyday of *dirigisme* and a social transformation of unprecedented dimensions in France: the farming population fell from nearly a third to under a tenth of the total, large-scale urbanisation took place, a chronic housing shortage was gradually ended, and French industry was substantially modernised. This did not happen without widespread unrest among both farmers and industrial workers: the near-general strike of May 1968 bore witness to the discontent of a working class too long excluded from a fair share of the fruits of growth. But in a country as prone to political conflict as France, such events took on a relatively minor dimension. That such massive and rapid change took place so speedily, and with relatively little human suffering and social dislocation, testifies in part to the success of the *dirigiste* model.

The state: image and reality

Both its admirers and its critics tend to cultivate an image of the state as monolithic, tentacular and animated by a single purpose. The reality is very different. As Tocqueville noticed in the mid-nineteenth century, the rules in France are rigid, but their implementation is often flexible. The rhetoric of the state often conceals a reality of grubby compromises with those very interests on which the state is supposed to keep a stern and watchful eye; the state's own servants, far from acting as a single co-ordinated body, often behave as a group of warring factions, with nothing to learn from the politicians about the darker arts of their trade; while the industries under the state's ownership could often escape the control of their shareholder altogether.

- The centralisation of the French state, a legal certainty before the decentralisation reforms of 1982, was nevertheless a practical impossibility. Centralisation was only a French obsession because of the centuries-long struggle to create a state in the face of powerful centrifugal tendencies in the provinces. In most cases, though, local dignitaries, or *notables*, who represented a potential threat to the unity of the state, were domesticated rather than destroyed. The *notables* exacted a continuous price for their co-operation, in the shape of political arrangements, or even subsidies, that allowed them to retain their local ascendancy and pursue their cherished projects while practising a largely formal deference to the central authorities. Candidates at local elections frequently claimed to stand for the 'defence of local interests', by implication against a state considered as interfering and rapacious. The different gradations of *notables* – in small or large municipalities, in *départements* and finally in regions – and the multiplicity of state services under the prefect's notional supervision created a complex web of clientship and complicity stretching from the small provincial *mairie* to Parisian ministries and the National Assembly. The most important *notables*, men like Jacques Chaban-Delmas, mayor of Bordeaux, or Pierre Mauroy, mayor of Lille, enjoyed regular access to government members (even when they were not prime minister, as each of these two was for three years) and commanded obedience of a more or less obsequious variety from all in their local strongholds, including the representatives of the state: a degree of authority that earned them the feudal nicknames of the Duke of Aquitaine and the Count of Flanders.
- The Jacobin claim that the state represented the 'general interest' and remained aloof from those 'partial interests', constituted by associations and pressure groups which threatened to perturb the serene and enlightened deliberations of government, was always based more on myth than on fact. The better-organised groups were able to buy influence, more or less discreetly. At local level, all six Deputies elected to the National Assembly in 1951 for the *département* of Calvados (famous then as now for its apple brandy) had promised in their personal manifestos to

defend the interests of the *bouilleurs de cru*, the home distillers' lobby. More tragic-ally, the Algerian policy of successive Fourth Republic governments, whether Left- or Right-leaning, was prey to the activities of the colonial lobby, constituted around large farming and wine-growing interests in the fertile valley south of Algiers, which opposed every concession to the Muslim population of Algeria until it was too late.

- The claim to represent the 'general interest' was further undermined by the ten-dency of strategically placed groups of the state's servants to negotiate privileged conditions of employment. Teachers, rail workers or employees of Électricité de France (EDF), for example, won benefits in kind such as a 'thirteenth month' of pay, shorter working hours, or early retirement. Observers like François de Closets have pilloried such privileges, often unfairly: but it has sometimes been the case that the 'defence of French-style public services' cited as justification of strike action by public employees has corresponded to the defence of their own perks, or *avantages acquis*.

- Even the Church has been able to impose itself as a necessary interlocutor of the secular state. A stout anti-clerical like the Interior Minister Georges Clemenceau felt obliged to intervene to ensure that the inventory of Church property under-taken in the aftermath of the Separation of 1905 was done with a minimum of respect for Catholic sensitivities. Nearly eighty years later, Pierre Mauroy's Social-ist government sought the Church's agreement to his proposed reform of Catholic schools (he sought in vain, and intense Catholic pressure sank the reform and helped destroy the Mauroy government). The Church at local level has been a necessary link in the networks of *notables* in Catholic areas.

- *Dirigisme* was often operated with much more flexibility than the *dirigiste* model suggests. The substantial state presence in the economy should not obscure con-tinued private involvement even in sectors considered elsewhere, at least in the post-war period, as 'natural' public-sector domains. The social security system, for instance, was officially administered by the 'social partners' – unions and employ-ers – with only periodic interventions from the state (chiefly in the form of bail-out packages, which became ever more frequent). Water was never nationalised. Local authorities were free to choose between direct control of water purification and distribution, a concession to a private firm, or a mixed solution; and France duly built up world-class private water companies. Motorways, largely built by private firms in return for toll concessions, are another example. The *sociétés d'économie mixte*, firms combining public and private finance, were a commonplace in the large-scale urban development of the post-war generation. Outside economic sec-tors in crisis, *dirigisme* rarely took the form of detailed state intervention; more frequently it took the form of a statement of ambition plus a set of financial inducements, or even, as in the aerospace industry, simply a general framework.

- The unity of the state was a judicial fiction, not a practical reality, its effectiveness often more mythical than tangible. At local level, for example, successive laws reaffirming the prefects' primacy at the head of the state's services in the *départe-ments* testified to the constant difficulty they experienced in making that primacy effective. Industrial *dirigisme*, meanwhile, was constantly hindered by the density of the institutional structure. Most major industrial policies required the interven-tion of several ministries, the Commissariat au Plan, DATAR, the banks and other credit organisations, and subnational field services and funding agencies.

Moreover, France's tightly knit and expert civil service elite was often riven with vicious rivalries between and within ministries, banks and other bodies, while the expertise was often of the wrong sort, placing the state at a disadvantage in relation to private industry. As to the vast public industrial sector, it became an incoherent patchwork created by political acts but extended by the acquisition policies of nationalised firms. It included lame ducks in need of constant and often ineffective subsidy, but also highly profitable firms like the state-owned oil companies CFP and Elf, or EDF, which tended to run themselves, on more or less conventional business lines, independently from the ministries that supposedly supervised them. The result was an industrial policy that was cumbersome, time-consuming and politicised, as well as inconsistent both over time and between different institutions in the process (so that the allocation of credit, for example, often bore little relation to the priorities of the Plan). Though a handful of flagship *grands projets*, such as Caravelle, succeeded, others, such as the Plan Calcul, were spectacular and expensive disasters.

Less ubiquitous and less effective than often alleged, France's state remained more ubiquitous (and, much of the time, more effective) than many of its West European counterparts. And the state tradition has been as much a part of France's political culture as the legacy of political division. Both, however, have been endangered, to a greater or lesser extent, by the changing context of French, of European and of global politics.

The changing context of French political traditions

Over the six decades since World War II, France, like most other West European countries, has sustained the impact of, first the long post-war boom, second, the complex series of developments known as globalisation, and third, the European integration process. Each of these developments transformed the context of political conflict in France. The second and third also represented direct challenges to many aspects of France's state tradition.

Post-war boom: *the* trente glorieuses

The *trente glorieuses* is a somewhat misleading but widely used term describing the post-war boom: it took six post-war years simply to return to the levels of production of 1929, and the boom was over by 1975. That France experienced quite unprecedented growth levels, however, is beyond dispute. At an average of over 5 per cent, growth was faster than in Britain or the United States throughout the period; towards the end of the boom it was even faster than West Germany's. In economic terms, the *trente glorieuses* involved three distinct processes that flowed into one another without interruption: post-war reconstruction, the completion of France's industrial revolution, and the beginning of a transition towards a service-based, post-industrial economy. In social terms, the *trente glorieuses* wrought transformations of unprecedented scope and speed, which had the potential to transform the bases of political alignments. These transformations included: a drop in the agricultural population; a rise in the numbers of almost every other occupational category, both blue- and (especially) white-collar; the arrival of new entrants to the labour market, notably immigrants and women;

urbanisation and a generation-long housing crisis; dechristianisation; a rise in educational attainment; and a growth in personal consumption.

- The agricultural population fell from well over a quarter in 1945 to under 10 per cent (and falling) thirty years later, the rural population from 46 per cent to under 30. The proportion of the French who were self-employed fell from nearly a third at the Liberation to 18 per cent in 1962 (and 12 per cent in 1982): France became, overwhelmingly, a nation of wage- and salary-earners. The France of the small family firm and the small family farm, fundamental bases of French politics for a century and a half, shrank at an unprecedented rate – not without provoking vigorous, at times violent, protests both from farm unions and from small traders (briefly organised, during the Fourth Republic, as the Poujadist movement).
- With industrial growth, in sectors as varied as petrochemicals, automobiles, aerospace, or building and public works, went a corresponding increase in the number of blue-collar workers, which peaked in 1970 at just over 9 million. This growth, though significant, was still limited: the Left in France never had a working-class base as large as that of, say, Britain at its peak. Moreover, unskilled labour was increasingly recruited from former African colonies, and first-generation immigrants lacked the vote.
- The fastest-growing occupational categories were white-collar workers of all kinds, in both public and private sectors; managers; and professionals. This development corresponded to a threefold development in the economy; the 'managerial revolution' within firms; the growth of the private service sector; and the growth of areas of the public sector such as healthcare and education. The new, salaried middle classes became more numerous than the old ones (professionals and independent business people) which had formed the recruiting ground for the political elites of the Third Republic.
- Women entered the labour market in ever larger numbers, filling many of the new white-collar jobs in both public and private sectors: some 45 per cent of women of working age did paid work in 1970, compared with just 25 per cent a generation earlier (the figure would rise to 80 per cent by 1999). This growing economic integration was barely matched by progress towards political equality: women only won the vote in 1944, and were still woefully under-represented in both parliament and government thirty years later.
- The labour shortage that France experienced until the late 1960s was filled partly by women, but also partly by immigrants, who often took over low-income, low-status jobs that French people were able to refuse. In 1931, France had been home to nearly 3 million immigrants, mostly from the Iberian peninsula, Italy and Central and Eastern Europe. The new immigrants came from Iberia but also from the Maghrib, the former North African colonies of Morocco, Algeria and Tunisia. At first they were working men and were expected to return to their country of origin. But by the end of the *trente glorieuses*, many had been joined by their families. Temporary immigration became permanent, adding a new element to France's already varied racial mix and raising the question of the integration of immigrants and their families and their accession to at least some of the rights of French citizens.
- The France of the *trente glorieuses* suffered from a chronic housing crisis, caused by low levels of construction in the inter-war years, wartime damage, population

growth (by nearly 30 per cent, from 40.5 to 52.5 million, between 1946 and 1975) and the rural exodus. The state's response, as elsewhere in Europe, was to build fast and cheap: over a generation, the Nissen huts and shanty towns that had accommodated poor families were replaced by *habitations à loyer modéré* (HLMs). Initially, this improved the quality of the housing stock dramatically: three-quarters of French homes had indoor toilets in 1975, against a mere 40 per cent in 1962. The cost, however, was that the HLM estates, typically built on cheap land on the peripheries of cities, were often surpassingly ugly and disagreeable to live in, and aged badly. If the quantitative housing crisis was over by the mid-1970s, a qualitative crisis was just beginning, as some estates began to show concentrations of delapidation, unemployment and crime of all kinds.

- As the cities and the hastily built suburban housing estates filled, the churches emptied. While about 70 per cent of the French still consider themselves to be Catholics, weekly attendance at Mass fell from just under 40 per cent in the immediate post-war years to some 9 per cent by 1998. The number of priests fell by nearly a third, from 41,000 to 28,000, between 1960 and 1982, and the average age of those remaining rose to nearly 60. The crisis of priestly vocations reflected a wider loss of Church influence in the wider French society, with mainstream attitudes to a variety of questions, especially those relating to sexuality, increasingly at odds with the teachings of the Church.

- The *trente glorieuses* were marked by a rapid general expansion of education, with the Fouchet reforms of 1963 guaranteeing at least some secondary education for all. As late as 1965, barely 10 per cent of French school leavers possessed the *baccalauréat*, the high school certificate that guarantees entry into university. By 1975, the figure was 25 per cent. Student numbers rose from 186,000 in 1959 to 615,000 a decade later. The result, in terms of overcrowding and poor facilities in both secondary and tertiary education, contributed to the student unrest of May 1968. But the expansion continued with barely a pause, and with little change to the centralised model established under Ferry. In a context of full employment with a growing number of qualified jobs available, the education system appeared to be more than ever filling its Republican role of *ascenseur social*, offering growing opportunities for upward social mobility.

- If there was less God in the France of the *trente glorieuses*, there was also a great deal more Mammon, for with growth went hitherto undreamt-of levels of personal consumption. There were a million television sets in France in 1960, for example, but ten times that number by 1970. The fruits of growth were unevenly distributed, but everyone got a share of sorts. The working class, therefore, was not only more numerous than in the pre-war years; it was also, by 1970, significantly more prosperous. The workers whose strikes nearly toppled the régime in May 1968 could still be placated by a larger slice of the cake – whatever the strictures of the students who rioted at the same time against the empty values of *la société de consommation*.

In the 1970s, French electoral sociologists suggested that these developments opened new opportunities for the Left: the Right's traditional bases in farms and small businesses, or among Catholics, were shrinking fast, while typically left-voting groups, such as schoolteachers or other white-collar public servants, were growing. Events from the end of the *trente glorieuses* revealed a more complex reality: a working class whose size and loyalty to the Left began to diminish; and a better-educated population that showed a growing scepticism about the more ideological claims of both Left and Right, and indeed about the notions of Left and Right themselves. As we shall see, the major long-term effects of the *trente glorieuses* were to soften the old divide between Right and Left while opening up new areas of political conflict. Those effects were accelerated in many ways by the economic crisis that followed.

Globalisation

The West's post-war boom was abruptly closed by the oil price rise of 1973–74. What had initially appeared as a temporary inflationary crisis lifted the curtain on three much more durable phenomena, which persisted long after real oil prices had returned to their pre-1973 levels. These were, first, the end of the industrialised capitalist world's very high post-war growth rates along with their causes – post-war reconstruction and the productivity gains attendant on the completion of industrialisation; second, a world of permanently free-floating exchange rates, heralded by America's effective destruction, in 1971, of the Bretton Woods system of fixed rates that had underpinned the boom; and third, the intensifying worldwide capitalist competition known as globalisation.

Globalisation may be seen as having four dimensions – technological, ideological, commercial and cultural. All are linked, and all have the effect of diminishing the capacity of individual nation states to implement fully independent economic policies – especially when such policies incline to *dirigisme*.

- *The technological dimension* to globalisation, at its simplest level, means that big reductions in transport costs have made it far cheaper to move goods around the world. More important, perhaps, has been the revolution in information technology which has made it incomparably cheaper and quicker to generate, access and transfer around the world all manner of data. Five effects of that deserve to be highlighted, since they have clearly impacted on the French economic model. First, technology has made a major contribution to opening up the world's financial markets, allowing decisions to buy or sell financial products to be implemented instantaneously across continents. Second, technology has transformed some 'natural' national monopolies into sectors susceptible to both domestic and international competition, undermining one of the main arguments in favour of state control: telecommunications and electricity supply are good examples of sectors in which barriers to competition are slowly, if reluctantly, being removed. Third, technology has changed the perception among policy-makers of what a 'strategic' industry is: no longer steel but electronics, no longer ship-building but computer software. Fourth, technology has brought far greater flexibility to formerly rigid aspects of the manufacturing process such as car assembly lines, and facilitated the 'outsourcing' of any number of formerly core activities. It is now possible to envisage a car manufacturer that makes no cars at all, but puts out to tender the whole succession of processes from design to manufacture, from marketing to distribution. Fifth, rapid technological change plus complacent management can quickly transform national champions (of whatever nation) into international lame ducks, as the painful lessons of America's IBM, Holland's Philips, or France's Bull show.
- *The ideological dimension* of globalisation arises from the progressive rejection by Western policy-makers, from the mid-1970s on, of the post-war Keynesian

economic consensus which favoured extensive state intervention in capitalist economies via regulation or ownership of firms, managed exchange rates and the use of demand management (through, for example, budget deficits) to moderate the fluctuations of the business cycle. By the mid-1970s, Bretton Woods had collapsed, state-owned firms were increasingly criticised as inefficient, and, above all, Keynesian techniques offered no remedy to the inflation which ravaged the major capitalist economies from 1973. The ideological paradigm shift away from Keynesianism and towards neo-liberal economic policies established new orthodoxies, each more favourable to capital than to labour. These included deregulation and trade liberalisation (within the financial markets, liberalisation was inseparable from the process of technological change); the encouragement by governments of direct inward investment from abroad; prudent exchange rate policies (in a world where the markets determine the value of currencies from day to day, with often brutal fluctuations); stricter fiscal discipline, with a greater inclination to balance budgets; tight controls on public spending (even at the cost of demolishing parts of the post-war welfare state); privatisation; tax reform (often in the direction of lowering tax rates on the wealthy and on corporate profits); more flexible labour markets (even at the price of withdrawing elements of social protection for employees); and wage cost containment (if necessary, via restrictions on the activities of trade unions).

- *The commercial dimension* of globalisation is the outcome of the technological and ideological changes noted above. Trade liberalisation (notably through the successive rounds of tariff reductions organised under the auspices of the General Agreement on Trade and Tariffs (GATT), but also the extension of capitalist trading relations to the former Communist countries of Eastern Europe and to China) has combined with technological change to expand the volume of world trade. Deregulation plus new technologies have rendered the financial markets busier (in terms of the volume of transactions handled), more rapid and more powerful. Flows of inward and outward investment have grown. And major enterprises have been increasingly obliged to become multinational in terms of turnover, domestic content, research alliances and production ventures – effectively shedding part or even all of their national identity. Regulation of these processes, finally, has become increasingly transnational.

- *The cultural dimension* of globalisation is closely related to the commercial one. With the growth of world trade have come the homogenisation of consumption patterns and the spread of world brands such as Coca-Cola, McDonald's, Levi's or Microsoft, as well as of world (typically American, or at least 'Anglo-Saxon') products in film, TV and popular music. The growth of world trade has also confirmed English as the international language of business, and as a necessary tool of communication for growing numbers of non-native English speakers.

France has undergone this complex series of processes with varying degrees of willingness. Successive French governments, through the intermediary of Europe since 1960, have been signatories to successive tariff-reducing GATT agreements; efforts to route imports of Japanese video cassette recorders through an obscure customs post in Poitiers (in 1982) or to negotiate quotas on Japanese cars (through the 1980s) had the air of rearguard actions. Nationalised French firms – especially EDF (electricity) and GDF (gas) bought into their privatised counterparts abroad, but retained their own protected status until after 2002. The technological aspects have been experienced less as an actor (aside from detours like the Minitel, a precocious but very slow French precursor of the Internet) than as a consumer; French firms have been neither especially quick nor hopelessly slow to apply information technologies. The cultural dimension of globalisation is clearly perceived by many French policy-makers as a threat. Hence, for example, the legal requirement that at least 40 per cent of songs broadcast on French radio stations should be in French, and that proceedings of conferences and seminars conducted on French territory should be in French; and the French government's readiness, in 1993, to delay or even to wreck the Uruguay Round of tariff cuts in order to preserve the 'cultural exception' of film and TV from the dangers of wholly free trade; or the heroic, if largely futile, attempts of the Académie Française to prevent the purity of the French language from being sullied by the incorporation of English words. The ideological paradigm shift, finally, developed among France's administrative elites from the late 1970s onwards, but was slower to affect the political elite or the wider population. This was hardly surprising. If globalisation imposed painful adjustments away from the post-war consensus on every developed capitalist economy, its implications for France were peculiarly wide-ranging. Without a return to protectionism, an economic model centred on state-led projects, subsidised and undercapitalised national champions, whether government-owned or not, and a thicket of national regulations could not long compete in a world of multinational corporations, free capital flows, acquisitions and mergers, and multilateral trade regulations; globalisation, in other words, threatened the whole edifice of *dirigisme*. A return to protectionism and an alternative national economic policy was seriously considered by President Mitterrand during the monetary crisis of March 1983, but decisively rejected. To have done otherwise would have been to reverse the process of European integration, the third of the long developments that has transformed the context of French politics.

Europe

France, along with Italy, West Germany and the Benelux states, was a signatory to the Treaty of Rome, creating the European Economic Community (EEC), in March 1957. The 'construction of Europe', towards which the Rome Treaty was the most decisive step, has been seen as an opportunity by the French in three ways. First, it has been the framework for a new relationship with Germany. Reconciliation, after three wars in the space of a single lifetime (in 1870, 1914 and 1939), was a major achievement, but paralleled by two less lofty aims: the 'containment' of an economically resurgent Federal Republic and the use of what became a special relationship to dominate the EEC. Second, French governments, with some misgivings, viewed Europe and the free trade it promised as an engine of economic growth: most obviously, as a market for France's burgeoning farm exports, but also as a means to force modernisation on French industry, newly exposed to the bracing winds of competition from other member states. Third, Europe offered France an opportunity, in de Gaulle's (private) words, to 'regain the status she lost at the battle of Waterloo, as the first among nations'. If this grandiose ambition appears fanciful, Europe has nevertheless enabled France to 'punch above its weight' in diplomatic terms. Of the other two large founding members of the EEC, Italy has not aspired to take on a role of leadership in Europe since Mussolini, and Germany was both divided and diplomatically disabled by the legacy of World War II: an economic giant but a political pygmy. By a process of elimination France, as one of the victors in World War II and (from 1960) as an atomic power, could therefore aspire to speak for the original six.

Such opportunities had a price: the partial surrender of national sovereignty. France was more sensitive than any other original member state to this issue. The 'ever-closer union' inscribed in the Treaty of Rome challenges the sovereignty of member states in five ways. First, its institutional processes offer at least the theoretical possibility, since the introduction in 1986 of qualified majority voting on the EEC's chief law-making body, the Council of Ministers, that a member state may be outvoted, thereby being forced by 'Europe' to implement policies it has opposed. Second, the EU is distinguished from most other international organisations in its possession of a body of law with a system of courts able, in principle, to sanction member states and businesses for infringements of EU law. Third, the range of policies in which Europe now has a hand – including, for example, regional aid, scientific research, the environment, immigration and foreign policy – has forced governments to include a European division in almost every national ministry and to take the European framework into account in almost every major political decision. Although the extent of Europe's involvement in different policy areas varies (and may, in some sectors, even diminish over time), the exercise of core EEC competences in the areas of free trade and competition has become steadily more invasive, especially since the late 1980s. The 1992 Maastricht Treaty on European Union represented a new threshold in this respect, when member states (other than the UK) agreed to establish a single European currency, to surrender monetary policy to a new European Central Bank, and to respect a constraining set of 'convergence criteria' aimed at limiting inflation, public debt and budgetary deficits. Fourth, member states can no longer fix their own trade policy. Since the Rome Treaty the European Commission has undertaken international trade negotiations, and notably the various rounds of multilateral reductions under the GATT and more recently of the World Trade Organisation (WTO), on behalf of member states. While only the Council of Ministers can set the final seal to any such agreement, the pressures on an individual member state, both from European negotiators and from other member states, to sacrifice national interests to the collective good, are considerable. Finally, while a big member state like France could be confident, in the early, small, EEC, of defending its national interests in Europe by simple self-assertion, such a calculation is less readily made in a European Union of twenty-five states.

All European heads of state and government, including the French, have had to weigh the benefits of European integration against the costs. Guy Mollet, the Fourth Republic prime minister who signed the Rome Treaty in 1957, took care to limit its supranational provisions in order to be sure of his parliamentary support: the Treaty was ratified by just 59 per cent of French Deputies (342 to 239). De Gaulle was prepared to halt both the 'enlargement' of Europe (by his veto of British entry into the EEC) and its 'deepening' (by preserving the national veto on all European legislation), in order to preserve his conception of French sovereignty. His successors have been less reserved. Each has agreed to the entry of new member states, to the reinforcement of European institutions and to the extension of European competences. France has not thereby been integrated into a new federal super-state, but the untrammelled exercise of national sovereignty, viewed by de Gaulle as a central aim of policy, has nevertheless been constrained in important ways. It was characteristic, moreover, of much of the first half-century of European integration that the initiatives and debates were carried on chiefly at elite level, rather than being brought into the hurly-burly of democratic politics. When the voters were involved, however, their generally favourable predisposition towards 'building Europe' often gave way to mistrust – of the specific European measures proposed, of the politicians proposing them, or both. The referendum of September 1992 on the Maastricht Treaty passed by the narrowest of margins. That of May 2005, on the European constitutional treaty, provoked a decisive no from the French electorate, much to the discomfiture of the president, Jacques Chirac, who proposed it.

Together, these three large-scale developments – two successive economic transformations, plus France's integration into an increasingly supranational form of polity – challenged the models both of political conflict and of the state with which the French of the post-war generation had grown up. But the transformation was a partial one; one of the tensions in contemporary French politics is between the novelty of many of the stakes of politics and the survival of the landmarks and shibboleths of an earlier age.

Political conflict and the state: transformations

The political changes undergone by France can be summarised under three headings. First, several conflicts inherited from the Third Republic have been laid to rest, or at least moderated to a significant degree. Second, a variety of external and internal factors have combined to undermine important aspects of France's state tradition, whether the Republican triptych or the *dirigiste* edifice. Third, these two developments have meant a redrawing of the lines of political conflict, but not their complete transformation.

Zones of consensus

France's traditional lack of consensus on the nature of the régime was effectively ended halfway through the *trente glorieuses* (though as Chapter 2 will show, this owed more to the crisis in Algeria than to France's economic development). The referendum establishing the Fifth Republic, and with it a strengthened presidency, was passed in September 1958 by 79.2 per cent of the voters. Four years later, de Gaulle's revision of his 'own' constitution, establishing the direct election of the president, was approved by 62 per cent. For a while François Mitterrand continued to refer to the régime as a 'permanent coup d'État'; and the constitution has been revised, sometimes in important ways, sixteen times since 1962. But in retrospect, the referendum of 1962 can be seen as a closure of debates over the fundamentals of the régime. In particular, it signalled the acceptance, first by the electorate and then, more slowly, by the political elite (including Mitterrand), that the Republic was compatible with a strong presidency: a striking reversal of the older tradition that equated the Republic with a parliamentary régime. The Fifth Republic survived de Gaulle's resignation in April 1969. Five years later, it survived the election of a president from the non-Gaullist Right (Valéry Giscard d'Estaing), following Georges Pompidou's sudden death in office. In 1981, the constitution passed the ultimate test of allowing peaceful alternation in power when François Mitterrand led the Socialists to victories in both presidential and parliamentary elections. Constitutional debate continues, notably over questions as important as the independence of the judiciary or the practice of multiple (national and local) elective office-holding. But it has lost the passion and urgency it provoked in the 150 years after the Revolution. Nearly 70 per cent of the electorate abstained at the September 2000 referendum that reduced the presidential term from seven years to five; opinion polls found that a majority of abstentionists considered high petrol prices a more important issue (though interestingly, it was in the debates over the European constitutional treaty in 2005 that some of the old passions over institutional questions were revived).

The political stability afforded by the new régime contributed to the acceleration of growth in the 1960s, but also to the (near-)resolution of the question of Church–state relations. The Debré Law of 1959, allowing state subsidies to Church schools under certain conditions, was, it is true, opposed by a vast petition that attracted the signatures of over 70 per cent of the voters in twenty of France's ninety-six *départements*. But once passed, it stuck. Subsequent attempts to modify the delicate balance it established between public (secular) and private (religious) education provoked mass demonstrations on either side, notably in 1984 and 1994, and were abandoned. France's remaining practising Catholics went on voting disproportionately to the Right. Yet the religious issue has lost the power to envenom political debate that it undoubtedly possessed at the start of the twentieth century. And the notion of *laïcité* has been transferred, as we shall see, to the quite different issue of headscarves on Muslim girls.

The resolution of the questions of the régime and the Church emptied France's Left–Right division of part of its substance. Late twentieth-century opinion polls showed that at least three out of five of the French – 62 per cent in 1996 – thought the Left–Right division 'out of date'. Even the division centred on class and the management of the economy had blurred somewhat after the great U-turn of 1983, when François Mitterrand turned away from the Socialist policies on which he had been elected and accepted the full implications of living in an open economy. Despite the revival of the far Left from the late twentieth century, it is unlikely that any new Socialist campaign would promise a 'rupture with capitalism'; no election would be seen, as those of 1978 and 1981 were by both politicians and observers, as entailing a *choix de société* – a *systemic* choice between capitalism and socialism. All governments will govern within capitalism, using their limited margins of manoeuvre in somewhat different ways, but also in unexpectedly similar ones: by 2002 the Left, for example, had been responsible for a greater volume of privatisations, in money terms, than the Right.

The blurring of the traditional divisions has been compounded by the unprecedented frequency of *alternance*, of the handover of power between Right and Left after elections. In 1981 this was a novelty for the French. The Third and Fourth Republics saw coalitions, usually of Centre-Right or Centre-Left, form and re-form according to the shifting balance of parliamentary arithmetic. The Fifth Republic translated the Left–Right division into practical politics, notably by providing for the direct election of the president at two ballots, with only two candidates present at the run-off. But for the first twenty-three years of the Fifth Republic the Right ruled without interruption. The *alternance* of 1981, on the other hand, was the first of many: in 1986, 1988, 1993, 1997 and 2002, the voters threw out an incumbent government and replaced it with one of the opposite political stamp. Moreover, the time lag between the presidential term of seven years and the parliamentary one of five ensured that in 1986, 1993 and 1997, the president and the parliamentary majority, and hence the government, were on opposite sides: a left-wing president (Mitterrand) with right-wing governments in 1986 and 1993, a right-wing president (Chirac) with a left-wing government in 1997. This 'cohabitation' between president and government combined with the frequency of *alternance* to render the Left–Right division banal. Despite regular skirmishes between the two sides on each occasion, cohabitation also obliged the leaders of Right and Left to work together from day to day over months or years. In doing so, it definitively buried the notion of 'civil war by other means' which had marked Left–Right political relations, with more or less intensity, for two centuries.

The configuration of Left–Right relations was also altered by the decline of the two great political forces to have emerged from the years of Occupation: Communism and Gaullism. The Communists' share of the vote fell from a quarter to a fifth at the outset of the Fifth Republic in 1958, but then stabilised. The real decline began two decades later: in the 1980s the Communist electorate shrank from over 20 per cent to well under 10. The consequences reached far beyond the realm of electoral politics. Marxists lost the high ground of intellectual debate that they had occupied – almost alone, it seemed at times – since 1945. And the non-Communist Left was no longer obliged to accept the limits on the range of acceptable policies imposed by an alliance with a powerful Communist partner, a change that in turn contributed to the ideological shift away from *dirigisme* discussed above. The Gaullists, for their part, lost both their hegemony on the Right and much of their political distinctiveness after de Gaulle's resignation in 1969. Their share of the vote halved from some two-fifths in 1968 to one-fifth ten years later. And the necessity of alliance with the non-Gaullist Right, plus the progressive replacement of the Resistance generation in the party leadership by younger men, turned the Gaullists into something closer to a commonplace conservative party than they had been in the General's day – an evolution carried to its term with the creation of the UMP, a party combining both Gaullists and much of the non-Gaullist moderate Right, in 2002. Widely different causes fed into the decline of the two parties: for example, the shrinkage of the blue-collar working class and the progressive discredit of the Soviet model for the Communists, and the progressive diffusion of the General's legacy throughout the political system for the Gaullists. But there were elements in common, too: the passing of the Resistance generation, and the rejection, after 1968, of an authoritarian style of politics that each party, in its own way, represented. The double decline meant not the disappearance, but the weakening, of elements that had shaped the singularity of French politics in the post-war generation.

The dismantling of dirigisme

The decline of Communism and Gaullism was paralleled by that of the economic structure that they had done much, between them, to create; for much of the apparatus of *dirigisme* was dismantled after the turning point of March 1983. On the Left, the emblematic figure of this policy shift was Pierre Bérégovoy, Socialist finance minister from 1984 to 1986 and 1988 to 1992, and prime minister from April 1992 to March 1993 (he committed suicide shortly after the Left's electoral defeat in 1993); on the Right it was Édouard Balladur, Gaullist finance minister from 1986 to 1988, and prime minister from 1993 to 1995. Firms nationalised by Socialists in 1981, or even in the Liberation era of 1944–46, were first freed to manage their affairs as they wished and then privatised in successive waves, under governments of the Right (1986–88 and 1993–97) but also of the Left (1997–2002). Practically no state-owned firm remains in what had been seen as the 'competitive' sector; not only industrial companies like St-Gobain or Renault but also banks and insurance firms like BNP or UAP that had underpinned the state's former *de facto* control of credit passed into the hands of private shareholders, many of them foreign; they became less and less tied to the state, and indeed, as they sought and found overseas partners and shareholders, less and less national too. More-over, under European pressure, state monopolies formerly seen as 'natural' had to be progressively opened to competition: by the late 1990s that had happened, for example, to telecommunications, electricity distribution, airlines and even, to a limited extent, rail transport. The Paris stock market was liberalised from 1984 to allow undercapital-ised French firms to build up their equity; the Socialists also began a steady build-down of corporate taxation rates. Budgetary constraints as well as the increasingly vigilant eye of Europe meant that national champions were less likely to be bailed out by public subsidy if they turned into lame ducks; rescues, commonplace in the 1970s and early 1980s, were progressively scaled down, though not before some particularly costly cases (Air France and Crédit Lyonnais) in the mid-1990s. The regulatory structures of the *dirigiste* model were cut back: the Left ended the automatic link between the minimum wage and inflation while the Right abolished controls on prices and foreign exchange. Controls on hiring and firing, abandoned by the Right after 1986, were never fully restored under the Left. Meanwhile the Plan, in decline by the mid-1970s, fell into even greater oblivion (before being abolished altogether in October 2005). Some of the *grands projets* characteristic of the *dirigiste* model were transferred to Europe for reasons of cost. Within the state machine, finally, there was a reshuffling of power, with a strengthening of the two major bastions of financial orthodoxy, the Finance Ministry and the Bank of France (independent from 1993, though superseded in its essential role by the European Central Bank from 1999), and the weakening of the Industry Ministry, DATAR and, of course, the Commissariat au Plan, all of *dirigiste* leanings. Not surpris-ingly, this was reflected in policy, and especially in the abandonment of the 'inflationary social compromise' which had provided a safety valve for the rapid transformations of the *trente glorieuses*. From 1983 the priorities of successive governments, of both Left and Right, shifted from the maintenance of something close to full employment, and the protection of the purchasing power of the employed, to the elimination of inflation and the limitation of both budgetary and trade deficits.

On orthodox criteria, both the policy of 'competitive disinflation' and the progressive dismantling of *dirigisme* were a resounding success. From 1992 to 2003, France ran a consistent trade surplus averaging nearly 1.7 per cent of GDP. Inflation has fallen to levels close to or below those of Germany. France under Mitterrand won praise from the London *Financial Times* for the soundness of its economic policies. The value of the franc stabilised against the deutschmark, after a last crisis in August 1992, and France's passage to the euro in 1999–2002 passed off smoothly. Meanwhile, French firms rose to the challenge of liberalisation by looking abroad and diversifying. The growth in the number and size of French multinationals has been remarkable. In 1994, France had the largest number of multinational firms after Germany, Japan, Switzerland and the USA, with companies like AXA (which took over its sleepy French competitor UAP) or Total-Fina-Elf being clearly world-class. French firms have been particularly active in the international mergers and acquisitions market: happily in the case of Renault's links with Nissan, disastrously in that of the takeover in 2000 of Seagram's, owners of Hollywood's Universal Studios, by Vivendi, whose core business was water distribution in France. And among major European Union countries, France was second only to Britain, over the years 1990 to 2003, in its capacity to attract foreign direct investment, from the Far East but also from the United States.

But the dismantling of *dirigisme* and the policy shift that went with it have had costs. Chief among these has been unemployment, which doubled from just under 1.5 million at the Left's victory in 1981 to some 3 million by the time of the Socialist defeat twelve years later. This record had several linked causes: slow growth resulting from the high real interest rates required to maintain the franc–deutschmark parity; the loss of industrial jobs, common to the developed world, to countries with low labour costs; the curtailment of bail-outs; the 'delocalisation' of such jobs away from developed countries by multinationals; the continuing perception of France as an over-regulated, over-taxed, high-wage-cost economy. Unemployment has now persisted at 9 per cent or more of the workforce for nearly twenty-five years; it has contributed, along with part-time working and fixed-term contracts, to a poverty level of some 5 million in France. And it has been disproportionately cruel to women, immigrants, the unskilled and the young, with between a fifth and a quarter of the workforce aged 18 to 25 out of work. That development undermined a crucial element of the republican model, the *ascenseur social*: for the rising generations, education, ever more widely available, was no longer a guarantee of a job, let alone of upward social mobility. Opinion polls from the early 1990s on showed that for the first time since 1945, most French parents expected their children to live no better, and possibly less well, than they did. The popularity of books such as Viviane Forrester's *L'horreur économique* illustrates a widespread sensitivity to the threats posed by globalisation, whether to agriculture, to industrial jobs, to public services or to non-'Anglo-Saxon' cultures. 'Delocalisations', though minor in the statistics of job losses, loom large in the public imagination and invite politicians to demand their prevention. And there is no counterbalancing discourse of comparable popular influence in France to argue that globalisation can bring benefits, or that it is inevitable, or even that France could adjust to it while preserving its essential values.

The state tradition: challenges from within

Under external pressure from Europe and from the markets, the French state has been quite radically, and painfully, redefined by comparison with the recent *dirigiste* past. But it has also faced internal challenges which have eroded some of its strongest 'Jacobin' characteristics. Three are worth mentioning briefly here.

- *Decentralisation*, or failing that the 'defence of local liberties', is an aspiration as old as the French state itself, typically invoked by oppositions and ignored by parties in power. The Left, condemned to twenty-three years of national opposition under the Fifth Republic but still retaining important local positions, had ample opportunity to meditate on, and attack with more or less sincerity, the intrusiveness of central government. Unusually, it also chose to act once in power, after the presidential and parliamentary election victories of 1981. The decentralisation legislation of 1982–83 brought substantial modifications to the Jacobin model. Directly elected regional councils were established. The powers of prefects, both as supervisors able to accept or reject all municipal acts and as the chief executives of the hundred *départements*, the middle tier of French local government, were severely clipped. Local authorities enjoyed new freedoms to finance their own projects without seeking project-specific grants from the state. The Right denounced the reforms nationally but soon benefited from them locally, after a series of local election victories in 1983–85. That helped to ensure a consensual basis for the main thrust of decentralisation. More generally, what had in principle (though not always in practice) been a hierarchical set of relationships with the state, acting through the prefect and other representatives on the ground, as the supreme arbiter of local destinies, turned into a more complex, and more equal, set of partnerships in which the co-operation of local and regional authorities with the state had to be sought rather than demanded or simply assumed. Subnational government has thereby been strengthened as an economic player: certain regions and *départements* and a small number of urban areas have emerged as economic actors and arenas in their own right. In terms of service delivery, on the other hand, subnational government continued to play a lesser role than in many other European states. In 2003, for example, total spending by local and regional author-ities, at about 163 billion euros, was well under half the amount spent by central government (excluding the social security system). The Raffarin government appointed in 2002 (Raffarin, significantly, was a former president of Poitou-Charentes regional council) sought to engage a second phase of decentralisation. This entailed both a constitutional amendment stating (in Article 1) that France was not only an 'indivisible, secular, social, and democratic Republic', but that it was henceforth 'organised on a decentralised basis', and practical measures to transfer new responsibilities to subnational government. Justified by the govern-ment in terms of greater flexibility and responsiveness to local needs, this move was opposed by public-sector unions in the name of the sacrosanct uniformity of provi-sion (they were also worried about job losses), and viewed with scepticism even by France's local and regional elites, who feared new tasks without corresponding resources.

- *The judiciary* occupies a clearly subordinate position in the Jacobin tradition of the state, according to which the nation and its representatives, invested by universal suffrage with the power to make and unmake laws, rightfully take precedence over the judiciary, whose task is merely to administer law. Any questioning of this subordination was considered to open the road to 'government by judges', viewed as a dangerous Anglo-Saxon (and more specifically American) innovation which conferred exorbitant powers on an unelected judiciary. This, however, has begun to change since the 1970s, as a result of several convergent pressures. One is external: France's increasing involvement in a network of European and international bod-ies, including some (such as the EU and the World Trade Organisation) with a judicial or quasi-judicial authority to resolve disputes and if necessary impose or agree penalties on member states for non-respect of its rulings. But France has also, like other major democracies, generated an increasing range of its own regulatory agencies whose very *raison d'être* lies, in principle, in their independence from the political authorities and thus from universal suffrage. They can only be controlled via judicial means. A third impulse tending to diminish the subordination of the judiciary has been the activism of the Constitutional Council, France's (very) approximate equivalent to the United States Supreme Court, which from 1971 incorporated the 1789 Declaration of the Rights of Man and the Citizen into the 'bloc of constitutionality' when it assessed the constitutionality of new laws. Fourth, judges within the ordinary courts, and especially examining magistrates, displayed an unwonted persistence, from the early 1990s, in investigating politically sensitive cases which in former times would have been smothered without difficulty by a word from the Justice Ministry. In doing so they opened an unprecedented debate about the desirable relationship between the judiciary and the political authorities, and prompted modifications to the law. Laurent Cohen-Tanugi, a leading specialist in this area, has referred to these changes as a 'silent revolution' that has transported France 'from the Jacobin state to the law-governed state' ('*de l'État jacobin à l'État de droit*').

- *Military service*, symbol of the link between France's citizens and the national aspiration to a world role, was phased out between 1997 and 2002, with a diminution in the strength of France's armed forces from 381,000 to under 240,000. Militarily, professionalisation made perfect sense, allowing levels of expertise and flexibility impossible in a conscript army – sixty-five years after de Gaulle had called for an *armée de métier*. Politically, the call-up had ceased to exercise much of its integrative role, not least because of the widespread exemptions for young middle-class men who, in return for teaching the children of France's former colonies or occupying a variety of civilian desk jobs vaguely linked to France's overseas interests, never saw a parade ground. But its end set a final seal on what had been a central component of the Republican synthesis.

Redefining political conflict

The last quarter of the twentieth century saw three more or less new splits take form within French political debate. The first, and in some ways the most familiar, turned around issues of globalisation and liberalism. The second opposed the new libertarian Left and the new authoritarian Right. The third concerned Europe. None reproduced the old frontiers of Left and Right.

The debate around the globalisation issue was conducted between a part of the Right and a part of the Left. On the Right, neo-liberalism in France (as elsewhere) fused ideas emanating from Austrian economics, monetarism, new classical macroeconomics and public choice theory. It was propagated by an alliance of 'nouveaux économistes' (such as Guy Sorman, Jean-Jacques Rosa and Florin Aftalion), philosophers (notably Jean-François Revel and Jean-Marie Benoist) and industrialists (notably Michel Drancourt and Yvon Gattaz), and given influential expression by journalists, by gurus such as Alain Minc (a somewhat unorthodox former member of the Inspection des Finances, an elite civil service corps, *directeur des finances* at St-Gobain and *chargé de conférences* at the École de Hautes Études en Sciences Sociales). Within politics, neo-liberalism was particularly influential within the non-Gaullist moderate Right, helped shape the programmes on which the Right won the parliamentary elections of 1986 and 1993, and in a more general sense was part of the ideological paradigm shift discussed above, affecting even Gaullists and Socialists in varying degrees. Balladur's account of the early privatisations was symbolically called *Je crois en l'homme plus qu'en l'État* ('I believe in Man more than in the state'). Yet neo-liberalism never captured the whole of the Right in France as it did in Britain. It had vigorous opponents among Gaullists like Philippe Séguin, while the mainstream of the Chirac camp handled it with great caution, at least after 1988. Its most committed political exponent, Alain Madelin, scored a mere 3.9 per cent of the vote at the 2002 presidential elections.

The anti-liberal opponents of globalisation have enjoyed wider general popularity and have made significant inroads into the political elite. France's 'alterglobalisation' movement, a term coined to reconcile left-wing internationalism with opposition to the neo-liberal globalisation process, has been centred around the Attac association (formed in 1997 to advocate the so-called Tobin tax on international capital movements, but articulating a much wider range of demands) and the *Monde Diplomatique* monthly. Led by intellectuals such as its president Bernard Cassen, the editor of *Monde Diplomatique* Ignacio Ramonet, and the late sociologist Pierre Bourdieu, the alterglo-balisation movement has also attracted less cerebral figures such as José Bové, leader of the Confédération Paysanne and tireless campaigner for real French food, and activists from the ranks of former Communists, Trotskyists and Greens. It has been at the forefront of such international antiglobalisation events as the World Social Forum, and won at least the nominal support of over 100 French Deputies in 2000, while the Tobin tax has been supported, at various times, by such mainstream figures as Jacques Chirac, Lionel Jospin and Laurent Fabius. Attac is popular because it expresses deep-seated French worries about globalisation (55 per cent of respondents to a poll in 2001 viewed globalisation as a threat to French firms and jobs, against 37 per cent who saw it as an opportunity), plus a sense of France's universal mission for humankind, leavened with anti-Americanism. But beyond the creation of commissions to study the feasibility of the Tobin tax or something like it, its policy impact was slight – at least until the fusion of the European and globalisation issues in the 2005 European referendum campaign.

The second opposition has been characterised as setting 'universalist' against 'anti-universalist' values, or libertarians against authoritarians. Ronald Inglehart has shown how the developed capitalist world saw the rise of a new libertarian Left from the late 1960s onwards. New movements mobilised, outside the confines of mainstream parties, on issues hitherto at the margins of political debate: the environment, the rights of women and of minorities such as immigrants or homosexuals, sexuality and family life (and the right to divorce, contraception and abortion), and the defence of civil liberties. In France, the liberties promised by the Republican triptych, as mediated by the rather heavy-handed authoritarianism of the Gaullist régime, seemed hopelessly limited to many activists in the wake of the upheaval of May 1968. Similarly, the formal equality before the law guaranteed by the constitution offered little hope of real equality in the face of discriminations on the basis, most notably, of race and sex. Finally, the frater-nity offered by the French model of integration ignored the *droit à la différence* – the right of provincial groups to preserve their own distinctive culture and language (be it Breton, Occitan, or Corsican) from the standardising juggernaut of the French state, and of immigrants to integrate into French society on their own terms rather than those traditionally dictated by the Republic. In the decade after May 1968, mobilisation on these issues was rather slow in France by comparison with other European countries, though not negligible (France saw some large-scale anti-nuclear demonstrations). By the 1990s, on the other hand, it had found expression both in a panoply of new social movements and in a Green party of respectable size and support, though of divided and quarrelsome temperament.

The new authoritarian Right, present in most West European countries by the late 1980s, has been viewed by Piero Ignazi as an equal and opposite reaction against the libertarian Left: autocratic in its organisation, patriarchal, racist, anti-gay and indiffer-ent to the environment. If France had been a laggard, by European standards, in the mobilisation of the libertarian Left, it was at the forefront in the rise of the new Right: the electoral breakthrough of the Front National in 1983–84 was an inspiration to its European counterparts. Although the immigration issue has been the FN's main stock-in-trade, it has drawn support from France's less educated, and often most economic-ally vulnerable, voters over issues as varied as high unemployment, rising crime, the decay of HLM estates, corruption among the mainstream parties, and what is presented as the sell-out of French interests by remote 'cosmopolitan' elites.

The question of European integration, finally, has repeatedly cut across the Left–Right division. The ratification of the Rome Treaty was supported by most parliamentarians of the central governing parties: Socialists, Christian Democrats and most Radicals and mainstream conservatives. It was opposed on the Left by the Communists and a minority of Radicals and on the Right by most Gaullists and the far right-wing Poujadists. A generation later, the referendum on the Maastricht Treaty reproduced almost the same alignment: the treaty was opposed from the Left by Communists and a small number of the Socialists, from the Right by the far-Right Front National, most of the Gaullists and a small section of the non-Gaullist conservatives; Socialists, Christian Democrats and a minority of Gaullists (including Jacques Chirac) supported it. A comparable division reappeared with the 2005 referendum on the European constitutional treaty. The fact that it was now the Left, not the Right, in opposition, the success of the far Left and Attac in mobilising against the treaty, and the willingness of Socialist leaders such as Henri Emmanuelli or Laurent Fabius to join them in the no campaign, ensured that the Left's weight in the no vote would be greater, and the Right's smaller, than in 1992; but the division between centre and extremes still applied.

None of these areas of conflict is unique to France; each, though, stands in sharp relief against past divides because of the traditional strength of the state in all its aspects and of the Left–Right division. The weakening of old Left–Right divisions, coupled with the appearance of other issues that divided Left and Right internally more than one from the other, suggested a new divide within French politics from the 1990s. The 'parties of government' – Socialists, the non-Gaullist moderate Right, and most neo-Gaullists – accepted, with reservations, France's steady integration into the world capitalist economy, and favoured, in varying degrees, further European integration. The forces 'outside the system', on the other hand, questioned or rejected both globalisation and Europe and, in the case of the FN, placed an inward-looking *nationalisme de repli*, which sought to protect the identity of France against the 'invasion' of immigrants, at the centre of their electoral appeal. The division was clearest at the first round of the 2002 presidential elections, when a third of votes cast went to candidates of the far Right or Left – and when these votes plus abstentions and spoilt ballots accounted for over 54 per cent of the registered electorate. It has also been observed that new divisions have generated new voter loyalties, with blue-collar workers from formerly loyal Communist neighbourhoods voting massively for the FN, and so-called *bourgeois bohêmes*, well-off, educated, and sensitive to libertarian Left values, supporting Socialists or Greens where their parents would have supported the moderate Right.

This is, however, an oversimplification. Divisions over Europe, over the libertarian–authoritarian divide and over globalisation may overlap at times, but they certainly do not coincide perfectly. Anything relating to Islam, in particular, tends to sow confusion in relation to both old and new boundaries. In 2005, debates over European integration were complicated by the distinct issues of the European constitution and Turkish entry; supporting the former did not necessarily entail accepting the latter; indeed, their Christian loyalties ensured that some of the most passionate European integrationists were among the most vigorous opponents of Turkish entry. An even more striking example was supplied a year earlier by the 'Muslim headscarf affair', the conflict over a law banning signs of religious faith in schools and directed chiefly against the wearing of headscarves by Muslim girls. The issue divided the French: 57 per cent of respondents to a poll in January 2004 considered that the public display of religious affiliation represented 'a danger for the cohesion of the Republic', against 41 per cent who took the opposite view. Each side had serious arguments: the *droit à la différence*, the right of young people to express a cultural identity, and pragmatic concerns about the risk of alienating France's four million or so Muslims, were set against the traditional principle of *laïcité* and the right of young Muslim women to escape religious pressures from their families or neighbourhood fundamentalists. The law, recommended by a committee headed by a Christian Democrat, and supported by the conservative president Chirac, was voted by nine-tenths of the conservative UMP Deputies – and opposed by two-thirds of the (much smaller) Communist group, nominally more attached than any to the principle of *laïcité*.

To summarise, for nearly two centuries after the Revolution, two elements distinguished France's political traditions. First, the Left–Right division served as a matrix for a variety of conflicts, particularly over the nature of the régime, Church–state relations, and questions of the distribution of wealth and income, and gained thereby in persistence and intensity. Secondly, France's state tradition had its roots in the *ancien régime*, but was reinforced by the Jacobins of the Revolution and above all by Napoleon. It was underwritten by all the main political families of Left and Right, albeit for different reasons, and gained a new lease of life with the advent of a more interventionist state after World War II. Third, in the half-century after 1945, the intensity of the Left–Right division was attenuated by the consequences of the *trente glorieuses*, especially dechristianisation; by the development of consensus over the nature of the régime, the new regularity of *alternance* and the practice of cohabitation; by the emergence of new issues that proved difficult to accommodate into the Left–Right matrix; and by the forced reconciliation of the Left with the capitalist economy after 1983. Fourth, the state tradition, having reached an apogee in the 1960s, with the combination of the strong leadership supplied by the de Gaulle presidency and a near-universal acceptance of *dirigisme*, was then challenged both by the constraints of globalisation and of Europe and by challenges to the internal Jacobin tradition as it bore down on subnational authorities and on judges. It remains to be seen how much of both traditions has survived these multiple assaults.

The survival of traditions

France was for long considered 'exceptional' by foreign (chiefly 'Anglo-Saxon') observers by virtue of the combination of an original, complex and intense pattern of political conflict with a powerful, intrusive state, at once depended upon and resented by the French ('a vulture with teats' was how the peasants saw it, according to Gordon Wright). Those two aspects of the French political tradition have been much attenuated under the impact of internal and external developments. They have not, however, disappeared.

The state tradition

The survival of France's state tradition can be highlighted in four ways. France continues to claim the status of a world power. Individuals and groups within the French state continue to resist the modification from within of the Jacobin model, whether by decentralisation or through greater judicial independence. Policy-makers, whether politicians, civil servants or leaders of the private sector, have had difficulty abandoning the habits of *dirigisme*. And the state's share of GDP has remained stubbornly high, as social spending has climbed.

France's continued ambition to remain a world power is best illustrated by the continued extent of its military commitments. France was the last European state to cut military budgets at the end of the Cold War, and the last of the older nuclear powers to abandon nuclear testing – after a resumption of tests, in 1995–96, which provoked hostility among the Pacific states nearest to the Muroroa atoll where they took place, as well as opposition in France, to the apparent surprise of President Chirac. As of 2004, France had 33,000 troops stationed overseas, from Afghanistan (where a French officer took command of the international force in summer 2004) to the Ivory Coast, from Haiti to Kosovo. France supplied the second largest contingent, after the USA, of troops and aircraft in the 1999 Kosovo war, and is still the largest contributor to UN peacekeeping missions. The question of France's return to the integrated NATO command structure from which de Gaulle withdrew in 1966 has been regularly posed, and in both the 1991 Gulf war and the Kosovo war, French troops did indeed come under American command. For the moment, though, France remains inside the Atlantic alliance but notionally free to deploy its defence forces independently – an aspect of the Gaullist legacy which is hard for any French leader overtly to abandon. By comparison, Britain, the only European nuclear power integrated into the NATO command structure, is regularly, and contemptuously, referred to in France as America's 'nuclear vassal'. France was not alone among European countries in opposing the 2003 Iraq war: it was joined by Belgium, Germany and, after the 2004 elections, by Spain as well. But the flamboyance of French opposition can only be fully understood in the context of the Gaullist tradition: it was intended to set an example to the world.

France also remains a 'one and indivisible Republic' – very far, despite the decentralisation reforms of the early 1980s or even those of the Raffarin government, from a federal state on the German model. Compared with the German *Länder*, France's regions control miserable budgets and limited areas of competence. The smaller local authorities remain heavily dependent on the state's field services for their technical support. A concern to safeguard the 'one and indivisible' Republic was revealed by the Constitutional Council's ruling of 1991 which required the words 'Corsican people' to be removed from a bill giving greater autonomy to the island of Corsica. The European directive setting standards for the wider use of regional languages was similarly perceived, chiefly on the nationalist Right but also among sections of the Left, as a threat to the Republic.

The Jacobin model also survives in the relations between the political authorities and the judiciary. Despite their greater assertiveness from the 1990s, France's judges still enjoy considerably less independence than, say, their Italian counterparts. The promotion system for prosecuting magistrates remains in the (political) hands of the Justice Ministry; attempts to change it, at the end of the Jospin premiership in 2002, collapsed in the face of opposition from the Senate. Cohen-Tanugi's transition from *l'État jacobin* to *l'État de droit* is far from complete.

Third, *dirigisme* remains embedded in the institutions and culture of the French state despite the transformations of French capitalism and its context noted above. *Dirigisme* survives, more specifically, in five ways.

- *As a dense institutional architecture.* The complex network of interministerial committees set up to intervene in the economy at the end of the *trente glorieuses* is still largely in place, albeit often with rather shorn powers. And France retains a distinctive fiscal system, industrial relations and wage bargaining systems, labour market regulations, educational and training systems, and financial and corporate governance frameworks.

- *As an expression of the character of France's interlocking elites.* One illustration of the continuing hold of the civil service elite on French capitalism was supplied by the takeover battle between the Banque Nationale de Paris (BNP) and the Société Générale in the summer of 1999. Both of these banks had been nationalised after the Liberation, in 1945. Both had been privatised, Société Générale in 1986 and BNP in 1993. On the BNP side, nine of the sixteen board members were graduates of elite civil service schools, and eight had started their careers as civil servants. For the SG, the equivalent figures were twelve out of seventeen graduates of elite civil service schools, of whom eleven were ex-civil servants. The conflict between the two banks was fed, not merely by the competition between two management teams seeking to convince shareholders of their superior ability to run a merged firm, but by political rivalries between members of the SG board whose career paths were closely intertwined with the neo-Gaullist party, the RPR, and those of the BNP, whose affinities lay with the non-Gaullist Right but whose president had served on the Socialist Prime Minister Pierre Mauroy's staff in 1981–84. Ernest-Antoine de Seillière, head of the MEDEF, France's main employers' association, is a graduate of the École Nationale d'Administration (ÉNA) who started his career as a civil servant; so were three out of the five captains of industry tipped as Seillière's possible successors. The domination of the civil service elite is not confined to the business world: of the five prime ministers appointed since 1993, four (Édouard Balladur, Alain Juppé, Lionel Jospin and Dominique de Villepin) have been ÉNA men.

- *As a policy style.* The *dirigiste* policy style has not deserted France. The behaviour of Lionel Jospin's left-wing government after 1997 offers plenty of examples of its rude health: the manifesto commitment to reduce unemployment by instituting a 35-hour week, and the rapid move to do this by law; the use of partial privatisations to raise capital for the public purse, while retaining the maximum possible measure of public control over the firms concerned; the slow and minimalist implementation of the European directive to open electricity markets to competition, conceived in such a way as to offer maximum protection to the national supplier EDF; the successful creation of a French national champion in the oil sector, with the takeover of Elf by Total; the successful reorganisation by the Socialists of the banking sector to favour the mutual banks; the botched attempt to produce a single national banking champion out of the BNP–Société Générale battle. Although Jospin admitted, after the latter setback, that in a modern, post-*dirigiste* economy the state could not 'impose its will' on the market, his record indicated that he still thought it worth trying. Nor was this propensity confined to the Left. When Jospin's conservative predecessor Juppé (another former civil servant, like Jospin, but one who had written a pamphlet on the need for France to break away from the state-led economy of the post-war generation) set out to tackle the gaping hole in the finances of France's social security system, he chose to reinforce the state's control. Whereas prior to 1995, the social security budget had been negotiated by employers and trade unions, with periodic injections of state money to cover the deficit, the Juppé plan involved the government and parliament fixing the social security budget annually. Free-market solutions, such as partial privatisation or even measures to encourage the development of pension funds, barely entered the debate. Some of the Juppé government's privatisations (notably of the arms and electronics firm Thomson) also came to grief owing to the inclination of the government, and especially of the president, to treat privatisations as a means to reward political friends. More recently, Nicolas Sarkozy as finance minister stepped in twice in the space of a few months to recapitalise the troubled Alstom engineering firm and save it from the unwelcome embraces of Germany's Siemens, and to arrange a merger between two French pharmaceutical firms, Aventis and Sanofi, so as to head off a financially more attractive bid from the Swiss firm Novartis. In 2005, Prime Minister Dominique de Villepin also made clear his hostility to any foreign takeover of food giant Danone, although less than a quarter of the firm's business was now done in France. These were small-scale interventions compared to the great days of *dirigisme*, but indicative of a state of mind still attached to the ideal of national champions.

- *As a myth.* Since the 1980s *dirigisme* has been depicted, at worst, as a habit that France has outgrown and, at best, as a major contributor to the golden age of the *trente glorieuses*. There appears to be a mismatch between the persistent omnipresence of state officialdom with its dense institutional architecture and the dilution and reshaping of the nature of *dirigisme*. There is another mismatch between the espousals of the market and a lingering hankering after the benefits of *dirigisme*. The fate of two reports on France's economic difficulties illustrates the point. The first, by former International Monetary Fund chief Michel Camdessus, insisted on the need to reduce the number of civil servants and the state's share of GDP, and received a lukewarm reception from president and government at its publication in October 2004. Three months later, by contrast, a very different report was published by a second committee led by Jean-Louis Beffa, head of the St-Gobain glass group. Its recommendations, including a state-led industrial policy, with a new Industrial Innovation Agency and plans for new *grands projets*, were enthusiastically taken up by President Chirac in a speech that explicitly harked back to the *dirigiste* heyday of his early political career as a model.

- *By public demand.* Even when the French Right's free-market faith was at its apogee in 1986, French opinion remained unconvinced. By the end of Chirac's second premiership in 1988, a majority of the French took the view that the economy needed more state intervention, not less. Both of the two leading candidates at the 1995 presidential election, Chirac and Jospin, promised greater state intervention, notably to tackle problems of inequality and social exclusion in France. If the typical reflex of the American pressure group is to sue or to give money to campaigns, its French counterpart is still more likely to take to the streets and demonstrate for action (and, typically, money) from the state. In successive polls run by SOFRES, some 46–48 per cent of respondents have stated that the state 'does not intervene enough' in economic and social affairs, against 26–27 per cent who take the opposite view. Even among right-wing sympathisers, the figures are evenly balanced, with about 40 per cent demanding more intervention and 40 per cent wishing for less. The crucial argument that the left wing of the no campaign brought to bear in the 2005 referendum was that the European constitutional treaty would rule out French-style public service monopolies or industrial policies; but it was even more revealing that the treaty's supporters, from Chirac down, chose to present the Europe of the treaty as a 'shield' against globalisation, a sort of France writ large.

Fourth, despite the dismantling of *dirigisme*, the French state of the early twenty-first century remained larger than ever, whether in terms of the number of public employees (between 25 and 30 per cent of the workforce, depending on where the public–private frontier is drawn) or the share of GDP taken by the state, at central and at local level. In 1981, the French state's fiscal revenue amounted to some 42 per cent of GDP – the same, given the balanced budget, as government spending. By 2003, on the other hand, fiscal revenue amounted to 46 per cent of GDP, fiscal plus non-fiscal revenue stood at 50.4 per cent, and government spending at 54.5 per cent, thanks to a deficit of 4.1 per cent of GDP.

The paradox, therefore, is that over a period when many among France's administrative and political elites were converted to the idea of a less interventionist state and to financial orthodoxy, the size of the French state continued to grow and the size of France's deficit to grow faster, while public debt rose from some 20 per cent of GDP to 63 per cent. The explanation lies largely in social spending. In 1980, France's levels of social spending, at 21.1 per cent of GDP, was close to the average for the EU15 countries (20.6 per cent). In 2001, by contrast, while the EU15 average had risen to 24.0 per cent, driven in part by Europe-wide factors such as ageing populations, the French figure had risen to 28.5 per cent and ranked third behind Denmark and Sweden. Part of this growth was caused by the expansion of France's excellent healthcare system. Much, however, was spent on palliating the consequences of joblessness, via unemployment benefits, early retirement packages (two-thirds of French workers have retired by the time they reach the age of 60), work experience programmes and minimum income programmes – plus, since 1997, the 35-hour week, heavily subsidised from public funds. Humane insofar as they spread part of the cost of joblessness away from its immediate victims and onto the wider community, such remedies suffer from the twin drawbacks of tying up growing amounts of scarce resources and doing so in ways that do little to promote France's wider economic competitiveness.

The dismantling of *dirigisme*, therefore, while it has rendered France's prosperity dependent on business performance more than on technocratic decision, has diminished neither the role of the state nor the reliance of the population, in all manner of ways, upon its largesse. Similarly, the 'Jacobin' model of strong central authority at home and assertive independence abroad, inherited from the *ancien régime*, consolidated under Napoleon and renovated by de Gaulle, has been modified and challenged, but remains a basic operating principle among the political and administrative elite.

Patterns of political conflict

If the vigour of the state tradition has represented one half of the 'French exception', the other has consisted in patterns of political conflict that were fiercely ideological; marked by emotional references to historic memories of bloodshed and civil strife; structured by the Left–Right divide, but also with a tendency to fragmentation, incoherence and government instability. Here too the changes have been substantial, with governments lasting longer and governing more under the Fifth Republic than under its predecessors. But the survivals are also significant.

The Left–Right division survives, if in muted form. If more and more of the French find it outdated, polls show that they are still perfectly willing to assign a definite position on a Left–Right axis both to themselves and to well-known politicians. The political institutions of the Fifth Republic, which, unlike its predecessors, furthers the bipolarisation of politics, also sustain the division, at least at the second ballot of national and municipal elections. But the Left–Right division does not survive merely as a function of institutions. Its traditional origins still leave traces. The tendency to vote for the mainstream Right still increases with frequency of church attendance, even though it is increasingly rare to go regularly to Mass. Onto this old cleavage new divisions have superimposed themselves. Issues such as abortion liberalisation, the rights of homosexuals, gender parity of women in politics, and ecology have mostly, though not always, appealed more to the Left than to the Right. Similarly, the new salience of immigration or law and order as political issues has tended to offer more opportunities to the Right. The 'new' Left–Right division, therefore, might be seen as corresponding to the more moderate bipolarisation of 'Anglo-Saxon' countries: no longer the barely healed wound of a nation set against itself, but the banal division between two clusters of interests, sharing a consensus on basic values and accustomed to alternating in, or even sharing, government office. The problem with this view, however, is that it leaves out the persistence of less domesticated forms of political mobilisation, particularly among those who feel excluded from the French economy as it has developed since the mid-1970s and from mainstream French politics. On the far Right, the combination of resentment at North African immigration, burgeoning crime rates and rising unemployment fuelled a powerful revival of *nationalisme de repli* from 1984, in the form of the Front National. The growing solidity of the FN's hold on its voters – many of them young unqualified working-class men, who would have been strongly left-wing a few years earlier – led specialists such as Grunberg and Schweisguth to argue that the binary division of the French electorate had been replaced by a 'tripartition' into Left, Right and far Right. On the far Left, the Communist Party was integrated, by the late 1990s, into a broad left-wing coalition and had all but shed its revolutionary pretensions, as well as most of its members and voters. But the vitality of 'new social movements', partly, but only partly, inspired by the Trotskyist far Left, testified to the continuing strength of an insurrectionary tradition stretching back to 1789. When public-sector workers went on strike against Prime Minister Juppé's social security reform in December 1995, they paralysed the country, forcing countless Parisians to walk several miles to work in the snow. After three weeks, a majority of the French, albeit a narrow one, still approved of the strikes. For many private-sector workers, unable to take industrial action themselves for fear of losing their jobs, they were surrogates for their own discontents. As public-sector employees prepared to walk out again in January 2005 over wages and a series of reforms proposed by the Raffarin government, they again enjoyed the support of two-thirds of poll respondents, a typical figure for most of the (many) intervening disputes. This campaign spilled over into the European referendum campaign, with the most successful 'day of action', on 10 March, setting the scene for a decisive shift towards a no majority. While the 1995 movement is the most striking case, examples abound of groups of French men and women – farmers in 1990, fishermen in 1994, the unemployed in 1998 – taking to the streets, causing varying degrees of disruption, to defend more or less narrow interests, justified in terms of the ideals of the Republic, and sometimes enjoying widespread public support. The insurrectionary tradition, though now usually played out without bloodshed and without threatening the régime, retains much of its force.

Two further points need to be made about the survival of distinctive political traditions in France. The first concerns the fragmentation of French parties, much noted by observers of the Third and Fourth Republics. For such a highly politicised country – whether one refers to the (generally high) turnout at elections, or to the tendency of interest groups to show party-political preferences, or to the extent to which politics permeates associative and cultural life – France has small and weak political parties. For the first generation of the Fifth Republic, the party system appeared to be undergoing consolidation into two broadly unified coalitions, on Left and Right. This is no longer the case. In the 1990s, *every* French party, bar the Communists, suffered a split. The survival of governments was not directly affected, partly because the Fifth Republic's institutions were constructed to supply stability in government in a context of unstable, undisciplined parties. But the splits aggravated the difficulty for ordinary citizens to find anything in the political system with which to identify.

Second, while the Gaullist party is weakened, diluted in its ideology, and, since 2002, merged into a wider entity, the UMP, Gaullism remains an important political reference point. As a historic individual, de Gaulle (like the Republic) now commands a near-universal reverence, even from those who were his bitterest enemies during his lifetime. Both the constitution and the foreign policy which he left to France are practically immune to frontal criticism, even if they have undergone piecemeal modifications over the years. On the Right, Gaullists nostalgic for past glories identify the heyday of Gaullism with national independence, *dirigisme* and the 'social' dimension of Gaullism. This continued penchant for state control within a major force on the French Right contrasts with the bases of the success of the 'Anglo-Saxon' Right in the 1980s, which lay in an ability to wrap economic neo-liberalism in the flag of patriotism.

French political conflict, in short, is no longer the 'civil war by other means' (or indeed, civil war *tout court*) that it was, on and off, for nearly two centuries after the Revolution. But it remains structured by its historical roots: by the Left–Right division, partially modernised; by the tradition of insurrection, transmuted into street demonstrations of a more or less peaceful character; by the Gaullist legacy, integral to the persistence of the state tradition; and by the striking inability of French parties to attract a large, stable membership or to avoid splits. Those elements often lend an apparently impenetrable character to political conflict in France: one recent dictionary of European parties left France out altogether for that reason. But here, as in the case of the state tradition, change has not meant the end of French 'exceptionalism'.

Concluding remarks

The rest of this book follows the development of France's political traditions through particular sections of the political system. Chapter 2 analyses the overall constitutional framework of the Fifth Republic, and the attempts of its founders to find a synthesis between the parliamentarianism of the republican tradition and the strong leadership beloved of Bonapartists and anti-democrats. Chapters 3 to 5 then examine in more detail the workings of France's executive, through the personal contributions of Fifth Republic leaders (Chapter 3), the resources available to president and prime minister (Chapter 4), and their respective roles in policy-making (Chapter 5). Chapter 6 considers the attempts of the French parliament to break out of the modest position assigned it by the constitution. Chapters 7, 8 and 9 cover patterns of political conflict, from the point of view both of individual parties and of the party system as a whole.

Chapters 10 to 13 deal with the state tradition and the challenges it faces, whether in the new demands being placed on the administration, the new and less predictable configuration of French interest groups, the transformation of central–local relations since the decentralisation legislation of 1982, and the new assertiveness of the French judiciary. Chapter 14 analyses France's commitment to Europe, and in particular the attempt to build a strong and activist European Union while at the same time safeguarding French sovereignty. If there is a common theme that runs through all these chapters, it is of a political system that has been the repository of old, independent and often idiosyncratic traditions being forced to reinvent itself in response both to the evolution of French society and to external constraints. That process of reinvention, incomplete though it certainly is, may have made French politics somewhat less 'exceptional'. It has certainly not made it any less interesting.

Further reading

General historical and political works

Fenby, J., *On the Brink: The Trouble with France*, 2nd edition, London, Little, Brown, 2002.
Gildea, R., *France since 1945*, Oxford, Oxford University Press, 1996.
Larkin, M., *France since the Popular Front*, 2nd edition, Oxford, Oxford University Press, 1997.
Sowerwine, C., *France 1870–2000*, Basingstoke, Palgrave Macmillan, 2001.

On French political cultures

Berstein, S., *Les cultures politiques en France*, Paris, Seuil, 1999.
Cohen-Tanugi, L., *La métamorphose de la démocratie française: de l'État jacobin à l'État de droit*, 2nd edition, Paris, Gallimard, 1993.
Debray, R., *La République expliquée à ma fille*, Paris, Seuil, 1999.
Hazareesingh, S., *Political Traditions in Modern France*, Oxford, Oxford University Press, 1994.
Hewlett, N., *Modern French Politics: Analysing Conflict and Consensus since 1945*, Cambridge, Polity, 1998.
Jenkins, B., *Nationalism in France: Class and Nation since 1789*, London, Routledge, 1990.
Portier, P., *Église et politique en France au XXe siècle*, Paris, Montchrestien, 1993.
Weber, E., *Peasants into Frenchmen*, London, Chatto and Windus, 1979.

On the trente glorieuses

Cole, A. and Mendras, H., *Social Change in Modern France*, Cambridge, Cambridge University Press, 1991.
Fourastié, J., *Les trente glorieuses*, Paris, Fayard, 1979.
Hoffmann, S., *Decline or Renewal? France since the 1930s*, New York, Viking Press, 1974.
Shonfield, A., *Modern Capitalism*, London, Oxford University Press, 1965.

On economic change since the 1980s

Cohen, E., *L'État brancardier*, Paris, Calmann-Lévy, 1989.
Flynn, G. (ed.), *Remaking the Hexagon: The New France in the New Europe*, Boulder, CO, Westview Press, 1995.
Forrester, V., *L'horreur économique*, Paris, Fayard, 1996.
Hayward, J., *The State and the Market Economy*, Brighton, Wheatsheaf Books, 1986.

Juppé, A., *La double rupture*, Paris, Économica, 1983.

Minc, A., *www.capitalism.fr*, Paris, Broché, 2000.

Schmidt, V., *From State to Market? The Transformation of French Business and Government*, Cambridge, Cambridge University Press, 1996.

On the changing boundaries between Right and Left

Boy, D. and Mayer, N., *The French Voter Decides*, Ann Arbor, University of Michigan Press, 1993.

Cautrès, B. and Mayer, N., *Le nouveau désordre électoral: les leçons du 21 avril 2002*, Paris, Presses de Sciences Po, 2004.

Martin, P., *Comprendre les évolutions électorales*, Paris, Presses de Sciences Po, 2000.

2   From Fourth to Fifth Republic

A constitution is a set of rules governing the relationships between the various institutions – most obviously the executive, the legislature and the judiciary – within a political system, and (often through a bill of rights) between the political institutions proper and the body of citizens. The rules are fundamental both in the sense that they govern the basic conduct of a wide range of players and because they are harder to change than the ordinary run of laws: amendments typically require reinforced majorities to be passed, and possibly ratification by subnational government or even referendum. They are usually codified (the United Kingdom is an exception in this respect), and may offer, to the unwary, a guide to the locus of political power in a given state. They are certainly a necessary part of any guide. But all constitutions are creatures of circumstance, and all admit of more than one reading: it is revealing, for example, that Woodrow Wilson's *Congressional Government* and Arthur M. Schlesinger's *Imperial Presidency* were about the same country, the United States, and nearly the same constitution. The present constitution of France is no exception to either rule. It aimed to establish the executive leadership that the Fourth Republic had conspicuously failed to supply – a failure that had brought the country to the brink of civil war by May 1958. By giving France not one executive leader but two, however, it offered both limitless opportunities for debate among constitutional specialists and a variety of possible practical applications.

Ultimately, a failure: the Fourth Republic (1946–58)

The Fifth Republic was born of its predecessor's inability to provide France with stable government, to implement any consistent policy towards Algeria and to command either the support of the people or the obedience of its own servants. It is easy to sneer at the Fourth Republic; most Frenchmen did. But it is also unjust. During the period 1945 to 1958 France achieved an extraordinary feat of reconstruction after five years of war and enemy occupation which had destroyed much of the country's industry and transport system (including, for example, half of its locomotives, a third of its merchant shipping, three-quarters of its port installations and every bridge over the Loire downstream of Nevers), as well as large swathes of its housing and even agriculture. Reconstruction was followed by the start of France's 'economic miracle', a revolutionary period of modernisation (punctuated, it is true, by bouts of inflation and of financial instability) which geared the French economy to meet international competition. In the area of social policy, the Fourth Republic laid the foundations of a comprehensive social security system and gave the working population a third week of paid holiday, a minimum wage and a measure of trade union recognition. France was firmly linked to Europe through the Coal and Steel Community, and, by the Treaty of Rome in 1957, through Euratom and the European Common Market. The country was integrated into the NATO alliance, and relations with Germany, the traditional enemy, were much improved. Even in the colonial field, progress was made: slowly, grudgingly and with more or less bloodshed as independence was granted to Indo-China (1954) and to Morocco and Tunisia (1956); more smoothly, if only partially, with the Defferre Law of 1956 which set up a framework for autonomy for sub-Saharan Africa. Only a solution for Algeria, the most intensively settled of the colonies (with a million white *colons* to 9 million Muslim Algerians) and the only one to have been organised as if a part of mainland France, proved beyond the political capacities of the Fourth Republic. Even in the strictly political arena, the régime's record was defensible. Its talented and (usually) honest leaders took France through this period of unprecedented economic and social transformation, while assailed from the Left (by the Communist Party, subservient to Moscow) and from a Right (notably, though not exclusively, the Gaullists) that clamoured for 'order' but disrupted government and fanned subversion among settlers and the military in Algeria.

In spite of its real achievements, the Fourth Republic remained unloved – *la mal aimée*. It was born of indifference: just 36 per cent of the registered electorate voted it into being at the referendum of October 1946 (32.5 per cent abstained; 31.5 per cent voted no). By 1951 nearly half the voters were supporting parties opposed to the existing régime. They thereby helped to ensure the political instability that was one of the Fourth Republic's salient, and unpopular, features. Hemmed in within parliament by the régime's enemies, the parties within the 'system' – Socialists, Radicals, Christian Democrats and conservatives, plus sundry minor groups – were too divided between and within themselves to form consistent majorities or stable governments. The constitution, with the weak executive and 'strong' parliament required by the French republican tradition, did little to alleviate the problem of weak parties and divided majorities. The average lifespan of a Fourth Republic government was under seven months; only two prime ministers, Henri Queuille and Guy Mollet, lasted more than a year. Ministerial crises, those periods between the fall of one government and the investiture of the next, lasted longer and longer: in the final year, caretaker governments ran France for a total of one day in four. By the time that settlers in Algiers rose in opposition to the appointment of a new government in May 1958, the régime's legitimacy – that intangible yet essential ingredient of any political system – was fatally undermined: it simply could not call upon the loyalties of its citizens.

Nor could it rely on the obedience of its own servants, whether civil or military. For civil servants on the ground, subjected to changing or contradictory instructions from Paris, the temptation to make their own policies was overwhelming. This was the case, above all, in the colonies. Here, representatives of the government such as General Leclerc and Admiral Thierry d'Argenlieu in Indo-China, Jean de Hautecloque in

Tunisia and General Juin in Morocco (each of them a French protectorate, the first two established in the 1880s and the third in 1912) shaped policy and faced Paris with embarrassing *faits accomplis*. The arrest of the Tunisian Prime Minister in March 1952, the deposition of the Sultan of Morocco in August 1953, the forced landing of the aircraft carrying leaders of the Algerian independence movement, the FLN, and their subsequent arrest, in October 1956, were all initiatives taken locally, often greeted with consternation in Paris, but finally covered by the government. Civil servants dispatched to the colonies with a liberal, reforming brief were regularly seduced or bullied into submission by local forces whose sole concern was the maintenance of colonial rule. The resulting policies, and the surrounding tissue of lies, evasion and irresponsibility, were uniformly disastrous. In Indo-China, France was forced to withdraw after the military humiliation of Dien Bien Phu, in spring 1954, had closed an inglorious war that cost the French 92,000 dead (including 15,000 Africans and 46,000 'local troops') and 114,000 wounded (the American willingness to take over from France the protection of the pro-Western south of the henceforth divided republic of Vietnam prepared an even greater humiliation for the United States twenty years later). The Algerian war, which began in November 1954, claimed fewer French lives (the Algerian dead were another matter: they numbered at least 250,000). But it was more costly in other ways, resembling, in many respects, the American experience in Vietnam. It caused governmental and financial instability; it weakened the country's already feeble diplomatic position; it drained the moral probity of the régime, as it became clear, for example, that French troops were making systematic use of torture to extract information from FLN fighters and summary execution to dispose of them. The Algerian war did more than any other single cause to sap the bases of the French state and the loyalty of its servants and of its citizens. Most dangerously, civil authority gradually relinquished power to the military, with a civilian 'resident-general' in Algiers being replaced by a soldier in 1957. This process accelerated in 1958. In February the French air force bombed the Tunisian village of Sakhiet, suspected of harbouring an FLN base. The raid killed sixty-nine Tunisians including twenty-one schoolchildren. Prime Minister Félix Gaillard, who had been neither consulted nor informed, chose to condone the bombing after the event, out of fear of army reactions. On 13 May, the army leaders in Algiers went one step further. By supporting the settlers' revolt against the appointment to the premiership of Pierre Pflimlin, who was suspected of being 'soft' on Algeria, the army effectively sought to dictate the composition and the form of the government in Paris. It was this act of open rebellion that opened the final crisis of the régime.

The Gaullist agenda

When René Coty, second and last president of the Fourth Republic, warned in January 1958 that 'our basic institutions are no longer in tune with the rhythm of modern times', he was probably expressing a consensus view. But the régime's most persistent and bilious critics were General de Gaulle and Michel Debré, his faithful lieutenant whose verbal violence exceeded even that of his master. De Gaulle attributed much of the weakness of the Fourth Republic to a lack of executive authority, which made governments a constant prey to a divided and unpredictable parliament. Parliament itself, the argument ran, was at the mercy of France's many and divided parties, which were, by their nature, the defenders of sectional interests rather than the national good (it was partly out of exasperation at what he saw as the petty squabbling of parties that de Gaulle had resigned as leader of the post-war Provisional Government, in January 1946). France's parties were divided, the Gaullists went on, because French society was so fragmented: territorial unity had been achieved slowly and painfully; the French people as a whole carried within them 'ferments of dispersion' and unruly individualism that made them supposedly less governable than the socially virtuous British or the regimented Germans. The weakness of the executive translated into the inability of the state to retain the esteem of its citizens, the respect of France's rich variety of vociferous interest groups, or the loyalty of its own servants. The 'reform of the state' that de Gaulle had demanded for twelve years (notably in speeches at Bayeux and Épinal in 1946) would therefore necessarily include the reinforcement of the government at the expense of the legislature, and thence of the parties. Thus, the Gaullists claimed, the authority of the state would be re-established, the nation's fissiparous tendencies reversed, and the obedience of the state's servants, notably the army, enforced.

There was a further dimension to the Gaullist agenda. In many ways the formative experience of de Gaulle the politician had been the fall of France in 1940. What had turned a military setback into a national disaster then, in his view, was the absence of any provision in the Third Republic's institutions for the exercise of national leadership in a crisis – still less at any other time. The Fourth Republic did nothing to remedy this. De Gaulle was determined to give the authority of the state a personal embodiment in a *chef* with far wider powers than those available to the consensual figures whom the parliamentarians of the Third and Fourth Republics elected to the presidency. Moreover, if such leadership was necessary to deal with France's pressing internal and colonial problems, their resolution was itself a means to a wider end: the restoration of France's national independence and the reinforcement of its position in the world.

De Gaulle had waited twelve years for his moment, conscious that it might never come (he had, after all, been born in 1890), before the army *coup* in Algiers. By then his attractiveness as national saviour was almost universal, though for widely varying reasons: as the anti-Fascist former leader of Free France (to good republicans); as the general who had defied an illegitimate civilian authority to save France (for the army rebels); and as the one major public figure who had said nothing about Algeria since 1954, and who could therefore be invested with the most varied and contradictory expectations (for everybody). But if he sought reform and strong leadership, de Gaulle insisted that it should be achieved 'within the context of republican legality': there could be no recourse to vulgar dictatorship, which he abhorred for reasons based on historical experience and on a tactical reading of contemporary French politics. Whatever the complicity and connivance between Gaullists and some of the Algiers rebels (notably General Massu), de Gaulle himself insisted on going through the regular processes of forming a Fourth Republic government, and seeking, at the invitation of President Coty, the votes of the National Assembly. These he obtained, on 1 June 1958. His conditions of accepting the premiership, that he should be given special powers to govern in Algeria and to draft a new constitution, became law two days later. The constitutional text, adopted by the government on 3 September, won a ringing endorsement from the French people at the referendum of 28 September 1958: four out of five voters, and two-thirds of the registered electorate (nearly twice the proportion that had supported the Fourth Republic), voted yes, and there was a majority for acceptance in every one of the then ninety *départements* of metropolitan France.

Between Washington and Westminster

If the referendum result seemed clear (though many voters supported de Gaulle, or French Algeria, rather than a constitutional text), this was more than could be said for the document it ratified. For the various constitution-makers were, as Olivier Duhamel observes, 'hostile cousins brought together over a summer's brief period of calm', men with conflicting views on the distribution of political power. Directly involved in the drafting of the constitution were Debré (now justice minister, an admirer of the West-minster system who aimed at reinforcing the prime minister and government in relation to parliament); de Gaulle (intent on reinforcing the presidency he was shortly to occupy); a handful of senior ministers (*ministres d'État*) drawn from the major Fourth Republic parties (who saw the president as a crisis manager, to be put out to grass once the Algerian emergency was over); and a group of parliamentarians (whose role, for the first time in the drafting of a republican constitution in France, was a merely consulta-tive one, but who were still, understandably, concerned to safeguard the prerogatives of parliament). Dialogue was possible because de Gaulle, anxious to respect due process, was still currying favour with parliament, while the parliamentarians and ministers, with the Algerian war still threatening France, could not afford to alienate the General. So both sides made concessions. The result, however, was not a happy compromise but a constitutional mess. The unfortunate constitutional experts of the Conseil d'État who assisted Debré in the drafting were called upon to juxtapose and superimpose conflict-ing ideals, and in the resulting lengthy text confusion competed with contradiction and ambiguity with obscurity. In essence, the lawyers were trying to fuse two ultimately incompatible notions: on the one hand, the principle of governmental responsibility to parliament (which implied a parliamentary régime); and, on the other, the separation of powers with a strong head of state (which smacked of presidentialism). To schematise somewhat, a 'Debré constitution', drawing on the British model, coexisted with a 'de Gaulle constitution', inspired by the General's obsession with leadership, both being moderated by the Fourth Republic politicians whose approval was necessary to a successful referendum.

- The 'Debré constitution' is most evident in the numerous articles reinforcing the position of government and prime minister *vis-à-vis* parliament. While admiring the Westminster model, Debré knew that no French premier could count on a disciplined single-party parliamentary majority on the British pattern. He therefore aimed to create constitutional substitutes for party discipline, drawing on some of the principles of 'rationalised parliamentarianism' that had inspired the constitu-tion of West Germany. Henceforth, the government would control the parlia-mentary agenda. Governments would be able to refuse parliamentary amendments to their own bills. They could only be voted out of office by a censure motion carried by an absolute majority of all Deputies in the National Assembly. Such a censure motion would also be necessary to refuse any specific bill that the govern-ment chose to make into a question of confidence. Individual parliamentarians would no longer be able to propose extra spending or tax cuts at will. The budget, if not agreed by parliament, could be adopted by decree after seventy days of parlia-mentary debate. Parliamentary sessions were restricted to a total of six months a year, to be extended only by consent of president and prime minister. Limits were placed on the (general) domains in which parliament could legislate, more specific legal provisions being reserved for ministerial decrees. A Constitutional Council was created, with the initial purpose of ensuring that parliament did not overstep its new legislative powers. In order to limit parliamentarians' appetites for governmental office, ministerial posts were made incompatible with office as Deputy or Senator. The prime minister was, for the first time, referred to as prime minister (not, as under the Third and Fourth Republics, *Président du conseil des ministres*), and given the clear role of 'directing the work of the government'. Articles 20 to 51 of the new constitution were, in short, nails in the coffin of the French republican tradition of parliamentary sovereignty.

- The 'De Gaulle constitution' appears, above all, in the fifteen articles concerning the president of the Republic. The new head of state would no longer be chosen, as his predecessors of the Third and Fourth Republics had been, by a joint session of the two houses of parliament; instead, he would be elected by a college of some 80,000 parliamentarians and representatives of local councils from throughout France and the French Community (as what remained of the empire was now known). This provision, justified in the name of the separation of powers, was designed to cut the umbilical cord between the president and parliament, and to raise the quality of presidents above that of those worthy but second-rank parliamentarians who had typically filled the office under the old system. The president's role was defined, broadly, as being to 'ensure, by his arbitration [*arbitrage*], the proper functioning of the public authorities and the continuity of the State' and to guarantee France's 'national independence, territorial integrity and observance of treaties'. To fulfil the role as guarantor effectively, and to avoid the dispersal of authority that had proved so fatal in 1940, the president was entitled to take sweeping powers in any grave crisis (one of the relatively few constitutional provisions included at the behest of the parliamentary consultative committee was that parliament should sit as of right when emergency powers were in force). The new constitution also gave the president powers to intervene in internal politics in less dramatic situations. The choice of prime minister was his (though at the behest of the *ministres d'État*, the president enjoyed no corresponding right to sack his premier). He could dissolve the National Assembly and call new elections (and the replacement of proportional representation by the two-ballot majority electoral system, though adopted as a regular law rather than as an article of the constitution, increased the possibility of minor vote swings producing big changes in party strengths in parliament). And, with the agreement of the government or parliament, he could call a referendum on questions relating to the 'organisation of the public authorities' or the ratification of a treaty.

It is the juxtaposition of these two sets of rules that gives the constitution its unique, and uniquely problematic, character. Comparative political scientists, beginning with the Frenchman Maurice Duverger, have taken to referring to France as a semi-presidential régime, one of a species including such European countries as Austria, Finland, Iceland, Ireland and Portugal, as well as (more recently) Romania, Poland, Russia, Ukraine and Moldova, as well as a number of South American, African and Asian states. Within this general category, however, France still occupies an unusual place by virtue of the distribution of political power within the executive. Ireland, for example, has a directly elected but largely ceremonial president who leaves the business of governing to the Taoiseach. In Russia, on the other hand, the president is indubitably the nation's political leader. But in the Fifth Republic, the central question of any constitution – who rules? – is fudged. Is it the prime minister, who 'directs the operation of the government', which itself 'determines and conducts the policy of the Nation'? Or is it the president of the Republic, who appoints the prime minister and who can make a direct appeal to the voters by dissolution or by referendum? In more detailed matters, too, the French Constitution of 1958 gives a sense of the world not of Descartes but of Lewis Carroll. Article 15 reads 'The President of the Republic shall be commander-in-chief of the armed forces. He shall preside over the higher national defence councils and committees.' Yet Article 20 indicates that the government 'shall have at its disposal . . . the armed forces', and Article 21 states that the prime minister 'shall be responsible for national defence'. Article 13 gives the president the right to appoint to certain military posts, while Article 21 empowers the prime minister to appoint to others. In other words, in the crucial area of defence, powers are shared but power is ill-defined. The constitution clearly establishes a diarchy at the top, a twin-headed or bicephalous executive unique in Western democracies, but it does not clarify the respective roles of president and prime minister. Such clarification was left to the interplay of personality and political circumstance.

Some further definition, it is true, was given by the major constitutional amendment of October 1962. This replaced, as the method of electing the president, the college of 80,000 *notables* with direct universal suffrage (on two ballots). Like the constitution it amended, the change was born of a specific context. De Gaulle's unique historical legitimacy and the peculiar dangers of the Algerian war, far more than his election by *notables* in December 1958, had established his presidential primacy during his first three and a half years in office. Now, in the summer of 1962, he sought to perpetuate that primacy for himself and his successors. The Algerian war was over, and with it a sort of internal political truce: many leaders of the Fourth Republic parties were keen to send the septuagenarian General into a retirement which he was in no hurry to begin. The French Community had disappeared, and with it the danger that a directly elected president would owe his position, not to metropolitan Frenchmen, but to colonials. France's explosion of an atom bomb in 1960 gave a terrifying new responsibility to whoever ran the armed forces. De Gaulle's relations with the *notables* of France's local councils had soured after the Senate, the upper house of parliament elected and peopled entirely by such *notables*, had offered unexpected opposition to his policies. The spread of television opened new possibilities for campaigning in a direct presidential election. Inspired by this combination of lofty rationales and base political calculation, de Gaulle seized the occasion offered by a botched assassination attempt (which came close enough to success to remind the nation of his mortality, and thus of the question of his successor's designation) and invited the French people to adopt his reform by referendum. They did so on 28 October 1962, albeit by a narrower margin (62 per cent of voters, 46.6 per cent of registered electors) than in 1958. The constitutional change gave no new *powers* to the president, but it nevertheless greatly enhanced his *power*. From 1965, the date of the first direct presidential election, each successive president could (and did) claim, through his unique position as the only *élu de la nation*, directly elected by the whole French people, a democratic legitimacy at least equal to that of the National Assembly. The political significance of the October 1962 reform cannot be overestimated, for it upset, in favour of the president, the uneasy and ambiguous balance established in the 1958 constitution.

This was all the more the case as the following month saw the emergence of what none of the constitution-makers of 1958 had imagined possible, a stable parliamentary majority. A majority of Deputies of the National Assembly had opposed the 1962 constitutional revision for reasons both of substance (the Deputies rightly saw the change as a threat to their own prerogatives) and of legality (de Gaulle was violating his own constitution, since Article 89 requires amendments to be agreed by both houses of parliament before referendum, rather than being submitted direct to the people). The Deputies therefore took the most ready means of protest to hand, passing a motion of censure against the government on 4 October. De Gaulle reacted by using his new power to dissolve the Assembly and call new elections: he was rewarded, on 25 November 1962, with an absolute majority for the Gaullists and their allies. Stable majorities, familiar to the British, were quite new to the French, accustomed as they were to what David Goldey and Philip Williams have called the 'shifting and shifty coalitions' of the Third and Fourth Republics. *Le fait majoritaire* became part of France's 'political constitution', never written into the texts but always underlying their application. And for a quarter-century it, as much as the October amendment, enhanced presidential power.

   Crucial as they were to the subsequent workings of the Fifth Republic, the events of autumn 1962 removed none of the possibilities of rich variation that were afforded by the texts. Why this was so may be illustrated by reference to Figure 2.1, which depicts the heart of the constitution of the Fifth Republic, as amended in 1962, and Figure 2.2, which represents its electoral chronology, and presidents, prime ministers and parliamentary majorities.

- *The electorate* may be asked by the president (usually in accordance with government and parliament) to vote in referendums, of which there have been nine since June 1958 (five of them under de Gaulle's leadership). More regularly, voters have two opportunities to choose their national rulers, at presidential and parliamentary elections. But the two were not synchronised until 2000. A president, unless he resigned (as de Gaulle did in 1969) or died in office (as his successor Georges Pompidou did in 1974), enjoyed a *septennat*, a full, and indefinitely renewable, seven-year term, longer than any comparable Western leader. A parliament, on the other hand, lasted (and lasts) a maximum of five years (less, in the event of a dissolution, as in 1962, 1968, 1981, 1988 and 1997). The constitutional reform of September 2000 shortened the presidential term to five years starting from the presidential election of 2002, and as this took place five weeks before parliamentary elections, a degree of synchronisation can normally be expected in future. On the other hand, voters will still be free in principle, as they were before the reform, to choose whether or not to elect a president and a parliamentary majority from the same political camp.
- *The National Assembly* majority may therefore be broadly supportive towards the president (as in 1962–86, 1988–93 and 1995–97) or hostile (as in 1986–88, 1993–95 and 1997–2002). There are many lesser possibilities of variation too. A broadly supportive National Assembly may contain a large single-party majority, as in 1968–73 or 1981–86, a deeply divided one, as in 1973–81, or no overall majority at all, as in 1988–93. A hostile majority may be tiny, as in 1986–88, or very large, as in 1993–95.
- *The prime minister and government* are responsible to the National Assembly and must therefore command a majority there (or at least, as in 1988–93, a plurality

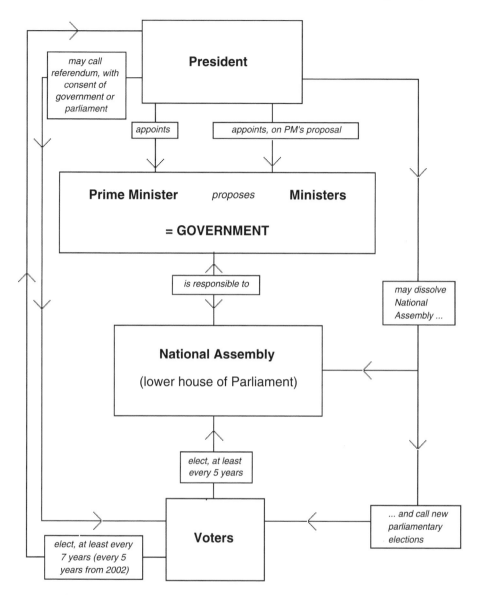

Figure 2.1 The heart of the Fifth Republic Constitution.

sufficiently large to be able to fend off an opposition censure motion). A president with a friendly majority will enjoy a wide choice of possible prime ministers from his own camp. Such a premier will therefore be beholden to the president for his appointment. Where the president faces a hostile parliamentary majority, however, he has no choice but to appoint a prime minister acceptable to that majority – usually the effective leader of the parliamentary opposition to himself. The parliamentary elections of 1986, 1993 and 1997 therefore opened periods of uneasy 'cohabitation' within France's twin-headed executive: between a left-wing president (Mitterrand) and a right-wing premier (Jacques Chirac in 1986, Édouard Balladur

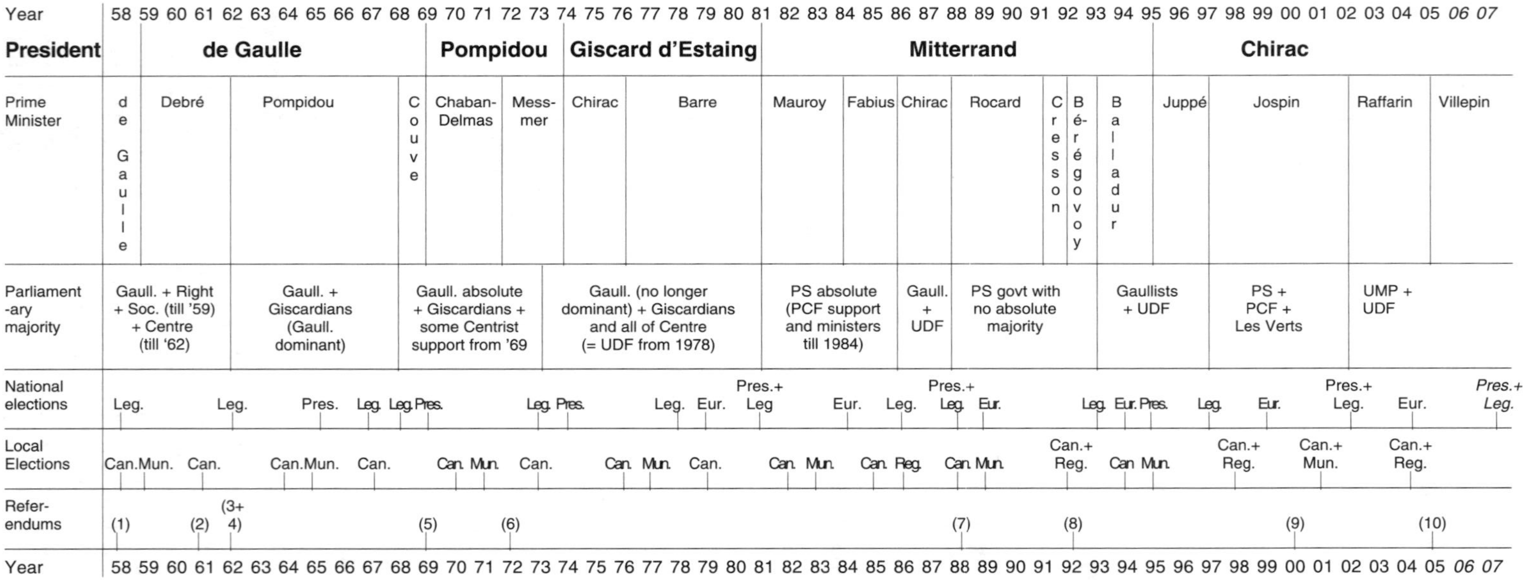

Figure 2.2 — The Fifth French Republic, 1958–2005: a chronological framework.

Year: 58 59 60 61 62 63 64 65 66 67 68 69 70 71 72 73 74 75 76 77 78 79 80 81 82 83 84 85 86 87 88 89 90 91 92 93 94 95 96 97 98 99 00 01 02 03 04 05 06 07

	de Gaulle	Pompidou	Giscard d'Estaing	Mitterrand	Chirac
President	de Gaulle	Pompidou	Giscard d'Estaing	Mitterrand	Chirac
Prime Minister	Debré; Pompidou; Couve	Chaban-Delmas; Messmer	Chirac; Barre	Mauroy; Fabius; Chirac; Rocard; Cresson; Bérégovoy; Balladur	Juppé; Jospin; Raffarin; Villepin
Parliamentary majority	Gaull. + Right + Soc. (till '59) + Centre (till '62); Gaull. + Giscardians (Gaull. dominant)	Gaull. absolute + Giscardians + some Centrist support from '69	Gaull. (no longer dominant) + Giscardians and all of Centre (= UDF from 1978)	PS absolute (PCF support and ministers till 1984); Gaull. + UDF; PS govt with no absolute majority; Gaullists + UDF	PS + PCF + Les Verts; UMP + UDF
National elections	Leg. / Leg. / Pres. / Leg. Leg. / Pres.	Leg. Pres. / Can.	Pres.+Leg. / Leg. Eur.	Pres.+Leg. / Leg. / Eur. / Pres.+Leg. / Leg. Eur. / Leg. Eur. Pres.	Pres.+Leg. / Eur. / Pres.+Leg. / Pres.+Leg.
Local Elections	Can.Mun. / Can. / Can.Mun. / Can.	Can.Mun. / Can.	Can. / Can.Mun. / Can.	Can.Mun. / Can. Reg. / Can.Reg. / Can.+Reg. / Can. Mun.	Can. Mun. / Can.+Reg. / Can.+Mun. / Can.+Reg.
Referendums	(1) / (2) / (3+ 4) / (5)	(6)		(7) / (8)	(9) / (10)

Key

Elections
Leg. = Legislative (parliamentary)
Pres. = Presidential
Eur. = European
Mun. = Municipal
Can. = Cantonal (*conseils généraux*)
Reg. = Regional

Parties
PCF = Communists
PS = Socialists
UDF = moderate Right (non-Gaullist)
UMP = Gaullist and non-Gaullist moderate Right

Referendums (all passed, except no. 5, 1969, and no. 10, 2005)
1 = Referendum on Fifth-Republic Constitution (15.4% abstention: 79.3% of valid votes yes)
2 = Referendum on self-determination for Algeria (23.5% abstention: 75.3% of valid votes yes)
3 = Referendum on independence for Algeria (24.4% abstention: 90.7% of valid votes yes)
4 = Referendum on election of President by direct universal suffrage (22.8% abstention: 61.8% yes)
5 = Referendum on Senate and regional reforms (19.4% abstention: 46.8% of valid votes yes: **53.2% no**)
6 = Referendum on entry of Britain and Ireland into the EEC (39.6% abstention: 67.7% of valid votes yes)
7 = Referendum on future status of New Caledonia (62.7% abstention: 80.0% of valid votes yes)
8 = Referendum on ratification of Maastricht treaty on European Union (31.8% abstention: 50.82% of valid votes yes)
9 = Referendum on reduction of presidential term from 7 to 5 years (69.7% abstention: 73.2% of valid votes yes)
10 = Referendum on ratification of European constitutional treaty (32.40% abstention: 45.3% of valid votes yes; **54.7% no**)

in 1993); or between a right-wing president (Chirac) and a left-wing premier (Lionel Jospin) from 1997. These cohabitation prime ministers, having won the job thanks to their support within the parliamentary majority, have been politically much stronger than their counterparts of 'normal' times, raised to the premiership by the president's choice. But once again, there is wide scope for variation within the two categories of 'coincidence' and 'cohabitation'. A president and prime minister from the same camp may be extremely close, like Chirac and Alain Juppé, or endure execrable personal and political relations, as Mitterrand did with Michel Rocard; cohabitation, on the other hand, may see a civilised *modus vivendi* develop, as it quickly did between Mitterrand and Balladur.

- *The president*, with his unique legitimacy as the people's direct choice, unmovable during his term except by trial for high treason, and able to appoint the prime minister and call parliamentary elections (though not more than once a year) and referendums (under certain conditions), is normally master both of France's politics and of its policies, internal and external. Faced with a hostile parliamentary majority, however, he ineluctably loses many of his powers (and notably the freedom to choose his prime minister, and control over domestic policy); and he has to struggle to retain many of the rest, and to avoid returning to the relative impotence of his predecessors of earlier republics.

Given the range of scenarios available on the basis of the same text, it is not surprising that the constitution itself has been subjected to different interpretations. These are discussed in the rest of this chapter.

Readings of the Fifth Republic

Debré presented the 1958 constitution to the Conseil d'État, rather confusingly, as a 'parliamentary régime' in which the presidency was 'the keystone'. For a generation, political practice and academic commentary stressed the second half of this ambiguous equation. Only the approach of cohabitation, in the mid-1980s, provoked a rediscovery of the first.

The republican monarchy

The specific new powers granted to the presidency were rather few: to dissolve parliament, to appoint the prime minister (both without any countersignature), to call a referendum (with the agreement of the government), to take emergency powers in a crisis. Presidential primacy was not, therefore, explicitly written into the 1958 constitution; it depended, in the first instance, on what David Bell has called 'an act of political levitation', and then on the revision of 1962. The principal architect of presidential primacy was, of course, de Gaulle, whose personal determination to extend presidential power up to, and indeed beyond, its constitutional limits was underpinned by five political assets. First, his wartime role as leader of Free France gave de Gaulle a unique historical legitimacy at least equal to that of his directly elected successors. Second, the wide-ranging powers he was granted as the last prime minister of the Fourth Republic, and which he exercised to the full from June 1958, gave him a tight grip on the reins of the state well before his inauguration as president in January 1959. Third, the real dangers presented by the Algerian war, which lasted till March 1962, ensured a degree of tolerance for strong executive leadership. Fourth, the still vivid popular memories of the confusion of the Fourth Republic offered de Gaulle corresponding opportunities to mobilise support for himself and for the Gaullists, and against the 'old' parties – whose failure to present a positive appeal to voters was well summarised by the name of the alliance they created to oppose the direct election of the president at the October 1962 referendum: the 'Cartel des Non'. Finally, the stable, Gaullist-led National Assembly majority that emerged from the elections of November 1962 ensured that parliament would offer no effective opposition to presidential primacy.

Presidential primacy meant, in essence, that the president would not only be head of state and crisis manager, but also the nation's chief policy-maker and its first politician. The policy-making role was evoked early on by the president of the National Assembly, Jacques Chaban-Delmas, in November 1959. Chaban coined the term *domaine réservé* to denote those areas – Algeria, the French Community, foreign affairs and defence – in which the government should merely 'execute' presidential policies. Devoid of any official place in the texts, the *domaine réservé* has still acquired quasi-constitutional status as a shorthand for the foreign policy and defence concerns at the heart of the president's policy-making role.

The president's role as France's leading politician was given striking practical demonstration, often in defiance of the spirit and even the letter of the new constitution, in 1962. During the eight months following the end of the Algerian war, de Gaulle:

- sacked a prime minister (the absence of any constitutional provision for such an act was circumvented by the ever-loyal Debré's acceptance of the presidential request for his resignation in April 1962);
- called a referendum, on the direct election of the president, under conditions of more than dubious legality;
- reappointed a government that had just lost a no-confidence vote in the National Assembly, in violation of the spirit of Article 50 of the constitution;
- dissolved parliament, exercising the right to do so granted in Article 12;
- won both the October referendum and the November parliamentary elections, thereby extending his own primacy beyond the Algerian crisis, creating a basis of legitimacy for his successors, and inaugurating *le fait majoritaire*.

De Gaulle turned the practice of presidential primacy into doctrine at his press conference of January 1964 – days after a decree had palliated the constitutional ambiguities in defence questions by putting the president in charge of France's new nuclear deterrent. There could, de Gaulle declared, be no 'diarchy' at the summit of the French state. He interpreted the profoundly ambiguous term *arbitrage* in Article 5 to mean, not a neutral referee's role suggested by the commonest use of the word *arbitre*, but rather the much stronger role of arbiter of the nation's destiny. Vested with this unique responsibility, the president was the sole source of political authority – a reading which, in principle, opened all domains of policy-making to presidential intervention. De Gaulle's assertiveness was echoed and exceeded by subsequent presidents. Pompidou argued in his short book *Le nœud gordien* that de Gaulle's successor would have to be *more* interventionist than the General in order to preserve presidential primacy while lacking de Gaulle's unique legitimacy: his subsequent record in the job confirmed his own prognosis. Giscard d'Estaing, having criticised de Gaulle's 'solitary exercise of power' while out of office, asserted his policy-making role as president by publicly giving his governments six-monthly programmes of work. Most strikingly of all, François Mitterrand, who had denounced the Fifth Republic in a celebrated pamphlet of 1964 entitled *Le Coup d'État permanent*, admitted once in power that 'these institutions, which I did not create, suit me well enough' – adding, more brutally, that 'it is up to me to decide in what areas the president should decide'. Far from being confined to Chaban's *domaine réservé*, presidential policy-making could extend to any sector. Combining many of the powers of the American president (a secure term of office, and for seven years not four) and of the British prime minister (a stable parliamentary majority, and the right to dissolve), the French president appeared as more powerful, within his own political system, than any Western leader: a 'republican monarch', in the expression of French commentators.

A 'parliamentary régime'

Debré's presentation of the 1958 constitution as a 'parliamentary régime' was largely forgotten as long as the presidential reading was confirmed by daily political practice. Giscard d'Estaing first conceded the possibility of an alternative interpretation early in 1978, when he reminded voters that if the Left won the elections due that March, its programme would be applied; he could do nothing to stop it. But the Communist–Socialist opposition aborted the experiment by losing. The issue only re-emerged seriously after the Left itself, after its dazzling presidential and parliamentary victories in 1981, had lost popular support and faced defeat at the 1986 parliamentary elections. The debate then showed the absurdities to which a fully presidentialist view of the constitution could lead. A number of commentators, citing the dubious precedent of de Gaulle's brusque departure after his defeat in the 1969 referendum, claimed that the only course of action consistent with the 'spirit' of the constitution would be for President Mitterrand to resign. Even the respectable former Prime Minister Raymond Barre argued that a right-wing parliamentary majority should force Mitterrand out by opposing any government, of whatever complexion, appointed by him. Seven years later, as the Right prepared for its landslide parliamentary victory of 1993, similar arguments were wheeled out: Jacques Chirac declared that Mitterrand would be morally (though not, he conceded, constitutionally) bound to go. But curiously, Chirac himself, once president, felt no such call of duty. In 1997 he chose to remain in the Élysée after dissolving the National Assembly and seeing his right-wing majority crash to defeat in the ensuing elections – a clear disavowal from the voters. By staying, appointing a prime minister acceptable to the new majority and embarking on a period of 'cohabitation', Chirac was acting consistently with both the letter of the constitution and the practice of his predecessor Mitterrand. A parliamentary majority opposed to the president, then, neither forces the president's departure nor permits the continuation of the republican monarchy. It therefore invites a dusting-off of the 'parliamentary' reading.

- The president's role as the nation's chief politician is severely circumscribed. His power to choose the prime minister becomes largely formal; he is effectively obliged to appoint the leader of the new parliamentary majority or another candidate enjoying that leader's support. His power to dissolve parliament, limited in any case to once a year by the constitution, is also limited politically, since few presidents would court two successive electoral defeats of their parliamentary supporters.

The power to call a referendum can only be exercised with the consent of the government. Nevertheless, the president has more control than anyone else over the political calendar.

- In domestic matters, the president's role as chief policy-maker passes to the prime minister. Unlike his American counterpart, France's president has no veto: while he can ask parliament to 'reconsider' a law (under Article 10), his request must have the prime minister's countersignature, and parliament is free in any case to vote the same law again by a simple majority. The battery of dispositions in the 1958 constitution limiting the powers of parliament now function to the exclusive benefit of the prime minister and government. For example, the Right's privatisations in 1986–88 and 1993–95, or the left-wing government's laws to establish a 35-hour week after 1997, were major domestic initiatives carried through in the face of presidential opposition. The president may place minor technical obstacles in the government's path, as Mitterrand did when Chirac's right-wing government attempted to legislate by decree in 1986. And he may voice his disapproval in the Council of Ministers, through the media, or both. But as long as the government's majority remains loyal, its domestic programme will be applied.
- The president retains a greater or lesser role in the *domaine réservé*, thanks notably to his constitutional position as head of the armed forces, guarantor of the nation's territorial integrity and negotiator of treaties. But parliament votes the budget, including defence spending; European affairs are a large and growing border zone between foreign and domestic policy; and, as we have seen, the prime minister is 'responsible for national defence'. So the *domaine réservé* cannot be fenced off. Indeed, Édouard Balladur, prime minister from 1993 to 1995, redefined it as a 'shared' area, the *domaine partagé*. Despite regular disagreements between the two heads of the executive, the broad consensus between Right and Left in France over foreign and defence policies has prevented really damaging conflicts over foreign or defence matters. The respective importance of president and prime minister in these sectors depends very much on the political context of each cohabitation. Mitterrand, for example, largely resisted Chirac's attempted incursions, but proved more flexible with Balladur, in part because of his own political and physical weakness at the end of his second *septennat*.
- Other responsibilities, and notably the highly sensitive area of appointments to senior posts in the civil service, the public sector and the military, are negotiated more or less fiercely between president and prime minister.

As will be clear from the above, a 'parliamentary' reading does not mean a return to an all-powerful parliament – as some Cassandras who saw the first cohabitation as a 'return to the Fourth Republic' predicted. Rather, it implies a partial and temporary transfer of many presidential powers to the other chief of the political executive, the prime minister, and to the government. How temporary depends on circumstance. The first cohabitation was seen as a blip, an interruption to the norm of republican monarchy. By the end of the third one in 2002, however, cohabitation represented something more than an aberration, having accounted for nine of the Fifth Republic's forty-four years. The public had apparently grown more relaxed about it, too, at least on the basis of opinion poll responses. But the experience of the first round of the 2002 presidential elections, when President Chirac and Prime Minister Jospin won a mere 35 per cent of the vote between them, suggested to the political elite that cohabitation had damaged French democracy by blurring the lines of political conflict. And in any case, the move to the five-year presidential term makes it very likely that voters in future will choose their parliamentary majority in the wake of a presidential race: on each of the three past occasions when this has happened (in 1981, 1988 and 2002), as well as in 1962, when the October referendum represented a vote of confidence in de Gaulle, voters have opted for a legislature to support the president. On that basis, the return of cohabitation is technically possible but politically improbable.

The Constitutional Council and the État de droit

Le gouvernement des juges is still a bogeyman in French political discourse; mistrust of the judiciary is integral to the Jacobin tradition (Chapter 1). The terminology of the constitution reflects that mistrust: the judiciary is referred to as an 'authority', not a 'power'. Nevertheless, the constitution of 1958 did innovate by introducing into France a body that has been compared – with, it is true, very partial justification – to the United States Supreme Court. The Constitutional Council has the power to rule on the constitutionality of new laws that are referred to it before they are promulgated, and to strike down those laws found wanting. Its composition reflected its chief purpose for the constitution-makers, which was to prevent parliament from overstepping the tight limits for legislation set by Article 34. Of its nine members (who may be wholly political appointments, as no judicial background is required of them), three, including its president, are chosen by the president of the Republic, and three each by the presidents of the National Assembly and the Senate. Only these individuals, plus the prime minister, had the right under the 1958 constitution to refer cases to the Constitutional Council (though it also has a standing duty to rule on the regularity of elections and on the internal rules of the two houses of parliament).

Two developments elevated the Council from its status as the executive's watchdog over the parliament to a quasi-judicial authority. First, after a dozen largely inactive early years (only nine cases were referred to it between 1959 and 1974), the Council was seized by a momentous attack of independence. In the 'freedom of association' decision of 1971, it specified that it henceforth took the constitutional text, which is the yardstick of its decisions, to include the preamble to the constitution, which itself includes the 1789 Declaration of the Rights of Man and the Citizen. At a single stroke, it effectively incorporated a bill of rights into the Constitution of the Fifth Republic. The second development was initiated by President Giscard d'Estaing: in 1974, a constitutional amendment allowed any sixty Deputies or sixty Senators to refer a law to the Council. The Left sneered at the measure as a *réformette*, although its parliamentarians used it to refer forty-three laws to the Council during the Giscard presidency alone. By the 1980s, it was a safe working assumption that every major law could be referred. Those who draft laws are therefore likely to take this into account by anticipation. This is, of course, still very far from being *le gouvernement des juges*. Once promulgated, a law cannot be touched by the Council: there is no question, as there is in the United States, of long-standing legislation arriving for a ruling after being fed upwards through the ordinary courts. But the Council's power to irritate the executive has been well illustrated by the regular attacks on its supposedly 'political' rulings from successive governments of both Right and Left. To this extent, therefore, no future 'republican monarchy' can hope to be absolute.

The constitution in flux

The rise of the Constitutional Council is one illustration of the way in which debate over 'presidential' versus 'parliamentary' readings fails to capture the full range of variation within the constitution. There are other examples. Chapter 1 described a context in which the prerogatives of the strong nation state on the Jacobin or Gaullist model are increasingly being challenged by both globalisation and Europeanisation, while the decentralisation undertaken in 1982 has transferred some powers out of Paris to the provinces. Theorists of multilevel governance argue that such developments require us to replace traditional conceptions of national governments with more flexible approaches based on networks and partnerships rather than sovereignty and hierarchies. Even if their case is at times overstated, it is clear that insofar as the French state as a whole has become less sovereign and more interdependent with European and other partners, so the working context of the leading French players, president and prime minister, government and parliament, has been transformed.

This transformation, indeed, has affected the constitution itself. Its revision is a relatively simple affair, unencumbered, in the unitary state that France remains, by a prolonged ratification process. After being voted in identical terms by National Assembly and Senate, amendments either go to referendum or are agreed by a three-fifths vote of the two houses of parliament meeting together in congress, for which purpose the parliamentarians are loaded into buses and transported to Versailles. Rare over the first three decades, these excursions have been almost annual since 1992. In less than half a century, indeed, the Constitution of the Fifth Republic has undergone nineteen amendments, two more than the Constitution of the United States has in the two and a quarter centuries since the incorporation of the Bill of Rights in 1791. Amendments can be divided into three categories (Table 2.1). The first (type a) includes a total of four technical amendments, either adjusting France's relations to overseas territories and former colonies (in 1960 and 1998) or effecting minor changes to France's own institutions (in addition, the amendment of 1995 also removed some of the constitution's obsolete articles, particularly relating to the French Community). The second (type b) consists of six adjustments to bring the constitution into line with new international, and more specifically European, commitments. The Maastricht Treaty on European Union of 1992, the Amsterdam Treaty of 1997 and the European constitution of 2004 all required constitutional amendments, some of them important (the most recent were passed by parliament in February 2005 before the text of the European constitution was put to a doomed referendum in the following May). To these should be added three amendments linked to a common European immigration policy (1993), to a European arrest warrant (2003), and to France's recognition of the International Criminal Court (1999). The third and final group (type c) is that of nine 'spontaneous', and more or less substantial, changes to core institutions. Of these, the two most significant concern the presidency – the direct election amendment of 1962 and the shortening of the presidential term in 2000. Three concern the legislative process: the 1974 amendment referred to above, that of 1995 initiating the single parliamentary session and extending the possible domains of the referendum (though no referendum has yet been held under the new provision), and that of 1996 bringing the social security budget into the legislative domain. Two softened the contours of the Jacobin state by acknowledging the penal responsibility of ministers (in 1993) and constitutionalising the principle of a decentralised Republic (in 2003). One, in 1999,

Table 2.1 Constitutional amendments since 1958

Type*	Date	Nature of amendment
a	4 June 1960	Reforms to French Community, allowing newly independent former colonies to retain membership
c	6 November 1962	Direct election of president
a	30 December 1963	Minor change to dates of parliamentary sessions
c	29 October 1974	Provision for 60 Deputies or 60 Senators to refer newly passed bills to Constitutional Council for verification of constitutionality
a	18 June 1976	Provisions in case of incapacity, resignation or death of a president
b	25 June 1992	Provisions allowing ratification of Maastricht Treaty on European Union (EMU, votes for EU citizens at municipal elections, common visa policy, parliamentary resolutions on EU legislation)
c	27 July 1993	Criminal responsibility of ministers: creation of Court of Justice of the Republic
b	25 November 1993	Changes to asylum legislation allowing reciprocal legislation with other (principally EU) states
c	4 August 1995	Single parliamentary session; extension of area of possible application of referenda to include economic and social questions
c	22 February 1996	Provision for parliament to vote law on finance of social security system
a	20 July 1998	Transitional arrangements for vote on future government of New Caledonia
b	25 January 1999	Provisions allowing ratification of Amsterdam Treaty (1997), especially relating to free movement of persons between EU states
b	8 July 1999 (a)	Recognition of jurisdiction of International Criminal Court
c	8 July 1999 (b)	Legislation permitted to promote gender parity in politics
c	2 October 2000	Presidential term shortened from seven years to five
b	25 March 2003	Minor adjustments allowing transfer of competences to EU relating to European arrest warrant
c	28 March 2003	Decentralisation incorporated into constitution
b, c	1 March 2005	Provisions allowing ratification of European Constitution and Charter of the Environment

Source: Constitutional Council.

Note
* Types a–c refer to classifications given in the text.

allowed future legislation to promote 'parity' of political representation between men and women. The most recent amendment, finally, incorporates a Charter of the Environment into the constitution, though it is uncertain to what extent its impact will be more than symbolic.

Although the broad lines of de Gaulle's legacy are still there, in significant ways the constitution is no longer his. France's institutions are in constant flux; this dynamic character of the institutional framework constructed in a few short summer weeks of 1958 will be one theme of the chapters that follow. Change may be reversible, as with the switch from presidential leadership to cohabitation and back again, or it may be more permanent. It may result from constitutional amendment, from altered political or electoral circumstance, or from developments outside France. And it is likely to be much bound up with individual personalities – the subject of the next chapter.

Further reading

Andrews, W. and Hoffman, S. (eds), *The Fifth Republic at Twenty*, Albany, NY, State University of New York Press, 1981.

Bell, D., *Presidential Power in Fifth Republic France*, Oxford, Berg, 2000.

Duhamel, O., *Vive la VIe République!*, Paris, Éditions du Seuil, 2003.

Duhamel, O. and Parodi, J.-L. (eds), *La constitution de la Ve République*, Paris, Presses de la Fondation Nationale des Sciences Politiques, 1985.

Duverger, M., *Les constitutions de la France*, 9th edition, Paris, Presses Universitaires de France (collection Que Sais-Je?), 1971.

Duverger, M., *La monarchie républicaine*, Paris, Robert Laffont, 1974.

Fondation Charles-de-Gaulle, *L'avènement de la Ve République: entre nouveauté et tradition*, Paris, Armand Colin, 1999.

Fontvielle-Alquier, F., *Plaidoyer pour la IVe République*, Paris, Robert Laffont, 1976.

Horne, A., *A Savage War of Peace: Algeria 1954–1962*, London, Macmillan, 1977.

McRae, D., *Parliament, Parties, and Society in France, 1946–1958*, New York, St Martin's Press, 1967.

Pouvoirs, no. 76, 1996, 'La IVe République'.

Revue de Droit Public, special issue, May–June 1998, 'Les 40 ans de la Ve République'.

Williams, P. M., *Crisis and Compromise: Politics in the Fourth Republic*, London, Longman, 1964.

Williams, P. M., *French Politicians and Elections, 1951–1969*, Cambridge, Cambridge University Press, 1971.

3 Presidents and prime ministers

The personal factor

The Fifth Republic was attacked by its early opponents as a régime of 'personal power'. This was inaccurate. As Olivier Duhamel observes, the institutions have worked in broadly the same way under very different presidents (de Gaulle and early Mitterrand, for example), but very differently, because of the change of parliamentary majority, under the same president (Mitterrand 1981–86 *versus* Mitterrand 1986–88). But neither presidents nor (with a few exceptions) prime ministers are mere vehicles of forces external to themselves. Their vision of their own role and of France's future has, at least, marked their periods in office and, at most, led to lasting institutional change.

Charles de Gaulle (1890–1970)

General de Gaulle's political career, which he began in 1940 after three decades as a professional soldier, was shaped by the collision between a jealous and passionate love of his country (depicted in the opening pages of his *War Memoirs* as a 'princess in a fairy tale' and a 'Madonna in a medieval fresco') and the searing experience of France's abject collapse in the face of Hitler's invasion. His two fixations thenceforth

Table 3.1 Presidents of the Fifth Republic

President	Dates of presidency
Charles de Gaulle	8 January 1959–28 April 1969
Georges Pompidou	19 June 1969–2 April 1974
Valéry Giscard d'Estaing	24 May 1974–21 May 1981
François Mitterrand	21 May 1981–15 May 1995
Jacques Chirac	15 May 1995–

were *autorité de l'État* and *indépendance nationale*. Their intensity was, if anything, increased by events of the thirteen post-war years – his own acrimonious relations with party politicians in the provisional government which he headed until his resignation in January 1946, and the Fourth Republic's failure to provide stable government and to handle colonial conflicts. All confirmed his view that in the absence of a strong state and a presidency allowing the exercise of vigorous leadership, the *ferments de dispersion* of the French would be given free rein and France would drift to catastrophe. De Gaulle's obsession with national independence sprang from the concrete experience, between 1940 and 1944, of having to rely totally on his British and American allies for France's liberation (a dependence that he forgave the 'Anglo-Saxons' much less readily than he pardoned the defeated Germans for the Occupation). It led him to withdraw France from NATO, to veto British entry into Europe, to boycott European institutions for six months rather than see them constrain France's sovereignty and to wage a battle – quixotic or visionary – against the Cold War division of the world into two blocs. The recovery of France's position in the world also served domestic ends, as a goal that would divert the French from petty internal squabbles. To further his vision, de Gaulle deployed an inflexible determination with regard to ends, but pragmatism bordering at times on cynicism as to means; a mastery of rhetoric combined with a willingness to resort to silence, secrecy or deceit where circumstances demanded (as they repeatedly did during the Algerian war); a grasp of the political arts, including the basest of them, combined with constant self-presentation as being above the political fray; a talent for theatre, shown in the broadcast call of 18 June 1940 to continue the fight against Germany, or the unannounced disappearance from Paris at the height of the 'events' of May 1968; a genius for touching a responsive chord in the national consciousness, whether by the pen or (remarkably for one born in 1890) through the new medium of television; an elevated conception, nurtured since childhood, of his own historic role (he never stooped to run for any elective office below the presidency) combined with a commitment to democratic, republican institutions. No vulgar dictator he, as shown by the readiness, indeed brusqueness, with which de Gaulle left office twice, first as head of the provisional government in January 1946, and then as president after defeat at his last referendum (over reforms to the Senate and the regions) in April 1969. The reluctance of the French to share his lofty purpose rarely ceased to disappoint de Gaulle; the scale of the student riots and workers' strikes of May 1968 left him, on his own account, temporarily with no grip at all on the situation. Yet even at his final defeat, he was still backed by a higher percentage of the voters than have supported any British prime minister since the war.

De Gaulle's institutional legacy includes not just the constitution of 1958, but the major reform of 1962 and a practice, building on his own unique historical legitimacy, which gave the presidency more prestige and more power than were explicitly provided in the ambiguous constitutional text. Over a decade-long presidency, he lent more than a touch of the heroic to the office. None of his successors has seriously sought to imitate the General's style; all, though, have been determined to preserve and build on the institutional legacy.

Georges Pompidou (1908–74)

There was little of the heroic about the first successor, Georges Pompidou, unless it was his manner of facing the appalling illness that was to kill him on 2 April 1974, after two years of painful and public suffering. Pompidou had never joined the Resistance – a source of tension with some of his fellow-Gaullists (he later explained, rather lamely, that he had never known the right person to ask). His three careers outside politics are typical of the talented, ambitious, upwardly mobile elite of the Republic: the son of a socialist schoolteacher, born in 1908 in the Cantal, one of the poorest parts of France, he rose via his local *lycée* in Albi and the École Normale Supérieure in Paris to become first a *lycée* teacher of Latin, Greek and French literature (in the pre-war years and the Occupation), then a distinguished civil servant in the Conseil d'État (for a brief period in 1946–50), and finally and most lucratively a banker with Rothschild's. But Pompidou was also a trusted confidant of General de Gaulle, who appreciated his discretion, his literary ability and his managerial efficacy. He worked on de Gaulle's staff first under the provisional government, from September 1944 to January 1946; then, on a part-time basis, from 1948 to 1953, in the years of the first, unsuccessful, Gaullist party, the Rassemblement du Peuple Français; and finally as the General's chief of staff (*directeur de cabinet*) at Matignon, the prime minister's office, during the last months of the Fourth Republic in 1958. After de Gaulle's move from Matignon to the Élysée (the presidential palace) in January 1959, Pompidou returned to his bank. But he accepted a seat on the new Constitutional Council, and carried out several confidential missions for the new president, connected with the Algerian war.

Pompidou's appointment to succeed Debré as prime minister in April 1962 was thus based on a close relationship with de Gaulle of nearly two decades' standing. For the French, however, he was an unknown figure who had never held elective office – something unprecedented for a prime minister of the Republic – and had barely even spoken in public. That made his success as prime minister all the more remarkable. At over six years, Pompidou's tenure in Matignon was of a length unequalled in French republican history. During this period he developed formidable political skills. He became a convincing parliamentary orator; an able party and coalition manager, forging a Gaullist-led majority which he led to victory at parliamentary elections in 1962, 1967 and 1968; a careful party organiser, winning the respect of initially sceptical activists and steadily consolidating a leadership position that was consecrated at the party's Lille conference in November 1967. That, as well as his capable handling of the May 1968 crisis, earned Pompidou the status of *dauphin*, the legitimate and apparently inevitable successor to de Gaulle. For the General this was an intolerable situation; and in July 1968 Pompidou's resignation, proffered in a moment of fatigue, was accepted with alacrity by the President. Pompidou spent nine months as a backbench Deputy before de Gaulle's resignation, when he immediately declared his own candidacy for the presidency and won the Gaullist party's backing. This was fitting, for Pompidou found himself defending the institutions of the Fifth Republic against a leading opponent, the centrist president of the Senate Alain Poher, who had made clear his inclination to return to the institutional practices of the Fourth. Pompidou won handsomely.

Le nœud gordien, Pompidou's highly personal volume of reflections written just after May 1968, argued for enhanced presidential intervention by de Gaulle's successor in order to safeguard the General's legacy. Once installed in the Élysée, Pompidou was true to his text and considerably extended the presidential sphere of government – though his attempt, a few months before his death, to shorten the presidential term to five years failed through opposition from orthodox Gaullists (the reform was finally passed, under the presidency of Pompidou's protégé Jacques Chirac, in September 2000). Pompidou also shared de Gaulle's preoccupation with the fragile and divided character of French society, of which May 1968 was merely the latest proof. But he differed from de Gaulle as to the remedy. Where de Gaulle sought to remind the French of their country's lofty mission ('When I talk to them of France, the French forget their divisions'), Pompidou was more down to earth, seeing material prosperity as the key to social stability. Where de Gaulle dreamt of a 'third way' between the free market and Soviet-style socialism, Pompidou possessed a banker's certainty of the wealth-creating virtues of capitalism: France's transformation, by 1974, into one of the world's great economic powers probably owes more to Pompidou than to any other single politician. He was not, it is true, merely a pro-business conservative: *Le nœud gordien* actually cites social democratic Sweden as a social model, and his presidency was marked by measures to spread the benefits of capitalist growth to every household. But he was always a more orthodox right-wing politician than his heroic predecessor: a better European (and ready, unlike de Gaulle, to allow British entry), less inclined to attack American leadership in the West, or to seek to transcend capitalism, or to upset the conservative instincts of his core voters. This ensured two partial reconciliations: at home, with most of the non-Gaullist Right, and abroad, with the 'Anglo-Saxons' (Pompidou is the only Fifth Republic president to have enjoyed good relations with a British prime minister, Edward Heath). Under Pompidou, in short, Gaullism was almost normalised.

Valéry Giscard d'Estaing (1926–)

The third president of the Fifth Republic, Valéry Giscard d'Estaing, comes, like Pompidou, from the Auvergne. There all resemblance ends. Pompidou's ancestors were peasants; Giscard can trace his forebears on both sides to a long line of political and industrial *notables* – or even, according to some ingenious genealogists, to the royal house of France. He inherited from his family great wealth, many political contacts and a ferocious intelligence: unusually, he is a graduate of *both* the two schools which form much of France's political, administrative and business elites, the École Polytechnique and the École Nationale d'Administration (ÉNA), whence he followed his father into the prestigious Inspection des Finances. The transition from the civil service to politics was effected, as so often, via a ministerial *cabinet* – that is, the small, often very political, private staff which every minister uses to help him run his department and liaise with colleagues. Giscard's post in the *cabinet* of Finance Minister Edgar Faure in 1953 opened a meteoric political ascension: Deputy of the Puy-de-Dôme in 1956 at the age of 30 (his maternal grandfather Jacques Bardoux retired from his parliamentary seat to make way for the ambitious young man); junior minister in the Finance Ministry from January 1959; finance minister from January 1962. In the meantime he was building a secure political base for himself, both locally as Deputy and as mayor of Chamalières (a wealthy suburb of Clermont-Ferrand) and nationally as leader, after 1962, of the newly created movement of Républicains Indépendants, the only group on the non-Gaullist Right to support de Gaulle after the October 1962 referendum. But by January 1966, having become both an obvious scapegoat for de Gaulle's unpopular economic policies and a potential rival to Pompidou for the succession, he was dismissed as finance minister – 'like a common servant', he complained.

It was a costly separation for the Gaullists. Without leaving the Gaullist-led majority, Giscard criticised what he called the 'solitary exercise of power', showed no loyalty in the May 1968 crisis, and in April 1969 helped to oust de Gaulle by announcing 'with regret' that he would not be voting for the General's referendum proposals. In the presidential elections of June 1969 he declared for Pompidou after some hesitation, and was rewarded with the Finance Ministry for the full duration of the Pompidou presidency. When Pompidou died, Giscard took full advantage of the Gaullists' disarray, trouncing Chaban-Delmas, his Gaullist rival, at the first round and beating Mitterrand, the left-wing candidate, by a wafer-thin majority at the second.

Whereas the first two presidents of the Fifth Republic, though not successful in every field, displayed considerable consistency in both aims and means, this is much less true of both Giscard and his successors. Central to the record of the Giscard presidency is the contrast between early reformism and late conservatism. The contrast concerns both substance and style: between the wide-ranging societal reforms of the first year and the authoritarian police and criminal evidence legislation of the last; between the early promises to improve the quality of life and material well-being of manual workers, and the austerity and rising unemployment of the closing period; between the Kennedy-like informality of a new, 48-year-old president, and the monarchical pre-occupation with protocol and brooding hostility to the press of the same man five or six years later. This evolution can be explained in economic, political and personal terms. Giscard faced a far less favourable economic situation than his predecessors: the first oil shock had ended the West's long post-war boom in the last months of the Pompidou presidency. Like other Western leaders, Giscard first failed to get the measure of the crisis and then paid a heavy price for the unpopular economic measures he finally took (Giscard's defeat in 1981 is paralleled by James Callaghan's in Britain in 1979; Jimmy Carter's in the United States in 1980; and Helmut Schmidt's in Germany in 1982). The often brutal insensitivity of Raymond Barre, the prime minister who had the job of administering the painful medicine after 1976, did not help; and the second oil price rise ensured that by 1981, when he stood for re-election, the indicators for both unemployment and inflation were very poor. Politically, Giscard suffered from having been elected on a reform programme but with essentially conservative backing both in the country and in the political elite. His reforms thus often lacked support within the right-wing National Assembly majority. The Gaullists, in particular, viewed the president with extreme suspicion and his reforms as gimmicks: Giscard's inability to define an adequate relationship with them helped seal his fate in 1981. Nor, however, did his reforming efforts win him any credit on the Left: both Socialists and Communists remained firmly in a frosty opposition from which they emerged briefly to vote a very few reforms (most notably the legalisation of abortion). In the end, therefore, Giscard was condemned to follow the increasingly conservative instincts of a cantankerous majority. As an individual, finally, Giscard suffered from a degree of both political *naïveté* and personal brittleness. The view, expounded in his 1976 book *Démocratie française*, that the growth of a 'vast central group' of French wage- and salary-earners with stable jobs and rising incomes rendered the old dynamics of class struggle obsolete, had a basis in the social dynamics of the recently ended post-war boom. But it flew in the face of the deepening economic crisis, while the bipolarising institutional dynamics of the Fifth Republic rendered Giscard's ambition to 'govern France from the Centre' highly problematic. Similarly, the president's stated commitment to a more 'pluralist' society was revealed to be less than total when confronted with political opposition: his discrimination against certain politically unsympathetic pressure groups, his assiduous use of patronage to place his own loyalists in key public-sector jobs, his surveillance of the state media and his interference in certain press matters are proof of that. On a more personal level, there was something rather pathetic about this impeccably well-bred man displaying his aristocratic knees on the sports field of Chamalières or his talents as an accordion-player in a local bar, or dining with garage mechanics and dustmen. It was noticed and ridiculed, provoking a withdrawal into regal *hauteur*. More seriously, a series of scandals in the late 1970s involving the president and his entourage (including the gift of diamonds to Giscard from Bokassa, the mad and bad Emperor of Central Africa) permanently soured his relations with the press. Giscard later claimed that for seven years after his defeat in 1981, he could not bear to open a French newspaper or watch the French television news for fear that he would happen upon a hurtful comment about himself.

Despite Giscard's failure to 'break the mould' of French politics, he left several important legacies. The series of early reforms, paralleled by similar measures in other Western countries but mostly refused or delayed by de Gaulle and Pompidou, brought France's legal framework abreast of social change, at least partially: women were given equal rights to own and dispose of property (this change did follow on from reforms initiated under de Gaulle), divorce was facilitated, contraception made widely available for the first time, abortion legalised (France's birth rate saw a rapid and spectacular drop). The age of majority was lowered to 18 (France's youth showed its gratitude by voting massively against Giscard in 1981). The constitutional amendment of 1974 transformed the role of the Constitutional Council by allowing referrals by Deputies or Senators (see Chapter 2). Parisians saw plans for the Left Bank expressway dropped and the maximum height of new buildings in their city limited; the Montparnasse Tower stands as a ghastly reminder of what might have been had Pompidou lived. They were also, for the first time in over a century, partially liberated from direct rule by central government and given a mayor like any other French city (Jacques Chirac, who was elected to the office in 1977, found the Paris town hall an admirable base from which to pursue a political vendetta against the president). Beyond France's frontiers, Giscard was a founder of the European Monetary System, the fruit of a particularly good relationship with Germany's Chancellor Schmidt and the forerunner, for two decades, of monetary union. Giscard has also, despite himself, inaugurated a new role in Fifth Republic politics, that of ex-president, for he has survived his defeat by nearly twenty-five years. About ten of these were spent in unfruitful attempts to get his old job back, but two of his more recent initiatives have almost as much potential significance for French politics as anything he undertook as president. In 2000, as a simple Deputy, he initiated the process that led to the shortening of the presidential term to five years. The final role in a career spanning half a century was as chair, in 2002–3, of the Convention on the Future of Europe which drafted the European constitutional treaty. That the resulting document lacked the concision and elegance of a well-crafted national constitution reflects less on Giscard than on the difficulty of the Convention's task: producing a set of rules for a new type of political entity, with limited (and therefore precisely *de*limited) competences, in such a way as to satisfy the Eurosceptical British and Danes and the federalist Belgians and Luxembourgeois. That a document was produced at all was remarkable. But the no result at the French and Dutch referendums on the constitutional treaty, and the subsequent stalling of the ratification process, suggested that Giscard would be remembered less as a European founding father than as an actor at one of the many European turning points at which nothing turned.

François Mitterrand (1916–96)

Giscard's defeat, though partly his own fault and partly the result of circumstances beyond his control, may also be explained by the presence of a viable and attractive alternative in the person of François Mitterrand. Giscard's senior by ten years (he was born in 1916), Mitterrand was the last president of the Resistance generation: like many of his contemporaries of all parties, he owed his start in politics to having had a good war. Brought up in a middle-class Catholic family, he began a legal career before being conscripted in 1939 and captured by the Germans in the *débâcle* of 1940. He then managed not only to escape but to found a Resistance network of former prisoners of war like himself. Over the long term, the network provided Mitterrand with reliable friends in the most unexpected corners of French society. In the short term, his record launched a political career; by 1947 Mitterrand, a leading member of the small but pivotal Union Démocratique et Sociale de la Résistance (UDSR) was minister for ex-servicemen, the first of eleven government posts he would hold under the Fourth Republic. At the same time he honed his formidable talents as an incisive, at times caustic, parliamentary orator, and consolidated a strong local base, becoming president of the *conseil général* of the left-wing Nièvre *département* and mayor of the small town of Château-Chinon. That was to stand him in good stead after 1958, when the advent of the Fifth Republic halted his ministerial rise and deprived him temporarily of a seat in the National Assembly. Mitterrand was unusual among politicians of the old régime in that he both rejected the Fifth Republic utterly and understood its central dynamics very quickly. In particular, he realised that the presidency was the centre of political competition, and that parties without allies were doomed to impotent opposition. His first presidential candidacy, in 1965, neatly expressed that understanding, as well as his considerable political skills: he won the backing of both Socialist and Communist parties without being a member of either. His achievement in forcing the apparently unassailable de Gaulle to a second ballot earned him a place in the pantheon of the Left. He then used this position to pursue two aims with great consistency: the rejuvenation of the non-Communist Left and the negotiation of a binding electoral alliance with the Communists. In 1971 he took over and relaunched the Socialist Party; the following year he signed a Common Programme of Government with the Communists; in 1974 he stood again for the presidency, backed by both big left-wing parties, and came within an ace of winning. The road to power thereafter was more difficult. The Communists began to distance themselves from an alliance which had done far less for them than it had for the revived Socialist Party, provoking a quarrel that spoiled the Left's chances of victory in the 1978 parliamentary elections. Within his own party, Mitterrand's strategy and leadership were challenged, most notably by his long-term rival Michel Rocard. But through most of the Giscard presidency, Mitterrand contrived to enhance the standing both of his party, which became the most popular in the country, and of his own person, as he cultivated the image of a literate and humane Socialist sage in the mould of Jaurès and Blum. Most importantly, perhaps, he managed to remain firm in his disputes with the Communist leadership while keeping the Communist electorate committed to the union of the Left. The firmness, and the inner self-assurance that underlay it, lent credibility to his moderate, reassuring campaign slogan of 1981, 'La force tranquille', and helped him win over the Centre voters whom he had failed to attract in 1974 or 1965; his continued self-presentation as a man of the Left ensured him a reserve army of some 4 million Communist voters when he needed them to beat Giscard at the second round.

Mitterrand's long presidency (he is the only French president to have served two full seven-year terms) saw France undergo profound social, economic and political transformations, but the changes were not always the ones he intended. The promise of 1981, to solve France's economic problems and achieve social justice through classic left-wing methods of nationalisation and high public spending, was dropped after the crisis of March 1983 (see Chapter 1). Far from undergoing a socialist transformation, France under Mitterrand saw a period of deregulation, privatisation and adaptation to global capitalist competition, with all the widening of inequalities that such processes involve: unemployment doubled (by 1993) to 3 million, France's city streets and doorways filled up with the 'new poor', while the stock market, liberalised under Mitterrand's Finance Minister Pierre Bérégovoy, offered unprecedented gains to those with money to invest. By November 1984, the contrast between rhetoric and reality had made Mitterrand the most unpopular president of the Fifth Republic (which he remained until the advent of his successor Chirac); the slow recovery of his poll ratings thereafter was not enough to prevent the Left's defeat at the March 1986 parliamentary elections. The period of cohabitation that followed saw a virtuoso display of Mitterrand's political genius. Posing simultaneously as the fair-minded elder statesman (by appointing a right-wing government with apparent good grace) and the defender of the underprivileged (in well-judged criticisms of the same right-wing government), uniting his own camp while playing on Centre voters' suspicions of his opponents, he ran circles around his main adversary, the Gaullist Prime Minister Jacques Chirac, and was comfortably re-elected in May 1988. The major ambition of the second *septennat*, European integration, was more successfully pursued than the earlier aspiration to social justice. The 1992 Maastricht Treaty on European union, above all, testifies to Mitterrand's determination to lock France and Germany irrevocably into the same political and economic structure. But the European ambition, and the commitment to the strong franc that went with it, also led to deep unpopularity: the recession that followed German unification in the early 1990s hit France particularly hard and combined with revelations about corruption among the Socialists to ensure a second parliamentary election defeat for the Left in 1993. Now there was to be no comeback for Mitterrand, who ended his presidency weakened politically by the size of the Right's victory and physically by age and cancer.

Mitterrand could be as monarchical as any French president. Like de Gaulle, he cultivated distance and aloofness when it suited him, and kept one eye permanently fixed not so much on his transient popularity as on his place in history. If left-wing supporters gave him the familiar nickname of *Tonton*, those closer to the Élysée referred to him as *Dieu*. Perhaps no other democratic leader has been personally responsible for so many grandiose public buildings, from the vast library that bears his name to the Louvre pyramid, from the Cité de la Musique at La Villette to the Bastille opera. Yet the Mitterrand years also softened the rigid hierarchies of French society which de Gaulle and Pompidou had perpetuated and which Giscard had only hesitantly begun to alter. France's noisy, anarchic midsummer music festival was as much a part of the Mitterrand legacy as the grand monuments; so was the profusion of newly legalised independent radio stations, and the significant relaxation of state controls on television. The ferocious police and criminal evidence legislation passed at the end of the Giscard presidency was repealed. The death penalty was abolished. France's

Jacobin state also ceded powers to the localities: the decentralisation laws, referred to by Mitterrand as the *grande affaire* of his first term, relaxed central government controls over mayors and *départements*, and gave directly elected councils to France's twenty-two regions (see Chapter 12). Change also resulted from circumstance. Mitterrand's election in 1981, together with the parliamentary elections that followed, was in itself a new departure: the first experience of alternation in power under the Fifth Republic, and indeed the first time in French history that the voters had completely replaced a governing coalition with the former opposition. Over the next twenty-one years, the French were to overthrow their rulers, peacefully, on every available occasion: in 1986, 1988, 1993 and 1995, as well as 1997 and 2002; by voting in a right-wing government under a left-wing president in 1986, they ensured the innovation of cohabitation, but also demonstrated the flexibility of the Fifth Republic's institutions. Equally significant were the revelations about political corruption that tainted the later Mitterrand years and the long-running debate about the justice system that resulted. Hitherto, governments had usually succeeded in managing the administration of justice so as to avoid embarrassment to themselves; in 1990, however, faced by a newly investigative press and a group of examining magistrates ready to press their powers to the limit, even at the risk of official disapproval, the Justice Ministry proved unable to hold the line. The 'judicialisation' of French politics (see Chapter 13) dates from the Mitterrand presidency.

Giscard had left the Élysée unpopular; Mitterrand left it in a climate of scandal and discredit which was only partially lifted at his death eight months later. His last years had revealed the darkest sides of a deeply ambiguous personality. Some of the ambiguities were widely known, if often forgotten. Mitterrand the apostle of the union of the Left had been a ferocious anti-communist thirty years earlier. Mitterrand the scourge of the Fifth Republic, author of a polemical attack on the régime entitled *Le Coup d'État permanent*, used its institutions to the full. Mitterrand the crusader against racism, who led a solemn march to condemn the desecration of a Jewish cemetery at Carpentras in 1990, also gave significant assistance to the far right-wing Front National, probably to embarrass the mainstream Right: he helped ensure air time for the FN leader Jean-Marie Le Pen in 1984, and changed the electoral system to allow FN Deputies into the National Assembly in 1986. More surprising were details of Mitterrand's private life, long cloaked in a secrecy that British and American politicians might envy: he housed his mistress and their daughter at the expense of the state for well over a decade, and published false health bulletins from the day in October 1981 when he was told of his cancer. More sinister were the large-scale, and illegal, phone-taps Mitterrand organised from the Élysée on a wide range of journalists and political rivals. Most damaging, though, were the revelations about his war record published in 1994. Before becoming a Resistance hero, Mitterrand had worked for, and been decorated by, the collaborationist Vichy régime: his handshake with the Vichy ruler, Marshal Pétain, was immortalised by photographers. Worse, he maintained a lifelong friendship with René Bousquet, under the Fourth Republic a banker who helped finance Mitterrand's party but under Vichy a police chief responsible for handing over hundreds of Jewish children to the Germans. Mitterrand's subsequent pleas of ignorance of Vichy's activities, or of Bousquet's role in them, sit ill with the extraordinary intelligence that he demonstrated over a half-century in politics.

One of Mitterrand's fiercest critics, after his death, was his former prime minister and long-term Socialist rival Michel Rocard. For Rocard, Mitterrand 'was not an honest man'; he dealt with people on the basis of 'trickery and violence'. The French people were more indulgent. By 1997, 53 per cent of them judged his overall record as positive, rating him highest in those areas where his major ambitions had lain – foreign policy and the 'reduction of inequalities'. He was even considered, by 31 per cent, as the best President of the Fifth Republic: a proportion only exceeded by de Gaulle.

Jacques Chirac (1932–)

Giscard and Mitterrand present a record of large presidential purposes frustrated, in part at least, by events. In the case of Jacques Chirac, the purpose itself is hard to discern: he has always displayed more energy in the pursuit of power than vision in its exercise. Like Mitterrand, Chirac won the presidency, at the third attempt, in his early sixties. Unlike him, he is a pure product of the Fifth Republic. The son of a Parisian banker, and a graduate of ÉNA like Giscard, Chirac saw military service as an officer in the Algerian war. Interestingly, he regards this period as the happiest of his life, and contemplated joining the *Algérie française* army rebels. Instead, however, he returned to France and took jobs in the Cour des Comptes (Court of Accounts), the General Secretariat of the Government, and, late in 1962, in Pompidou's Matignon *cabinet*. Chirac quickly established an almost filial relationship with the prime minister, who appreciated his formidable energy, referred to him affectionately as his 'bulldozer' and groomed him for active politics.

The constituency of Ussel in the *département* of Corrèze borders Pompidou's Mauriac constituency in the Cantal, and is just as backward. Chirac's ancestral roots are there (within ten miles of Ussel is a village called Chirac-Bellevue). But it had a tradition of left-wing voting. Chirac targeted the constituency from 1964, making frequent visits, getting himself elected a municipal councillor, squaring the local (and mostly ageing) political class, and above all showering the largess of the state, made available through his position in Matignon, on the fortunate voters. The systematic exploitation both of patronage and of his own considerable physical presence, energy and human warmth have been Chirac campaign trademarks ever since. In 1967 they won him the Ussel seat (as they did in every parliamentary election up to and including 1993). Pompidou immediately gave him a government post as junior minister for social affairs, a job that proved more eventful than expected: in the May 1968 'events', Chirac, along with the Matignon adviser for social affairs Édouard Balladur, was part of Pompidou's crisis team: photographs of the Grenelle negotiations that ended the strikes show Chirac seated on the prime minister's left. His ministerial progress thereafter was rapid: he became agriculture minister in 1972 and interior minister in February 1974. Barely six weeks later, Pompidou's death deprived him of a patron.

His behaviour in the subsequent election campaign earned Chirac a reputation for political treachery which has never quite left him. With forty-three Gaullist Deputies, he called for a Giscard vote at the first ballot, in preference to the Gaullist candidate Chaban-Delmas. He was rewarded, when Giscard won the presidency, with the premiership at the age of just 41. Six months later, he used his office to seize the Gaullist party leadership from under the noses of the older Gaullist 'barons'. The president expected Chirac to 'Giscardise' the party; Chirac wanted it for his own use; the mutual fascination that the two men had exercised upon one another turned to fierce rivalry; and Chirac resigned as prime minister in August 1976. He spent most of the next four and a half years preparing his first presidential bid, relaunching his party as the Rassemblement pour la République (RPR), winning election as mayor of Paris in 1977, and regularly attacking Giscard while never quite leaving the presidential majority. Chirac's second act of treachery came with the 1981 elections, when he campaigned more vigorously against the sitting president than against Mitterrand. Then, after he was eliminated at the first ballot, he gave Giscard the most oblique and unenthusiastic endorsement for the run-off, contributing materially to Mitterrand's victory.

As the vigorous leader of a still intact party, Chirac found himself in 1981 as the effective head of France's opposition – and, as Mitterrand's popularity waned in 1983, France's most likely next president. It was the growing competition from Giscard's other former prime minister, Raymond Barre, that led Chirac to envisage a return to Matignon as a way of preparing a second run at the presidency. As leader of the first government of cohabitation, from 1986 to 1988, he began a range of liberal economic reforms, including a large privatisation programme, before being defeated by Mitterrand's superior political skills in 1988. Chirac could have repeated the experiment after the Right's landslide parliamentary victory of 1993; instead he stayed out of government to prepare his third presidential bid, leaving the premiership to his trusted adviser and former finance minister, Édouard Balladur. Treachery now nearly worked against Chirac, for Balladur discovered popularity and with it a presidential vocation. But Chirac's overall strategy was successful: starting from a marginal position in the polls, but free to exercise his considerable campaigning talents, he overtook Balladur two months before the first ballot, against all predictions. He then benefited from the Left's disarray in the late Mitterrand years to win the run-off against the Socialist Lionel Jospin by a comfortable 53 per cent to 47.

Whereas Mitterrand was never quite what he seemed, Chirac has had trouble seeming anything in particular for very long. In a political career spread over nearly three decades before the 1995 presidential election, Chirac had been a Euro-enthusiast (as Giscard's prime minister), a Eurosceptic given to histrionics (attacking Giscard as the agent of a foreign power in 1978), a Euro-enthusiast again (signing the Single European Act with Mitterrand), and a Euro-pragmatist (deciding, reluctantly, to vote yes in the referendum on the Maastricht Treaty). He had sung the praises of a 'French-style Labourism' in 1977, and of the neo-liberalism of Thatcher and Reagan six years later. His reliance on advisers – Pierre Juillet and Marie-France Garaud in the 1970s, Balladur in the 1980s, and his chief of staff Dominique de Villepin after 1995 – has been seen as compensating for the lack of a consistent personal vision. As one leading member of his party put it, 'Chirac is like Beaujolais: there's a new one every year.' He has been most in his element as a clientelist politician in the mode of the old Radical Party of the Third Republic, working a Corrèze cattle fair or a Parisian street market (the most favoured group of all in Chirac's world are *corréziens* living in the capital). Paris, it should be added, was more than an excellent electoral base for Chirac. His real dynamism over eighteen years as mayor, the greater accessibility of his administration compared with the prefectoral régime that had preceded it, and a big public relations budget kept not only his popularity within Paris but also his visibility outside it persistently high. The town hall also offered an unrivalled source of patronage, bigger than most ministries. Under Chirac's stewardship, loyal supporters like Alain Juppé were given high-level town hall jobs and attractive housing at peppercorn rents; firms were invited to contribute to the RPR in return for municipal contracts; full-time party workers were paid out of municipal funds; and electoral rolls were falsified – though these practices only became widespread public knowledge, and in some instances reached the courts, after he had left the town hall for the Élysée.

The conditions of Chirac's victory in 1995 flawed his first presidential term from the start. The election had split the parliamentary majority between his supporters and Balladur's, but Chirac attempted neither a serious reconciliation with the *balladuriens* nor a fresh start through early parliamentary elections. Worse, having taken up ground vacated by the disgraced Left in order to beat Balladur, lamenting what he called *la fracture sociale* and promising to make employment his highest priority, he proceeded to do nothing of the sort once in the Élysée. Instead, he instructed Juppé, now his prime minister, to reduce France's public-sector deficits in line with the economic convergence criteria of the Maastricht Treaty. The resulting tax rises helped choke off a timid economic recovery. Economic malaise was compounded by sleaze (as details emerged of the rent reductions that Juppé had given himself and his son on their Parisian apartments) and by political error, notably the sacking of most of the women members of the government. The announcement of a major reform to the social security system provoked strikes and completed the divorce between Chirac and French opinion. By the end of 1995, polls showed that 71 per cent of the French were disappointed by his record, compared with just 16 per cent who claimed to be satisfied – a steeper, deeper drop in popularity even than Mitterrand's in 1983. The Chirac–Juppé tandem never recovered; and when, in 1997, Chirac seized on a modest improvement in the polls to dissolve the National Assembly, the Right's vast parliamentary majority was replaced by a narrow but adequate left-wing one. Chirac thus became the first president to face a hostile parliamentary majority as a result of elections he had called himself.

Like Mitterrand in 1986, Chirac now faced a period of cohabitation, stretching out to the next presidential election, with the prime minister forced on him by his majority's electoral defeat – in this case, his Socialist rival Jospin. Again, the leading challenger for the presidency was widely expected to be the prime minister. But Chirac's task was harder than that of his old enemy Mitterrand. He had five years to wait for the presidential election, not two. He faced a prime minister whose popularity, assisted at least for three years by an unexpectedly buoyant economy, remained persistently popular. And Chirac's own party, the RPR, practically escaped his control in the wake of the 1997 defeat. In the face of these difficulties, Chirac owed his re-election in 2002 to four factors. The first was the paternalistic appeal of a president under cohabitation: the genial host at France's 1998 World Cup victory enjoyed solidly positive popularity ratings, precisely echoing Mitterrand's return to favour after 1986. The second was the lack of serious competition on the Right: Chirac's success in undermining potential rivals in his own camp meant that by 2001 both the RPR and most of the non-Gaullist moderate Right had drifted back to supporting him, with more or less enthusiasm, as the only contender with a chance of stopping Jospin. The third was Jospin's own difficulties, both circumstantial (the economy began to slow down, and unemployment to rise, from mid-2001) and self-made (his campaign was a compendium of strategic and tactical errors). The fourth was the unexpectedly strong showing by Le Pen, who, with 16.9 per cent of the first-ballot vote in April 2002, pushed Jospin into third place, eliminating him from the contest and leaving the French with a second-round choice between 'a crook (an allusion to Chirac's stewardship of the Paris city hall) and a fascist'. Overwhelmingly, they chose the former. No Fifth Republic president has achieved a lower first-ballot score than Chirac in 2002 (at under 20 per cent); none, however, has managed a better showing at the run-off (with over 82 per cent, including well over three-quarters of all left-wing voters).

This lopsided victory proved a solid base for that of the moderate Right, largely but not wholly reorganised in a new party, the UMP, at the parliamentary elections that followed in June 2002. By the end of September, Chirac held a more commanding institutional position than any of his predecessors: absolute majorities for the UMP in both National Assembly and Senate, and a broadly supportive majority even in the Constitutional Council. Translating institutional advantage into political momentum, however, was another matter. Elected in 1995 on the basis of promises he could not keep, Chirac had been re-elected seven years later on the basis of a fundamental ambiguity: had he won on his own moderately free-market first-ballot programme, or merely on the 'republican reflex' of the vast majority of the French who preferred him to Le Pen but who had no wish to see the state rolled back? The former interpretation largely prevailed in the policies of Chirac and his new prime minister, Jean-Pierre Raffarin (significantly, a figure from the non-Gaullist wing of the UMP). They set out to reverse the hitherto almost continuous expansion of France's civil service, to transfer more of the state's responsibilities onto regional and local authorities, to lengthen both the working week (undermining a flagship Jospin reform, the 35-hour week) and the working lifetime (by raising the years of work required to earn a full pension), and to ration access to specialist medical care in order to reduce the social security deficit. Such reforms made a deeply unpopular prime minister of Raffarin, and cost the Right two heavy defeats at the regional and European elections of 2004. They also contributed to the no victory at the 2005 referendum on the European constitutional treaty.

Summing up an as yet unfinished political career is beset with difficulties, especially one as long as that of Chirac, whose first premiership began when Richard Nixon was still in the White House and Harold Wilson in Downing Street. His *achievements* are disparate. He moved France towards a less *dirigiste* economy, both as prime minister in 1986–88 and as president after 1995. But this was part of a wider general movement, in which leaders as varied as Mitterrand, Fabius, Bérégovoy, Balladur and even Jospin participated; it is hard to identify Chirac as a prime mover in the process, on the model of a Thatcher or a Reagan. He announced the phasing-out of military service in 1996, and France's last conscripts ended their duties in November 2001. In 1997 he courageously accepted the share of responsibility of France, even if represented by the dubious legitimacy of the Vichy government, in the Holocaust. After his re-election, he placed his full authority behind three very practical goals: a tough road safety campaign, better treatment for cancer patients and improved facilities for the handicapped – hardly the stuff of a visionary presidency, but policies that have already saved thousands of lives (on France's notoriously dangerous roads) and, arguably, have improved many others. He also ensured, by sponsoring, via his Élysée advisers, the creation of the UMP out of the remains of the RPR and a chunk of the non-Gaullist moderate Right, that for the first time under the Fifth Republic no major party claimed to draw its inspiration from Gaullism. And he may go down as the president who – reluctantly – prepared France for the single currency after 1995, and who, with the support of over two-thirds of the French public, briefly took the leadership of nations opposed to the 2003 Iraq war.

This mixed record suggests a common, and not unfounded, view of Chirac as a superb tactician, a political survivor with no overarching vision. He has, at best, reflected the conflicts and contradictions with which the French faced the world at the turn of the twenty-first century. Chirac is a Gaullist-turned-European, committed to the 'construction of Europe' but dismissive of smaller member states inclined to question France's leadership on the continent; a persistent advocate of lower taxes and higher spending; a rhetorical environmentalist, ready to incorporate a Charter of the Environment into the constitution but reluctant to impose constraining environmental legislation on his own voters; a proponent of a worldwide tax to overcome Third World poverty, but a committed defender of European agricultural subsidies that create it; a consistent enemy of the FN, who remained capable as late as 1991 of racist lapses, quite worthy of Le Pen, in his own discourse.

As far as the presidency is concerned, however, Chirac's record appears reasonably clear: he has weakened it. This is true in terms both of presidential *power* and of presidential *powers*. In the former domain, Chirac has failed to articulate and to mobilise the French behind a long-term vision of France's future – no easy task, but one which de Gaulle saw as essential to the presidential function. In the area of *powers*, Chirac has allowed the reduction of the presidential term to five years, confirming that the presidential function is henceforth bound to the parliamentary calendar. More disastrous, perhaps, has been his inept use of the two new tools of presidential leadership provided by the 1958 constitution. Chirac's dissolution of parliament in 1997 (under Article 12) was rewarded with the opposition's victory; his referendum of 2005 (under Article 11), over the European constitutional treaty, with a decisive no vote. De Gaulle's record suggests that either of these defeats would have prompted his resignation; Chirac, by contrast, stayed put on both occasions. His successors will nevertheless think twice about using Articles 11 and 12 again. This will not deprive future French presidents of all means to exercise political leadership. But they will probably have to use tools that are more political and less regal – the tools, in fact, of the average European prime minister.

Prime ministers

Entrusted, according to the conventional wisdom of the Fifth Republic, with the day-to-day running of the country, prime ministers have no call to display any personal vision of France's longer-term destiny. Some conform perfectly to this model. Neither Maurice Couve de Murville, nor Pierre Messmer, nor Édith Cresson presented any clear goal distinct from those of their masters. Of Chirac's first, youthful, premiership under Giscard, his adviser Marie-France Garaud later said 'it wasn't that you were a bad prime minister, Jacques; you weren't prime minister at all'. Juppé was a comparable, though not precisely similar, case. He enjoyed a broad delegation of powers from Chirac, but partly because his views corresponded so closely to those of his president: he said later that not even the most hostile observers had been able to put a cigarette paper between them. The symbiosis between the two men is unique in the annals of the Fifth Republic – with the result that Juppé's lack of political sensitivity (he has been referred to as 'a computer without any politics software') helped drag Chirac's popularity down as well as his own. Jean-Pierre Raffarin, the prime minister Chirac chose after his re-election in 2002, lacked Juppé's personal closeness to the president, and was also unusual in having made his career largely in provincial France (as president of the Poitou-Charentes regional council) rather than Paris. But he corresponded, more or less, to the model of the self-effacing executant rather than the policy entrepreneur.

Table 3.2 Prime ministers of the Fifth Republic

Prime minister	Date of appointment
Michel Debré	8 January 1959
Georges Pompidou	14 April 1962
Maurice Couve de Murville	10 July 1968
Jacques Chaban-Delmas	20 June 1969
Pierre Messmer	5 July 1972
Jacques Chirac	27 May 1974
Raymond Barre	25 August 1976
Pierre Mauroy	21 May 1981
Laurent Fabius	17 July 1984
Jacques Chirac	20 March 1986
Michel Rocard	10 May 1988
Édith Cresson	15 May 1991
Pierre Bérégovoy	2 April 1992
Édouard Balladur	29 March 1993
Alain Juppé	17 May 1995
Lionel Jospin	2 June 1997
Jean-Pierre Raffarin	6 May 2002
Dominique Galouzeau de Villepin	31 May 2005

Other prime ministers, by contrast, have had the opportunity to make more of a personal impact, for one of two reasons. Either the president – whether out of a conception of the most effective division of labour, or because of their own political weakness, or both – allowed them to play a significant role; or he was forced, under cohabitation, to concede the major policy-making role to his prime minister. In the former category, Michel Debré used the full powers of the new Republic to resolve questions which had proved beyond the reach of his predecessors, including subsidies to Church schools and curbs on home-distilled spirits. The central priorities of Pompidou's premiership, to industrialise France and to build up the Gaullist party, both received de Gaulle's approval, the former wholeheartedly, the latter more guardedly. Chaban-Delmas gave a grandiose label – the 'New Society' – to diverse liberalising reform plans. That provoked the displeasure of Pompidou, who found the tone too vague, too left-wing and too presidential; but he supported his prime minister on many of the concrete measures involved. Raymond Barre, appointed by Giscard as 'the best economist in France', made a trademark of pursuing economic orthodoxy at the expense of popularity, and won much respect for it – retrospectively, after his policies had contributed to Giscard's defeat. Mitterrand's first prime minister, Pierre Mauroy, represented a French version of Old Labour, his uniquely good relations with the Communists helping to tie the Communist Party into the left-wing majority of 1981. His successor, Laurent Fabius, appointed as the Communists left government, was the opposite: young, technocratic, a symbol of the Left's modernity more than of its social conscience. Michel Rocard, the first prime minister of Mitterrand's second term, was chosen for his apparent ability to widen the left-wing majority towards the Centre. His approach to policy, which became known as the *méthode Rocard*, involved widespread consultation and consensus politics leading to long-term reforms. It won some significant successes, notably a settlement in the troubled Pacific territory of New Caledonia, but was also attacked from the Left, and by Mitterrand, for its apparent timidity. Pierre

Bérégovoy was a Socialist converted to financial orthodoxy, a doctrine that dominated his behaviour both as finance minister and, between 1992 and 1993, as premier. His 'strong franc' policy helped earn France the plaudits of the world financial press, not usually prolix in its approval of socialist governments. It also laid him open to the reproach of having lost sight of left-wing goals. That, and the more important accusation that he had compromised his integrity by accepting a dubious loan from one of Mitterrand's lifelong associates, fuelled the depression that led to his suicide after the Left's defeat in 1993. Dominique de Villepin, like Bérégovoy, was appointed at a time of great political weakness for the president: France had just voted no at the 2005 referendum on Europe. Initiatives such as tax reform, the easing of restrictions on hiring and firing in small firms, and as an attempt to revive state-led industrial policy and protect 'strategic' French firms like Danone from foreign takeover were identified as de Villepin's policies. The new decisiveness, even flamboyance, of the de Villepin style (which had been most tellingly displayed in 2003, in a speech as foreign minister to the United Nations against plans for war in Iraq) was a welcome change from his uninspiring predecessor Raffarin and ensured a brief honeymoon period over the summer of 2005. How much of that popularity would survive the setbacks of the autumn – a series of damaging strikes and the riots of November – and keep de Villepin as a credible *présidentiable* – was of course uncertain.

Of the prime ministers under France's three periods of cohabitation, the first, Jacques Chirac, pledged himself to a wide-ranging programme of liberal economic reforms in 1986, and was able to implement some of them. In some respects, for example the privatisation programme, the Balladur premiership from 1993 to 1995 was simply the continuation of this: Balladur had, after all, been in charge of economic policy under the second Chirac government. But he also tried to conceptualise what he called 'le nouvel exemple français', a way of reconciling the particularities to which the French remain highly attached with the demands of the global marketplace.

The longest period of cohabitation corresponded to the premiership of Lionel Jospin. With nearly five full years in office, Jospin was the Fifth Republic's longest-serving prime minister after Pompidou, and arguably the most powerful bar none. A Protestant and an ÉNA graduate like Rocard, Jospin is unique among French premiers in having made his political start in the ranks of the extreme left-wing Organisation Communiste Internationaliste (OCI). Indeed, he first joined the Socialists as a Trotskyist mole, and retained links with the OCI until 1987, by which time he had been the Socialists' first secretary for six years. But by then he had long since been turned, chiefly by Mitterrand, into a loyal Socialist, retaining from the OCI a penchant for doctrinal rigour and austerity that in any case sat well with his Protestant background. Education minister under both Rocard and Cresson, Jospin was dropped from the government in 1992 and lost his parliamentary seat in 1993. These setbacks proved to be blessings in disguise, dissociating him from the dark twilight of the later Mitterrand years and positioning him as a credible candidate for the Socialists in 1995. His performance at this election – losing to Chirac at the run-off, but nevertheless achieving a remarkable recovery for the Socialists, with the best first-round score of any candidate – made Jospin easily the Left's leading politician. He used this position to build a triple alliance with Communists and Greens; the construction of the *gauche plurielle*, as it was known, was sufficiently advanced to secure victory at the 1997 parliamentary elections, with a National Assembly majority for the Left as a whole and the premiership for Jospin.

Unlike Tony Blair, who had won the UK elections for Labour just a month earlier,

Jospin was not interested in setting out a 'third way' between social democracy and neo-liberalism. Rather, he aimed to show that social democratic policies could work in an open, globalised economy. The record of his government in this light was impressive. It included the 35-hour working week and universal health cover, benefiting those who had so far fallen through the social security net. Small-scale changes to the tax and welfare system redistributed income towards poorer groups, reinforced consumption and ensured that France benefited from the European economic upturn following 1997; unemployment dropped by nearly a million between 1997 and 2001. While the Jospin government sold off shares of publicly-owned companies on a large scale, sales were often limited to a minority stake and often ceded to the mutual sector, protecting the firms from international markets. The policy record is matched by a political one: not the least of Jospin's achievements lay in maintaining a sense of common purpose in a disparate government under the abnormal pressures of cohabitation. Significant failures, however, remained: the Jospin government neither took the opportunity offered by strong growth to tackle France's chronic public sector deficits, nor addressed the nation's serious pensions overhang. Higher-income groups, not the working class, benefited most from the 35-hour week. Environmental measures remained low on the agenda (a bill regulating France's ever scarcer and more polluted water supplies failed through lack of parliamentary time). And law and order, a growing preoccupation throughout the electorate, remained the weak suit of the *gauche plurielle*. But Jospin's elimination from the 2002 presidential election after a first-round score of just 16.2 per cent was due less to gaps in his record than to a poor campaign in an unfavourable context. The context was unfavourable both economically – slower growth and rising unemployment had demonstrated conclusively, by early 2002, that Jospin had not engineered a lasting recovery – and politically: like Chirac before him in 1988, Jospin faced the near-impossible task of holding the solidarity of a government coalition together in the competitive context of a presidential election, when each candidate seeks to maximise an individual score, at the expense of coalition allies; and of converting the record of a government, chiefly preoccupied with domestic affairs, into a platform for national leadership, against a president with unlimited opportunities to tread the world stage. To these were added a campaign that combined most of the errors available in the circumstances.

On the evening of his defeat, Jospin announced his retirement from politics. He did not quite keep his promise, and would turn up as an 'ordinary activist', rather in the manner of Aircraftman Shaw, to (usually well-reported) meetings of the Socialist Party in the 18th *arrondissement* of Paris. The voters, too, were unsure whether they welcomed his departure: indeed, successive polls from 2003 placed him as the most credible Socialist candidate. It would take a surprising turn of events for these brief encounters to turn into a serious presidential candidacy; or, indeed, with a five-year presidential term, for any prime minister to govern France for five years in a comparable context of cohabitation. Jospin's therefore stands as a unique premiership, flawed certainly, but nevertheless creative in many aspects and unlikely to be matched in the post-2000 Republic.

Concluding remarks

Raymond Aron remarked of the defeated Giscard in 1981 that he had 'forgotten that History is tragic'. Each president has, of course, sought to exercise his authority to the full – to 'go to the limits of his power', in the words of Mitterrand at the start of cohabitation in 1986 (and of Thucydides 2,400 years earlier). But every Fifth Republic presidency to date has ended in public disenchantment or lassitude, physical diminution, or both; not for these men the elegantly timed departure or the serene retirement. Presidents have been steadily less successful in achieving their goals: growing obstacles, whether in the shape of a public opinion less inclined to be led from the front, or the constraints of a European polity or a global economy, stand in the way of a heroic presidency in the de Gaulle mould. Worse, they have, in times of cohabitation, had to share the mantle of national leadership with prime ministers not of their choosing. The relationship between presidents and prime ministers is at all times a complex one. The elements that structure it are considered in Chapter 4.

Further reading

Bell, D., *Presidential Power in Fifth Republic France*, London, Routledge, 2000.
Cole, A., *François Mitterrand: A Political Biography*, London, Routledge, 1994.
de Gaulle, C., *Memoirs of Hope*, London, Weidenfeld and Nicolson, 1971.
Favier, P. and Martin-Roland, M., *La décennie Mitterrand*, 4 vols, Paris, Seuil, 1990–99.
Frears, J., *France in the Giscard Presidency*, London, Hurst, 1981.
Giscard d'Estaing, V., *Deux Français sur trois*, Flammarion (Livre de Poche), Paris, 1985.
Lacouture, J., *De Gaulle*, 3 vols, Paris, Seuil, 1984–86 (English translation, in 2 volumes, HarperCollins, 1990).
Lacouture, J., *Un destin de Français: François Mitterrand*, 2 vols, Paris, Seuil, 1998.
Madelin, Philippe, *Jacques Chirac*, Paris, 2002.
Modern and Contemporary France, vol. 10, no. 3, August 2002: special issue on the Jospin Government, 1997–2002.
Peyrefitte, A., *C'était de Gaulle*, 3 vols, Paris, Éditions de Fallois/Fayard, 1994–2000.
Pompidou, G., *Le nœud gordien*, Paris, Plon, 1974; Paris, Flammarion, 1984.
Roussel, E., *Georges Pompidou*, 2nd edition, Paris, Jean-Claude Lattès, 1994.
Williams, P. and Harrison, M., *Politics and Society in de Gaulle's Republic*, London, Longman, 1971.

4   The sources of executive power

The Constitution of the Fifth Republic reinforced both halves of France's dual executive: the prime minister and government in straightforward ways, the presidency in more complex and variable ways. These changes placed the relationship between president and prime minister at the heart of the new executive. That relationship is an unstable, volatile compound of competition (always), conflict (almost invariably) and co-operation (even at the most conflictual of times). To an extent unparalleled in other major democracies, the political situation affects the constitution's basic workings, and in particular the functions and the policy-making responsibilities of the two heads of the executive. Their relationship is structured by the resources available to each: both relatively fixed constitutional and administrative resources, and highly variable political resources (especially the support of the parliamentary majority, or the lack of it) which determine the usefulness of the others. This chapter will discuss the resources; Chapter 5 will consider the results in terms of policy-making by president, prime minister and government.

Constitutional resources

Though both president and prime minister wield power according to political circumstance, their powers remain grounded in the constitutional text.

Prime minister and government

The government, according to Article 20 of the constitution, 'shall have at its disposal the administration and the armed forces' and 'shall determine and conduct the policy of the Nation'. In relation to the president, its real policy-making capacity is variable. In relation to parliament, on the other hand, the constitution gave the government important new powers, as outlined in Chapter 2 (p. 53). When the National Assembly majority is not positively hostile, a Fifth Republic government, unlike its predecessors of the Third and Fourth, has the means to remain in office and to ensure a relatively smooth passage for its legislation.

The constitution also reinforces the specific powers of the prime minister, whose title alone, as opposed to the Fourth Republic's more modest *président du Conseil des ministres*, indicates enhanced authority.

- The prime minister proposes the members of his or her government for appointment by the president (Article 8). This task involves defining the government's size and the shape and responsibilities of ministries, as well as the choice of men and women.
- Article 21 establishes the prime minister's primacy over his or her ministerial colleagues by stating that s/he 'shall direct the operation of the Government'.
- The constitution also gives the prime minister specific powers that designate him or her as more than *primus inter pares* among ministers. According to Article 21, s/he may deputise for the president in chairing the Council of Ministers; s/he 'shall be responsible for national defence', shall 'ensure the implementation of legislation' and 'have power to make regulations', signing (with the president, in the most important cases) the decrees that implement legislation (about 1,500 decrees and 7,000–8,000 prime ministerial orders (*arrêtés*) every year, according to Philippe Ardant); and 'shall make appointments to civil and military posts'. Under Article 61, s/he may refer a bill to the Constitutional Council before its promulgation, a right also enjoyed by the president of the Republic, the presidents of the two houses of parliament, and sixty Deputies or sixty Senators, but by no other government member.
- The constitution makes the prime minister the leading manager of government business through parliament. Aside from the parliamentarians themselves, s/he is the only possible initiator of legislation (Article 39) and of extraordinary sessions of parliament (Article 29). It is the prime minister, under Article 49, who asks the National Assembly (the lower house of parliament) for a vote of confidence in the government, or makes a specific bill a question of confidence, which the Assembly can only reject if an absolute majority of its members pass a vote of censure. It is the prime minister, as head of the government, who wields the battery of constitutional provisions designed to curb the activities of parliament: the request for delegated legislation under Article 38, for example, or the procedure of the *vote bloqué* (Article 44), under which parliament may be obliged to vote on the government's version of a bill. It is the prime minister, finally, who controls the complex procedure under which bills are shuttled between the two houses of parliament (National Assembly and Senate) for successive readings before an agreed version (or failing that, the Assembly's version) is passed.

Few of these powers, it is true, can be exercised independently by a prime minister under an interventionist president supported by a loyal parliamentary majority; some, such as the responsibility for appointments or defence, are shared with the president in a wholly ambiguous manner. At the same time it should be noted, first, that this is a significantly greater array of powers, in relation both to government and to parliament, than those granted to premiers of the Third and Fourth Republics; secondly, that under the constitution it is the prime minister who engages directly with parliament, and not the president (whose official communications with parliament are limited, under

Article 18, to messages); and, third, as we shall see below, that the prime minister's constitutional role in managing and co-ordinating government business is underpinned by considerable administrative resources.

The president

Clemenceau claimed that the Third Republic presidency was as useless as the prostate gland; of Fourth Republic presidents it was said that their main task was opening flower shows. Like all caricatures, such views combine exaggeration with accuracy. Both Fourth Republic presidents, Vincent Auriol and René Coty, readily voiced strong views on policy matters, and played a key role during the régime's frequent government crises (Coty, indeed, was instrumental in engineering de Gaulle's return to power, and thus his own premature departure from the scene). But in neither Republic did a president exercise strong executive leadership for any length of time; indeed, with rare exceptions, the parliamentarians who elected presidents kept strong figures out of the job; and without strong figures, the president's formal powers, hedged about with the requirement for the countersignature of the prime minister, or the presidents of the two houses of parliament, or both, were worth little.

The Fifth Republic, together with the political context and the personalities surrounding its foundation, changed that. The president's role was now widely defined, by Article 5; he was given certain completely new powers; other powers were transformed by the removal of the need for any countersignature; still others were transformed, first by the exceptional personal status of de Gaulle, and then by the enhanced legitimacy of a directly elected president under the constitutional amendment of 1962.

- Article 5 states that the president 'shall see that the Constitution is observed', and 'shall ensure, through his arbitration, the proper functioning of the public authorities and the continuity of the State'. It also makes him 'the guarantor of national independence, territorial integrity, and observance of treaties'. Vague though much of this article is, successive presidents have regularly invoked their role as constitutional guarantors, and de Gaulle was the first (but not the last) to give an activist interpretation to the word 'arbitration'.
- Of the president's completely new powers, one resulted from de Gaulle's determination to ensure adequate crisis leadership. Under Article 16, if France's institutions, territorial integrity or even treaty commitments are under 'serious and immediate threat', the president may take 'the measures required by the circumstances'. Article 16 may be invoked by the president without countersignature (though it does include some limited safeguards, notably the right of parliament to sit and for the Constitutional Council to be consulted on measures taken). De Gaulle was given an early opportunity to use his emergency powers by the 'generals' putsch' in Algiers in April 1961. He stretched them to the limit, though, by keeping Article 16 in force for five months (the putsch had lasted less than a week) and by taking the opportunity to sack or transfer army officers, policemen and civil servants suspected of supporting the rebellion, to extend detention without trial to fifteen days, and to set up a military court to try offences against state security. Before he won the presidency, Mitterrand undertook to abolish Article 16. He did not do so. But emergency powers have not been invoked since 1961.
- The other completely new presidential power, the right to call a referendum, arose

from de Gaulle's concern to bypass unrepresentative parties (in other words, for his adversaries, to prepare his own dictatorship). Under Article 11 of the 1958 text, referendums were limited to questions concerning treaties and the 'organisation of the public authorities', though an amendment of 1995 allowed them to cover social, economic and public service issues too. They have also served political purposes: to establish a direct line of communication between president and people (especially under de Gaulle), to reinforce the unity of the governmental coalition, to divide the political opposition. Article 11 may be invoked without the prime minister's countersignature; the constitutional requirement that a referendum should be proposed to the president by the government or parliament has often (though not always) meant in practice that the Council of Ministers is notified of the presidential decision. Of the ten referendums since 1958, the first four – ratifying the constitution itself in 1958 and amending it in 1962, as well as agreeing first the 'self-determination' of Algeria (in 1961) and then its independence (in 1962) – may be rated successes, with turnouts of at least 75 per cent and yes votes of at least 61 per cent. The other six were less kind to their initiators. The voters rejected proposals to reform the Senate and the regions in April 1969, provoking de Gaulle's immediate resignation; a wafer-thin majority ratified the Maastricht Treaty on European Union in September 1992; turnout was too low to indicate clear public approval of the proposals put at referenda on the enlargement of the European Community in April 1972, on the future of the troubled Pacific territory of New Caledonia in November 1988, and above all on the five-year presidential term in September 2000, when barely a quarter of the electorate cast a valid vote. The referendum of May 2005 mobilised the French public, but chiefly against the European constitutional treaty. Nearly 55 per cent of voters rejected the treaty, delivering a further blow to Chirac's already troubled presidential term and demonstrating to him and to his successors the considerable risks entailed by this type of consultation.

- Less spectacular among the president's new powers, also requiring no countersignature, are powers relating to the Constitutional Council: the right to refer bills and treaties to it, and to appoint three out of its nine members, including its president. Presidents have eschewed referring bills, preferring more indirect methods of challenging legislation, though they have referred several treaties signed by themselves, including Maastricht and the European constitutional treaty of 2004, for verification. All presidents, on the other hand, have used the power of nomination to place their friends on the Council. Of François Mitterrand's two appointments to its presidency, the first was his former justice minister, the liberal Robert Badinter, and the second his former foreign minister, Roland Dumas (who resigned from his post in March 2000 after being placed on charges of corruption). Similarly, Chirac appointed a 'historic' Gaullist, Yves Guéna, to succeed Dumas, and a Gaullist of his own generation, Pierre Mazeaud, to succeed Guéna (unlike Guéna, Mazeaud has a significant background as a constitutionalist). The president enjoys a similar right to appoint, without countersignature, one member of the Higher Council of the Judiciary (indeed, all of its members before the constitutional reform of 1993).

- More important in many ways than the president's wholly new powers have been long-standing ones now exercised with no required countersignature, and thus freely, for the first time: to appoint the prime minister (under Article 8, Clause 1) and to dissolve parliament (under Article 12, which limits dissolutions to one a year). In prime ministerial appointments, successive presidents have made the most of their freedom to make surprise choices: de Gaulle with Georges Pompidou in 1962 and Giscard with Raymond Barre in 1976 (surprises because they had never held elective office), Mitterrand with Laurent Fabius in 1984 (a surprise because he was only 37), and with Édith Cresson in 1992 (a surprise because she was a woman). Moreover, the choice of prime minister is a preliminary to the appointment of the whole government, officially by the president on the prime minister's proposals, often by the president after the briefest of consultations with his premier. Presidents have also regularly used their right to dissolve parliament: de Gaulle in 1962 and in the crisis of May 1968, Mitterrand after his election and re-election in 1981 and 1988, Chirac, finally, in 1997. Their purpose, to win a favourable parliamentary majority, has usually been well served by the two-ballot majority electoral system which, unlike proportional representation, tends to produce large swings in terms of seats and clear parliamentary majorities. The dissolutions of 1962, 1968 and 1981 were all resounding successes; in 1988 Mitterrand saw his Socialists returned to government, but only with a relative majority; in 1997, however, Chirac managed to throw away the right-wing majority he already had, opening the way for the appointment as prime minister of the Socialist Party leader Lionel Jospin. The coincidence, since 2002, of five-year presidential and parliamentary terms makes a future dissolution on the whole unlikely. But the threat of such action may help to focus the loyalties of wayward parliamentarians.

- The president does not set foot in parliament and, unlike his American counterpart, has no legislative veto. Nevertheless, he has a real if indirect role in the legislative process. He chairs the Council of Ministers (Article 9), like his predecessors of the Third and Fourth Republics, and may do so more actively than they. He may request the 'reconsideration' of laws passed by the parliament (Article 10), though as a simple majority remains sufficient to carry any resulting vote, this right is rarely invoked. He may put a legislative proposal to referendum. He signs *ordonnances* (that is, primary legislation delegated to the government by parliament) and decrees (which implement primary legislation) under Article 13 – though the constitution does not state whether he may refuse to do so. Extraordinary parliamentary sessions are summoned by the president, at the request of the prime minister or a majority of members of the National Assembly (Article 30). Under Article 61, the president may refer bills or treaties to the Constitutional Council, though, as we have seen, this right has only been used for treaties to date. The president is also guaranteed a role in any plan for constitutional amendment. He may initiate such amendments (as may members of parliament). He decides, under Article 89, whether an amendment should be adopted by a joint meeting of the two houses of parliament (where a three-fifths majority is necessary), or whether it should go to referendum. And he has a potential right to block any amendment he feels to be wholly inconsistent with the spirit of France's institutions, of which, under Article 5, he is the guarantor. Finally, he may communicate with parliament by means of messages. Taken together, these provisions ensure that even a hostile parliamentary majority cannot wholly ignore the president's views.
- Other presidential powers were held by Fourth Republic presidents but have been transformed by a more active use that de Gaulle and his successors have been able to make of them thanks to their enhanced legitimacy and to the blanket provisions

of Article 5. The chairmanship of the Council of Ministers has already been mentioned. Fifth Republic presidents have the right to make key appointments, though these do require ministerial countersignatures. The constitution (Article 13) specifically mentions ambassadors, members of the Conseil d'État, the Grand Chancellor of the Légion d'Honneur, prefects and government representatives in French overseas territories, rectors of academies (the heads of the state education system in the provinces), ambassadors and special envoys, senior members of the Cour des Comptes, and *directeurs d'administration centrale* (heads of divisions in the ministries), as being appointed by the president in the Council of Ministers. This list, though, is not exhaustive, and in practice the president may propose candidates for a wide range of other state or public-sector posts, for example public prosecutors, secret service chiefs, senior broadcasting chiefs or heads of France's remaining nationalised industries and public utilities. Few of these requests are refused. In some cases even ministerial *cabinets*, in principle in the personal gift of ministers or of the prime minister, have been subject to presidential influence. Finally, and very importantly, presidents have expanded, through an activist interpretation inaugurated by de Gaulle, their roles in receiving and accrediting ambassadors (Article 14), as head of the armed forces and chairman of the key national defence committees (Article 15), and as chief negotiator of treaties (Article 52). These, together with the president's responsibilities for France's territorial integrity under Article 5, are a constitutional basis for the leading foreign and defence role played by all presidents.

- A final 'constitutional' resource relates to the president's role as France's representative on the European Council. Though initially conceived (from 1974) as a regular informal gathering of Europe's heads of state and government, the European Council soon acquired a more clearly defined leadership role, defined *ex post facto* by the 2004 European constitutional treaty: 'The European Council shall provide the Union with the necessary impetus for its development and shall define the general political directions and priorities thereof.' Even in the most unfavourable domestic political context, therefore, a French president participates in the setting of the European Union's policy framework – and thus, indirectly, in the definition of policies and legislation which affect all member states, including France.

Jean-Luc Parodi remarks that presidential power is reinforced under the Fifth Republic not so much by new powers considered individually as by their cumulative effect: the combination, for example, of the legitimacy flowing from direct election with the right to appoint a prime minister and the right to dissolve parliament. Parodi also, however, includes the majority electoral system – a key part of the institutional structure, but not a part of the constitutional text – in his explanation of presidential power; for it is this that allows the president to entertain realistic hopes of a favourable parliamentary majority when he uses the right of dissolution. That underlines the dependence of presidential power upon such a majority. When the majority is favourable, the president can, as it were, manipulate the government machine from outside. When it is not, however, his power to do so is very limited, not least because the heart of France's administrative machine has never been in the Élysée, but at Matignon.

Administrative resources

If more means better, then the advantage in staffing lies with Matignon, the prime minister's office. Matignon is at all times the centre of the government machinery. What varies is the president's ability to use his own much smaller staff, as well as his wider networks of support, to penetrate it.

The Matignon machine

Every developed democracy faces two structural problems: the articulation between politicians and bureaucrats within each ministerial department, and the central co-ordination of the government machinery as a whole. In France, ministers run their departments through personal staffs, or *cabinets*, each combining, within a total membership of twenty to thirty for a full ministry, a majority of high-ranking civil servants and a leavening of the minister's close political friends (the total tally of official *cabinet* members for any government typically runs to about 500). Central government co-ordination is officially ensured, at the highest level, by the Wednesday morning meetings of the Council of Ministers, chaired by the president. In practice, however, the main role of the Council of Ministers is to set an official stamp on decisions already taken (its unofficial role, very often, is as an opportunity for both president and ministers to catch up on their mail or other reading while colleagues are talking). More important is the dense thicket of meetings that prepare and decide policy. These can be divided into three categories, only one of which is run by the presidency.

- *Conseils restreints* are meetings of small groups of ministers, convened and chaired by the president to discuss a specific issue. In the early Mitterrand years, when presidential interventionism was at its height, there were as many as 100 *conseils restreints* a year. The minimum annual figure, though, is nearer twenty.
- The prime minister chairs a small number of *comités interministériels*, whether formally constituted (such as the committees on urban affairs and regional planning) or organised ad hoc to decide specific questions between a limited group of ministers: there were 118 such meetings in 1961, 121 in 1971, 120 in 1982, 57 in 1983, 51 in 1984 but only 20 in 1985, since when the total has varied between 20 and 40. *Comités interministériels* are most regularly used for the prime minister to make his final decisions on the budget before it goes to parliament.
- The bulk of the co-ordinating work takes place in the *réunions interministérielles*, which are ad hoc meetings of members of ministerial *cabinets*. Their number grew from 142 in 1961 to a peak of 1,836 in 1982, and ran at some 1,400 a year under the Jospin premiership.

Both *comités interministériels* and *réunions interministérielles* are run by the two key components of the Matignon machine: the General Secretariat of the Government, responsible for administrative co-ordination, and the more political *cabinet* of the prime minister. The General Secretariat of the Government, founded in 1935, is manned by some forty to fifty senior civil servants, and is the rough equivalent of the British Cabinet Office. It is headed by a secretary-general, a high-ranking civil servant usually from the Conseil d'État. There have been just eight holders of the office since 1944, an indication of the political neutrality and continuity associated with the post (only one, a secretary-general of declared Socialist sympathies, has been replaced for political reasons, by Jacques Chirac when he became prime minister in 1986). The General Secretariat prepares all ministerial meetings (even those chaired by the president of the Republic, from the Council of Ministers down). Its members assist at such meetings and take their minutes (for example, the so-called *bleus de Matignon* which record the decisions taken, as well as those left outstanding, at each *réunion interministérielle*). They supply advice on questions of administrative law, ensure that decisions are translated into administrative action, guide their administrative passage into law and ensure their implementation. The General Secretariat also co-ordinates the vast array of administrative agencies (from the Atomic Energy Commissariat to the High Council on Horses) which are under the prime minister's direct authority.

The prime minister is also assisted by junior ministers attached to his or her office, usually numbering three or four. Usually more important, however, is the role of the prime minister's *cabinet*. Like a typical ministerial staff, the prime minister's *cabinet* is composed of young, able, politically sympathetic civil servants with a sprinkling of close political friends. But it is larger (at up to 100 members, including the unofficial advisers) and has more to do. Its members are the prime minister's eyes and ears: they are expected to build networks around their area of specialisation, both within the ministry concerned and in the relevant interest groups and political parties, in order to maintain a constant supply of high-grade information. It is they who chair the *réunions interministérielles*, and who maintain the day-to-day pressure on their counterparts in ministerial *cabinets* to press policy forward. They prepare the ground for major policy initiatives by the prime minister. Some of them also undertake more wholly political tasks: speech-writing, preparing the presentation of policy, or servicing the prime minister's parliamentary constituency. They are headed by a *directeur de cabinet*, the chief manager of interministerial co-ordination: it is he who chairs weekly meetings of the *directeurs de cabinet* of all ministries, plans the programme of *réunions interministérielles* and chairs the most important of them, and maps out the agenda for government bills in parliament. The *directeur de cabinet* usually, though not always, has a further crucial role as the prime minister's chief political adviser.

The growing influence of the prime minister's *cabinet* was a major institutional innovation of the Fifth Republic. As such it has been criticised as constituting a parallel government. The style of overt, ruthless interventionism set by Michel Debré's *cabinet* has been imitated by many, though not all, of its successors of both Right and Left: relations between individual ministers and their opposite members in the Matignon *cabinet* often involve intense competition for control of policy-making. Under Chirac's 1986–88 government, for example, the very right-wing higher education adviser, Yves Durand, initiated, against the opposition of the higher education minister, a university reform that provoked enormous student demonstrations and ultimately the resignation of the hapless minister. Chirac's successor, the Socialist Michel Rocard, recruited a *cabinet* described by President Mitterrand as 'men without pity ... barbarians'. The activism of Alain Juppé's *cabinet* between 1995 and 1997, combined with the low calibre of many of his ministers, helped to concentrate the burden of policy-making, and thence the intense unpopularity of his government, on the person of the prime minister. Olivier Schrameck, the *directeur de cabinet* under Jospin, wrote a book on ministerial *cabinets* two years before his appointment, and came to Matignon with rigorous ideas about how to organise them: no 'unofficial advisers' (Jospin's *cabinet* was limited to about fifty members, all official), a clear hierarchy (Schrameck's ascendancy, and role as arbiter of many second-level policy decisions, were clear from the start) and no impinging on the political responsibilities of ministers. These laudable rules do not appear to have been fully respected. One of the complaints of Jean-Pierre Chevènement was that devolution plans for Corsica – the issue on which he resigned as interior minister in August 2000 – had been prepared behind his back by Matignon insiders such as Alain Christnacht. At the same time, however, it is unlikely that this would have been possible if the *cabinet* members had not had the full backing of a prime minister who was determined not to leave the Corsican question in the sole hands of the Interior Ministry.

Two other important co-ordinating bodies under the prime minister's responsibility deserve mention. One is the General Secretariat for National Defence, numbering some 250 officials and responsible for a range of defence-related issues including the preparation of meetings of the High Council of Defence (chaired by the president), interministerial co-ordination on defence issues, strategic planning, and the management and protection of defence secrets. The other is the secretariat for European affairs, or SGAE (Secrétariat Général des Affaires Européennes, formerly the SGCI, or Secrétariat Général du Comité Interministériel pour les questions de coopération économique européenne), charged with co-ordinating France's positions in day-to-day European affairs and issuing instructions to the French permanent representation in Brussels. Each of these bodies, as well as the General Secretariat of the Government, though technically under the prime minister's authority, are in practice responsible to the president as well, whether because the president chairs the bodies they service (the Council of Ministers and the High Council of Defence) or because of the key presidential role in European affairs.

When the various administrative agencies, as well as a small military *cabinet* (which does not change with the government), are added to these bodies, the total prime ministerial staff numbers over 5,000. It serves a prime minister directly responsible for the progress of government business and able, in principle, to intervene at every stage of policy-making. Everything lands on the prime minister's desk. This is not, however, an unmixed blessing. Chaban-Delmas described his period at Matignon as 'two hundred weeks of work, six days a week, fifteen hours a day'. Part of this effort is certainly entailed by the need to co-ordinate, and on occasion fight battles with, the president's office. It is a physically exhausting burden which makes it hard for a prime minister, even with able assistants, to rise above the day-to-day pressure of events. The president, by contrast, can afford to be more selective.

The Élysée

While Matignon is palpably a hive of activity surrounded by an intense traffic of people and vehicles, the visitor to the president's residence in the Élysée palace (the *château*, as it is known to insiders) may well hear no sound louder than the crunching of his or her own feet on the gravel as they cross the courtyard. Under the Fourth Republic, the political staff at the Élysée numbered about ten, along with a military household of four. De Gaulle doubled this total: an increase that in no way reflected the vast growth of presidential power. Since 1959 the military staff, which has a specific and limited sphere of competence, has never numbered more than thirteen, the civilian political staff never more than forty (and at times as few as eighteen). More uncertain is the size of the off-budget presidential staff. A Socialist Deputy, Armand Dosière, claimed in

2004 that no fewer than 714 staffers were seconded to the Élysée from ministries – 65 per cent of them from Defence and 13 per cent from Culture. The Élysée has denied these assertions. What is certain is that no president has wanted a very large full-time establishment. Derisory as the figures for full-time staff may appear compared to the personnel available to the White House, they suffice to meet what are seen as limited needs for, as we have seen, the essential work of governmental co-ordination is done from Matignon.

The precise organisation of the civilian staff varies between presidencies, but it is generally divided into two, the *cabinet* and the General Secretariat of the presidency (not to be confused with the General Secretariat of the government). A third element, the General Secretariat for African Affairs, was created by de Gaulle, reflecting France's recent colonial past, headed by the shadowy Gaullist baron Jacques Foccart, but wound up after Pompidou's death in 1974. The *cabinet* has a generally limited role, managing the president's diary and travels within and outside France. The General Secretariat is therefore the largest and the most important component of the Élysée staff. It includes three types of adviser, grouped, under Chirac, into three 'cells': the *politiques* proper, entrusted with relations with the president's party and its allies, and with the president's political and communications strategies; a small foreign policy group, consisting (in 2000) of four diplomats; and the internal policy group, with experts corresponding to the main ministries. The head of the Élysée staff is the secretary-general. He is, in the first place, an administrative co-ordinator, preparing the weekly Council of Ministers agenda in tandem with the secretary-general of the government and managing the staff (Chirac's secretaries-general, Dominique Galouzeau de Villepin till 2002, Philippe Bas from 2002 to 2005, and Frédéric Salat-Baroux since May 2005, have held daily meetings with the whole staff). He is also, usually, a more political animal as well. Both de Villepin and his predecessor under Mitterrand, Hubert Védrine, have been career diplomats, illustrating the combination of political sensitivity and discretion required of the secretary-general. At the very least, he is the final screen between the president and the outside world: the 'eyes, ears and arms' of an absent president, in Jean Gicquel's words, and the daily interlocutor of a present one. The fact that three out of five presidents have suffered significant medical problems – de Gaulle with a prostate operation, and Pompidou and Mitterrand with the cancers that killed them – underlines one aspect of the secretary-general's role. The secretary-general is also, usually, one of the president's three or four most important political advisers, and has often assumed a higher profile in recent years than that of the rather self-effacing holders of the office under de Gaulle. Since de Gaulle's departure, indeed, three former secretaries-general of the Élysée (Édouard Balladur, Pierre Bérégovoy and Dominique de Villepin) have become prime ministers; four (Michel Jobert, Jean François-Poncet, Hubert Védrine and Dominique de Villepin) have become foreign ministers. Jean-Louis Bianco became minister for social affairs in 1992 after a decade in charge of the Élysée staff; Philippe Bas also moved to Social Affairs, though at a more junior level, in May 2005.

Like many of their Matignon counterparts, most of the Élysée staff are both members of the *grands corps*, the most prestigious divisions of the civil service, and graduates of the highly competitive *grandes écoles*, which train most of France's administrative elite (and indeed most of the nation's political and business elites as well). These two qualifications are considered to guarantee quickness of mind and familiarity with the workings of the state. They also assist networking, a practice as essential at the Élysée as at Matignon. But the choice of Élysée staffers is also very personal to the president: the appointments by Mitterrand of his own son (Jean-Christophe Mitterrand, or 'Papamadit' as he was soon known in African capitals) as adviser on African affairs, and by Chirac of his daughter Claude as communications adviser, are only the most extreme instances of this. It is not surprising, then, that the most influential advisers are not always the highest placed in the hierarchy. De Gaulle's foremost political adviser was not any of the three secretaries-general who served him, but Foccart. Under Pompidou, the ultra-conservative Pierre Juillet had an official status as a special presidential adviser outside the staff hierarchy. Under Giscard, any one of half a dozen staffers were said to be as influential as the secretary-general. Mitterrand's secretaries-general, Bérégovoy (1981–82), Bianco (1982–92) and Védrine (1992–95), had to vie for influence both with the official special adviser, Jacques Attali, and with a variety of unofficial advisers, or *visiteurs du soir* as Prime Minister Pierre Mauroy ironically called them: Roger-Patrice Pelat, the millionaire businessman who had known Mitterrand since their days as prisoners of war together in Germany (and who died in 1989, three weeks after being charged with insider dealing offences); Roland Dumas, Mitterrand's former lawyer (who became foreign minister in 1984 and was president of the Constitutional Council from 1995 until his constrained resignation in March 2000); or François de Grossouvre (who committed suicide in his Élysée office after being slowly downgraded to the post of Master of the Presidential Hunts). Only under Chirac, perhaps, did the secretary-general until 2002, Dominique de Villepin, have the reputation of being the single most influential adviser.

While the Élysée staff are many fewer than their Matignon counterparts, they share some of the functions of the Matignon *cabinet*: as suppliers of information via well-constructed networks (in this their efforts complement the more discreet ones of the secret services, as well as the gleanings of the illegal telephone-taps in which all presidents have indulged), as technical and political advisers, as speech-writers and communications consultants. The Élysée staff have also been attacked for wielding power without responsibility. Chaban-Delmas ascribed his own removal from Matignon in 1972 to the malign influence on Pompidou of the 'devilish duo', Pierre Juillet and Marie-France Garaud (who had taken to producing regular notes on 'How to annoy Chaban today'). More recently, Villepin was blamed both for Chirac's decision to dissolve the National Assembly in April 1997 and for the president's erratic treatment of his own party thereafter. Such views are exaggerated. Élysée staffers have no formal decision-making powers (their Matignon counterparts at least have a formal role in *réunions interministérielles*). While they are consulted on everything, they are seldom the *only* people consulted on anything; there are too few of them to be able to determine, or even affect, more than a few decisions; and their advice is not always followed (Juillet, for example, would retire to his sheep farm in the hills of the Creuse when he felt that his views were not receiving the presidential attention they merited). The power of the Élysée staff also, of course, depends on their ability to engage with the government machine; and this in turn is conditioned by the president's possession or lack of political resources.

President and prime minister: political resources

De Gaulle, as noted in Chapter 2 (p. 59), commanded a unique range of resources as he moulded the institutions of the Fifth Republic in the early 1960s, including the legitimacy procured by his wartime role as leader of Free France, the trust he commanded as the only man capable of handling the Algerian emergency and the lasting discredit into which the Fourth Republic had fallen. None of his successors (still less any prime minister) has accumulated a comparable basis of political capital. Nevertheless, the two heads of France's executive wield important political resources, including political legitimacy; the power of political communication; personal networks; and patronage. To these should be added one that conditions all the rest: the support, or hostility, of the parliamentary majority.

Political legitimacy is first and foremost a presidential resource. The president is always France's head of state, and always, since 1965, the only individual to have been elected by the whole nation (rather than a single parliamentary constituency). As Mitterrand declared in November 1984 (at a historically low point in his popularity), 'the president of the Republic incarnates the nation, the state, the Republic. Everyone should remember that more. In any case, I do not forget it.' The president is also France's national leader, a role revealed above all at moments of crisis: it was President Chirac, for example, who took the lead in broadcasting to the nation on the progress of the Kosovo war in 1999 – despite his political weakness at the time. More routinely, the president always heads the French delegation at major summits – the G8, the European Council and the regular bilateral meetings organised with other EU states. The prime minister, by contrast, is the president's appointee, not the public's favourite. Jean-Pierre Raffarin, at his appointment to the post in May 2002, was an (indirectly elected) senator but had never faced a direct election to any body more elevated than the regional council of Poitou-Charentes. Most strikingly, neither Pompidou nor Barre (two of the Fifth Republic's longest-serving prime ministers) nor yet de Villepin, had ever been elected to anything when they first stepped into Matignon. But the relationship between president and prime minister inevitably changes under cohabitation: then, the prime minister is effectively the people's choice, not the president's. Chirac in 1986, Balladur in 1993 and Jospin in 1997 were all their respective coalitions' acknowledged candidates for Matignon. Each could claim a 'fresher' electoral mandate than the sitting president. Even then, though, the president's residual legitimacy remains considerable. Prime ministers under cohabitation have always manifested respect, even deference, towards the presidential office, partly out of consideration for public opinion, which has always supported the president's continuation in office, and partly out of self-interest as aspirants to the presidency themselves.

The second political resource is the ability to communicate with the public, either directly or via the media. De Gaulle's monarchical *hauteur* and distance were paradoxically combined with a constant wish for direct contact with the French, often in the form of *bains de foule*, or walkabouts. These were the nightmare of his security staff and of the prefects and other local officials responsible for the smooth running of the provincial tours that took de Gaulle to every *département* and every major city during his presidency, as well as to many smaller towns and villages. De Gaulle's successors have, each in his own style, followed his example. Chirac's provincial visits express an undiminished zest for election campaigns; his past as agriculture minister and as mayor of Paris is reflected in a taste for photo opportunities in bars and at agricultural shows (a penchant that has obliged all his political rivals to be photographed with one or another of the farm animals gathered annually in Paris at the *salon de l'agriculture*). De Gaulle also initiated the intensive presidential use of the press and broadcast media. De Gaulle's press conferences, effectively speeches framed around the questions of the assembled Élysée press corps, were grandiose affairs, at which spectators were often treated to surprise announcements such as his veto of Britain's entry into Europe in 1963. Though he came to television late in life and used it in what would now be considered a hopelessly theatrical manner, at his best he was unsurpassable. The appeal to the nation after the army revolt in Algeria in April 1961, for example, was as moving and resolute as it was effective, a rare combination of high drama and deep sincerity. His successors, albeit in a less heroic style, have never forsaken the small screen. Not always, it is true, with the results hoped for: de Gaulle's televised attempt to halt the rioting of May 1968, Mitterrand's unconvincing exhortations to national effort in the financial crisis of spring 1982 and Chirac's laments over his countrymen's 'conservatism' in December 1996 or his attempts at 'dialogue' with young voters during the 2005 referendum campaign, are all well-documented presidential flops. But there have been successes enough: the studied informality of Mitterrand's interviews with Yves Mourousi at Élysée garden parties on 14 July and the well-orchestrated good humour of Chirac's reception of France's victorious World Cup football team at the same occasion in 1998, both helped to portray the president in a much-needed sympathetic light. De Gaulle was also able to rely on a broadcasting system under tight government control, insisting (as did Pompidou after him) that television and radio should be 'the voice of France' (by which they meant the president and the Gaullist party). This iron grip has slackened, slowly after 1974, more rapidly after 1981. It remains the case that a French president can intervene on television where and when he likes, that he can count on a degree of deference from his interviewers that a British or American politician could only dream of and that opposition politicians have no automatic right of reply.

If presidents use the media to *remind* the French of who they are, prime ministers set out to *acquire* a presidential stature through their appearances. This is a more difficult exercise: the prime minister must neither seem to usurp the presidential function nor behave (even under cohabitation) as a mere opposition politician. Nevertheless, all prime ministers since the mid-1980s have appeared on television at least once every two months. For Chirac and Balladur (both under cohabitation), the frequency was closer to once every two weeks. Chirac's appearance after the terrorist bombings of September 1986 and the poised, elegant interviews in which Balladur informed the French of the parlous state of their economy from his chalet in Chamonix, were notably successful exercises in the genre. Jospin innovated in the seriousness with which he approached prime minister's questions in the National Assembly. Although these televised appearances often betrayed the tension (and the polemics) natural to the exercise, Jospin placed sufficient value on them, as a means to rally his own majority and to explain himself to a wider public, that he sometimes regretted it when important political events occurred outside parliamentary sessions.

Third, both president and prime minister will bring a range of personal networks to their offices. Such networks may have been built in a variety of ways: through the Resistance (in the case of de Gaulle, Mitterrand and Prime Minister Chaban-Delmas); through business connections (particularly important for the former banker Pompidou, but also significant for Chirac); via ministerial office (Giscard's solid base at the Finance Ministry); via local office (the officials from Lille and the Nord *département* who moved into the *cabinet* of Mitterrand's first prime minister Pierre Mauroy in 1981, or the enormous reserve of loyal Chirac supporters in the Paris town hall, or Raffarin's reserve of Poitou-Charentes supporters); or through the main majority party. A president will have to have built such networks to win election; if wise, he will cultivate them once in the Élysée, both to diversify sources of advice beyond his staff and to ensure more or less discreet backing for his initiatives within civil society. Prime ministers may also have very diverse networks: Chaban-Delmas, for example, was a leading *résistant*, a rugby international and president of the National Assembly before his appointment, and he continued as mayor of Bordeaux throughout his time at Matignon. Others may be less well endowed. Édith Cresson's lack of networks in the political, administrative and media communities, and her apparent indifference to building them once appointed to Matignon, was one reason for the rapid failure of her premiership. Dominique de Villepin was widely viewed as being handicapped by his failure to build strong relations with parliamentarians of the conservative majority, whom he had treated with ill-concealed contempt over the previous decade. Unlike Cresson, he was prepared to correct this: one of the major political successes of de Villepin's first months in office was to build bridges with the National Assembly president Jean-Louis Debré.

The opportunity to reinforce and extend networks is supplied by the patronage that comes with office, the fourth political resource. Both president and prime minister wield, jointly, very substantial powers in this area: most obviously in relation to the government itself under Article 8 of the constitution, but also to high-ranking posts in the military, the civil service and the shrinking but still important public sector. Pompidou, both as prime minister and as president, assiduously created a network of grateful clients within what became known as the 'Gaullist state'. His successor's attempts to replace them with his own people explains part of the acrimony generated between Gaullists and Giscardians. And Mitterrand was not slow to follow what had become, by 1981, the standard practice of the Fifth Republic, provoking a spate of articles analysing the 'Socialist nomenklatura'. Chirac's early presidency was distinguished from others chiefly by the fact that many of the victims were not Socialists but right-wingers who had been imprudent enough to support his rival Balladur. Prime ministers, outside cohabitation, have had a secondary but far from negligible role in this area: Pompidou, Chaban-Delmas, Mauroy and Rocard were all able to place their own in strategic state positions. During cohabitation, the prime minister has a much stronger hand to play, and can get most of his appointments through the Council of Ministers, though always with preliminary negotiation and the promise of suitable alternative positions for the displaced.

Patronage extends to money as well as to jobs. For the first forty-four years of the Fifth Republic, this included the 'special funds', amounting to some 45 million euros, voted annually by parliament to the prime minister. The disposal of this money escaped all further control. Some of it served to pay ministerial staffs: it was a curious anomaly of the supposedly structured, formalised French state that for decades the status within the civil service of *cabinet* members led to their being paid via brown envelopes full of cash. Special funds were also used for various secret service operations; and roughly a fifth was commonly used for political purposes. Although technically the prime minister's resource at all times, the special funds were under the effective control of the president outside periods of cohabitation. This changed after 2001, when the Jospin government replaced the special funds system with a regular vote for president and premier, and taxable salaries for staffers. Largely as a result of these changes, the presidential budget for 2005 amounted to 32 million euros, some six times more than the figure for 1994.

On a larger scale, patronage covers the many opportunities afforded by control of the budget: the spending programmes that may make the reputation of a rising minister, the constituency favours that may make the difference between defeat and re-election to a sitting Deputy. Again, the budget, nominally determined by the prime minister and government, is controlled in the last instance by the president outside periods of cohabitation – and by the prime minister within them.

The fifth political resource is popularity with the electorate. Tables 4.1 and 4.2 show average levels of support for the two heads of the French executive from 1978 to mid-2005, based on monthly SOFRES surveys of 'confidence' and 'no confidence' (other polling institutes such as IPSOS or IFOP, asking slightly different questions, give rather different levels of support, but with comparable trends). These averages can, of course, mislead. The figure for Mitterrand's first term conceals a deep trough from June 1983 to March 1986, between the buoyant periods of the early presidency and the first cohabitation; his second term divides into two equal halves, with his popularity turning negative in October 1991, never to recover while he was in office. Both Giscard and Jospin had the ill luck to see sharp dips in their popularity in the last months before the presidential elections, respectively of 1981 and 2002.

If there is one clear trend to emerge from the tables, it is that France's presidents have commanded more or less steadily declining levels of public support (figures for de Gaulle and Pompidou, both popular through most of their presidential terms, would broadly confirm this). This reflects a wider growth of distrust of political institutions generally among electorates of all developed Western countries since the 1970s, and has obvious implications for the capacity of presidents to reproduce de Gaulle's 'heroic' style of leadership. This judgement should, however, be qualified by the much less linear

Table 4.1 Presidential popularities, October 1978–June 2005

Giscard d'Estaing	October 1978–April 1981	10.53
Mitterrand I	May 1981–April 1988	5.96
Mitterrand II	May 1988–April 1995	−1.48
Chirac I	May 1995–April 2002	−1.35
Chirac II	May 2002–June 2005	−13.22

Source: average of monthly positive minus negative opinions, calculated from SOFRES website, http://www.tns-sofres.com/archives_pol.htm

Table 4.2 Prime ministerial popularities, October 1978–May 2005

Barre	October 1978–May 1981	−23.03
Mauroy	June 1981–June 1984	−1.89
Fabius	July 1984–March 1986	8.37
Chirac	April 1986–April 1988	−0.64
Rocard	May 1988–May 1991	22.14
Cresson	June 1991–April 1992	−30.18
Bérégovoy	May 1992–March 1993	3.00
Balladur	April 1993–May 1995	22.19
Juppé	June 1995–May 1997	−23.13
Jospin	June 1997–May 2002	21.48
Raffarin	June 2002–May 2005	−15.97
Overall average		2.57

Source: average of monthly positive minus negative opinions, calculated from SOFRES website, http://www.tns-sofres.com/archives_pol.htm

trend observable for prime ministers. More directly linked to the grubby details of unpopular policies, prime ministers outside cohabitation often serve to shield presidents from the voters' hostility. This has been true, for example, of Debré under de Gaulle, of Barre for Giscard and most recently of Raffarin for Chirac. Such prime ministers, moreover, are no masters of their term of office: presidents regularly dismiss them when they have outlived their usefulness – and with their unpopularity intact. On the other hand, some prime ministers have been capable of establishing their own basis of public support independent of the presidents who appointed them. This was true of Rocard, whose popularity matched Mitterrand's (much to the latter's irritation) during his three-year premiership, and of two of the three cohabitation prime ministers, Balladur and Jospin.

Popularity is, nevertheless, the most relative of political resources and the hardest to convert into tangible successes. It is relative in relation both to the political opposition (or to competitors within one's own camp) and to the electoral calendar. To take two recent examples, Juppé was politically paralysed within less than a year of his appointment by his deep unpopularity during a pre-election period; Raffarin, his successor but one, though almost equally disliked by the public, survived and launched cautious reform projects because the voters' sanction was further off (although by the time of his resignation in May 2005, with levels of unpopularity now matching those of Juppé or Cresson, he was politically played out). Moreover, election results have shown that popularity does not readily translate into votes. Of the three most popular prime ministers in the list on Table 4.2, none even reached the second ballot of a presidential election; Rocard never even tried the first (the legion of highly popular non-*présidentiables* also includes the two health ministers Simone Veil and Bernard Kouchner). And it was Chirac, not the 'more popular' Jospin, who won the 2002 presidential elections. Balladur was attacked for courting popularity too deliberately, and postponing necessary reforms; Juppé for his indifference to public opinion in engaging them. The issue of popularities highlights the idiosyncracies of the French case: their embedding within both the competitive relationship of president and prime minister (during and outside cohabitation) and an uncertain electoral calendar which rarely left more than two or three years before allowing the voters to make a new choice. In principle, the switch to a five-year presidential term may open the curtain on a more conventional four-to-five-year democratic rhythm, in which a newly elected government spends much of its early capital of support in controversial reforms, suffers mid term setbacks, but seeks to regain the voters' favours in time to be returned to office; but it is now hard to fit the record since 2002 into this pattern.

The sixth political resource is the support of a majority coalition and (normally) of the leading party within it. The links of mutual dependence that bind the president to the parliamentary majority have been a central feature of Fifth Republic politics before 1986, from 1988 to 1993, from 1995 to 1997, and since 2002. The president needs the parliamentary majority to enact legislation; the majority normally looks to the president as its political locomotive. The severance of these links, and the transfer of majority support to the exclusive benefit of the prime minister, have defined the periods of cohabitation, from 1986 to 1988, 1993 to 1995, and 1997 to 2002. Control of the majority is the most decisive resource because its possession conditions the use of virtually all others.

The constitution-makers did not foresee it thus. De Gaulle wanted a presidency 'above parties'. Newly elected presidents display an outward respect for his wish by shedding any party offices they may have held before polling day, the better to don the mantle of president of all the French. The reality, though, is that a president will have needed the solid backing of his own party to reach the second ballot of the presidential election, and the support of a coalition beyond his own party to win. Thus Pompidou had both built up a strong Gaullist party under his leadership, and established good relations with some of the centrists, before his election in 1969. Mitterrand's victory in 1981 crowned a long-term strategy based on the relaunch (under his leadership) of the Socialist Party ten years earlier and on an alliance with the reluctant Communists. Chirac, similarly, used a relaunched Gaullist party and an alliance with the non-Gaullist moderate Right to further his long march to the Élysée (and a reconstructed moderate right-wing party, the UMP, to back his re-election campaign in 2002). The other two presidents were the exceptions that proved the rule, though in very different ways. De Gaulle's attempt to pitch his presidential campaign 'above parties' in 1965 led to a disappointing first ballot, after which the Gaullist party entered the fray on his behalf. Giscard won the presidency at the head of a small party, his Républicains Indépendants. This was the only occasion on which the president's party has been the smaller partner within the majority coalition. The organisational and electoral weakness of the RI, and Giscard's inability to achieve a satisfactory relationship with the larger Gaullist party, blighted his presidency and contributed to his defeat in 1981.

Table 4.3 presents the level and type of majority support available to presidents throughout the Fifth Republic. On the most basic level, this ranges from the four parliaments in which the president's party has held an absolute majority ('Type 1') – though even then it has always shared power in a coalition with one or more smaller groupings – to the opposite extreme, when the parliamentary majority is opposed to the president (Types 6 and 7). While the domination of the National Assembly by friendly forces is certainly an important asset for any president (and its absence, as the Giscard case (Type 4) shows, a distinct handicap), it is by no means a guarantee of an easy ride, for neither the loyalty of the president's party nor *a forteriori* that of his coalition are automatic. Table 4.3 therefore suggests other factors affecting party support for the president. Presidents who are expected to run for re-election command more loyalty than those who do not; of these, presidents who are popular and expected to win attract more support than those about whom there are doubts (in fact only one incumbent who has sought re-election, Giscard in 1981, has failed to secure it; none has yet been defeated by a competitor from within his own camp). At the same time, parties and coalitions may be hard to manage, not because they become the focus of competing presidential ambitions for the future, but because they bear the scars of the past: the trauma of de Gaulle's departure in 1969, for example, or that of Chirac/Balladur competition in 1995. Fourth, the order and offensiveness of the opposition may also affect the cohesion and loyalty of the majority. Even when these elements are taken into account, however, the loyalty of parties and coalitions to the president is subject to circumstance. The Algerian war and de Gaulle's unique usefulness at a time of acute national crisis were crucial assets in managing the disparate, shifting majorities of 1958–62. On the other hand, the big Gaullist majority returned in June 1968 was very hard to manage. This was true in de Gaulle's last nine months, because of the widespread perception that he had managed the 'events' of May 1968 less well than had his prime minister Pompidou; opposition from within the ranks of the Right lost the General his last referendum in 1969. It was then true under Pompidou, because many Gaullists felt an obscure sense of betrayal after the General's departure. More

Table 4.3 Party and majority support for presidents under the Fifth Republic

President and period	Parliamentary majority	President to stand for re-election?	President's popularity	Unity of majority party/coalition	Opposition	Observations
de Gaulle 1968–69	**Type 1**: Overall National Assembly majority for president's party (but other parties still in majority coalition)	No: de Gaulle aged 75 in 1965	Damaged	Mediocre	Weak and divided	de Gaulle weakened after May 1968; Pompidou appears a viable alternative for conservatives
Pompidou 1969–73	**Type 1**: Overall National Assembly majority for president's party (but other parties still in majority coalition)	Uncertain (Pompidou visibly ill from 1972)	Generally good	Mediocre	Increasingly credible after 1972	Gaullists factionalised after de Gaulle's departure and (in 1970) death
Mitterrand 1981–86	**Type 1**: Overall National Assembly majority for president's party (but other parties still in majority coalition)	Probable, but parliamentary elections to precede presidential election	Good to 1983, then mediocre to poor	Socialists cohesive; Communists out of coalition from 1984	Increasingly credible after 1982	Left's popularity dips in 1983–85, recovers partially by 1986
Chirac 2002–	**Type 1**: Overall National Assembly majority for president's party (but other parties still in majority coalition)	Uncertain (Chirac aged 70 in 2002)	Mediocre	Mediocre	Credible	Chirac faces eligible younger competitor, within own camp, in Nicolas Sarkozy

de Gaulle 1962–68	**Type 2:** Overall majority for president's coalition: president's party the 'majority of the majority'	Yes (to 1965), no (post-1965)	Generally good	Good, though some coalition difficulties between Gaullists/Giscardians	Divided	Gaullist ascendancy; unprecedented government stability
Pompidou 1973–74	**Type 2:** Overall majority for president's coalition: president's party the 'majority of the majority'	No: Pompidou's illness known from 1972	Generally good	Mediocre	Credible	Uncertainty in view of Pompidou's failing health
Chirac 1995–97	**Type 2:** Overall majority for president's coalition: president's party the 'majority of the majority'	Probable, but parliamentary elections to precede presidential election	Generally poor	Mediocre in both majority parties	Credible	Majority party divided by legacy of Chirac/Balladur contest in 1995 presidential election
Giscard 1974–81	**Type 3:** Overall majority for president's coalition: president's party the 'minority of the majority'	Probable (Giscard aged 55 in 1981)	Generally positive, but with dips in 1976–77 and 1980–81	Poor, and non-Gaullist moderate Right only federated into UDF in 1978	Broadly credible, though divided after 1977	Increasingly bitter rivalry between Gaullists and Giscardians
Mitterrand 1988–93	**Type 4:** President's coalition a few seats short of absolute majority	No (Mitterrand aged 75 in 1991)	Good to 1991, then poor	Poor	Credible from 1991	Majority party factionalised in view of impending succession to Mitterrand

(Continued overleaf)

Table 4.3 Continued

President and period	Parliamentary majority	President to stand for re-election?	President's popularity	Unity of majority party/coalition	Opposition	Observations
de Gaulle 1958–62	**Type 5**: No overall majority: president's party strongest in Assembly	Uncertain (de Gaulle aged 70 in 1960)	Good	Mediocre	Weak and divided	Algerian crisis serves as cement for potentially undisciplined majority
Mitterrand 1986–88 (Cohabitation with Chirac)	**Type 6**: Narrow overall majority opposed to the president	Probable	Good	Limited	Credible, loyal to president	Impending presidential election damages unity of right-wing majority; cohesion maintained in parliamentary votes
Mitterrand 1993–95 (Cohabitation with Balladur)	**Type 7**: Clear overall majority opposed to the president	No (Mitterrand aged 75 in 1991, and illness public from 1992)	Poor	Good but declining by 1995	Weak, divided, and increasingly distant from president	Right-wing majority increasingly divided by Chirac/Balladur rivalry
Chirac 1997–2002 (Cohabitation with Jospin)	**Type 7**: Clear overall majority opposed to the president	Probable	Variable to good	Fair	Weak, but increasingly supportive of president	Cohesion of left-wing majority increasingly tested by impending presidential election

generally, therefore, although the configurations of the National Assembly majority in relation to the president may be repeated (with four examples of Type 1, three Type 2 cases, and so on), there are no two cases in Table 4.3 where the wider configurations are the same.

The importance of party and coalition control as a presidential asset can be gauged from what happens when the grip loosens. De Gaulle's post-May 1968 lame duck status was reproduced under the obviously ailing Pompidou after 1972; the November 1973 Gaullist party congress almost openly transferred its allegiance from the terminally ill president to Chaban-Delmas, seen by delegates as the most promising candidate for the succession. Giscard's failure to secure the loyalty of the Gaullists has already been referred to. An equally clear case was that of Mitterrand, whose triumphant election to a second *septennat*, in 1988 at the age of 71, immediately opened a succession struggle among Socialists. Twice, in 1988 and 1990, the president's preferred candidate for the party leadership, Laurent Fabius, was blocked by rival Socialist factions, provoking the violent internal party strife which contributed powerfully to the Socialists' catastrophic defeat of 1993. Chirac's party and coalition were badly divided at his election in 1995 by the bitter rivalry between himself and his Gaullist rival, former prime minister Édouard Balladur. His failure either to crush or to co-opt the *balladuriens* was to weaken both party and majority at the 1997 parliamentary elections. The difficulties of his second presidential term have arisen in part from the greater attractiveness to many activists and parliamentarians of Nicolas Sarkozy, senior government minister and then, from November 2004, leader of the UMP, as a presidential candidate for 2007. Chirac's defeat in the 2005 referendum and subsequent unpopularity, Sarkozy's efforts to secure the UMP's loyalty to his own person, and his combination, from May 2005, of the two posts of party leader and interior minister, compounded the president's lame duck status.

Hence the importance, for presidents, of working to sustain party support once elected. Day-to-day party management is typically delegated to trusted lieutenants. De Gaulle and Pompidou were discreet about this, using advisers, respectively Foccart and Juillet. Their successors have had more open contact with leading party officials, such as Michel Poniatowski for Giscard and Jospin (the Socialist Party's first secretary from 1981 to 1988) for Mitterrand. An important role, too, is played by the leader of the parliamentary group of the presidential party. Mitterrand gave his role in party management a semi-official status early in his presidency by holding weekly breakfasts with Socialist Party leaders. Party leaders are also often chosen unofficially by the president and ratified by the party: this was true of the Gaullist party's secretary-general in 1967 and 1971; of all the leaders of Giscard's Républicains Indépendants (which became the Parti Républicain after its relaunch in 1977); of Jospin for the Socialists in 1981; and of Juppé, Chirac's successor to the Gaullist party leadership in 1995. Parliamentary candidates are also vetted by presidents. Foccart's diaries reveal the extent of the General's personal involvement in candidate selection: deciding disputed cases, choosing the constituencies where the Gaullists' allies would be allowed a free run and even agreeing to find money for his own son-in-law's campaign in the islands of St-Pierre et Miquelon. De Gaulle's successors have followed his example. The majority candidacies in 1997, for example, were vetted by Chirac after being drawn up in the music pavilion in the Matignon garden by presidential advisers and party leaders. Rocard's description of Mitterrand's hold over the Socialist Party is only partially exaggerated: he 'was able to appoint everyone, and to control a whole pyramid of men'.

As well as choosing candidates, presidents have also, typically, been their parties' leading campaigners in parliamentary elections. De Gaulle's famous request, in 1958, that his name should not be invoked by any party 'even in the form of an adjective' during the election campaign was a dead letter from the start. By 1962, having just won the referendum on the direct election of the president and used his power of dissolution against a hostile National Assembly majority, he quite logically expressed the hope that the yes vote could be 'confirmed' at the following month's parliamentary elections. That inaugurated a regular tradition of presidential interventions in campaigns for parliamentary elections, whether caused by an early dissolution or not. In 1973 Pompidou evoked the red peril to frighten Centre voters away from the left-wing opposition; in 1978, Giscard, more obliquely, reminded voters that if the Left won, he would be unable to prevent the full application of the Socialist–Communist Common Programme; in 1986, the Socialists used the slogan 'Avec le Président'. Indeed, the dissociation of the president from the majority's parliamentary campaign, as in 1993, is a sure sign that both president and party are in trouble.

Presidents also cultivate a wider range of political support, both to maintain the coalition that brought them to power and to diversify their political bases. Perhaps the clearest case of this is the Parti Républicain's federation with centrists and Radicals as the Union pour la Démocratie Française in 1978. But Mitterrand's channelling of funds to the SOS–Racisme group, his contacts with the maverick businessman Bernard Tapie and his wooing of leading Trotskyist activists – small in number, but influential with the rising generation because of their role in student politics, and so an important influx of new blood when they arrived in the Socialist Party in 1986 – are also important cases in point. It was also Mitterrand who decided that the Communists were a dispensable component of the ruling left-wing coalition in 1984, and who limited the experiment with a Socialist–centrist alliance in 1988 to the inclusion of centrist ministers in the government rather than a full-scale coalition.

That the president enjoys majority party support does not preclude the prime minister from doing so as well. Indeed, the first prime minister of a presidential term is often chosen precisely because his own political base, within the president's party or with its allies, is expected to reinforce the presidential coalition. Debré owed his appointment in 1959 as much to the support he commanded among the large group of conservative, *Algérie française* Deputies as to his own unfailing loyalty to de Gaulle. Chaban-Delmas, as a historic Gaullist who had built good relations with the parliamentary centrists over a decade as president of the National Assembly, was an obvious choice for Pompidou in 1969. Five years later, Chirac's appointment was intended by Giscard to ensure presidential control of the Gaullist party (Chirac did not see matters in the same light). In 1981, Mitterrand chose Pierre Mauroy not only as an experienced Socialist Party power broker, but as one of the few Socialist leaders trusted by the Communists whom Mitterrand was determined to lock into the government majority. At the start of his second term he chose his long-standing rival Michel Rocard as a prime minister capable of 'opening' the Socialist majority towards the Centre. Chirac appointed Raffarin in 2002 because of his strong local and regional record, supposedly a guarantee of strong affinities with the concerns of ordinary French voters. But the fate of each of these prime ministers illustrates the president's political primacy and the prime minister's inability to use his political resources independently. Debré was discarded within weeks of the Algerian war ending, Chaban dismissed when Pompidou came to see him as a rival for control of the parliamentary majority. Chirac, having refused to emasculate the Gaullist party for Giscard's benefit, resigned angrily in 1976 after repeated humiliations by the president. Mitterrand let Mauroy go once the Communist alliance had outlived its usefulness; Rocard lost his job because Mitterrand suspected that he was cultivating the centrists (and, incidentally, his own presidential chances) at the expense of the core Socialist electorate – a suspicion fuelled by deep personal loathing on both sides; the politically wrung-out Raffarin left in 2005 once he had begun to drag Chirac's own ratings down. Alain Juppé, finally, was an unusual choice for a first prime minister: although he had succeeded Chirac as president of the Gaullist party when Chirac began his 1995 presidential campaign, he was more a creature of Chirac than an independent politician with his own base, and noticeably lacked supporters outside his own party. This relative lack of independent weight, more typical of 'second' prime ministers (Pompidou at his appointment in 1962, Messmer in 1972, Barre in 1976, Fabius in 1984 and Cresson in 1991), told against Juppé; but it was the voters, not the president, who ended his premiership by destroying the Right's majority in 1997.

Under cohabitation (Types 6 and 7 in Table 4.3), the distribution of political resources is radically altered to the benefit of the prime minister. The prime minister is appointed as the leader of the largest party in the new majority and the main winner of the elections (Chirac in 1986, Jospin in 1997) or as his agreed delegate (Balladur, with Chirac's blessing, in 1993). This resource is nevertheless fragile. The prime minister must continuously convince the majority parties that he is their best electoral asset: a difficult task, because he faces not only the pressure of events, but also both a determined adversary in the Élysée and rivals within his own camp. Hence the considerable efforts deployed by prime ministers under cohabitation; Chirac and Balladur held 'majority lunches' to clear major issues both with key ministers and with party leaders outside the government, while Jospin took a weekly breakfast with Socialist leaders, and all three used patronage to try and keep their coalitions onside.

A president under cohabitation can only find party support in the opposition. This is a meagre consolation compared to the clout offered by a majority. But it must be husbanded carefully: it is essential, in the long term, to any prospect of a presidential comeback, and thus, in the short term, to the preservation of some vestiges of presidential authority. Mitterrand's continuing ascendancy over the Socialists, and the perception that he had limited the damage to his party in the 1986 parliamentary elections, preserved his chances of re-election and strengthened his hand against Chirac during the first cohabitation (1986–88). In 1993, by contrast, Mitterrand was too old and too ill to contemplate a third term; he had all but lost control over his party since 1988; and the Socialists had suffered a defeat of historic proportions in 1993. That ensured an easier cohabitation for Prime Minister Balladur, who faced more difficulties from his own camp (and especially from Chirac) than from the Élysée. Chirac, finally, found himself in an unprecedented position after the Right's defeat at the 1997 parliamentary elections: facing a cohabitation of five years, not (as in 1986 and 1993) two; widely blamed within his own party for calling the elections ten months early; unable to keep his own protégé Juppé at the head of his own party; and confronted by a plethora of rival right-wing *présidentiables*. Chirac's first priority from 1997 was to eliminate such competitors. To do so, however, he practically destroyed his own party, the neo-Gaullist RPR. Only a complex process of orchestrating supporters throughout the moderate Right provided a substitute in the shape of the electoral network that would become the UMP.

Concluding remarks

Early interpretations of the Fifth Republic tended to view it, whether approvingly or not, as a 'republican monarchy' in which presidential primacy was assured. They also tended to overestimate the significance, in the basis of this primacy, of permanent, constitutional provisions, and to underestimate both the importance to presidential power of parliamentary majority support and above all the contingent, conditional character of that support. Hence the perplexity with which France's political science community viewed the approach of cohabitation in 1986, as well as the widespread notion that a majority opposed to the president was somehow contrary to the 'spirit' of the Fifth Republic. The two further cohabitations, of 1993–95 and 1997–2002, suggested that the 'republican monarchy' could no longer be taken as the normal institutional practice. And even if the future possibility of cohabitation is now relatively remote, there is a sense in which the key measure taken to render it less likely, the shortening of the presidential term, also reduces the likelihood of a return to the 'republican monarchy' because the presidential term is now so closely tied to the fortunes of a legislature.

Nor, however, should the possession or lack of parliamentary support by the president be viewed as the only important variable in the distribution of executive power, entailing a simple, binary model. For the resources available to president and prime minister are varied and complex, act upon one another, and may be used or misused in a variety of ways. The patterns of policy-making that result are equally diverse.

Further reading

See also list for Chapter 5.

Ardant, P., *Le Premier ministre en France*, Paris, Montchrestien, 1991.
Claisse, A., *Le Premier ministre de la Ve République*, Paris, La Documentation Française, 1972.
Cohen, S., *Les conseillers du président: de Charles de Gaulle à Valéry Giscard d'Estaing*, Paris, Presses Universitaires de France, 1980.
Duhamel, O., *Le pouvoir politique en France*, 2nd edition, Paris, Seuil, 1999.
Fauvet-Mycia, C., *Les éminences grises*, Paris, Belfond, 1988.
Institut Charles de Gaulle, *'L'entourage' et De Gaulle*, Paris, Plon, 1979.
Jobert, M., *Mémoires d'avenir*, Paris, Grasset, 1974.
Jobert, M., *L'autre regard*, Paris, Grasset, 1976.
Long, M., *Les services du Premier ministre*, Aix-en-Provence, Presses Universitaires d'Aix-Marseille, 1981.
Massot, J., *La présidence de la République en France*, 2nd edition, Paris, La Documentation Française, 1986.
Pouvoirs, no. 68, 1994, 'Qui gouverne la France?'
Py, R., *Le secrétariat général du gouvernement*, Paris, La Documentation Française, 1985.
Quermonne, J.-L., *Le gouvernement de la France sous la Ve République*, Paris, Dalloz, 1980.
Rials, S., *Le premier ministre*, Paris, Presses Universitaires de France, 1981.
Schifres, M. and Sarazin, M., *L'Elysée de Mitterrand: secrets de la maison du Prince*, Paris, Alain Moreau, 1985.
Schrameck, O., *Les cabinets ministériels*, Paris, Dalloz, 1995.
Schrameck, O., *Matignon rive gauche, 1997–2001*, Paris, Seuil, 2001.

5 Executive policy-making

The variable diarchy

This chapter seeks to show how policy-making powers are shared within the political executive. The issue is complex because France has a dual executive of variable geometry: although some of its characteristics, such as the president's role as France's head of state and the prime minister's as chief processor and co-ordinator of government business, are fixed, others vary with political circumstance. In particular, the variable relationship between the parliamentary majority and the president has been of crucial importance to the distribution of power. For that reason, the two basic scenarios – a majority favourable to the president and a hostile majority – will be treated successively. But the sharp distinction that such a treatment implies should be qualified in three ways. First, many powers are exercised jointly by both heads of the executive (though not always in the same way inside and outside cohabitation). Second, variations in the resources available to the two main actors, explored in Chapter 4, and in the use made of them, entail variations of policy-making powers within the two main scenarios, as well as between them. Third, while attention is primarily focused on the president and the prime minister, there are important instances, discussed later in the chapter, where ministers have contributed substantially to the policy-making process.

Presidential government

A president with the support of the parliamentary majority is both *de facto* head of the governing coalition and the effective, if not the constitutional, leader of the government. Nowhere, indeed, is the gap between constitutional theory and presidential practice greater than here. Constitutionally, the government is a collective body of ministers, responsible to the National Assembly, which 'determines and conducts' national policy, and whose members are appointed by the president on the proposal of the prime minister; in practice, outside cohabitation it has usually been an instrument of presidential government, its members reduced to the role of advisers responsible to the president alone. In that sense, the French government came to resemble the cabinet of an American president.

Presidential control of the government

Presidential control of the government outside periods of cohabitation may be seen in several ways.

- *The president appoints and dismisses its head, the prime minister.* To the constitutional right freely to appoint prime ministers (of however unexpected a stamp, where Pompidou in 1962, Barre in 1976 and Cresson in 1991 were concerned), successive presidents have added the right to sack them – or rather, since the dismissal of the prime minister appears nowhere in the constitution, to force their departure. De Gaulle inaugurated this practice by requiring undated letters of resignation from his nominees to the premiership. His successors have continued it, usually without resorting to such crude methods: given their ascendancy over the parliamentary majority, a simple request is enough. Seven prime ministers – Debré, Pompidou, Chaban-Delmas, Mauroy, Rocard, Cresson and Raffarin – have lost their jobs in this way. Rocard, for example, was asked to go by Mitterrand, at 9.30 a.m. on 15 May 1991; the resignation letter was sent by noon on the same day, directly after the meeting of the Council of Ministers (which was kept completely in the dark about the matter). Although prime ministers since Cresson have fallen to the voters, not to the president (with the partial exception of Raffarin, who was blamed for defeats at the regional and European elections of 2004, and the referendum of 2005, but was under no obligation to resign), there is no doubt that Chirac could freely dispose of Dominique de Villepin as and when he wished.
- *The president determines the size and shape of the government.* However much discussion takes place between president and prime minister over the composition of the government, the president has the last word. Pompidou's creation of an environment ministry, Giscard's appointment of junior ministers for penal reform, 'the feminine condition' and immigrant affairs were examples of new posts fitted to presidential priorities. The unwieldy size of Rocard's government in 1988, of Juppé's in 1995 and of Raffarin's in June 2002 resulted more from the wishes of presidents Mitterrand and Chirac to pay the debts of the presidential elections (and, in the latter case, to open up the government to more women and to representatives of 'civil society') than from a direct concern with effective policy-making.
- *The president intervenes directly in the choice of individual ministers.* Pierre Messmer records in his memoirs that all three of the governments he headed were in large measure chosen by Pompidou. Chirac's first government, in 1974, was concocted by Giscard and his henchman Michel Poniatowski in a manner almost calculated to displease his Gaullist party; Giscard's habit of presenting 'his' governments on television, and reshuffling them, as he did in 1975 and 1976, without even pretending to consult his prime minister, merely extended and made more open the practice of his predecessors. Rocard, in 1988, was allowed to include a handful of his own protégés like the Health Minister Claude Évin, but was also forced to accept the old guard of Mitterrand loyalists, such as Roland Dumas, Louis

Mermaz, Pierre Joxe or Michel Charasse. Raffarin was quoted in May 2002 as telling a right-wing parliamentarian anxious for preferment that it was not he, but Chirac, who was forming the new government. It was Chirac who ruled that ministers should not hold major executive office at local level (a continuation of a practice established under Jospin, to which a certain number of exceptions were allowed); Chirac again who negotiated Nicolas Sarkozy's place in each of the Raffarin governments, who ruled in 2004 that Sarkozy could not combine ministerial office with the presidency of the UMP, and who decided in May 2005 that, after all, he could.

- *The president determines the political balance of the government.* The inclusion of only four Gaullists, none of them heavyweights, in the 1974 Chirac government was clearly the choice of Giscard and Poniatowski, rather than of the prime minister. It was Mitterrand who, in 1981, decided to include Communists in the government and who determined the representation of the various factions of the Socialist Party in it. The exclusion of all but two Balladur supporters from the 1995 Juppé government was Chirac's decision (influenced, in the case of one unhappy *balladurien*, by the new president's wife).

- *The president treats the government not as a collective body responsible to the National Assembly, but as a group of individuals responsible to himself.* Indeed, General de Gaulle in his *Memoirs* was specific on this point: 'when one is a minister, it is to de Gaulle and to him alone that one is responsible'. Pompidou, Giscard d'Estaing and Mitterrand never failed to act upon that unconstitutional assumption. More than his predecessors, Chirac delegated some of this responsibility to his prime minister Juppé (though not to Raffarin), but the effect was broadly similar.

As we have seen, the president's official powers of patronage extend well beyond the political executive. While the existence of a fully developed spoils system has been limited by the requirement for continuity and experience in top posts, presidents enjoying the support of the parliamentary majority have routinely used these powers to reward the faithful, tempt the waverers, punish the recalcitrant and the hostile, and get rid of the embarrassing. De Gaulle cleansed the army of dissident elements, and purged the Quai d'Orsay of diplomats suspected of being too pro-European or pro-American; Pompidou rewarded younger followers; Giscard removed recalcitrant Gaullists; Mitterrand created the 'Socialist nomenklatura'; Chirac rewarded his loyalists within the RPR after 1995 and punished the hapless *balladuriens*.

Processes of presidential policy-making

Master of the parliamentary majority and the government, and to a significant extent of the administration, the president is also the nation's chief policy-maker. In the first place, he may intervene at all stages of the policy-making procedure.

- *The president determines the overall programme of the government.* The overall shape of government policy is determined by the president, a fact of which the public is left in no doubt. To take two recent examples, Prime Minister Raffarin's general policy declaration of July 2002 took as its starting point, not the Right's victory at the June parliamentary elections, but the programme on which Chirac had been re-elected to the presidency the previous May. Again, the Military Programme Law for 2003–8 was explicitly based on Chirac's presidential commitments. Presidents periodically remind governments publicly of presidential election pledges, whether via regular 'directive letters' (as under Giscard), or through Mitterrand's and Chirac's more periodic instructions.

- *The president fixes the agenda and timetable of the Council of Ministers.* From week to week, the president fixes, via orders passed through the secretary-general of the Élysée to the secretary-general of the government, the agenda of the Council of Ministers and the timetable of government business.

- *He is in regular direct and indirect contact with ministers,* whether on formal occasions, such as *conseils restreints,* or informally through personal meetings, meals, telephone calls (much favoured by Chirac, though not by his predecessor) or outside visits – undermining the fragile collective identity of the government.

- *He acts as a final court of appeal,* over the prime minister's head, on policy issues (and particularly questions of resources). Rocard's careful budget calculations, for example, were often upset by the last-minute appeals for more money made to the president by ministers such as Jack Lang or Pierre Joxe who were particularly close to Mitterrand.

- *He signs the decrees essential to the implementation of government legislation.* Though the prime minister and ministers both control implementation documents, the *arrêtés,* the major decrees, are signed by the president as well as the prime minister in the Council of Ministers.

- *His advisers extend his personal policy role.* Crucially, Élysée advisers attend inter-ministerial meetings to transmit presidential wishes and to verify compliance. They also liaise with parliamentary majority leaders and committee chairmen to ensure that if parliamentarians do amend or distort governmental projects, they do so only in ways approved by the Élysée.

- *He may also meet with leading representatives of pressure groups* – 'intermediary' organisations viewed with deep mistrust by de Gaulle but more openly accommodated in the policy process by his successors.

- *The president has regularly played a role of government spokesperson,* most frequently on television, defending governmental policies and criticising those of the opposition.

Domains of presidential policy-making

The president is the master of the substance as well as of the processes of policy-making. This was first acknowledged in November 1959, when Chaban-Delmas invented the *domaine réservé* over which the president had more or less exclusive control. Chaban was seeking chiefly to deflect criticism within the Gaullist party of de Gaulle's moves towards Algerian independence. His term is political; it lacks any constitutional status. But it has stuck, and has been taken to include foreign affairs, defence matters and questions relating to the French Community – or, more recently, to the vestiges of empire in Africa. In practice, though, the president controls as much or as little of policy-making as he wishes: when Mitterrand observed in 1983 that 'it is up to the president to decide which policies should be decided by the president', he was merely echoing his old enemy de Gaulle's claims of 1964.

Imperial and post-imperial matters

Presidential supremacy in this area was quickly established: de Gaulle had, after all, returned to power in order to end the Algerian crisis. This he did, with little regard either to the government or to parliament, by imposing his policies on a rebellious army, a divided parliament and a deeply reserved Gaullist party. The Council of Ministers was consulted only once, in August 1959, and Prime Minister Debré, a strong *Algérie française* supporter up to his appointment, was constantly bypassed, and dismissed as soon as the war was over. When the president appealed to the French people for support on the issue, he always stressed the personal nature of his policies. Just as personal, but without the popular consultation, has been the conduct of African affairs by both de Gaulle and his successors: policy has typically been decided by the president himself, by close personal advisers with their own networks (Foccart for de Gaulle, Pompidou and even, until his death, for Chirac; his own son Jean-Christophe for Mitterrand) and by the heads of the client states concerned. This extends to the use made of the troops France has stationed in several of its former colonies of sub-Saharan Africa since their accession to independence in 1962. Neither de Gaulle's despatch of troops to save the Bongo régime in Gabon in 1964, nor Giscard's use of paratroopers to pacify Zaïre (a former Belgian colony, but increasingly a French sphere of influence) in 1978, nor the interventions of French forces in the Chad civil wars of the 1980s under Mitterrand were discussed by the government. The same was true of Chirac's intervention against an army mutiny in Central Africa in 1997. The obscurity surrounding African policy has fuelled claims that behind a façade of development aid and the promotion of Francophone culture lurked more sinister practices: the pillage of mineral resources by an alliance between French firms, backed by the French state, and local dictators; or money-laundering through the scandal-ridden Elf oil company. African affairs came to haunt one president, Giscard d'Estaing, whose re-election campaign in 1981 was damaged by the revelation that he had accepted a gift of diamonds from Jean-Bedel Bokassa, the tyrant whose lavish coronation as Emperor of Central Africa had been financed by France. By the 1990s, however, there was every sign that time was running out for such highly personalised relations, as states of the former empire found other foreign sponsors, notably the United States. Symbolically, it was Chirac, heir to de Gaulle and Pompidou, who announced an end to interventionism and a scaling-down of France's military presence in Africa from 8,500 to 5,000 men. It was Chirac, too, who managed France's troubled relations with the Ivory Coast, and the use of the French military force there, after civil war broke out in 2003.

Foreign policy

Foreign policy in the wider sense has also been part of the 'reserved domain' (indeed, there were precedents for presidential foreign policy activism under earlier Republics, notably that of Raymond Poincaré in 1913–14, but they were of brief duration). Among de Gaulle's many personal acts were his policy of *détente* with the Soviet bloc, his recognition of Communist China in 1964, the decision not to sell arms to Israel, the outrageous proclamation about 'free Quebec' in 1967, or the decisions that progressively extracted France from NATO between 1959 and 1967. Giscard travelled to Warsaw to discuss the Afghan crisis with the Soviet President Brezhnev in 1980 – a much criticised visit that was only announced to the foreign minister after the President's personal emissary had settled all the details. Mitterrand disconcerted his two first prime ministers by receiving visits from two pariah leaders, South Africa's P.W. Botha and Poland's Wozzeck Jaruzelski, and undertook secret trips to meet Morocco's King Hassan II and Libya's Colonel Kadhafi; no one disputed his right to engage in this type of personal diplomacy. When Mitterrand consulted his government on the issue of French participation in an international force to be sent to the Gulf after the Iraqi invasion of Kuwait in 1990, the great majority of ministers were opposed; the president immediately committed French troops to the force. Chirac's personal initiatives include an offer to take France back into NATO if a European could be given the alliance's southern command – a move quickly rebuffed by the Americans. He has also attempted to improve France's economic relations with China, Japan and the Pacific Rim states, and like Mitterrand has often included cohorts of French business executives in his delegations on overseas visits. Though he was the first European leader to visit New York after the attacks of 11 September 2001, Chirac also made France's refusal to countenance the 2003 invasion of Iraq very much his own.

European affairs

Presidential supremacy has been equally manifest here as long as the president has been supported by the parliamentary majority. The so-called 'Fouchet plans' for European political union were really de Gaulle plans. De Gaulle announced his first veto of British entry into the Common Market at a press conference, just three days after his own foreign minister had assured the British negotiating team that 'no power on earth' could prevent a successful outcome to their efforts. His decision to boycott European institutions for six months in 1965 was equally personal, a fact underlined by the timing of the eventual compromise (just after de Gaulle's re-election). President Pompidou reversed several of de Gaulle's European policies, 'relaunching' Europe at a summit in The Hague in December 1969 and lifting the veto on British entry, but the methods remained the same, with the decisions largely escaping ministerial scrutiny. Giscard's major European initiatives – the creation of the European Council, the European Monetary System and direct elections to the European Parliament – owed more to his close relationship with the German Chancellor Helmut Schmidt than to any discussions with government ministers. Similarly, Mitterrand's major European legacy, the Maastricht Treaty, arose above all from his personal conviction, shared with Chancellor Kohl, that reunited Germany must be irrevocably attached to Europe, and that the best way to achieve this was the single currency; specific points such as the role of the European Central Bank were managed personally by Mitterrand, who took assistance from his foreign and finance ministers but excluded his prime ministers. Chirac, though a less constant European than either of his two predecessors, has overseen the negotiation of no fewer than three European treaties – Amsterdam in 1997, Nice in 2000 (when he was chiefly remembered for his fierce defence of France's parity of voting rights on the Council of Ministers with Germany) and the European constitutional treaty of 2004. He also took the ill-fated decision to submit the last of these to a referendum.

Defence policy

The president's constitutional position as commander-in-chief and chairman of the National Defence Committee ensures a central role in defence policy at all times, especially but not exclusively when he occupies his normal political position as head of the executive. This applies equally to major strategic initiatives and to the budgetary choices that ensure their implementation. De Gaulle's pursuit of the full panoply of a nuclear deterrent, including bombs, warheads, missiles and submarines, as independent as was possible from NATO, was the most striking early instance of this. It set a framework for de Gaulle's successors over a generation. The defence decisions taken by Mitterrand shortly after his election, to continue work on France's neutron bomb, to retain the length of military service at one year, to replace the old generation of ballistic missiles by a new one and to build a seventh nuclear submarine, were all presidential choices, announced from the Élysée. In 1992, when the end of the Cold War had placed the issue of future defence postures before all Western nations, the announcements that France would sign the nuclear test ban treaty and declare a moratorium on nuclear tests signalled a move away from the *gaullien* defence posture, but was still a wholly presidential move. Chirac's resumption of testing in 1995, albeit for a brief period, was announced in characteristic Gaullist fashion, at a press conference, and provoked reactions in the world comparable to those that greeted the General's more extravagant initiatives. But Chirac was also responsible for two more lasting changes, both visible in the 1997–2002 Military Programme Law: the professionalisation of the armed forces, ending a two-centuries-old tradition of compulsory military service, and the downgrading of France's nuclear deterrent from over 31 per cent of the defence budget to under 20 per cent. The creation of a Rapid Reaction Force in Bosnia, finally, though announced by the Defence Minister Charles Millon, was very much the president's work.

Economic, financial and industrial policy

These core sectors of internal policy-making fall less obviously in the president's 'reserved domain'. Even here, though, few really major decisions do not bear the presidential stamp. The currency reform and austerity package that opened the de Gaulle presidency, though inspired by the orthodox economics of Jacques Rueff, were decided by the president in *conseils interministériels*. So was the unpopular economic 'stabilisation' plan of 1963. It was de Gaulle's decision that the Bank of France should sell dollars and buy gold in order to challenge American monetary hegemony, and that France should build Concorde (for prestige, and for the supposed spin-off onto the rest of French industry) and develop a home-grown computer industry: such matters were the economic face of de Gaulle's foreign policy, and as such adjacent, at least, to the 'reserved domain'. The presidential refusal, in November 1968, to devalue a franc made weak by the events of the previous May astounded not only the financial world but also the prime minister and government: it is significant that the last pages of de Gaulle's unfinished memoirs are taken up by an almost lyrical apologia for monetary orthodoxy. When Pompidou reversed the General's decision and devalued in August 1969, he kept his Prime Minister Chaban-Delmas completely in the dark. He regularly arbitrated between the Finance Ministry and the spending departments in disputes over the budget; his view that France should seek high growth even at the price of (modest) inflation, and that major French private firms should merge to constitute national champions both marked the economic record of his five-year presidency. Giscard, a former finance minister at a time of great economic and financial instability, was more interventionist than either of his predecessors. The French franc's periodic entries to and departures from European monetary structures during his presidency were decided by him, as was the controversial capital gains tax bill of 1976. While the appointment, in August 1976, of Raymond Barre as prime minister and minister for economic affairs signalled a distancing of the president from direct involvement in these questions, in practice Barre's prescription of neo-liberal remedies for France's economic ills often ran up against Giscard's electorally motivated veto, particularly when jobs were at risk: the late Giscard years were especially active ones for the interministerial committee responsible for bailing out lame duck industries. Mitterrand's relative ignorance of economic affairs compared with his predecessor did not prevent him from intervening extensively. The non-devaluation of May 1981, and the three devaluations that followed over the next two years, were his choices – including the last one, in March 1983, with the sea change in economic policy implied by his decision to keep the franc in the European Monetary System. It was Mitterrand who decided that the nationalisations that launched his first *septennat* should cover 100 per cent of shares of the firms involved, and not 51 per cent as ministers like Rocard had suggested; Mitterrand who announced a policy of neither nationalisation nor privatisation for his second term, and who then agreed to partial exceptions, picturesquely referred to as the 'breathing of the public sector'; Mitterrand again who took responsibility for the major restructuring of the steel industry in 1984. Mitterrand also intervened in budgetary matters, requiring taxation to be kept to no more than 43 per cent of GDP in the 1985 budget (a demand made without the consent of either finance minister or prime minister, which meant that some 80 billion francs, or 12 billion euros, suddenly had to be 'found'). In his second term, Élysée advisers were despatched to verify that Mitterrand's priorities of education, overseas development and research were being respected in the 1990 budget, and to ask Prime Minister Rocard for an extra 300 million francs for the gendarmerie. A year later, in the face of demonstrations by secondary school students, Mitterrand threw out the careful balance of Rocard's 1991 budget by demanding an extra 4.5 billion francs (686 million euros) for education. Above all, perhaps, the 'strong franc' policy of the second *septennat* might not have survived without Mitterrand's backing for Finance Minister Bérégovoy. Chirac's first set-piece intervention in this area came in his television broadcast of 26 October 1995, when he reaffirmed France's commitment to the euro, and thus to the Maastricht convergence criteria, at the expense of his own election promises. Thereafter, he was less openly interventionist, though always ready to fly rhetorically to the aid of his increasingly beleaguered government. Behind the scenes, it is clear that Chirac took particular interest in the privatisation programme, though not with very conclusive results: the sale of Thomson, for example, needed the capable (Socialist) touch of Jospin to be carried through. Chirac's second term was marked by his insistence that election promises to cut income taxes were (more or less) kept, even at the cost of flouting France's commitment to European requirements to keep public-sector deficits down to 3 per cent of GDP.

Cultural and broadcasting questions

These areas too have been an object of interest for four presidents at least. Here again, de Gaulle set a framework, appointing France's first culture minister, the novelist André Malraux, who was given a respectable budget with which to promote Maisons de la Culture that would dissipate the obscurity of the philistine provinces. Pompidou paved the way for the national museum of modern art that bears his name; Giscard did the same for the nineteenth-century museum in the former Orsay railway station.

Mitterrand both backed his flamboyant minister, Jack Lang, and pressed ahead with his own ambitious and expensive *grands chantiers* which have changed the face of Paris. Only Chirac, despite personal cultural interests ranging from primitive art to Japanese haikus, has given the sector relatively little attention, appointing second-rank ministers and allowing budget cuts. Broadcasting has also witnessed direct presidential intervention, such as de Gaulle's decision to allow advertising on France's two public television channels in 1967. Both de Gaulle and Pompidou saw radio and (in particular) television as the 'voice of France', and demanded favourable coverage for themselves and their governments: Pompidou notably stalled Chaban-Delmas's attempts to liberalise the sector. Giscard broke up the state broadcasting monopoly in 1974, giving the three stations and the production company a (modest) measure of autonomy. Mitterrand delivered on electoral promises to allow private radio stations and to create an arm's-length broadcasting authority, took the final decision on who should appoint the members of the new body, the Haute Autorité de l'Audiovisuel, opened two television channels to private operators and was instrumental in choosing those operators (one of whom was Silvio Berlusconi, the future right-wing prime minister of Italy).

Political reforms

These have always been, in varying degrees, a presidential concern. The referendum on a constitutional amendment allowing direct election of the president was announced by presidential broadcast in 1962; and if de Gaulle left office in 1969, it was because the reform of the Senate and the regions proposed in his last, unsuccessful referendum was a presidential project. Pompidou too suffered a setback when he had to abandon his plan to shorten the presidential term to five years owing to opposition within parliament. Giscard left a more lasting legacy with the liberalisation of conditions in prisons and barracks, the lowering of the age of majority to 18 and the reform giving parliamentarians the right to refer bills to the Constitutional Council. Mitterrand's early years were marked by a vast range of political changes, including the decentralisation reforms, the abolition of the death penalty and the detested State Security Court set up by de Gaulle, and the repeal of some of his predecessors' more repressive criminal justice legislation. Although the president did not present all of these reforms as his own initiatives, he ensured backing for them by arbitrating publicly, usually on the liberal side, in disputes between his ministers. Chirac, as well as accepting several constitutional changes during his cohabitation with Jospin, pressed for decentralisation to be given constitutional status through the amendment of 2003, and was identified personally with a constitutional 'charter' that aimed to guarantee a right to a decent environment for all. This reform, of symbolic appearance but with far-reaching implications if broadly interpreted, aroused such grave suspicions within the UMP majority that it had to await a final parliamentary vote until February 2005.

Circumstantial interventions

In addition to the policy sectors outlined above, there remain countless examples where presidential interventions have been provoked by a specific political context. Such a context may result from disputes within the government: President Mitterrand's decisions to abandon the military camp at Larzac and the planned nuclear power station at Plogoff are cases in point. Or a decision at the highest level may be needed to face down entrenched interest groups, as when de Gaulle decided to move the wholesale meat and vegetable markets from Les Halles in Paris to the wind-swept wastes of Rungis, or Giscard forced a recalcitrant École Polytechnique from the fifth *arrondissement* of Paris into the suburbs, or Mitterrand chose to locate a major nuclear research installation at Grenoble, not Strasbourg. The president may also get involved in issues that are, or threaten to become, politically explosive. This has repeatedly been the case with education. De Gaulle had to give strong personal backing to his Education Minister Edgar Faure's plans to liberalise French universities in the wake of the May 1968 'events', since the reform plans faced strong opposition within the Gaullist-led parliamentary majority. Giscard intervened in the drafting of the 1975 Education Act, which aspired to promote social equality in education in a manner that many of his core middle-class electorate would have found suspect. Mitterrand appeared on television to announce the withdrawal of his government's controversial bill on private education which had brought hundreds of thousands of Catholics onto the streets. In doing so, he provoked the resignation of Education Minister Alain Savary, whom he had told of the decision an hour before going on air, and indeed of the whole Mauroy government. But the situation was defused. Chirac, too, intervened more than once after 2002 to 'advise' his education ministers, Luc Ferry and François Fillon, on concessions to make to demonstrators opposed to education reforms; and he placed his personal weight behind the reform of 2004 banning the wearing of religious signs or garb at school. Finally, presidents may intervene because of their personal attachment to a particular policy area, or because they judge their intervention to be necessary in order to fulfil election pledges or to react effectively to a new situation. Many of Giscard's interventions fall into these categories. He gave his strong backing to the early measures of social liberalisation – the legalisation of abortion and the facilitation of contraception and divorce. He reacted to the 1973 energy crisis by backing a nuclear power programme of unprecedented scope, and to the architectural excesses of the de Gaulle and Pompidou eras by demanding, and getting, the incorporation of much tighter environmental criteria into France's building regulations. But, while Giscard expanded presidential intervention into hitherto unexpected areas, he is not wholly alone in this. The example of culture has already been mentioned. The concern of Pompidou and, more recently, Chirac, with agricultural policy, for example, has been proverbial.

Presidential policy-making: limitations and models

Presidential government does not mean, and cannot mean in the French context, that the president governs alone. The sheer volume of government business, and the small numbers of the Élysée staff, see to that. Nor does it mean that the president decides alone. Before the economic U-turn of March 1983, for example, Mitterrand spent nine days not only reflecting in private but also holding numerous meetings with advisers and ministers (though these never ran to a formal round-table discussion in the Council of Ministers). Nor yet does it mean that the prime minister is marginalised. As the articulation between the president and the government and between the government and its majority, as the chief presenter of government policy in parliament and as the individual most responsible for ensuring the implementation of that policy by the administration, the prime minister is at the very least a presidential tool of the first importance. It was, for example, Mitterrand who committed French forces to the Gulf war, but Rocard who had to 'sell' the war to a deeply sceptical National Assembly;

it was Chirac who signalled the need to bring France into line with the Maastricht criteria, but Juppé who conceived, developed and announced an unpopular rationalisation of the social security system. Similarly, the major reforms of Chirac's second term, covering pensions and the rollback of the 35-hour week, though followed closely by the president, were developed by Prime Minister Raffarin and the ministers directly concerned. And the prime minister is usually more than merely the president's man. In areas where the president has no pressing personal interest, prime ministers may feel free either to drag their feet (as Pompidou did over de Gaulle's dream of workers' 'participation' in industrial management) or to develop their own policies (as Rocard did, with partial success, in his attempts to reform France's public services). In that sense, policy-making may be said to be 'segmented', with some sectors being run directly by the president, others by the prime minister, and others still by individual ministers. But there are two important qualifications to this view. The president may take direct control of any sector at any time that he chooses. And the prime minister may be dispensed with at any time, and notably when he becomes either unpopular enough to drag the president down with him, or, worse, successful enough to be a political rival to the president.

Presidential power should not be confused with presidential activism. The economic and financial interventions of de Gaulle, for example, were rare, but crucial. Otherwise he left much of economic policy-making to Pompidou, subjecting him to periodic grillings in the Council of Ministers. Giscard, on the other hand, as well as taking large decisions like the franc's entry into the European monetary snake, was more inclined to detailed interventions as well – the specifics of subsidies to particular firms, or the level of value- added tax on certain products. But it is far from certain that Giscard was thereby more in control of policy than de Gaulle.

Variations in the level of presidential activism, indeed, could be said to delineate different models within the overall pattern of presidential government. Three such models may be identified for the years since 1981. The first corresponds to the highly interventionist period of the early Mitterrand presidency – itself both a continuation of the Giscard period in this respect, and the result of the lack of governmental experience suffered by all but two ministers. During this period, Élysée advisers were frequently present at interministerial meetings, where they spoke regularly: at meetings to prepare the nationalisation legislation, for example, they expressed suspicions of ministers, and especially of civil servants, whose commitment to the expropriation of the capitalists they doubted. The drawback of such interventionism was that Mitterrand, like his predecessor, was held responsible for policy failure: Prime Minister Mauroy's popularity (according to SOFRES polls) went negative in September 1982, Mitterrand's nine months later. Under the second model, on the other hand, the president is more distant from much of the policy-making process. Under the Rocard government (1988–91) for example, Mitterrand usually, though not always, kept to his stated resolution to intervene less. Élysée advisers were less present, and less vocal, in interministerial meetings, and both Matignon and individual ministries were less inclined to seek advice from the Élysée. However, this period was also marked by the intense and growing mistrust between president and prime minister, and at times by a lack of presidential backing for government policies, and by continued presidential interventions in sensitive areas. Individual ministers sought and sometimes obtained changes of policy by appealing to the president over the prime minister's head; the same was even true of pressure groups, as when Mitterrand insisted more money for education after receiving protesting *lycée* students in November 1990. The third model corresponds to the Juppé premiership (1995–97). Here, too, the president had promised institutional self-restraint – the 'modest presidency' of Chirac's campaign. Here, too, Élysée staff were discreet at interministerial meetings. On the other hand, relations between president and prime minister were exceptionally close, to the point of being symbiotic. Chirac tried to concentrate on the traditional 'reserved domain', left Juppé a freedom of action such as very few prime ministers have enjoyed, save under cohabitation, and backed his prime minister against critics from both opposition and majority. Again, though, the Chirac–Juppé tandem encountered major difficulties. The relatively low calibre of many of Juppé's ministers led their *cabinets* to seek direction from the Élysée. Worse, the strike wave of late 1995 inevitably drew the Élysée into policy-making, establishing the link between the presidency and policy failure that Chirac had sought to avoid.

It is tempting to discern a pattern to the different models of presidential government. After the establishment of presidential prerogatives under de Gaulle, a growing range of policy challenges caused a crescendo of presidential activism till approximately 1984. This was followed by a degree of disengagement as first Mitterrand, then Chirac, sought, with only partial success, to distance the presidency from day-to-day policy-making and the unpopularity associated with it in times of economic difficulty. As suggested in Chapter 4, generally declining levels of popularity since the 1970s may act as a political constraint on presidents. The room for 'heroic' leadership, quite extensive in the 1960s, shrank in the more complex environment of the 1980s and 1990s, leading to a system characterised by Olivier Duhamel as 'rationalised presidentialism'. Such a linear view should, however, be treated with caution because other elements affect the working of France's executive tandem; the variables outlined in Table 4.3 do not change in any linear manner.

Chirac's relationship with the Raffarin governments of his second term offers an illustration of Duhamel's argument and its limitations. On the one hand, France's economic position was mediocre, with slow growth and stubbornly high unemployment, while the government was more or less obliged to enact unpopular reforms, notably to pensions and healthcare, in order to rein in what had become structural public-sector deficits. None of this invited heroic presidential leadership; on the contrary, it suggested that the president, while allowing himself heroic gestures in the 'reserved domain' of foreign affairs, for which opposition to the 2003 Iraq war offered ready opportunities, should maintain an arm's-length presidential relationship to a government doomed to lose voter support (as indeed it did, most clearly in the regional and European elections of 2004 and the following year's referendum). On the other hand, unpopularity was only one of the government's problems. Others included Raffarin's failure to establish his own personal authority over it as prime minister, the political ineptitude of two high-profile ministers chosen from 'civil society' to run Education and Finance, and Sarkozy's open use of his ministerial office to grab media attention and establish his personal credentials as a *présidentiable*. All of this required Chirac to become more directly involved in policy-making than he might have wished. For example, Education Minister Luc Ferry suffered the humiliation of having the introduction of his bill on university reform delayed in June 2003 after an announcement by a member of the Élysée staff. And at the start of 2005, Chirac used a series of New Year's messages to outline the government's programme for the year – a return, albeit in a somewhat more relaxed style, to Giscard's six-monthly instructions of thirty years earlier. In other words, while the economic and international contexts may have reduced (though not ended) the scope for presidential leadership, unpredictable domestic developments may reinforce the need for presidential interventionism.

Cohabitation: prime ministerial government?

Faced with the prospect – eventually unrealised – of a left-wing victory in 1978, President Giscard d'Estaing publicly contemplated retreating to the presidential residence at Rambouillet, outside Paris. In practice, he would quickly have found such an internal exile constitutionally impossible and politically suicidal. Even presidents who lack a supportive parliamentary majority, as in 1986–88, 1993–95 and 1997–2002, remain a vital part of France's system of government. President and prime minister require each other's countersignatures for many important acts, including appointments and the promulgation of laws. Without a majority, the president remains both commander-in-chief of the armed forces and a central foreign policy player, but cannot exercise either role without reference to the prime minister. The prime minister, for his part, has no interest as a presidential aspirant in assaulting the institutions of which he hopes, eventually, to become the guarantor. The two heads of the executive need each other to function, and both know that the French public would be inclined to penalise any attempt to upset the delicate institutional balance that became known, after an anticipatory article by Balladur in 1983, as cohabitation. These points highlight the difference between the situation of a French president without a supportive National Assembly majority and that of an American president facing a hostile Congress. In the United States, thanks to the separation of powers, the challenge to the president is to prevail over the legislature: an acute version of what is a delicate task under the most favourable conditions. In France under cohabitation, by contrast, the fault-line runs within the executive itself. It has never resembled a grand coalition or a government of national unity; it has never been used as an opportunity to undertake large-scale reforms on which all parties broadly agree. For despite the constitutional requirement of a minimum of co-operation, especially clear in foreign and defence policy, and whatever the public's perception (especially strong in early 2002) of complicity between the two heads of the executive, cohabitation remains fundamentally adversarial.

President and prime minister are therefore obliged to learn new roles, different in many ways from those used when the majority supports the president. Under the new division of labour, the president is always obliged to concede much enhanced powers to the prime minister both in appointments and in policy-making. But the constitution ensures a partial segmentation of policy-making, with the president retaining a significant role in foreign and defence policy. And the three experiences of cohabitation have all been quite dissimilar in some respects, showing how the political resources possessed by the two major actors affect the division of power between them.

Cohabitation and party politics

By definition, cohabitation arises from the leadership of the parliamentary majority passing from the president to the prime minister. For the president, this intensifies the characteristic ambiguity of his role, as the 'president of all the French' who is also a party politician. The partial resolution of this ambiguity in 'normal' times, whereby president and majority alike could be identified with state power and thus, in the French political tradition, the 'general interest', no longer works. To have any chance of retrieving his fortunes and winning a further presidential term, the president under cohabitation must be the clear leader of the opposition; yet he must also give prominence to his other role, defined by Article 5, as impartial guarantor of France's institutions. These two roles were most successfully combined in 1986–88 by Mitterrand. Enjoying more or less unanimous support within the Socialist Party, he cloaked fiercely partisan criticisms of the Chirac government in the rhetoric of statesmanlike impartiality, and went into the presidential elections of 1988 enjoying all the advantages of incumbency with none of its dreary responsibilities. Seven years later, on the other hand, having largely forfeited his leadership of the Left and with no prospect of a third term, Mitterrand largely concentrated on his consensual role as head of state. Chirac, as a cohabitation president from 1997, clearly planned for his own re-election in 2002. His task was, however, complicated both by the length of the cohabitation period – five years not two – and by his partial loss of control over the RPR following the 1997 election defeat. Chirac's struggles to reassert his leadership over his own party, and over the right-wing opposition generally, chimed badly with his attempts to play the role of 'president of all the French'; his criticisms of the Jospin government (as when he referred to legislation for the 35-hour week as a 'dangerous improvisation') ran the risk of appearing both partisan and impotent. Nevertheless, his identification, during his traditional 14th July interview in 2001, of law and order as the government's weak suit adroitly combined the partisan and (at least apparently) statesmanlike roles, helping to set the agenda for April 2002.

The prime minister's partisan role in times of cohabitation is scarcely easier. As leader of the government and of the parliamentary majority, the prime minister must keep together a diverse coalition within which groups and individuals will demand a price for loyalty. But as a presidential candidate in waiting (as all three prime ministers under cohabitation have been) the prime minister may have to engage in pre-campaign competition with at least one other member of that majority. Both Chirac in 1986–88 and Balladur in 1993–95 hoped to win the presidency on the strength of their governmental record; both faced serious competition from within their own camp (Chirac from Barre, Balladur from Chirac); both found it physically very difficult to combine the burdens of the premiership with the rigours of campaigning; neither won the presidential election following his premiership. The position of Jospin from 1997 was somewhat easier: there were five years, not two, to establish a governmental record; his party dominated the government majority; and within that party, he had no rival in sight. That, however, encouraged complacency on Jospin's part: assuming (like almost all observers of the presidential election) that he was guaranteed to face Chirac at the run-off ballot, he neglected to develop a vigorous partisan strategy for the first round, aimed at maximising his own vote at the expense of his coalition partners'. This strategic oversight contributed substantially to Jospin's elimination from the race on the night of 21 April 2002.

Cohabitation: oiling the wheels

The political necessity of cohabitation for the two main partners involved has ensured the development of procedures that contain their mutual hostility and ensure the relatively undisturbed running of the state machinery. This lends predictability to the day-to-day processes: Balladur even wrote that he and Mitterrand had 'a mutual commitment not to take each other by surprise'. Where the president is not involved in policy-making, for example, he is at least informed of it. The *bleus de Matignon* – the records of decisions taken at interministerial meetings – are still sent to the Élysée. So are copies of the intense diplomatic correspondence, much of it electronic, received by the Foreign Ministry (an early interruption in these in 1986 led to vigorous protests by Mitterrand, and a swift resumption of the normal service; by 1993, the president had taken the necessary technical measures to ensure they reached him automatically). Certain rituals, too, continue more or less unchanged under cohabitation. The secretary-general of the government visits the Élysée every Monday, when he meets successively the Élysée secretary-general, the assistant secretary-general and finally the president, putting the final touches to the agenda for that week's Council of Ministers. The president holds weekly meetings with the prime minister on Wednesdays before the Council of Ministers, as well as with the defence minister on Mondays and the foreign minister on Tuesdays. Informal contacts function in addition to these formal routines. Balladur's *directeur de cabinet* Nicolas Bazire recalls daily telephone conversations and generally good relations with the Élysée secretary-general Hubert Védrine during the second cohabitation. Working relations between their two successors from 1997 to 2002, Olivier Schrameck in Matignon and Dominique de Villepin in the Élysée, were comparable, despite an often more politically charged context. Schrameck has observed that cohabitation depends dangerously on the ability of a small number of people to act sensibly. So far, though, they have.

Cohabitation: patronage and policy-making

Despite this general commitment to civilised procedures, there is no concealing the fact that when the parliamentary majority is opposed to the president, a sizeable part of power within the executive tandem crosses the Seine from the Élysée to Matignon. This is obvious, in the first place, in the area of appointments. However much presidents faced with a hostile majority may attempt a show of considering several candidates for the post of prime minister, they have effectively had no choice, as the appointments of Chirac in 1986, Balladur in 1993 and Jospin in 1997 show. The president also has no effective voice in the choice of other ministers: although Chirac claimed, in 1986, that Mitterrand had vetoed both Jean Lecanuet for the Foreign Affairs portfolio and François Léotard for Defence, this 'veto' was wielded with the connivance of the prime minister, who was himself lukewarm about both appointments but found it convenient to blame the president for the two men's disappointed ambitions. No such controversy, real or apparent, over the choice of individual ministers troubled the formation of the Balladur government in 1993 or that of Jospin in 1997. Nor has the president any way of circumventing the constitution in order to sack his prime minister – except by dissolving the National Assembly in the hope of a changed majority, something that no president has yet attempted in time of cohabitation. In negotiating the wide range of other appointments, in the administration or the public sector, which the two heads of the executive constitutionally share, the president may have to accept the displacement of his own men by the prime minister's choices. Strictly speaking, as Olivier Schrameck observes, the president can veto appointments but cannot propose his own candidates. Under the Jospin premiership, these appointments were negotiated between the Élysée and Matignon, typically as packages involving concessions on either side: the most difficult cases involved public prosecutors and the security services. Presidents have also, and usually with success, insisted that suitable alternative employment is provided for persons displaced for political reasons. It is true that the prime minister's hand in appointments during cohabitation is less free than the president's is in 'normal' times. In particular, the prime minister's dependence on the parliamentary majority makes it indispensable to lock in the support of the party leaders within that majority, which can most obviously be done by giving them ministerial office. The prime minister's power of patronage at all levels is nevertheless vastly enhanced by cohabitation.

The president's policy-making role is also, not surprisingly, much curtailed. This is clear, in the first place, at the level of procedures. More than ever, the Wednesday Council of Ministers is a formality: during Chirac's 1986–88 government, Mitterrand spent the meetings perusing catalogues of rare books (but never for very long: one of the ministers timed a meeting at just twelve minutes). Matignon both fixes the agenda and settles the decisions well in advance. This is done both at a party level (the breakfasts and lunches with party leaders referred to in Chapter 4) and within the government as a whole (through regular meetings of the whole government without the president, to which Jospin added fortnightly government 'seminars', lasting from 10 a.m. till 3 p.m., at which wide-ranging discussion was allowed). Underlying the different techniques is a common concern to establish a collective sense of responsibility and to lock the president out of the discussions and disputes that typify any policy-making process. Outside the Council of Ministers, contacts beween individual ministers and the president are rare and, in principle, all are channelled through Matignon. Presidents may try to circumvent the rule by inviting ministers on official trips, and may even get on friendly terms with individual ministers, as was the case between Mitterrand and Charles Pasqua or, more recently, Chirac and Education Minister Claude Allègre; but in no case can a president under cohabitation become an alternative focus of ministerial loyalty, still less a court of appeal against prime ministerial decisions. The presidency is also largely disconnected from the Matignon machine. Élysée advisers are kept out of interministerial meetings, except for a minority concerned with foreign and defence policy (and even there, the advisers remain silent). Contacts between officials pass between the secretary-general of the government and the prime minister's *directeur de cabinet* on the one hand, and the Élysée secretary-general on the other. In many respects, therefore, Matignon functions freely and independently.

Policy-making under cohabitation is typically *segmented* – that is, divided by sector between different parts of the executive. This happens because the actors' resources vary between sectors. In the whole vast area of domestic policy – taxation, spending (with the partial exception of the defence budget), borrowing, private and public ownership of industry, industrial relations, education, the environment and social policy – the prime minister is, by and large, the supreme arbiter. Thus the Chirac government of 1986–88 launched France's first major programme of privatisations, tightened immigration legislation, reformed the broadcasting sector (privatising one station and changing the supervisory body) and restored the two-ballot system for parliamentary elections after the brief experiment with proportional representation in 1986 – all against the president's more or less explicit opposition. Balladur continued broadly the same range of policies. Jospin gave France the 35-hour week, a huge youth employment package, universal health cover and the Civil Solidarity Pact (PACS), a lightened version of civil marriage available to homosexual as well as heterosexual couples, against presidential opposition that varied from the explicit (for the 35-hour week) to the muted (for the PACS). Such measures corresponded to clear manifesto commitments which neither president was in a position to block. Indeed, Mitterrand defined the president's domestic role as that of a 'notary', doing no more than recording the government's decisions and promulgating its laws. In practice it is rather more than that, as Mitterrand's own record demonstrates: as we have seen, the constitution offers the president some expedients, especially when a government in a hurry resorts to special procedures. Mitterrand used the ambiguity of Article 13 to refuse to sign the delegated primary legislation (*ordonnances*) which parliament had allowed the Chirac government to draw up in 1986, on the ground that questions as important as privatisations and a change in the electoral law required a parliamentary debate (the *ordonnances* were abandoned, but the legislation went through parliament in the most rushed way imaginable). The following year, Mitterrand refused to call an extraordinary session of parliament to modify the legal status of the Renault car firm; in 1993, he agreed to an extraordinary session, but insisted that it should only discuss bills referred to in manifesto commitments (as prime minister, Jospin only used *ordonnances* after getting preliminary clearance from Chirac).

In the general run of domestic affairs, however, the president can do little but make solemn pronouncements, inside or outside the Council of Ministers, about the damaging character of government policy, or engage in the sort of gesture politics that led Mitterrand to invite striking railwaymen to his Mediterranean residence in 1986, or Chirac to refuse (before bowing to Jospin's insistence) to put reforms to the legal status of Corsica on the agenda of the Council of Ministers. Such interventions may serve to highlight policy differences between president and government, but they cannot be described as participating in policy-making.

Two partial exceptions can be cited to prime ministerial supremacy in domestic policy. One concerns those domestic policies which are shaped by Europe, and where the president's role as a member of the European Council may come into play. The reform of European and French agriculture after 1999, in which Chirac successfully fought for the commercial interests of France's major cereal farmers, is a case in point. A second partial exception is represented by the area of institutional reforms, as the president holds a potential veto over any constitutional amendment (Chapter 4, p. 89). This institutional position is enhanced, in the case of a right-wing president, by the permanent right-wing majority that has existed in the Senate since 1958, allowing effective obstruction not only to amendments but also to new 'organic laws'. These govern such issues as size of and eligibility for the Senate and the National Assembly, and must be voted in identical terms by both chambers if they affect the Senate. Presidential behaviour towards institutional reform projects has been varied. None arose in 1986–88 (other than the reform of the parliamentary electoral system, a matter dealt with by ordinary law in France). In 1993, Mitterrand was able to effect a modest softening of the Right's constitutional amendment concerning asylum seekers. Between 1997 and 2002, Chirac gave his co-operation to two amendments, one on male–female parity (with every appearance of willingness), the other on the reduction of the presidential term to five years (clearly unwillingly, but faced by such broad public and parliamentary support for the change that it would have been costly to obstruct it). On the other hand, the Jospin government's attempts to ban parliamentarians from holding important executive offices at local level (for example, as city mayors or presidents of regional councils) fell foul of the Senate's refusal, while a planned constitutional amendment to remove the appointment of public prosecutors from the control of the Justice Ministry, agreed to in principle by Chirac in the summer of 1999, was withdrawn in the face of Senate opposition – orchestrated, according to Schrameck, from the Élysée.

It is in foreign and defence policy, however, that the constitution guarantees an important role for the president in all circumstances (as guardian of France's territorial integrity, as commander-in-chief and chair of France's national defence committees, as negotiator of treaties and accreditor of ambassadors), and politics normally indicate that he insist on his own primacy in this 'regalian' domain of his office. But the prime minister also has constitutional prerogatives in this area: he is 'responsible for national defence' and leads a government that 'determines and conducts the policy of the nation'. There is also a political incentive for the prime minister, as candidate-in-waiting, to acquire a presidential stature by asserting these prerogatives. One of Chirac's major innovations on entering Matignon in 1986 was to create a 'diplomatic cell' responsible to the prime minister: he even called back de Gaulle's former *éminence grise*, Jacques Foccart, as an adviser. In no area, therefore, does cohabitation appear to contain more potential for conflict. In practice, however, conflict is rare: the traditional 'reserved domain' becomes, in Balladur's expression, a 'shared domain', but only occasionally a disputed one. The reasons are threefold. First, there are clear disincentives to public bickering over foreign and defence policy: loss of credibility abroad and of respect among opinion at home. For the prime minister, the supreme office to which he aspires would be diminished by a public victory in this area at the president's expense. Second, the measure of consensus over foreign and defence policy in France is considerable – far greater, for example, than existed in Britain or Germany in the 1980s. Third, the widespread acceptance, within the defence and foreign affairs policy communities, that 'France should speak with one voice' at all times has generated institutional mechanisms by which initiatives can be co-ordinated and conflicts defused. In European affairs, for example, the SGAE (Secrétariat Général des Affaires Euro-péennes, formerly the SGCI) plays a crucial co-ordinating role, and reports both to the president and to the prime minister. In the area of defence, a comparable role is played by the General Secretariat for National Defence. As we have already seen, the regular presidential meetings with both foreign and defence ministers, and the presence of members of the Élysée staff at interministerial meetings on foreign and defence matters, constitute exceptions to the general isolation of the presidency from the processes of government. Perhaps the clearest symbol of continuing co-operation at the top of the executive, even in times of cohabitation, are the regular *conseils interministériels* held in the Élysée, normally just after the formal Council of Ministers. These meetings typically include the president and prime minister, the foreign, defence, European affairs, and overseas development ministers, as well as the chief of the defence staff, the secretary general of the national defence committee, and Élysée advisers. The government side of this group normally meets to co-ordinate its positions on the previous day. But unlike the Council of Ministers, these *conseils interministériels* are more than rubber stamps, and offer the chance for real discussion. Issues of urgent military importance always become the object of such *conseils interministériels* (during the third cohabitation, they covered the crises in Iraq, Kosovo, East Timor and Central Africa). So, frequently, does Europe: every meeting of the European Council has been preceded by a *conseil interministériel*.

For the outside world, the most visible sign of cohabitation is the joint appearance of president and prime minister at major summits, ever since Chirac sought to establish a precedent by accompanying Mitterrand to the Tokyo G7 meeting in 1986. Jospin, it is true, preferred (as Balladur did) to leave G7 (or G8) meetings to the president and the foreign and finance ministers, after taking part in the preparatory meetings to define the French position. However, Jospin (again like Balladur) was more assiduous in attending the regular European summits, and the periodic bilateral meetings with major European partners. More importantly, prime ministers have managed significant areas of foreign policy. It was Chirac who, by somewhat questionable methods, obtained the release of the French hostages in Lebanon in April 1988, as well as playing a significant role (with Foccart's help) in African policy and in the promotion of France's foreign trade. Balladur and his government managed both the European monetary crisis of summer 1993 (for which they received Mitterrand's public congratulations) and the world trade negotiations of the same year, with rather little intervention from the Élysée. On a day-to-day basis, the means for Matignon to influence policy exist in the budget (particularly important, of course, in the area of defence, even though the president's interest in this area is still regarded as legitimate even in periods of cohabitation), in the European 'cells' that now exist in every ministry, in the links between Matignon and the SGAE, and through personal links to other European and international leaders. Both president and prime minister have from time to time used symbolic occasions, such as speeches to the Higher Defence College, to set out their own doctrines and to assert their own primacy in specific areas. Where conflict has occurred, it has generally been resolved by the maintenance of the *status quo ante*. For example, Balladur was unable to overturn the moratorium on nuclear testing declared by Mitterrand in 1992 (though the Defence Ministry budget contained provision for tests, conveniently for Chirac when he entered the Élysée in 1995).

Models of cohabitation

While the constitution clearly determines the contrast, under cohabitation, between the 'shared domain' of foreign and defence questions and the great autonomy of prime minister and government in domestic policy, it only determines the general workings of cohabitation, not the detail. And indeed, there have been very significant variations between the three periods of cohabitation according to the circumstances and the political resources controlled by the two main players.

- *The first cohabitation*, from 1986 to 1988, was the period in which the president's residual power was at its greatest. Mitterrand's personal popularity, already recovering by the time of the Left's defeat in March 1986, was increased dramatically by his observance of the forms of fair play vis-à-vis Chirac's new government. The president was also still in firm control of France's strongest single party. By turns falsely emollient and (as when refusing to sign *ordonnances*) genuinely combative, he successfully drew benefits both from his own legitimacy as head of state and from the discomfitures of Chirac and his government, particularly the student unrest and the strikes of late 1986. Chirac, by contrast, was handicapped by his majority's extreme narrowness (just three seats), and by divisions within it that grew as the presidential election approached. Too many of Chirac's decisions, especially in the crisis of late 1986, which did enormous damage to his government, were defined by the need to hold his coalition together. His personal capacities within his new role were also questionable. One minister later described Chirac as 'an amateur playing against a professional'. Mitterrand claimed that his relations with Chirac were 'all right, except that he would lie to me so often'. The television debate between the two men five days before the second round of the presidential election revealed a mutual hatred that had built up during two years of intense competition.

- *The second cohabitation*, from 1993 to 1995, was in many ways the opposite of the first. The Right's victory in 1993 had been a landslide, with 497 right-wing Deputies to 57 Socialists and 23 Communists. Mitterrand was 76 years old, sick and discredited by revelations about his Vichy past. He had no prospect of a third term and minimal control over his own party, and was increasingly preoccupied by merely surviving to the end of his second *septennat*. Relations between the two heads of the executive were undisturbed by future electoral competition and generally good, in the retrospective estimation of both men. As well as handling the 1993 franc crisis and the world trade negotiations, Balladur and his government were active in African policy, taking the decision to devalue the currency of France's former African colonies, which is linked to the franc, and managing – not necessarily to their credit – the Rwandan crisis with Mitterrand. France's policy on former Yugoslavia was also jointly managed: Balladur claims to have created the European contact group, ordered changes in troop deployments and conceived the idea of a European stability pact. Mitterrand, in short, allowed the prime minister an almost unprecedented freedom of action, even in the 'shared domain', but on two conditions: that his own decisions taken before 1993 were not reversed, and that his outward prerogatives were respected.

- *The third cohabitation*, which began in 1997, differed from the other two in being relatively open-ended, with the possibility of five full years before the elections of 2002. Both protagonists had incentives to play a long game. Jospin wanted as much time as possible to establish a convincing governmental record. President Chirac, widely blamed within his own camp for provoking the Right's defeat with his dissolution of parliament in April 1997, needed time to rebuild his own credibility before seeking re-election. This longer timescale discouraged early or open confrontation between the two men. Jospin was in any case more concerned with applying an ambitious programme of domestic reform than with carving out a foreign policy role (his rare attempts to do so were marked by some memorable reverses, as when he was chased by stone-throwing Palestinians after an ill-calculated speech at Bir Zeit university). The Kosovo war in spring 1999 provided the clearest case of joint management of a crisis: interestingly, the fairly close identity of views in this area between Chirac and Jospin contrasted with the reservations expressed openly by several government ministers, notably the Communists. Cohabitation also, on this third occasion, became almost normalised, having accounted for nine of the twenty-one years after Mitterrand's election in 1981. In 1987, most of the French public had hoped that cohabitation would be a short-term episode in politics: in 1998, by contrast, two-thirds of poll respondents considered cohabitation a positive experience, and over half hoped it would have lasting effects.

Looking back towards the end of the Jospin government, Olivier Schrameck observed two advantages to cohabitation: it forced a consensual approach to France's relations with the world, and it allowed the presence of checks and balances within a political system that had too few of them in normal times. These advantages, however, were outweighed by the drawbacks: the amount of time wasted in both the Élysée and Matignon on mutually hostile political manoeuvres, whether offensive or defensive, and the lack of accountability or clear alternatives for voters. There was a risk, argued

Schrameck, that the appearance of consensus on the two sides of the executive and by extension on the two sides of the mainstream political spectrum would leave discontented voters to seek solace at the political extremes – a forecast amply fulfilled at the first round of the 2002 presidential election. Having come close to 'normalisation', the experience of cohabitation may now, thanks to the five-year presidential term, be viewed as of largely historical interest.

The dichotomy of 'presidential' government in 'normal' times and 'prime ministerial' government during cohabitation is an oversimplification, for a number of reasons. Even when the parliamentary majority supports the president, Matignon has a considerable role to play. Even under cohabitation, the president retains important powers. Moreover, each of the two major configurations allows for substantial variation. Relations were at times more strained between Mitterrand and Rocard, for example, than they were between Mitterrand and Balladur – a state of affairs that prompted Pierre Servent to observe that 'cohabitation is merely a tougher version of what happens usually'. Government, finally, or even the operation of the political executive, cannot be reduced to the tandem at the summit; there are other ministers than the first one.

Ministers and government

The concentration of power within political executives in the hands of their leaders has been almost as widely observed as the transfer of power towards executives and away from parliaments. The ever-increasing need for co-ordination within a complex government machine, both to achieve 'joined-up government' at home and to present a common position to partners abroad (for example, within Europe), is the most obvious reason. In France, the change of constitution also furthered this reinforcement of chief executives at the expense of ministers.

The role of ministers under the Fifth Republic

Under the Fourth Republic, many ministers were appointed for the party support they would bring with them to the government. They were more or less indispensable because their resignation would weaken or even bring down governments. As Deputies or Senators, they retained strong parliamentary and local power bases. And the prime minister, designated only by the term *président du conseil* – a curious term, as François Goguel has pointed out, since the premiers of the Third and Fourth Republics almost never chaired a Council of Ministers – was often no more than *primus inter pares*. Under the Fifth Republic, on the other hand, the president and prime minister enjoy far greater freedom in their choice of ministers: indeed, as Table 5.1 shows, between a quarter and a third of most ministries have consisted of ministers without parliamentary office at their first appointment. The emergence of stable parliamentary majorities ensured that, other than in exceptional circumstances (such as the 1986–88 Chirac premiership), no minister was indispensable because no ministerial resignation would threaten a government's survival. The incompatibility between governmental and parliamentary office, enshrined in Article 23, was intended to cut ministers off from merely parliamentary politics. And the prime minister was given a clear hierarchical superiority over his colleagues. In relation to the president and prime minister, therefore, the constitution appeared to cut ministers down to size.

It also, however, reinforced their powers in other respects, and especially in relation to

Table 5.1 Percentage of ministers without any parliamentary seat on their appointment, 1958–2005

Year	Prime minister	%	Year	Prime minister	%
1958	Debré	37	1986	Chirac	27
1962	Pompidou	27	1988	Rocard	39
1968	Couve de Murville	3	1991	Cresson	29
1969	Chaban-Delmas	2	1992	Bérégovoy	28
1972	Messmer	6	1993	Balladur	3
1974	Chirac	33	1995	Juppé	14
1976	Barre	29	1997	Jospin	17
1981	Mauroy	23	2002	Raffarin	31
1984	Fabius	31	2005	Villepin	34

Sources: O. Duhamel, *Le Pouvoir Politique en France* (Paris, Seuil, 1999); *Le Monde* (for 2002); official site of the Prime Minister (for 2005).

parliament. Fifth Republic governments have lasted longer than their predecessors. While this does not always mean greater longevity for individual ministers (especially as some ministers of the Third and Fourth Republics held the same portfolio through several governments), on balance there is a greater chance of stability and thus of achieving something in office. Ministers are much less vulnerable to parliamentary interpellations, their bills less prone to disappear in the quicksands of parliamentary committees, their time therefore freer – in principle – for policy rather than politics. And even if they cannot threaten to bring governments down single-handed, some ministers are still appointed, and retained, because of their political weight, especially during periods of cohabitation; the strictures of Article 23 have not, in practice, cut ministers off from their own political bases; and even those with no parliamentary seat at their appointment may acquire independent political weight by running for local or national office.

Profiles of the ministers of the Fifth Republic before 1981 revealed few surprises: like their counterparts elsewhere in Europe, they were overwhelmingly male, married, middle-aged, bourgeois (with a sprinkling of aristocrats) and well educated (generally at the Paris Law Faculty or the Institut d'Études Politiques), and they had good links with established political, administrative and economic elites. Socialist ministers since 1981 have been very similar in many respects, although they have tended to be less wealthy, more southern in origin and less connected with the financial elites. The 1990s saw attempts at the 'feminisation' of governments, with the appointment of France's first woman prime minister in 1991 (Cresson, a less than successful choice), of a strong contingent of middle-ranking women ministers in the May 1995 Juppé government (most were sacked the following autumn) and of nine out of twenty-nine women in the Jospin ministry, including several of its key members (Martine Aubry at Labour and Social Affairs, Élisabeth Guigou at Justice and the Green Dominique Voynet at Regional Planning and Environment). Women represented a quarter of the June 2002 Raffarin government (they included France's first female defence minister, Michèle Alliot-Marie) – though the figure for Villepin's government of 2005, just 16 per cent women, does not suggest an irresistible tide of feminisation.

Compared with ministers of the Fourth Republic, those of the Fifth have lacked parliamentary experience. As Table 5.1 shows, some have had no parliamentary experience at all, and although the late 1990s saw a fall in the number of these 'technician' ministers, this does not appear to represent a trend. Just as important, though, is the number of ministers who, while holding elective office at their appointment, have come to politics from a civil service background. Of prime ministers since 1981, this has been true of Fabius, Chirac, Rocard, Balladur, Juppé and Jospin, as well as of leading ministers like Jacques Delors and Jean-Pierre Chevènement on the Left, and Jacques Toubon, Dominique de Villepin, Dominique Perben and Hervé Gaymard on the Right.

French ministers tend to view their role more in individual than in team terms. As prime minister in July 1995, for example, Alain Juppé claimed to have inherited a 'catastrophic' financial situation from the previous government – of which, as foreign minister, he had been a senior member just weeks before. Collective responsibility is generally no more highly valued within Fifth Republic governments than collective decision-making. Two other factors reinforce ministerial individualism. One is the fairly segmented policy structure of the French government, in which individual ministries (and indeed individual directorates of ministries) are jealous of their independence and, in some cases (such as Agriculture), the centre of a policy community which regards the ministry, and the minister, as in some sense its property. The second factor is the varying loyalty of ministers. A French government outside cohabitation, as well as being a coalition, is typically composed of president's people first and prime minister's people second, plus, possibly, some from a necessary coalition partner. President's people are not invariably bound by any sense of loyalty to the prime minister. During the 1974–76 Chirac government, for example, several *giscardien* ministers made openly patronising comments about the prime minister, with the president's support. It was no secret that many senior members of the Rocard government were imposed on the unwilling prime minister by Mitterrand, to whom they would regularly pay (individual) visits at which they acted practically as informers. Cohabitation did little to reinforce ministerial solidarity. Both the Chirac government of 1986–88 and the Balladur government were divided within weeks of their formation by the preferences of individual ministers for one or another right-wing candidate for the rapidly approaching presidential elections. To prevent these loyalties tearing their governments apart, both prime ministers had to allow ministers considerable freedom to express individual views about government policy, however negative they might be. As interior minister in 2005, de Villepin thought aloud, in public, about the need for a 'bolder, more decisive' government to take over from Raffarin's after the European referendum of 29 May; after his appointment to succeed Raffarin, he had to cope with the public disagreements of his own interior minister, Nicolas Sarkozy, over immigration quotas and a range of other subjects.

The variable nature of ministerial power

Under the Fifth Republic, then, it would be misleading to refer to the power of the government, since, in practice, it exercises no *collective* power at all. Yet individual ministers can exercise considerable power, whether as policy-makers or as wielders of patronage. First, a minister will normally have the primary responsibility for drafting his ministry's legislation. Secondly, ministers usually control the implementation of laws, especially the *décrets d'application* without which so much legislation remains a dead letter. Third, they may have significant powers of patronage, putting forward names for *directeurs* in their ministries, or for the holders of important posts both in the provinces (for example the *recteurs* of the different *académies* of the state education system) and in organisations associated with ministries (such as France's remaining nationalised firms). They may also have subsidies to distribute in the sectors of their concern. None of these powers may be exercised in complete independence. President, prime minister, their staffs, or other ministries intervene in the course of interministerial meetings over bills or even decrees; the proportion of a budget which is not already allocated to ongoing programmes is usually minute; appointments to the most senior posts are usually the object of bitter negotiations with other parties, including Matignon and the Élysée. Nevertheless, ministerial office offers opportunities to those able to seize them. Their success in doing so depends upon the interplay of several factors:

- *The degree of interest displayed by the president or the prime minister in the affairs of the ministry*. The existence of a 'reserved domain', or indeed the 'shared domain' under cohabitation, ensures that foreign and defence ministers are rarely policy-makers in their own right. Even Couve de Murville suffered the humiliation of assuring the British of the imminent success of their application to enter Europe on a Friday, only to hear de Gaulle veto British entry on the Monday. Presidents have intervened to keep Latin in school syllabuses (Pompidou) and to stop urban road plans (Giscard). But there have also been important cases when ministers have enjoyed considerable freedom in working to their brief. Peyrefitte's penal reform under Giscard and Barre and Defferre's decentralisation legislation under Mitterrand and Mauroy, and the 35-hour week managed by Aubry under Jospin were among such instances.

- *The support of the president or prime minister*. Some ministers have clearly enjoyed a special relationship with the president. Both de Gaulle and Mitterrand had a *faible* for their ministers of culture, respectively André Malraux (who initiated the large-scale clean-up of France's ancient façades, and created a network of Maisons de la Culture to enlighten what was then the cultural desert of provincial France) and Jack Lang (under whom the culture budget doubled as a share of national income, the new money being spread between small, neighbourhood-scale projects and Mitterrand's *grands chantiers*). Edgar Faure's education reforms of 1968 and Simone Veil's legalisation of abortion in 1974 would never have passed the right-wing majorities of the day without support from the top. Justice Minister Badinter enjoyed the Élysée's full support in his abolition of the death penalty. Chirac gave full backing, and considerable freedom, to Balladur as his minister for the economy and finance between 1986 and 1988, much to the chagrin of Balladur's many enemies. As prime minister, Balladur established especially close relations with the youthful Nicolas Sarkozy, who enjoyed a key position as both budget minister and government spokesman. The importance of personal links should not be over-estimated, however. Jospin's closeness to Interior Minister Jean-Pierre Chevène-ment, Finance Minister Dominique Strauss-Kahn and Education Minister Claude Allègre did not prevent the resignation of all three men before 2002 – Strauss-Kahn over his (undeserved) implication in a financial scandal in 1999, Allègre as a result of opposition from education unions in 2000 and Chevènement over a disagreement on Corsican policy later the same year.

- *The minister's conception of his/her role*. Some ministers view their role as essentially technical and managerial, and become the faithful and faceless executors of the presidential will. In foreign affairs they have rarely had much choice, and the job has tended to suit the self-effacing professional diplomat more than the rising politician (in this de Villepin was an exception, as a flamboyant professional diplomat, whose speech at the United Nations in 2003 gave eloquent expression to Chirac's opposition to the invasion of Iraq). Other ministers, however, have left reputations as able and active reformers, and a determined and skilful minister with an ambitious programme can easily establish a reputation. Such cases include Pisani at Agriculture or Faure at Education under de Gaulle, Defferre at Interior, Badinter at Justice and Fabius at Industry under Mitterrand. Under Jospin, Aubry came to Labour and Social Affairs, and Guigou to Justice, with ambitious reform plans as well as the prime minister's backing.

- *The political weight of the minister.* Giscard's influence as minister of finance arose not only from the fact that he did a technically brilliant job in a key ministry for a long time (four years under de Gaulle and five under Pompidou), but because of his leadership of the Républicains Indépendants, a small but important group in the governing coalition. Interior ministers like Raymond Marcellin, Gaston Defferre, Charles Pasqua, or Jean-Pierre Chevènement have also been political heavyweights. The case of Nicolas Sarkozy after May 2005 is unique: no other government minister has combined this post with the leadership of the principal majority party exercised in his own right, with the declared intention of running for the presidency in less than two years. By contrast, non-parliamentary ministers lack this sort of political punch, and have often come to grief as a result: Claude Allègre under Jospin, or Francis Mer and Luc Ferry under Raffarin, all lost office in part because of their lack of political networks and skills. Survivors among non-parliamentary ministers tend to overcome an initial reluctance and seek election.

- *The minister's tenure of office.* Successful policy-making often goes with ministerial longevity. Here too, Malraux and Lang were fortunate, each occupying the Culture Ministry for ten years (Malraux from 1959 to 1969, Lang from 1981 to 1993 with a break in 1986–88). Marcellin left an indelibly nasty impression in his five years at Interior under de Gaulle and Pompidou, while Bérégovoy managed, during a total of six years at Finance, to become a symbol to the money markets of the Socialists' conversion to financial orthodoxy. Rather less, on the other hand, is remembered of the four industry ministers from the short (though crucial) 1981–83 period, or of the four women – Corinne Lepage, Françoise de Panafieu, Élisabeth Hubert and Colette Codaccioni – appointed by Juppé in May 1995 and brutally ejected by him the following November. And the considerable continuity at Finance of the Mitterrand presidency's first eleven years (with just three ministers, Delors, Balladur and Bérégovoy) has given way to much less stable times since 1992, with eleven ministers in thirteen years. Of these, several (Michel Sapin, Edmond Alphandéry, Alain Madelin and Jean Arthuis) made a limited impression and one (Hervé Gaymard) lasted only three months in post; by way of comparison, the British and German finance ministers in early 2005 had been in their jobs for eight and six years respectively.

- *The prestige and power of the ministry.* Certain ministries, notably Interior, Foreign Affairs, and Justice, enjoy a very high reputation and confer upon their political head an undeniable prestige. Finance is in a class of its own, the power of the purse being critical in all routine affairs at least. Other ministries suffer from a weak or non-existent administration, low budgets, an ill-defined scope of action and the scepticism of other ministries. Urban Affairs and the Environment both represent pressing policy concerns; neither ministry has been able to attract the resources and clout that correspond, or indeed to establish a strong institutional identity. In between are well-established ministries with big budgets, graveyards for some politicians but springboards for others: Agriculture, for example (occupied by Chirac from 1972 to 1974), or Education (a good ministry for Jospin in the Rocard and Cresson governments, a much less happy one for Jospin's *protégé* Claude Allègre a decade later or for Luc Ferry or François Fillon in the Raffarin governments).

- *The strength of the ministry's administrative services.* The administrative services of some big ministries are strong and resistant to changes they dislike. Finance, for example, succeeded for forty years in evading requests from ministers for a simple list of the ministry's senior officials with their salaries and bonuses. Agriculture and Education are both heavily infiltrated by the powerful unions in their sector (which helped to explain the removal of Cresson from Agriculture in 1983 and of Allègre from Education in 2000). Such administrations may be powerful opponents of ministerial plans for reform; it requires a minister with ambition, ruthlessness and longevity to impose policies upon these ministries. On the other hand, administrations may be equally strong allies in defending the ministry's long-term interests. One key to Juppé's largely successful record as foreign minister from 1993 to 1995 was his ability to establish good working relations with directors at the Quai d'Orsay through weekly meetings; these helped him undertake significant administrative reform there. At the other extreme, the rudimentary administrative services accorded to the Environment Ministry in over three decades of its existence have been a handicap to any minister seeking to make a serious impact in this area.

- *The efficiency of the ministerial* cabinet. A well-organised, determined and sensitive *cabinet* may be a powerful support for a minister, in achieving co-ordination within the ministry's services, in representing the minister effectively in interministerial meetings, and in building and maintaining networks with other ministries and with interest groups. Successful ministers usually have strong *cabinets*: another incentive to political experience and ministerial longevity.

Institutionalised tensions and the elusive goal of co-ordination

Early accounts tended to characterise the Fifth Republic as a 'monocratic' regime characterised by overwhelming presidential power. This description contained an element of truth compared both with preceding French Republics and other democracies. Security in office, significant constitutional powers, plus party and parliamentary support, afford French presidents outside periods of cohabitation an enviable freedom to intervene at all levels of policy-making. They have also contributed to executive crimes. The blowing-up of the Greenpeace vessel *Rainbow Warrior* in Auckland harbour, New Zealand, in 1985 testifies at the very least to failures in co-ordination between president, prime minister, the defence minister, and the secret services and defence staff. The behaviour of an 'anti-terrorism' unit in the Élysée, which undertook widespread illegal telephone taps (always knowingly denied by Mitterrand) in order to protect not France from terrorism but the president from political embarrassment, reflected the culture of impunity associated with great power.

But the 'monocratic' accounts always underestimated the degree to which that power depended on a favourable parliamentary majority, as cohabitation was to reveal. That the voters thrice refused to supply an incumbent president with a supportive parliamentary majority weakened the presidency both temporarily, for obvious reasons, but on a more lasting basis by helping to desacralise the president. The republican monarchy was welcome in the context of 1958; nearly five decades later, the spectre of a 'return to the Fourth Republic' has lost much of its power to frighten.

Despite the improbability of any recurrence of cohabitation since the shortening of the presidential term to five years from 2002, few would be ready to bet on a return of the republican monarchy in all its Gaullist splendour. In the first place, the president's 'reserved domain' is increasingly subject to constraint: globalisation and European integration have both limited France's ability to pursue independent economic, industrial, fiscal, trading and monetary policies in the manner of de Gaulle (see Chapter 1). The fact that the European Council enhances the policy-making role of heads of state and government within the EU, does not, on balance, compensate for this. Within France, a range of developments, some very actively shaped by the executive (decentralisation, and the shrinkage of the public sector and of the opportunities for patronage that go with it) and some less so (the increased activism of the Constitutional Council) have conspired to limit the untrammelled exercise of power from the top downwards. To some extent these are developments that affect the whole executive, prime minister as well as president. Nevertheless, just as the president's power under the Fifth Republic has been more visible than that of the prime minister, so has its diminution. The voters, too, have helped limit presidential power, and not only by inducing cohabitation. They appreciate presidents less: Giscard in 1976 and 1980, Mitterrand in 1984 and 1993, and Chirac in late 1995 and mid-2005 all reached depths of unpopularity unknown to de Gaulle or Pompidou; the overall decline is clear from Table 4.1. The referendum, once the ultimate tool of heroic presidential leadership, was transformed by the voters, successively, into de Gaulle's nemesis in 1969, a damp squib in 1972 and 1988, a near-disaster for Mitterrand and for Europe in 1992, a collective snub to the whole political class in 2000. Though Chirac successfully obtained a constitutional amendment to extend the area of application of referendums, he eschewed their use during his first five years in office, only bringing the issue of the five-year term before the people after outside pressure. Practically in a class of its own in the series was the 2005 referendum on the European constitutional treaty. This had three main purposes: to rally French voters behind a European project, to demonstrate presidential leadership and to split the Socialist opposition. It achieved the third aim so well that it produced a no vote of nearly 55 per cent, wrecking the constitutional treaty project and doing possibly fatal damage to Chirac's credibility as president. It seems unlikely that future presidents will rush to use a constitutional tool that, in practice, only worked to its user's benefit in the early de Gaulle presidency.

This record gave rise to the (exaggerated) comment by Georgette Elgey and Jean-Marie Colombani in 1998, that 'the president is becoming one actor among others'. But other available models of executive power, as Robert Elgie observes, give partial and therefore inadequate accounts of the French case. The 'segmented' government model, under which president and prime minister each govern distinct, complementary areas of policy, fails to take account of the president's ability to intervene, outside periods of cohabitation, in any sector. The model of 'executive co-operation' between president and prime minister leaves out the often fierce political competition between the two, particularly during cohabitation. 'Prime ministerial government' is at best a partial account of cohabitation, and no account at all of the Fifth Republic at other times. The 'ministerial' government model, emphasising the control of individual ministers over their departments, will not do for a system in which this control is very uneven indeed.

'Bureaucratic co-ordination', finally, certainly exists within and between ministries, but is deeply imperfect (with, for example, a culture of information-sharing that is patchy at best), susceptible to intervention by politicians, and thus quite inadequate as a general account of the French case.

It is more convincing to characterise executive power in France as a system of institutionalised tension, a system encouraged, either actively or tacitly, by successive presidents and prime ministers. This tension, which may be amplified or muted by individuals in what remains a highly personalised system of government from the president down, manifests itself at a minimum of five different levels:

- *Between the president and the prime minister*. Even outside cohabitation there have been well-publicised differences between the two heads of the French executive. Debré had deep reservations – expressed privately – both about de Gaulle's Algerian policy and about his somewhat cavalier interpretation of the constitution. Pompidou dragged his feet over de Gaulle's dreams of 'participation', threatened resignation in order to save a general involved in the 1961 army putsch in Algeria from execution and committed the ultimate crime of *lèse-majesté* by appearing as a viable successor. As president, he clashed with Chaban-Delmas over the form and, in part, the content of the 'New Society' programme, and accused Chaban of neglecting the Gaullists' conservative core in a bid for Centre-Left votes. Chirac, as prime minister after 1974, reproached Giscard with the same strategic error, engaged in a bitter struggle with the president over the leadership of the majority in general and the Gaullist party in particular, and finally became the only prime minister to date to resign of his own accord, stating publicly that he had not been given the means to do his job properly. Mitterrand's relations with Rocard were notoriously bad: the president (again) reproached his prime minister for neglecting core voters, in this case left-wing ones, in favour of centrist ones, and for cultivating his own popularity as a *présidentiable* at the expense of tough decisions, while the prime minister resented the president's habit of overturning government decisions after appeals by individual ministers over Rocard's head. Perhaps the most harmonious relations between the two heads of the executive were between Chirac and Juppé, but this did Chirac little good as Juppé was widely detested within his own majority.
- *Between the prime minister and the ministers*. The history of the Fifth Republic has also been punctuated by unseemly squabbles between the prime minister and his 'subordinates', especially when the latter have been not his nominees but the president's. Tense relations between Pompidou and Giscard during de Gaulle's first term, for example, arose, characteristically, from multiple causes: 'turf' (the respective roles of finance minister and prime minister in the control of economic policy), policy (Pompidou found Giscard's economic policy too restrictive) and personal rivalry (both men hoped to succeed de Gaulle). Both Chirac in 1974–76 and Rocard in 1988–91 had reason to complain that they were being bypassed and indeed undermined by ministers who enjoyed the confidence of the president. Juppé sacked Alain Madelin, his independent-minded finance minister, three months after appointing him, although Madelin was an important figure in Chirac's majority coalition. With his other ministers, Juppé's relations were simple: he held all of them in contempt, and said so publicly. Most recently, Nicolas Sarkozy, successively interior minister and finance minister between 2002 and 2004,

used his energy and his talent for publicity, as well as his popularity within the right-wing coalition and the wider civil society, to promote his own stature as a *présidentiable*, within but not quite of the Raffarin government. This, unsurprisingly, was the source of constant tensions with his fellow ministers, especially the first among them. The same pattern seemed likely to intensify after Sarkozy's reappointment in the de Villepin government, in a period that would be dominated by the approach of the 2007 presidential elections.

- *Between the prime minister's* cabinet *and the ministers.* There is always institutional tension between ministers and members of the Matignon *cabinet* who follow their work. Philippe Séguin once claimed that his main achievement as Chirac's social affairs minister from 1986 to 1988 was having blocked the initiatives of Marie-Hélène Bérard, the right-wing Matignon adviser for his sector. Jean-Pierre Chevènement's disagreements with members of Jospin's *cabinet* were one reason for his resignation.

- *Between individual ministers.* Ministerial rivalries develop even as a government is being formed: the precise attributions of ministries, the junior posts and even in some cases the premises that go with them, are the object of hard-fought battles. As has been underlined, too, there is no tradition of collective solidarity and responsibility within Fifth Republic governments. Clear disagreements with government policy do, it is true, sometimes lead to resignations: de Gaulle's Algerian and European policies provoked the early departure of several ministers, Rocard resigned from the Agriculture Ministry over Mitterrand's reform of the electoral system; Chevènement left the Industry Ministry in opposition to Mitterrand's economic policy in 1983, the Defence Ministry through opposition to the Gulf war in 1991 and the Interior to protest against Jospin's Corsican policy in 2000. A handful of ministers have also been dismissed, whether because of verbal imprudences (Jean-Jacques Servan-Schreiber over nuclear testing in 1974, Alain Madelin over civil service numbers and employment conditions in 1995) or because they faced criminal charges (Bernard Tapie in 1992, Alain Carignon, Gérard Longuet and Michel Roussin in 1994, Dominique Strauss-Kahn in 1999). In general, though, Chevènement's dictum that 'a minister shuts up or resigns' has been but imperfectly applied, and ministers have often felt free to stay in government and talk out of turn. Some disputes between ministries run on regardless of who is minister, because they reflect structural competition for the leading role in specific policy areas. The many clashes between Justice and Interior have involved issues as various as the seizure of *La gangrène*, a book depicting the spread of torture in Algeria (1959); the degree of autonomy allowed to judges (1975); identity controls (1982); and the reform of the justice system (1999). Under the post-1981 Socialist governments, some disputes reflected the political heterogeneity of a government ranging from Communists to mild Social Democrats. They included social security coverage, the financial extent of nationalisations (51 per cent was seen as adequate by moderates, but nothing less than 100 per cent would do for hardliners), the successive wage and price freezes, the de-indexation of public servants' pay, and the issue of France remaining in the European Monetary System in 1983. Divisions within Chirac's 1986–88 government were accentuated by rivalries between *présidentiables* and their respective supporters. Séguin and Balladur clashed over the long-running problem of the social security deficit; Albin Chalandon, the justice minister, and Michèle Barzach, the health minister, over the criminalisation of drug addiction. François Léotard, the culture minister, referred to his RPR colleagues as 'soldier-monks', while Michel Noir, the foreign trade minister, said it would be better for the Right to lose the elections than to lose its soul through any form of deal with the far Right. Perhaps the most spectacular display of internal governmental disagreement was over the handling of the students' revolt of November–December 1986: the open demand by Léotard and Madelin that the university reform bill that had provoked the demonstrations be withdrawn left Chirac 'foaming at the mouth' (according to Léotard's account) but unable to sack either minister for fear of bringing down the entire government.

- *Between ministers and their junior ministers, and within ministries more generally*. A further complication in the debacle over the 1986 university reform arose from the notoriously poor relations between Education Minister René Monory, his junior minister for universities, Alain Devaquet (who ultimately had to resign), and the Matignon adviser on universities, Yves Durand. The problem was partly a structural one: similarly acrimonious relations had prevailed a decade earlier between Education Minister René Haby and his junior minister for universities, Alice Saunier-Seïté. More broadly, difficulties often arise from the fact that ministers and their juniors are not necessarily chosen for their capacity to work in harmony; indeed, many junior ministers are appointed in order to 'mark' a minister who, whether because of different party origins or other reasons, is distrusted by the president or the prime minister. Personal relations may also come into play: as finance minister in the 1986–88 Chirac government, Balladur humiliated both of his junior ministers, Juppé and Noir, in ways that were minor but damaging to their working relationship. The Balladur–Juppé relationship was to some extent smoothed over by close collaboration between their respective *cabinets*, which allowed the privatisation programme to proceed relatively smoothly. Just as often, however, conflicts at ministerial level may be reproduced or compounded by long-running bureaucratic feuds, as competition for scarce resources takes place not only between ministries but between directions within the same ministry.

As the republican monarchy has declined, so the other tensions within France's executive, though present from the start, have become more visible and thence more damaging both to the image of the governing team and to effective co-ordination in policy-making. The outcome can make the policy outcomes of the Fourth Republic appear as a model of stability: for example, according to one study undertaken by the École Nationale d'Administration, French employment policy 'changed doctrine each year for the last ten to fifteen years'. More generally, as Hayward and Wright have observed, policy co-ordination tends to focus on routine conflict avoidance more than on strategic planning; there is, in general, too little time, too little political will, too few established and effective instruments to overcome entrenched conflicts and long-established habits. Perhaps the most sustained effort to overcome these tensions was made under the Jospin premiership from 1997. Jospin was in no position to lessen tensions between president and prime minister, embarking as he was on a long period of cohabitation with a president who would rather have kept Juppé. But with his *directeur de cabinet* Olivier Schrameck, Jospin did attempt to limit the impact of the last three sets of tensions – between prime minister and ministers, between ministers, and between ministers and their juniors. Their remedies were threefold: the appointment to key ministries of political heavyweights (Chevènement to the Interior, Strauss-Kahn to Finance and Economic Affairs, Guigou to Justice, Aubry to Social Affairs); the delegation to them of considerable autonomy and thus relative immunity from interventions by Matignon advisers, freeing the prime minister from much involvement in policy detail; and the use of fortnightly government meetings (including, on alternate occasions, junior ministers) to ensure co-ordination and, crucially, to air and resolve disputes. It was a formula that resembled, in outline, a traditional view of cabinet government; applied, albeit imperfectly, it helped reinforce the cohesion of Jospin's disparate ministerial team. Government cohesion was, however, also helped by common opposition to President Chirac at a time of cohabitation, by the government's popularity under favourable economic conditions and by Jospin's own unchallenged status as its leader and political 'locomotive'. Its success, in retrospect, appears brief, and dependent on personalities: by March 2001, with Strauss-Kahn, Chevènement and Aubry all out of government for diverse political reasons, the bases of the Jospin formula looked much less solid.

More generally, as Hayward and Wright's study observes, policy co-ordination was never as effective as it looked in the early Fifth Republic, and has become less so since. In the first place, they argue, France's highly centralised administration was increasingly Balkanised as it took on the full range of post-war peacetime activities during the *trente glorieuses*, with some crucial policy areas, such as the social security system, escaping it partially or totally. The pyramidal model of government idealised in France since Napoleon and beyond was ill-adapted to these complexities, to which duplication and overlapping, however untidy, were intrinsic and even healthy as failsafe mechanisms.

Secondly, policy co-ordination has become more difficult since the de Gaulle presidency, not only because of the type of political factor outlined above, but also for reasons intrinsic to the nature of policy-making in a contemporary West European state. Some of these have been considered in Chapter 1. The policy agenda has become more complex, both because of the addition to it of new priorities (the environment, food standards, and the curtailment of racial and sexual discrimination, to name three) and because of a growing awareness of the interrelatedness of different policy issues. That ought to encourage more co-ordination, but at the same time a number of developments have made decision-making more diffuse and a traditional state-centred policy approach, which came readily to the (many) Jacobins among France's politicians and civil servants, harder to sustain. Privatisations coupled with globalisation and Europeanisation have generated new independent regulatory agencies, not only nationally but also at the European and international levels. Meanwhile many of the traditional props of an older style of government, such as political parties, have become weaker as relays of public opinion, while traditional networks and interest groups have mutated or (in some cases) collapsed under the impact of multinationalisation and competition from other activists; and the cracks in the traditional structures of the state have become harder to paper over as French journalism has become less deferential and more investigative.

It is time to move beyond France's political executive to the world that surrounds it: the other branches of government and France's parties, interest groups, and bureaucracy. We begin with the deeply flawed but still indispensable forum for connecting government to the wider civil society, the French parliament.

Further reading

See also list for Chapter 4.

Antoni, P. and Antoni, J.-D., *Les ministres de la Ve République*, Paris, Presses Universitaires de France, 1976.

Balladur, E., *Deux ans à Matignon*, Paris, Plon, 1996.

Cohen, S., *La monarchie nucléaire*, Paris, Hachette, 1986.

Cohendet, M.-A., *La cohabitation: leçons d'une expérience*, Paris, Presses Universitaires de France, 1993.

Elgey, G. and Colombani, J.-M., *La Vᵉ République, ou la République des phratries*, Paris, Fayard, 1999.

Favier, P. and Martin-Rolland, M., *La Décennie Mitterrand*, 4 vols, Paris, Seuil, 1990–99.

Foccart, J., *Journal de l'Élysée*, 3 vols, Paris, Fayard/Jeune Afrique, 1997–2000.

Giroud, F., *La comédie du pouvoir*, Paris, Fayard, 1977.

Hayward, J. and Wright, V., *Governing from the Centre: Core Executive Coordination in France*, Oxford, Oxford University Press, 2002.

Institut Charles de Gaulle, Fondation Nationale des Sciences Politiques, *De Gaulle et ses Premiers ministres*, Paris, Plon, 1990.

Nay, C., *La double méprise*, Paris, Grasset, 1980.

Peyrefitte, A., *C'était de Gaulle*, 3 vols, Paris, Fayard/de Fallois, 1994–2000.

Pfister, T., *La vie quotidienne à Matignon au temps de l'Union de la gauche*, Paris, Hachette, 1985.

Pfister, T., *Dans les coulisses de pouvoir: la comédie de la cohabitation*, Paris, Albin Michel, 1987.

Pompidou, G., *Pour rétablir une vérité*, Paris, Flammarion, 1982.

Prate, A., *Les batailles économiques du Général de Gaulle*, Paris, Plon, 1978.

Schneider, R., *La haine tranquille*, Paris, Seuil, 1992.

Schrameck, O., *Matignon rive gauche, 1997–2001*, Paris, Seuil, 2001.

Servent, P., *Œdipe à Matignon: le complexe du premier ministre*, Paris, Balland, 1988.

Tuppen, J., *Chirac's France*, Basingstoke, Macmillan, 1991.

6 The French parliament

Decline – and resurgence?

One of the most striking characteristics of the Fifth Republic is the relatively weak position of parliament. Indeed, it has been argued that from its all-powerful position during the Third and Fourth Republics parliament has now been relegated to a position of total impotence. Such a view is misleading. In the first place, the decline of the French parliament dates not from 1958 but from some four decades earlier. Secondly, while the decline of the French parliament cannot be denied, its weakness should not be exaggerated: in some respects the 'decline' resembles a convergence towards a more general European model of a parliament neither supreme nor insignificant. Third, weakness at the start of the Fifth Republic has since been followed by a partial recovery of parliamentary influence as a result both of institutional reforms and of changing political practice.

Most historians distinguish four phases in the evolution of parliamentary power in France. The first, starting with the restoration of the monarchy in 1814, was marked by the sporadic but apparently inexorable extension of parliamentary power, culminating in the establishment of the 'republican Republic' after the elections of October 1877. During the second phase, from 1877 to 1914, parliamentary supremacy was entrenched, becoming a core component of the republican tradition. The government was reduced to the role of a mere committee whose main task was to implement parliament's decisions. Within parliament, individual members exercised great power: weak party discipline allowed them to create havoc with governmental proposals, and to badger unstable governments into budgetary concessions in favour of their constituencies. Parliamentary initiatives delayed the adoption of the budget and all too often compromised the balance between revenue and spending. It was small wonder that one critic (Gaston Jèze) could describe the parliamentary assemblies as 'wasteful, incompetent and irresponsible'.

The third period, 1918 to 1958, was characterised by parliament's progressive decline. The impact of foreign and colonial wars, of military occupation, of the growing weight and technicality of legislation and the rise of well-organised pressure groups all had their impact, reducing parliament's capacity to initiate or effectively control legislation. After World War I, important policies in foreign affairs, defence and economic planning often completely escaped parliamentary attention. This development was facilitated on the specific occasions, from 1924 onwards, when parliament formally granted the government powers to legislate by decree in certain areas. But while conceding a government's right to legislate in its place, parliament still questioned the political responsibility of the executive. Powerful, specialised parliamentary committees harassed ministers and earned a status as alternative governments. And none of the well-intentioned constitutional devices introduced in 1946 by the makers of the Fourth Republic were able to break the habits of generations.

While steadily abdicating many of their positive policy-making capacities, the parliaments of 1918–58 retained all their power to question and obstruct the workings of government, for parliamentary sovereignty continued to be recognised in important ways. Parliament had complete control of its own rules and agenda; it had the exclusive right (though it often chose to delegate it) to legislate in any domain; it enjoyed a near-monopoly on supplying ministers; its members enjoyed power and prestige at the local level. Parliament frequently paralysed governments by denying them its support. In other words, parliament was a declining yet ultimately all-powerful body, while governments, though powerful in certain circumstances, were generally short-lived. In these conditions neither parliament nor the government had real power.

The fourth and final phase in the development of the French parliament opened in 1958 as parliament was first put in a subordinate place by the framers of the new constitution and then kept there by the political practice of successive Gaullist-led governments. Curiously, Michel Debré called the Fifth Republic, of which he was the prime architect, a 'parliamentary régime'. He had in mind a 'true' parliamentary régime, on British lines, in which parliament could control but not destroy or supplant executive power. In Britain, party discipline supplies the restraint necessary to this balanced state of affairs. As a Gaullist, Debré believed that to be impossible in a country like France, where deep social divisions were reflected in an unstable multi-party system. Hence the notion of *rationalised parliamentarianism*: the idea that new institutional arrangements should compensate for the traditional absence of a parliamentary majority. The Fifth Republic *is* a parliamentary régime insofar as any government needs the goodwill of the National Assembly, the lower house, to survive. But its constitution also contains a battery of provisions designed to reduce the parliament's powers, prerogatives and prestige.

Since 1958, parliament has been both more and less subordinate than Debré envisaged. It has been more so because the unexpected appearance of a stable majority reinforced his constitutional restrictions. It has been less subordinate, especially since the 1970s, because a reaction in favour of parliament has enabled it to recover a little, though far from all, of its old institutional power and political assertiveness.

The constitutional assault upon parliament: the provisions

Among the least ambiguous passages in the constitution of the Fifth Republic are those that limit the powers of parliament. Most, though not all, have been activated by the executive.

The separation of powers

The framers of the new constitution sought a rigorous separation of executive and legislative powers. This separation was inspired by de Gaulle himself, and included in the constitution (Article 23) against Debré's advice. De Gaulle had always insisted that 'executive power should not emanate from parliament . . . or the result will be a confusion of powers which will reduce the government to a mere conglomeration of delegations'. The separation of legislature and executive has been underlined by the regular appointment of ministers from outside parliament: over a third of the total in some governments (see Table 5.1). Article 23, moreover, requires any parliamentarian who becomes a minister to relinquish his or her seat, which passes to a replacement (*suppléant*), who has been elected, along with full parliamentarians, at the legislative elections. This 'incompatibility rule', it was thought, would curb the appetites of those parliamentarians, common under earlier republics, who overthrew governments in the hope of winning office for themselves (they would now have to sacrifice their parliamentary seats for a portfolio); it would also make temperamental ministers think twice before leaving the government (they could face a long wait, possibly till the next general election, before returning to parliament).

The practice of Article 23 has never, it is true, worked as intended. De Gaulle himself positively encouraged his extra-parliamentary ministers to enhance their legitimacy by standing at parliamentary elections in 1967 and 1968. Only his culture minister, André Malraux, resisted; many of the others needed little prompting, since they saw the attractions of a secure constituency, and delegated members of their *cabinets* to cultivate support on the ground. Moreover, newly resigned ministers wishing to return to parliament easily found ways to persuade their *suppléants* to stand down and provoke by-elections. On the other hand, Article 23 did break parliament's stranglehold over ministerial recruitment. Prime ministers Pompidou (1962–68) and Barre (1976–81) had never been elected to parliament when they were appointed. The same is true of de Villepin, appointed on 31 May 2005. Both Couve de Murville and Messmer had served for several years, as foreign and defence minister respectively, before they first stood for the National Assembly (unsuccessfully on the first occasion, in both cases). No longer is a parliamentary apprenticeship a necessary preliminary to winning a portfolio; a successful period in a ministerial *cabinet* may do just as well, or better; nearly half the ministers appointed between 1958 and 1974 had been in a *cabinet*. Even among those who held parliamentary seats before being appointed to government, the *cabinet* route is common. Jacques Chirac offers an excellent illustration of this: his conquest of the Ussel seat in Corrèze, though striking, was a mere staging-post between five years in Pompidou's *cabinet* at Matignon (1962–67) and nine years of continuous ministerial and prime ministerial office (1967–76).

Restrictions on parliamentary sessions

The new constitution drastically reduced the time parliament was allowed to meet. Previous republican constitutions guaranteed a *minimum* period for parliamentary sessions; that of the Fifth Republic imposed a *maximum* period: two ordinary sessions, one in autumn and one in spring, for a total of no more than five and a half months (Fourth Republic parliaments had sat for ten months on average). Special sessions were limited to a fortnight, and only to debate a specific agenda. When a majority of the

National Assembly demanded a special session in 1960, de Gaulle turned them down, in violation of his own constitution according to most jurists. A similar request was accepted by Giscard in 1979, but in terms that underlined that he could have refused. Usually, special sessions are called by *governments* unable to find time in ordinary sessions to enact their programme. Socialist administrations have been particularly prone to this: there were nineteen special sessions from 1958 to 1980, but seventeen under the Mauroy and Fabius governments between 1981 and 1986, and thirteen under Rocard, Cresson and Bérégovoy between 1988 and 1993.

The limitation on parliament's law-making powers

The new constitution severely curtailed parliament's monopoly on law-making. Article 34 defines the area of law (i.e. legislation which has to be passed by parliament) in two ways.

- Parliament determines the rules on a range of specified subjects, which include fundamental liberties, civil status and civil rights, liability to taxation, conscription, penal procedures and electoral laws.
- It also lays down the general principles and the framework of laws relating to another range of subjects, comprising local government, education, property rights, trade union law, social security and finance bills. The detailed implementation of such laws is left to the government.

Any area not covered by these two categories is left to the discretion of the government (Article 37), which may rule any parliamentary bill or amendment out of order (Article 41), subject to confirmation by the Constitutional Council, if it falls into this 'regulatory domain'. The constitution limited parliament's law-making monopoly in two further ways: the referendum provision in Article 11, and the formalisation, in Article 38, of Third and Fourth Republic practice allowing the government to ask parliament for powers to legislate by decree (*ordonnance*).

In principle, the constitutional restriction of the law-making domain represents a massive breach of parliamentary sovereignty, a central component of the British tradition that Debré was apparently trying to emulate. The application has been somewhat less spectacular. Bills or amendments have been ruled out of order in the Assembly on the basis of Article 34 just 41 times, all but two of them before 1981 (on the most recent occasion, in January 2005, the industry minister used it to refuse some 11,000 opposition amendments to a government bill revising legislation on the 35-hour week, tabled more to cause delay than as a serious attempt to amend). Rulings of the Conseil d'État and the Constitutional Council in this area have proved more liberal than restrictive. The referendum has been used on only 10 occasions. On the other hand, Article 38 was used 15 times from 1958 to 1981, 11 times from 1981 to 1997 and 6 times during the 1997–2002 parliament; de Villepin revived it, largely as a public relations device, to effect changes to employment law after his appointment in 2005. Perhaps the most important routine implication of Articles 34 and 37 has been that laws need decrees – *décrets d'application* – before coming into force, enhancing the possibility of delay and distortion of the legal text.

The passage of government business

The government acquired new and draconian means under the constitution to ensure the speedy passage of its own business. Parliaments of the Third and Fourth Republics often relegated government bills to the bottom of the agenda, buried them in committee, amended them out of recognition, or, if all else failed, defeated them. The Fifth Republic, by contrast, gives governments the procedural means to get most of their measures enacted in the form they choose. These include their mastery of the agenda; the limitation of the power of parliamentary committees; the right to override and ignore amendments; the right to turn any bill into a question of confidence; the control of the 'shuttle' procedure by which bills pass between the two houses of parliament; and special provisions for finance bills.

- *The agenda*. Article 48 of the 1958 constitution gave government measures priority on the parliamentary agenda. Other business, including private members' bills (*propositions de loi*) and the (necessary) election of officials of the two houses of parliament, not least the president (speaker) and vice-president of each, was left to a 'complementary' agenda, to be discussed only if time was available. Usually it was not: in the first twenty-five years of the Fifth Republic, the 'complementary' agenda occupied barely four days a year on average. The main casualty was private members' bills, whose share of total legislation enacted fell from nearly a third under the Fourth Republic to an average of 13 per cent between 1958 and 1981. And the French opposition, unlike its British counterpart, technically has no right at all to time in which it can determine the nature of parliamentary business.

- *Committees*. Committees in the French parliament consider bills, and amendments to them, before they are presented for general debate. They therefore have the chance to define the terms of that debate, to approve some amendments and to reject others. The nineteen specialised National Assembly committees under the Fourth Republic tended to savage government bills beyond repair; they also monitored the activities of a particular ministry with a zeal often enhanced by the chair coveting the portfolio he was controlling. Debré did away with these 'permanent anti-governments'. Indeed, he envisaged that in the new régime most bills would be sent for consideration by non-specialist ad hoc committees, analogous to the Standing Committees of the British House of Commons, provided for in Article 43 of the new constitution. This did not happen; both the National Assembly and the Senate (the upper house) preferred most bills to be sent to the permanent committees. But Article 43, crucially, allows only six such committees in each house. The National Assembly now has four committees of 72 members (Defence; Finance; Foreign Affairs; and Legal and Administrative Matters) and two of 144 members, described as 'two big dustbins in which the least prestigious areas of parliamentary activity are thrown': Production and Trade, and Cultural, Social and Family Affairs. Less specialised, more unwieldy than their Fourth Republic predecessors, these new committees are far less capable of detailed interference in legislation. Moreover, the government's mastery of the agenda means that it fixes the time available to a committee to discuss a bill. Not surprisingly, many parliamentarians, including successive presidents of the National Assembly, believe that there is far too much legislation for too few committees. But no proposal to increase their number has yet come close to adoption.

- *Amendments.* Both Deputies (members of the National Assembly) and Senators may propose amendments to legislation, but under Article 44–3 the government may, at any time, insist on a single vote on the whole bill with only such amendments as it has proposed or accepted. This 'package vote' (*vote bloqué*) procedure has been invoked, on average, more than 7 times a year in the National Assembly since 1958, with peaks under the de Gaulle presidency (114 times in ten years), the Chirac government of 1986–88 (43 times in two years) and the minority Socialist governments of 1988–93 (82 times in five years) (see Table 6.1).

- *The question of confidence.* Under Article 49–3 of the constitution, the government may also make any bill a question of confidence in the National Assembly, halting parliamentary discussion. To defeat it, the bill's opponents must table a motion of censure against the government within twenty-four hours and vote it *by an absolute majority of all members of the National Assembly* (currently 289 out of 577). This last provision means that abstentions count, in effect, as votes for the government. If no censure motion is voted, the bill is considered as passed. If such a motion is carried, on the other hand, the government must resign; a dissolution of parliament will probably follow. In effect, the use of Article 49–3 invites Deputies to back the government's measure, whether explicitly or tacitly, or overthrow the government and face the uncertainties of a general election. It is the ultimate weapon in the government's armoury, conceived for parliaments without stable majorities. Under the Fifth Republic there have been two such parliaments, those of 1958–62 and 1988–93: between them, they account for 45 of the 81 occasions to 2005 on which Article 49–3 has been invoked (see Table 6.1). Major issues have sometimes been at stake: the funding of France's atomic weapons programme (under Debré) and the Contribution Sociale Généralisée, an unpopular but necessary measure to shore up the social security system under Rocard, are two measures that owe their passage to this Article 49–3. Rocard, Cresson and Bérégovoy all used it (as had Barre before them) to adopt the budget. But Article 49–3 was also used to accelerate procedure by governments with secure majorities – by Mauroy over

Table 6.1 Use of Articles 44–3 and 49–3 in the National Assembly, 1958–2004

	Article 44–3 (*vote bloqué*)	Article 49–3 (*question of confidence*)	
	Times used (*all readings*)	Times used	Bills concerned
1958–62	23	7	4
1962–67	68	0	0
1967–68	17	3	1
1968–73	13	0	0
1973–78	17	2	2
1978–81	18	6	2
1981–86	3	13	9
1986–88	43	8	7
1988–93	82	38	19
1993–97	24	3	3
1997–2002	13	0	0
2002–4	6	1	1
Total	**327**	**81**	**48**

Source: Assemblée Nationale.

nationalisations after 1981, and Chirac over privatisations five years later (both had previously been delayed by the Constitutional Council). No censure motion tabled under Article 49–3 has succeeded, though two, one under Chirac in 1986 and one under Rocard in 1990, came within five votes of the majority.

- *National Assembly and Senate.* All bills pass through both the National Assembly and the indirectly elected upper house, the Senate. In the last resort, the National Assembly vote may override the Senate's. Before this happens, however, the bill is shuttled between the two houses for at least one reading; in case of disagreement, a joint committee of Deputies and Senators tries to reach a compromise which is then debated again by both houses. The government is master of this complex procedure. It may choose whether to present a bill in the Senate or the Assembly (though finance bills must go to the Assembly first); whether to make a bill a matter of urgency (shortening the shuttle procedure, something done no fewer than 272 times between 1958 and 1981 and 35 times between 1999 and 2002); and whether to include Senate amendments in a revised bill or give the National Assembly the last word.

- *Finance bills.* Two constitutional provisions restrain what had been the proverbial propensity of Deputies to hold up the budget so as to extract concessions from a desperate and precarious government. Article 40 bans private members from proposing measures that would entail an increase in government spending or a drop in revenue. A total of 415 private members' bills were ruled out of order between 1958 and 1981 by virtue of this provision. Under Article 47, parliament must debate and vote the budget in seventy days, failing which the government has the right to impose it by ordinance. No government has used this provision, largely because other articles rendered it unnecessary: the *vote bloqué* was used in *every* budget from 1959 to 1970, except for 1961, while Article 49–3 was invoked to close budgetary debates on 27 occasions between 1958 and 2004.

A less accountable executive

The new constitution severely limited parliament's opportunities to call the executive to account. In the first place, the real *de facto* head of the executive became (outside periods of cohabitation) the president, who is no longer responsible to parliament: it is tempting to wonder how long either President Mitterrand or President Chirac might have survived persistent parliamentary questioning, the former about his war record, the latter about his stewardship of the Paris town hall. But the explicit provisions of the Fifth Republic constitution also limit parliament's ability to call the government, which theoretically remains responsible to it, to account. It became more difficult not only to overthrow governments, but also to question them, and to scrutinise their performance through committees of enquiry.

Votes of censure and of confidence

A Fifth Republic government may be overthrown in one of three ways. It may fall to a motion of censure under Article 49–3, as outlined above. It may fall to a vote of censure put down spontaneously in the Assembly, under Article 49–2. Such a vote also needs an absolute majority of Deputies to pass – and, moreover, requires signatures of one-tenth of all Deputies to be *tabled*. The signatories could not then, under the 1958 constitution, table another vote of censure during the same session of parliament – a significant restriction if opposition Deputies were few. Parliament may also, finally, defeat a government's request for a vote of confidence on a general policy declaration, under Article 49–1, under which motions are decided by a simple majority of those voting. But Fifth Republic governments, unlike their hapless predecessors of the Fourth, are under no obligation to request the National Assembly's confidence in this way: the Messmer government, for example, was in office for three months after being appointed on 5 July 1972 without parliament even sitting. Governments may request a vote of confidence to discipline their majorities: Mauroy with his Communists in 1982, for example, or Chirac during the first cohabitation. They will not do so, however, if they risk losing. Thus Rocard and Bérégovoy, with no absolute majority, limited their requests for confidence to relatively consensual foreign policy issues where their support transcended the narrow confines of the Socialist Party.

Only one government since 1958 has been brought down by parliament: that of Pompidou on 4 October 1962. What followed was the most successful month for the executive in the history of the Fifth Republic (cf. Chapter 2, p. 60): the victorious referendum on the direct election of the president on 28 October, and the emergence of a stable Gaullist-led majority at the parliamentary elections in November. Pompidou, reappointed as soon as he had resigned, remained at Matignon for another sixty-seven months; parliament fell under the new constraint of stable majorities.

Questions

At least as important, under the new system, as changes to the procedures of formal censure votes (which had never brought down Fourth Republic governments anyway) was the limitation of opportunities to question the government. The restrictions were both quantitative (Article 48 of the 1958 constitution limited questions to one sitting a week) and qualitative (questions lost their power to threaten the government). Under the Third and Fourth Republics the procedure of *interpellation* had allowed questions to be followed by a debate and a vote at which the Deputies could record their dissatisfaction at the government's answer. A government defeated on an interpellation, though not constitutionally required to resign, often felt politically bound to go. There were 316 interpellation debates under the Fourth Republic; they brought down five governments (ironically, the practice, long the sole preserve of the lower house, was introduced and regularly used in the Senate by Michel Debré). Interpellations in this form were banned in June 1959; National Assembly Standing Orders state that they are considered as equivalent to, and subject to the same rules as, votes of censure. The Deputies were left with two procedures, both cumbersome and lacking in the element of speed and surprise needed to catch a minister off balance: oral questions – put down in advance in the Assembly's agenda for a Friday morning, and answered, if at all, weeks later and at the rate of half a dozen per sitting; and written questions, typically answered by members of ministerial *cabinets* and thus useless as a means of holding a minister personally to account.

Committees of enquiry

Under the Third and to a lesser extent Fourth Republics, the creation of special parliamentary committees of inquiry, especially on issues relating to political scandals, could destabilise governments. However, a government decree of November 1958 specified that no committee was to work for longer than four months; proceedings were to be held in secret; and they were to be halted in the event of a judicial inquiry: all powerful disincentives to vigorous public investigation.

The Constitutional Council as anti-parliamentary watchdog

The constitution's anti-parliamentary provisions were given teeth by the creation, in Article 56, of a new body, the Constitutional Council (see Chapter 2, p. 63), with the explicit task of reviewing new legislation for constitutionality. It meant, for example, that successful private members' bills, or amendments to government bills, could be referred to the Council by the prime minister or president and ruled unconstitutional on the basis of Article 37 (limitation of the domain of parliamentary legislation) or Article 40 (the ban on parliamentarians proposing higher spending or lower taxes). That the Council was set up, above all, to restrain parliament is also indicated by the obligation placed on both assemblies to refer their own standing orders to it before bringing them into force. That measure was used, for example, to ban interpellations in 1959.

These provisions added up to what has been described as a 'constitutional corset' designed to restrict parliamentary initiative and control. As Professor François Goguel pointed out, the framers of the constitution created a form of parliamentary régime without parliamentary sovereignty. And its restrictions were compounded by more political factors.

The decline of parliament: factors unconstitutional and extra-constitutional

Tight though it was, the corset left some margins of manoeuvre available for exploitation by a resolute parliament. But the parliaments of the early Fifth Republic were far from resolute in their opposition to the executive. Locked, from 1962, into newly stable majorities which made the whole notion of 'opposition' to government on the part of parliament as an institution (as distinct from left-wing opposition parties within parliament) deeply problematic, cowed by presidents and governments that often treated them with arrogance and contempt, and hamstrung by their lack of technical resources, many Deputies chose to be assiduous in their constituencies but docile (even when present and awake) in the Palais-Bourbon, seat of the National Assembly.

An overbearing executive

Parliament has suffered from cavalier treatment at the hands of successive presidents and governments, especially as few early leaders of the executive were inclined to redress the new constitutional balance in favour of parliament. De Gaulle had never belonged to parliament, and blamed it for many of the shortcomings of earlier republics. Pompidou sat as a Deputy for a total of one autumn session between his stints at Matignon and the Élysée; aside from honing his debating skills during his prime ministerial visits to the Palais-Bourbon, he treated parliament with benign indifference. Among the early prime ministers, only Chaban-Delmas, president of the National Assembly for a decade before entering Matignon, showed sympathy towards his former parliamentary colleagues, and even this was largely cosmetic. Debré, although (or perhaps because) he was a former parliamentarian, treated the institution with barely disguised impatience; Messmer was apprehensive, Chirac petulant and Barre patronising, didactic and irritable.

The cavalier treatment of parliament consisted in a combination of spectacular affronts – de Gaulle's refusal of a special session in 1960, or his bypassing of the Senate in the constitutional reform proposals of 1962 and 1969 – and routine humiliations. The latter included the regular use of the *vote bloqué* and urgency procedures outlined above, and, to a lesser extent, of Article 49-3. Parliaments also had to endure the bunching of bills into the ends of sessions: on 23 and 24 June 1970, for example, the Senate sat for 24 hours and 40 minutes, almost as long as it had sat in the whole of the previous April (such practices were not confined to the early years: of the 134 texts adopted in 1994 by the National Assembly, 60 were passed in December). Bills delivered late in sessions were typically sprawling, hold-all texts, with such informative names as *diverses mesures d'ordre social*; others were poorly drafted and incorporated last-minute flurries of government amendments. Parliamentarians have also seen government bills stuffed with detailed regulation, in violation of Articles 34 and 37. Needless to say, the quality of legislation suffered.

Three areas illustrate the government's behaviour to parliament especially well: the gap between laws and their implementation; the annual budget; and the government's responses to questions.

Implementation

Fifth Republic governments – and not only the early ones – have often rushed legislation through parliament, and then waited months or even years to implement it. Contraception, for example, became *legal* in 1967, but only *available* when the decrees were published in 1974. In another egregious case, decrees instituting a new penalty system for driving offences were hurriedly watered down in June 1992 after causing a lorry drivers' strike, a crisis that might have been avoided had parliament been given time to debate the law properly during its passage (under the urgency procedure) in July 1989. Prime Minister Rocard once estimated that a third of all laws were without their *décrets d'application* six months after their adoption, and a tenth were never implemented at all – quite aside from those repealed when the parliamentary majority changed. In October 2003, the secretariat-general of the government noted that only 10–15 per cent of *décrets d'application* had appeared for laws voted since the start of the legislature in 2002; moreover, some pre-2002 legislation voted under the Jospin government, including, for example, a law on joint ownership of residential property that affected 6 million people, still lacked the necessary decrees to bring it into force. Rarer, but no more satisfactory, is the opposite case illustrated by the Juppé government: it decided to abolish military service in 1996, and advertised the *rendez-vous citoyen*, a substitute patriotic rite of passage for young men, *before* parliament had even debated the changes.

The budget

The government takes nine months to prepare the annual budget, producing a finely balanced product of economic forecasts (which have the genius of being invariably wrong), rationally quantifiable models (whose 'rationality' often disguises some very irrational political choices) and nice calculations of party and pressure group interests. Parliamentarians have then been given three months to debate it. They have suffered both from an overload of information (receiving each year over 120 separate official budget documents representing some 30,000 pages, as well as 9,000 pages of reports and opinions produced by themselves) and a dearth of it (all too often crucial data, like year-on-year comparisons, transfer of unused credits from one year to the next, matching funds from elsewhere, or transfers between ministries, have not been available; the budget's 850 chapters, organised under headings such as personnel, information technology, or jobs by corps and grade, have made it impossible to read or assess programmes). Few governments have looked kindly upon parliamentary amendments to their delicately tuned document. The debates on the budget for 2000, for example, changed the disposal of just 7.6 billion francs (1.2 billion euros) out of a total of 1,500 billion (229 billion euros). Even then, it should be borne in mind that most budget amendments have originated with the government (one recent study showed that government spokespersons regularly exceeded their allotted time in the finance committee by over 100 per cent), and that the government has always been free to invoke the *vote bloqué* procedure, or even Article 49–3. Implementation of the budget has largely escaped parliament. Changed circumstances could lead ministers to alter important details of their expenditure. Credits might be frozen or cancelled by the Finance Ministry. Significant spending items have been 'debudgetised', or moved to external bodies. Parliament's control over these, and over France's still numerous public and semi-public enterprises (numbering over 600 at their peak in the 1980s), has been largely fictitious. While reforms to budgetary procedures initiated in July 2001 will change many of these arrangements, parliamentary scrutiny of the budget over the first half-century of the Fifth Republic will have been very limited indeed.

Questions

The attitude of early Fifth Republic governments reinforced constitutional barriers to effective questioning of the executive. Of the 1,416 'oral questions without debate' – the commonest type of oral question – tabled between 1967 and 1973, for example, just 323, fewer than a quarter, received *any* reply. A question about the Ben Barka affair (the leader of Morocco's left-wing opposition, kidnapped in broad daylight in Paris, then murdered with the complicity of elements in the French secret services), put down in November 1965, received an answer (as the government euphemistically described it) in May 1967. Ministers' routine disrespect for questions was illustrated by the appearance, on 28 November 1975, of the junior minister for *housing* to reply, perfunctorily, to parliamentary questions concerning atomic energy, the French car industry, the crisis in the textile industry and the speed limits of heavy lorries. The appropriate ministers were not in parliament, despite rules stipulating that they should be.

Domaine(s) réservé(s)

Even in comparatively uncontentious matters like professional training or regional health funds, parliamentarians have faced obstacles in seeking information from governments. More sensitive areas, including almost anything linked to foreign or defence policy, are treated as off-limits to parliamentary scrutiny. Sixty per cent of all treaties signed by France are ratified without any parliamentary debate at all. This was true, for example, of defence agreements signed with Togo in 1963 and Cameroon in 1974, as well as the agreements to 'maintain order' in Côte d'Ivoire, Gabon and Chad between 1961 and 1963. Parliament has often been told of France's periodic military interventions (notably in former African colonies) only after the event, when it is presented with the (financial) bill.

Parliament was also, initially, excluded from any discussion of European legislation, which came to represent a direct constraint on its activities and a breach on its legislative monopoly as important as anything in the constitution. The Gaullist position, which remained effective for twenty years, was that all European legislation amounted merely to implementation of the 1957 Treaty of Rome, and was therefore no concern of parliament's.

Le fait majoritaire

The existence of stable majorities greatly enhanced the executive's control over parliament. Indeed, their appearance from 1962 meant that the basic premiss on which the constitution was framed – a fragmented and undisciplined legislature – proved unfounded. Majorities have ranged from the precarious (1967–68, 1986–88) to the comfortable (1962–67, 1973–78, 1978–81, 1997–2002) or the massive (1968–73, 1981–86, 1993–97, 2002–). For governments lacking a majority, as in 1958–62 and 1988–93, the constitutional safeguards were a necessity of survival. For the others, they have been a convenience. The real opposition under the Fifth Republic (typically of a parliamentary régime) has not been between the executive and legislative branches but between party majority and party opposition.

This has been so because majorities have not only existed; they have generally been disciplined. That was not automatic. Parliamentary groups had been notoriously weak under the Third and Fourth Republics, especially on the Right and Centre. The Gaullists broke with this tradition and gave the new Republic its prototype disciplined majority group. Their cohesion had five bases: rules requiring discipline on major votes; the fact that most Gaullist Deputies owed their seats to the party ticket; the removal, with the end of the Algerian war, of the one critical issue that had divided them; the Gaullist political culture, receptive to strong leadership and, now, mindful that indiscipline had nearly destroyed Gaullism under the Fourth Republic; and the patronage of a government in a secure position to offer the chance of office, constituency favours (the budget includes a small 'parliamentary reserve' to accommodate these) or even a small amount of liquid cash, from the prime minister's 'special funds', to help with election expenses. The group chairman was elected by a show of hands (and often unopposed), took his orders in the Élysée from Jacques Foccart, derived a part of his legitimacy from his status as the General's anointed and won obedience from the Gaullist Deputies in consequence. And the Gaullists, with 233 seats out of 482 in 1962, could generally dominate their Giscardian majority allies, who had 35 seats. The Socialists, the Fifth Republic's other great majority party, have always been more open to discipline than the Right. Their rules require absolute voting discipline: indeed, no group member may table a motion, an amendment or even a question without obtaining the permission of the group's governing *bureau*. In 1999, their group literature stated that 'the primary role of Socialist Deputies is to get government bills passed, in accordance with commitments made to the French people'. This was reflected in their behaviour in the 64 roll-call votes taken during the 1997–2002 National Assembly, when an average of 94.7 per cent of Socialist Deputies voted with the group position, 5.1 per cent abstained or stayed away, and only 0.2 per cent opposed their comrades. This was nothing exceptional: the overall average support for the group position within all six parliamentary groups, majority and opposition, in 1997–2002 was 92.9 per cent.

Debré had expected governments to discipline parliament from without, with new constitutional powers; but disciplined majority groups allowed governments to colonise parliament from within. Deputies backed by president or government have won election, not only as majority group leaders, but also to the presidency of the National Assembly (Edgar Faure under Giscard, Louis Mermaz under Mitterrand and Jean-Louis Debré under Chirac are good examples) and to committee chairmanships. This control of key posts in the National Assembly is all the more important because neither the constitution nor parliamentary standing orders ensure a formal status or safeguards for the opposition. The National Assembly president remains clearly identified with the majority, unlike the politically neutral speaker of the British House of Commons; and he may, in some conditions, rule bills and amendments as unconstitutional and thus out of order. The Conference of Presidents, which makes key decisions about the agenda (such as which private members' bills and even, in some cases, which questions are discussed), has a built-in majority because the group chairmen who sit on it, with the president and vice-presidents of the National Assembly, have block votes in proportion to the size of their groups. Taken to its limits, therefore, the *fait majoritaire* has the potential to allow government control, not only of legislation, but even of how governments are held to account by parliament.

Opposition clearly offers more opportunities to criticise the government, which is why many Deputies have preferred it. But there are frustrations here too: without a formal status, for years the opposition disposed of no allocation of days in which it could decide business and lead debates. Group discipline, moreover, applies here too, and the meagre opportunities available for opposition politicians to shine are often monopolised by party 'tenors', however unbriefed, at the expense of backbenchers, however expert. Even more than in other parliaments, the opposition risks being confined to a role of impotence and negativity.

Parliament's lack of resources

Parliament has generally lacked the technical means to act as an effective check on government, despite improvements since 1958. It is true that between 1956 and 1995, the staff of the National Assembly grew from 602 to 1,260. The number of senior staff – *directeurs, administrateurs* and *administrateurs adjoints*, highly competent officials, recruited, like senior civil servants, by a fierce competitive examination – rose from 150 to 266. Parliamentary groups are funded from the National Assembly budget, which reached 2.5 billion francs in 1995 (the Senate budget was 1.4 billion francs). Individual Deputies have had their own offices since the early 1970s. Their monthly pay is now comparable to that of a fairly senior civil servant: 5,231 euros in 2004, in addition to a staff allowance of 8,511 francs, enough to employ a secretary and one or two researchers, and general expenses of over 7,000 euros.

French parliamentarians are thus much better provided for than British Members of Parliament. But they remain poorly off in relation to their American or even

German counterparts and, crucially, in relation to their tasks: the passage of sixty-seven laws a year on average since 1958, as well as budgets, scrutiny of a growing volume of European legislation, and whatever attempts are made to monitor government performance. Above all, their capacity to obtain high-quality information independently of the executive departments they seek to monitor is both slight and uncertain. Parliamentary staff tend to possess legal skills (suitable for drafting legislation) rather than social or economic ones. And their numbers are still few. In 1990 the president of the committee for cultural, family and social affairs complained that for an area of responsibility covering education, training, culture, broadcasting, employment, social security, pensions, health, family and children's affairs, and youth and sport – about a third of the Assembly's total agenda – he had just seven *administrateurs* at his disposal: about a quarter of a single ministerial *cabinet*.

Absenteeism and impotence

Parliamentarians' absenteeism has compounded parliamentary impotence. When Jacques Chirac met the newest Deputies of the huge right-wing majority elected in 1993, he told them to look after their constituencies first and attend sittings second. Every parliamentarian has to balance roles as national legislator and as constituency factotum; Fifth Republic parliamentarians have had every encouragement to confine themselves to the latter. High levels of absenteeism were facilitated for over thirty-five years by the non-enforcement both of Article 27 of the constitution, which states that all parliamentary votes are made in person, and of the parliamentary standing orders setting financial penalties for repeated absences from votes. The National Assembly regularly presented the unedifying spectacle of group leaders and their assistants clambering over benches to turn the keys at literally scores of empty desks, thereby registering the electronic votes of their absent colleagues, illegally but with impunity.

A further encouragement to absenteeism has been the practice, unique to France in its scope and extent, of multiple office-holding – the *cumul des mandats*. Most of France's national politicians are local politicians as well. In every Assembly since 1958, about half of all Deputies have also been mayors – some of villages and country towns, others of major cities, including (in Chirac's case) Paris (see Table 12.2). About half have been councillors for the *départements* or the regions (of which there are respectively ninety-six and twenty-two in metropolitan France). As many as a quarter have held their parliamentary seats at the same time as two major local offices. For a Deputy, local office, especially as mayor, offers a concentration of the scarce goods politicians crave: a high profile in the constituency; a reserve of loyalty (opinion polls regularly show that the public places far more confidence in mayors than in national politicians); the chance to make a larger personal impact than most legislators can; local patronage (town halls are major employers and control access to much low-cost housing as well); and a car, an office and expenses. The *cumul des mandats* has also been seen as a counterweight to France's traditional centralisation, giving well-established local figures the chance to intercede directly in Paris on behalf of their localities. But neither the decentralisation laws of 1982 nor the modest limitations placed, from 1988, on the *cumul* have diminished its attractions. In 1990 Laurent Fabius, president of the National Assembly, denounced its 'absurd and paralysing' effects and claimed that too many parliamentarians saw national office as a mere complement to their local functions. Fabius himself nevertheless ran, successfully, for the post of mayor in the big Rouen suburb of Grand-Quevilly at the next municipal elections, in 1995.

The clearest consequence of the *cumul* is that many Deputies are in their constituencies from Thursday evening till Tuesday at lunchtime. Meanwhile the benches in the Chamber are empty, as a few examples from the early 1990s – all relating to issues that had raised high levels of public interest – illustrate: 12 Deputies at Interior Minister Joxe's presentation of a reform of immigration law, 10 when Education Minister Jospin outlined the government's policy on the wearing of Islamic veils by schoolgirls, 17 for an important debate on the nuclear industry. The *cumul* also encourages Deputies to cultivate good relations with the government in the hope of constituency favours rather than using the opportunities available to them to question the government's performance; or to concentrate questions on matters of local concern rather than broader issues. As one observer claimed with some exaggeration, 'La Ve République a infantilisé le Parlement.'

A resurgent parliament?

The weakening of parliament written into key provisions at the heart of the 1958 constitution now appears irrevocable. Even among Deputies, according to a poll in 1990, a clear majority wanted to keep the *vote bloqué* and Article 49–3. Public demand for parliamentarians to assume a greater legislative or policy-making role has been slight: only 17 per cent in a 1985 poll. Yet there has been a reaction against the corseting of parliament under the early Fifth Republic; and polls show a continuing demand, among Deputies and voters, for parliament to be more active in holding the government to account.

The reaction against the weakening of parliament under the Fifth Republic opened with the Senate's defeat of de Gaulle's attempt to reform it out of existence at the referendum of April 1969. Parliament was strengthened by important reforms under Giscard; since 1988, that process has been furthered by the independence and determination of two National Assembly presidents, the Socialist Laurent Fabius (1988–92 and 1997–2000) and the Gaullist Philippe Séguin (1993–97). Parliamentarians now show greater freedom in blocking, amending and even initiating legislation, and they have become bolder in monitoring the performance of governments.

The survival of the Senate

Through most of the Fifth Republic, the Senate has been a conservative, curmudgeonly institution (second in this respect only to the British House of Lords), resistant to the reforming energies of Gaullists and Socialists alike. The Senators, whose number rose from 273 in 1962 to 321 in 1989, were chosen (for a nine-year term, a third of the Senate being renewed every three years) by an electoral college of approximately 150,000 delegates from among France's half-million regional and local councillors. The gross over-representation of rural areas among local councillors and Senators alike gave the upper house an impressive contingent of farmers and the reputation for representing *la France du seigle et de la chataigne* (literally, the France of rye and sweet chestnuts): a Senator for the rural *département* of Creuse represents 62,000 inhabitants, while a Senator for Seine-St Denis, in the grubbier Paris suburbs, represents a population of 230,000. With a minimum age for Senators of 35, and a leisurely pace of deliberation, the Senate has never been a youthful body: Alain Poher, its president from 1968 to 1992, left his post at the age of 83.

Recent reforms, accepted with more or less good grace by the Senators, have altered this picture somewhat. A law of 2003 reduced the senatorial term to six years and the minimum age to 30, as well as providing for a modest reapportionment of seats which will bring the total membership to 346 by the time implementation of the reform is completed in 2010. Parity legislation has also reached the upper house: the Senate of 2004 included 56 women, or 17 per cent of the total, compared to 12.7 per cent for the National Assembly. The ranks of the more obviously rustic Senators have dwindled: the 28 farmers and 8 veterinary surgeons of 2004, though still a generous proportion by comparison with their place in the working population, were massively outnumbered by over 80 teachers of various descriptions. The Senate has also tried to dynamise its image both by building links with business leaders and by organising art exhibitions, jazz concerts and operatic productions.

These changes, however, fall far short of what Jospin had in mind when he referred to the Senate as an 'anomaly' in a democracy. And in two respects there is rather little sign of change. First, the Senate remains a fairly elderly body: 198 senators, or 60 per cent, are aged 60 or over; 65, or 20 per cent, are 70 or over; there are 7 octogenarians; and the average age is 62. Second and more importantly, the Senate has never seen a left-wing majority; indeed, right-wingers typically outnumber the Left by about two to one. This does not ensure the Senate's passive compliance with the designs of right-wing governments, for the Senators tend to behave more independently than their colleagues in the National Assembly. It does mean, however, that the upper house will generally present greater difficulties for governments of the Left.

The constitution-makers of 1958, seeing rural notables as potential allies against an unruly National Assembly, gave the upper house back the name, and some of the prerogatives, that it had lost under the previous régime. The ungrateful Senators, urged on by their president, Gaston Monnerville, responded by leading resistance to the 1962 reform providing for direct presidential elections. De Gaulle's delayed rejoinder was the 1969 referendum proposal. This envisaged a Senate confined to a merely consultative role and including representatives of economic and social interests. The French voted no at the referendum, de Gaulle resigned and the Senate survived. Thereafter, as the Gaullists' reforming energies ebbed, their positions in both local government and the Senate grew; their reconciliation with the upper house was sealed in 1998 with the first election of a Gaullist (Christian Poncelet) to its presidency.

Governments are not responsible to, and therefore cannot be overthrown by, the Senate. But Senators can affect legislation in significant ways. They can, notably, block constitutional change: according to Article 89 of the constitution, constitutional amendments must be voted in identical terms by both houses of parliament, and then passed either by referendum or by a three-fifths majority of a Congress composed of both houses. De Gaulle deliberately ignored these provisions by proposing referenda directly to the voters in 1962 and 1969; but according to the letter of the constitution, the Senate's blocking powers are absolute. Parliamentary (chiefly senatorial) opposition has torpedoed a number of cherished presidential projects, some of them quite radical: under Pompidou, the reduction of the presidential term to five years, in 1973; under Mitterrand, the extension of the area of application of the referendum, in 1984, the extension to private citizens of the right to refer bills to the Constitutional Council, in 1990, and the inauguration of referenda by popular initiative in 1993; under Chirac, the independence of prosecuting magistrates (opposed by conservatives in both houses) in 2000. The Senators have also been able to block organic laws (laws of a semi-constitutional status, entailing special conditions of debate and requiring the Senate's consent in any matters relating to itself) aimed at radically reforming the inequitable system under which they are elected, and at limiting the *cumul des mandats*.

Over ordinary legislation, the Senate has more limited control: it may refuse bills or propose amendments, but can be overridden by the National Assembly. It has used its powers in two different ways. Under the left-wing governments of 1981–86, it practised a systematic, politicised opposition, obstructing bills, referring them to the Constitutional Council, or both. The National Assembly overrode the Senate over 38 bills under the de Gaulle presidency, 17 under Pompidou, 6 under Giscard – but 140 between 1981 and 1986. At other times, however, it has acted as a less political 'chamber of second thoughts'. No government persistently disregards the Senate's views. Even in the 1981–86 parliament, 46 per cent of Senate amendments were retained in legislation, and the National Assembly overrode the Senate on only a quarter of bills (under the Jospin government, corresponding to the 1997–2002 parliament, the lower house had the 'last word' on 68 bills, out of a total of 432 texts voted). Other governments have been notably friendly to the Senators: under Balladur, for example, half of government bills were debated in the Senate before the National Assembly, and 87 per cent of Senate amendments were retained.

Parliament's institutional reinforcement since 1974

The partial revival of parliament owes much to two waves of institutional reforms, initiated first by Giscard d'Estaing, the Fifth Republic's first non-Gaullist president, and then, since 1988, by the two National Assembly presidents, Fabius and Séguin. The reforms have not affected the core of the 1958 constitution: the government can still control most of the parliamentary agenda, and use the *vote bloqué* and Article 49–3. But the changes have gone some way to redressing the balance.

Parliament and the Constitutional Council

Giscard's constitutional reform of October 1974 extended the right to refer bills to the Constitutional Council (limited under the 1958 constitution to the prime minister and the three presidents of the Republic, the Senate and the National Assembly) to sixty Deputies or sixty Senators. This change transformed the Constitutional Council from a government weapon against an unruly parliament, as envisaged in 1958, to a tool of the parliamentary opposition. Deputies and Senators are now responsible for almost all referrals of bills; and though only about one bill in ten is actually referred, most of the rest are drafted with the constraint of the Council's scrutiny in mind (see below, Chapter 13).

Questions

The procedure of 'questions to the government' was initiated in 1974 with Giscard's blessing, on an informal basis without being included either in the National Assembly's standing orders or the constitution (an anomaly not corrected in the constitution till 1995, and still unresolved in the Assembly's standing orders). It differs from the older 'oral questions' formula in four respects: it is more spontaneous (with ministers being informed of questions just two hours in advance), quicker (with shorter time limits on both questions and answers), less controlled by the Conference of Presidents (which allocates time to the different groups, but does not select questions) and better publicised (being televised, and timetabled on a Wednesday afternoon, unlike oral questions, which continue on Friday mornings). The first year of operation saw ministers who had never deigned to answer oral questions in person appearing to face the Deputies. Interestingly, the greater consideration attached to the new format increasingly appeared to extend to the old ones as well: where fewer than a quarter of the 1,091 'oral questions without debate' tabled during the 1968–73 parliament had received any response at all, the proportion rose to over 90 per cent in the 1981–86 parliament.

As National Assembly president, Séguin further reinforced the characteristics of 'questions to the government' in 1994 by splitting them over two one-hour sittings, ending advance notice of questions, and limiting the time for both questions and answers to two and a half minutes. Their number has therefore risen. From an annual average of 250 during the Giscard presidency, they reached 668 per year during the 1997–2002 parliament, thirty-eight of them answered by the prime minister; questions took up nearly 12 per cent of the 4,615 hours that the National Assembly sat. Like question time in the British House of Commons, 'questions to the government' are criticised as ritualistic confrontations. But they are an indisputable improvement on what passed for questions before.

Monitoring and evaluation

Fabius, as National Assembly president from 1988 to 1992, sought to extend parliament's role in the evaluation of policy and of its implementation. Changes to standing orders allowed National Assembly committees to set up their own *missions d'évaluation*, charged with monitoring the implementation of laws, and to hold public hearings. The regularity with which National Assembly committees now call government members directly to account may be indicated by the fact that during the 1998–99 session, they held 84 hearings with ministers, 13 of them in public, as well as 118 hearings (32 in public) with other individuals. Perhaps the most spectacular case was the mission set up in 1998 by the foreign and defence committees to examine France's role in the Rwanda genocide of 1994. However cautious the committee's conclusions were, the fact that it interviewed 88 people in public over such a sensitive issue, including Édouard Balladur and François Léotard, respectively prime minister and defence minister at the time of the massacres, and obtained access to confidential documents, illustrates the growth in this area of parliamentary activity since de Gaulle's time. Another mission, on the prison system, was set up in 2000 and promised to be just as controversial: Deputies undertook to make unannounced visits to prisons, as the government inspectors notionally responsible for the penal system had conspicuously failed to do. Committees have also won the right to give a consultative opinion on *décrets d'application* of laws before they are published. Both Fabius and Séguin sought to palliate the lack of expertise available to parliament by formalising links with the Cour des Comptes (Court of Accounts) (whose role in monitoring public finances is specified in Article 47 of the constitution) and by setting up evaluation offices, with regular access to panels of experts, on a model inspired by the US Congress. The first of these, the Office Parlementaire d'Évaluation des Choix Scientifiques et Technologiques, had been set up as early as 1983, and has conducted studies into such issues as ozone depletion and the disposal of radioactive waste. It was followed in 1996 by the Office d'Évaluation des Politiques Publiques and the Office d'Évaluation de la Législation, both grouping Deputies, Senators and experts, and in 1999 by the Mission d'Évaluation et de Contrôle. These offices did not make a striking debut on the political scene: they lacked the resources of their American counterparts, and their reports, on subjects such as the situation of French cinema, public-sector pensions, on incentives to inward investment, passed relatively unnoticed. It remains to be seen whether, like many other institutions of the Fifth Republic, they will acquire importance only after a number of years; or whether the relationship with the Cour des Comptes, headed since 2004 by Philippe Séguin, a former president of the National Assembly, will be reinforced.

The importance of formal committees of inquiry has also grown. They were allowed to sit over six months, instead of four, in 1977, and to conduct public hearings from 1991; in 1988, under the first Fabius National Assembly presidency, opposition group leaders were given 'drawing rights' to one committee of inquiry a year. Both houses have been bolder in appointing committees: there were 14 for the National Assembly (and 8 for the Senate) in the first two decades of the Fifth Republic, but 36 for the National Assembly (and the same number for the Senate) from 1979 to 2002. In the 2002–3 session, subjects of inquiry included Pyrenean wolves, decision-making in publicly owned firms, maritime transport, the troubled airline Air Lib and the vexed question of the wearing of religious symbols in schools. There are certainly limits on what they will do: for example, both the Socialists and the Right have too much to lose to agree to an inquiry into the use of the former state-owned oil company Elf for purposes of political funding. But the committees have uncovered a range of other scandals, including property speculation in Paris, the lucrative but unpatriotic practices of the Dassault aircraft company, the financial black hole of the Crédit Lyonnais and the corrupt management of France's bankruptcy courts.

Private members' bills

These have been facilitated by the constitutional reform of 1995, under which one sitting a month is reserved for parliamentary, not government, business, in addition to sittings devoted to questions. As in the British parliament, time is short (213 hours out of 4,615 in 1997–2002, or 5 per cent of the total sittings), and inconveniently placed (typically on a Friday); majority Deputies have had the lion's share of it (especially before 1997 and since 2002, when the majority has been large). The government may plant potentially controversial bills with private members (the Juppé government did this with a bill to limit liability to prosecution for misuse of company funds, the Jospin government with the civil solidarity pact (PACS), Raffarin with reforms to the 35-hour week). And bills generally need the government's support to survive the shuttle procedure between National Assembly and Senate. Nevertheless, the new provision, enshrined in Article 48–3 of the constitution, allowed for the passage of twenty bills in its first two years. And it was a striking reversal of the constitution-makers' priorities: Michel Debré had firmly refused such a reservation of time for private members' bills in 1958.

Parliamentary amendments

One of the priorities of Séguin's presidency of the National Assembly was to make more time for committee work, ensuring a fuller scrutiny of a text between its tabling and the final vote, if necessary at the expense of plenary debates. The 1994 changes to standing orders ensured that committees were allowed to sit outside parliamentary sessions, and recommended that at least one committee a week held a public hearing with a minister. They also allowed the authors of amendments to present their amendments to committees, whether or not they belonged to the committee themselves.

The single parliamentary session and personal voting

The constitutional amendment of 1995 replaced the two three-month parliamentary sessions established in 1958 by a single nine-month session lasting from October till June. Total parliamentary time was not extended, as the new Article 28 of the constitution sets a maximum 120 days of sittings within the single session (the number of hours sat actually fell from 1,015 in 1993–94 to an average of about 930 between 1995 and 2002). But the single session both limits the parliamentary recess, when government is free of any immediate control, to three months in the summer, and allows most sittings to be held on midweek days when most Deputies and Senators are in Paris. The reform also allowed individual Deputies to sign up to three censure motions a year instead of two as under the 1958 constitution.

The corollary of the single session was that Deputies, whose attendance in parliament it facilitated, should really be there. To this end Séguin insisted, much to the irritation of Deputies, that parliamentary votes should be personal, as the constitution requires. Séguin admitted, after the first single session (1995–96), that absenteeism was still too high. But the new arrangements did at least end the dishonest practice under which proxies cast, and recorded for the *Journal Officiel*, hundreds of votes for their colleagues.

Extended competences

Parliament's competences have also been extended by two institutional reforms. First, control over European questions has been modestly reinforced: in 1979 by the creation of a parliamentary delegation for European affairs in each house, and in 1992 and 1999, more importantly, by constitutional amendments under which parliament, under Article 88.4 of the revised constitution, gives its opinion on proposed European legislation in a formal report and resolution before the government expresses its position to the European Council of Ministers. Although such resolutions are not binding on governments, they have generally taken account of them – not least because they can be presented by France's representation in Brussels as a national constraint that limits their ability to make concessions to European partners.

Secondly, the amendment of 1996 allowed a parliamentary debate, for the first time, on the annual budget for the social security system, notionally financed by contributions negotiated between employers and employee representatives, in practice increasingly heavily subsidised out of taxation. Both of these changes established, at least notionally, an element of parliamentary control in important areas where there had previously been practically none.

Parliament's legal and material capacities, then, were substantially greater in the year 2000 than they had been at the outset of the Fifth Republic. It was better able to monitor the government's performance, whether through questions (more numerous and better publicised), *missions d'information* or committees of inquiry; better able, thanks to the 1974 reform, to challenge the constitutionality of government measures; better able, too, to propose and amend legislation. Just as important has been a reinforcement of independent behaviour.

The loosening of parliamentary discipline

There has been no return to the anarchy of the Fourth Republic, as the figures (p. 153) for roll-call votes in the 1997 parliament show; but few parliamentary groups have quite matched the discipline of Gaullist Deputies at the height of the de Gaulle presidency. The non-Gaullist moderate Right and Centre have always retained the relaxed habits of earlier régimes. The Gaullists themselves now inflict no penalties on their own dissidents (Roselyne Bachelot incurred vicious sarcasm, but no formal sanction, from her fellow Gaullists when she supported the Socialist PACS bill in 1999). The formerly monolithic Communist group had become so (relatively) lax by early 2000 that its president Alain Bocquet was able to quip that 'exceptionally', they would all vote together on one government bill. Even Socialists, though still subject to strict and (broadly) enforced discipline, have been prone on occasion to absenteeism (as, notably, in a key vote on the PACS in 1998) and, above all, inclined to negotiate their support rather than concede it without question. For Socialists as for others, the ultimate sanction for dissent, deselection at the next election, is difficult to apply to incumbents with the strong implantation that goes with local office – an asset possessed by the great majority of Deputies and Senators.

Presidents of parliamentary groups typically emerge, no longer from a show of hands, but from elections held by secret ballot and often fiercely contested. Matignon or the Élysée may affect the result (Jean-Marc Ayrault, president of the Socialist group in the 1997 parliament, was an early Jospin supporter, while his Gaullist counterpart, Jean-Louis Debré, was close to Chirac); but group presidents' long-term authority depends less on blessings from above than on an ability to address Deputies' constituency problems, to listen to their policy concerns and to balance competing factions within the group. That in turn implies the capacity of Deputies of the majority to establish the parameters of government action. The thwarting of much of Chaban-Delmas's 'New Society' programme, for example, was as much the work of the conservative Gaullist parliamentary majority as of the Élysée. Mitterrand's preference for a return to proportional representation for parliamentary elections after 1988 was blocked by the Socialist Deputies, who disliked the enhanced dependence on party that would have resulted. If French governments have so far failed to apply the European directive on bird conservation, it has been because of parliament's tendency to bow to pressure from the bird-shooting lobby. Junior groups in the majority, moreover, may require attention as strategic partners: the Jospin government's reluctance to apply certain European measures relating to competition in electricity or rail markets, for example, resulted in part from the reservations of the Communist group. Finally, cohabitation, while placing a premium on majority solidarity in the face of presidential hostility, also requires the prime minister to be very attentive to his majority. Balladur, for example, recalls fortnightly meetings with each of the two majority groups (UDF and RPR), as well as visits to the Senate's majority intergroup.

A final indication of the moderation of discipline has been the behaviour of recent National Assembly presidents. The poor relations between Laurent Fabius and Prime Minister Rocard, or between Philippe Séguin and both Balladur and Juppé, ensured that they were far from compliant links in a disciplinary chain stretching from government to individual Deputies; Jean-Louis Debré, president of the National Assembly since 2002 (and son of Michel Debré), has showed a concern to respect and to reinforce the rights of parliament (including the opposition) that bely his past record as a highly partisan minister. Their independence both served as an example to Deputies and helped to press forward the institutional changes to parliament outlined above.

Obstructions, amendments and private members' bills

Despite the threat of the *vote bloqué* or Article 49–3, parliament has made increasing use of its powers to obstruct and delay legislation. These include a variety of procedural devices: points of order of several types, filibustering and, above all, the right of amendment. The tabling of parliamentary amendments has exploded since the de Gaulle presidency: as Table 6.2 shows, nearly five times as many amendments were tabled during the 1997–2002 parliament than in that of 1968–73. Oppositions have regularly used amendments to slow down government measures since 1980, when the Socialists fought a pitched battle against Peyrefitte's repressive *Sécurité et liberté* law. The Right responded in kind with the nationalisation legislation of 1982; under Rocard, right-wing and Communist oppositions joined to put down 4,703 amendments to a bill changing the legal status of Renault with a view to facilitating its partial privatisation. Although such tactics can be halted by the use of Article 49–3, they may gain in effectiveness when the bill in question is under fire from within the parliamentary majority as well. Giscard's capital gains tax bill of 1976, for example, was so amended by the more conservative elements in his majority that it was finally promulgated in a form that was emasculated and unworkable. The Socialist Culture Minister Catherine Trautmann's broadcasting bill was so disliked by the left-wing majority that it ran into the sand in parliament in 1998 and had to be reintroduced in amended form. Her colleague Dominique Voynet's bill implementing a European directive on the shooting calendar provoked intense hostility in the hunting lobby and enough absenteeism among Socialist and Communist Deputies to be defeated. Such instances are, it is

Table 6.2 Amendments in the National Assembly, 1968–73 and 1997–2002

Amendments proposed by	Amendments tabled		Amendments passed		Success rate of amendments (%)	
	1968–73	*1997–2002*	*1968–73*	*1997–2002*	*1968–73*	*1997–2002*
Government	1,329	3,141	1,104	2,682	83.1	85.4
Committees	4,425	12,405	3,041	10,784	68.7	86.9
Deputies	4,829	35,305	814	3,334	16.9	9.4
Total	**10,583**	**50,851**	**4,959**	**16,800**	**46.9**	**33.3**

Source: Assemblée Nationale.

true, rare. But they show that governments hesitate to use their panoply of consti-tutional powers to force through measures which have aroused real hostility among their own supporters.

But obstructionism only partly explains the explosion of amendments. If the indi-vidual Deputies of the 1997–2002 parliament were putting down amendments at over seven times the rate of their forebears, they were also getting more passed, at least in absolute terms. And the Deputies' amendments passed in 1998–99 included 313 put down by the opposition (in parliaments where they are or may be necessary to form a majority, the centrists are especially influential, with success rates for amendments exceeding 50 per cent in both 1967–68 and 1988–93). Committees have also become more active. While not free from party discipline (Socialist Deputies, for example, may not sign a committee amendment without their group's approval), they are less prone to party confrontation than the full sittings of the Assembly. Amendments adopted in committee often have cross-party support, and, as Table 6.2 shows, a high and growing success rate. Of the 94 bills passed by the Assembly in the 1997–98 and 1998–99 sessions, only 19 went through without amendment; 48 incorporated between one and fifty amendments, and 27 included over fifty amendments. The importance of this aspect of parliamentary business gives the *rapporteur*, the committee member respon-sible for presenting a bill and its amendments to the Assembly, a particularly sensitive role in consulting with interest groups, parliamentarians and ministerial *cabinets* and in deciding which amendments to favour: a careful *rapporteur* can make a significant difference to legislation.

Many amendments, it is true, are of little real importance; but not all. Robert Elgie has documented the debate on the 1987 budget, during the first cohabitation, in which the Giscardian Michel d'Ornano extracted a substantial reduction of the local business tax from the government. He was able to do this thanks to his post as chairman of the Assembly's Finance Committee, to his strategic position as a senior UDF Deputy able to influence support for Chirac at the presidential election and to a political context particularly favourable to tax cuts. The mirror image of that instance was the Commun-ists' success, in 1999, in winning changes to the implementation of a European directive opening the electricity market to competition: they obtained tighter controls on when electricity can be cut off, and reduced charges for the worst-off, again thanks to their strategic position in the majority and a broadly favourable ideological climate.

Parliamentarians are, finally, increasingly able to get their own bills passed, even though the two major caveats – that some private members' bills are disguised govern-ment bills, and that government co-operation is usually needed for a bill to survive – still apply. Parliamentarians' share of legislation has risen: six out of 90 texts passed, or 7 per cent, in 1988–89, but nineteen out of 93 texts, or 20 per cent, ten years later: a figure comparable to that of the German Bundestag, rather than to the British House of Commons where the share is generally under 10 per cent. The rise has been due in part to the 1995 reform reserving a sitting a month to parliamentary business. Such laws are not confined to minor issues. France's main law against incitement to racial hatred was put down by Jean-Claude Gayssot, a Communist Deputy, during the Rocard government; the banning of political contributions from businesses, after a brief period of legality, was Séguin's initiative, and was initially treated with reluctance by the Balladur government. Perhaps most important for France's institutions, however, the July 2001 reform of budgetary procedure was a joint initiative of the National Assembly and the Senate. This law, to be implemented over a three-year period from

2005, will facilitate scrutiny by reducing the previous 850 budgetary chapters to some 150–200 programmes, which will include year-on-year comparisons and may themselves be pluriannual. It will also enhance the role of parliament by requiring government adjustments to budgetary commitments to be agreed by the relevant parliamentary committees, and by setting up an Evaluation and Control Mission in parliament.

Concluding remarks

When, in 1988, new limitations on the *cumul des mandats* obliged roughly 150 politicians to resign one or more elective posts, only one chose to leave the National Assembly (and he sought re-election in 1993). The politically eminent, if kept out of government, still seek important parliamentary posts, such as the National Assembly presidency or committee chairmanships: in 1997 Foreign Affairs, the most prestigious committee (which meets rarely but travels often), included a former president (Giscard) and four former prime ministers (Balladur, Fabius, Barre and Juppé); former culture minister Jack Lang succeeded Giscard as chairman in 1997 before becoming education minister in 2000; the committee of 2002, though somewhat less lustrous, was still chaired by Balladur and included Fabius and Lang among its distinguished members. Parliament, and more specifically the National Assembly, remains central for French politicians because it retains significant powers and high visibility. It is a significant transformer, and occasionally initiator, of laws. It defines at least some of the limits of what governments can do. It serves, still, to reveal political talent: a whole generation of right-wing leaders, including Philippe Séguin and Alain Madelin, won their spurs opposing left-wing government bills round the clock in 1981. Moreover, a political consensus has come to favour parliament's rehabilitation and reinforcement after the corset years of the early Fifth Republic. That consensus includes heirs of de Gaulle like Chirac or Séguin; only a handful of surviving first-generation Gaullists (such as the former president of the Constitutional Council, Yves Guéna) oppose it. It has enabled parliament to regain some of its lost prerogatives: enough, certainly, to render the term rubber stamp as inappropriate in the twenty-first century as it was plausible in the 1960s. Developments such as a reform of the parliamentary committee system (sought by Jean-Louis Debré), or a growth in the activities of parliament's evaluation offices, would extend the process further. The five-year presidential term could have a large impact on the context of parliament's work. The near-continuous institutional reform in which France has been engaged since the late 1980s, to the disquiet of observers like Guéna, shows few signs of halting. And it has tended, on balance, towards the reinforcement of parliament.

If parliament is central for politicians, however, it seems less so for the wider population. No parliament can hope to be a mirror image of its voters; all, in Western democratic countries, give undue space to middle-class, middle-aged, white men. But the French National Assembly is especially unrepresentative. The proportion of women, at 10.9 per cent in 1997 and 12.7 per cent in 2002, was barely above that of Greece, and only 6 per cent higher than the level reached in France in November 1946. The 2002 figure was despite recent legislation setting out penalties (in terms of public funding) for parties that failed to ensure gender parity among candidates: while minor parties respected male–female parity quite carefully, for the sake of the financial reward, the major ones sought to maximise their parliamentary representation (which in their view required the reselection of almost all sitting male Deputies who wished to run), and took the penalty for ignoring the law. Again, the growing population of second-generation immigrants is entirely left out: just one black Deputy represented a mainland French constituency in 1997, a number that fell to zero when he was beaten in 2002. The National Assembly's composition is further skewed by the generous facilities enjoyed by public employees to swim in and out of careers according to electoral fortune; hence, in part, the over-representation of teachers – and the very low numbers of blue-collar or even white-collar workers. Many of France's most eminent politicians, moreover, are products of the senior civil service, who use parliament merely as a transit point between ministerial *cabinets* and government office.

The unrepresentativeness of parliamentarians might matter less if the electorate appreciated their work. But voters are far from unanimous in doing so. Fifty-two per cent of respondents to a poll in 1989 considered that Deputies did not do their jobs conscientiously; two years later, 43 per cent thought that parliament in general was not doing its job well, against 37 per cent who took a more positive view. Deputies themselves were unsure: according to a survey in 1990, 69 per cent thought that the parliament was not adequately filling its function of calling the executive to account.

In part, the public's view reflects the fact that, despite recent reforms, parliament has lost powers (and power) since the advent of the Fifth Republic and of the *fait majoritaire*. The executive retains, and still uses, formidable means with which to get its own way (in January 1996, the Juppé government invoked Article 49–3, decree powers under Article 38 and the accelerated legislation procedure of Article 48 *at the same time* in order to enact controversial reforms to the social security system). The president of the Republic, head of the executive outside periods of cohabitation, is beyond parliamentary scrutiny unless accused of high treason. And, crucially, the uniquely French phenomenon of the *cumul des mandats* still encourages parliamentarians to neglect their role as national legislators for a more rewarding one as local barons.

Both a cause and a consequence of the public's dissatisfaction with parliament has been its loss of ground, as a major forum of political debate, to the media and, more recently, to the judiciary. In all the big crises of the de Gaulle presidency – the 'barricades week' in Algiers in 1960, the 'generals' putsch' the following year and the 'events' of May 1968, parliament was reduced to the role of impotent spectator. Mitterrand's economic U-turn of 1983, in many ways the economic turning point of the post-war half-century, was done without any reference to parliament. The 1991 Gulf war presented a notable contrast between the frequent appearances of generals and government officials before congressional committees in Washington, and the absence from the Palais-Bourbon of their French counterparts, who preferred the television studios. The rise of the extreme right-wing leader Jean-Marie Le Pen is also a revealing case in this respect. His appearance on a flagship television interview programme early in 1984 greatly increased both his recognition and his approval ratings. By contrast, his two years at the head of the Front National group in the National Assembly made little difference to public perceptions of him. More generally, ministers are more likely to announce policy initiatives in interviews or press conferences than in parliament; governments do not even have to justify policy in the ritual of a Queen's Speech debate, still less in the rigour of a congressional hearing. And their adversaries in opposition are at least as likely to rush to the television studios to reply. Parliament's continuing shortcomings as a forum within which to hold the government to account have also meant that the judiciary has taken over part of its role as exposer of scandals, most notably in the political funding cases that became all too numerous from the late 1980s. The French parliament, despite recent reforms, is neither an arena for aggressive questioning of the executive, on the model of the British House of Commons, nor a 'working' parliament (*arbeitsparlament*) dedicated to the serious processing of legislation, like the German Bundestag.

Finally, while parliament has certainly regained some power within a strictly French context, the outside world has not stood still in the meantime. The growth of European law has restricted parliament's role as law-maker more than the formal provisions of Articles 34 and 37 of the constitution. Europe decides questions ranging from the amount of permissible state aid to Renault to the specifications of automobile motors, or the levels of competition required in the electricity or rail industries. Parliament's legislative role is thereby limited and constrained – despite the opportunities for scrutiny of European legislation provided by Article 88-4 of the constitution. The Jacobin notion of law as a sovereign act establishing universal obligations binding on citizens, still plausible in 1958, has been increasingly open to question. Both the sources of law (Europe and judges, as well as parliament) and its applications (as one part of an interlocking framework of obligations between institutions, for example) have become more complex.

The French parliament's further recovery will still require it to reinforce its position vis-à-vis the executive, as a proposer and amender of legislation and, above all, as a body able to call the executive effectively to account on any issue. For it to fulfil these functions requires both legal and technical means, and a change of focus which would be best achieved by the further limitation of the *cumul des mandats*. Even if it achieved this, it could not hope, in a more polycentric structure of government, to recapture the 'centrality' it enjoyed under earlier Republics. But the competent fulfilment of more limited functions might regain a respect and interest on the part of voters that it currently tends to lack.

Further reading

Abélès, M., *Un ethnologue à l'Assemblée*, Paris, Odile Jacob, 2000.
Ameller, N., *L'Assemblée Nationale*, Paris, Presses Universitaires de France, 1994.
Avril, P., *Les Français et leur parlement*, Paris, Casterman, 1972.
Baguenard, J., *Le Sénat*, 2nd edition, Paris, Presses Universitaires de France, 1996.
Belorgey, J.-M., *Le parlement à refaire*, Paris, Gallimard, 1991.
Camby, J.-P. and Servent, P., *Le travail parlementaire sous la Cinquième République*, 4th edition, Paris, Montchrestien, 2004.
Cayrol, R., Parodi, J.-L. and Ysmal, C., *Le député français*, Paris, Armand Colin, 1973.
Chandernagor, A., *Un parlement pour quoi faire?*, Paris, Gallimard, 1967.
Chrestia, P., 'La rénovation du parlement, une œuvre inachevée', *Revue française de droit constitutionnel*, 30, 1997, pp. 293–322.
Duhamel, O., 'Députés sondés', in SOFRES, *L'état de l'opinion 1991*, Paris, Seuil, 1991, pp. 163–80.
Frears, J., 'The French parliament: loyal workhorse, poor watchdog', *West European Politics*, 13(3), July 1990, pp. 32–51.
Jan, P., *Les Assemblées parlementaires françaises*, Paris, La Documentation Française, 2005.
Kimmel, A., *L'Assemblée Nationale sous la Cinquième République*, Paris, Presses de la Fondation Nationale des Sciences Politiques, 1991.
Mastias, J., *Le Sénat de la Cinquième République*, Paris, Economica, 1980.

Maus, D., *Le parlement sous la Ve République*, Paris, Presses Universitaires de France (collection Que Sais-Je?), 1996.

Pouvoirs, no. 34, 1985, 'L'Assemblée'; no. 44, 1988, 'Le Sénat'; no. 64, 1993, 'Le parlement'.

Revue Française de Science Politique, 31(1), February 1981, special issue on 'Le parlement français sous trois présidents, 1958–1980'.

Smith, P., *The French Senate*, 2 vols, Lampeter, Mellen Press, 2005.

Williams, P., *The French Parliament, 1958–1967*, London, George Allen and Unwin, 1969.

The National Assembly (126, rue de l'Université, 75007 Paris) publishes a series of booklets entitled 'Connaissance de l'Assemblée', with titles including *Les principales étapes de la procédure législative* (1997), *L'Assemblée Nationale et les relations internationales* (1998), *L'Assemblée Nationale et l'Union européenne* (1998), *Les questions à l'Assemblée Nationale* (1997), *Le statut du député* (1997), as well as the Assembly's own rules of procedure (in French and English).

The National Assembly's website, at http://www.assemblee-nationale.fr, posts an annual statistical review of parliamentary activity (*Bulletin de l'Assemblée Nationale, Statistiques*), as well as a recapitulation for each parliament, from which most of the statistics in this chapter are drawn. It also supplies biographies of individual Deputies and links to the progress of specific bills.

7 The Left and the Greens

The dilemma of government

For de Gaulle, '*Le régime des partis, c'est la pagaille*': a party-dominated régime meant a mess. Parties might, at best, represent partial, sectional interests in society with more or less integrity. By definition, however, they could never be trusted with the national interest. Indeed, he blamed the failures of the Third and Fourth Republics – governmental instability, policy immobilism and, in 1940, national collapse in the face of the German invasion – on the unchecked power of parties. Notwithstanding an attitude that varied from barely concealed mistrust to active contempt, in 1958 he was prepared – not least in order to reassure those who saw him as a dictator preparing to suspend all normal political activity – to include a grudging constitutional guarantee of their freedoms. Article 4 of the 1958 constitution (the first such passage to appear in a French constitutional text) states that: 'Political parties and groups shall play a part in the expression of universal suffrage. They shall be formed, and shall carry on their activities, freely. They are obliged to respect the principles of national sovereignty and democracy.'

Little that has happened since then has made French party politics any less messy. This makes France a difficult environment for the study of political parties and electoral behaviour, but also an attractive one. France offers an almost unrivalled range, for a single country, of what Klaus von Beyme called *familles spirituelles*: the far Left, Communists, Socialists, Greens, liberals, Christian Democrats, conservatives and the extreme Right are all present, more or less, in force. It is true that France has no agrarian party and that regionalist parties, in such areas as Brittany, Corsica, Alsace and Savoy, tend to be electorally very weak; on the other hand these lacunae have been compensated by the presence of other political forces, whether sublime (Gaullism) or ridiculous (the birdshooters of Chasse, Pêche, Nature, Traditions (CPNT)) that are more or less recalcitrant to von Beyme's broad classifications. To the interest offered by this varied political bestiary should be added the liveliness of political polemic, the wide range of organisational types, the diversity of electoral competition and the paradoxes that this complex environment throws up.

The tendency of the French to articulate political argument in strongly ideological terms has been noted in Chapter 1; although its intensity has decreased since the Fourth Republic, it may still lend a vigour to polemic that is lacking in other political systems, as the referendum campaign of 2005 demonstrated. The range of different types of party organisation deserves closer attention. It was a French political scientist, Maurice Duverger, who pioneered the classification of parties into organisational types by drawing a contrast between 'mass' and 'cadre' parties. The mass party, in Duverger's profile (dating from 1951), is a highly structured entity with a large, regular, dues-paying membership, strong discipline (applying notably to its elected officials) and a large and not very flexible body of (usually left-wing) doctrine. The cadre party, on the other hand, is a very loose network of elected officials, with no rank-and-file membership to speak of: though their political views may be broadly similar, the elected officials are unconcerned with the fine points of doctrine, and enjoy considerable independence from the (rudimentary) party organisation thanks to their personal, localised, bases of support. Two other archetypes may to be added to Duverger's. The 'catch-all' party, theorised in the 1960s by the American Otto Kirchheimer and, as the *parti d'électeurs*, by the French political scientist Jean Charlot, combined the discipline and structured organisation of the mass party with the doctrinal flexibility of the cadre party – and added both a broad electoral appeal to a very wide range of social groups and a fixation on the personal qualities of the party leader. Finally, the 'cartel' model outlined by Katz and Mair in 1995 highlights the growing material dependence of parties on the state, especially through the spread of public financing of parties and elections; the weakening, not only of ideological confrontation, but of the roots of parties and politicians in civil society; and the inability of parties to offer the voters more than a choice of very similar managerial options for public policy-making. Each of these models corresponds to one or more parties or aspects of party competition in Fifth Republic France. However, because French politics is often localised and personalised, parties that seek a large membership, structure and discipline may nevertheless find themselves subject to a sort of gravitational pull towards the cadre model.

The diversity of electoral competition in France is structured by the diversity of electoral systems. There are six levels of direct electoral competition in France: European, presidential, parliamentary, regional, cantonal and municipal. To these should be added the indirect elections to the Senate (via the electoral college of 150,000 local and regional councillors) and referenda. French electoral laws, which have frequently been changed in the course of the twentieth century (usually as a function of a narrow but inept calculation of self-interest on the part of the incumbent parliamentary majority), have generally selected one of two main options, the two-ballot system or *proportionnelle départementale*. The two-ballot system, with single-member constituencies, has been used for every parliamentary election of the Fifth Republic except that of 1986. A wide range of candidates stand at the first ballot, which is only decisive if one of them wins both an absolute majority of votes cast and the votes of at least a quarter of registered electors. If (as is usually the case) no candidate achieves such a first-round win, then a second ballot is held a week later, which is won by the leading contender as in a British first-past-the-post election. In practice, many victorious candidates at this run-off ballot win by an absolute majority, because they have fewer opponents than at the first round. Some first-round candidates are eliminated by the electoral law: the run-off is open only to candidates who have obtained a set number of votes at the first ballot, fixed by law at 5 per cent of votes cast in 1958 and 1962, 10 per cent of registered voters in 1967, 1968 and 1973, and at 12.5 per cent of registered voters from 1978. Moreover, most parties narrow the field further by concluding pre-election agreements providing for mutual withdrawals of candidates after the first ballot in favour of better-placed allies; the system therefore rewards parties that conclude such alliances and penalises those (usually on the political extremes) that do not. A variant on the two-ballot system is used for cantonal elections (to the councils of France's 100 *départements*) and for direct presidential elections: at the latter, only the two leading contenders are present at the run-off and the interval between ballots is two weeks instead of one. At regional elections, however, and at a single parliamentary election (in 1986), *proportionnelle départementale* has applied. This is a single-ballot proportional list system, under which each *département* is a multi-member constituency. Seats are shared out proportionally to the score of each list within the *département* (with some majoritarian correctives in the detailed rules, and an extension of constituencies to cover whole regions in 2004). A variation of this system is used for European elections, but the constituency base is different. From 1979 to 1999, the whole of France was a single constituency for the election of the nation's MEPs; in 2004 the country was divided into eight super-regions to elect French MEPs, who currently number seventy-eight. Finally, a hybrid two-ballot system is used for municipal elections in France's towns and cities, combining sufficient safeguards to ensure a clear municipal majority with a 'dose' of proportional representation to allow an opposition voice on the council.

The relationship of the electoral system to the configuration of parties is a complex one in any state. What is clear in the French case is, first, that the various electoral systems in force allow the space for multiparty competition (to a far greater extent than does the British system) and, secondly, that the coexistence of several systems at different levels of election have led to differing patterns of competition and co-operation between parties: for example, *proportionnelle départementale* does not include the same incentives as the two-ballot system for pre-election alliances between parties. The situation is further complicated when a referendum is called, for then the question at issue may cut across party divisions – especially if it concerns Europe. This was true of the referendums held in 1972, 1992 and (especially) 2005.

The position of parties in France is paradoxical in two senses. In the first place, they are simultaneously ubiquitous and weak. De Gaulle's ambition to create a presidency 'above parties', to be won by direct competition before the voters between individuals free of partisan ties, was quickly revealed as an uncharacteristically naive dream. The first direct presidential election in 1965 quickly became an occasion for partisan confrontation; the presidency has been the object of party (as well as personal) strategies ever since. Moreover, as is shown in Chapter 11, party divisions pervade (and thereby weaken) a very wide range of French interest groups, from trade unions to anti-racist groups to lawyers' or doctors' professional associations. If it is unsurprising that no aspect of politics is a party-free zone, it is more remarkable that parties have penetrated to other aspects of society where in other countries their intrusion would be considered unwelcome. In other ways, however, French parties can be considered weak. In the first place, parties command little respect among a public that is generally inclined to share de Gaulle's view of them. Successive surveys since 1985 have found between 18 and 24 per cent of respondents trusting 'parties in general', compared with ratings of 44–52 per cent for parliamentarians, 49–59 per cent for the civil service, 67–77 per cent for mayors – and even 25–32 per cent for 'politicians in general'. Anti-party sentiment was an important factor in the dramatic first ballot of the 2002 presidential elections, when candidates representing the mainstream 'parties of government' of Left and Right were supported by less than 46 per cent of the registered electorate between them, compared with 20.5 per cent for the extremes of Right and Left and 30.8 per cent for abstentions and spoilt ballots. This result allowed the far Right candidate (and fierce critic of established parties) Jean-Marie Le Pen to win a place at the run-off ballot. Secondly, parties are bad at attracting members (Table 7.1) – and worse at keeping them. Membership density in France (the ratio between the total number of party members and the total number of registered voters) has been among the lowest in Europe for half a century: a comparative study by Mair and van Biezen, based on figures from the late 1990s, put France, with a density of 1.3 per cent, nineteenth out of twenty European countries – ahead only of Poland, behind the UK, and well behind countries such as Germany (with a membership density of 2.9), Spain (3.4), or Italy (4.1). With the exception of the Communists, no French party has sustained a membership of over 200,000 on anything but an ephemeral basis; few have managed much over 100,000 for very long. All parties have difficulty sustaining activity among those members that they have. And even the Communists were known as a *parti-passoire*, a 'colander party', for the speed at which members passed through and out after the first flush of idealism. The third aspect of party weakness in France is electoral. Parties structure political competition, but they do not monopolise it: dissidents with local roots, who might be crushed by party machines elsewhere, may thrive in France. Finally, and partly for this reason, parties are impermanent. Splits and mergers occur with a regularity and an unscrupulousness that recall the world of business. Of all French parties in 2005, only the (much weakened) Communists could boast an unbroken existence since the fall of the Fourth Republic in 1958; all the others had either been founded for the first time since then (like the Greens, or the Front National) or relaunched one or more times (like the Socialists, the Gaullists, and the various incarnations of the non-Gaullist moderate Right). This instability exasperated Katz and Mair to such an extent that they chose simply to leave France out of their 1992 data book on party organisations in Western democracies.

A second paradox is that the untidiness and instability that characterise the landscape of French political parties coexist with a remarkable stability of the division between Left and Right. The ideological parameters of this division, and its limitations, were discussed in Chapter 1; some of its electoral dimensions will be considered in Chapter 9. The Left–Right divide is still easily recognised and readily used by the French when they talk about politics; it has shaped the successive *alternances* of different political forces in government since 1981; it will therefore structure the main division between the chapters on parties.

The divided Left

The defining event in the twentieth-century history of the French Left took place in December 1920 at Tours on the Loire. Here, at its first congress since World War I, France's Socialist Party (the SFIO, or Section Française de l'Internationale Ouvrière), which had been created out of several different socialist organisations just fifteen years earlier, split on the issue of whether to affiliate to Lenin's Communist International. A minority of the delegates (but a majority of parliamentarians) voted to remain in the

Table 7.1 France: party membership since 1945

	Communist		Socialist		Green		Centrist		Non-Gaullist moderate Right		Gaullist		Euro-sceptic Right	Extreme Right (Front National)		Est'd total*	Total as % of electorate
	Claimed	Estimated	Claimed	Estimated	Claimed	Estimated	Claimed	Estimated	Claimed	Estimated	Claimed	Estimated	Claimed	Claimed	Estimated		
late 1940s	1,000,000	800,000		340,000				125,000		50,000		400,000				1,675,000	6.7
late 1950s	425,150	300,000	85,000	60,000				40,000	10,000		280,000	20,000				430,000	1.7
early 1960s	420,000	330,000	74,000	55,000			40,000	20,000	7,500		150,000	86,000				498,500	1.8
late 1960s		380,000	84,000	60,000			25,000	15,000			180,000	160,000				615,000	2.2
early 1970s		450,000	146,000				25,000			3,000	238,000	100,000				724,000	2.4
late 1970s	632,000	520,000	200,000					17,500	145,000	8,500	760,347	160,000			900	906,900	2.6
early 1980s	600,000	380,000	200,000	180,000			43,000	12,500	60,000	10,000	850,000	200,000		65,000	10,000	792,500	2.8
late 1980s	604,285	330,000	180,000				49,000			20,000	142,113				50,000	771,113	2.1
early 1990s		220,000	150,000	125,000				12,500		25,000	148,000			48,000		578,500	1.5
late 1990s	210,000	100,000	148,795			10,000	40,000		33,000	10,000	80,424		33,000	60,000	42,000	464,200	1.3
post-2000	133,767		120,027			8,525	44,000**				180,858†		15,000	60,000		562,177	1.4

Sources: C. Ysmal, 'Transformations du militantisme et déclin des partis', in P. Perrineau (ed.), *L'Engagement politique: déclin ou mutation?* (Paris, Presses de la Fondation Nationale des Sciences Politiques, 1994), pp. 48–9; A. Knapp. *Le Gaullisme après de Gaulle* (Paris, Éditions du Seuil, 1996), p. 391; Y. Mény and A. Knapp, *Government and Politics in Western Europe* (3rd edition, Oxford, Oxford University Press, 1998), p. 55; P. Bréchon, *Les Partis politiques* (Paris, Montchrestien, 1999), pp. 107–8: *Le Monde*, 23 November 1999, 23–24 January 2000, 22 February 2000, 18 October 2004, 28 November 2004, 22 January 2005; http://www.pcf.fr (results of members' vote for 32nd congress, dates 28 February 2003); http://www.u-m-p.org/site/index.php, visited 13 July 2005; http://www.frontnational.com; press office, Mouvement pour la France.

Notes

* Annual totals are calculated on the basis of estimates where available, and of claimed figures where no estimates have been made.

Years for data
Communist: 1947, 1959, 1964, 1969, 1974, 1978, 1984, 1987, 1990, 1998, 2003
Socialist: 1946, 1958, 1963, 1968, 1974, 1978, 1983, 1988, 1992, 1999, 2004
Green: 1999, 2004
Centrist: 1946, 1958, 1962, 1968, 1974, 1979, 1983, 1986, 1992, 1997, 2005 (**New UDF)
Non-Gaullist moderate Right: 1947, 1958, 1961, 1970, 1979, 1983, 1986, 1992, 1999
Gaullist: 1947, 1958, 1963, 1969, 1973, 1978, 1985, 1989, 1994, 1999, 2005 (†UMP)
Euro-sceptic Right: 1999 (RPF), 2005 (MPF)
Front National: 1979, 1985, 1992, 1999, 2004 (claim for members 'and sympathisers').

old SFIO. Attached to a certain Marxist discourse about class struggle, but also steeped in the French republican tradition and respectful of the democratic rules of 'bourgeois' politics, they did not carry internationalism to the point of taking orders from Moscow. The majority of the delegates (though a minority of parliamentarians), on the other hand, voted for affiliation, and formed the Communist Party (Parti Communiste Français, or PCF). Though often unaware of the full implications, they were voting to become a Leninist party, and soon a Stalinist one: subordinate to Moscow's directives, contemptuous of 'bourgeois' political systems and freedoms, committed to creating a disciplined, hierarchical revolutionary vanguard organisation, and ready to use both open political processes and clandestine activities to smash the bourgeois capitalist state and replace it by a socialist republic of workers' councils.

For nearly half a century, the most important originality in the configuration of France's left-wing parties was the coexistence and competition of a Communist Party and a Socialist Party of something close to comparable strength, split by deep ideological divisions which have made alliances invariably problematic. Their stormy relationship has varied between fierce enmity (1920–34, 1939–41 and 1947–62); minimal, tactical alliances (1977–81 and 1984–96); and co-operation, more or less close (1934–38, 1941–47, 1962–77, 1981–84 and 1996 to the present). One major theme of this chapter is the struggle for predominance, inside and outside alliances, between these two *frères ennemis* of the Left. That struggle, as well as the fear of Communism among moderate voters in the context of the Cold War, helped to keep the Left out of power from the foundation of the Fifth Republic until May 1981. Both were attenuated (but not ended) by that year's victories and by the catastrophic decline of Communism thereafter, first within and then, from 1989, beyond France.

Even in a close and credible alliance, however, the Socialist and Communist Left has rarely commanded an electoral majority. In order to win elections, other, albeit smaller, elements have usually been necessary. Some votes, at second ballots, have come from the various Trotskyist and far left-wing groupings which between them have commanded anything up to 10 per cent of the vote, though usually a much lower figure (Tables 7.2 to 7.4). Support has also come from more moderate sources: from anti-clerical Radicals, the remains of the great governing party of the Third Republic; from left-wing Catholics, some of whom gravitated to the little Parti Socialiste Unifié; or, most recently, from the ecology movements. Such support is usually, though not always, secured via inter-party agreements. The most recent example of this is the *gauche plurielle* alliance which won the 1997 parliamentary elections and carried the Socialist leader, Lionel Jospin, to the premiership: it incorporated a relatively new player, the Greens, into the established party system, but with a cost in additional intra-coalition rivalries that were to lose Jospin his place at the second ballot of the presidential election in 2002.

A third theme, far from unique to France, concerns the difficulties of left-wing parties in delivering on their promises in an international capitalist context which has rarely been favourable. This was as true in 1936, when the Socialist Léon Blum took office at the head of a Popular Front coalition of Socialists, Communists and Radicals, as it was in 1981 when Mitterrand brought a comparable coalition to power with a particularly heavy burden of hopes and promises. The favourable economic context of the first four years of the Jospin premiership, including, briefly, an embarrassment of unexpectedly high tax receipts, was unusual. But even this benign environment did not dispel a tension between the need to meet voter expectations on social issues (and, for

Table 7.2 Results of National Assembly elections under the Fifth Republic[1]

Date	Extreme Left		Communists		Socialists		Other moderate Left[2]		Greens		Non-Gaullist moderate Right[3]		Gaullists		Extreme Right		Others		Total Left including Greens		Total moderate Left		Total Right		Total moderate Right		Total		Valid votes cast	Blank and spoilt ballots
	% of vote	seats	% of vote	seats	% of vote	seats	% of vote	seats	% of vote	seats	% of vote	seats	% of vote	seats	% of vote	seats	% of vote	seats	% of vote	seats	% of vote	seats	% of vote	seats	% of vote	seats	% of vote	seats	% of total electorate	
1958	0.0	0	18.9	10	15.5	43	10.9	39	n.c.[5]	0	31.1	172	20.6	216	2.6	1	0.5	0	45.2	92	26.4	82	54.3	389	51.7	388	100.0	481	75.2	2.0
1962	2.0	0	21.9	41	12.4	66	7.4	44	n.c.	0	23.0	98	32.4	233	0.8	0	0.0	0	43.8	151	19.9	110	56.2	331	55.4	331	100.0	482	66.6	2.1
1967	2.2	0	22.5	73	18.9	123	0.0	0	n.c.	0	23.7	91	32.1	200	0.6	0	0.0	0	43.6	196	18.9	123	56.4	291	55.8	291	100.0	487	79.3	1.8
1968	4.0	0	20.1	34	16.5	58	0.0	0	n.c.	0	20.8	102	38.0	293	0.1	0	0.5	0	40.6	92	16.5	58	59.0	395	58.9	395	100.0	487	78.6	1.4
1973	3.2	0	21.4	73	19.1	102	2.1	3	n.c.	0	29.0	129	24.6	183	0.5	0	0.0	0	45.8	178	21.2	105	54.1	312	53.6	312	100.0	490	81.3	1.8
1978	3.3	0	20.6	86	22.8	115	3.5	0	2.0	0	23.9	136	22.8	154	0.8	0	0.2	0	52.2	201	28.4	115	47.5	290	46.7	290	100.0	491	81.6	1.6
1981	1.2	0	16.1	44	36.1	289	2.2	0	1.1	0	21.7	70	21.2	88	0.3	0	0.0	0	56.7	333	39.3	289	43.2	158	42.9	158	100.0	491	69.9	1.0
1986[4]	1.5	0	9.7	35	30.8	212	2.0	4	1.2	0	44.6[4]	136	[4]	155	10.1	35	0.1	0	45.2	251	34.0	216	54.7	326	44.6	291	100.0	577	75.1	3.4
1988	0.4	0	11.3	25	34.9	275	2.6	5	0.3	0	21.3	141	19.2	130	9.8	1	0.2	0	49.6	305	37.9	280	50.3	272	40.5	271	100.0	577	64.7	1.4
1993	1.7	0	9.1	23	17.8	57	2.4	13	11.1	0	23.8	227	20.3	257	12.9	0	0.3	0	42.7	93	31.8	70	57.0	484	44.1	484	100.0	577	65.8	3.7
1997	2.6	0	9.9	36	23.8	250	4.0	26	6.9	8	20.7	116	15.4	140	15.3	1	1.2	0	47.3	320	34.8	284	51.4	257	36.2	256	100.0	577	65.1	3.3
2002	2.8	0	4.8	21	24.1	141	3.8	13	5.7	3	10.1[3]	30[3]	33.3[6]	369[6]	12.7	0	2.7	0	41.2	178	33.6	157	56.1	399	43.4	399	100.0	577	63.0	1.4

Sources: Based on A. Lancelot, *Les élections nationales sous la Vᵉ République* (3rd edition, Paris, Presses Universitaires de France, 1998); *Le Monde*, 12 June 2002, for 2002.

Notes

1 All figures for *votes* are given as a percentage of the first-ballot vote in metropolitan France only, except those for 2002, which include overseas *départements* and territories. All figures for *seats* are total numbers, including seats for both metropolitan France and for overseas *départements* and territories (except for 1958, where Algerian seats have been excluded). Deputies not registered with any parliamentary group (normally between ten and twenty in an average Assembly) are classified in the table according to nearest partisan proximity.

2 'Other moderate Left': chiefly Radicals and 'various Left'. Radical candidates were part of the Socialist-led federation in 1967 and 1968, and their votes are classified under the Socialists' for these years. From 1973 to 1993, Radicals ran under their own colours but joined the Socialist parliamentary group. For 1997, 'Other moderate Left' includes the Radicals and Jean-Pierre Chevènement's Mouvement des Citoyens, which together with the Greens formed the Radical-Citoyen-Vert group.

3 Up to 1973, this classification includes both the Centrists outside the Gaullist-led majority and those other groups of the non-Gaullist moderate Right that supported the government, chiefly Valéry Giscard d'Estaing's Républicains Indépendants and, for 1973, the majority Centrists. From 1978 to 1997, the non-Gaullist moderate Right consists of the UDF and 'various Right'. For 2002, it includes all moderate right-wing candidates not bearing the endorsement of the Union pour la Majorité Présidentielle.

4 The 1986 elections, unlike all others listed here, were run on a proportional list system with a single ballot. Gaullists and UDF ran joint lists in most *départements*, making their respective votes impossible to separate. The 44.6 per cent under non-Gaullist moderate Right therefore includes the whole of the moderate right-wing vote, Gaullist and non-Gaullist.

5 No candidates.

6 The 2002 figures are for the Union pour la Majorité Présidentielle, a broad right-wing group with the RPR as its core component, but including substantial forces from the non-Gaullist moderate Right as well.

Table 7.3 Results of presidential elections (first ballots), 1965–2002

	Extreme Left	Communist	Socialist	Other moderate Left	Greens/ Ecology	Total Left including Greens	Non-Gaullist moderate Right	Gaullist	Other moderate Right	Extreme Right	Others	Total moderate Right	Total Right
1965	n.c.	n.c.	31.7	n.c.	n.c.	31.7	15.6	44.7	1.7	5.2	1.2	62.0	67.2
1969	1.1	21.3	5.0	3.6	n.c.	31.0	23.3	44.5	1.3	n.c.	n.c.	69.1	69.1
1974	2.7	n.c.	43.3	n.c.	1.3	47.4	32.6	15.1	3.7	0.8	0.4	51.6	52.4
1981	2.3	15.4	25.9	3.3	3.9	50.8	28.3	21.0	n.c.	n.c.	n.c.	49.3	49.3
1988	4.5	6.8	34.1	n.c.	3.8	49.1	16.5	20.0	n.c.	14.4	n.c.	36.5	50.9
1995	5.3	8.6	23.3	n.c.	3.3	40.5	18.6	20.8	4.7	15.0	0.3	44.1	59.1
2002	10.4	3.4	16.1	7.6	5.3	42.3	12.6	19.9	1.2	19.2	4.2	33.7	52.9

Sources: Based on A. Lancelot, Les élections nationales sous la Ve République (3rd edition, Paris, Presses Universitaires de France, 1998); Le Monde for 2002.

Note

n.c. = no candidate.

Table 7.4 Results of presidential elections (second ballots), 1965–2002 (all figures as percentage of votes cast, including overseas *départements* and territories)

	1965	1969	1974	1981	1988	1995	2002
Left	44.8 (Mitterrand)	n.c.	49.2 (Mitterrand)	51.8 (Mitterrand)	54.0 (Mitterrand)	47.4 (Jospin)	n.c.
Centre-Right	n.c.	41.8 (Poher)	n.c.	n.c.	n.c.	n.c.	n.c.
Right	55.2 (de Gaulle)	58.2 (Pompidou)	50.8 (Giscard)	48.2 (Giscard)	46.0 (Chirac)	52.6 (Chirac)	82.2 (Chirac)
Extreme Right	n.c.	n.c.	n.c.	n.c.	n.c.	n.c.	17.8 (Le Pen)

Sources: Based on A. Lancelot, *Les élections nationales sous la Ve République* (3rd edition, Paris, Presses Universitaires de France, 1998); *Le Monde* for 2002.

Note

n.c. = no candidate present at second ballot.

the Greens, on environmental ones as well) while establishing credibility as economic managers – 'managers of capitalism', in Communist parlance – which has inevitably fuelled conflict and competition both between and within the parties of the Left.

The Parti Communiste Français (PCF)

With a quarter of the vote and the status of France's biggest party under the Fourth Republic, a fifth of the vote for the first twenty years of the Fifth Republic, but under 10 per cent at almost every election since 1984, the PCF has undergone such an accelerated decline that it now requires an effort of imagination to recall the attraction it held for former generations of French men and women, and its critical importance within the French party system. It owed its attractiveness to five main elements. First, the PCF succeeded early on in adapting its Marxism-Leninism to a more home-grown French revolutionary tradition, thereby winning the support of 'red peasant' areas of France, where the vote had always gravitated towards the far Left. Second, this reconciliation of the Moscow-led PCF with French tradition was greatly reinforced by the PCF's own role as the major force in the French internal Resistance, and from the Soviet Union's role in the defeat of Germany in World War II. The Soviet Union's prestige lasted far longer in France than in Britain, America or Germany; a large swathe of the left-wing intelligentsia contrived to be wilfully ignorant of the existence of show trials and labour camps until the 1970s. Third, for its main target group, the French working class, the PCF offered not only a mythical Communist future free of the familiar daily round of poverty and exploitation, but also an alternative present, with associations (anything from the Communist-led trade union, the Confédération Générale du Travail, to the Union des Femmes Françaises, the Secours Populaire, the Mouvement de la Jeunesse Communiste, the Fédération Sportive Générale du Travail, or Tourisme et Travail, a Communist-run travel operator specialising in trips to the Soviet Union and Eastern Europe) and political activities that gave self-respect or simply affordable enjoyment to those who participated in them, as well as a chance of upward social mobility for the most gifted through party or union organisations. Fourth, the Communists' local elected officials, and especially mayors in working-class suburbs, won support, in the words of Denis Brogan, 'by methods that recalled Joseph Chamberlain in Birmingham rather than Lenin in Petrograd': they showed dynamism, honesty and competence in getting housing, schools, and health and leisure facilities built and properly run at a time when such achievements were novelties. Finally, the creation during the 1920s, at Moscow's insistence and almost certainly with Moscow's money, of a hard-core revolutionary vanguard, able to operate openly or underground, combined with an expanding base in civil society and in local government to give the PCF France's only real mass party organisation. At its peak in the immediate post-war years, it probably attracted some 800,000 members; under the Fifth Republic it oscillated between a quarter and a half million, at least until the early 1990s.

The Fifth Republic and the decline of the PCF

The PCF opposed the Fifth Republic and suffered for it: its vote dropped from 25.9 per cent in 1956 to 18.9 per cent in 1958 (see Figure 7.1), while the two-ballot system and the party's lack of electoral allies ensured that the number of Communist Deputies fell from 150 to just ten. The next two decades, however, saw a modest recovery, with the

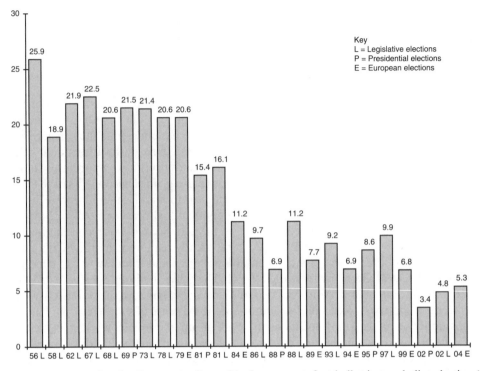

Figure 7.1 Votes for the Communist Party (% of votes cast, first ballot in two-ballot elections), 1956–2004.

party settling to a steady 20-plus per cent of the vote (see Table 7.2). The electoral decline under the Fifth Republic only started after 1979. Four sets of figures illustrate its dimensions. First, in the parliamentary elections of 1978, the PCF attracted 5.8 million voters, or 20.6 per cent of the vote; by the 1997 parliamentary elections both figures had more than halved, to 2.5 million voters or 9.9 per cent of votes cast; five years later, at the parliamentary elections of June 2002, they had halved again, to 1.26 million, or 4.8 per cent. At the presidential election of the same year, the Communist candidate Robert Hue had attracted fewer than a million voters, and a vote share, at 3.4 per cent, lower than that of two of his three competitors from the extreme (Trotskyist) Left. Second, whereas in 1978 the PCF won over 20 per cent of the vote in forty-five – nearly half – of the ninety-six *départements* of metropolitan France, in 1997 it reached this figure in just three *départements*. By the 2002 parliamentary elections, not only did it fail to win 20 per cent of the vote in even one *département*; it was obliged, in order to keep the handful of seats needed to form a parliamentary group, to enter into unprecedented swaps of constituencies with Socialist and Green allies from the first ballot. Third, whereas in 1978, with 39 per cent of the blue-collar vote (more than any other party), the PCF could still justify its claim to be the party of the working class, by 1997 its share of the blue-collar vote had shrunk to 15 per cent, barely half that of the Socialists – and two-thirds that of the far right-wing Front National. In 2002, Hue was supported by fewer workers than was Jean St-Josse, the candidate of Chasse, Pêche, Nature, Traditions; even at the June parliamentary elections that ensued, the PCF share of the blue-collar vote was a mere 6 per cent, a fifth that of the Socialists. Finally, although the sharpest drop occurred in the six years after its score of 20.8 per cent in 1978, with Georges Marchais, the party's secretary-general since 1972, managing just 15.4 per cent as a presidential candidate in 1981 and then leading the party's list at the European elections of 1984 to a mere 11.2 per cent, the decline has continued since 1984, and even steepened between 1997 and a modest and partial recovery in 2004. The party has been increasingly thrown back on its most resilient bastions, often sustained by control of municipal office; even here, it is now threatened, and dependent in most years on support from Socialists and even Greens.

Many of the sources of the Communists' decline are to be sought in the reasons for the party's success. They may be discussed under six headings.

The passing of the Resistance generation

The prestige that its role in the Resistance brought to the PCF was inevitably a wasting asset. It affected, above all, the age cohort that underwent its formative political experiences – normally in early adulthood – at the time of the Occupation. By the late 1970s, that generation was a minority nearing the upper end of the age pyramid. Newer voters, baby-boomers born after 1945, were less sensitive to the appeal of *anciens résistants*. The same applied to the Communists' elected officials: again by the late 1970s, a generation of men (and women) whose popularity with voters had been founded on their Resistance role was nearing retirement. Equally appealing successors were at times hard to find. The other great party of the Resistance, the Gaullists, also experienced the difficulties of generational change in the 1970s.

The numerical decline of the party's core electorate of workers and peasants

By the late 1970s, the PCF's electoral reserves – blue-collar workers, especially if unionised and in big firms, and, on a more regional basis, small peasants – had begun to shrink. The numerical decline of the peasantry is easily demonstrated: the number of French men and women working on the land fell by two-thirds between 1954 and 1982. The issue of blue-collar workers is more complex: the absolute decline of the whole class, from about 8 million to about 7 million since the 1970s, counts for less than the shrinkage of the big battalions of industrial workers with stable jobs in large enterprises (such as steel plants), unionised and long favourable to the PCF, plus the replacement, in some of the worst-paid or least attractive jobs, of French people by immigrants who did not have the vote. In addition, a declining proportion of voters retained a subjective identity as members of the working class. These slow social changes, like the passing of the Resistance generation, did not signal the PCF's inevitable eclipse; but they did require the party to appeal to new groups and generations.

The collapse of the prestige of the Soviet Union (and then of the Soviet Union tout court)

The PCF's defining characteristic at its foundation was its subordination, as the 'Section Française de l'Internationale Communiste', to orders from Moscow, determined by the interests of the 'international workers' movement' – in other words, of Soviet foreign policy. Maurice Thorez, party leader from 1930 till his death (on holiday by the Black

Sea) in 1964, and the generation who surrounded him at the top of the PCF, had been hand-picked from Moscow. To a greater extent than the leaders of almost any other Western Communist Party, they were Stalinists and proud of it. Their reaction to Khrushchev's denunciation of Stalin in 1956 was one of stunned disbelief. When first China and then Italy challenged the claims of the Soviet Union to lead the world Communist movement, the PCF energetically backed the Russians.

A slow and discontinuous process of de-Sovietisation of the PCF nevertheless opened after Thorez's death. Party leaders, and the PCF daily *L'Humanité*, cautiously criticised the crushing of the 'Prague Spring' by Warsaw Pact forces in August 1968, and voiced disapproval of the treatment of selected Soviet dissidents over the ensuing decade. The PCF leadership stopped referring to the Soviet Union as a model, instead claiming their attachment to *un socialisme à la française* and stressing the independence of their own policies from Moscow's dictates (which probably had an element of truth, if only because the Soviet leadership had long since renounced any dreams of revolution in Western Europe and was quite comfortable with de Gaulle, Pompidou and Giscard, none of whom was precisely pro-American, in the Élysée).

But for the party leadership, de-Sovietisation was always a tactical, and therefore reversible, choice. As both international *détente* and the alliance with the Socialists in France turned sour at the end of the 1970s, the old Soviet links were reaffirmed. At the PCF's Twenty-third Congress in 1979, Marchais declared the overall record of the Soviet bloc to be *globalement positif*; early the following year, he proclaimed his support for the Soviet invasion of Afghanistan on live television from Moscow; the year after that, the French Communists declared their support for the military *coup* against the Solidarity movement in Poland. The timing could not have been worse, for the Soviet Union was speedily losing what credit it had among the French, and even among PCF sympathisers. A survey in December 1972 showed 28 per cent of respondents, and 62 per cent of the PCF's own supporters, agreeing with the *globalement positif* view of the Soviet achievement; ten years later, the figures had fallen to just 11 per cent overall and 35 per cent of PCF sympathisers. Marchais, in other words, succeeded in reviving the Communists' reputation as Moscow's men at precisely the moment when such a reputation had become electorally fatal. Nor did the softer image of Gorbachev's Soviet Union improve matters, for the PCF was noticeably reserved about the Gorbachev reforms. Not surprisingly, the end of the Soviet Union forced the PCF into an independence for which its ageing leadership was wholly unprepared. In a broader sense, too, the discredit into which Marxism fell meant that the PCF lost its ideological bearings.

The decline of counter-societies and subcultures

In its heyday, roughly from the mid-1930s to the mid-1960s, the PCF was able to lock some at least of its supporters into what Annie Kriegel called a Communist 'counter-society', a subculture in which the party's press and wide range of satellite associations took care of the dedicated Communist's every free moment. Control of local government helped too, especially in working-class bastions in the suburbs of Paris and other cities, with their *rues Lénine*, their *avenues Maurice-Thorez* or their *centres sportifs Youri Gagarine*. But from the 1960s, the counter-society began to fall apart under the impact of a wider society that was more individualist and more consumerist – and where, with 10 million televisions in France (as there were by 1970), the 'dominant' (capitalist) culture could be beamed into almost every living room. By the late 1980s, *L'Humanité* was seeking, like any other daily newspaper, to cut costs and make do with fewer journalists, while the party's provincial press had almost ceased to exist. The Communist subculture was not alone in fading away in this manner; it was paralleled by the withering of a whole range of Catholic organisations, which had still been thriving in the 1950s among groups ranging from students to farmers.

The changing stakes of urban governance

'Municipal Communism' reached a peak in 1977, when the party elected or re-elected mayors to 72 out of France's 221 biggest towns. No major town had been lost to the PCF since 1959. But in the municipal elections of 1983, 1989 and 1995, 33 of the party's major municipalities were lost (Table 7.5). This reversal of fortunes is partly linked to the PCF's overall decline. But it also resulted from the changing demands being made on local government. While at a time of more or less full employment, Communist mayors were purposeful and competent at building housing, schools, clinics, sports halls and cultural centres, they were far less successful at delivering the economic development that became the key voter priority as joblessness rose in the 1980s. Many Communist mayors, moreover, lost patience with what they saw as their party's lack of realism in its attitude to local government: some, like Robert Jarry of Le Mans or Fernand Micouraud of Vierzon, left the PCF altogether, while others like Jacques Rimbault of Bourges, maintained a 'semi-detached' existence. In either case, the PCF's reputation as a supplier of good local government had been badly damaged by the mid-1980s.

The decline of authoritarian organisational models

At Moscow's behest, the PCF of the 1920s adopted the Leninist model of party organisation known as 'democratic centralism'. Based on the cell in the factory or neighbourhood, the section in the firm, town or canton, the federation in the *département*, and the central committee, *bureau politique* and general secretariat at national level, the system was highly centralist and hardly at all democratic. It had three major principles: the presentation at elections to party office, at all levels, of a single candidate for each

Table 7.5 Party control of towns of over 30,000 inhabitants (total number 221, at 1977 population figures) after local elections, 1971–2001

Mayor's party	1971	1977	1983	1989	1995	2001
PCF	50	72	53	45	39	28
PS	46	81	60	72	68	65
Other Left	7	6	2	8	13	10
Les Verts	0	0	0	0	0	1
Total Left	103	159	115	125	120	103
Gaullists	35	16	44	43	47	55
Non-Gaullist moderate Right (UDF from 1983)	83	46	42	44	42	42
Other Right	0	0	20	9	11	20
Extreme Right	0	0	0	0	1	0

Sources: P. Martin, *Les élections municipales en France* (Paris, La Documentation Française, 2001); *Le Monde*.

post, vetted (and usually chosen) in advance by the immediately superior level of the party; a ban on all horizontal contacts between, for example, two cells or two sections without reference to the superior level, ensuring the effective isolation of dissidents; and the presentation of a single policy text for discussion at the party's congresses. The party's dissidents in the 1940s and 1950s were subjected to ritual humiliations reminiscent of Stalin's show trials. For a dedicated full-time party official, the punishment of expulsion, though less severe than the gulag or the bullet, entailed loss of livelihood and, frequently, psychological trauma. Perhaps more than anything else, this rigid style of organisation cut the PCF off from the young revolutionaries of May 1968. From the 1970s, though, dissidence began to lose its terrors and was embarked upon by increasing numbers of leading party members, including Jean Elleinstein, official historian of the party, Henri Fiszbin, head of the Paris federation, Claude Poperen, emblematic figure of the Renault workers, and Pierre Juquin, official party spokesman from 1976 to 1985. And at a time when the PCF was trying to demonstrate its democratic credentials in other areas (for example, by abandoning another Leninist concept, the dictatorship of the proletariat, at the Twenty-second Congress in 1976), democratic centralism was regularly used as evidence by opponents seeking to deny the sincerity of the party's commitment to real democratic values. By the early 1980s, in short, the PCF's authoritarian style of organisation had become an electoral liability without even fulfilling its main function of ensuring a single party line. Once again, the PCF was not alone in this case. The Gaullist party, also described by its own more mischievous members as functioning on the democratic centralist model, had difficulty, from the 1970s, in adapting to the open and public expression of several different viewpoints.

In all of these respects, then, the bases of the PCF's earlier strength became sources of weakness by the late 1970s or early 1980s. But two other causes of decline should also be added.

The new strategic environment of the Fifth Republic

The new constitution, which the PCF opposed in 1958, placed the Communists in a hostile institutional environment. The loss of 140 out of 150 Deputies in the November 1958 parliamentary elections was a brutal demonstration of the dangers of isolation in a two-ballot electoral system. Moreover, it became clear that, against the cohesive Gaullist-led coalition, the opposition would need an equally cohesive programme. Those two factors pushed the PCF towards alliance with the only possible partners, the Socialists, in a slow, discontinuous process beginning with second-ballot withdrawal agreements in the 1962 parliamentary elections, and culminating in the signature of the Common Programme of the Left a decade later, in June 1972.

Unlike earlier alliances of the Popular Front or Liberation periods, the union of the Left benefited the Socialists more than it did the PCF. It did so for two reasons. First, the PCF was handicapped by direct presidential elections. Everyone knew that no Communist had a chance of winning the support of over half the voters at a run-off ballot. Communists implicitly acknowledged this fundamental disqualification in 1965 and again in 1974: on both occasions they backed François Mitterrand from the first round. Second, Mitterrand himself managed to establish a revived Socialist Party (of which he became first secretary in 1971) as the more credible and more modern partner in the union, and thereby succeeded in his (openly expressed) ambition of using the union of the Left to poach 3 million of the PCF's 5 million voters. His supreme political achievement was to lock the PCF into a dynamic of union, despite the party leadership's growing misgivings; to establish the Socialists as the larger party of the Left as early as 1974 (for the first time in over three decades); and thereby to create the bases of the left-wing victory of 1981. These developments were observed with dismay by the PCF leadership, which tried to get out of the union while placing the blame on their allies. But the hunger for change among Communist as well as Socialist voters, after two decades of right-wing government, prevented this. After the PCF leadership demanded the radicalisation of the Common Programme in 1977, and effectively sabotaged the Left's chances at the 1978 parliamentary elections, Mitterrand therefore simply relied on the voters' support and behaved as if the alliance still existed. The result was that at the first round of the 1981 presidential elections, not only did Mitterrand win 3 million more votes than Marchais, he had also ensured that he would get the second-round support of Marchais's voters. After 1981, the Communist leadership faced two possible strategic choices, neither of them palatable: to join the Socialists, as they did from 1981 to 1984, as the junior partner in government, masters of none of the major choices (and especially not of the 1983 economic U-turn); or to leave government, as they did in 1984, but maintain the minimal tactical alliance necessary to safeguard at least some parliamentary seats and town halls.

Leadership failure

No West European Communist Party prospered in the last quarter of the twentieth century. And many of the causes of the PCF's decline listed above, such as sociological and institutional change or the discrediting of the Soviet Union, may be seen as beyond the party's control. Equally, however, it is clear that Marchais himself accelerated the PCF's decline, notably by reinforcing rather than severing the umbilical cord with Moscow, and by failing either to drop the liability of democratic centralism or to pitch the party's appeal to a wider range of social groups as core social bases of Communist support shrank. In particular, the party's apparent inability, in the generation after May 1968, to win the loyalty either of women or of second-generation immigrants – two groups who suffered quite disproportionately from the onset of recession from the late 1970s on, at the same time as their capacity for mobilisation and political expression grew – can be ascribed at least partly to leadership failure. When the 73-year-old Marchais relinquished the post of secretary-general to Robert Hue at the Twenty-eighth Congress in 1994, he was handing over a party damaged almost as much by his own leadership as by outside circumstances.

The PCF's mutation: too little, too late?

Hue, though very much a Marchais protégé, rapidly embarked on a process of party 'mutation' (which he detailed, characteristically for a French party leader, in a book). This at least attempted to address the causes of the PCF's decline.

Democratic centralism

This was abandoned officially at the Twenty-eighth Congress, and to a significant extent in practice over the years after 1994. A series of top-level changes spread over the following decade saw the party secretary-general replaced by the national secretary, the *bureau politique* by the executive committee, and the central committee by the national council, while the party secretariat disappeared. At the same time the cell structure at the base of the party, which was functioning with steadily greater difficulty as activism declined, gave way at Hue's behest to 'thematic networks'. Such changes were not merely cosmetic. Activists were invited to comment on the texts for discussion at the Thirtieth Congress, held in March 2000, not within the confines of their cells or through the carefully vetted columns of *L'Humanité*, but on the party's website; at the Thirty-second Congress in 2003, members were, for the first time, invited to vote for competing motions (that of the leadership won, but with a fairly modest 55 per cent of the vote). Factions – a European wing led by the economist Philippe Herzog, the *refondateurs* who considered that change had not gone far enough and orthodox groups of varying degrees of conservatism – were tolerated as quasi-autonomous organisations, some even claiming public party funding in their own right; Communists opposed to the 'mutation' held their own public meetings to attack it and the new leadership, and went unpunished. Well-entrenched local officials chose often ambiguous relationships with the party, discreetly downplaying or even dropping their party affiliation, demanding the PCF's endorsement of their electoral candidacies, but being prepared to run against official Communist candidates if necessary; one PCF dissident even ran in June 2002 against an incumbent Communist in the Paris suburb of Aubervilliers. The former iron cohesion of the PCF's parliamentary group has crumbled, with several of the Jospin government's bills, such as the 35-hour week, provoking deep controversy. Hue was in no position to impose the old disciplines on parliamentarians like Maxime Gremetz or Alain Bocquet, president of the National Assembly group, who had served for many years under Marchais and retained a significant following in the party. But he did succeed, at the Thirtieth Congress, in achieving a (relative) liberalisation of the party's structures while at the same time weeding out the more Stalinist office-holders in its middle and upper ranks, and replacing them with younger members and more women. Two-thirds of the forty-six members of the executive college elected in March 2000, for example, were new to high party office (and two-fifths were women, a proportion that roughly reflected the membership as a whole). At the same time there was always an element of window-dressing about the end of democratic centralism: whatever the changes in the PCF's leading bodies, dissidents claimed that nine-tenths of them still consisted of full-time officials beholden to the leadership. A true gauge of the PCF's democratisation might be a wholesale purge of the top leaders responsible for its dismal electoral performance. This has not happened.

The record of the Soviet Union

The Soviet experience was now described as *globalement négatif* and past 'errors' in this area were officially acknowledged. The timing of these discoveries, however, was hardly such as to restore the PCF's credibility (especially given the dissent of the Stalinist minority). And Communists still had difficulty coming to terms with the full extent of the crimes committed under Soviet rule.

The 'revolutionary' label

The PCF has virtually dropped its identity as a revolutionary party and now claims merely to seek a peaceful and progressive evolution to a more just society (the neologism *révolutionnement* was briefly used in 2000 to express this); Hue went on record as saying that 'Communists are not adversaries of the market', appeared in a dinner suit among the glitterati of the Cannes film festival – a brief but powerful symbol – and hired out the party's headquarters, built in the prosperous 1970s, for smart fashion shows. These excesses have been abandoned since the defeats of 2002, but without any serious return to the 'revolutionary' label.

The special relationship with the working class

The prime revolutionary class for Marxists, still the fixation of the PCF in the late Marchais era, has also been effectively abandoned. Party documents prefer the term *salariés* (meaning wage- and salary-earners) to 'workers'. And blue-collar workers now count for barely a quarter of those party members who are economically active. At the same time, the party under Hue began to pitch for support among groups often left out by the old workerism, including second-generation immigrants, women, sexual minorities and (to judge from the enthusiasm of the PCF's support for protests against high petrol taxes in September 2000) motorists.

The alliance with the Socialists

The union of the Left was effectively revived in a series of negotiations following the 1995 presidential election, and came to fruition in the victory of the *gauche plurielle* in June 1997. The PCF was rewarded with two middle-ranking ministries in the Jospin government, Jean-Claude Gayssot at Transport and Marie-Georges Buffet at Youth and Sport, as well as a further junior post. They were popular ministers in their respective spheres, in particular Buffet when she spearheaded a campaign against doping in the Tour de France. And whereas in 1981–84 Marchais had remained highly critical of the Socialist-led government, even when it included four Communist ministers, Hue was noticeably moderate in his reservations; the PCF remained a *gauche plurielle* partner, and the ministers stayed in office, until the electoral defeats of 2002. Jospin responded with the necessary appropriate gestures on details of policy-making, ensuring, for example, that Communist views were taken into account when France's electricity market was partially opened to international competition. Even Hue's presidential campaign of 2002, while clearly differentiated from Jospin's (it was more Eurosceptical, more focused on the defence of French public services and on new legislation to prevent redundancies), was not noticeably critical of the government's record.

The group's preservation was also due to incumbency, whether local or national; the PCF's sitting Deputies and local office-holders, all of them elected at second ballots with Socialist votes, accounted for the totality of the increase of a quarter of a million votes in the PCF's June 2002 score against Hue's presidential support two months earlier. The withdrawal of Socialist co-operation, therefore, would remove Communists from national and local elective office – depriving the party both of the nationwide presence and visibility that office procures, and of income: vital assets that (for the moment) distinguish the PCF from a small far-left grouping.

Hue's initiatives quickly improved the PCF's general popularity: the percentage of poll respondents declaring a 'good opinion' of the party, and of its leader, rose from the mid-teens (under Marchais) to the high twenties. The Communist vote, on the other hand, continued to drop like a stone. Hue not only registered a record low presidential result in April 2002; he lost his parliamentary seat the following June, and moved to a dignified retirement at the Senate, leaving the party leadership to Buffet at the Thirty-second congress in April 2003.

Buffet's PCF, predictably after an electoral defeat, was inclined to return to its traditional values, the defence of jobs and public services, and critical of the Jospin government's record. In 2005, Buffet found the campaign against the European constitutional treaty a perfect issue on which to mobilise, centred as it was on core concerns (opposition to a free-market Europe) and full of opportunities both to highlight differences with the Socialist leadership and to bring Socialist 'dissidents' into the Communist orbit. The soundness of her instincts was confirmed when some 95 per cent of Communist supporters who voted said no to the treaty. But the PCF had competitors for the anti-capitalist, Eurosceptical, anti-globalisation, left-wing vote both in non-party groups like Attac and in the Trotskyist parties, long dismissed by the PCF leadership as irresponsible *groupuscules*. In purely electoral terms, indeed, the party that Buffet inherited was hardly more important than the Trotskyist organisations, now courted as comrades as well as competed against as rivals.

In other respects, however, the party remained something more. It has a unique place in France's political culture that the Trotskyists lack – though this is both ambiguous and hard to turn to electoral advantage. More importantly, it retained, in 2005, 21 Deputies, 11 Senators and 3 MEPs, as well as a significant number of mayors and other local elected officials, something resembling a nationwide organisation with several dozen full-time employees, and *L'Humanité*. The difficulty for the PCF, however, is that these assets are shrinking – as is shown by the repeated rounds of redundancies among the party's officials and the falling circulation of *L'Humanité*, which has had to call in capitalist shareholders like Bouygues or Lagardère to bail it out. Worse, these assets depend to a significant degree on the PCF's ability to win elective office and to attract the public finance that goes with it, as well as the contributions it has usually been able to extract from those elected on the Communist ticket. Winning elective office requires allies, and bigger ones than the Trotskyists; and material survival depends on the PCF's willingness to keep its radicalism within bounds acceptable to such allies. The Communists' political strategy, in short, is framed by their state of dependency on the goodwill of their much larger partner in the former *gauche plurielle*, the Socialist Party.

The Parti Socialiste (PS)

The Socialist Party at the outset of the Fifth Republic was small, ageing, divided and discredited. Membership of what was still called the SFIO had fallen from a peak of 335,000 in 1946 to some 70,000, most of them elderly mayors or local councillors. The party's share of the vote fell from 23.4 per cent in November 1946 to 15.5 per cent in 1958 and 12.4 per cent in 1962. Wedded, in principle, to Marxist ideas of class struggle, the Socialists showed no haste, in practice, to smash capitalism, and based much of their left-wing self-image on an archaic and insular anti-clericalism, itself rendered less credible by the 'Third Force' governing alliance with the Catholic Mouvement Républicain Populaire (MRP). No party was more tainted than the SFIO by the compromises and chaos of the Fourth Republic. The SFIO leader, Guy Mollet, won the premiership in 1956 on a platform of peace in Algeria, but promptly escalated the war by sending conscripts to fight. Dissent on the Algerian issue, and on the question of support for the new constitution, led a minority to leave the party in September 1958 to form the Parti Socialiste Autonome (which united with other small groups to form the Parti Socialiste Unifié (PSU) in 1960).

Yet the late twentieth-century Socialists could make some claim to be France's 'natural' governing party. For fourteen of the twenty-one years after 1981, the refounded Parti Socialiste was in government (1981–86, 1988–93 and 1997–2002). For fourteen years too, a Socialist was in the Élysée (Mitterrand's second term ended in 1995). The PS overtook the PCF vote in the 1970s, has dominated the Left throughout the period since 1981, and for most of it has also been France's largest single party. However, as Tables 7.2 and 7.3 show, the Socialists' fortunes since 1958 have been extremely varied. Chronologically, they can be divided into six periods.

- *The 1960s*, a decade of internal conflict and confusion, at the end of which the Socialist presidential candidate, Gaston Defferre, achieved barely more than 5 per cent of the vote.
- *The 1970s*, a period of revival, as the newly refounded PS renewed its organisation under the leadership of François Mitterrand and won increasing electoral support, overtaking the PCF and ultimately winning the presidency and a parliamentary majority in 1981.
- *The 1980s*, when the PS established itself as a party of government, staying in power for the whole decade (except for two years of cohabitation between Mitterrand and a right-wing government in 1986–88) but failing to achieve its ambitions to transform France's economy and society.
- *The early 1990s*, when a combination of scandals and recession drove the Socialist vote below 20 per cent, the PS out of office and the defeated Prime Minister Pierre Bérégovoy to suicide, in 1993.
- *The later 1990s*, when a partial electoral recovery secured the Socialists' return to government, with Communist and Green allies and under the leadership of Lionel Jospin, in 1997.
- *The period since 2002*, when the PS, now in opposition, won significant electoral successes (notably at the 2004 regional and European elections) against the incumbent right-wing government, but without developing a coherent strategy for a return to government or avoiding its most damaging split since 1971 over the referendum of 2005.

The pivotal figure in this chequered record remains Mitterrand. In the crucial early 1970s, he fixed a clear alliance strategy, built a majority out of the Socialists' endemic factional strife, gave the party the leadership required to win power, renewed its membership and elites, transformed its ideology and policies, placed its finances on a sound (but unfortunately illegal) footing, and enhanced its electoral appeal. These seven themes remain central to understanding the development of the PS over the past thirty-five years.

Alliances

The non-Communist Left of the 1960s was troubled above all by its search for an alliance strategy to oppose what was the quite new phenomenon (for France) of a stable governing majority. One line, represented by Gaston Defferre, former minister and mayor of Marseille, was to revive the 'Third Force' alliance with the MRP and the Radicals but not the Communists. The other strategy was advocated by François Mitterrand, initially a member, not of the SFIO, but of a small Centre grouping, the Union Démocratique et Sociale de la Résistance (UDSR). Mitterrand, though an early opponent of the Fifth Republic, understood its logic quickly enough to see that no left-wing victory at a presidential or parliamentary second ballot was possible without the Communists. In the mid-1960s, Mitterrand's strategy prevailed. He sidelined Defferre at the 1965 presidential election and ran with the support of the PCF, the SFIO and other small left-wing groupings, winning 31.7 per cent of the first-ballot vote and forcing the seemingly invincible de Gaulle into a run-off ballot, at which he won a respectable 45 per cent. Mitterrand brought together an alliance of the non-Communist Left, the Fédération de la Gauche Democrate et Socialiste (FGDS), that included the SFIO, the Parti Radical, the UDSR and a number of political clubs formed to promote the renewal of the Left, including his own Convention des Institutions Républicaines (CIR). The FGDS delivered significant gains, both in votes and in seats, for the Communist and the non-Communist Left at the 1967 parliamentary elections. But it fell apart the following year under the impact of the 'events' of May 1968: the FGDS had signally failed either to make any connection with the workers' and students' movement or to prevent a right-wing landslide at the following month's snap elections, while Mitterrand had temporarily discredited himself by an ill-judged offer to lead a 'provisional government' at the height of the crisis. His eclipse, and de Gaulle's sudden resignation from the presidency in April 1969, opened up Defferre's chance for a presidential bid. But Defferre had the support of neither the Communists, nor the Centre, nor even the whole SFIO; he won a humiliating 5 per cent at the first ballot, just 1.4 per cent ahead of the PSU candidate Michel Rocard and over 15 per cent below both the Communist Duclos and the centrist Poher.

Defferre's rout put the Mitterrand strategy back onto the agenda. Mitterrand became First Secretary of the re-founded PS at the Épinay congress in June 1971; the Common Programme with the Communists was signed barely a year later, and attracted the support of the left wing of the Radicals shortly afterwards. Mitterrand's fight for an alliance with the PCF was not, however, motivated by any fellow-feeling for Communists: on the contrary, he openly declared his aim to use the Common Programme to attract 3 million of the 5 million PCF voters over to the PS. He knew that while the PCF was necessary for electoral victory, such a victory could only be secured with a weakened PCF that had ceased to frighten the moderate Centre-Left voters whose support was also vital.

The goal of an electable Left with a weakened PCF was achieved by 1981. At the 1974 presidential election, Mitterrand reinforced his personal credibility by carrying the colours of the united Left and coming within less than 400,000 votes of beating the right-wing candidate, Valéry Giscard d'Estaing, at the run-off. By September 1974, by-elections showed that the Socialists were overtaking their Communist allies. That inevitably strained relations between the two parties. The Communists had no wish to take office as junior partners in a Socialist-led government, and spoiled the Left's (initially quite good) chances at the 1978 parliamentary elections after the quarrel over the 'updating' of the Common Programme. But the Communists were, at least temporarily, locked into the alliance by their need for the Socialists' second-ballot support to win parliamentary seats and town halls, and by their own voters' wish to see the Left win. Hence Marchais's declaration of support, however reluctant, for Mitterrand after the first round of the presidential election in April 1981, and the entry of four Communist ministers into Pierre Mauroy's government the following June. At the 1981 presidential elections, Mitterrand was over ten points ahead of Marchais; at the June parliamentary elections, the gap between the two parties was over twenty points. The Socialists' leadership of the Left was definitively established in 1981, and was not called into question even during the very bad period of the early 1990s. By the time that the Communists left the government in 1984, after growing tensions over policy, they had permanently lost over half their 1978 electorate. Relations between the two left-wing parties again became acrimonious, with the briefest periods of co-operation for elections.

The Socialists' problem, however, was that Mitterrand had succeeded almost too well at weakening the Communists, whose voters not only gravitated to the PS, but also dispersed towards abstention, spoilt ballots and even the far-Right Front National. These electors were lost to the Left as a whole, depriving the Socialists of reserves needed to win second ballots; as Tables 7.2 and 7.3 show, the Left, even including its most extreme fringes, has never won 50 per cent of the vote at the first round of a parliamentary or presidential election since 1981. In his second presidential term, Mitterrand therefore attempted to replace the union of the Left with a new majority alliance – something resembling the Third Force coalition he had prevented in the 1960s. His first attempt was the bid to bring the centrists into the majority after his second presidential victory in 1988; it foundered on the reluctance of most centrists to change sides so rapidly, as well as on extreme suspicion of such a move within the PS. Other alternative allies included ecologists (hence the inclusion of Brice Lalonde, ecology candidate in 1981, in the Rocard and Cresson governments) and dissidents from the PCF. Mitterrand's attempts at diversification were, therefore, largely a failure and an irritant to the PS. The groups he targeted tended to prosper in proportion to the Socialists' weakness (the various Green movements never did so well as in the Socialists' black years of 1992 and 1993). And as allies, they were needed in addition to the Communists – not instead of them.

The *gauche plurielle* coalition that Jospin led to victory in 1997 responded to this arithmetic. Its bases were laid after the 1993 defeat at a series of meetings grandly named *assises de la transformation sociale*. The basis of alliance was common interest, especially from 1994: the Socialists needed all the allies they could get; the short-lived pretensions of ecology groupings to replace the Socialists as the main force of the non-Communist Left had been punctured by their insignificant result at the 1994 European elections; and Marchais had handed the PCF leadership to the more conciliatory Hue. Jospin's strong performance at the 1995 presidential elections (and the poor ones of Hue and of the Green candidate, Dominique Voynet) re-established the Socialists' claim to lead a left-wing coalition; the relative success of joint lists at the 1995 municipal elections enhanced the credibility of such a coalition. Further discussions led to a Socialist–Green agreement in January 1997 (with a view to parliamentary elections expected in 1998) and to an accord with the PCF at the outset of the 1997 election campaign. There was no official common programme, but the Socialist programme contained enough elements – the 35-hour week, better job opportunities for the young, changes to immigration laws passed by the right-wing government and a moratorium on the construction of new nuclear power stations – to win the support of the two partner parties. The *gauche plurielle* also included two other small groups, the Left Radicals (close allies of the Socialists since 1972) and the Mouvement des Citoyens (MDC), a former current of the PS led by Jean-Pierre Chevènement, who had left the party in 1993.

The dynamic of the *gauche plurielle* differed from that of the old union of the Left. The Socialists' status as the strongest party was uncontested, but the smaller allies remained indispensable to any left-wing victory. Where Mitterrand had used the union of the Left to poach Communist votes, Jospin's PS needed to maintain the strength and credibility of its allies – so long as they remained within the tent. Indeed, a major asset of the *gauche plurielle* was its ability to offer voters both choice and the coherence and credibility of a united coalition. This was, inevitably, hard to do over a long period; the interest of each partner in the coalition's overall victory was balanced by its own interest in maximising its own distinctiveness, and thence its own electoral audience, at its allies' expense.

This ambiguity was central to Jospin's first-round defeat in the 2002 presidential race. Practically all observers and participants in the election took it as a foregone conclusion that Jospin would go through to the run-off ballot as the Left's candidate against Chirac. In the meantime, therefore, each component of the *gauche plurielle* could afford to run its own candidate, stressing its own individuality with a view to securing the strongest possible bargaining position within the coalition: Hue for the Communists, Noël Mamère for Les Verts, Chevènement for the MDC and Christiane Taubira for the Left Radicals. Between them, these four won 16.3 per cent of the vote, to Jospin's 16.1; the Left's support was further split by the 10.4 per cent of votes that were spread between the three Trotskyists, Laguiller, Besancenot and Gluckstein. The total score, for all eight candidates, of under 43 per cent would in any case have ruled out a left-wing victory at almost any imaginable run-off. What pushed Jospin into third place behind Chirac and Le Pen, and thus, under the rules for presidential elections, out of the run-off, was the insouciant fragmentation of the left-wing vote.

Something resembling the *gauche plurielle* will be needed if the Left is to govern France again. The alliance was indeed reconstituted, on a partial and tactical basis, for the June 2002 parliamentary elections and the regional elections of 2004. While Chevènement effectively chose to stay out (and lost his parliamentary seat as a result), the Socialists, Left Radicals, Communists and Greens were able to share out candidacies well enough to limit the damage in 2002 and to win a striking success in 2004, when twenty out of the twenty-two regions of metropolitan France elected a left-wing majority.

Much more difficult, however, will be the building of a credible coalition aimed at governing France. Such an alliance would have to overcome the long-standing tension between those forces that seek to reaffirm a strong left-wing identity, if need be against both European and global constraints, and those that accept the global capitalist economy and an integrated Europe as part of the environment within which they must work. This division widened into a yawning gulf during the 2005 referendum campaign on the European constitutional treaty. To some extent, this tension corresponds to party divides and sets the 'revolutionary' Communists and Trotskyists against the 'reformist' Socialists. But it also reflects the struggle of ideas, and the continuing vivacity of factional strife, within the PS.

Factions

The PS as it emerged from the congresses of Issy-les-Moulineaux, which began the process of refoundation in 1969, and Épinay in 1971, was a conglomerate of factions. The largest of these was the now defunct SFIO, initially divided between followers of Mollet (who died in 1975) and of Pierre Mauroy, mayor of Lille. Mauroy served as prime minister from 1981 to 1984, and as first secretary of the PS from 1988 till 1992, having played a pivotal role at the congresses of the 1970s, generally in support of Mitterrand. This core was joined by the various left-wing clubs associated with Alain Savary (first secretary of the PS from 1969 to 1971) and Jean Poperen, and the CERES, led by Jean-Pierre Chevènement, a ginger group of left-wing intellectuals, former members of the SFIO, which formed the most pro-Communist wing of the party. At the Épinay congress in 1971, Mitterrand joined the new PS with his CIR, and indeed wrested the post of first secretary from Savary; by dint of skilful and shifting alliances with other groups, he made the *mitterrandiens* into the party's dominant faction. Three years later, Michel Rocard led a contingent of former members of the PSU into the PS. Despite their left-wing origins, the *rocardiens* represented, within the PS, a moderate faction, sceptical about the alliance with the Communists in the 1970s, mindful of the constraints imposed by the market economy, less confident in the transforming possibilities of the Jacobin state and more aware of those within civil society.

Each faction or *courant*, alone or in alliance with others, has the right to compete for members' support by presenting a motion for consideration at the congresses held by the party about every three years. Members' votes on the different motions then determine the composition of the Socialists' 300-member National Council, and thus indirectly that of its top leadership, including the first secretary. Factions tend to have strong territorial bases, based on control of the federations (the party organisation in each *département*), itself often a function of the preferences of a powerful party figure in the locality.

From 1974 to 1981, Mitterrand maintained his majority in the party, in a sometimes difficult environment (notably the aftermath of the 1978 defeat) by playing off *rocardiens* against *chevènementistes* and vice versa. Largely suspended after 1981 (when almost everyone became a *mitterrandien* out of reason if not sentiment), factional activity broke out again, with a vengeance, after 1988, with the succession to Mitterrand as the main prize. Since then, the PS has been divided between a left-wing minority and a mainstream majority, each of which in turn is often divided. On the Left, CERES and the *poperénistes* were complemented, in the late 1980s, by the Gauche Socialiste, a group of former Trotskyists who emerged from the student and anti-racist movements of the mid-1980s under the leadership of Julien Dray; with Chevènement out of the party after 1992 and the *poperénistes* in steady decline, the Gauche Socialiste was the dominant left-wing faction for a decade until it split in September 2002, with Dray joining the mainstream. After 2002 two left-wing factions, the more traditionally left-wing Nouveau Monde under the leadership of former party treasurer Henri Emmanuelli and former *chevènementiste* Jean-Luc Mélenchon and the more innovative Nouveau Parti Socialiste led by Arnaud Montebourg and Vincent Peillon, opposed the Socialist majority, winning 31 per cent of the votes between them at the Dijon congress in 2003 and controlling seventeen federations. From 2004 onwards, however, they faced competition from Laurent Fabius, who had cast himself in the role of left-wing opposition leader. In the general switch of alliances that followed, Nouveau Monde disappeared while the Nouvau Parti Socialiste attracted the support of Emmanuelli and won 24 per cent of the members' votes during the preparations for the November 2005 Le Mans congress – better than Fabius's 21 per cent, but less than half the number backing the First Secretary François Hollande.

The party mainstream, meanwhile, has always been dominated by the various Socialist *présidentiables*, potential presidential candidates. One of these has been Laurent Fabius: born in 1947, Mitterrand's young prime minister from 1984 to 1986, first secretary of the PS from 1992 to 1993, finance minister from 2000 to 2002, Fabius is in principle eminently *présidentiable* – and will only turn 60 in 2007. He is also mistrusted within and outside the party as being too ambitious, too tactical and too clever by half, and for a long period – at least until cleared in court – was damaged by a scandal over the distribution of HIV-contaminated blood to haemophiliacs during his premiership. Whether openly or within a broad majority tent, the Fabius faction has existed since the Rennes congress of 1990. The non-*fabiusiens* in the mainstream were dominated first by Rocard – prime minister from 1988 to 1991 and first secretary from 1993 to 1994, but out of front-line national politics since the humiliating defeat of the Socialist list he led at the 1994 European elections – and then, from 1995 till 2002, by Jospin. Once installed in Matignon from 1997, Jospin left the day-to-day care of the party to his protégé François Hollande, who took over as first secretary in 1997 and who retained the post at the congresses of Grenoble in 2000 and – after Jospin's eclipse following the 2002 defeats – Dijon in 2003 and Le Mans in 2005.

The Hollande majority, incorporating (until 2005) the supporters of Fabius, who had been in no position to contest Jospin as prime minister even indirectly, won 61 per cent of the votes at Dijon – a respectable tally for a party majority that had just suffered a major electoral defeat, and one that owed something to Hollande's patience, good humour and penchant for consensus-building. Hollande's run of successes continued with strong Socialist results at the regional and European elections of 2004. The same year, however, saw the reappearance of serious intra-party strife. The immediate cause of this was Chirac's announcement in mid-2004 of a referendum on the European constitution. Within the PS, the no camp centred on the supposed free-market bias of the text and was led not only by the left-wing factions but by Fabius, hitherto considered a right-wing, modernising pro-European. Although an internal PS referendum of December 2004 resulted in a yes victory of 56 to 44 per cent of party members, the no leaders, and especially Emmanuelli, Mélenchon and Fabius refused to be bound by it; their campaign continued up to polling day, when some 59 per cent of Socialist *supporters* voted no. The fierceness of the campaign exchanges underlined, not only strongly-held views about Europe, but also a renewed struggle for control of the party against the backdrop of future elections. The National Council meeting following the referendum result saw Fabius's dismissal from his post as the party's no. 2, and his reconstitution of an independent faction called Agir à Gauche.

Preparations for the Le Mans congress of November 2005 thus saw Hollande fighting for his political life against a possible union of the opposition forces that had backed the no vote. This failed to materialise. The alliance between Nouveau Parti Socialiste and Emmanuelli became the main opposition force with the support 24 per cent of members, the *fabiusiens* attracted 21 per cent, but Hollande kept his majority with 53.7 per cent. Sufficient for Hollande to keep control of the party in the short term, this result would probably not be enough to prevent a damaging fight for the Socialist presidential candidacy in the run-up to 2007.

Factionalism has been part of the price paid by the Socialists for federating disparate tendencies. Voting by factions at party congresses offers several advantages in principle. It helps to structure debate, since the various motions offer different views on key questions such as alliances with other parties, the role of the state in society and electoral strategy. It enables each faction to take stock of its position. And it allows the party's National Council (formerly *comité directeur*), elected in proportion to votes for each motion, to represent the shifting balance of views in the party – even though the party secretariat is firmly controlled by the majority. However, factionalism has always been about interest as much as about principle. Mitterrand, for example, enlisted the support of CERES in 1979, and invited Chevènement and his friends to write a very left-wing programme for the PS, in order to marginalise the *rocardiens*. And from 1988 factional competition increasingly appeared as an unprincipled struggle for control of the party in succession to the ageing Mitterrand. The nasty spectacle of the *fabiusiens* and their opponents squabbling live on television over party jobs at the Rennes congress in 1990 was perhaps the low point of this, and contributed significantly to the party's lack of credit in the following years; it also reached down into every federation, demoralising activists (though sometimes artificially increasing their numbers, as votes were rigged with cards issued for non-existent members). The Socialists' organisational difficulty in the aftermath of the 2005 referendum will be not only to manage their serious internal differences over Europe and, more generally, over their relationship to an open capitalist economy, but also to ensure that the exercise of party democracy does not appear merely as an unseemly scramble for jobs.

Leadership

A great part of the Socialists' success in the 1970s was due to Mitterrand's leadership. His talent as an organiser and as a negotiator, as well as a boundless ambition served by long experience (he first won ministerial office in 1947), enabled him to grasp the party leadership at Épinay in June 1971 and to see off all challenges (notably from Rocard in 1979) thereafter. This was also, however, made possible by his credibility as a presidential candidate after the respectable defeats by de Gaulle in 1965 and Giscard in 1974. A stature unequalled by any Socialist leader since Léon Blum in the 1930s helped him to dominate the Communists within the left-wing alliance and to win the presidency in May 1981. Within the PS, he earned the nickname of 'the Prince' and 'the Pope'; after a few years in the Élysée, he was promoted simply to *Dieu*.

Once elected to the presidency, Mitterrand ceased to hold any party office. But he continued to dominate the PS, both through the positioning of his own people in key jobs (as first secretary from 1981 to 1988, Jospin showed unwavering loyalty), and because he himself remained an excellent 'locomotive' for his party. It is doubtful, for example, whether the Socialists would have salvaged a respectable 30.6 per cent at the long-expected defeat of 1986 had not Mitterrand campaigned in their support. There were differences between president and party during Mitterrand's first term: the party was uneasy about the deflationary economic policies adopted in 1983–84, unhappy about the withdrawal of the 1984 Savary bill designed to integrate (Catholic) private schools more closely into the state system and troubled, in 1985–86, by the continued nuclear testing in the South Pacific. But there was never any serious question, once Mitterrand had declared his intention of seeking a second term, that the party would not rally to his support and campaign for him.

After 1988, however, relations between president and party became more strained. The septuagenarian Mitterrand, who had fought his last election, had less need of the party, while the party took to fighting over the succession. During his second *septennat*, Mitterrand's political interventions in the life of his own majority were more irritating than inspiring to many Socialists: the botched attempt to open out his majority to the Centre in June 1988; the persistent support for the elevation of Fabius to the party leadership, which contributed not a little to the disaster at the Rennes congress in 1990; the attempt to engineer a return to proportional representation for the 1993 legislative elections (blocked by the Socialist parliamentary group); the flirtation with Brice Lalonde's ecologists; and the behind-the-scenes backing for Bernard Tapie's Radical list at the 1994 European elections, which helped bring Rocard's Socialist list to disaster. Motivated partly by a genuine wish to diversify the Left's sources of support in changed times, but also by a long-standing enmity for Rocard (which Rocard's stint as prime minister from 1988 to 1991 only reinforced), and an old man's reluctance to see any stong successor emerge, these initiatives damaged the party Mitterrand had done so much to create. Finally, the revelations about Mitterrand's war record were deeply troubling to all but the most unconditional Mitterrand loyalists.

Jospin's emergence as a successor occurred largely by default in the first instance, as the party cast around for a presidential candidate for 1995. Rocard was disqualified by the abysmal election result of 1994, Fabius ruled out by the contaminated blood scandal and Emmanuelli was under investigation for corruption during his period as party treasurer. Jacques Delors, Mauroy's finance minister from 1981 to 1984, and then president of the European Commission for a decade, was briefly seen as a saviour in the autumn of 1994; but he decided not to run. That left Jospin, who had built up personal networks during his seven years as first secretary, and had had the sense to stay out of the political limelight during the Socialists' bad years since 1993. With the choice of candidate open to individual members, diminishing the power of the Fabius organisation, the rank-and-file chose Jospin against Emmanuelli by a two-to-one majority. Despite a general lack of charisma, Jospin was brought to life by his own campaign in 1995, insisting on the Socialists' right to criticise the negative elements of the Mitterrand record as well as applauding his achievements, and he succeeded in projecting an image of integrity, a commodity seen by the voters to be in short supply after the scandals of the late Mitterrand years. His stylish presidential defeat (particularly his leading position at the first ballot) restored the credibility of the PS, making the 1997 victory possible; Jospin himself was unassailable as leader (even with Hollande in the formal post of first secretary) for seven years, until the evening of his defeat in April 2002 and his abrupt withdrawal from politics.

Jospin's departure did not leave the PS leaderless, at least not in formal terms. Hollande proved a good party manager in the difficult aftermath of 2002. His unremitting cheerfulness coupled with his determination to bounce back from every reverse won him real affection among members. As a *présidentiable*, however, he suffers from serious handicaps. He has never held ministerial office, has so far lacked charisma and has never articulated a clear presidential vision of France's future. These are serious drawbacks, especially compared with as determined a right-wing probable adversary as Nicolas Sarkozy. Hollande also faces a plethora of potential competitors within the PS. These include his own long-term partner Ségolène Royal, president of Poitou-Charentes regional council and the candidate most favoured by opinion polls late in 2005; former finance minister Dominique Strauss-Kahn; the eternally popular (but rather lightweight) former culture minister Jack Lang; the mayor of Paris, Bertrand Delanoë; and, above all, the most experienced and most determined (if not, for the moment, the most popular) contender, Laurent Fabius. No major French party can do without a leading *présidentiable*: the challenge to the PS in the period before 2007 will be to agree on one without tearing itself apart.

Members and elites

The PS organisation of the 1970s was probably a more dynamic force than at any time since the immediate post-war period. Membership more than doubled, to over 150,000, between the Épinay congress and 1975. Since then it has fluctuated between 100,000 and 200,000, leaning more to 100,000 in the twenty-first century. Many of the new members of the 1970s were young, middle-class (the proportion of blue-collar members fell by half, to 19 per cent, in the two decades to 1973), imbued with a soft version of the ideals of May 1968, and active. They were the pool from which the party's elite was completely renewed. Already under Savary's leadership (1969–71), 70 per cent of the secretaries of local federations had been replaced; the average age of the holders of these posts fell by twenty years. At the Nantes party congress in June 1977, over half of all delegates were under 40, only a quarter had belonged to the pre-1969 SFIO, and over half had university degrees. Renewal was also seen among mayors and local councillors, and in the National Assembly, where half the Socialist Deputies elected in 1978, and again in the big contingent of 1981, were newcomers.

Three decades on, the PS membership was still marked by the generation of 1970. In 1998, just 7 per cent of PS members were under 30, compared with 40 per cent who were over 60. Only a quarter were women (a small improvement on 1985, when the figure had been a fifth). Only a quarter had joined since 1985. With age had come diminished activism (indeed, Mitterrand tended to discourage activism outside election campaigns after his election in 1981): by 1998, 64 per cent of members gave five hours or less to the party every month – the time for one or two meetings. Similarly, the (former) young elite remained and aged. Of delegates to the Rennes congress of 1990, four-fifths were men, two-thirds were over 40; only a quarter had joined since 1981; two-thirds had at least one university degree; over half came from the liberal or higher managerial professions. The main difference between this comfortable assembly of middle-aged men and a party of the Right was the Socialists' strong links with the public sector.

This picture of a stagnating turn-of-the-century party deserves some qualification. In particular, some elite change was discernible by the late 1990s under Jospin's leadership. The inner circle of *jospinistes*, constituted between 1988 and 1994, was younger than the generation of 1970, had risen (often through ministerial *cabinets*) during the 1980s, included some particularly able and senior women like Martine Aubry, Élisabeth Guigou and Ségolène Royal, and was drawn from a wide range of currents. One in three secretaries of federations were changed at the Brest congress of November 1997. Of PS parliamentary candidates in 1997, 60 per cent were new and 30 per cent, an unprecedented figure, were women.

But in the defensive context of June 2002, the 30 per cent figure was not exceeded, despite parity legislation; the PS preferred to keep its sitting, mostly male, Deputies, even at the cost of a penalty in public finance, than approach male–female parity. More generally, the Socialists have failed to renew and replenish their membership as they would have wished. The brief surge of members in the aftermath of the 2002 defeat was of short duration; and the attempt, early in 2005, to attract '*adhérents du programme*', registered sympathisers paying minimal dues in return for an opportunity to be consulted on the future party programme, testified to a breakdown in conventional party recruitment and activism. That was common, to a degree, with all parties, but owes something too to the Socialists' lack of a self-renewing organisational reservoir. Unlike Britain's Labour Party, the PS has no organic links with the trade union movement (in 1998, the proportion of blue-collar workers among party members was just 5 per cent). Relations with groups such as feminists or ecologists have remained generally distant and suspicious. So were links with the various social movements, whether related to housing rights or the unemployed or immigrants 'without papers' which gathered momentum in the second half of the 1990s. With second-generation immigrants, while organisations close to the PS, such as SOS–Racisme, existed, they were frequently accused of being the party's tools within ethnic minority communities. And except in a handful of industrial areas (notably in the Nord–Pas-de-Calais region), the PS has had few links with the subcultures that made up the natural terrain of great parties elsewhere. The PS could still, therefore, become as old, sclerotic and out of touch with voters as the SFIO of the 1960s. One ambition of leaders of the no campaign in 2005 in the aftermath of the referendum result was to reverse that, and to transform the very real public mobilisation against the European constitutional treaty into lasting activism within a rejuvenated PS committed to left-wing policies and alliances – something similar, in fact, to Mitterrand's party of the early 1970s.

Ideology and policies

SFIO policies in the early Fifth Republic were an unappealing package of negatives: anti-Gaullism, in the name of a strictly parliamentary view of the Republic; anti-Communism, inherited from the early Cold War; anti-clericalism, inherited from the early struggles of Socialist and Republican parties against the Right at the turn of the century. These appeals to doctrinaire loyalties reinforced the SFIO's image as an ageing and increasingly irrelevant party. It was the achievement of the relaunched PS to supply a more positive vision; and it did so largely by giving full rein to the young, radical, left-wingers who filled its ranks in the wake of May 1968. Mitterrand himself, indeed, declared in 1971 that 'anyone who does not accept . . . a rupture with capitalist society cannot be a member of the Socialist Party'. The party's National Convention in May 1972 adopted a new programme – *Changer la vie* – whose title revealed both its ambition and its *naïveté*. More or less soft varieties of Marxism, together with New Left ideas like *autogestion* (workers' self-management), continued to dominate the policy debates of the 1970s. Solid tactical reasons, as well as the spirit of the age, also pulled the party leftwards. The main doctrinal deal in the Common Programme signed with the PCF in 1972 was that the Communists should accept the basics of Western 'bourgeois' democracy while the Socialists committed themselves to large-scale nationalisations. *Autogestion* served to show up the authoritarian and hierarchical view of society that still prevailed in the PCF. And Mitterrand's tactical alliance with the CERES faction against the *rocardiens* inspired the radical *Projet Socialiste* of 1979.

Mitterrand therefore won the 1981 elections burdened not only with his own, fairly restrained, '110 propositions', but also with the background of his party's more revolutionary commitments and expectations. The collision with economic reality was painful for the Socialists: the spirit of the campaigns of the 1970s was increasingly left behind as unemployment was allowed to rise and ailing firms to go bankrupt, while business taxes were reduced, the purchasing power of households stagnated and the 'new poor' appeared, lacking either jobs or benefit entitlements and reduced to begging on the streets.

Any party of the centre-Left in Western Europe faces the challenge of reconciling ideals of social protection, full employment, equality of opportunity and decent living standards for all both with the reality of a global economy that thrives on competition and inequalities, and with the constraints of EU membership. But the Socialists' doctrinal debates since the 1980s have also been shaped by the strongly anti-capitalist tradition of a current of French socialism and by the apparent victory of that current in the years just before the conquest of power. The reluctance of activists to engage in any root-and-branch modernisation was demonstrated at the Toulouse and Lille congresses of 1985 and 1987; even at the La Défense congress of 1991, where much anti-capitalist and workerist baggage was dumped, the contours of the Socialist project remained vaguely defined by references to 'humanism' or a 'critical relationship' to capitalism. It was also noticeable that doctrinal disputes did not, on the whole, correspond to divisions between currents, with the exceptions of the left-wing *gauche socialiste* and the *poperénistes*. The Socialists' return to office in 1997 owed less to any major ideological advances than to a new impression of modesty and integrity combined with the deep unpopularity of the ruling conservative coalition.

During his five years in power, Jospin tended to avoid doctrinal controversy, beyond general claims to accept a 'market economy but not a market society', concentrating instead on concrete measures: the 35-hour week, the *emplois-jeunes* (creating government-assisted jobs for under-25s), the provision of universal health care (taking in, for the first time, those whose contributions did not qualify them for healthcare under the social security system), the re-examination of the cases of immigrants left 'without papers' as a result of the previous government's immigration legislation (and the granting of leave to remain in France for about a third of them), and the Civil Solidarity Pact (see above, p. 124) served two related functions. First, they sought to anchor the Jospin government's left-wing credibility and reputation for integrity (the later left-wing governments of the Mitterrand presidency, under Cresson and Bérégovoy, had been viewed as short on both). Secondly, they allowed the government to pursue, without any very substantial opposition, a number of policies more congenial to the markets than to the Left's activists: a greater financial volume of privatisations than under the Chirac, Balladur and Juppé governments put together, and the progressive opening to competition, with considerable prodding from Europe, of a number of traditionally protected public service enterprises.

By most standards, the Jospin government's achievements were impressive: most of the programme was fulfilled and a million jobs were created in four years, bringing the jobless total briefly to just 9 per cent, after a peak of over 12.5 per cent in the mid-1990s. As the basis of a future programme, however, it suffered from the fact that too few of the benefits had reached the working-class and routine white-collar categories who could, in the past, have been expected to support the Left. Indeed, many among these groups suffered negative effects from the shorter working week: less convenient working hours, tougher production targets and stagnant or falling purchasing power. Such grievances were compounded when Jospin argued his inability to stop unemployment creeping back up from mid-2001, and the campaign focused on law and order, one of the Socialists' weaker suits but an important issue for many working-class voters. Jospin then dug himself a deeper hole by announcing, in a bid for centre voters at a future second ballot, that although his political loyalties were Socialist, his manifesto for 2002 was not – a statement that encouraged the increasingly widespread perception that there was little to choose between the Jospin and Chirac programmes. The widespread availability of alternative candidates who claimed to offer more, in terms either of job protection or security from crime, completed the dispersal of the left-wing vote at the first round and led to Jospin's elimination.

Jospin claimed to offer a 'realism of the Left' – a policy package in which the necessities of France's insertion into a global capitalist economy were acknowledged but avowedly left-wing objectives such as full employment, strong public services and wealth redistribution were still pursued. Critics like Henri Rey, on the other hand, turn this argument inside out. The contemporary PS, in their view, falls between two stools. On the one hand, it has not embraced the market in a Blair-style third way, abandoning key Socialist shibboleths like monopoly public services owned and managed by the state, posing difficult questions about the aims of state intervention, drawing reform lessons from other developed countries, and if necessary challenging the vested public-sector interests within what remains of the core Socialist electorate in the name of the wider benefits Jospin outlined. On the other, however, it has not embarked on a radical left-wing path, aimed at mobilising the Left's historic supporters among the working class and modifying the European and international constraints that supposedly tie the hands of French policy-makers. The party, argue its critics, is therefore thrown back on essentially defensive positions, themselves vulnerable to the constraints of office, about shielding ordinary wage-earners (and pensioners) from the worst effects of unrestrained capitalist competition – an uninspiring mix, especially for those (often younger) voters already left unprotected for lack of a stable record of employment and social contributions.

While somewhat exaggerated (Jospin's record was better than merely defensive), this view highlights the continuing difficulty of the PS, even out of office. The party's opposition to the Raffarin government's conservative reform programme, which aimed to empty the 35-hour legislation of much of its substance and to prolong the working lifetime via pension reforms, certainly contributed to a partial recovery at the regional and European elections in 2004. But the PS remained vulnerable to attack both from the Left, which claimed it had done too little when in office, and from its own right-wingers, such as Rocard, who argued that on issues such as pensions a Socialist government would have had to engage comparable reforms to Raffarin's.

In 2005, the debate over the European constitutional treaty became a matrix for the Socialists' dilemma. The leadership and the majority of party members were ready to accept the treaty in order to maintain the forward march of Europe, to which the Socialists had generally been favourable in the past. The party's left wing, joined by Fabius, protested that the text locked Europe into a neo-liberal economic future, and refused to be bound by the majority after the party's internal referendum held in December 2004. In the ensuing campaign, the dissenters compared Hollande and the leadership to the Socialist Deputies who had signed over full powers to Pétain in 1940, while their adversaries accused the no camp of xenophobia. The venom of these exchanges is to be explained not only by the power of Europe to mobilise and to divide, but also by the fact that this debate was in part a cipher for something older – the tension between a culture of government and a culture of activism, mobilisation and opposition which has troubled the Socialists since the earliest days of the SFIO.

Money

With neither a mass membership nor trade union backing, the Socialists lacked stable sources of lawful income before the public finance of parties was introduced in 1988. They were not alone in this (only the Communists have had a membership exceeding 200,000 during the Fifth Republic); and like other parties, they resorted to business funding, which was illegal. They attracted (or extracted) money from firms by the time-honoured method of levying percentages on public works contracts signed with the local authorities – cities, above all – that they controlled. Unlike other parties, however, the Socialists limited the freedom of their mayors and councillors to raise and use such cash as they saw fit. They created a national system, run through a front organisation of 'planning consultants' called the Urba group, which ensured the delivery of false invoices for cash raised and channelled some of it to the party's central office. This both ensured some central financial control on local office-holders (although parallel systems on a smaller scale were soon funding the party's different factions) and pre-vented, at least in principle, the use of these illicit funds to fill individual pockets rather than party coffers. Reinforced by the big municipal victories of 1977, the Urba system gave the PS a sound financial underpinning for its campaigns up to and beyond 1981, in a world of increasingly sophisticated and expensive political communication tech-niques. But in such a centralised structure, the discovery of a part could readily reveal the existence of the whole. This happened between 1989 and 1991, when examining magistrates investigating false invoices cases first in Marseille, and then in Le Mans, found trails leading straight to the PS central office. Although elected officials of all parties had been found to be involved in corrupt financial practices, the PS was alone in having had its national funding system revealed as illegal in this way. This was a disaster for a party that had always taken the moral high ground when discussing this type of issue, and it contributed much to the Socialists' 'disgrace' in the early 1990s. From 1995, however, the taint of corruption was transferred from the PS to its opponents on the moderate Right. Although two recent investigations, one involving payments for plan-ning decisions to allow the construction of hypermarkets and another concerning the student insurance firm run by the (Socialist-controlled) Union Nationale des Étudiants Français, involved PS personalities, neither uncovered clear proof. For the present, thanks to the generous (and legal) public subsidies, the PS appears to be living within its means and within the law.

Electoral support

By the 1960s, the SFIO's electorate had not only been shrinking for nearly two decades, but was increasingly limited both socially and geographically: the typical Socialist voter was a male, middle-aged, anti-clerical teacher or other public employee, living in the south-west. It was the indispensable achievement of the renewed party both to halt the overall decline and to diversify its electoral audience. The overall recovery, shown in Table 7.2 and Figure 7.2, began with the score of 19.1 per cent at the 1973 parliamentary elections; five years later this had risen to 22.8 per cent – ahead of the PCF. At the 1981 presidential elections, Mitterrand put 10 percentage points

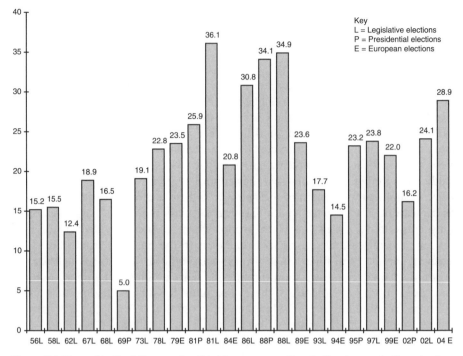

Figure 7.2 Votes for Socialist parties (% of votes cast, first ballot in two-ballot elections, not including allies), 1956–2004.

between himself and the Communist candidate Marchais: at no national election since, except for the disastrous parliamentary elections of 1993, has the gap been less than this.

A diffuse public sympathy accompanied this electoral recovery: except for the periods 1983–85, 1991–95 and a few months in the aftermath of the 2002 defeats, the PS, alone among French political parties (until the Greens were included in surveys), has enjoyed a consistent majority of positive over negative poll ratings. And the earlier sociological and geographical shrinkage was corrected. Mitterrand had particularly sought to give the party a solid base among the growing numbers of white-collar workers in both the public and the private sectors, many of them women, and this goal was achieved; in June 1981, the PS won 45 per cent of the vote among white-collar workers and middle managers. The gender gap was also narrowed (and closed completely in 1986). But the PS had also successfully challenged the Communists in their working-class heartlands (with 44 per cent of the blue-collar vote), and attracted the young (45 per cent of the under-35s); it even made progress among upper management (38 per cent) and Catholics (often through contacts in the Catholic-influenced trade union confederations); only among farmers and self-employed artisans and shopkeepers did it remain weak. Moreover, far from being confined to traditional bastions of the south-west, the PS of June 1981 was the biggest party in twenty-one of France's twenty-two regions (all except Corsica), and in seventy-nine of the ninety-six metropolitan *départements*, while in only four *départements* did its vote fall below 30 per cent; it had built strength in areas like Brittany and Alsace, which had hitherto been almost impregnable strongholds of the Right. Like the Gaullists of the 1960s, the Socialists of 1981 attracted the votes of a cross-section of the population. To use Otto Kirchheimer's term, it had succeeded in becoming a 'catch-all' party.

This was a remarkable and unprecedented achievement for a Socialist party in France; it was one in which the leader and the party had helped each other to victory in remarkable complementarity; and it was more or less repeated in 1988, though this time with an incumbent president whose popularity depended rather less on his party. Yet the Socialists' electoral ascendancy has always been brittle. PS support at European elections has only once (in 2004) risen above 24 per cent. In 1994 Rocard's European list sank to 14.5 per cent, a result that came at the worst point of the Socialist 'disgrace', brought on by a combination of the dreadful image offered at the 1990 Rennes congress, economic recession, the Urba scandal and revelations about Mitterrand's war record. It was the third disaster in three years, after a mere 18.3 per cent at the 1992 regional elections and 17.7 per cent at the 1993 parliamentary elections (a loss of 4 million out of 8.4 million votes, and 215 out of 282 seats compared with 1988).

The recovery under Jospin, though effective at winning office, was limited in purely electoral terms: 23.2 per cent at the 1995 presidential elections, 23.8 per cent at the parliamentary elections two years later; in only 25 seats out of 577 did Socialists win over 40 per cent of the vote. Jospin's 16.2 per cent in 2002 may charitably be considered as below the Socialist norm, the two most recent scores – in June 2002 and June 2004 – as defining the typical range of the PS, in the mid- to high twenties. By way of comparison, Tony Blair's New Labour won the British May 1997 election with 43.2 per cent of the vote, in 2001 with 41.7 per cent and even in 2005 with 37 per cent, while Gerhard Schröder's SPD returned to power in Germany in September 1998 with 40.9 per cent. The PS vote, in other words, is low for a European social democratic party; even if the vote for the Socialists' closest allies, the Left Radicals and the Greens, against which they ran no candidates in selected constituencies, is included, the total in 1997 was still barely 30 per cent.

Moreover, the 'catch-all' composition of the Socialist vote may be a handicap as well as an asset. No social group, and no region, is wholly impenetrable for the PS: in its weakest region (Alsace) and its most difficult social groups (the self-employed and practising Catholics), the Socialist score is in the 15–16 per cent range. Conversely, though, there are few groups or regions where the Socialist hegemony is unchallenged. In particular, the PS inherited the Communists' special relationship with the working class on a fleeting basis, essentially confined to the period from 1981 to 1988. Mitterrand's blue-collar vote at the first round in 1988, at 42 per cent, exceeded his average by 8 points; Jospin's in 1995, at 25 per cent, by 2 points only; in 2002, Jospin's share of the blue-collar vote was 13 per cent, or 3 points *below* his average. The same applies, albeit to a somewhat lesser degree, to routine white-collar groups at presidential elections and to the blue-collar vote at legislative elections – a good 6 points clear of the national PS average in June 1988, but between 2 points below and 3 points above in 1993, 1997 and 2002. That the Socialists have made inroads since 1988 into professional and executive groups – where they now do as well as or better than their average score – scarcely compensates for losses elsewhere, for these gains still count for less in terms of absolute numbers of votes.

In a bad year, the PS leaks votes on all sides: to abstention, to the far Right (the Front National has been the leading party among blue-collar workers since 1993), to the moderate Right, to the Greens, to the extreme Left. Moreover, a catch-all party needs to satisfy a wide range of groups. For a West European social democratic party, this may mean a difficult balancing act between the wishes of its blue-collar voters (conservative on many societal issues, less than enthusiastic about Europe, anxious to defend the welfare state and fearful of unemployment) with those of more cosmopolitan supporters in professional and managerial groups (pro-European, liberal on societal issues, resistant to high taxation). The referendum of 2005 illustrated the gulf that could open between those groups. Polls taken in its aftermath, on the Le Mans congress in November 2005, illustrated the party's loss of credibility. On a whole range of domestic policy issues, including the reduction of social inequalities, education, housing, the environment, public services, purchasing power, law and order, or unrest in France's suburbs, respondents who thought a Socialist government would do better than de Villepin and the Right were clearly outnumbered by those who considered it would do no better, or even worse. Fifty-nine per cent of respondents, and 50 per cent of Socialist sympathisers, considered that the party was doing its job as an opposition force poorly or very poorly. If the Socialists appear certain to retain their hegemony on the Left, therefore, their role as France's 'natural' party of government appears much less secure. For a party as electorally modest as the PS, winning and retaining office will always require allies, but the dynamics of alliances may themselves help to pull the PS in opposite directions.

The far Left

If the French Left as a whole is divided, the far Left is splintered into a profusion of warring factions, clans and *groupuscules*, among which unity (especially among the working class) is proclaimed as vital in principle yet frequently eschewed as opportunist in practice.

For three decades, the most original grouping of the far Left was the PSU (Parti Socialiste Unifié), founded in 1960, a mixture of Marxists, disillusioned Socialists, left-wing Catholics and followers of the Fourth Republic Prime Minister Pierre Mendès-France. Composed chiefly of intellectuals, the PSU supplied some of the Left's more innovative ideas, but was also prone to byzantine internal disputes. It fielded two presidential candidates: Michel Rocard won 3.6 per cent of the vote in 1969 (the high point of the PSU's influence was just before and just after May 1968) and Huguette Bouchardeau managed just 1.1 per cent in 1981. Weakened by the departure of Rocard and his associates to join the PS in 1974, and uncertain about its relationship with Mitterrand's majority after 1981, the PSU finally disbanded in 1990.

The far Left has also included anarchist groupings (the Fédération Anarchiste being the strongest) and Maoists (the Parti Communiste (Marxiste-Léniniste), then the Gauche Révolutionnaire, then Pour une Alternative Communiste). More important have been the various Trotskyist groups, descendants of movements attached to (or split from) the Fourth International founded by Leon Trotsky in 1938. Of these, the 'Lambertiste' tendency, successively incarnated as the Organisation Communiste Internationaliste (OCI), Parti Communiste Internationaliste (PCI), Mouvement pour un Parti des Travailleurs (MPPT) from 1985, and most recently Parti des Travailleurs, has been long-lived but electorally weak. Its leader Pierre Boussel won a mere 0.4 per cent at the 1988 presidential elections; fourteen years later, Daniel Gluckstein did better – with 0.5 per cent. The Ligue Communiste Révolutionnaire (LCR) is led by Alain Krivine, a veteran of May 1968 who ran in two presidential elections, winning 1.06 per cent in 1969 and 0.4 per cent in 1974. It recruits its members (2,000 are claimed) and voters

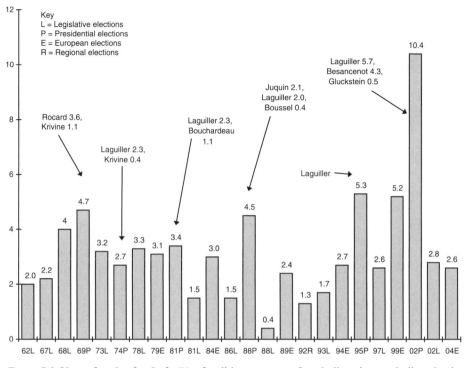

Figure 7.3 Votes for the far Left (% of valid votes cast, first ballots in two-ballot elections), 1962–2004.

chiefly among teachers and students in universities and schools. The LCR's profile, and vote, were raised in 2002 when it presented France's youngest presidential candidate. Olivier Besancenot, a personable 27-year-old postman, won an unprecedented 4.25 per cent for his party (and 9 per cent among French students) – more than Robert Hue for the PCF – and over the next three years steadily eclipsed Krivine. Lutte Ouvrière (LO), on the other hand, is perhaps the only Trotskyist party to attract significant numbers of 'ordinary French people', typically white-collar public-sector workers but also, in 1995 and 2002, blue-collar workers in traditional industries. Its spokesperson, the indefatigable Arlette Laguiller, is the only candidate to have run in all five presidential elections since 1974, and has won over 5.2 per cent at the last two (including over 10 per cent of the blue-collar vote – just 3 points behind Jospin – in 2002).

Far Left voters are a mixed group, far from all of them convinced Trotskyists: fully 16 per cent of them switched their vote to Chirac at the run-off in 1995, and nearly one in twenty appears to have supported Le Pen in the Chirac–Le Pen run-off of 2002. Electorally, the far Left vote is able to surprise, but also prone to collapse: most strikingly, from the 10 per cent plus (spread over the three presidential candidates) of 21 April 2002 to below 3 per cent at the parliamentary elections seven weeks later. This suggests that many, perhaps most, far Left voters seek to express their disappointment with other parties (especially with the mainstream Left) rather than their attachment to Trotsky (or indeed to Besancenot). All of the far Left's best scores have been achieved with the Socialists in power.

Though they are capable of inspiring levels of membership activism that put other parties to shame, the far Left groups are disdainful of, and correspondingly bad at, electoral strategy. Both doctrinal differences and very distinct organisational cultures – counter-cultural and non-conformist for the LCR, dour and sectarian for LO – have helped keep the Trotskyists divided. Their achievement at the 1999 European elections, when LO and the LCR ran a joint list that won 5.2 per cent of the vote and propelled Krivine and Laguiller into the Strasbourg parliament for five years, was unique; far more typical has been squabbling before elections (typically over the issue of whether to withdraw at second ballots in favour of Socialist candidates) and disunity during campaigns. Small wonder, then, that Krivine and Laguiller lost their seats in 2004, and that the far Left has almost no seats on local and regional councils.

Despite this weakness at the crucial local level, the far Left retains a threefold importance for French party politics. First, its electoral significance, though small, is far from negligible; 5 per cent at a parliamentary or presidential election could make the difference between victory and defeat for the Left, if transferred into second-ballot votes. Second, the far Left has supplied activists to the mainstream of French politics. This is true of the left-wing press (many of the brightest journalists on *Le Monde, Libération*, or public-service radio have seen service with one or another of the far Left groups) and of parties, especially the PS: some of the latter have been 'moles', planted by far Left groups into mainstream parties, who then repudiate their Trotskyists origins. Julien Dray and much of the *gauche socialiste* came out of Trotskyism via SOS–Racisme. Jean-Christophe Cambadélis, the Socialists' deputy leader from November 1997 till 2002, led a whole group of *lambertistes* over to the PS in 1985 after direct talks with Mitterrand; they were a highly attractive catch for the PS as they controlled the Union Nationale des Étudiants Français. Henri Weber, another senior PS leader (and a Senator since September 1995), is a former leader of the May 1968 students' movement. The Socialists' biggest single prize, however, was Jospin himself – a *lambertiste* infiltrator when he joined the PS in the early 1970s, still technically a member of the MPPT while serving as first secretary of the PS, but definitively a mainstream Socialist from about 1987.

Third, the far Left has been both active (its supporters being few but committed) and influential at the grass roots of left-wing politics. In the early 1970s, its campaigns achieved an unexpected degree of mobilisation over issues which the mainstream Left was reluctant to touch – the living conditions of soldiers, abortion, prison reform, the plight of immigrant workers and the eviction of tenants by property speculators. Trotskyists have also been active in SOS–Racisme and in the two big student movements of December 1986 and autumn 1995. They have an audience in some academic circles (the late sociologist Pierre Bourdieu, while not a member of any far Left group, was considered a guru) and in pockets of the (otherwise staid) Force Ouvrière union. And the far Left has been very well implanted (far better than the PCF) in France's many social movements since the mid-1990s – the Paris squatters' movement of 1994–95, the big strikes of December 1995, the *sans-papiers* movement, the unemployed movement of 1997–98 and the succession of protests against the Raffarin government's reforms since 2002. That capacity to mobilise was also evident during the 2005 referendum campaign, when Besancenot held meetings alongside Buffet for the PCF and Mélenchon for the no camp in the PS – and was by no means a second-rank speaker. The Trotskyist groups, in short, have been able to play the role of the Left's radical conscience, always ready to outbid their mainstream competitors: a living link with France's centuries-old tradition of protest and insurrection, and a standing (and self-righteous, and quite possibly utopian) reproach to those on the Left who consider that achieving left-wing goals requires the acceptance, however unpalatable, of the constraints of government.

Citoyens et Radicaux

The left-wing majority returned in 1997 consisted of three parliamentary groups: Communists, Socialists and a motley assortment called Radicaux-Citoyens-Verts (RCV). One component of the latter was Jean-Pierre Chevènement's Mouvement des Citoyens (MDC), the successor to the Socialisme et République current (itself a successor to CERES) which Chevènement had led out of the PS in 1993. Chevènement's successful political career after 1993 (including three years as Jospin's interior minister from 1997 until his resignation in 2000) was an excellent illustration of the capacity of individual politicians with strong local bases (in Chevènement's case, Belfort) to survive and even prosper outside major party organisations. The Marxism of the early CERES had increasingly given way, from the 1980s, to an old-fashioned left-wing Jacobinism, allergic to transfers of sovereignty to Europe, deeply suspicious of Greens and positively apoplectic about plans for further decentralisation to Corsica announced in 2000. The fact of being too few to form a parliamentary group on their own was almost the only thing the seven MDC Deputies had in common with their Radical and Green colleagues.

As it developed towards 2002, however, the Chevènement case illustrated something further: the destructive centrifugal potential of a presidential campaign. Half detached from the *gauche plurielle* after 2000, Chevènement as a presidential candidate became much the bitterest critic of Jospin on the Left, using the names Chirpin and Josrac to underline his claim that little differentiated the president and the prime minister as candidates – and that both wanted to sell France out to multinational business, Europe, or both. Early in the campaign, with the FN still partially disabled, this made Chevènement attractive to voters of the far Right, and he was briefly credited with over 12 per cent of voting intentions. In the event, most of the far Right voters returned to Le Pen, but Chevènement still managed to mobilise enough disgruntled, Eurosceptical Socialists with a leavening of Gaullists to attract over 5 per cent of the vote on 21 April 2002. Disappointing compared with initial expectations, this was still more than enough to keep Jospin out of the second ballot. Unlike the other groups of the *gauche plurielle*, Chevènement refused to return to the left-wing fold after the presidential defeat. At the June 2002 parliamentary elections, MDC candidates were therefore in outright competition with Socialists – and lost: not even Chevènement kept his seat. Renamed the Mouvement Républicain et Citoyen, the *chevènementistes* retain a distinct identity and organisation, and receive public party finance, and were active in the no campaign for the 2005 referendum. But with no parliamentarians and few other elected officials, they gave every impression of being a spent force; in alliance with the PCF and the Left Radicals at the 2004 regional elections, for example, they were easily outdistanced by the Socialists even in Chevènement's (former) stronghold of Belfort.

The Parti Radical, the great governing party of the Centre under the Third Republic, was reduced by 1958 to a small group commanding under 10 per cent of the vote and uncertain whether to join forces with the Gaullists or the Left or to try to maintain a central position between them. Left-wing Radicals, known from 1972 till 1994 as the MRG (Mouvement des Radicaux de Gauche), as Radical from 1994 to 1996, as the

Parti Radical Socialiste (PRS) from 1996 to 1998 and as the Parti Radical de Gauche (PRG) since 1998, are the group that chose to sign the Left's Common Programme in July 1972. Most of the MRG's history was played out as a satellite of the PS, though its first leader, Robert Fabre, defected in 1978 to accept the post of Mediator from Giscard. Fabre's successor Michel Crépeau always acknowledged that his 1981 presidential candidacy (which won 2.2 per cent of the votes) was chiefly designed to bring moderate voters into the Mitterrand camp. When the MRG tried more independent action, its results were not encouraging: 3.3 per cent at the 1984 European elections in alliance with some ecologists and dissident centrists, and a miserable 0.25 per cent of the national vote for its lists in the 1986 parliamentary elections (though it did manage to negotiate ten safe places on the Socialist lists as well). But the Left Radicals have been an asset to the Left, because their voters are geographically rather concentrated. If the Socialists leave them a clear run in selected towns and constituencies in the south-west and Corsica, the Left Radicals are therefore capable of electing mayors (for example, Crépeau in La Rochelle until his death in 1998), local councillors and a handful of Deputies, who have usually (though not in 1997) chosen to join the Socialist parliamentary group.

This picture was complicated by the irruption onto the political scene of Bernard Tapie, a flamboyant self-made millionaire businessman, owner of the Olympique de Marseille football club, who had led the non-Communist left-wing list at the 1992 regional elections in Bouches-du-Rhône. Tapie was briefly minister for urban affairs in the 1992 Bérégovoy government before being forced to resign in the face of imminent bankruptcy proceedings. Temporarily undeterred by these, he joined the MRG, and won election as Deputy for Marseille in 1993. He then bought his way into the party's leadership, aiming at Marseille town hall, the Strasbourg parliament and even the Élysée itself. In this he was probably encouraged by President Mitterrand, who admired Tapie's energy and was seeking an alternative left-wing force to Michel Rocard and the demoralised Socialists. Tapie's, and the Radicals', high point came at the 1994 European elections, when their list attracted over 12 per cent of the voters, most of them discontented Socialists, especially from the ranks of blue-collar workers alienated from the PS since 1992. But Tapie's plans for a presidential candidacy foundered after an avalanche of legal proceedings were initiated against him for offences ranging from fixing a football match to failing to declare his private yacht to the tax inspectorate; he went, not to the Élysée, but (albeit briefly) to prison. Under Jean-Michel Baylet's leadership the PRG resumed the MRG's more tranquil course, with one middle-ranking and one junior minister in the Jospin government. Like all the other components of the *gauche plurielle*, the PRG ran a presidential candidate; Christiane Taubira, Deputy for French Guiana, was the first black woman to contest the presidency. She did so in a much less aggressive manner than Chevènement, and won 660,000 votes, or 2.3 per cent, including a significant black ethnic vote in the Paris suburbs. Again unlike the *chevènementistes*, the Left Radicals have retained their close ties with the Socialists. Most of their nine Deputies elected in June 2002 enjoyed Socialist support from the first ballot; seven sit as associate members of the Socialist group, the other two as independents.

The ecology groupings

Like their counterparts elsewhere in Europe, France's ecologists have had to grapple with three structural problems. First, there is an intrinsic electoral problem, because the benefits of Green policies tend to be very long-term, or localised, or costly, or all three. Diffuse voter concern with the environment, readily expressed in opinion polls and (to a lesser extent) at 'inconsequential' European and regional elections, rarely extends to a readiness to put Greens into government. Secondly, they have an organisational problem, arising from the reluctance of many ecology groupings to accept the hierarchical structures and clearly identifiable leaders of conventional political parties, and the loss of effectiveness and media impact that has tended to follow from more collective styles of decision-making. Third, ecology movements, like any new entrants into a party system, face a strategic choice between remaining isolated and impotent or joining alliances and risking unacceptable compromises. Indeed, although ecology voters have always been more inclined to support the Left than the Right at second ballots, it is only since the mid-1990s that Les Verts, the main ecology grouping, could be said to have joined the left-wing camp by entering into the *gauche plurielle* alliance.

There has been an ecology candidate at every French presidential election since Friends of the Earth supported René Dumont in 1974; only in 2002, however, did one attract more than 4 per cent of the vote (Table 7.3). Results of ecology groupings in parliamentary elections were no better (Table 7.2 and Figure 7.4), until 1993 (when they won 11.1 per cent) and 1997 (with 6.9 per cent). Ecology candidates have done best at European elections and regional elections (2.8 per cent in 1986, but 13.9 per cent in 1992) – both held on proportional representation and both considered relatively unimportant for national policy-making. In 1992, some 200 regional councillors (out of a total of 1,700) were elected among ecology candidates. Crucially, however, and with the two important exceptions of the 1989 and 1999 European elections, the allegiances of ecology candidates have been divided – between at least three groupings in 1993, for example, and two in 1997.

The history of the (political) ecology movement since 1974 can be divided into four periods corresponding, roughly, to presidential terms.

- *During the Giscard presidency*, the ecologists' electoral audience was low (the peak was 4.4 per cent in the 1979 European elections). They were handicapped by the fact that neither the French Friends of the Earth, nor the Mouvement Écologique, created in 1974, nor the Mouvement pour l'Écologie Politique, founded five years later, resembled a structured party; indeed, most ecologists were allergic to the very notion. Brice Lalonde's 3.88 per cent in the first ballot of the 1981 elections owed more to his own falsely naive charm than to the solidity of his campaign organisation, Aujourd'hui l'Écologie. After some hesitation and some vague promises from the Socialist candidate to re-examine the nuclear energy issue, Lalonde's backers supported Mitterrand for the second ballot.
- *Mitterrand's first term* showed Lalonde's relative success in April 1981 to be short-lived, and ecology candidates achieved a negligible score at the June 1981 parliamentary elections. Moreover, the foundation in 1984 of Les Verts, a serious attempt at an ecology party, drove Lalonde into dissidence. This was perhaps the most important division within the movement for the next decade: the 1984 European elections confirmed the split between the 'neither Right, nor Left' line of the

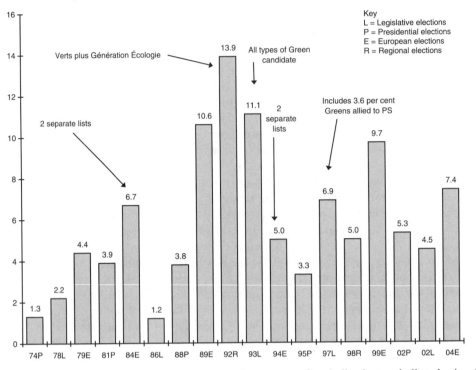

Figure 7.4 Votes for ecology movements (% of votes cast, first ballot in two-ballot elections), 1974–2004.

official Verts and the opportunism of Lalonde, who formed a joint list with Michel Crépeau of the MRG and a dissident former Gaullist, Olivier Stirn. Each of the two lists won some 3.3 per cent of the vote, but the two 1986 elections (regional and parliamentary) left Les Verts disappointed and in debt. At the 1988 presidential elections a new Green candidate, the somewhat dour Antoine Waechter, won 3.8 per cent of the vote – a creditable score as he was competing against a dissident Communist, Pierre Juquin, who had sought to create a 'Red–Green alternative' federation but achieved only 2.1 per cent.

- *Mitterrand's second term* saw both a new electoral peak and a strategic impasse for the ecology movement. The run of good election results, all over 10 per cent, in 1989, 1992 and 1993, appeared at the time as a breakthrough into mainstream politics. In fact they were flawed, for three reasons. First, they depended, like Green results elsewhere in Europe (especially in 1989), on an ephemeral public interest in the environment, speedily overshadowed by the onset of recession in the early 1990s. Second, in both 1992 and 1993, ecology candidates attracted votes from discontented PS supporters at the time of the Socialists' 'disgrace'. The Socialist recovery, when it came, was at the expense of ecology candidates. Third, the movement was still divided. Waechter still insisted on the absolute independence of Les Verts from both Right and Left; Lalonde, on the contrary, was junior environment minister from 1989 till 1992 and founded Génération Écologie in 1990 with the blessing of Mitterrand, who hoped for a Green 'satellite' for the PS. The cost of division was clear in March 1993, when the more sanguine Greens had hoped to replace the discredited PS as the major party of the 'non-Right' in France. Despite an electoral alliance between Les Verts and Génération Écologie, the two parties won a mere 8 per cent of the votes between them (4.1 per cent for Les Verts, 3.7 for Génération Écologie, to which were added votes from more dubious ecology and animal-lovers' candidates, some of them close to the far Right). On this basis, they failed either to win any seats or even to count for much in the second-ballot result. Both the Waechter and the Lalonde strategies seemed to lead nowhere, and the movement fragmented further: in the mid-1990s, some ten different groups competed for the support of ecology-minded citizens. Within Les Verts, the fallout of the 1993 elections saw Waechter placed in a minority by Dominique Voynet, a former far Left activist. But Voynet's result as a presidential candidate in 1995 (3.3 per cent) showed no obvious sign of a Green recovery.

• *The Chirac presidency* saw the ascendancy of Voynet in the Green movement and the breakthrough of Les Verts into parliamentary and ministerial office. Voynet survived her indifferent presidential result to confirm the change of strategy she had embarked upon before 1995: neither the opportunism of Lalonde nor the austere isolation of Waechter, but a negotiated alliance with the Left, with constituencies reserved for Les Verts and some joint policy commitments. Such a national agreement was reached with the PS in January 1997, with twenty-nine constituencies 'reserved' for Les Verts at the first round, in exchange for first-ballot support from Les Verts for 77 Socialist candidates; and on the strength of 3.7 per cent of the vote the following May, Les Verts won 8 parliamentary seats and a post for Voynet as minister for regional planning and the environment (a junior ministerial post for the party would follow). That eclipsed the other components of the disparate ecology movement, led by former presidential candidates, which accounted for a further 3 per cent of the vote: Waechter's Mouvement pour une Écologie Indépendante, and Lalonde's Génération Écologie (Lalonde's promiscuity after the presidential election had drawn him close first to President Chirac and then to the free-market conservative Alain Madelin). In April 2002 Noël Mamère, a former television presenter and mayor of Bègles, achieved the best ever result for an ecology candidate at a presidential election, but his score of 5.3 per cent was still below the heightened expectations of Les Verts. At the parliamentary elections two months later, back in harness with the Left (94 Socialists, as well as 12 Communist and 4 Left Radicals, were supported from the first ballot by Les Verts, who in turn benefited from Socialist backing in 59 seats and from backing of all *gauche plurielle* parties in 4 more), Les Verts lost all but 3 of their Deputies, including Voynet – but remained an indispensable part of the Left.

The two decades since the foundation of Les Verts have thus seen their partial integration into the political mainstream. By the end of 2004, the party could boast 47 mayors (mostly of smallish suburban municipalities), 168 regional councillors, 25 councillors for *départements*, 23 Paris councillors, 6 MEPs, 3 Deputies and – thanks to their alliance with the Socialists and the beginnings of their local implantation – 4 Senators (including Voynet). Limited compared to the record of the German Grünen, this still represented a foothold in the system. Les Verts should not, however, be viewed simply as a party of government; their experience of office within the *gauche plurielle* alliance has been at best a partial success, hotly debated after the event. They had rather little direct impact on government policy. It is true that convergence with the PS on institutional measures produced the five-year presidential term, gender parity, justice reforms and partial limitations on the *cumul des mandats* (significantly frustrated by the Senate), while Les Verts were also strong supporters of the 35-hour week. On the other hand, the only two major decisions in favour of the environment, the shutdown of the Superphénix nuclear reactor and the cancellation of the Rhine–Rhône canal, were already in Jospin's 1995 presidential programme. And a range of other measures, such as the continuation of the motorway programme and the abolition of the car licence fee, the re-opening of the Mont Blanc road tunnel after the disaster of 2000, the failure to raise taxes on diesel fuel, the announcement of a third airport for Paris, as well as the ambiguous attitude to genetically modified foods, went against the spirit of the 1997 agreement with the PS. Jospin's France still had one of Europe's worst records on implementing European environment directives, and was notably remiss on anything relating to the shooting season, thanks to the fear – or sympathy – inspired by the gun lobby among Socialist parliamentarians. Voynet's personal record as a minister was undistinguished, that of her successor (after 2000) Yves Cochet practically invisible; neither used the available opportunities to further the green cause.

Unsurprisingly in these circumstances, the experience of government has not reinforced the unity of Les Verts; even before the defeats of 2002, the party's endemic factionalism had led one Green Deputy to refer to Les Verts as a party of ageing and over-argumentative hippies, while Voynet remarked in private that 'our rules are daft, you have to head off a psychodrama every two years'. An inevitable result of this was weak leadership. At the November 2002 congress Voynet lost her post as national secretary to Gilles Lemaire, who had only joined Les Verts in 1999 and whose roots were with the far Left; in January 2005 Lemaire himself had to hand over to Yann Wehrling, a 33-year-old with no experience of elective office, who candidly described himself as the 'lowest common denominator' between the four factions that had fought the party to a near stalemate at the December 2004 congress. The party found it no easier to agree on the European constitutional treaty than on the leadership: while the membership of Les Verts supported the treaty by a narrow 53 per cent to 47 per cent in an internal referendum in February 2005, Green voters said no by 64 per cent to 36 at the real referendum three months later.

What would bring Les Verts greater leverage within the French Left would be the introduction, at least partial, of proportional representation to the legislative electoral system. This was one of the party's major goals, early in 2005, as it undertook initial moves towards the negotiation of a joint programme with the PS for the elections of 2007. Its achievement would depend on clear leadership, consistency of purpose and electoral muscle. Whether these were any more available than in the past among Les Verts, however, was open to question.

Concluding remarks

Even when out of national office, the Left has still held various forms of power. As Table 7.5 shows, Communists and Socialists have typically run half or more of France's major towns under the Fifth Republic. Nantes, Rennes, Grenoble, Lille and Le Mans all have left-wing mayors; they were joined by Paris and Lyon in 2001. The excellent results at the regional and cantonal elections of 2004 won the Left control of half of the ninety-five provincial *départements* of metropolitan France (a high level given the rural, conservative bias inherent in cantonal representation) and, in a striking reversal of earlier fortunes at the regional level, the presidencies of twenty out of twenty-two regions. At the national level, even with the Right in power, the Left has also retained sympathisers in government, within ministerial *cabinets* (it was Jacques Delors, for example, who drafted much of the 'New Society' speech with which the Gaullist Jacques Chaban-Delmas opened his premiership in 1969, while his daughter Martine Aubry became a Socialist labour minister three years after leaving the *cabinet* of a Gaullist social affairs minister) and even among ministers (Edgard Pisani, de Gaulle's agriculture minister, and Michel Jobert and Léo Hamon, both ministers under Pompidou, all subsequently joined the Left; Jean-Louis Borloo, Chirac's social affairs minister, would be at home in any centre-Left government in Europe). Indeed, it could be argued that left-wing sympathies, at least in some policy areas, penetrated to the very highest levels. De Gaulle's foreign policy was interpreted as dangerously pro-Soviet and Giscard's early societal reforms won the bulk of their popular support (as well as their parliamentary support in several cases) from left-wing sympathisers; the campaigns that elected Chirac in 1995, and to a lesser extent in 2002, had a distinct (if tactical) left-wing tinge, and his opposition to the Blairite agenda for Europe is well entrenched. The Left has also retained much of its ideological ascendancy. The alarming domination of much of France's intellectual life by Marxists and their fellow-travellers that reached a peak in the 1970s has, it is true, ended. It is also possible, as it was not before 1981, for politicians to declare their right-wing loyalties openly without being classed as Fascists. 'Conservative', on the other hand, remains a term of abuse in the French political lexicon, and the Left also retains a hold on the hearts and minds of the French in more substantial ways. The Gaullists, the largest current on the French Right both before and after the merger of the Gaullist party with part of the non-Gaullist moderate Right, has never fully sloughed off its penchant for a strong, interventionist state. The dominant ethos in a range of pressure groups, not only the obvious ones like the major trade unions, but others such as women's organisations, consumer groups or sports clubs, is progressive, egalitarian and leftish. The same is true of environmental groups, of influential sections of the press, of many Catholic lay organisations, and to a greater or lesser extent of economic planning agencies and of policy communities surrounding such areas as education, social security, health and housing. Finally, the remarkably wide sympathy inspired by rebelling students, striking railwaymen, or wider masses of wage-earners who challenged right-wing governments in 1986, 1995 and 2003–4, by the ideals of equality in education, the defence of the social security system and the preservation of public services that they claimed to stand for, has been a powerful brake on attempts to reform France's very large public sector. When a section of the Left considered that the European constitutional treaty threatened these ideals, it campaigned against it and won. That the treaty would be opposed by the nationalist Right and the extreme Left was a foregone conclusion. It was the size of the opposition within the mainstream Left, and particularly the PS, that set France's Socialists apart from their counterparts elsewhere in continental Europe and ensured a majority no vote on 29 May 2005.

The problem of the left-wing parties has always been to translate the diffuse sympathy they command into useful votes at the right moment. Only twice under the Fifth Republic, at the parliamentary elections of 1978 and 1981, has the Left commanded a first-ballot majority at a national election. On three occasions, moreover, the Left has won the support of fewer than a third of the voters: 31.7 per cent in the presidential election against de Gaulle in 1965; 30.9 per cent against Pompidou in 1969 (when no left-wing candidate survived to the second ballot); 30.8 per cent at the 1993 parliamentary elections, during the Socialist 'disgrace'. At another five parliamentary elections, in 1958, 1962, 1967, 1968 and 1986, and at the presidential election of 1995, the Left's first-round score has been so low (45 per cent or less) as to preclude any serious prospect of victory (the same would also have been true of the presidential elections of 2002, had Jospin not in any case been eliminated at the first ballot). And even François Mitterrand's presidential victories were preceded by at least relative right-wing majorities at the first round.

   This record raises the question of how the Left has won power at all. The answer lies in a performance that usually (though not invariably) improves at second ballots, owing to five main elements, most readily discernible in the transfers of votes between ballots at presidential elections.

- *The Left's 'republican discipline' at second ballots.* As the left-wing alliance took shape from the mid-1960s, most voters of the two big left-wing parties grew accustomed to supporting one another's candidates. Even when relations between them were poor, as in 1981, 1988 and 1993, Communist voters overwhelmingly supported Socialists at the second ballot. Socialists were somewhat more reluctant to vote for Communists, but about three-quarters of them could still usually be expected to do so.
- *Absentionists.* At some second ballots the Left has mobilised significantly more first-ballot abstentionists than the Right. At the 1981 presidential elections, for example, a number of left-wing voters, disenchanted by the Left's squabbling and pessimistic about the outcome of the election, stayed away at the first round, but rallied to Mitterrand at the second.
- *Ecologists.* Both Mitterrand in 1981 and 1988, and Jospin in 1995, attracted a clear majority of first-round ecology voters at the run-off, without any formal agreement with Les Verts or any other group, at a time when ecology groupings were formally situated, by themselves and by electoral statisticians, as neither Right nor Left. Many of such voters, indeed, especially in the early 1990s, were disappointed Socialists who could be expected to return to the PS at the decisive round. In the 2002 parliamentary elections, with Les Verts fully integrated into a left-wing damage limitation strategy, as many as 89 per cent of their voters backed left-wing candidates at the second ballot.
- *The moderate Right.* The Left has sometimes been the beneficiary of splits and quarrels within the mainstream Right. Mitterrand was elected in 1981 with the help of about an eighth of Chirac's voters from the first round. Seven years later, a similar proportion of Barre supporters helped him beat Chirac. And some 9 per cent of Balladur voters switched to Jospin in 1995.
- *The far Right.* The willingness of some far right-wing voters to support a left-wing candidate at second ballots was clear from the presidential election of 1965, when many voters who had supported the far Right candidate Jean-Louis Tixier-Vignancour chose to back Mitterrand at the run-off in order to punish de Gaulle for his 'loss' of Algeria. Similarly, as many as a quarter of Le Pen's voters switched to Mitterrand in 1988 and to Jospin in 1995. However, this is more likely to happen at presidential elections, where only two candidates go through to the run-off, than at parliamentary ones, where the Front National always keeps as many candidates as possible in the running for the second ballot. Some analysts have argued that the

survival of 76 Front National candidates to the second round in 1997 ensured the Left's victory; for 61 of these constituencies were won by the Left.

Between them, these elements give the Left a somewhat better chance of victory than the usual level of its first-ballot support would suggest. But two conditions also have to be met at the first ballot: a PCF too weak to frighten away crucial Centre voters at the run-off, and a score within striking distance of a majority (over 45 per cent). The first of these conditions, insuperable for the Fifth Republic's first two decades, has been fulfilled at every election since 1981. The second, on the other hand, has been met under the two-ballot system on just five occasions since then: the presidential elections of 1981 and 1988 and the parliamentary elections that followed in each case, and the parliamentary elections of 1997.

The Left's return to government in 1997 bore witness to a remarkable restoration both in the strength of the PS and in the credibility of the left-wing alliance after the disasters of the early 1990s; it therefore suggested the possibility of a similarly rapid recovery under the widely unpopular rule of Chirac and Raffarin. But the defeats of 2002 offer two harder lessons. The first is the Left's difficulty in retaining (winning back might now be more accurate) what went almost without question for half a century – the support of the bulk of the French working class. Whatever the Jospin government's achievements, it failed to convince enough of this still large and crucial group either that it could deliver its historic goal of a radical transformation of society (that had been abandoned in 1983), or that it could even reform capitalism in accordance with the Left's values of equality and of economic and social as well as political citizenship. The deep divisions of the Left, and especially the Socialists, over the European constitutional treaty should be understood in this light. Supporters saw the treaty as a means to reinforce the position of Europe (including its social model) in the world. For many of its opponents, by contrast, the treaty's adoption would have closed off the prospects of serious left-wing reform for the forseeable future; the Left would thereby be permanently cut off from its natural constituency. France's no vote of May 2005, on the other hand, seemed (to them, though to few others) to hold out the hope of a Europe-wide mobilisation in favour of a renegotiated treaty.

The second lesson of Jospin's, and then the Left's, defeats, might be called catch-2002. It is that the Left needs to be as inclusive and diverse as possible, to compensate for the PCF's catastrophic decline and the failure of the PS either to retain working-class support or even to win 30 per cent of the vote on a lasting basis; but that inclusiveness and diversity have a cost, in terms of coherence, which risks pulling the whole alliance apart at the crucial moment. A succession of studies, most recently by Daniel Boy and others, have underlined the presence of rather different cultures – the 'worker-ist', the 'pragmatic' and the 'post-materialist' – within the Left. These are regularly projected into a context of intense party competition within the alliance by party leaders mindful of their home bases, and prove difficult to manage in consequence. This poses the question of leadership. And from that perspective, not the least achievement of François Mitterrand, despite his failings, was to allow the Left to transcend its longstanding differences for long enough to win.

Further reading

Amar, C. and Chemin, A., *Jospin & Cie. Histoire de la gauche plurielle, 1993–2002*, Paris, Seuil, 2002.

Bell, D. S. and Criddle, B., *The French Socialist Party*, 2nd edition, Oxford, Clarendon Press, 1988.

Bell, D. S. and Criddle, B., *The French Communist Party in the Fifth Republic*, Oxford, Clarendon Press, 1994.

Bergounioux, A. and Grunberg, G., *Le long remords du pouvoir: le Parti socialiste français 1905–1992*, Paris, Fayard, 1992.

Boy, D., Platone, F., Rey, H., Subileau, F. and Ysmal, C., *C'était la gauche plurielle*, Paris, Presses de Sciences Po, 2003.

Bréchon, P. (ed.), *Les partis politiques français*, 2nd edition, Paris, La Documentation Française, 2005.

Clift, B., *French Socialism in a Global Era*, London, Continuum, 2002.

Cole, A. and Doherty, B., 'France: *Pas comme les autres* – the French Greens at the crossroads', in D. Richardson and C. Rootes (eds), *The Green Challenge: The Development of Green Parties in Europe*, London, Routledge, 1995, pp. 45–65.

Courtois, S. and Lazar, M., *Histoire du Parti communiste français*, 2nd edition, Paris, Presses Universitaires de France, 2001.

Duverger, M., *Political Parties: Their Organisation and Activity in the Modern State*, London, Methuen, 1964.

Evans, J. (ed.), *The French Party System*, Manchester, Manchester University Press, 2003.

Hazareesingh, S., *Intellectuals and the French Communist Party*, Oxford, Clarendon Press, 1991.

Hewlett, N., *French Politics since 1945: Conflict and Consensus*, Cambridge, Polity, 1998.

Johnson, R. W., *The Long March of the French Left*, London, Macmillan, 1981.

Katz, R. S. and Mair, P., 'Changing models of party organization and party democracy: the emergence of the cartel party', *Party Politics*, 1(1), 1995, pp. 5–28.

Kirchheimer, O., 'The transformation of West European party systems', in J. LaPalombara and M. Weiner (eds), *Political Parties and Political Development*, Princeton, NJ, Princeton University Press, 1966, pp. 177–200.

Knapp, A., *Parties and the Party System in France: A Disconnected Democracy?*, Basingstoke, Palgrave Macmillan, 2004.

Kriegel, A., *The French Communists*, Chicago, University of Chicago Press, 1972.

Lancelot, A., *Les élections nationales sous la Cinquième République*, 3rd edition, Paris, Presses Universitaires de France, 1998.

Lavabre, M.-C. and Platone, F., *Que reste-t-il du PCF?*, Paris, CEVIPOF/Autrement, 2003.

Mair, P. and van Biezen, M., 'Party membership in twenty European democracies, 1980–2000', *Party Politics*, 7 (1); January 2001, pp. 5–21.

Nick, C., *Les Trotskistes*, Paris, Fayard, 2002.

Perrineau, P. (ed.), *L'engagement politique: déclin ou mutation?*, Paris, Presses de la Fondation Nationale des Sciences Politiques, 1994.

Pingaud, D., *La gauche de la gauche*, Paris, Seuil, 2000.

Portelli, H., *Le Parti socialiste*, 2nd edition, Paris, Montchrestien, 1998.

Rey, H., *La gauche et les classes populaires*, Paris, La Découverte, 2004.

Sainteny, G., *L'introuvable écologisme français?*, Paris, Presses Universitaires de France, 2000.

Schain, M., *French Communism and Local Power*, London, Frances Pinter, 1985.

Touchard, J., *La gauche en France depuis 1900*, Paris, Seuil, 1991.

von Beyme, K., *Political Parties in Western Democracies*, Aldershot, Gower, 1985.

Ware, A., *Political Parties and Party Systems*, Oxford, Oxford University Press, 1996.

Party websites

Parti Communiste Français	http://www.pcf.fr/accueil/php
Parti Socialiste	http://www.parti-socialiste.fr
Ligue Communiste Révolutionnaire	http://www.lcr-rouge.org
Lutte Ouvrière	http://www.lutte-ouvrière.org
Les Verts	http://lesverts.fr

8 The Right

Domination and division

On the Left, the major division can be dated from the Socialist–Communist split at Tours in 1920. No equivalent point of separation can explain the divisions between Gaullists, the non-Gaullist moderate Right and the far Right. René Rémond, however, has related them to three separate traditions running through the French Right since the Revolution, corresponding to the dynasties that competed with the republicans for control of the régime in the nineteenth century. These are: the 'ultra' Right, which rejected all republican values and sought to restore the pre-revolutionary Bourbon monarchy; the moderate, 'Orleanist' Right, ready to compromise with moderate republicans, and attached, in the nineteenth century, to the British virtues of moderate constitutional monarchy and free trade; and the 'Bonapartist' Right, which stressed the virtues of strong leadership with direct links to the mass of the people, a strong state and an assertive foreign policy. In contemporary terms, Rémond suggested, the inheritors of the 'Orleanists' were the non-Gaullist moderate Right, while the heirs of Bonaparte were the Gaullists; others have cast the Front National in the role of the latter-day 'ultra' Right. The reality is much less tidy. The sources of policy division have been transformed; and the French tradition of Christian Democracy (weaker than in Germany or Italy, but still significant) finds no easy place in any of the categories. But Rémond's triad remains a useful reminder of the different temperaments, repeatedly encountered among right-wing parties and leaders, which help to explain their recurrent failure to unite.

Linked to, but distinct from, ideological traditions are traditions of party organisation. In the France of 1900, nearly half the active population worked on the land. Rural networks and hierarchies marked much of the country well after the emergence of universal suffrage and free elections in 1871. They, not the emerging industrial mass society, shaped the organisation of right-wing parties. In Duverger's terms (see Chapter 7), they were 'cadre' parties, formed essentially of local notables and with little or no formal membership. Social changes and the institutions of the Fifth Republic (notably the direct election of the president) have encouraged more structured, nationwide forms of party organisation. But politicians of the Right remain divided between those who value the flexibility and independence found in the cadre party, and those (chiefly among the Gaullists) who value a more disciplined organisation and clearer leadership, whether within a 'mass' or a 'catch-all' party.

The two moderate components of the French Right are also divided because France's various electoral systems allow space for competing forces on the Centre–Right. The failure of merger attempts between the moderate Right's two main components, Gaullist and non-Gaullist, in the late 1980s did not prevent the comfortable electoral victories of 1993 and 1995; when a merger did take place, with the formation of the UMP, it *followed* rather than preceded the victories of 2002, was incomplete and did not prevent major setbacks in 2004. In a broader political sense, however, the moderate Right has repeatedly been damaged by its own internal divisions and rivalries. These were compounded, from 1984, by the challenge posed by the rise of the Front National. This chapter first covers the Gaullists and the non-Gaullist moderate Right (NGMR), and their partial merger in the UMP in 2002, before turning to the problems posed by the extreme Right.

The Gaullists

Though Gaullism has always attracted conservatives, it did not start life merely as a variety of conservatism. De Gaulle's central concern with France's place in the world's affairs; his insistence on strong leadership and robust institutions as the necessary conditions of France regaining and keeping its rightful 'rank'; his readiness to engage the power of the state, often in a manner that could only be described as *dirigiste*, to the same end; his refusal to compromise on his conception of national sovereignty, but his readiness to be pragmatic, and often radical, about much else (including Algeria); all of these marked him apart from the dominant, Orleanist, conservative current of the time. Indeed, the General's three decades in politics were replete with clashes with conservatives of every stamp. The founding act of Gaullism, the refusal to accept France's defeat in 1940, was a gauntlet thrown down as much to the conservative elites who fell in behind Marshal Pétain in the collaborationist Vichy government as it was to the occupying Germans. De Gaulle clashed with conservatives on the constitution both in the immediate post-war period and in 1962, when he engaged the constitutional reform on the direct election of the presidency; his relations with France's Christian Democrats were at best chilly and at worst, notably over European issues, downright hostile. And it was his final challenge to the conservative France of local notables, in his plans for Senate and regional reforms, that led to de Gaulle's downfall in the referendum of 1969. The quirkiness that set Gaullism apart from mainstream conservatism led Klaus von Beyme, in his classification of Western Europe's political families, to place it in a category almost of its own – shared only with Ireland's Fianna Fáil.

De Gaulle always claimed for himself personally a special relationship with France, and argued that as France was beyond Right and Left, so he was above parties. It is therefore one of the great ironies of the Fifth Republic that General de Gaulle endowed France with its first great organised, disciplined party of the Right. The Union pour la Nouvelle République developed, unusually, from the top downwards: on de Gaulle's return to power in 1958, the Gaullists enjoyed the benefits of office while barely existing at all as a party. For that reason, many observers forecast the party's imminent demise once its creator was out of the way. These expectations (or hopes) were confounded. De Gaulle's resignation, in April 1969, and his death, in November 1970, came and went; Pompidou died in April 1974, and a non-Gaullist succeeded him in the Élysée; the premiership was lost in 1976, and all remaining government positions in 1981. But the party refused to disappear. Its survival depended ultimately on building the internal organisation which it had lacked at the start of the Fifth Republic. Chirac's election in 1995 as the first president in twenty-one years to claim allegiance to the Gaullist family testifies to both his and his party's success at doing this. But the process, neither smooth nor easy, involved a progressive surrender of the 'pure' Gaullist identity. Indeed, the Gaullists changed their official party name six times under the Fifth Republic (for the sake of convenience, all the party's incarnations – given in full in Appendix 6 – before the party adopted the RPR label in 1976 are referred to here simply as the Gaullist party, even though the word 'party' aroused such loathing among Gaullists that it appeared in none of the titles), until they merged, in 2002, into a new party without any open Gaullist reference, the UMP (Union pour une Majorité Présidentielle from May to November 2002, Union pour un Mouvement Populaire since then).

The vicissitudes of Gaullism under the Fifth Republic, and its progressive dissolution into a wider conservative identity, were spread over seven distinct phases.

The search for identity: 1958–62

It was in this period that the party transformed itself from a small group of Gaullists scattered amid the ruins of the Fourth Republic into a centralised organisation. Pro-*Algérie française* elements were purged, and the party became a subservient instrument of the president of the Republic. After the referendum and elections of autumn 1962, it had become an indispensable one too. But the party membership remained small, partly to prevent *Algérie française* infiltration and partly because de Gaulle had mistrusted mass organisations ever since the unsuccessful experience of the first big Gaullist party, the Rassemblement du Peuple Français (RPF), between 1947 and 1953.

Growth, consolidation and hegemony: 1962–73

The decade between the referendum and elections of autumn 1962 (see Chapter 2, p. 60) and the March 1973 parliamentary elections, just a year before Pompidou's death, can be counted the Gaullists' golden age, during which they enjoyed a position of dominance unequalled under any French republican régime. This dominance in this period rested on six pillars.

- *The propagation of a set of doctrines*, a form of Gaullism for the masses, based on the primacy of national unity and a denial of the Marxist notion of class struggle; the defence of a powerful state and a strong executive authority, as written into the new constitution; the creation of a modern industrial economy; and the assertion of national independence in foreign and European affairs. To the doctrines corresponded policy outputs that voters valued and appreciated. These included peace and reconciliation after the Algerian trauma; political stability; economic growth; and an agreeable sense of France's renewed stature in the concert of nations.
- *The party's symbiotic relationship with the president* made it the buttress and

guardian of the presidency, and the main defender of presidential policies in parliament and in the country, especially at election times. This role was a subservient one; the party's secretary-general, for example, was effectively a delegate of the president, who also vetted its parliamentary candidates. At the same time de Gaulle found he needed the party's support, notably to ensure his own re-election to the presidency in 1965.

• *The penetration of the state apparatus.* The party's reward for loyalty to the president was the lion's share of the patronage available to the executive: not only the premiership and most government portfolios, but also the key posts in ministerial *cabinets*, in the state broadcasting networks and in nationalised industries and banks went to Gaullists. This tentacular spread of political patronage led the visceral anti-Gaullist Jean-Jacques Servan-Schreiber to coin the phrase 'l'État-UDR' – the Gaullist state.

• *Electoral strength.* At the start of the Fifth Republic, the Gaullists relied almost wholly on their association with General de Gaulle for their electoral support. But in later parliamentary elections, as Figure 8.1 (and Tables 7.1 and 7.2) show, their level of support converged with de Gaulle's own: a fifth of the voters in 1958, over a third in 1962 and 1967, and nearly two-fifths in June 1968, when a conservative reaction against the (perceived) Communist threat of the previous month secured the Gaullists 293 out of 487 seats – the first single-party parliamentary majority in the history of the Republic. Gaullists always claimed to represent a cross-section of the electorate – 'the rush-hour crowd on the Paris metro', as André Malraux

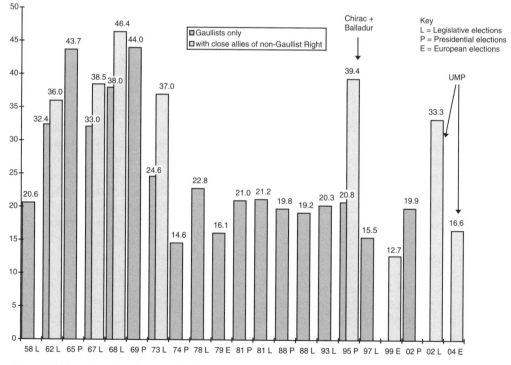

Figure 8.1 Votes for Gaullist parties (% of votes cast, first ballot in two-ballot elections), 1958–2004.

put it. This was always less true of the party than of the General himself, and also less true as time went on and the Gaullist ranks swelled with traditionally conservative groups – the elderly, women, higher income groups and practising Catholics. But it remained more socially representative than most earlier right-wing parties: a 'parti d'électeurs' in Jean Charlot's term, a 'catch-all' party in Otto Kirchheimer's.

- *The domination of the presidential majority*. Outside the unusual circumstances of 1968–73, the Gaullists depended on allies – notably, from 1962, on Valéry Giscard d'Estaing's Républicains Indépendants – for their parliamentary majority. They shared out the government ministries with Giscardians and, from 1969, with Jacques Duhamel's Centre Démocratie et Progrès. But they were the dominant partners. One indication of this was the Gaullists' share of the majority's parliamentary candidacies. These *investitures* were shared out between the different components of the majority before each election, often after long negotiations, but according to a general rule that sitting Deputies faced no competition from other majority candidates. The Gaullists, with plenty of sitting Deputies from the elections of 1962 and then 1968, dominated the *investitures*, to a degree which opinion polls suggested was disproportionate to their support in the country by 1973.

- *Organisational strength*. De Gaulle's reservations about creating a big, structured, party organisation were balanced, from 1965, by an awareness that he needed such an organisation to revive his sagging presidential campaign. In 1966, he therefore allowed his prime minister Georges Pompidou to take the party in hand. By the time of de Gaulle's resignation, many leaders and cadres of Resistance pedigree had given way to a newer generation, and party membership had probably doubled since the early 1960s (to about 160,000, many of them recruited in reaction to May 1968). It would take an indulgent observer to call this a 'mass' party, but it was still considerably more structured than the cadre model typical of earlier parties of the Right. Its existence helped save the party during *l'après-de Gaulle*. It also, of course, helped elect Pompidou to the presidency, with a record 58.21 per cent at the second ballot against the centrist Poher.

Jean Charlot argued that in the 'parti d'électeurs', the Gaullists gave France a new kind of party, free of attachments to particular ideologies or interest groups, which won elections by delivering policy goods the voters wanted. He also claimed that Gaullism changed the multiparty landscape of the Fourth Republic into a 'dominant-party system' during the 1960s. Comparison with other democracies makes such claims look overstated; all democratic parties must satisfy voters, after all, and a party that wins a string of elections over fifteen years, though impressive, has no more created a 'dominant-party system' than Thatcher's Conservatives in Britain or Kohl's Christian Democrats in Germany. But when the comparison is with the parties and party system of the Fourth Republic, Charlot's analysis does indeed point up a dramatic contrast.

Other observers compared the Gaullists to the Radicals, the quintessential governing party of the Third Republic, pointing to their pragmatic doctrine, their solid, durable position in parliament and in ministries, their electoral spread south of the Loire where Radicals had always done well, their steadily growing local roots. True, there were also differences: the Gaullists' love of strong leaders, anathema to the Radicals; their assertiveness in foreign policy, an area which had left the Radicals indifferent; their imperviousness to the anti-clericalism which animated so many Radicals. But the most striking resemblance was that by 1972, the Gaullists appeared to many, as the Radicals had in the 1930s, as a party that had grown fat on patronage and been in power too long.

The loss of power: 1973–76

By 1972 it was clear that the Gaullists were in serious difficulties. Discipline, traditionally their strength, had declined since 1969. Deputies had criticised the 'opening' of the majority, and had found Pompidou's first prime minister, Jacques Chaban-Delmas, too liberal. Gaullist dissidents had helped turn Pompidou's 1972 referendum on enlargement of the European Community into a damp squib; in 1973, they would sabotage his plan for a constitutional amendment to limit the presidential term to five years. Property development scandals had engulfed several leading Gaullists and passed close to several more. The March 1973 parliamentary elections saw the party's support fall back to a quarter of the voters, a drop of 2 million and a lower percentage than in 1962 (see Table 7.2). That meant a loss of over 100 Deputies. Although Gaullists held on to two-thirds of the majority's parliamentary seats, this was largely thanks to their continued hold on the majority's *investitures* rather than to their inherent electoral strength. Opinion polls suggested that their real support in the country was now no greater than that of their allies, the Centrists and Giscard's Républicains Indépendants. The special relationship with the whole of France, the essence of de Gaulle's style of politics, had largely vanished; the Gaullists had become simply the largest component of a conservative coalition.

Pompidou's illness, visible by mid-1973, prompted the Gaullists to look for a successor. Perversely, they adopted Chaban-Delmas, whom they had mistrusted before Pompidou had sacked him as prime minister in 1972, as the rightful heir. But they were still caught unprepared by Pompidou's death on 2 April 1974 – unlike Giscard, who had chosen not to run in 1969 but was now swift to seize this opportunity. Chaban's poor electoral showing accelerated rather than contained his party's decline; he was eliminated at the first round of the presidential elections, with less than half of Giscard's vote. Defeat was rendered all the more bitter for the Gaullists by the 'treason' of Interior Minister Jacques Chirac, who, with forty-three other leading Gaullists, had campaigned for Giscard from the first ballot (and whose reward, once Giscard was safely elected, would be the premiership). A handful of left-wing Gaullists called for a Mitterrand vote at the run-off in 1974, and joined the Left. Michel Jobert, who could not stomach Giscard, left the Gaullist party in 1975 to found the Mouvement des Démocrates. But for those Gaullists – the vast majority – who refused to throw in their lot with the Left, support for Chirac was the only viable option. His treachery towards Chaban, and his complicity with the liberal, reforming president inspired unease; but at least he offered leadership, especially from December 1974, when he took over the top party post of secretary-general in a spectacular coup. Chirac's equally spectacular resignation, in August 1976, came as a relief to many Gaullists as it cut the link with Giscard. But it also 'lost' the premiership to the party, and thus completed the severance of that close association between president, prime minister and the dominant party in the parliamentary majority which had been such an important cement during the Fifth Republic's early years.

Organisational renovation, electoral and strategic impasse: 1976–81

To compensate for their loss of power the Gaullists then attempted to build a mass party, relaunched as the RPR in December 1976. Chirac was elected, with Soviet-style ease (96.5 per cent of the votes), to the new post of party president. Grossly inflated membership figures were claimed: 550,000 at the end of 1977 and 750,000 (with 776 workplace sections) a year later; but if the true figure was probably nearer the 160,000 recorded after May 1968, this still brought the party back to its best levels of the Fifth Republic. Party elites were renewed. Chirac's election as the first twentieth-century mayor of Paris in March 1977 (after a law of 1975 had relaxed the former tight central government control over the capital) equipped him with a powerful logistical base, better in many ways than the premiership, or than a mass party organisation. In the parliamentary elections of March 1978, with 22.8 per cent of the votes cast and 154 Deputies elected, Chirac could still, just, claim to head France's largest party. Survival was no longer in serious doubt – as it clearly had been in 1974.

But the 1978 vote was still lower than that of 1973, and much lower than those of 1962, 1967 or 1968. The Gaullists were also in a strategic impasse: since joining forces with the Left was unthinkable, they had no choice but to stay in Giscard's majority – as long, that is, as Giscard was president. Before 1981, Chirac's (frequent) attacks on Giscard were thus reminiscent of a Caesar who repeatedly rushed his troops at the Rubicon, only to tell them to take out their fishing-rods. Above all, the Gaullists never voted a motion of censure against the government; voters would not have forgiven such an act of open complicity with Communists. Chirac was less restrained, however, at the campaign for the 1979 European elections, when he practically accused the Giscardians of being agents of a foreign power. And at the 1981 presidential election the need for Gaullist self-restraint applied not at all; a defeat for Giscard here would allow the Gaullists to regain their leadership on the Right.

Chirac's first-round vote in 1981, at 18 per cent, though insufficient to reach the run-off, was nearly three points ahead of Chaban in 1974 and thus respectable, especially as he had faced two dissident Gaullists, his own former adviser Marie-France Garaud and de Gaulle's first prime minister Michel Debré, who polled 3 per cent between them. But his charge that 'a change of policy requires a change of president' also mobilised pent-up Gaullist discontent against Giscard, legitimised the attacks of the more dangerous challenger, the Socialist François Mitterrand, and thus helped to destabilise the incumbent president. The Right's total first-round vote, at 49.8 per cent, was nearly three points down on 1974 (with Giscard himself dropping nearly four points from 32.6 per cent to 28.8). Giscard therefore needed all the right-wing votes he could get at the run-off. Chirac helped ensure he would not have them by declaring that while he himself would cast his ballot for the incumbent, his voters should follow their own consciences. Small wonder that Giscard, having lost the run-off by 48.24 per cent to Mitterrand's 51.76, accused Chirac of 'premeditated treachery'.

May 1981 saw the Right's first defeat in a national election under the Fifth Republic. June 1981 saw the second: at the parliamentary elections called by the newly elected Mitterrand, the Right lost 132 out of its 287 seats – and thus its majority. But the right-wing alliance continued. Among voters, while a quarter of Chirac's supporters had either abstained or voted Mitterrand at the run-off, the other three-quarters had loyally supported the incumbent. And the Right's leaders, after Giscard's temporary removal from the scene, made some effort to limit the impending disaster of the June elections by backing a joint candidate in 385 out of 487 constituencies, compared with 158 in 1978.

Chirac's two defeats: 1981–88

The defeats of 1981 left Chirac as the effective leader of the right-wing opposition and obliged him to reverse his political strategy. Since 1976 he had pursued a 'first-ballot' strategy, seeking to survive by highlighting his differences with his Giscardian 'allies' of the UDF in every possible way. Now he needed a 'second-ballot' strategy to secure the UDF's support for any future presidential bid. He therefore sought reconciliation with the wounded UDF, treating it as an equal partner in all pre-election negotiations. He undertook a major revision of the Gaullists' programme, and included elements of the New Right agenda – privatisations, business deregulation, law and order, as well as a degree of support for the Atlantic alliance and for Europe that would have been unthinkable four or five years earlier; these then became the basis for the joint RPR–UDF platform of 1986. Before 1981, it had still been possible to make a clear distinction between Gaullist policies (more attached to national sovereignty, more Eurosceptical, more *dirigiste* on the economy, more authoritarian, more inclined to dramatise politics) and those of the NGMR (more liberal on social issues, less *dirigiste*, more pro-European, Atlanticist within limits). From roughly 1983 onwards, this distinction was blurred, as the RPR converged on (and even overtook) its allies' neo-liberal economic positions. Meanwhile Chirac led a crusade against the 'Socialo-Communists' with as much gusto as he had recently employed in his attacks on Giscard. Elections in municipalities and *départements* brought big gains for the Right, allowing the Gaullists to reinforce their positions in local authorities and the Senate – both traditionally weak points. These successes left little doubt as to the outcome of the 1986 parliamentary elections, which produced a victory for the RPR–UDF coalition, with the Gaullists winning 155 seats to the UDF's 131, and won Chirac a second stint as prime minister.

Despite a respectable economic record, this second premiership failed in its purpose of convincing enough voters of Chirac's presidential qualities. Chirac was working under very difficult political conditions: a parliamentary majority of three, his most dangerous opponent (Mitterrand) still in the Élysée, pressure on the majority coalition's Right from the FN and on its moderate wing from Raymond Barre, who divided the coalition's loyalties – and two years to show a convincing record before the 1988 presidential elections. Chirac's failure to reach 20 per cent at the first ballot, and his 46 per cent at the second, were a humiliation. At the parliamentary elections that followed, the Gaullists even lost their majority of right-wing seats, with 130 Deputies to the non-Gaullist moderate Right's 131.

Disarray and victory: 1988–95

These defeats plunged the Gaullist party into a three-year post-electoral crisis, in which the party's elite aired grievances and doubts which had been building since 1981. The leadership was attacked for aligning itself too readily on the UDF's positions and straying too far from historic Gaullism. The very acceptance of cohabitation could be viewed as contrary to de Gaulle's vision of how the Fifth Republic should work. The dismantling of part of the apparatus of *dirigisme* was attacked as a betrayal that favoured the interests of a narrow elite but neglected those of the nation; Édouard

Balladur, finance minister from 1986 to 1988, was an emblem of this *embourgeoisé* Gaullism, remote from the reflexes of the party rank and file. The RPR's response to the threat from the FN was also questioned, though Gaullists disagreed as to the best solution, with some arguing for a rapprochement with the far Right, and others seeking a more aggressive attitude drawing on the anti-Fascist legacy of the Resistance. Finally, voices suggested that the Gaullist party had been sacrificed on the altar of Chirac's presidential ambitions and that past policy errors might have been avoided by a greater tolerance of internal debate and dissent than the party's autocratic structures had permitted. Some dissidents, indeed, began to refer to the RPR as 'the last Stalinist party in France'.

Underlying each of these questions was an unspoken doubt about Chirac's leadership and electability. The February 1990 congress saw a dissenting motion (a novelty in itself) presented jointly by Charles Pasqua on the party's Right and Philippe Séguin on the Left in the name of a return to Gaullist values: it lost by a two to one margin, probably rigged, but showed that the leadership could not take the rank and file for granted. The Pasqua–Séguin duo went on to supply the backbone of the no campaign for the referendum of 1992 on the Maastricht Treaty; they won the support of two-thirds of RPR voters, placing Chirac in a minority in his own party and highlighting his distance from traditional Gaullist values (de Gaulle had viewed currencies as central to the exercise of national sovereignty; the Maastricht Treaty spelt the end of the French franc). Despite this detour, however, Chirac's own leadership was not in doubt after 1991, and the prospect of a handsome win in the 1993 legislative elections was a force for cohesion.

Chirac could have embarked on a third premiership after the moderate Right's landslide victory (in terms of seats, more than of votes) in 1993. Instead, he left this job to Balladur and concentrated on preparing his presidential campaign for 1995, expecting Balladur's support when the time came. This did not materialise; Balladur's metamorphosis, in 1993, from understated prime minister into a credible presidential candidate ensured that Chirac's third presidential candidacy would divide the Right, and even the RPR. Competition with Balladur also dictated the conditions of Chirac's election: a vicious first-round battle where none had been expected, and a campaign that combined, with scant regard for any sort of coherence, the free-market, anti-tax rhetoric of Alain Madelin (Chirac's leading supporter from the ranks of the UDF) with Séguin's Gaullist discourse on social solidarity (Séguin claimed that the key phrase of Chirac's 1995 campaign, *la fracture sociale*, referring to the need to eliminate social exclusion, was his own). If that helped ensure Chirac's first-ballot lead of over two points over Balladur and thus, practically, to guarantee victory at the run-off, it also gave hostages to fortune for the Chirac presidency.

Victory and disarray: 1995–2000

By mid-1995 the elements of the Gaullists' lost 'dominance' – the presidency, the premiership (Alain Juppé became Chirac's first prime minister) and the largest group in a huge right-wing majority in the National Assembly – had fallen back into place. RPR membership, at about 140,000, was comparable to post-1968 levels: low compared with European conservative parties, but quite respectable in the French context, and big enough to represent a real national organisation. The party was good at attracting business money in the brief period in the early 1990s when business funding was legal and open (and probably also in all other periods, when it was neither). The Gaullists' local positions, moreover, with the presidencies of 7 out of metropolitan France's 22 regions and 28 out of 96 *départements*, as well as the control of Paris and 47 out of the 221 largest towns, were incomparably stronger than in the 1960s. The Senate, a persistent thorn in the side of de Gaulle, now contained 92 Gaullists out of a total of 321 Senators – nearly three times as many as in the General's time; they won enough allies, in September 1998, to win the presidency of the Senate for the first time under the Fifth Republic.

Yet, despite appearances, the equation of the 1960s no longer applied. First and foremost, the Gaullist electorate had shrunk. The victories of 1993 and 1995 were based on levels of first-ballot support for the RPR of about 20 per cent – little over half what it had been thirty years earlier. The 'catch-all' party of the 1960s had lost its (significant) working-class support to the rising forces of the Left after 1968, while many of the dynamic elements of the earlier electorate – the *forces vives* beloved of de Gaulle – defected to Socialism or the UDF. Chirac became president with a lower first-ballot score than any of his four Fifth Republic predecessors, and parts of this electorate – the young people attracted by the discourse on the *fracture sociale* – had grown disillusioned by 1997. His victory was flawed in other respects, too. The battle with the *balladuriens* created a lasting rift in the right-wing coalition generally and the RPR in particular which Chirac did nothing to heal. The promises of the campaign, lower taxes and an end to the *fracture sociale*, were dumped within months in the name of the Maastricht convergence criteria. Of the two pillars of the campaign, Séguin was sent back to his old job as president of the National Assembly, while Madelin was sacked as finance minister within three months of his appointment. When Juppé ran into political difficulties, he had few sure supporters, and Chirac had no alternative prime minister. The disastrous dissolution of 1997 was at least in part a bid to find a way out of a situation which the very logic of the 1995 campaign had rendered impossible.

The defeat of 1997 not only cost the Gaullists office and nearly half their 257 Deputies; it also plunged the party into its worst crisis since 1958. But the crisis had long-term roots, which can be summarised under three headings.

President and party

Relationships between presidents and their parties under the Fifth Republic have never been straightforward. Thanks to the Gaullist myth of a head of state 'above parties', the president cannot afford to be *seen* to be a party leader. He must *be* a party leader in order to manage his own support in the country; but he can only be so covertly. Presidential parties tolerate this as long as the president is a 'locomotive' for his party, as de Gaulle and Pompidou were. But Chirac in 1997 was a locomotive in reverse, whom many leading Gaullists considered had lost any right to support at the presidential elections due for 2002. Hence Chirac's temporary loss of control over the RPR in 1997: the party elected Séguin, whom Chirac had never trusted, as its president, and Séguin appointed Nicolas Sarkozy, Balladur's budget minister and presidential campaign director, as his secretary-general. The following two years saw a curious struggle as Chirac sought to destabilise Séguin as RPR leader while Séguin tried to undermine Chirac's re-election prospects – with neither daring to fight openly. Chirac won: Séguin resigned from the party leadership in the middle of the 1999 European election campaign, and Sarkozy, who took his place on a temporary basis, also left his party office after the poor result of the European list he had led. By the year's end the RPR had its first woman leader in Michèle Alliot-Marie, not Chirac's first choice but sufficiently weak politically to be increasingly dependent on him. But Chirac's victory had a cost in terms of the demobilisation of his party; by the end of 1999, the RPR counted an official total of 80,000 members – a drop of nearly half in five years.

A longer-term problem was the broader question of leadership in the party. More than any other political force, Gaullism had lived in symbiosis either with an incumbent president (de Gaulle and Pompidou) or with an aspiring one (from Chirac's relaunch of the party as his own instrument in 1976). From the 1980s, however, this link had been loosened by the Gaullists' stronger local positions, and by the fact that individual RPR politicians had to make their own way without any of the perquisites that may come from being the country's governing party. Political circumstances, as well as the institutional changes that attenuated the presidential character of the 'one and indivisible Republic' since 1958, had also 'depresidentialised' the RPR. The party's viability as a tool of Chirac's re-election ambitions, in terms both of loyalty and of organisational muscle, was badly damaged.

Ideology and policies

What Gaullism stood for was relatively clear in the 1960s: support for de Gaulle and for the (still controversial) Fifth Republic Constitution, for a state that was strong at home and assertive and independent abroad. Within those general perspectives, Gaullists could take pride in their pragmatism and diversity, describing their party as 'a movement of Frenchmen from a wide range of political horizons, agreed on a few essentials and sharing a common ideal of France'. That allowed the cohabitation between different Gaullisms: the Gaullism of the Resistance generation, loyal above all to 'the man of 18 June 1940'; a *gaullisme de gauche* focused on the General's social preoccupations; a *gaullisme droitière*, first seen in the RPF days under the Fourth Republic, steeped in a virulent anti-Communism; a *gaullisme pompidolien*, of which Balladur became the salient latter-day representative, obsessed by France's need to adapt to an increasingly competitive world while preserving social peace; and later a *gaullisme chiraquien* (mark 1), which revelled in the aggressive, populist, anti-European, anti-free-market rhetoric of the late 1970s (some of which was given a further outing in the 1995 campaign), and a *gaullisme chiraquien* (mark 2), inspired by the aggressive pro-free-market rhetoric of the mid-1980s. At all epochs, too, the party has had its opportunists, conservatives for whom it represented the best organised expression of their views and interests at a given moment. The party has harboured economic liberals and economic *dirigistes*, social liberals and social conservatives, and pro- and anti-Europeans.

This unity in diversity, however, became increasingly hard to sustain. First, none of the General's successors has had de Gaulle's ability to bind people to him; leadership is no longer the same counterweight to diversity. Secondly, the core Gaullist values of the 1960s began to appear either banal (loyalty to the Fifth Republic Constitution, now accepted in its broad outline by all parties) or problematic (a vigorous independent foreign policy, or an interventionist state). It was far harder to say what Gaullism was for in 2000 than it was in 1960; in 1999, indeed, polls indicated that 63 per cent of the French thought of Gaullism as 'a notion that no longer means much today' – a view shared by 57 per cent of RPR supporters. Within the party, the most divisive issue was Europe. For Gaullist diehards, the transfers of sovereignty to which Chirac consented in the treaties of Maastricht and of Amsterdam were breaches of the essential Gaullist value of national independence. Hence, in part, Pasqua's departure from the RPR in 1999 to form the Rassemblement pour la France, as well as the distancing from the party of many survivors of the Resistance generation.

Paris

For eighteen years between 1977 and 1995, Paris was Chirac's showcase and his power base, his international platform and the bastion on which he fell back in the event of defeat. Judicial investigations have also shown that it was the centre of much illegal activity. Full-time RPR officials were on the municipal payroll, housing distributed on a clientelistic basis, tenders for municipal contracts rigged in return for cash payments to the party, electoral rolls tampered with. After 1995, these scandals engulfed Jean Tiberi, Chirac's uninspiring successor as mayor, and France's capital elected a Socialist mayor in 2001. But senior party figures, including Juppé, were also placed under investigation. From an incomparable asset, Paris became a symbol of the RPR's rotten heart.

Chirac himself remained remarkably untouched by the stench of corruption emanating from his former bastion. The courts extended his constitutional immunity to prosecution for acts committed as president to his activities before his election. Moreover, polls two years before the 2002 elections showed that he had at least an even chance of beating his expected opponent, Jospin – and that no other right-wing candidate would come close. Under the Fifth Republic, however, it is axiomatic that a successful presidential candidate requires the solid backing of a party. The RPR, with its shrunken electoral support, its uncertain ideological base and its dislocated organisation, and its sleazy public image, scarcely seemed to meet this requirement.

The non-Gaullist moderate Right (NGMR)

If Gaullists trace their origins to de Gaulle's London broadcast which launched the Free French movement in 1940, their allies of the NGMR have a less heroic pedigree: their ancestry may be sought in the parties of the Right and Centre that ruled France for most of the Fourth Republic. The Parti Radical, the Christian Democrats of the MRP and the conservatives grouped in the Centre National des Indépendants et des Paysans (CNIP) all supported de Gaulle in 1958; all, however, had fallen out with him by the end of 1962, with the exception of Giscard and his Républicains Indépendants (RI), who stayed in the Gaullist-led majority. Defeated in that year's elections, squeezed between the Gaullists and the Left, most of the 'old' parties' members and leaders gravitated slowly towards Giscard, joining the federation launched as the Union pour la Démocratie Française (UDF) in February 1978.

The sluggishness of this process, which spread over fifteen years, was due to the difficulties of the parties concerned in adapting to the politics of the Fifth Republic. Although the MRP had tried to recruit a mass membership in the 1940s, it and the other groups of the non-Gaullist Right were really cadre parties. Their 'members' were notables whose support derived as much from their own networks in constituencies, towns and *départements* as from party labels and whose recalcitrance towards strong party discipline or leadership was legendary. Even Giscard preferred a 'light' party organisation – or rather two: on the one hand the RI, credited in 1970 with just 3,000 members (mostly mayors and local councillors), and on the other the select Clubs

Perspectives et Réalités, half-party and half think-tank, which he had founded in 1965. These were the tools with which he had won the presidency. In tranquil times he would probably have stuck to them, negotiating electoral agreements with partners as necessary. But from 1976 onwards, the continued strength and growing hostility of the Gaullists (notably their relaunch as the RPR, and Chirac's dramatic capture of the Paris town hall), as well as the real danger of a left-wing victory, offered powerful incentives for more formal structures. The name given to the new federation left little doubt as to the source of its inspiration: *Démocratie française* was the title of the book in which Giscard had laid out his political credo two years earlier.

The president's own party was also the largest single component of the UDF, and supplied half of UDF Deputies from 1978 to 1997. From 1962 the RI played two roles: as one of Giscard's own political networks, and as a 'place of welcome' for conservatives (not all of them fervent Giscardians) who wished to join the Gaullist majority without submitting to the discipline of the Gaullist party. Its structures and organisation remained rudimentary. In May 1977, however, the competition from Chirac's Gaullists prompted a change of style. The RI, renamed the Parti Républicain (PR), began actively to recruit members. Successive secretaries-general (Jean-Pierre Soisson from 1977 to 1978, Jacques Blanc from 1978 to 1981, François Léotard after the defeats of 1981) sought to project an image of youth and energy, as opposed to outmoded provincialism of the traditional notables or the brutalism favoured by the RI secretary-general Michel Poniatowski. Preposterous membership figures were claimed for the PR – as many as 145,000 in 1979. Outside estimates indicated 10–12,000 members in the early 1980s, and perhaps 20,000 ten years later: less than a fifth of the Gaullists' total. But it was still a more structured organisation than the RI of the 1960s, and incorporated other Giscardian groupings, for example its well-heeled youth and student movements (the Mouvement des Jeunes Giscardiens, the Mouvement Génération Sociale et Libérale and the Collectif des Étudiants Libéraux de France) – though the Clubs Perspectives et Réalités remained outside the new party, Giscard preferring some diversity among his supporters. Both names changed in the 1990s. In September 1995, Hervé de Charette, foreign minister in the Juppé government, converted the Clubs Perspectives et Réalités into the Parti Populaire pour la Démocratie Française (PPDF). And when the former finance minister Alain Madelin took over the PR from Léotard in 1997, he relaunched it as Démocratie Libérale (DL).

The second party to join the UDF was the Centre des Démocrates Sociaux (CDS), headed by the Deputy and mayor of Rouen, Jean Lecanuet, who also became president of the whole UDF. Lecanuet had run for the presidency against de Gaulle in 1965, and won a respectable 15.6 per cent of the vote, with backing from the MRP, the CNIP and some Radicals. On the strength of that he formed a new 'centrist' party, the Centre Démocrate, to group these supporters. From 1969 to 1974 these centrists were split between Jacques Duhamel's Centre Démocratie et Progrès (CDP), which had backed Pompidou and joined the majority after his election, and Lecanuet and the rest of the Centre Démocrate, who stayed in opposition. But Giscard's election led to the incorporation of both Centre parties inside the enlarged presidential majority. Their reunification as the CDS followed, with the encouragement of Giscard's factotum Poniatowski, in May 1976. Unlike the PR, the centrists have not claimed a large membership: the modest official figure of 30,000 members claimed in both 1979 and again in 1997 was probably double the real total – a tiny exaggeration by French standards. As the successor to the MRP, the CDS represented the Christian Democratic tradition in

French politics; it accounted for between a quarter and a third of the non-Gaullist moderate Right Deputies from 1978 to 1993; and among the main components of the UDF, it was the most hesitant (particularly after Mitterrand's second victory in 1988) about its position in the alliance of the Right. The Education Minister François Bayrou relaunched the CDS as Force Démocrate in 1995.

The UDF's third component, the Parti Radical, had been France's most important party from its foundation in 1901 till the defeat of 1940. Though much diminished under the Fourth Republic, the Parti Radical retained its pivotal role, but both shrank and split under the impact of the Fifth, acquiring the status, and the fragility, of a historical relic. Its opportunists joined the Gaullists; its left-wingers formed the Mouvement des Radicaux de Gauche (MRG) and signed the Socialist–Communist Common Programme in 1972; the rest sought salvation in the mercurial leadership of Jean-Jacques Servan-Schreiber, co-founder and editor of *L'Express* and the party's president from 1969 till 1978. He rallied to Giscard at the second ballot in 1974, and to the UDF in 1978, but was unable to stem his party's decline. By the eve of their centennial year, the Radicals had become a regionalised party with a few thousand members at most and three Deputies, centred on a few localities including Nancy (where Servan-Schreiber had been Deputy). They were also susceptible to the influence of Jacques Chirac: two successive presidents of the party, Didier Bariani and Yves Galland, were Chirac's assistant mayors in the Paris town hall.

Several very small groups or parties also joined the UDF. The Carrefour Social Démocrate consisted of left-wing centrists, the Mouvement Démocrate Socialiste of right-wing anti-Communist Socialists. They were to join the Parti Social-Démocrate (PSD), which voted in 1995 to join the centrists in Force Démocrate. Finally, the group of *adhérents directs* included members of the UDF who eschewed links with any of its individual components.

The UDF started well: the amalgamation of the weak, the unimportant and the plainly derisory produced something more than the insignificant. With 20.6 per cent of the first-round votes and 123 Deputies in the 1978 parliamentary elections, and 27.5 per cent in the 1979 European elections (the highest score of any list), the confederation could challenge the Gaullists' claim to be the Right's largest party. As well as these positions the UDF had many councillors in France's municipalities, *départements* and regions, and thus in the Senate (local office-holding has always been the non-Gaullist Right's strong suit), while the leadership of the president of the Republic offered patronage and even financial backing. But the UDF lacked the Gaullists' organisational muscle, and when Giscard sought re-election in 1981 he preferred to organise his campaign through his Élysée staff and personal 'support committees' in the country, in an attempt to downplay his links with any one party.

Giscard's defeat was nevertheless a traumatic blow to the party he had founded. Not that the UDF vote collapsed (Figure 8.2): the drop in the 1981 parliamentary elections, from 22 per cent to 20.6, was hardly catastrophic (though the loss of 57 out of 120 Deputies was more serious). More important was the fact that the three main constituent parties had come from quite different traditions – the Radicals' heritage of anti-clericalism versus the centrists' Christian Democracy, the PR's free-market leanings versus the Centrists' concern for 'social' goals – and were held together largely by support for the president of the Republic. An ex-president was a much less effective cement. From 1981 until its breakup in 1998, the UDF accordingly fell prey to constant divisions over policies, strategy and personalities.

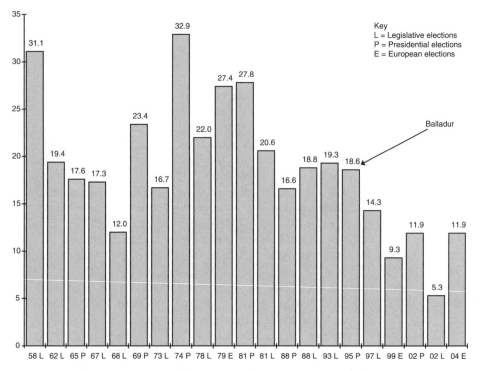

Figure 8.2 Votes for the non-Gaullist moderate Right (UDF from 1978; % of votes cast, first ballot in two-ballot elections), 1958–2004.

- *Policy divisions* centred, in the first instance, on the Right's economic programme. While the Parti Républicain, and especially the *bande à Léo* – François Léotard and his two lieutenants, the former extreme right-wing activists Alain Madelin and Gérard Longuet – was in the vanguard when it came to incorporating 'New Right' themes such as privatisation into the opposition's agenda in the 1980s, the centrists of the CDS were much less sure. As ministers in the second Chirac government, on the other hand, Léotard, Madelin and Longuet were among the most sympathetic to protesting students in December 1986, lacking all solidarity with René Monory, the CDS education minister who had prepared the reform the students were protesting against. A more surprising split came later, in 1992, when the UDF, hitherto seen as the most solidly pro-European element on the Right, split over the Maastricht referendum, with a minority under Philippe de Villiers campaigning against the treaty and eventually leaving the UDF altogether.
- *Strategic divisions* concerned, in the first instance, the wisdom or otherwise of 'cohabitation' between a government supported by a right-wing majority and President Mitterrand in 1986. Raymond Barre, Giscard's second prime minister, opposed such an experiment in the name of a more Gaullian interpretation of the constitution than the Gaullists themselves adhered to, until events overtook him. Other strategic divisions centred on relations with other parties, notably the FN. A minority of leaders in the PR, notably the arch-conservative Alain Griotteray as well as Gérard Longuet, periodically suggested ending the 'quarantine' of the far Right; and the UDF's leader in Marseille, Jean-Claude Gaudin, co-operated with

the FN to save a handful of seats from the Socialists in the parliamentary defeat of 1988. By contrast, the centrists, led by Pierre Méhaignérie after Lecanuet gave up the CDS leadership in 1982, appeared genuinely tempted by an alliance with the Socialists in 1988; they formed a separate group from the UDF in the National Assembly, and helped keep Rocard's Socialist government in office by supporting it on a number of key votes – though they returned to the main UDF group in 1993.

A final strategic division concerned relations with the Gaullists, whose superior organisation has always inspired a mixture of admiration and resentment in the UDF. This was especially apparent as the 1995 presidential elections approached. The UDF was torn between support for a candidate from within its own ranks (Giscard and Barre, as well as the president of the UDF parliamentary group, Charles Millon, all suggested they might run, before being dissuaded by a glance at the opinion polls); support for Balladur, the line which won a majority in each of the UDF's three main parties and was actively promoted by government ministers including Léotard, Longuet and Simone Veil; and support for Chirac, voiced openly by Madelin and by Hervé de Charette, President of the Clubs Perspectives et Réalités, and more discreetly by Giscard. For a major party in a 'presidentialised' system, the UDF in late 1994 presented an extraordinary picture of disarray.

- *Personalities* and their competing ambitions inevitably lay behind disputes over policy and strategy. Giscard, in particular, cast a long shadow, embarking on what he may have hoped was a long road back towards his old job, via the council of his *département* of Puy-de-Dôme (in 1981), the National Assembly and the presidency of the regional council of Auvergne (in 1986), and the European Parliament in 1989. He also took over the presidency of the UDF in 1989, and reinforced its central institutions. But except during a brief period between 1989 and 1992, Giscard never appeared in the polls as a serious presidential contender. The chief effect of his continued influence was therefore to help spoil the chances of his rivals in the UDF, especially Barre and Léotard. The Chirac–Balladur battle divided the UDF almost as much as it did the RPR. It completed the breakup of the *bande à Léo*, as Léotard and Madelin ended up on different sides, and left a legacy of division well beyond 1995. A prolonged struggle for control of the CDS in succession to Pierre Méhaignérie was waged through the early 1990s between Dominique Baudis and Bernard Bosson; the Education Minister François Bayrou, one of the rare *balladuriens* to survive Chirac's victory, defeated both of them in October 1995.

These three sources of division – policies, strategy and personalities, combined with the lack of an adequate organisation to contain them – caused the breakup of the UDF, twenty years after its foundation, over the FN's proposal of alliance after the 1998 regional elections. This offer was especially tempting to the UDF, a federation of cadre parties for which local and regional office had always been very important. Four regional presidents chose to accept FN votes: two were former secretaries-general of the Parti Républicain, Jean-Pierre Soisson and Jacques Blanc, while Millon had been the UDF's leading parliamentarian. They were condemned by the UDF president François Léotard, but enjoyed widespread sympathy among rank-and-file UDF elected officials. At the same time the leaders of the UDF's two component parties used the occasion to further their own ambitions. François Bayrou, leader of Force Démocrate, called for 'a renovated party of the Centre and Centre-Right, refusing any alliances with the FN' – headed, presumably, by himself. That turned the debate over alliances with the FN and penalties against the four regional presidents into a debate about the future of the UDF itself and led to the departure from the confederation of Bayrou's main rival Alain Madelin, and of his party, Démocratie Libérale. The old UDF was liquidated at the end of May 1998, leaving an unedifying trail of debts and judicial investigations. By the year's end, Bayrou had formed a new UDF under his leadership: it included Force Démocrate, the Parti Populaire pour la Démocratie Française and the Parti Social-Démocrate, all now fully merged, as well as the Parti Radical, which maintained a separate identity chiefly in order to be able to celebrate its centenary in 2002.

There is a sense in which what has been the main strength of the non-Gaullist moderate Right has also been its main weakness. Through most of the Fifth Republic, it has been able to conserve its local positions despite national reverses. This is reflected in the fact that, although very much the junior partner of the moderate Right nationally, the UDF on the eve of its breakup still had 727 members of *conseils généraux* against the RPR's 670, and 32 presidencies of *conseils généraux*, against the RPR's 21. The result was that the non-Gaullist moderate Right remained under the domination of its local, and especially rural, elected officials, who were independent-minded and resistant to strong party organisation. That characteristic weakness of the cadre party was compounded by ideological diversity: probably no greater than that within the RPR, but without any central myths or symbols to bind the various elements together. In that context, the conquest of the presidency by Giscard in 1974 appears quite exceptional, the result of the Gaullists' divisions after Pompidou's death. The UDF's choices in 1995 were especially revealing of a party unable either to run a presidential candidate of its own or even to unite behind one of the two Gaullists on offer.

The split of 1998 was in some ways a clarification. France now had a free-market party of the Right in DL and a post-Christian Democratic party of the Centre-Right in the new UDF. Their leaders, Madelin and Bayrou, were open rivals for the presidency of France. But the breakup has also brought further weakness: surveys in 2000 showed the two candidates together attracting the support of barely 10 per cent of the voters – about 7 for the UDF and 3.5 for DL. For conservatives seeking a candidate to prevent a Jospin presidency and prepare the way for a restoration of the Right's parliamentary majority, neither man appeared remotely as credible as the incumbent.

Conflict, co-operation and the UMP

For most of the Fifth Republic, relations between the moderate right-wing parties have been closer than those between their adversaries of the Left. They have differed on the specifics of policy more than on fundamentals of doctrine; and since 1981 they have agreed on a single common parliamentary candidate in most constituencies.

Their greatest differences were early in the Republic. The government of national unity formed by de Gaulle on his return to power in June 1958, which included ministers from all non-Communist parties, suffered progressive defections over the next four years: the Socialists in January 1959 over budget-balancing austerity measures, the right wing of the conservative CNIP over Algeria by March 1962, the MRP over Europe the following May, and all remaining allies bar the Giscardians over the October 1962 referendum on the direct election of the president. The Gaullist victories of autumn 1962 saw 62.3 per cent of voters approve the constitutional reform, and the emergence of a stable parliamentary majority, with 233 seats for Gaullists and 35 for their Giscardian allies, out of a total of 482. The 'Centrists' – the remnants of the CNIP and the

MRP – were out of the majority, but not with the left-wing opposition either, for the rest of the decade, and more.

Table 8.1 charts their progressive return to the right-wing majority: first at the presidential election of 1969, when Pompidou persuaded Jacques Duhamel's group of centrists to support his presidential candidacy, then five years later, when the whole of the NGMR supported Giscard at the second ballot, and finally in 1978, when almost the whole of the NGMR grouped under the UDF umbrella. The closing point in this evolution may be placed at 1981, when the RPR and the UDF, in the wake of Mitterrand's election, chose common candidacies in most constituencies and a joint programme to minimise damage at the June parliamentary elections. They lost anyway, but the habits of close co-operation remained, surviving victories and defeats.

In this context it may be wondered why the moderate right had not merged into a single big conservative party by, say, 1984. Four reasons may be given. First, as we have observed, the Gaullists and the NGMR differed significantly, at least till the early 1980s, over policy, especially over Europe, sovereignty and the role of the state in the economy. Second, their organisational styles were radically different. The Gaullists, who aspired to build a mass party and loved a leader, derided what they saw as the disorganised character of the UDF parties, as well the effete, well-mannered character of its well-to-do elites; UDF activists returned the compliment by comparing the RPR, with its propensity to mass rallies, to a fascist movement. Third, the RPR and the UDF were used as vehicles for *présidentiables* whose ambitions clashed, and who preferred to take their chances with the voters at first ballots of real elections than to submit to the nomination rules of a hypothetical new party. Fourth, and most simply, the electoral benefits of a merger were not obvious: the institutions allow room for two parties of the Right (and of the Left) to compete against one another, so long as they conclude a working second-ballot alliance.

Each of these sources of division, however, except for the last, had diminished in

Table 8.1 The growth of the right-wing ruling coalition, 1958–81

Legislative elections 1958	Gaullists (UNR)
Legislative elections 1962	Gaullists (UNR-UDT) + Républicains Indépendants (RI)
Presidential election 1969	Gaullists (UDR) + Républicains Indépendants (RI) + Centre Démocratie et Progrès (CDP)
Presidential election 1974	Gaullists (UDR) + Républicains Indépendants (RI) + Centre National des Indépendants et des Paysans (CNIP) + CDP + Centre Démocrate (CD) + Radicals
Legislative elections 1978	Gaullists (RPR) + CNIP + Union pour la Démocratie Française (UDF): made up of Parti Républicain (ex-Républicains Indépendants) + Radical Party + Centre des Démocrates Sociaux (CDS, a fusion of CDP and CD) + Mouvement Démocrate et Socialiste de France + Clubs Perspectives et Réalités

importance by 2000. Few serious policy differences separated the RPR from the remains of the UDF. While such differences remained in plenty within the moderate Right, they barely coincided any more with party divisions. The gap in organisational culture, though still present, had narrowed as the RPR tended to become a collection of fractious notables. Presidential rivalries remained, but for the first time since 1965 a single candidate dominated the ranks of the Right: Chirac was over ten points ahead of any possible rival from the right-wing camp. As the only possible right-wing winner of the 2002 presidential election, Chirac wielded considerable attractive power, and not just for the elites of the RPR.

The realisation of a big and (more or less) united right-wing party was nevertheless a project that required deliberate action and not a little arm-twisting, especially between December 2001, when an RPR congress saw the party's star orators queue up to declare that the Gaullist movement 'did not want to die', and September 2002, when the RPR pronounced its own dissolution. Part of the initiative came from (mostly young) RPR, UDF and DL Deputies on the ground, such as Renaud Dutreil or Hervé Gaymard, who launched a succession of associations – first France-Alternance, then Alternance 2002, and from April 2001 the Union en Mouvement – deliberately aimed at creating a party that would replace the RPR and the UDF and monopolise the moderate Right's share of public political finance. Chirac did not endorse this initiative personally, and kept his own options open till the last minute; but the role played by senior members of his staff, notably Jérôme Monod, by a handful of senior figures from the RPR, DL, and the UDF, and by Juppé, indicated both that the project was taken seriously by the Élysée and that it could be activated at short notice. What precipitated the creation of the UMP was the result of the presidential first ballot on 21 April 2002. Chirac had confirmed his dominant position on the moderate Right, with 19.9 per cent of the vote to Bayrou's 6.8 and Madelin's 3.9. His defeated rivals were in no position to bargain or hesitate over their support for Chirac at the run-off, because Chirac's second-ballot opponent was not Jospin but Le Pen. And Le Pen's performance led to a perception, misplaced but real, among commentators and candidates that the FN would be in a position to decide the results of the June parliamentary elections in many constituencies – a consideration that brought many sitting Deputies of every stripe to seek the shelter of a broad *chiraquien* umbrella. Within two days of the first ballot, Juppé was therefore able to state terms, in what amounted to his founding act as provisional president of the UMP: at the parliamentary elections, the new party would endorse a single candidate in each constituency, who would be committed in return to sitting in the UMP group in the National Assembly – thus ensuring that the lion's share of the Right's political finance went to the UMP, not to the old parties. Two weeks later, with Chirac safely returned to the Élysée, and the parliamentary election campaign just beginning, the great majority of the Right's candidates were using standardised campaign material, featuring the UMP ticket and the new Prime Minister Jean-Pierre Raffarin (significantly a figure from DL, not a Gaullist).

With the newly elected Chirac and the newly appointed Raffarin as its locomotives, the UMP proved remarkably successful in the short term. With over eight million votes – a third of the first-ballot total – at the June 2002 parliamentary elections, it elected 369 out of 577 Deputies – nearly two-thirds of the National Assembly, and only the third-ever absolute majority in a Republic (after the Gaullists in 1968 and the Socialists in 1981). Of these, 205 had come from the RPR, 57 from DL and 77 from the UDF. This strong vote and representation would ensure a regular income from the state of some 30 million euros, or about 45 per cent of all public funding for parties. By November, moreover, 166 of France's 321 Senators had joined the UMP group, reflecting the extent to which the Right's local elected officials had gravitated to the new party and giving a breadth of institutional dominance, at both national and local levels, that even the Gaullists of the 1960s had not achieved. September 2002 also saw the dissolution of the RPR and DL; while the UDF continued an independent existence under Bayrou, it had the aspect of a rump party, with just 4.2 per cent of the first-ballot vote in June, 30 Deputies, and only one minister (Gilles de Robien at Transport).

These early triumphs were short-lived. Within two years of its creation, the UMP had paid a heavy price for the slump in popularity of the Raffarin government after August 2003, losing 11 out of its 13 regions in March 2004 and achieving just 16.6 per cent of the vote in the European elections of the following June – just half the vote share of two years earlier. Bayrou's UDF, by contrast, had adopted an increasingly critical view of Raffarin, and reaped the benefits; its 11.9 per cent at the June 2004 European elections – nearly three-quarters the UMP's level – was an impressive result for what had appeared as a residual party two years earlier.

Electoral setbacks were compounded by organisational weakness. Juppé's explicit ambition had been a big conservative party on the British, German, or Spanish models, a broad church with a big membership and a culture of debate. But the membership remained stubbornly close to the 100,000 mark – barely more than the RPR in the 1990s, for a party with a supposedly much greater political coverage. The so-called 'movements' within the UMP, initially announced as the framework for intra-party debate, were never set up. And no agreement was reached on the mechanism for choosing the UMP's presidential candidate when the time came. The original sins of French right-wing parties – low membership and weak institutionalisation – were not, therefore, ended with the launch of the UMP. And they were compounded by leadership problems. Juppé had been given the party presidency as a proxy for Chirac, the initial focus of the UMP's loyalties. But Juppé, never a very appealing politician nationally, was convicted in January 2004 for his role in financing RPR officials on the city of Paris payroll and banned from public office for ten years. Although an appeal reduced the length of this penalty, Juppé progressively withdrew from public political activities over the following year. The leadership contest opened by his impending departure attracted Sarkozy, the most popular minister in the Raffarin government and an open contender for the succession to Chirac.

Sarkozy won the succession to Juppé at the head of the UMP in November 2004 with the support of 85 per cent of the party's voting members, and quickly launched a drive to take membership above the 200,000 level (it claimed 180,858 by July 2005). His energy, gift for self-publicity, talents as a media performer and relative youth (born in 1955, he is Chirac's junior by twenty-two years) made him the favourite even of the long-standing activists, many of who preferred him to the sitting president; of the new members, younger and more right-wing than their elders, most were unequivocal *sarkozystes*. Sarkozy's control of the big UMP budget, of the development of a party programme and of the choice of parliamentary candidates, could all be used, not as supports for an incumbent president as under the traditional Gaullist model of the Fifth Republic, but as tools to promote his own future candidacy. His public visibility was also promoted by his position, held from May 2005 in addition to the party leadership, as interior minister. It was far from certain, on the other hand, that Chirac, even in his weakened state of mid-2005, would depart quietly. His personal interests outside politics are few; and his immunity from prosecution over his stewardship of the Paris city hall would end with his presidential term. Even if Chirac heeded the voice of reason and gave up on a third term, he would be more likely to back the more loyal de Villepin for the succession than to concede it to his turbulent interior minister.

The creation of the UMP did not, therefore, succeed in its aim to break the mould of politics on the moderate Right and create a single big party within which policy could be debated, and personal rivalries canalised, within a structured environment. The UMP of mid-2005 had failed to absorb the whole of the UDF and remained unpopular with the general public, with 55 per cent of negative opinions to only 29 per cent of positive ones according to SOFRES polls (the equivalent figures for the PCF were hardly different, at 58 and 25). This was a sort of RPR mark 2, with Sarkozy in the role of the aggressive leader that Chirac had played a generation earlier. But Sarkozy, paradoxically, was also France's most credible presidential candidate, enjoying a clear polling lead over all possible left-wing and right-wing rivals (with the single exception of Jospin). Whether he could use his polling advantage and his control of the party to supplant the incumbent without wrecking the Right's chances in a renewed bout of internecine warfare remained, however, uncertain.

Other right-wing groups

The UMP and the UDF do not have a monopoly of support in the moderate Right. Five other groups deserve brief mention.

- *The Centre National des Indépendants et Paysans (CNIP)* lingered on, despite the loss of Giscard's RI group in 1962 and of other leading members to the centrists. It was led initially by an ageing generation of Fourth Republic politicians, notionally independent but increasingly marginal. A flurry of renewal from the late 1980s came to an abrupt close in 1992 when the aircraft carrying the party's new young leader Yvon Briant flew into a Corsican cliff. In the mid-1990s it counted ten parliamentarians, mostly Senators. The CNIP's leaders had conceived the party's role as forming a bridge between the FN and the moderate Right, since unlike the RPR–UDF coalition, the CNIP never banned alliances with Le Pen's party. But a succession of leadership difficulties (Briant's successor but one, the poultry king Gérard Bourgoin, resigned after being placed under judicial investigation) diminished its ranks: by the time the party joined the UMP as an associated movement in October 2002 it had no national elected officials and claimed members in just forty *départements*.
- *The* divers droite. Some politicians, chiefly but not exclusively on the Right, go without party labels, especially if they have a strong local base. Some of these *divers droite* candidates are temporary dissidents who later return to a party loyalty. Others feel no need at all to belong even to a cadre party. At parliamentary elections, their numbers are small but not negligible: 4.5 per cent and thirteen seats in 1993, 1.6 per cent and seven seats in 1997. The *divers droite* Deputies were even necessary to the Right's overall majority in 1986. At local level, the *divers droite* are more powerful. This is especially true in France's ninety-six *départements*, where some 600 of the 3,857 *conseillers généraux* are *divers droite*. Their survival testifies to the continuing relative weakness of France's party structures, especially in France's rural cantons; it is still possible for a small rural *département* like Cantal to

be run by a *divers droite* majority. The *divers droite* have also tended to prosper in proportion to the unpopularity of the main right-wing parties. For this reason the late 1990s and the municipal and cantonal elections of 2001 were especially fruitful in (often successful) *divers droite* candidacies. In June 2002, *divers droite* candidates won over 10 per cent of the vote in over a hundred parliamentary constituencies, and carried the Right's colours at the second ballot in a dozen of them, winning in six; although they joined the UMP parliamentary groups once elected, their ability to win without the party label testifies to the vigour, at least in some constituencies, of a personal vote.

- *Chasse, Pêche, Nature, Traditions (CPNT)*. This group, the shooters' rights party, has run candidates in the European elections since 1989, at regional elections since 1992, as well as at the presidential and parliamentary elections of 2002 and at cantonal elections in a handful of cantons. CPNT started out as a single-issue group *par excellence*, seeking to frustrate the 1979 European directive limiting the bird-shooting season both by electoral means and by more or less rowdy demonstrations. Aided by proportional representation and at times high abstention rates, it had a significant electoral impact in the late 1990s: with 5 per cent of the vote at the 1998 regional elections, it held the balance of power in four regions (and used it to keep the Right in office); its 6.8 per cent at the following year's European elections secured five members at the Strasbourg parliament. Just as important, in areas where they enjoyed support, such as the Aquitaine region or the *département* of the Somme, they were able to frighten Deputies from the mainstream parties, of whatever political stripe, into backing their cause. CPNT has been termed the 'rural Front National', and while it claims to have drawn support from people of the Left as well as the Right, the frequent brutality of its methods recalls the far Right all too well. These have largely achieved its central aim, at least for the moment: France has never properly implemented the 1979 wildfowl directive.

CPNT proved less successful when it turned into something resembling a political party. It did this after its founding president, André-Henri Goustat, was convicted in 2000 of illegally diverting public money derived from the sale of shooting licences to further its campaigns. Deprived of this convenient source of income, CPNT constituted itself as a party in order to benefit from public finance. To do this, it had to run candidates at the June 2002 parliamentary elections, and to win a national audience for the party, Goustat's successor since 1999, Jean Saint-Josse, ran for the presidency. His campaign widened the earlier exclusive focus on shooting to take in wider issues of 'rurality' – notably the preservation of rural public services and the dangers of rural 'desertification'. This served him reasonably well at the presidential election: with 4.2 per cent of the first-ballot vote, Saint-Josse won nearly a quarter of a million more votes than Hue managed for the Communists. At the June 2002 regional elections, however, CPNT's lack of local elected officials or experienced candidates told against it: although it contributed to the defeat of at least two Socialist Deputies of whom it disapproved in the Somme, its overall vote share fell to just 1.7 per cent. The elections of 2004 spelt the near-annihilation of CPNT's elected positions: its refusal to join other parties in second-ballot alliances under the new system for regional elections ensured the elimination of all thirty-two CPNT regional councillors; it was left with just three *conseillers généraux* for France's *départements* out of a total 3,857; its low score of 1.7 per cent at the June European elections removed it from the Strasbourg parliament; and even at the referendum on the European constitution in 2005, which might have been the occasion for a revival, CPNT failed to win a leading position in the victorious no campaign. Claims that it represents a revival of an old urban–rural cleavage in France therefore appear overstated; but it retains an apparent veto over any serious attempts to protect migrating birds ill-advised enough to stray into French airspace.

- *The Eurosceptical Right.* The most consistent defender of a Eurosceptical Right is Viscount Philippe de Villiers, former UDF minister and political boss of the conservative, Catholic *département* of Vendée. De Villiers campaigned actively for a no vote at the 1992 Maastricht referendum (as he would thirteen years later against the European constitutional treaty) and left the UDF to form his own Mouvement pour la France (MPF) in 1994. His best electoral performances since then have been at European elections: 12.4 per cent in 1994; 13 per cent (in tandem with the Gaullist renegade Charles Pasqua) in 1999; and 6.7 per cent (enough to win three seats in the Strasbourg parliament) in 2004. The MPF is more than merely Eurosceptical; it articulates a rural, Catholic conservatism characteristic of de Villiers's home base. But neither de Villiers (who won less than 5 per cent at the 1995 presidential election, and did not stand in 2002) nor his party has converted these successes into a sustained national presence. La Droite Indépendante, the alliance formed with *divers droite* and CNIP candidates in 1997, performed indecisively in what was in any case a bad year for the Right. The alliance of 1999, despite its success at the polls, was complicated by the fact that Pasqua had hoped for a 'sovereignist' grouping of Eurosceptics of both Right and Left; only lack of interest among left-wing Jacobins had forced him into the arms of de Villiers in the first place. The two leaders of the Rassemblement pour la France quarrelled almost from the moment of its creation in the aftermath of the 1999 poll: over the political alignment (which de Villiers wanted to be firmly on the Right, against Pasqua's wishes), over jobs for their respective protégés and over the party's debts of 7–10 million francs. These split the Rassemblement pour la France in June 2000. Although clearly stronger than the Pasqua group (which retained the RPF label, but only scored 1.7 per cent in the 2004 European elections), the MPF remains massively dependent on its leader's local base: of its five national parliamentarians (three Deputies and two Senators), four represent the Vendée. One of the paradoxes of the 2005 referendum on the European constitutional treaty was that while the Vendée, along with six other *départements* of the Catholic west, was one of only thirteen metropolitan *départements* out of ninety-six to vote yes, Villiers had used the no campaign to make a national comeback. With the Front National playing an unwontedly discreet role in the campaign and the UMP's Eurosceptical wing torn between hostility to the treaty and loyalty to the president and government, the leadership of the right-wing no vote was de Villiers's for the taking. More than any other leader of the no camp, he linked the treaty to the separate question of Turkey's entry to the EU, no doubt calculating that this would appeal not only to his own conservative Catholic voters but also to xenophobic FN voters. Whether the 2005 campaign would allow the Viscount to make serious inroads into the FN's electorate in time for 2007 was, however, uncertain.

- *The Catholic Right.* Two other late twentieth-century groups have been just as marked by Catholic traditionalism as the MPF, without the same degree of Euroscepticism. The Droite Libérale et Chrétienne was launched (initially just as

La Droite) by Charles Millon after he had accepted FN support as president of the Rhône-Alpes regional council in 1998 and left the UDF. Still tainted by the controversy over the FN deal, Millon is an embarrassment to Chirac, who hoped to remove him to Rome by appointing him to the Food and Agriculture Organisation. Millon, however, has remained active in Lyon politics, with a view to running for mayor, though he has failed to build a national organisation. Another grouping, the Forum des Républicains Sociaux, was formed by Christine Boutin, a right-wing Catholic UDF Deputy who made a national reputation by filibustering the National Assembly debate on the Pacte Civil de Solidarité with a Bible in her hand. Boutin won 1.2 per cent of the vote at the 2002 presidential elections, merged her Forum with the UMP the following June, but was active in the no campaign in 2005.

The extreme Right: permanence and isolation of the Front National

France's far Right has a rich history, though one that has rarely been either successful or respectable. For much of the nineteenth century it was a shrinking band which remained loyal to the pre-1789 *ancien régime*. From the Dreyfus Affair of the 1890s, however, it emerged as a more 'modern' force, not just anti-republican but also nationalist and anti-Semitic. After a partial eclipse during World War I and the following decade, 'French Fascism', as authors such as Robert Soucy and Zeev Sternhell have called it, enlarged its audience during the crisis of the 1930s. In June 1940 the occupying German forces found French people who were ready to collaborate with them not only for reasons of expediency, but also out of conviction. Discredited at the Liberation, then briefly rallying to the RPF's visceral anti-Communism, the far Right found two main outlets in the later years of the Fourth Republic: the Poujadist movement of small traders threatened by economic progress, and support for France's increasingly hopeless colonial wars.

De Gaulle's return to power in 1958, provoked by a putsch by *Algérie française* groups in Algiers, was thus presented by the Communists and others as a Fascist victory. In fact, the far Right was progressively marginalised during the first generation of the Fifth Republic. *Algérie française* supporters lost the political argument and either made their peace with de Gaulle's régime or took to armed struggle before dispersing into prison, exile or oblivion. Their last sally was the presidential candidacy of Jean-Louis Tixier-Vignancour in 1965; he won 5.2 per cent of the first-ballot vote, much of it from discontented *pieds noirs*, former white settlers who had left Algeria at independence. Thereafter the extreme Right went into rapid decline, torn by bitter rivalries. There was no far Right candidate in the 1969 presidential elections. In 1974, Jean-Marie Le Pen, a former Poujadist Deputy who had founded the Front National (FN) two years earlier, ran for the presidency and won just 0.7 per cent of the vote. His second candidacy, in 1981, was even less successful; he failed to obtain the 500 signatures of mayors and councillors necessary to stand. FN candidates in the June 1981 parliamentary elections won a mere 0.3 per cent of the vote. Accounts of French politics written in the aftermath of Mitterrand's election to the presidency (including an earlier edition of this book) could therefore afford to neglect the extreme Right or dismiss it as a spent force.

The far Right's lasting breakthrough

Thereafter, however, the far Right's rise was very fast (Figure 8.3): local breakthroughs at municipal elections in 1983 were followed by a score of over 11 per cent at the 1984 European elections. From then until 1998, it won between one-tenth and one-seventh of votes at every election. FN candidates scored a consistent 15 per cent of the vote at the 1995 presidential elections, the 1997 parliamentary elections and at the 1998 regional elections. After setbacks due to a major party split in 1998, discussed below, Le Pen achieved a record 16.9 per cent at the 2002 presidential election, against his rival Bruno Mégret's 2.3 per cent. These were the best ever results for an extreme right-wing party in France: sufficient to establish the FN as more than a 'flash' party on the model of the Poujadist movement of the 1950s, and an inspiration to its counterparts elsewhere in Europe. In 2002, indeed, Le Pen won over 15 per cent in sixty out of ninety-six metropolitan *départements*, and over 20 per cent in twenty-five of those; in only three *départements* did he win under 10 per cent. It is true that the far Right did less well in 2002 parliamentary elections and at the European elections of 2004. Nevertheless, the regional results of the same year testified both to the continuing attraction of the party as well as its leader, and to the FN's increasingly nationwide appeal.

Any explanation of the sudden awakening of France's far Right must not only take into account the general conditions that helped generate and sustain support, but consider why the far Right, which had been available and active for decades, achieved a breakthrough in 1983–84 rather than earlier or later.

- *Economic* causes included, most obviously, the rise of unemployment. This had, it is true, been an issue through most of the Giscard presidency, which was also the flattest period in the far Right's history. But it was rather more than a mere 'background' factor in that during the three years from early 1981 to early 1984 it rose by

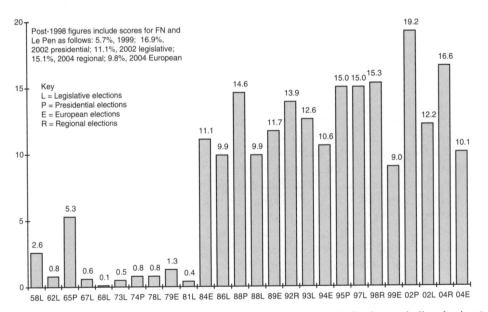

Figure 8.3 Votes for the extreme Right (% of votes cast, first ballot in two-ballot elections), 1958–2004.

half, from 1.5 million to 2.25 million. That enabled the FN to suggest, with implacably faulty logic, that the deportation of an equivalent number of immigrants would create enough vacancies to end joblessness among the French.

- *Social change* also favoured the rise of the FN, in a variety of ways. Immigration itself must be considered as a 'background' element. It was significantly slowed by the banning of primary immigration of workers from outside Europe in 1974, and the number of foreigners on French soil remained fairly stable, at about 4 million, through the 1980s. The Socialists' decision to give residence permits to some 130,000 clandestine immigrants in 1981 was certainly opposed on the Right, but did not constitute a qualitative change. But the perception of immigrants altered as men were joined by families and a second generation (the 'beurs') was born in the 1970s and 1980s, and as 'immigrants' (or people of North African origin) were seen to compete with native-born French for increasingly scarce goods: jobs and tolerable housing (it is notable that new low-cost housing construction fell sharply in the 1980s, at the same time as the vast estates built since the mid-1950s fell increasingly prey to physical as well as social decay). The fact that France's second industrial revolution had merged without transition into economic crisis from 1974 meant that by the 1980s French society had seen an unprecedented transformation lasting almost half a century. Other social factors included the weakening of subcultures which had given a framework to political activity in previous decades: the Catholic (with the decline in religious practice) and the Communist (with the spread of television and the disappearance of traditional working-class jobs). Both had generally inhibited xenophobia and assisted the 'integration' of immigrants. The FN also probably benefited as the experience of Nazi Occupation, and its links with the French extreme Right, faded into history.
- *Leadership* has also been crucial to the FN's success. Jean-Marie Le Pen was probably the West European far Right's ablest leader during the late 1980s and early 1990s. By 2000 his political longevity was greater than that of any active French politician except Giscard. First elected to the National Assembly in 1956 on the Poujadist list, a vociferous defender of *Algérie française* both in the Assembly and as a paratrooper, campaign manager to Tixier-Vignancour in 1965, founder of the FN in 1972, he had no major rival on the far Right for a generation until the (ultimately ineffectual) challenge from his lieutenant Bruno Mégret in 1998. After choosing, in 1972, to use legal methods to advance his cause rather than the violence to which the far Right had had ready recourse in earlier years, Le Pen made himself a master of the baser political arts. His speeches are direct, truculent, simplistic and plausible, spiced with humour, home-spun aphorisms, and the occasional learned reference or unexpected allusion (in 2002, he quoted from Martin Luther King's 'I have a dream' speech). He is also just as 'good' in the more intimate setting of the television studio as on a platform in front of his own supporters. Adept at exploiting fear and racial bigotry, he still makes a point of suing anyone who calls him a racist (and has sometimes won). Above all, he has been successful in polluting the political mainstream with 'his' issues (above all immigration) and his 'solutions', blurring the distinction between his party and its competitors and creating a corner of political debate in which his party is an obligatory reference point. Yet Le Pen's leadership talents are inadequate as an explanation for the FN's sudden success; they went unnoticed, after all, by the French public for over a decade after the party's foundation.

- *Political factors*, however, hold most of the immediate explanations for the break-through of 1983–84. The Left's victory in 1981 was clearly one of these. It disqualified the Communists as a protest party by putting them (however briefly) into government. It all but exhausted the governmental options available under the Fifth Republic, without any of them bringing a significant reduction in unemployment; the FN was attractive as a solution that had not been tried. It radicalised elements of the Right, just as the Gaullists were becoming less populist, less nationalistic, more bourgeois and more European; their decision, at the 1984 European elections, to join the list led by Simone Veil (female, Jewish, liberal and responsible, as health minister ten years earlier, for legalising abortion) was seen as offering a large political space for Le Pen to fill. Chirac's 1986–88 premiership, on the other hand, disappointed the hard Right, which had expected at least a significant change to the nationality law.

  If these political elements were all more or less 'accidental', the rise of the FN was also assisted by the active complicity of other political players. President Mitterrand contributed materially to the FN's transformation into a party of respectable appearances: he was responsible both for the enhanced television coverage given Le Pen from 1984 and for the change to proportional representation, allowing the election of FN Deputies in 1986. While these moves succeeded in their apparent goal of wrongfooting the moderate Right, they also helped create something the president had no means of controlling. Moreover, once the breakthrough had occurred, the mainstream parties responded to it ineptly. The moderate Right's indecision over the question of alliances is a good illustration. Established politicians of all parties spoke on Le Pen's issues in terms reminiscent, on occasion, of Le Pen's own. In a television debate in 1985, for example, the Socialist Prime Minister Laurent Fabius vied with Jacques Chirac to prove that he would be more effective in expelling illegal immigrants. During a few months in 1991 another Socialist premier, Édith Cresson, declared that she would happily hire charted aircraft to deport illegal immigrants *en masse*, Giscard spoke of a foreign 'invasion' of France, and Chirac claimed that immigrant households smelt. Opinion poll evidence suggests that such pandering to racism was counterproductive, since racists would always end up preferring the 'genuine article', Le Pen himself. Since then, mainstream politicians have treated the race issue with greater care. On the other hand, Chirac's decision to bring law and order (a weak suit for the Left) to the forefront of the 2002 presidential campaign almost certainly benefited Le Pen more than any other candidate.

The electorate attracted by the FN since 1984 differs radically from that of the mainstream Right. Where the map of mainstream right-wing support still resembles that of Catholic France, with strong points in Brittany, Alsace and the south-west, that of the FN has typically been a combination of Mediterranean *départements* (home to a sometimes explosive combination of *pieds noirs* and Algerian immigrants) and old industrial regions, where demand for unskilled labour had attracted immigrant populations; hence the concentration of the FN's best *départements* east of a line running from Le Havre to Perpignan. The suburbs of industrial France, in the Rhône valley and around Paris, with high-rise housing estates and big immigrant populations, inspired fear and loathing among small individual homeowners in surrounding zones; they proved among the firmest FN supporters in the 1990s. Yet to characterise the FN vote as 'eastern' is to underestimate its dynamic character. Some of Le Pen's biggest gains in 2002 were outside the traditional eastern areas of strength, in more western, often rural *départements* where older loyalties of conservative Right (Vendée) or Left (Aude and Ariège), and low levels of immigration, had hitherto minimised the FN's appeal.

The FN electorate is as socially distinct from that of the mainstream Right as it is geographically. Six out of ten of its voters are men. Traditionally conservative categories like the liberal professions or practising Catholics or the retired were attracted in 1984, but are now under-represented. Indeed, the list of social groups most resistant to the appeal of the Le Pen and his party contains more typically 'right-wing' categories (the elderly, the retired, regularly practising Catholics, the wealthy) than 'left-wing' ones (such as trade unionists). The FN electorate has usually included disproportionate numbers of small traders and artisans, the categories who gave birth to the Poujadist movement. They have been complemented, since the late 1980s, by blue-collar workers, typically from the private sector, often young, with few qualifications and vulnerable to unemployment. Indeed, with between 20 and 30 per cent of the votes of both blue-collar workers and the unemployed, Le Pen and his party have repeatedly held the leading position among these groups – the single most striking distinction between the FN electorate and that of the mainstream Right. Traditionally, such male working-class voters had provided the backbone of the Communist Party's rank-and-file support. While there is scant evidence of direct transfers of voters from far Left to far Right, it does appear certain that working-class voters who in an earlier generation would have been natural Communist supporters, but who reached voting age in the 1980s or early 1990s, immediately gravitated, not to the PCF, but to the FN. Some working-class FN voters retain a residual left-wing loyalty, which led analysts to coin the term '*gaucho-lepénistes*'. In 1995, for example, 28 per cent of Le Pen's voters switched to Jospin at the second ballot, against 21 per cent who abstained and 50 per cent who supported Chirac. Similarly, between 25 and 30 per cent of first-ballot FN voters at the 1997 parliamentary elections supported the Left at the run-off. Again, however, to highlight the FN's working-class vote at the expense of other groups is to miss its diverse and changing character; in 2002 the FN made headway among older voters, often retired, prosperous and quite remote from the threat or reality of joblessness that motivated its blue-collar supporters. The FN's spread across classes and social groups, now probably better than that of any other party, is likely to be a durable source of strength.

Individuals attracted to the FN are a similarly mixed group. The hard core are ideologically motivated: monarchists still fighting against 1789; Catholic fundamentalists, loyal to the Latin Mass and the memory of Joan of Arc; wartime collaborators and others nostalgic for Hitler's 'new order' (Le Pen himself ran a publishing house specialising in recordings of German marching songs of World War II); veterans of the *Algérie française* struggle, and even of the Organisation Armée Secrète (OAS); skinheads who have found in FN activities the inspiration to attack and kill men of the 'wrong' colour (although the FN is committed to legal methods, its membership, and especially its 'Protection and Security' service, have been found to contain members of smaller, more violent groups). A larger number of FN supporters, however, without having any very strongly articulated extreme right-wing views, have resented the economic and social evolution of France since the 1980s (especially rising crime and unemployment), despaired of the established parties' ability to address their problems and (in many cases) blamed them on immigrants. Their economic priorities are sharply opposed: support for free-market solutions for the self-employed and professionals in the FN electorate, but a continuing sympathy for *dirigisme* and state-run public services for Le Pen's blue-collar supporters. Two shared concerns of FN voters stand out, however: law and order and immigration. On law and order, Le Pen's voters found themselves close to the mainstream in 2002, when the issue – unusually – was at the centre of the presidential campaign: 74 per cent of them thought law and order a very important stake of the election, compared to an average of 58 per cent for all voters – but 73 per cent for Chirac supporters. On the other hand, they were highly distinctive in their concern over immigration: this was cited as a very important election issue by 60 per cent of Le Pen voters, against an average figure of only 18 per cent.

These priorities are reflected in the the FN's discourse. Le Pen and his lieutenants claim to have a general political platform. They have sought, at various times, to abrogate the Maastricht Treaty, to abolish the European Commission, to create a *Europe des patries* with the most minimal EU structures, or, during the 2002 campaign, to withdraw from the European Union; to lock up AIDS sufferers in institutions (Le Pen has now relented on this score, and has even moved on to express support for homosexual marriages); to punish the corruption that has tainted the other parties; and to create a 'Sixth Republic' with proportional representation, or stronger executive powers, or both; to apply free-market solutions to the economy, but to protect France's small businesses from 'unfair' competition. They opposed France's participation both in the 1991 Gulf war (arguing that Iraq's invasion of Kuwait was part of the normal process of nation-building) and in the 1999 Kosovo conflict, as well as (like everyone else) the 2003 Iraq war. But these concerns have been incidental to the main themes: more powers for the police, harsher prison sentences, the death penalty for murderers and drug dealers; and above all, 'La France aux Français', the application of 'national preference' in employment and social services, and in due course the forced 'repatriation' of 3 million 'immigrants'. Sending immigrants 'home', it is claimed, would at a stroke solve the problems of unemployment, of crime and of the costs of the welfare state. The logistics of this vast round-up and airlift of unwilling populations (equivalent to six jumbo jets daily for two years) are no more considered than the morality of the exercise. But the FN deals less in practical policies than in the designation of enemies and scapegoats. As well as immigrants (particularly those from North Africa), it is against intellectuals, bureaucrats, Eurocrats, liberal Catholics, mainstream journalists, judges, drug addicts, social 'do-gooders', trade unionists, Communists and (though not openly) Jews. This lengthy litany of dislikes and hatreds has fuelled the protest against established parties which is a key to the FN's growth.

The FN in the French political system

Le Pen's FN is an anti-party party, within the French political system but not of it. This is true of the public's view of its policies and of the party itself; of its electoral implantation; and of the party's own strategic perspectives.

Although FN voters are unusual in placing their resentment of 'immigrants' at the centre of their political preoccupations, the FN's views on its own core issues nevertheless win acceptance well beyond the FN's own electorate. Polls in May 2002, for example, showed over three-quarters of respondents supporting the propositions that the police should have greatly enhanced powers, or that the justice system was much too lenient with petty criminals. Two-fifths stated that they 'agreed with Le Pen's ideas' on law and order and justice, and a similar proportion that the death penalty should be restored. Even Le Pen's views on immigration have consistently attracted support beyond the FN electorate: the high point of 38 per cent in 1991 has not been reached since, but even the lower figure of 23 per cent in November 2003 exceeded the FN's voting strength. At the same time, however, Le Pen remains France's most unattractive politician. The simplest indication of this is the fact that in the straight second-round contest of May 2002 between Chirac, a deeply objectionable candidate for left-wing voters, and Le Pen, the incumbent president won by 82 per cent to Le Pen's 18. Similarly, the FN is France's most repulsive party. In poll after poll since 1985, nearly two-thirds of poll respondents have regularly claimed that the FN is a danger for democracy; between two-thirds and four-fifths say they could never in any circumstances vote for it; and unfavourable opinions of the FN exceeded favourable ones by an average of 67 percentage points in monthly polls between 1984 and 2003. No party, not even the PCF at the height of the Cold War, has done worse than this.

This combination of support and rejection is reflected in the FN's electoral performance. The core FN electorate, perhaps 7 per cent of France's voters, is extremely loyal, and the FN vote, aside from the dip of the late 1990s, has been among the more stable in France. At elections held under proportional representation, the FN has won seats. At the one parliamentary election under the Fifth Republic held under proportional representation, in 1986, the FN secured thirty-five Deputies. The FN has had European parliamentarians in Strasbourg since 1984 (the total in 2004 was seven). In 1998 it won 275 out of France's 1,722 regional council seats – a figure that dropped to 156 in 2004, thanks not to any drop in support but to a change of electoral system that had been designed to penalise it. However, at the (more important) elections held on two-ballot majority systems, the FN had been unable to win seats because of its isolation. Just one FN Deputy was elected in 1988 and 1997, none were in 1993 or 2002. There have been no FN Senators, and there were just two FN *conseillers généraux* for France's *départements* in 2004, out of 3,857. Even the municipal victories of 1995 in Toulon, Marignane and Orange, though much commented on, did not reflect the FN's influence in the country as a whole (among towns of over 30,000 inhabitants, the FN has only kept Orange).

Even if the FN's isolation cut it off from office, its nuisance value, to the mainstream Right in particular, has been considerable. In its good elections – 1993, 1995, or the parliamentary elections of 2002 – the mainstream Right has been confident of victory by virtue of a comfortable first-ballot lead over the Left. At more evenly balanced elections, however, there has been a perception that the FN's support or hostility could decide between victory or defeat for the Right as a whole. This was claimed in 1988 (at both presidential and parliamentary elections), and above all in 1997 (when the FN maintained candidates at the second ballot against the mainstream Right in 76 constituencies, and the Right lost in 47 of them – enough, it was claimed, to destroy its National Assembly majority). Worse, where the FN could win seats – at the 1998 regional elections, for example – it held the future of right-wing council presidents in its hands. The RPR and the UDF effectively banned local and national deals with the FN from 1988 (not least on the ground that such arrangements would alienate vital centre voters) – a policy which, though not fully respected, was sufficient to keep the FN in effective quarantine. Not surprisingly, the mainstream Right's standard-bearers in areas of FN strength have been the most vocal in demanding that their parties consider an alliance with Le Pen's party. We have seen how the issue effectively split the UDF in 1998; it may still return to haunt the mainstream Right in a future difficult election.

But if the FN's isolation presents difficulties for the mainstream Right, it also has considerable costs for the FN itself. The resulting tensions led to the split of 1998, and will almost certainly be an issue in future leadership struggles. They arise, above all, from the frustration of some members of the FN elite at their party's continued distance from office. Le Pen has usually tended not to seek accommodations with the mainstream Right, or at least, not on terms other than his own. His opponents have argued that he simply does not want to break into government, preferring to maintain the FN, in permanent opposition, as a family enterprise in which nepotism and favouritism are rife and the barrier between the party's money and that of the Le Pen family is distinctly porous. The split of 1998 was caused by conflicts over this issue, over party organisation and strategy, envenomed by a bitter personal dispute between Le Pen and his lieutenant Bruno Mégret.

The FN's structure has always reflected Le Pen's concern not to encumber himself with a potential successor: 'in the Front National', he has said, 'there is no Number 2 or Number 3, only a Number 1'. In particular, the coexistence, below the party presidency, of a secretary-general and a delegate-general, was designed by Le Pen as a tool to divide and rule; and the *bureau exécutif*, entirely appointed by Le Pen and described by the FN's press service as the 'most important body' in the party, was for a long time left out of the organisation chart. Mégret challenged this autocratic style. He had several assets in his favour. In 1997, after the annulment of a municipal election in the southern suburban town of Vitrolles, Mégret (himself temporarily banned from running for public office) secured the election of his wife as mayor, against the Socialist candidate. The Mégrets had been the darlings of the FN's congress, held at Strasbourg in March 1997 – much to Le Pen's annoyance. And while Le Pen was 70 in 1998, Mégret was still under 50.

The background to Mégret's challenge was the relative strategic impasse in which the FN found itself by early 1998: its vote appeared to have flattened out at 15 per cent, and the FN was still frozen out of the political mainstream. This situation was far more frustrating to Mégret and his like, who had joined the FN in the mid-1980s in the expectation that it would soon win a share of power, than it was to Le Pen, who had spent decades as a political outsider. Hence the different strategic lines backed by the two men, with Le Pen seeking to destroy the mainstream Right from without, and Mégret wishing to join alliances the better to subvert it from within. In the spring of 1998, Mégret's rising star forced Le Pen to accept, against his own preferences, his plans for minimal regional alliances with the mainstream Right. That further damaged Mégret's standing in the eyes of the party leader – especially as both men knew that, for mainstream right-wing politicians, Mégret, the former École Polytechnique student and son of a *conseiller d'État*, was altogether more acceptable as a possible alliance partner than the unpredictable Le Pen.

The *casus belli* between the two men concerned the leadership of the FN list at the 1999 European elections. Le Pen had led the lists in 1984, 1989 and 1994, and was expected to do so again; but he had punched a female Socialist candidate in the face in 1997, and risked being banned from elective office as a result. Le Pen announced that if he did not stand, his wife would take his place; Mégret claimed that the party's official bodies (where he had strong support) should meet and choose the candidate; by the end of 1998, Mégret was out of the FN and disputing the ownership of the FN's funds, name and logo with Le Pen in the courts. Le Pen won, leaving Mégret to call his new party the Mouvement National Républicain (MNR) and to seek cash wherever he could.

Mégret took with him most of the FN's middle-ranking cadres, as well as its more well-heeled and more ideological voters. There was little to choose between the programmes of the MNR and FN, and certainly no question that the MNR was more 'moderate'. What became clear within three years at most, however, was that the polished, well-spoken Mégret was no match for his former boss; the 2002 presidential elections condemned the MNR to political marginality. The qualities that make Le Pen an impossible ally – his unpredictability, boorishness and brutality – have also made him the greatest asset for voters who *want* their party to stand outside the norms of mainstream politics.

This victory did not, however, resolve the FN's longer-term strategic problem. The party still contains those who, like Le Pen himself, appear to enjoy its pariah status. Le Pen has regularly reinforced this by referring to the Holocaust as a 'detail' of World War II, or by referring (in January 2005) to the Occupation of France, including the role of the Gestapo, as 'not especially inhuman'; Mégret's successor as crown prince, Bruno Gollnisch, has also regularly espoused 'revisionist' views on the period, earning a suspension from his chair at Lyon University in 2004. Such declarations undermine the work of those in the party elite who would like to see the FN move closer to the mainstream. They include Le Pen's own youngest daughter, Marine, a member of the *bureau exécutif* and an MEP. Her association Générations Le Pen aims precisely at 'dediabolising' the FN, establishing its credentials as a respectable 'party of government', attractive in particular to women voters who have so far tended to withhold their support. A further split is unlikely as long as Le Pen remains at the helm. Biology, however, suggests that this is unlikely to continue much beyond the elections of 2007.

Concluding remarks

In or out of national office, France's right wing has well-established sources of power and influence. Throughout the Fifth Republic, it has held a comfortable majority in the Senate. It has controlled most of France's ninety-six *départements* except for a brief period in the late 1970s, and ran the great majority of regions from the first direct elections in 1986 until the defeats of 2004. It has held major cities such as Bordeaux and Toulouse for decades (the loss of Paris and Lyon in March 2001 was balanced by victories in other major cities such as Strasbourg, Blois and Orléans). Some of the most influential pressure groups in the country can be counted on to propagate right-wing ideas, despite periodic squabbles with right-wing politicians: they include the MEDEF which represents the business community; the FNSEA which is the main farmers' union, the UNAPEL which protects Catholic schools, and the PEEP, which defends a rightist viewpoint in the state school sector. France's intellectuals, more or less in thrall to Marxism during the post-war generation, now count fashionable right-wingers among their number; belief in any early replacement of capitalism by a socialist system has been marginalised, since the early 1980s, among politicians and political commentators alike. The Right has committed supporters in the administration and, as a consequence of *pantouflage* (see Chapter 10, p. 287), in key posts in business. Although its control of the state broadcasting system was broken after 1981, the Right is still influential both among private broadcasting stations and above all in the press; the late Robert Hersant, founder of the Hersant group which owns *Le Figaro* and a string of regional dailies, was a former RPR Deputy.

Despite these assets, the record of the French Right since the 1980s has been unimpressive compared with those of many foreign counterparts. In opposition for sixteen of the twenty-five years from 1981 to 2005, the Right often seemed hesitant even when in office. It has been no more able than the Left to secure the re-election of an incumbent parliamentary majority. And while it has (like the Left, though in a different manner) engaged in large-scale privatisations, in other respects it has been slow to aim at what right-wing governments elsewhere might view as obvious targets. The Right's record on eliminating France's chronic public-spending deficits (they rose in Raffarin's first two years), or on reducing the overall level of public spending (still in excess of 54 per cent of GDP), has been weak; targets for reducing civil service numbers are timid compared with those of Britain's New Labour; reform of the labour market, and of a taxation system which (especially at local level) actively penalises employment, has been slow; changes to an education system that is both prodigal (in terms of surplus school-teachers paid not to teach unwanted subjects) and starved (of funding for universities) have been virtually non-existent.

One reason for this uncertain performance has been institutional. For much of the Fifth Republic, the superposition of a seven-year presidential term onto five-year parliaments has meant electoral cycles of two to three years, too short for unpopular reforms (such as those indicated above) to show benefits in terms of competitiveness, growth and jobs. Governments looking to the next election are thus well advised to tread softly on reform. That difficulty should, in principle, be resolved by the likely synchronisation of presidential and parliamentary terms over five years. But the Raffarin government's reforms to pensions, health, taxation and the working week were more prudent than bold – despite his command of five clear years. Other reasons for this cautious record should therefore be sought – in the Right's electoral weakness, in its ideological predilections and in its internal divisions.

The mainstream Right's relative electoral weakness is most simply illustrated by the contrast between the period from 1958 to 1974, when the parties or candidates of the moderate Right *always* won over half of all first-ballot votes at presidential and parliamentary elections, and the years since 1978, when they have *never* done so. Victories since the 1980s have been won with shares of the first-round vote that fell far short of the comfortable majorities of old: 43 per cent in 1986, 44.2 in 1993, 20.8 per cent for Chirac in 1995 and 19.9 per cent in 2002, 43.7 per cent in the 2002 parliamentary elections. Defeats have taken the moderate Right to hitherto unimaginably low levels: 36 per cent in 1997. The most obvious reason for this step change was the rise of the FN, which rendered permanent what might initially have been viewed as the moderate Right's temporary loss of vote share in 1978–81. The FN's presence meant that a significant proportion of the total right-wing vote was practically unavailable to candidates of the moderate Right at the decisive second ballots of elections. Hence, in part, the paradox of a right wing (including the FN) commanding a consistent overall majority of first-round votes but staying so long out of power. It also meant that the moderate Right has regularly had to fight a war on two fronts. In doing so, it has conceded something to the FN agenda on law and order and immigration – but also something to the Left's defence of the public sector (indeed, on this issue Chirac and his prime ministers have appeared distinctly to the left of Blair's New Labour).

The French Right's hesitancy to engage in ambitious neo-liberal reforms also has ideological reasons, which electoral weakness compounded. Right-wing commentators castigate the Left's continuing ideological hegemony, exemplified, for example, by the widespread support for public-sector strike movements in 1995 and after 2002. To an extent, they were right. The view of the state as an active promoter of social equality has been current on the Right as well as the Left, especially among Gaullists and Christian Democrats. In 2002, some 40 per cent of Chirac's and Bayrou's voters did not accept the proposition that the number of public employees should be cut. When, at the same time, Alain Madelin gave the French the chance to vote for an unambiguously neo-liberal candidate, he was rewarded with under 4 per cent of the vote. A further difficulty is that neither of Chirac's presidential victories could be said to offer a clear mandate in favour of change from the Right. In 1995, his campaign was marked by a phrase – *la fracture sociale* – and a leftish, Statist, tonality, intended to contrast with Balladur, which appeared to offer a return to the interventionism of the de Gaulle years. In 2002, his re-election to the presidency was helped by the (anti-Le Pen) demonstrations and by millions of left-wing votes; the Right's parliamentary victory in June was assisted by the voters' wish to avoid any repetition of cohabitation and by Raffarin's emollient promises to listen to *la France d'en bas* (the France of ordinary working people). Little in these campaigns presaged any radical rollback of the state.

France's right-wing parties have also, finally, suffered from their divisions. They have drawn on different traditions, and have had different patterns of organisation and (to some degree) different electorates. They have argued about money (notably the prime minister's 'special funds'), about policies and about political strategy (and notably how to handle the FN). Yet many of these divisions had narrowed by 2000; they are probably not too deep to be accommodated within a single, diverse, right-wing party such as the UMP aspired to be. Perhaps harder to contain have been the divisions caused by presidential rivalries. The contests between Giscard and Chirac in 1981, or Chirac and Barre in 1988, though not sufficient on their own to ensure Mitterrand's two victories, did deny the leading right-wing candidate votes at the run-off. The damage at parliamentary elections was more limited; parliamentary seats could, after all, be shared out in a way that the (one) top job could not. Even here, though, the division between Chirac and Balladur supporters poisoned the right-wing majority between 1995 and 1997. More indirectly, however, the *querelles des chefs* caused widespread disenchantment with moderate right-wing parties among right-wing voters, rendering other options – for example the FN – more attractive and thus further increasing the moderate Right's handicaps. Hostilities between Sarkozy and Chirac, more or less open within weeks of the 2002 victories, have the potential to be similarly damaging in 2007 – unless, of course, they are supplanted by an equally bloody confrontation between Sarkozy and de Villepin.

Personal rivalries are the stuff of politics and it would be surprising not to find them on the French Right. The openness with which they are pursued is perhaps more remarkable; French politicians tend to stab one another in the front as well as in the back. What is most striking, however, is how bad the party organisations have been at containing such conflicts and canalising them to produce strong party leaders and election-winning candidates. No party of the moderate Right has an agreed procedure for making these choices that has operated regularly between several contenders. One result has been an often messy pattern of competition, regularly involving the most demagogic varieties of outbidding, at presidential elections: four candidates on the moderate Right (Giscard and three Gaullists) in 1981; two Gaullists but no UDF candidate in 1995; five candidates of the mainstream Right in 2002. Another has been the relative immunity of party leaders to sanction from below. Few parties in any democracy have hung onto so many unsuccessful leaders for so long. The problem of

French parties, notwithstanding De Gaulle's critique of their role under the Fourth Republic, is not that they are not too strong; it is that they are too weak.

Further reading

For general studies on French and European parties, see Chapter 7.

Anderson, M., *Conservative Politics in France*, London, George Allen and Unwin, 1974.
Bastow, S., 'Front National economic policy: from neo-liberalism to protectionism?', *Modern and Contemporary France*, 5(1), February, 1997, pp. 61–72.
Berstein, S., *Histoire du gaullisme*, Paris, Perrin, 2001.
Betz, H.-G., *Radical Right-Wing Populism in Western Europe*, Basingstoke, Macmillan, 1994.
Birenbaum, G., *Le Front National en politique*, Paris, Balland, 1992.
Bresson, G. and Lionet, C., *Le Pen, biographie*, Paris, Seuil, 1994.
Camus, J.-Y., *Le Front National: histoire et analyses*, Paris, Olivier Laurens, 1996.
Cathala, J. and J.-B. Prédall, *Nous nous sommes tant haïs. 1997–2002. Voyage au centre de la droite*, Paris, Éditions du Seuil, 2002.
Charlot, J., *L'UNR: étude du pouvoir au sein d'un parti politique*, Paris, Armand Colin, 1967.
Charlot, J., *The Gaullist Phenomenon*, London, George Allen and Unwin, 1971.
Chebel d'Appollonia, A., *L'extrême droite en France de Maurras à Le Pen*, 2nd edition, Brussels, Complexe, 1996.
Constanty, H., *Le lobby de la gâchette*, Paris, Seuil, 2002 (on CPNT).
Davies, P., *The National Front in France: Ideology, Discourse, and Power*, London, Routledge, 1998.
Davies, P., *The Extreme Right in France, 1789 to the Present*, London, Routledge, 2002.
de Gaulle, C., *Memoirs of Hope: Renewal and Endeavour*, New York, Simon and Schuster, 1971.
Dély, R., *Histoire secrète du Front national*, Paris, Grasset, 1999.
Dolez, B. and A. Laurent, 'Quand les militants RPR élisent leur président', *Revue Française de Science Politique*, 50(1), 2000, pp. 125–46.
Faux, E., Legrand, T. and Perez, G., *La main droite de Dieu: enquête sur François Mitterrand et l'extrême droite*, Paris, Seuil, 1994.
Fysh, P. and Wolfreys, J., *The Politics of Racism in France*, London, Macmillan, 1998.
Giscard d'Estaing, V., *Démocratie française*, Paris, Fayard, 1976.
Haegel, F., 'Faire l'Union: la refondation des partis de droite après les élections de 2002', *Revue Française de Science Politique*, 52(5–6), October–December 2002, pp. 561–76.
Hainsworth, P. (ed.), *The Politics of the Extreme Right: From the Margins to the Mainstream*, London, Pinter, 2000.
Hanley, D., 'Compromise, party management and fair shares: the case of the French UDF', *Party Politics*, 5(2), 1999, pp. 171–89.
Kitschelt, H., with A. McGann, *The Radical Right in Western Europe: A Comparative Analysis*, Ann Arbor, University of Michigan Press, 1997.
Knapp, A., *Gaullism since de Gaulle*, Aldershot, Dartmouth Publishing, 1994.
Madelin, P., *Les gaullistes et l'argent*, Paris, L'Archipel, 2001.
Marcus, J., *The French National Front*, London, Macmillan, 1994.
Martin, P., *La montée du Front National*, Paris, Fondation Saint-Simon, 1996.
Massart, A., *L'Union pour la Démocratie Française (UDF)*, Paris, L'Harmattan, 1999.
Mayer, N., *Ces Français qui votent Le Pen*, 2nd edition, Paris, Flammarion, 2002.
Perrineau, P., *Le symptôme Le Pen: radiographie des electeurs du Front National*, Paris, Fayard, 1997.
Rémond, R., *Les droites en France*, Paris, Aubier Montaigne, 1982.
Sirinelli, J.-F. (ed.), *Histoire des droites en France*, vol. I, Paris, Gallimard, 1992.

Souchard, M., Wahnich, S., Cuminal, I. and Wathier, V., *Le Pen: Les mots*, Paris, Le Monde Éditions, 1997.

Touchard, J., *Le gaullisme, 1940–1969*, Paris, Seuil, 1978.

Traïni, C., *Les braconniers de la politique*, Paris, Presses Universitaires de France, 2003 (on CPNT).

Tristan, A., *Au Front*, Paris, Gallimard, 1987.

Party websites

CNIP	http://www.cnip.asso.fr
CPNT	http://www.cpnt.asso.fr
Front National	http://www.frontnational.com
MPF	http://www.mpf-villiers.com/
UDF	http://www.udf.org/index.html
UMP	http://www.u-m-p.org/site/index.php

9 Transformations of the party system
Continuity and change

A party system in any democratic state consists of three sets of relationships. The first of these concerns the parties themselves. How many parties are there? Are there extreme parties of Right and Left, or is the ideological distance between the various parties small? And is there a pattern of alliances between the parties? Secondly, a party system is shaped by the relations between parties and society – by levels of membership, by public attitudes towards parties, but above all by levels of electoral support. A third aspect is the relationship of parties to government. Which party or parties govern? Do they do so alone or in coalition? And is there regular alternation in power, or does a single party or coalition monopolise governmental office over an extended period?

The time dimension is crucial because a party system is not just a snapshot of the configuration of political parties at a given moment – just after a major election, for example. On the contrary, the purpose of analysing party systems is to reveal long-term dynamics and continuities beyond the contingencies of any single electoral result, however dramatic. The analysis of party systems does not ignore change, whether involving the emergence, splitting or disappearance of parties, gains and losses in party support, or the conquest or loss of governmental office. But it does seek to place these things in a long perspective. Analysis of the British system, for example, sets the varied events of the late twentieth and early twenty-first centuries – the vicissitudes of the Conservative and Labour parties, the rise of centre-party politics, or the development of Welsh and Scottish nationalisms – within a more general context in which one or other of the big parties can normally be expected to win a House of Commons majority and occupy government office alone.

Such an exercise presents obvious problems in the case of France. The two previous chapters have demonstrated that French parties are numerous (no fewer than nine lists won 5 per cent of the vote or more at the European elections of 1999, and seven at those of 2004); that in the course of the Fifth Republic the level of electoral support of each of them has either halved (in the case of the Gaullists) or quartered (in that of the Communists) or both doubled and halved (in the case of the Socialists, Les Verts and the Front National (FN)); that most have split, in more or less dramatic ways, at least once, and some have merged; and, confusingly, that all except the Communists have changed their names at least once. No two post-election snapshots of the configuration of parties resemble one another very closely. With French parties as numerous, and their support as variable, as they are, it should be no surprise to find that the party system has defied any neat classification. Moderate pluralism, a dominant-party system, imperfect bipartism, the bipolar quadrille and a two-and-a-half party system are all expressions that have been applied to it during the Fifth Republic. At times, indeed, and especially since the 1980s, observers have come close to detecting a new party system with each election. Such successive characterisations are a useful reminder of how the configuration of parties has changed in the course of the Fifth Republic, and this chapter will start with them. But they miss out the longer-term dynamics, which is why an attempt at a more synthetic view of the party system over the full course of nearly five decades will follow.

Party configurations, 1956–2005

The party system of Fourth Republic France (Figure 9.1) presented an almost perfect case of what the Italian specialist Giovanni Sartori called *polarised pluralism*. This was a volatile and unstable mix of six major characteristics.

- The presence of strong and irresponsible 'anti-system' parties of the Left (the Communists) and the Right (the Gaullists in the late 1940s and early 1950s, the Poujadists thereafter), determined to bring down the régime, or at the very least to sow confusion among its supporters, hampered all attempts to find a coherent governing majority in parliament. The proportional electoral system allowed such parties to win parliamentary seats (a minimum of 100 for the Communists) without committing themselves to any form of alliance.
- Political conflict was fiercely ideological, even on issues that in other systems might have been resolved by negotiation and compromise (Chapter 1). The four main political forces which broadly supported the régime, and from which governments might be drawn, were themselves divided, in two different ways: on the clerical/anti-clerical issue which had traditionally separated Right from Left in France, and on issues of state intervention, taxation and spending. New issues that confronted the politicians of the Fourth Republic, notably European integration

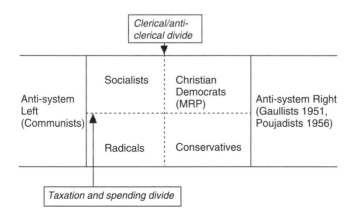

Figure 9.1 The party system of the Fourth Republic: a simplified view.

and decolonisation, also divided the governing parties. All parliamentary majorities were thus quarrelsome and precarious.

- Most parties, especially those of the Centre and Right, had difficulty in commanding the loyalty of their parliamentarians, rendering major votes in parliament unpredictable.
- Governments were therefore unstable, lasting an average of six months and a maximum of seventeen.
- The link between votes and the composition of the political executive was tenuous to the point of appearing non-existent. The composition of governing coalitions was determined not so much by election results as by negotiations between party leaders behind closed doors.
- Electoral competition led parties to outbid their competitors, including those with which they would later enter governing coalitions, on key policies at election time. In government, however, parties invariably disappointed their supporters because they were obliged to make compromises in coalition, and because few governments had the time to enact any major policy before losing office. Voter disappointment with parties led to disappointment with the political system as a whole.

The transition to the Fifth Republic between 1958 and 1962 offered an equally classic case of institutional change leading to party system change. The new constitution gave governments new safeguards against attack from parliament; it gave the president both new *powers*, including the right of dissolution and the right to call a referendum, and reinforced *power*, through the 1962 reform instituting direct presidential elections. The replacement of proportional representation at parliamentary elections by the two-ballot majority system with single-member constituencies, though not part of the constitution, was nevertheless a major institutional change. Polarised pluralism disappeared. But the new party system did not settle down to a pattern as predictable as those of, say, Britain or the Federal Republic of Germany. On the contrary, six different configurations of French parties can be observed since 1958. They may be read in conjunction with Figure 2.2, which shows the relationship between presidential terms, governments and parliamentary majorities under the Fifth Republic.

The transitional phase, 1958–62

The 1958 elections cut the Communists' parliamentary representation from 150 to ten, and gave the Gaullists much the biggest parliamentary group, with 216 Deputies, on the strength of just 20.2 per cent of the first-ballot vote (Table 7.2). But no group or alliance had a stable majority. The first government of the Fifth Republic, under Michel Debré, included conservatives and Christian Democrats, but lost support from *Algérie française* elements of both parties. In votes on Algerian policy, it depended, in part, on support from the Socialists, who opposed Debré on every other issue. This lack of a stable majority, and the use of different coalitions for different votes, resembled the politics of the Fourth Republic, though the government's new constitutional powers and the gravity of the Algerian crisis gave Debré greater staying power than his predecessors. From a post-1962 perspective, this period appears as a transition from the polarised pluralism of the Fourth Republic to the stable parliamentary majorities of the Fifth. But to representatives of what de Gaulle was to call the 'parties of yesteryear', it appeared as a mere interruption in the normal conduct of parliamentary government as it was carried on under any Republic. With the Algerian war over, Debré replaced by the inexperienced Pompidou, and de Gaulle's challenge thrown down in the shape of the constitutional referendum proposal on the direct election of the president, the old parties moved quickly to oppose the emergence of a new régime. Hence the motion of censure, which they won, and the 1962 elections that followed the referendum, both of which the old parties lost, laying the Fourth Republic finally to rest.

Gaullist 'dominance', 1962–74

The November 1962 elections gave the Gaullist–Giscardian coalition 36 per cent of the first-round vote and 268 out of 482 Deputies. They gave French voters that link between electoral choice and the composition of the executive which had been so conspicuously lacking under the Third and Fourth Republics. They gave France the first stable parliamentary majority in the history of any Republic: Pompidou lasted a record six years as prime minister, and commanded parliamentary forces sufficiently disciplined for him not to need the most draconian power in the constitutional armoury, Article 49–3, during the whole of the 1962 parliament (see Chapter 6). For Jean Charlot, the Gaullists of the de Gaulle and Pompidou presidencies represented France's 'dominant' party. In a French context this term is comprehensible, so remarkable was the contrast with the Fourth Republic, in terms of voting patterns, of the conduct of parliamentary business, and of the concentration of ministerial posts and patronage in the hands of one party. But as observed in Chapter 8, the Gaullists' 'dominance' was still relative. Their 44 per cent of the vote at the first ballots of presidential elections (de Gaulle in 1965 and Pompidou in 1969), and between 33 per cent and 38 per cent at parliamentary elections, were strong results, but no more indicative of 'dominance' than those of the German CDU or either of the big British parties. This was not Mexico's Institutional Revolutionary Party or Japan's Liberal Democrats. Moreover, the dilution of the Gaullists' positions in the parliamentary majority of 1973, and above all the very poor result of their candidate Chaban-Delmas in the first round of the 1974 presidential elections, drew a fairly speedy close to what had been the hegemony of little more than a decade. At least as important as the Gaullists' (partial) dominance was the slow process of bipolarisation of the party system, as the left-wing parties understood that, to beat the Gaullists, they needed an alliance at least as coherent as the governing coalition. Hence the signature of the Left's Common Programme in 1972. At the same time the centrists felt increasingly squeezed between the Gaullists and the Left.

The 'bipolar quadrille', 1974–81

The election of Valéry Giscard d'Estaing to the presidency opened a period which differed in two respects from the de Gaulle and Pompidou years. First, once the opposition centrists had rallied to Giscard at the run-off of the presidential election, practically the whole range of political forces had been absorbed into one of the two great coalitions of Left and Right; bipolarisation appeared complete. Second, within each of these coalitions, no single party was dominant. Each of the four parties – on the Left Communists and Socialists, on the Right Gaullists and the non-Gaullist moderate Right federated by Giscard into the UDF in 1978 – could hope to win between a fifth and a quarter of the vote. This 'bipolar quadrille' could appear as the natural product, in terms of the party system, of the institutions of the Fifth Republic, once the exceptional personality of de Gaulle had faded from the scene and the Communists and Socialists had become allies. But interparty conflicts within Left and Right were never so fierce as when the parties concerned were of roughly equal strengths. They rendered the 'bipolar quadrille' inherently unstable: for each of the two weaker parties – Communists and Gaullists – overall victory against the opposite camp became less important than regaining a dominant position against allies. The bipolar quadrille did not survive 1981.

Socialist 'dominance', 1981–86

The collapse of the Communist vote in 1981, amplified at the European elections of 1984, established the Socialists as the dominant party within the Left. This they have remained ever since, even at their low point of 1993 – a critical break with the Communist hegemony on the Left characteristic of the three post-war decades. Indeed, the PS could briefly appear as France's dominant party, for the June 1981 parliamentary elections brought them 36 per cent of the first-ballot vote and a single-party majority (the second out of three in French republican history) at the run-off. At the presidential elections of 1988 and 1995, and at the parliamentary elections of 1981, 1986, 1988 and 1997, the Socialists had the highest vote of any single party. But 'dominance' supposes, at the very least, governmental office, and the Socialists lost this to the Right in 1986.

The challenge to 'parties of government', 1986–97

In fact, 1981 led not to Socialist 'dominance' but to a period of instability without precedent under the Fifth Republic. Alternation in power, unknown from 1958 to 1981, suddenly became normal: the voters changed president, parliamentary majority, or both, in 1981, 1986, 1988, 1993, 1995, 1997 and 2002. Only Mitterrand, who survived two seven-year presidential terms and left the Élysée as a moribund 78-year-old in 1995, and Chirac, who won re-election under exceptional conditions in 2002, resisted the trend. Having rid themselves of Giscard and the Right in 1981, the French voted the Right back into government (though not the presidency) in 1986, inaugurating the experience of cohabitation between a president and a government of different camps. In 1988, the voters re-elected Mitterrand to the presidency, and when Mitterrand dissolved parliament, they duly removed the Right from government (though without giving the Socialists an absolute majority). Five years later, the Right's landslide victory at the 1993 parliamentary elections opened the second cohabitation, between Mitterrand and Balladur. But when Balladur attempted a presidential bid in 1995 he failed; it was Chirac who won the succession to Mitterrand. Chirac proceeded to sack his rival from the premiership and replace him with his own protégé Alain Juppé. But Chirac himself suffered a major reverse in 1997 when he called parliamentary elections a year early; Jospin's left-wing coalition won, opening a third period of cohabitation which lasted until a further reversal of fortunes at the parliamentary and presidential elections of 2002.

As the mainstream parties of Left and Right pursued each other in a revolving door leading in and out of office, they came to resemble one another to a degree unprecedented under the Fifth Republic. All became fixated (though not always to great effect) by the tedious goals of low budget deficits and low inflation at home and monetary stability abroad. All allowed unemployment to rise, with a brief pause in the late 1980s. All incurred the voters' displeasure – at their record on joblessness above all, but also on issues relating to France's urban malaise, including crime and immigration, and to corrupt political finance. The periods 1983–85 and 1991–93 for the Socialists, and 1995–97 for the Right, saw record levels of public dissatisfaction with governments and with parties. Frequent alternation in power was the most obvious expression of public disappointment. Another was falling party membership: total estimated party membership dropped from some 900,000 in the late 1970s to barely half that twenty years later, with the three major membership parties (Communists, Socialists and Gaullists) all struggling to keep their totals above 100,000. A third manifestation of disappointment was falling turnout, as abstentions at major elections rose by roughly half, from some 20 per cent of the electorate to 30 (see Table 7.2). A fourth manifestation was protest voting, or at least voting for parties that showed no aspiration to join a coalition with one of the mainstream parties of government. Traditionally, one party had been good at canalising working-class protest and opposition to 'the system': the Communists, who had left government in 1984 and returned to positions of truculent, workerist (and pro-Soviet) opposition, only contracting the most minimal electoral agreements with Socialists to save their parliamentary seats and town halls. But the Communists' credibility as a protest party, badly damaged by their period in office, was never revived by the return to opposition. To a significant degree the PCF was supplanted as a force of protest, after 1983–84, by the FN; the FN's vote rose from 10 per cent during most elections of the 1980s to 15 per cent in 1995, 1997 and 1998. Also outside the system were the ecology groupings, which won 10.7 per cent at the 1989 European elections; and the shooters' rights party (Chasse, Pêche, Nature, Traditions (CPNT)), which achieved at least 4 per cent at European and regional elections in the decade after 1989.

These parties won seats in the European Parliament and the regional councils (both elected by proportional representation) but not in the French National Assembly. The only exceptions were the 1986 Assembly, elected by proportional representation and including thirty-five FN Deputies, and those of 1988 and 1997, which included one FN Deputy each. Otherwise France's parliament consisted entirely of Communists, moderate Left and moderate Right, just as it had done in the 1970s, and in no way reflected developments among the voters. The resulting gulf between votes cast and seats won reached its widest point in the 1993 parliamentary elections. Of the total registered electorate then, 34 per cent abstained or spoilt their ballots; 23 per cent voted for a party outside the 'system' – the FN, the PCF or one of the various Trotskyist or ecologist groupings; 14.4 per cent supported the non-Communist Left; while just 29 per cent was enough to ensure the 'landslide' of the right-wing coalition, which took 80 per cent of the parliamentary seats. The 'parties of government' were supported by fewer than 44 per cent of the electorate. Some observers therefore suggested that the real division in French politics was no longer between Right and Left, but between parties of government and parties outside the system.

Full circle? 1997–present

The closing years of the twentieth century, on the other hand, appeared to demonstrate the integrative power of the Fifth Republic's party system. This was most obvious on the Left, where the *gauche plurielle* coalition of Communists, Greens and Socialists, constructed in the aftermath of Jospin's honourable defeat at the 1995 presidential elections, proved victorious in 1997. Both Communists and Les Verts, in other words, came in from the cold and became parties of government, albeit junior ones. For the Communists, the process was facilitated by the fall of the Soviet Union and by the leadership change of 1994; the PCF was rewarded with three posts in government, the first in thirteen years. Les Verts, in alliance for the first time with the Socialists and benefiting from their first-round support in twenty-nine constituencies, won seats for eight of their candidates and a ministerial portfolio for Voynet. Even after the defeats of 2002, it seemed probable that something resembling the *gauche plurielle* coalition would line up for future battles – as indeed it did, with considerable success, for the regional elections of March 2004.

Meanwhile the split of the FN in 1998–99 appeared to signal the retreat of protest politics on the Right. As we have seen in Chapter 8 (p. 246), the intense personal rivalry between Le Pen and his lieutenant Bruno Mégret that occasioned the split was under-pinned by a strategic difference about possible alliances with the mainstream Right. In a sense, the FN split and the entry of the PCF and Les Verts into the *gauche plurielle* had a comparable underlying cause: the difficulty for a Fifth Republic party to exist outside one of the main coalitions of Right or Left. These coalitions continue to dominate political representation at all levels in France, with some 90 per cent of seats on regional councils and among France's MEPs and nearly 100 per cent in municipalities, *départements*, National Assembly and Senate.

Yet these developments cannot be seen as signalling a return to any of the earlier party configurations of the Fifth Republic. No party is dominant: the Socialists, France's largest party before 2002, had an audience of some 25 per cent; the UMP, though enjoying an enviable hold on France's institutions since 2002, remains too electorally vulnerable (as its results in 2004 showed) to claim even the watered-down 'dominant' status often accorded to the Gaullists at their zenith. The 'bipolar quadrille' is rendered impossible both by the hegemony of the Socialists on the Left and the Gaullists (and then the UMP) on the mainstream Right, and by the proliferation of parties and candidacies. Above all, protest parties still count. The FN recovered from its split, against many expectations, propelling Le Pen into the second ballot of the 2002 presidential election. The Trotskyists have attracted hundreds of thousands of new voters, unfamiliar with Marxism-Leninism but lacking confidence in the mainstream Left's ability to address their concerns. At the first ballot of the 2002 presidential election, a third of the vote went to anti-system candidates (far Right, far Left and Saint-Josse for CPNT). This was an extreme, so far unique, case, but even at the lower levels seen since (about a fifth at June 2002 parliamentary elections and the 2004 European elections, a quarter at the 2004 regional elections), a significant bloc of voters (to which may be added the growing ranks of non-voters) remains outside the mainstream of Left–Right politics.

The referendum of 2005 (more fully described in Chapter 14) suggested something more: a division between extremes and centre, already seen in the Maastricht refer-endum of 1992 but intensified over the intervening thirteen years, and now skewed leftwards by the circumstances of the campaign (it was a right-wing president who had called the referendum) and its character (focused on the supposed neo-liberal thrust of the constitutional treaty). Observers in 2005 saw a durable division opening up between the Left's extreme wing (Trotskyists, Communists, and the large number of Socialists and Greens drawn into their orbit by the no campaign) and left-wing moderates (the rest of the Socialists and Greens). If sustained, this division would match that between moderate and extreme Right. The resulting party system would have four blocs (moderate and extreme Left, moderate and extreme Right), but would differ from the bipolar quadrille because of the extreme difficulty of forging alliances on Left or Right. Indeed, it would be closer to the polarised pluralism of the Fourth Republic. The outcome, of course, would not be identical. The institutions of the Fifth Republic would probably guarantee stable government, at least in formal terms. But governments would lack legitimacy, and thus that power of effective decision that de Gaulle so prized, because so many of the voters would have supported parties 'outside the system' on the far Left and the far Right. Moreover, there was no guarantee at all that the 'accident' of 2002 would not recur; indeed, the 2005 referendum result provoked speculation that the second ballot of the next presidential election, in 2007, might be held between Le Pen and the Trostkyist Besancenot. While such an analysis probably overstates the short-term divisions caused by the referendum, it tallies with the growing range of issues that cut across Left–Right barriers, and with the growing disenchantment of many voters with mainstream politics.

To understand these six stages, however, is not to understand the party system. Though an analysis by stages is necessary to appreciate the frequency and extent of change in party configurations, such an analysis characteristically lacks a long time span and therefore leaves us with too little comprehension of underlying dynamics. Understanding these requires an attempt at a more synthetic model of Fifth Republic party politics.

Bipolar multipartism

The salient feature of the French party system under the Fifth Republic, as presented in Table 9.1, is the balance between forces tending to bipolarisation, coalition and (relative) simplicity, and forces tending to multipolarisation, fragmentation and complexity. Both types of force exist in almost any party system, but most systems are marked by the predominance of one or the other: the British system is overwhelmingly bipolar, for example, while the French Fourth Republic or pre-1992 Italy incorporated few restraints to balance the forces of fragmentation and multipolarity. In the contemporary French case, on the other hand, both types of force are almost equally strong. Such relatively small variations in the balance as occur may therefore produce quite marked effects in the configuration of parties from one election to another – in other words, the changes over time noted above. The term bipolar multipartism attempts to capture this balance while remaining sufficiently loose-fitting to accommodate these variations.

Bipolarity: characteristics

The party system of the Fifth Republic can be characterised as bipolar, first, on the basis of the parties' relationship to government. The great unexpected development of the Fifth Republic was the emergence, from 1962, of the *fait majoritaire* – of stable majorities in the National Assembly, of either Right or Left, capable of sustaining a government in office for a whole parliament. Stable majorities have encouraged the development of more or less stable oppositions, capable at least of some measure of

Table 9.1 Bipolar multipartism: the party system of the Fifth Republic

Bipolar characteristics	Multiparty characteristics
• The norm of government is a stable coalition in office, supported by a clear majority for the whole duration of a parliament. • Alternation in power results from competition between Left and Right blocs, not, for example, from Centre parties changing partners: individuals may change sides, parties do not. • No 'grand coalitions'.	• Failure of '2-party system' to emerge (single-party majorities rare; all govts. are coalitions). • Up to 5 or 6 'relevant' parties (> 5% of vote), 1997: PCF, PS, (Greens), UDF, RPR, FN. • Some relevant parties outside the two main coalitions (Centrists before 1974, FN from mid-1980s). • Shrinking vote share of 'parties of government' from 1980s. • New entrants (Greens, FN, CPNT). • Party splits: PS/MDC, UDF/DL, RPR/RPF, FN/MNR.
Bipolarising dynamics	**Centrifugal dynamics**
Institutional • Direct presidential elections, second ballot. • Single-member two-ballot majority system at parliamentary elections penalises isolated parties. • Constitution stabilises parliamentary majorities (Article 49–3, etc.).	*Institutional* • Wide available choice at first ballots of parliamentary and presidential elections. • The coming of proportional representation (new: 1979, 1983, 1986): the 'accordion effect'. • Localism (and *cumul des mandats*) lowers costs of dissidence, weakens parties.
Voter-related • Right and Left are a readily accessible framework for French voters (1996: 37% Left, 32% Right, 24% don't know), which corresponds to party allegiance. • TV and 'nationalisation' of politics reinforced presidentialism.	*Voter-related* • Old suspicions within Left and Right. • Voter perception of failure in government (new). • Voters believe Right and Left distinction out of date (62%). • Divisive new issues: immigration, crime, Europe, environment. • Social change (e.g. decline of working class).
Party- and candidate-related • Competitive strategies deployed by parties and presidential candidates to meet institutional constraints — construction of presidential coalitions — 2nd-ballot discipline — programmatic alliances — exclusion of FN — absorption of Greens.	*Party- and candidate-related* • French parties' weak organisation causes difficulty in destroying new competitors, at least in short term. • Parties' competitive strategies *within* Right and Left.

co-ordination both within the Assembly and at the approach of elections. Governments do not fall, as they had under the Third and Fourth Republics, on the whim of a single party or even of a fraction of a party within the governing coalition. The departure of the MRP ministers in 1962, for example, led to no more than a reshuffle. On the contrary, alternation in power under the Fifth Republic has always been the outcome of competition between left-wing and right-wing blocs. These blocs have remained relatively stable. Although a handful of individuals, such as the former Giscardian ministers in 1988, may change sides, whole parties do not; the Centre – with the partial exception of the 1988 parliament, the only one since 1962 where there was no overall majority – has never played the pivotal role it enjoyed under the Third and Fourth Republics. Nor has the Fifth Republic seen a grand coalition, grouping socialists and conservatives (as, for example, the CDU–SPD coalition in West Germany from 1966 to 1969). De Gaulle's government of 1958 resembled one, but it fell apart as the new constitution came into force. Cohabitation involves an element of power-sharing by a president and a prime minister of opposed political camps, but the two heads of the executive are always in open competition and never present, as coalition partners do, a set of agreed policies and objectives. Nor have governments sought to negotiate a consensus on economic reforms with political adversaries and social partners. Serious competition for state power, then, is dominated by the two forces of Left and Right.

Bipolarity has therefore also been manifest at elections, especially at second ballots. Of the seven direct presidential elections under the Fifth Republic, five have produced what Jean Charlot called a 'great simplifying duel', a straight Left–Right fight at the second round (the exceptions were 1969, when Pompidou faced the centrist president of the Senate, Alain Poher, at the run-off, and 2002, when Chirac defeated Le Pen by a record total of over 82 per cent of the vote). At parliamentary elections, in those constituencies where no candidate won at the first round, the run-off was a straight fight between Left and moderate Right in 94 per cent of cases in 1988, 73 per cent in both 1997 and 1993, and 80 per cent in June 2002. At local level, although the Socialist–centrist alliance, so characteristic of the Fourth Republic, lasted longer on many city councils than it did nationally, joint Socialist–Communist lists have been run against the Right in 90 per cent of towns of more than 30,000 inhabitants since 1977.

Multipartism: characteristics

Yet France is *also* rather obviously a multiparty system, in four respects. The first concerns the number of parties. Despite periods of consolidation, nothing resembling a two-party system has ever emerged under the Fifth Republic. If, by rough rule of thumb, a party is said to be 'relevant', or to have the potential to affect the complex set of relationships that makes up a party system, when it has 5 per cent of the vote, then at the 1997 parliamentary elections there were five 'relevant' parties: Communists, Socialists, UDF, RPR and FN; the ecology groups, which won 6.4 per cent of the vote but did so partly thanks to the Socialists' goodwill, might conceivably be considered as a sixth, especially given Dominique Voynet's appointment to the government. The number fell to three (Socialists, UMP and FN) in June 2002, but it would be hasty to view this as an inexorable movement towards concentration: three other parties (Communists, Greens and UDF) all won over 4.5 per cent in June 2002, and moved back above 5 per cent at the European elections two years later. Moreover, the number of parties and candidates has tended to increase. The 1978 record figure of 8.9 candidates per constituency was comfortably exceeded in 1997, when the number was 11.5, and again in June 2002, when it reached 14.6. Almost as striking has been the tendency to inflation in presidential candidacies: six in 1965, seven in 1969, twelve in 1974, ten in 1981, nine in 1988 and 1995, and fifteen in 2002.

Second, some 'relevant' parties have remained outside the blocs of Left and Right: this was true of all the centrists between 1962 and 1969, and of most of them till 1974. It was half-true of the Communists between 1984 and 1997, since their links to the rest of the Left took the minimal form of second-ballot withdrawal agreements. More importantly, it has been true of the extreme Right since its electoral breakthrough in

1983–84. The ability of the FN to keep candidates in the running at second ballots was the main reason for the drop in the number of straight contests between Left and moderate Right in the parliamentary elections of the 1990s; its relatively poor first-ballot performance in June 2002 explains the rise in the number of straight Left–Right run-offs then. Whatever the position inside the National Assembly, a situation where, as in 1993 (or at the first ballot of the 2002 presidential elections), one-third of those voting supported forces outside the mainstream parties of government, it is hardly a manifestation of perfect bipolarity.

Third, the French party system leaves some room for new entrants. The period since 1980 has seen four such new forces emerge. Two, or possibly three, promise to have a significant long-term impact. CPNT affected the balance of power on four regional councils after 1998, qualified for 'relevance' at the 1999 European elections with a score of 6.8 per cent and exceeded the PCF score at the 2002 presidential elections, though its record has been much less impressive since this high point. Philippe de Villiers's Mouvement pour la France has occupied a conservative, Eurosceptical niche for over a decade and survived its brief, doomed merger with Charles Pasqua's dissident Gaullists as the Rassemblement pour la France between 1999 and 2000. The FN, with its 10–15 per cent of the vote, brought race, in the guise of the immigration issue, to the centre of political debate, posed serious strategic difficulties for the mainstream Right and to a lesser extent for the Left, and contributed at least partially to the mainstream Right's defeats in 1988 and 1997 – even before Le Pen's surprise result of April 2002. Les Verts, finally, contributed to the Left's victory in 1997 and now appear as indispensable partners in any future winning left-wing coalition.

Fourth, the French party system leaves some room for existing parties to split. The Communists maintain an uneasy relationship with their own organised dissidents, half in and half out of the party. The Socialists lost Jean-Pierre Chevènement and his Mouvement des Citoyens after 1992. The UDF lost de Villiers in 1994, Démocratie Libérale in 1998, and finally most of its Deputies and other elite groups, to the UMP in 2002. The RPR lost Pasqua to the Rassemblement pour la France. The FN suffered the departure of Mégret to form the Mouvement National Républicain. Each of these splits left room, at least for a limited period, for the original and the schismatic parties to coexist.

France is therefore characterised both by a simple, bipolarised form of party competition – within the National Assembly, or at the second ballots of (most) presidential elections and of parliamentary elections in the great majority of constituencies – and by an extremely untidy reality of parties on the ground. This Janus face of the French party system is shaped by two opposed sets of dynamics. Party systems are determined by the institutional framework; by the voters – both the composition of the electorate and its relationship to parties and politics; and by the choices and strategies developed by parties and candidates. On each of these dimensions, France has been pulled in opposite directions.

Institutional dynamics

The institutions of the Fifth Republic secure a measure of bipolarisation in four important respects. First, although the constitution, in limiting the second ballot of a presidential election to the two leading candidates, does not quite enforce bipolarity (as was made clear by the elimination of the left-wing candidates in 1969 and 2002), it at least strongly encourages it. Second, a parallel to the second rounds of presidential elections is provided by the elimination from second ballots of parliamentary elections of all candidates who have won less than the votes of 12.5 per cent of registered voters. In each case the voter, having chosen freely at the first round, is firmly invited to vote for the candidate (s)he finds least undesirable at the second.

This deserves close attention because the effect of the electoral law on the second ballots of parliamentary elections is not merely arithmetical. Agreements between parties lead to withdrawals by candidates who could legally stay in the race. Two simplified hypothetical cases, each referring to a single constituency, illustrate how the two-ballot system rewards alliances (Table 9.2) and penalises isolated parties (Table 9.3). In the first example, four candidates are present, but only those on the Right have a second-ballot withdrawal agreement. At the first round, both the Communist and the Socialist candidate win more votes than either of the right-wingers. As none wins a first-ballot majority, however, a second ballot is held, at which all candidates may be present (each has won the votes of over 12.5 per cent of registered voters). But the candidate of the non-Gaullist Right stands down in favour of his better-placed ally, leaving just three candidates present at the run-off. At this second round no absolute majority is needed to win, and the seat goes to the Gaullist, who has rallied the whole of the right-wing vote (40 per cent) to his cause, rather than to the Communist or the Socialist – although the Left as a whole has a clear arithmetical majority in the constituency. This type of scenario provided a powerful incentive for the union of the Left from the 1960s.

Table 9.2 The two-ballot system: alliances rewarded

	Left (no alliance)		**Right (alliance)**	
First ballot	Communist	Socialist	Non-Gaullist Right	Gaullist
	35%	25%	17%	23%
Between ballots	*Both left-wing candidates stay in the race and retain all their first-round votes*		*Non-Gaullist candidate drops out and calls for Gaullist vote: Gaullist candidate attracts all the Right's first-round votes*	
Second ballot	35%	25%	–	**40%**
Result	*Left loses with 60% of vote*		*Gaullist wins with 40% of vote*	

Table 9.3 The two-ballot system: isolation penalised

	Left (alliance)		**Right (alliance)**		**FN**
First ballot	Communist	Socialist	Non-Gaullist Right	Gaullist	FN
	18%	22%	12%	23%	25%
Between ballots	*Communist candidate drops out and calls for Socialist vote*		*Non-Gaullist candidate is eliminated and calls for Gaullist vote*		*FN candidate stays in race*
Second ballot	–	**40%**	–	35%	25%
Result	*Socialist wins with 40% of vote*		*Gaullist loses with 35% of vote*		*FN loses with 25% of vote*

Table 9.3 shows why the FN found it almost impossible to elect any Deputies. Here, the FN candidate, with 25 per cent of the vote, has a first-ballot lead on the four candidates of the mainstream parties. But whereas both Left and moderate Right operate second-ballot withdrawal agreements, allowing the leading candidate in each case to add to his or her first-round support, the isolated FN candidate has no way of improving on the first-ballot result, and comes in a poor third at the run-off. Table 9.3 also shows why the FN has posed difficulties for the moderate Right in many constituencies: without an FN candidate, the Gaullist might have expected to win most of the overall right-wing vote of 60 per cent in the constituency, and thus the seat.

The two-ballot system may, of course, be grossly distorting. In 1958, for example, the Communists, with 18.9 per cent of the first-ballot votes, won only 2 per cent of National Assembly seats; the Gaullists, with barely 1 per cent of the first-round votes more than the Communists, won 41 per cent of the seats. The Socialists in 1962 lost votes but increased their number of seats by well over half. In 1993 the right-wing coalition secured 80 per cent of the seats with 44 per cent of the first-ballot votes; in 2002, the UMP won a third of the first-ballot votes but nearly two-thirds of the seats. One reason for these apparent anomalies is widely varying constituency sizes. The largest constituency was four times as large as the smallest one in 1978. That was partly remedied by the redistricting law of 1986, but by 2003 the Constitutional Council underlined the need for another law by observing that the 34,374 people living in the second constituency of Lozère were well over *five* times better represented than the 188,200 inhabitants of the second constituency of Val-d'Oise. Another crucial source of distortion was the different capacities of parties to win second-ballot votes on top of first-ballot support – which will depend on their alliance capacity, noted above, but also on their wider acceptability to voters. That, for example, explained the Gaullists' remarkable successes in 1958 or 1962; they were the second-ballot choices of many Socialists as well as of right-wingers. This factor also helps explain why the Communists, in both June 1968 and June 1981, saw a relatively modest drop in their first-ballot vote (2.5 points in 1968, 4.5 points in 1981) but lost roughly half their seats despite having a working alliance with the Socialists: in either case, the Communists were especially unpopular (as a result of the May events in 1968, and of their Soviet links in 1981) and this hampered their ability to rally extra votes at the run-off.

A third institutional encouragement to bipolarisation was the two-ballot majority system used for municipal elections in towns and cities of over 30,000 inhabitants from 1965. At municipal elections, lists led by a mayoral candidate, with as many candidates as there are council seats, compete for control of town halls. Under the 1964 law, the winning list, on an absolute majority at the first ballot or a relative majority at the second, took all the council seats. Lists could drop out between ballots but they could not merge. This was a powerful incentive for parties to enter alliances and to run joint lists from the first round. The Left did this in a growing number of towns from 1965, and in 200 out of 221 of them in 1977, when its candidates won two-thirds of France's town halls. It is true that a new electoral law, applied to all municipalities of over 3,500 inhabitants from 1983, moderated the iron discipline of the earlier system. Lists were allowed to merge between ballots, and a minority of council seats was conceded to candidates from the losing lists – allowing extreme and isolated parties to win minority council representation. But both Left and Right have generally presented joint lists for elections since 1983, in order to give the impression of political harmony in each camp and avoid the need for potentially destructive last-minute haggling between ballots.

Finally, France's institutions encourage bipolarity in parliament as well as at elections, for the constitution includes a series of articles designed to force the behaviour of parliamentarians into a clear majority–opposition divide. The right of a government, under Article 49–3, to declare any bill a question of confidence, which may be rejected only by the vote of a motion of censure, is merely the most formidable of several possible means to compel compliance from a reluctant majority (see Chapter 6).

It should be emphasised, though, that the constitution and electoral laws do not produce any *automatic* bipolar outcome. Indeed, the broadly similar two-ballot electoral system used for most of the Third Republic produced a quite different result: unstable governments of the Centre. Much, therefore, depends both on the way in which the various institutional elements interact (there was no direct election of the president under the Third Republic) and on the behaviour of the voters and the political elite.

Moreover, the position is complicated by the fact that the institutional framework *also* tends to fragment politics in five ways. First, the constitution conceives presidential elections as a confrontation between *individuals* and the voters. Despite the requirement, in force since 1981, that candidates must have the signatures of 500 mayors (out of over 36,000 across France) before running, first ballots are crowded occasions: Chirac's campaign team claimed to have known, before the first round in 2002, that he was unlikely to win much more than 20 per cent of the vote (in fact he won less) simply because of the competition from fourteen other candidates, about ten of them national figures. Although it is normally necessary to have the backing of a major party in order to win (Giscard being the main exception to this rule), no party has a long-established institutional mechanism for choosing its candidate. The choice of Jospin, in 1995, by the Socialist Party on a one member, one vote basis, was an innovation; the UMP's arrangements for choosing a candidate are still obscure. Potential candidates, *présidentiables*, tend to plan their campaigns in highly personal terms, and sometimes run against competitors from their own party. The supposedly disciplined Gaullists, for example, have split their support at three out of the seven presidential elections: in 1974, when Chirac's friends supported Giscard against the official candidate Chaban-Delmas; in 1981, when three candidates, Chirac, Debré and Garaud, all claimed a Gaullist pedigree; and in 1995, when both Chirac and Balladur did so. The experience of 2002 showed that even very closely allied political allies, ready to negotiate share-outs of candidacies at any other election, will still back their own candidate for the presidency. This relative chaos at the first ballot is not automatically transformed into bipolar order at the second; indeed, in 2002 it skewed the whole system away from its 'normal' bipolar pattern. While the expectation of most observers, and of most polling institutes, was for a classic Left–Right second ballot in 2007, there was no guarantee that the 'normal' pattern would reassert itself.

Second, the two-ballot system for parliamentary elections provides the conditions for fierce first-ballot competition between 'allied' parties. The period of the 'bipolar quadrille' offers edifying examples of this on both Right and Left. Third, the first ballots of parliamentary elections also offer opportunities for candidates outside the control of major parties. Such candidates can hope for the support of voters prepared to make a fanciful first-round choice, or to address a 'warning' to the established parties, secure in the knowledge that they will still be able to cast a 'serious' or 'useful' vote at the run-off. Candidates from outside the main parties may also be assisted by the localism still prevalent in French politics, and especially by the phenomenon of multiple elective office-holding, the *cumul des mandats*, an extremely effective tool in constituting a personal local political base. A well-established local figure may do sufficiently well to reach the run-off ballot, and either seek final victory or bargain the price of their withdrawal with better-placed competitors. An outstanding example is Jean-Pierre Chevènement, who left the PS in 1994, converting his Socialist faction into a mini-party, the Mouvement des Citoyens (MDC), running his own Eurosceptical left-wing list at the 1994 European elections, and winning 2.55 per cent of the vote. In other systems, the political demise of a Chevènement and of his party would soon have followed. In France, however, the MDC's handful of strong local bases, notably in Chevènement's eastern stronghold of Belfort, pointed to an arrangement with the PS. Of the seven successful MDC candidates at the 1997 parliamentary elections, none had faced an official Socialist opponent; Chevènement, instead of sinking into oblivion, became Jospin's Interior Minister – until he resigned again, in August 2000. Even then, it was only Chevènement's destructive presidential candidacy of 2002, and his refusal to return afterwards to the fold of the *gauche plurielle*, that prevented his continuing his career as a relative independent allied to the PS.

Fourth, fragmentation has been encouraged financially. The introduction of public finance for political parties since 1988, and above all the party finance law of 1990 as amended on instructions of the Constitutional Council, guarantees state aid to any party able to field at least 75 candidates at parliamentary elections. Although the lion's share of this sum (which exceeded 80 million euros in 2000) goes to the biggest parties, because the share-out is determined by electoral support and by parliamentary representation, there remains enough to keep smaller groups afloat. During the 1997 parliament, for example, the taxpayer covered 60 per cent of the FN's budget, while Lutte Ouvrière received some 700,000 euros annually, or nearly a quarter of its annual income, from the bourgeois state. It is reasonably clear, moreover, that CPNT chose to fight parliamentary elections in 2002 precisely in order to regain the regular financial underpinning that it had lost when the courts stopped it from using the product of hunting licences. Other so-called parties, such as the 'Nouveaux Écologistes du Rassemblement Nature et Animaux', which received 97 per cent of its income (about 23,000 euros annually) from the public purse, were almost certainly founded with the sole purpose of siphoning off a share of the largesse. Public finance is the single most important cause of the proliferation of parliamentary candidacies since the 1980s.

Finally, while early Fifth Republic France employed two-ballot majority electoral systems at all levels, national and local, this has been diluted since 1979 by proportional representation. European elections were first held in France on a national list system with proportional representation in 1979. A somewhat more 'majoritarian' variety of proportional representation, using each of France's ninety-six *départements* as a multimember constituency, was introduced both for parliamentary elections and for the new regional elections in 1986. While the parliamentary electoral law was switched back to the two-ballot majority system for 1988, proportional representation – incorporating a majority element since 2004 – is still used for regional elections. A dose of proportional representation, finally, is also present in the list system used for municipal elections since 1983. Alain Lancelot has written of the 'irruption of a proportionalist logic' from 1979, which 'encouraged centrifugal tendencies and led to the return of division and instability'. This assigns too strong an influence to what is only one part of the overall institutional framework. More subtle is Jean-Luc Parodi's use of an impeccably French image, the 'electoral accordion', to describe the contrast between the majority system used for the most important elections – presidential and parliamentary – and the proportional representation used for elections regarded by the French as secondary – European and regional: a dispersed, multipolar distribution of votes at elections held on proportional representation (when the 'accordion' is open), versus a more disciplined, bipolar pattern at those held on majority systems (when it is closed). Parodi goes on to argue, though, that the habit of dispersal gained at European and regional elections may stick, so that the accordion becomes more difficult to close, encouraging long-term fragmentation in the system. There is no more striking illustration of this than the first round of the 2002 presidential election, when the proliferation of candidacies and the dispersal of votes resembled a European election more than a presidential contest.

Social developments, new issues and voting behaviour

If the institutional dynamics of the Fifth Republic point *both* towards bipolarisation *and* (especially since the partial introduction of proportional representation) towards dispersal, the same is true of developments within the electorate (cf. Appendices 3–5).

On the bipolar side of the balance, three points are worth highlighting. First, the division of politics into Left and Right is not an artificial creation of the Fifth Republic's institutions. On the contrary, they are notions with which the French are fairly comfortable: polls showed 73 per cent of respondents in 1981, and 69 per cent in 1996, willing to place themselves in one or the other category. Second, when invited to make a second-ballot choice between a left-wing and a right-wing candidate, the great majority of voters transfer their support to a party or candidate in a manner consistent with their first choice. Thus even when relations between Communists and Socialists were at their most strained, at the March 1978 parliamentary elections, two-thirds of Socialist voters supported a Communist at the run-off in those constituencies where a Communist was the leading left-wing candidate. In the 1981 presidential elections, 95 per cent of Communists voted for Mitterrand at the run-off, despite their party's incessant campaign against him since 1977 – a remarkable indication of the dynamic created within the electorate by the union of the Left. Just as striking in 1981 was the support for Giscard of an estimated 71.5 per cent of first-ballot Chirac voters, despite the Gaullist party's evident dislike of the sitting president. Moreover, polls taken after presidential elections show how support for the principal new entrants has fallen, albeit imperfectly, into the Left–Right framework. Of the ecology candidates, an estimated 68 per cent of Antoine Waechter's voters supported Mitterrand at the second ballot in 1988, and 75 per cent of Voynet's supporters preferred Jospin in 1995. Even sympathisers of that most problematic of new entrants, the FN, fitted in to some degree. An estimated 65 per cent of Le Pen's voters in 1988, and 51 per cent in 1995, supported Chirac at the run-off; even the lower figure was roughly twice as great as the level of support for Jospin, given that a quarter of Le Pen's voters also preferred abstention; in June 2002, 48 per cent of FN voters went on to support candidates of the mainstream Right, against 43 per cent who abstained – and only 9 per cent who switched to the Left. The much-noted phenomenon of *gaucho-lepénisme* should not, therefore, obscure the fact that most supporters of the far Right who voted were ready to support the mainstream Right as a second choice. At the other extreme, 60 per cent of far left-wing voters at the first ballot in June 2002 backed left-wing candidates at the run-off, compared with 33 per cent who abstained and 7 per cent who supported the Right. Among all other groups of first-ballot voters, at least 85 per cent made second-ballot choices consistent with their vote at the first round.

Third, for much of the Fifth Republic, there has been a certain consistency in the sociological bases of left-wing and right-wing support. Giscard in 1974, for example, enjoyed the backing of a disproportionately large number of women, the elderly, the wealthy, the well-educated and the religious, as well as of upper-managerial, professional and commercial groups and farmers. Chirac in 1995 also did particularly well among the over-65s and the retired, among top income groups and practising Catholics, among heads of firms and the self-employed, and among the ever-dwindling ranks of French farmers. Similarly, Mitterrand scored heavily in 1981 among manual workers (winning 72 per cent of their votes), lower managerial groups and white-collar workers; in 1988 he drew his support disproportionately from the unemployed (a group that the polls had only recently begun to notice), the working class, public-sector workers, the young (especially those between 25 and 34 years old) and the irreligious. These social bases of voting are paralleled by geographical ones. The two maps of right-wing voting, spread across twenty-one years – Map 9.1 representing second-round support for Giscard in 1974, and Map 9.2 showing second-round votes for Chirac in 1995 – show very broadly consistent areas of strength and weakness for the Right and Left. The Right is especially strong in Brittany and the 'inner west' belt of *départements* running from Manche in the north to Vendée in the south, in Alsace, in the south-eastern Massif Central, and in the Basque country in the far south-west; the Left has done best in the north and in central and southern France (except for the Basque country). Expressed numerically, comparisons between second ballots show high levels of correlation from one election to another: 0.97 (out of a possible maximum of 1) between 1974 and 1981, for example, or 0.96 between 1988 and 1995.

It has also been suggested that the bipolar patterns of voting behaviour observable during much of the Fifth Republic were assisted by the transformations of French society since the Fourth Republic, which tended to the simplification of political divisions. The decline of the farming population and of religious practice were two such major developments in the course of the post-war generation. Hopeful left-wing observers took these developments, among others, to augur a 'sociological majority' for the Left, and to celebrate its political expression with the Left's victory in 1981. This was largely wishful thinking (as contemplation of Mrs Thatcher's 1979 victory in irreligious, urbanised Britain might have suggested). Another change was the spread of television from the 1960s, said to 'nationalise' the stakes of politics, taking it out of the hands of local notables and placing it in the hands of national parties. While the reality of these developments is unquestionable, their political impact in terms of bipolarisation is less clear. It is more certain, on the other hand, that several of the most politically divisive issues of the Fourth Republic either disappeared or lost a part of their importance. Decolonisation, the question that killed the Fourth Republic, was itself laid to rest after 1962. The problem of the régime, which had periodically exercised the French since 1789, was sufficiently settled by the referenda of 1958 and 1962 for all the major parties to agree to work peacefully within the Constitution of the Fifth Republic, however critical they might be of certain of its aspects. The partial thaw in the Cold War in the 1960s rendered the East–West conflict in French politics less acute – a necessary, though not a sufficient, condition for the rapprochement between Communists and Socialists. All these issues, it should be noted, had created divisions *within*

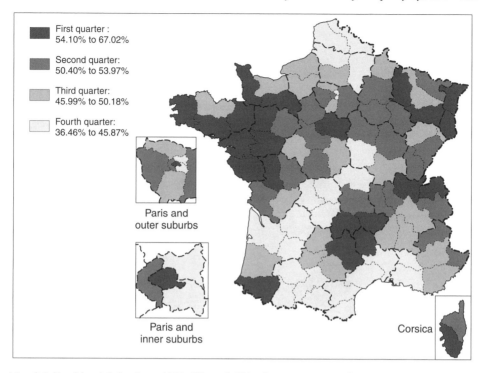

Map 9.1 Presidential elections, 1974: Giscard d'Estaing, percentage of votes cast at second ballot (overall result in metropolitan France: 50.67%).

the Right, the Left, or both. Their removal therefore had the potential to clear away some of the obstacles to a straight confrontation between Left and Right – at least if the politicians, who had been so ready to accentuate and dramatise political divisions under the Fourth Republic (see Chapter 1), allowed them to.

An equally strong case, however, can be made for the Left–Right cleavage among voters being undermined, especially since the 1980s, by developments within the electorate. Paradoxically, although voters may still be willing to position themselves as left-wing or right-wing, most have come to consider the distinction to be out of date. Only 33 per cent of poll respondents had taken this view in 1981, against 43 per cent who believed that Left and Right were still valid categories; by 1988 the figures were 48 per cent and 44 per cent respectively; in 1996, 62 per cent considered the distinction was out of date, against 32 per cent who thought it still useful – and 70 per cent agreed with the proposition that 'whether it's the Right or the Left in government, you always get the same thing'. The transfer of first-ballot to second-ballot votes, though broadly consistent with the Left–Right cleavage, is less so than in the 1970s, thanks largely to the impact of the FN. That can be illustrated, at the simplest level, in the variations of right-wing votes between first and second ballots. In the 1981 presidential election, the Right's total first-ballot vote was 49.3 per cent; Giscard's total at the run-off was 48.2, a drop of 1.1 per cent. Seven years later, Chirac, with 46 per cent at the run-off, dropped 4.9 per cent against the Right's first-ballot vote; in 1995, his share of the second-round vote, at 52.6 per cent, was 6.6 per cent lower than the Right's first-round potential.

Survey results since the 1990s have also showed a blurring in the social bases of left-wing and right-wing support. The religious variable, it is true, still operated; Chirac's

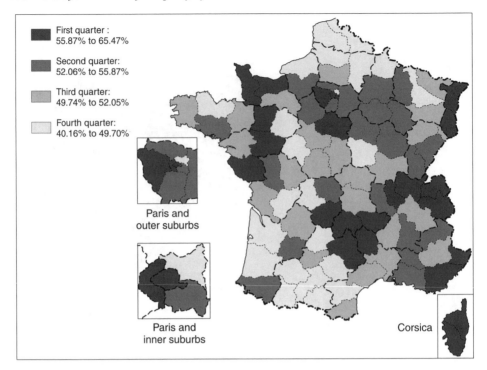

First quarter :
55.87% to 65.47%

Second quarter:
52.06% to 55.87%

Third quarter:
49.74% to 52.05%

Fourth quarter:
40.16% to 49.70%

Paris and
outer suburbs

Paris and
inner suburbs

Corsica

Map 9.2 Presidential elections, 1995: Chirac, percentage of votes cast at second ballot (overall result in metropolitan France: 52.69%).

and Jospin's votes at the second ballot in 1995 varied in direct proportion to the frequency of religious practice. But because there are fewer practising Catholics (rather fewer than 10 per cent of the adult population, against 40 per cent in 1945), religion counts for less in the overall shaping of voting behaviour. And in almost every other respect, old voting patterns had faded or even disappeared by the turn of the millennium. The tendency of women, who only won the right to vote in 1944, to support the Right had been considered as an immutable fact of electoral behaviour during the post-war generation; Mitterrand would have become president in 1965 with an all-male electorate. Yet this gender gap disappeared in the 1980s; in both 1988 and 1995, contenders at the second ballots of presidential elections won almost identical levels of support from men and women. Another gender gap had appeared in the meantime: among far Right voters, men outnumber women in a ratio of about six to four.

The most striking changes, however, have concerned the pattern of class voting. Blue-collar workers, among whom Mitterrand had exceeded his average vote by 20 per cent in 1981, were much less solidly behind Jospin in 1995, when the gap was only 10 per cent (with public-sector workers showing stronger left-wing support than those in the private sector). At the first round in 2002, a mere 13 per cent of blue-collar workers voted for Jospin. This was *below* Jospin's overall vote (16.2 per cent), below his level of support among professional and executive groups, no better than Chirac's share of the blue-collar vote, and barely half of Le Pen's 24 per cent share in this group. Even at the June 2002 parliamentary elections, when many electors reverted to bipolar patterns of voting, 47 per cent of the blue-collar vote went to the Left (including the extreme groups), compared with the moderate Right's 32 per cent and the far Right's 16 per cent (as well as 4 per cent for CPNT); the split among professionals and managers was 48 per cent for the Left, 42 per cent for the moderate Right and 9 per cent for the FN and MNR. The difference between the two groups, in other words, lay less in the overall shares of Left and Right than in the distribution of votes between moderate and extreme Right. Among routine white-collar workers in June 2002, the Right as a whole had a clear predominance: only 39 per cent voted for the left-wing parties, compared with 38 per cent for the moderate Right and 20 per cent for the FN and the MNR. This process of class dealignment does not mean that different social classes have begun to vote in more or less the same way. Blue-collar workers, for example, are more likely than other groups to abstain altogether, and to vote for the FN. Within broad class categories, there are also important differences: the left-wing vote has held up better among blue-collar workers in the public than in the private sector, in large plants more than in small firms, and in manufacturing more than in, say, the building trade. Nevertheless, a rather clear tendency has emerged since the late 1980s: the Left can no longer count on the allegiance of the blue-collar and white-collar working class as it broadly could over the four post-war decades, but has won partial compensation in increased support among professionals and managers, at the expense of the moderate Right. The result of the 2005 referendum (Appendix 5) was a revelation in this respect. With 81 per cent of blue-collar workers and 60 per cent of white-collar workers voting no, but 62 per cent of professional and managerial groups voting yes, the class cleavage could be said to correspond *better* to the divide over Europe – although it cuts across the Left–Right division between existing parties – than to the Left–Right division itself.

Similarly, the geography of left-wing and right-wing support, though still recognisable, has altered. Already from the 1970s the Left had been making inroads into the Catholic west and east, as well as the traditionally conservative regions of Burgundy, Lower Normandy and the Franche-Comté; this was evident in Mitterrand's results in 1981 and, even more, in 1988. On the other hand, Mitterrand lost support after 1981 in traditionally left-wing south-eastern *départements*. This development, even more pronounced in 1995 than in 1988, represents the largest single divergence from the classic Left–Right distribution observed in Map 9.1 which shows Giscard's 1974 vote. The statistical comparisons tell a similar story. Pierre Martin has shown how geographical correlations between left-wing support in one presidential election and the next are unusually low for the 1981–88 pair: 0.76, compared with 0.97 between 1974 and 1981, for example, and 0.96 between 1988 and 1995. He cites this as evidence that a realignment in French party politics, driven by the collapse of the PCF and the rise of the FN, took place during Mitterrand's first *septennat*. That explains some, though not all, of the phenomena noted above: the drop in the Left's share of the working-class vote, for example, or the Right's gains in the south-east, where the PCF had been strong, and the FN became so.

In short, what had seemed, in the 1970s, as a pattern of support for Left and Right that was fixed in terms both of voters' opinions and of their electoral behaviour came to appear much less settled. A growing number of voters, moreover, opted out of the electoral process by abstaining or spoiling their ballots. At the six parliamentary elections between 1958 and 1978, the proportion of abstentions and spoilt ballots only once exceeded 30 per cent – in 1962, a year when voters had already gone to the polls at two referenda. At the six parliamentary elections between 1981 and 2002, on the other hand, the proportion of abstentions and spoilt ballots only once fell *below* 30 per cent (see Table 7.2); and that was in 1986. Although presidential elections offer a less striking example, the proportion of abstentions and spoilt ballots at the second round in 1995, at 25.1 per cent, was a record, aside from the exceptional case of 1969, when the absence of a left-wing candidate at the run-off demobilised many voters. And the presidential first ballot of 21 April 2002 saw abstentions plus spoilt ballots exceed 30 per cent for the first time. Figures for municipal elections were comparable, while turnout at European elections fell below 50 per cent for the first time in 1999, and dropped below 43 per cent in 2004. Voting at the September 2000 referendum on the five-year presidential term reached a record low of just 30.3 per cent.

Yet the willingness of the French to place their trust in the ballot box, however diminished, might be considered high in the light of the growing disenchantment with politics and politicians that they manifested in the 1980s and 1990s. Surveys revealed that 64 per cent of respondents in 2000 believed that politicians were 'generally corrupt' (the figure had been 38 per cent in 1977); that 70 per cent considered that they personally were 'not well represented' by a party or a political leader in 2000, compared with half ten years earlier; that 81 per cent of respondents in 1997 (against 42 per cent in 1977) believed that politicians were 'not concerned with what ordinary people thought'. In a succession of polls since 1990, respondents asked to say which ideas they associate with politics have cited 'mistrust' twice as often as 'hope' ('boredom' and 'disgust' are also favoured choices). In this light, turnout at the referendum of 2005 – at 69.3 per cent, the highest level at any referendum since 1969 – could be viewed as the exception that proved the rule: the exceptional opportunity to give a resounding no to the constitutional treaty, and through it to the full range of mainstream politicians, mobilised unusual numbers of voters.

Two distinct though related phenomena, then, could be said to have weakened bipolarisation among voters since the 1980s: a generalised pessimism about politics, and a weakening of Left–Right loyalties. Social developments can be plentifully cited to explain both. The continuing decline of religious practice and the falling number of blue-collar workers (but above all, the falling numbers of blue-collar workers employed in big, unionised plants and identifying themselves as workers) helped to weaken the two classic variables of religion and class in the determination of the vote. Both pessimism and the desertion of old Left–Right loyalties were also furthered by mass unemployment. With a brief pause in the late 1980s, joblessness rose relentlessly from its 1981 rate of 7 per cent to 12.5 per cent in 1996; among under-25s, it was twice this level. The fear of unemployment, according to poll data, affected 35 per cent of the French in 1982, but 54 per cent in 1992. Even when the jobless total dipped between 1997 and 2001, voters gave politicians little credit for it; its renewed rise thereafter (it topped 10 per cent in March 2005, for the first time in five years) produced renewed levels of pessimism among voters. This perception of the failure of successive governments to deal with a problem that affected, directly or indirectly, as a reality or as a fear, the majority of French households, was the single most important reason for the defeat of successive incumbents since 1981 noted above. It also contributed powerfully to the disenchantment with politics, especially when coupled with other developments damaging to the image of parties and politicians, such as the corruption revelations of the 1990s (themselves renewed, early in 2005, by a big trial on corrupt tendering for the renovation of *lycées* in the Paris region and by a minor property scandal that forced the resignation of Finance Minister Gaymard).

At the same time the political debate between Right and Left was disturbed by three new bundles of issues. The first of these was race and immigration, used briefly by the Communists shortly before the 1981 presidential campaign and again by the mainstream Right in some cities during the campaign for the 1983 municipal elections. From 1983 the race issue both fed and was fed by the rise of the FN; it was also linked by the FN to the malaise of France's 1960s high-rise estates, where the deterioration of the built environment coincided with rising levels of crime (which rose by some 60 per cent between 1981 and 1993) and unemployment. These were former Communist heartlands in what had until recently been the 'red belt' suburbs of Paris and other cities; the neighbourhoods bordering the estates now gave the FN some of its best results. Researchers such as Nonna Mayer have shown how the 1980s and 1990s saw the emergence of a distinct electorate whose political choices were shaped by 'ethnocentrism', a combination of racist, nationalist and authoritarian views. The constitution of this electorate is the strongest reason for scepticism about any possible disappearance of the far Right from French politics, despite the tensions within the FN linked to the issue of the succession to its leader.

The second group of issues related to what the American observer Ronald Inglehart called the 'Silent Revolution', the rise of 'post-materialist' values among the more educated citizens of the baby-boom generation which came of age just before or shortly after May 1968. Such values included sexual tolerance, anti-racism, civil rights and the defence of the environment. They not only provided a base – more modest in France than in other European countries such as West Germany – for the rise of ecology groupings; they also divided both Left and Right, to some degree, between liberals and conservatives on societal questions.

Third, European integration emerged as a divisive issue as early as the enlargement referendum of 1972. This reproduced, among voters, the division observed within the National Assembly during the ratification votes on treaties during the Fourth Republic: not Left versus Right, but the Centre against the extremes on both sides. Twenty years later, the referendum of 1992 on the Maastricht Treaty saw how voters in one of Western Europe's two great old nation states began to doubt the wisdom of new transfers of sovereignty. The supporters of every major party, especially the Gaullists, split into pro- and anti-Maastricht camps. The 1992 referendum also served as a catalyst for the alienation, noted above, of much of the blue- and white-collar working class from the Left, and especially from the Socialists, who were strong supporters of the treaty their president had negotiated. The referendum of 2005 on the European constitutional treaty showed the potential of European questions to rekindle the same divisions, giving a neat, if left-skewed, extremes-versus-Centre pattern of voting (Appendix 5) and incidentally tearing the PS apart. It should be added that these three bundles of new issues had plenty of space to develop. The economic differences between Right and Left, which had turned in the 1970s on the very ownership of the heart of France's economy, had narrowed dramatically after the Left's forced reconciliation with capitalism from 1983: in the early twenty-first century a right-wing president (Chirac) could insist on the need to preserve the French model of social protection, while a left-wing finance minister (Fabius) could demand tax cuts.

From the late 1980s, the impact on the electorate of these changes in the political debate led commentators such as Philippe Habert to discern the emergence of a 'new voter', cut loose from old loyalties and inclined to behave as a consumer, voting on particular issues and switching between parties from one election to the next. Other observers were more inclined to stress the growing number of alienated voters, often with a minimal interest in politics but an increasing inclination to protest voting or abstention. Three figures illustrate the growing gulf between the voters and political representation in France. First, on 21 April 2002, the total 'protest' vote (for presidential candidates of far Left, far Right and CPNT), when added to the total number of abstentions and spoilt ballots, reached 54.3 per cent of the total electorate. Second, the 'protest' parties, whose candidates had attracted a third of votes cast on 21 April, won not a single seat in the National Assembly the following June. Third, while nearly 90 per cent of France's Deputies and Senators voted in favour of changes to the French constitution occasioned by the European constitutional treaty in February 2005, 55 per cent of France's voters rejected the treaty itself three months later. Perhaps unsurprisingly, the correlation between the protest vote in April 2002 and the no vote three years later was rather high, at 0.725.

Personal and party strategies

Candidates and parties, finally, have adopted a variety of political strategies which have reinforced both bipolarisation and multipartism at different times.

Presidential candidates have responded to the obvious incentives contained in the electoral system to build coalitions of Right and Left. This is most obviously true of second ballots. De Gaulle, it is true, appears genuinely to have considered that he could win, and win well, in 1965 with neither any semblance of a campaign nor active party support; it was only with some reluctance, and after failing to win at the first round, that he agreed to a series of three television interviews and accepted the open support of the Gaullist and Giscardian parties that formed the parliamentary majority. None of his successors, however, has had much hesitation about campaigning, or about accepting party support. Pompidou, in the first of two elections where a left-winger failed to reach the second ballot (he faced the centrist president of the Senate, Alain Poher, at the run-off), negotiated hard to secure the backing of Jacques Duhamel's group of centrists, the future Centre Démocratie et Progrès, in addition to the support that Gaullists and Giscardians had already guaranteed him. At the second ballot in 1974, Giscard had the support of every significant party of the 'non-Left': his own Républicains Indépendants, the Gaullists whose candidate he had roundly defeated at the first ballot (after negotiating Chirac's support), and the centrists of every stripe, the right-wing Radicals and the right-wing Socialists who were to join the UDF in 1978. Mitterrand in 1981 was similarly endorsed by the whole Left: by his own Socialists, by the Communists, the Left Radicals and the Parti Socialiste Unifié, and even by the Trotskyist Arlette Laguiller. He also made enough greenish gestures to pick up most of the voters who had supported Brice Lalonde, the ecology candidate, at the first round. In 1988 he attracted the votes of nearly all of the first-round left-wing voters (bar a small proportion of the extreme Left), a majority of Greens, and a minority of the centrist supporters of Giscard's second prime minister Raymond Barre (whose votes he had deliberately courted) and of Le Pen's voters (whose valuable support he had not openly sought). Chirac, finally, attracted most of the mainstream right-wing supporters of Balladur and de Villiers without any difficulty; just over half of Le Pen's voters also rallied to him (without any encouragement at all from Le Pen); and this, given the continued unpopularity of the Left as a whole among voters, was sufficient.

Successive presidents have also deliberately polarised opinion prior to second ballots (whether prior to their election, in parliamentary elections during their term of office, or in re-election campaigns), implying a division over one basic issue that transcended all other cleavages. De Gaulle presented every election, and all five of his referendums, as a choice between him and his régime on the one hand and 'chaos' on the other. Under Pompidou, the electors were asked to choose between 'peaceful change' and 'revolutionary adventurism' in no less Manichaean a fashion. Giscard confronted the electorate with a choice between his pluralistic, liberal, democratic, socially just and quietly reformist style of rule and the revolutionary, collectivist, bureaucratic, illiberal and undemocratic régime he associated with the Left. François Mitterrand presented the choice of 1981 as between social justice and the defence of the narrow, selfish interests of a privileged class that had failed the country; in 1988 it was between the consensual values of a united country and the sectarian designs of a partisan minority – Chirac and the RPR. In some respects the 1995 election was an exception: the second-round television debate between the two remaining candidates – a tradition since 1974 – was a low-key affair, with no dramatic moments that crystallised the opposition between the two men. Chirac's main aim was to highlight the (numerous) failures of the Socialist administrations between 1981 and 1993 and to convince the voters that social justice – a stronger theme of his 1995 campaign than in 1988 – had been and would be poorly served by a Socialist president. It remains to be seen if the elections of 2007 will see a return to an earlier style; in 2002, at Chirac's insistence, no debate took place between the incumbent president and Le Pen.

Bipolarisation has also been furthered by parties at different junctures. During the first thirteen years of the Fifth Republic, Socialists and Communists moved from outright enmity (in 1958) to partial co-operation at the second ballots of parliamentary elections (in 1962) to common support of Mitterrand as presidential candidate (in 1965) to a national second-ballot withdrawal agreement (in 1967) and to the Common Programme of government (in 1972). The Communists contributed substantially to this process, especially through their remarkable endorsement of Mitterrand from the first ballot in 1965 (and again in 1974). In the late 1970s, Mitterrand's tenacity in keeping the Socialists' commitment to the strategy of left-wing unity, in spite of their own misgivings and the open hostility shown by the Communists from 1977, was crucial in maintaining the bipolar dynamic. After 1996, the creation of the *gauche plurielle*, rebuilding the Socialist–Communist alliance and co-opting Les Verts for the first time, represented a comparable strategy of building a credible left-wing governing coalition. It should be added that the Left's Common Programme of 1972 set a precedent whereby, at most parliamentary elections, the main opposition forces produced a joint programme of government with which to oppose the incumbents, highlighting a bipolar majority–opposition divide. This was true, for example, of the mainstream Right in both 1986 and 1993, while in 2002 the process was carried a stage further with the merger of the RPR and most of the UDF into the UMP.

The mainstream parties have also sought, if at times indirectly, to preserve bipolarisation through the strategies they have deployed to deal with new entrants. One such strategy was to freeze them out. The moderate Right's ban on alliances with the FN after 1988 was crucially important in ensuring that FN Deputies did not return to the National Assembly to upset the duopoly there of moderate Right and moderate Left; it also contributed to long-term tensions within the FN that contributed to the split of 1998. Changes to the electoral laws governing European and regional elections in 2003 were designed to reduce the ability of extreme parties to win seats. The opposite strategy was to draw a new entrant into an alliance, as the Socialists did with Les Verts from 1997 – after over a decade of practically ignoring them.

Other party strategies, however, have been much less calculated to further bipolarisation. First ballots of elections are often viewed by parties and candidates as an opportunity to measure their strength, and possibly to acquire bargaining power in relation to larger allies. This was certainly true of many of the candidates at the first ballot of the 2002 presidential election, whose presence indirectly helped Le Pen to the second ballot. First rounds may, indeed, generate a dynamic of destructive competition capable of doing lasting damage to alliances or even to individual parties. The period of the 'bipolar quadrille', in particular, faced each of the four major parties with the choice between dominating its partner or facing junior status within the alliance and possible marginalisation. For the leaders of the most threatened parties, Communists and Gaullists, that stark alternative suggested that if the price of avoiding marginalisation was overall electoral defeat, it was a price worth paying. Hence the unacknowledged, indeed covert phenomenon of 'objective alliances' *across* the Left–Right divide that developed at the presidential elections of 1981. Although the Communist Marchais endorsed Mitterrand for the run-off ballot, and the Gaullist Chirac reminded his voters of the dangers that a Mitterrand victory would entail for France, neither did so with any great conviction, and each tolerated, if they did not actively promote, activities designed to favour the opposite candidate. The most trusted Communist Party members were instructed to vote for Giscard, while a leading left-wing Gaullist was allowed to mail every RPR member to call for a Mitterrand vote. Objective alliances did not end with the 1981 result. President Mitterrand actively, though quietly, favoured the emergence of the FN by encouraging television networks to give greater coverage to Le Pen and his party from late 1983, and by using proportional representation for the 1986 parliamentary elections in order to embarrass the resurgent right-wing opposition. It should be added, finally, that party strategies decided in Paris are not always fully applied on the ground, as the defiance, in 1998, by four right-wing presidents of regional councils of the Right's ban on alliances with the FN illustrated. At national level, established parties may see a new entrant as an enemy to be excluded and destroyed; at the grass roots, however, the weakness of established parties may lead their local representatives to see the new entrant as a necessary ally to be courted. And vice versa.

Concluding remarks

In each of these areas – institutions, developments among voters, and candidate and party strategies – the party system of the Fifth Republic is underpinned by a complex mixture of dynamics, some promoting coherence and bipolarity, others furthering fragmentation. Bipolar multipartism is thus a finely balanced party system. Since 1981, the balance has shifted from bipolarity towards multipartism. The introduction of proportional representation at European and regional levels, the weakening of older social cleavages of class and religion, the appearance of issues that cut across the boundaries of Left and Right, the (usually unwitting) promotion of the FN by mainstream politicians, all contributed to this. Many of the factors that contributed to the upheavals of the 1980s and 1990s were lasting rather than contingent: proportional representation at some elections, tensions over crime and race and divisions over Europe. There are therefore no reasons to expect an early return to the almost fully bipolarised configuration of the 1970s; the results of the 2002 presidential election and of the 2005 referendum offer ample evidence of that.

Nevertheless, the bipolar dynamic remains rooted enough in France's institutions to give a continuing structure to the whole system. So far at least, only the parties of moderate Left and Right that form the core of the two big coalitions – PS, UMP and, with some difficulty, the non-Gaullist moderate Right – have been able seriously to aspire to the presidency; the second round of the 2002 presidential election, when Chirac, an unpopular president especially on the Left, nevertheless won over 82 per cent of the vote against Le Pen, is a good illustration of that. The parties of government have also, since 1981, controlled at least 90 per cent of all seats in both the National Assembly and the Senate, as well as the great majority of France's *départements*, towns and cities. If the Communists and the Greens chose to join the *gauche plurielle*, and if first Bruno Mégret and more recently Marine Le Pen have sought to make the Front National an acceptable partner for the mainstream Right, it is because the Fifth Republic has offered a simple choice: either participation in one of two coalitions aimed at the conquest and exercise of state power, or political marginalisation or at best confinement to regional councils and the Strasbourg parliament. Some party leaders and activists will always prefer purity and marginalisation. Parties that prosper, however, will also attract others with an ambition to join the bipolar mainstream. The bipolar dynamics discussed above, though much assailed, are therefore unlikely to disappear altogether from France's political system.

The conditions thus remain for the continued uncertain balance of bipolar multipartism. But beyond the question of the party system lies the broader issue of the relationship between the French and party politics. Developments such as the rise of abstentionism and of protest voting, the drop in party membership, or the deterioration in the public's opinion of politicians (which had never been high in the first place) have led observers such as Janine Mossuz-Lavau to argue that France since the early 1990s has been experiencing a political 'crisis of representation' of a similar gravity to the economic crisis.

This argument should be set in a wider context, in three ways. First, the level of political mobilisation should not be confused with the health or stability of a political system. Party membership and activism were never stronger than in the Popular Front era of the 1930s, or in the five years after the Liberation; but the political climate was close to one of civil war. Secondly, France is far from unique in experiencing wide-ranging popular disenchantment with politics. A succession of comparative studies indicates that a comparable malaise has affected developed democracies from the United States to Italy and from Sweden to Japan. Third, whatever the difficulties of the French (and other nations) with political parties, they do not extend to a general disenchantment with democratic values. Successive polls suggest a vigorous attachment, especially among the young, to the basic rights and processes of democracy, in France and elsewhere. In France, the 2005 referendum expressed not only the public's alienation from the mainstream political system but also a concern that the political process was escaping democratic control and that the constitutional treaty would accelerate this tendency. With all of these caveats, however, it remains the case, in the most basic sense, that French parties, and governments, represent the French less well than in the recent past: the French say, in polls, that they do not feel represented, and fewer of them vote for parties that aspire seriously to government. These tendencies have survived Jospin's promise of a 'rehabilitation of politics' after 1997, and Raffarin's of his concern for *La France d'en bas*.

To the extent that political disenchantment is (even) more marked in France than in other democracies, this may be ascribed to a variety of French exceptions: in particular, to the long-term weakness of French parties outlined in earlier chapters, or to the collision between the unusually high expectations of politics that marked the first *alternance* of 1981 and the measures that followed the economic U-turn of 1983. What is certainly unique to France, however, is the institutional framework, outlined above, into which the relationship of citizens to parties feeds. On one interpretation, the framework provides both safety valves for protest parties (for example, the opportunity to win seats at European or regional or municipal levels) and the near-certainty that France will be governed by a clearly accountable majority with a clearly defined and responsible opposition. On a less optimistic view, however, the institutional framework in the context of wide-ranging disenchantment with parties has made France unusually difficult to govern. Abstentions and votes for anti-system parties mean that governments represent a declining proportion of the electorate, and thereby find it harder to mobilise a consensus, or even a solid majority, behind difficult policy decisions. As they lose popularity, the available scope for party fragmentation allows ample room for outbidding. This is encouraged by the personalisation of politics at all levels, from the presidency down. Personalisation offers plenty of scope for outbidding within each coalition and even each party, and favours, even more than other political systems, the presentation of politics as a contest for office between individuals rather than a confrontation of programmes, contributing further to the alienation of voters from the political process. The potential for fragmentation and outbidding further limits the government's freedom to manoeuvre and to reform, and it goes on to lose the elections by disappointing its own supporters. The opposition wins office, but more on the strength of a rejection of the opposite camp than on a positive appreciation of its own merits, and a further cycle is opened, leading to further disappointment, to a reinforced perception that there is nothing to choose between the mainstream camps of Right and Left, and to renewed protest voting. From this point of view, the result of 21 April 2002 was not an 'accident' resulting from the voters' erroneous belief that they could afford to vote for minor candidates, because Jospin and Chirac were certain to be present at the run-off of the presidential election; on the contrary, it was a logical expression of the political system's development, and could readily recur.

Constitutionalists of a (usually) Gaullist bent have regularly warned, since 1969, of a possible 'return to the Fourth Republic' – especially, but not exclusively, in times of cohabitation, when a part of the executive power moves from the Élysée to Matignon. This is perhaps to miss the point. The greater stability of the Fifth Republic has rested as much on the emergence of stable parliamentary majorities, underpinned by rejuvenated political parties, as it has on the new institutions. Stable majorities have not disappeared (there is little suspense about the voting behaviour of individual Deputies in the National Assembly), but part of their party underpinning has. *Some* familiar traits of the Fourth Republic – the presence of anti-system parties, the habit of outbidding – were visible in the Fifth in the early twenty-first century; but they appeared more in the country than in the Chamber, and hampered policy-making rather than bringing down governments. There is a sense in which this contemporary malaise is more dangerous than that of half a century ago. It is less susceptible to institutional reform; and the administration, often credited with holding France together through the Fourth Republic, is now far less able to fulfil the same role.

Further reading

For studies on individual parties and on the party system, see Chapters 7 and 8.

Bon, F. and Cheylan, J.-P., *La France qui vote*, Paris, Hachette, 1988.
Boy, D. and Mayer, N. (eds), *L'électeur français en questions*, Paris, Presses de la Fondation Nationale des Sciences Politiques, 1990.
Boy, D. and Mayer, N. (eds), *L'électeur a ses raisons*, Paris, Presses de Sciences Po, 1997.
Bréchon, P., *La France aux urnes: soixante ans d'histoire électorale*, 4th edition, Paris, La Documentation Française, 2004.
Broughton, D. and Donovan, M. (eds), *Changing Party Systems in Western Europe*, London, Pinter, 1999.
Capdevielle, J., Dupoirier, E., Grunberg, G., Schweisguth, E. and Ysmal, C., *France de gauche, vote à droite*, Paris, Presses de la Fondation Nationale des Sciences Politiques, 1981.
Cautrès, B. and Mayer, N. (eds), *Le nouveau désordre électoral*, Paris, Presses de Sciences Po, 2004.
Cole, A. and Campbell, P., *French Electoral Systems and Elections since 1789*, 3rd edition, London, Pinter, 1988.
Dalton, R., Flanagan, S. and Beck, P. (eds), *Electoral Change in Advanced Western Democracies: Realignment or Dealignment?*, Princeton, NJ, Princeton University Press, 1984.
Faux, E., Legrand, T. and Perez, G., *La main droite de Dieu: enquête sur François Mitterrand et l'extrême droite*, Paris, Seuil, 1994.
Gaffney, J. (ed.), *Political Parties and the European Union*, London, Routledge, 1996.
Gaffney, J. (ed.), *The French Presidential and Legislative Elections of 2002*, Aldershot, Ashgate, 2004.
Grunberg, G., Mayer, N. and Sniderman, P. (eds.), *La démocratie à l'épreuve: une nouvelle approche de l'opinion des Français*, Paris, Presses de Sciences Po, 2002.
Habert, P., Perrineau, P. and Ysmal, C. (eds), *Le vote éclaté: les élections régionales et cantonales des 22 et 29 mars 1992*, Paris, Presses de la Fondation Nationale des Sciences Politiques, 1992.
Habert, P., Perrineau, P. and Ysmal, C. (eds), *Le vote sanction: les élections législatives des 21 et 28 mars 1993*, Paris, Presses de la Fondation Nationale des Sciences Politiques, 1993.
Lancelot, A. (ed.), *1981, les élections de l'alternance*, Paris, Presses de la Fondation Nationale des Sciences Politiques, 1986.
Lancelot, A., *Les élections sous la Cinquième République*, 3rd edition, Paris, Presses Universitaires de France, 1998.
Lewis-Beck, M. (ed.), *How France Votes*, New York, Chatham House, 2000.
Lewis-Beck, M. (ed.), *The French Voter: Before and After the 2002 Elections*, Basingstoke, Palgrave Macmillan, 2003.
Leyrit, C., *Les partis politiques: indispensables et contestés*, Paris, Marabout, 1997.
Mair, P. and Smith, G. (eds), *Understanding Party System Change in Western Europe*, London, Frank Cass, 1990.
Martin, P., *Comprendre les évolutions électorales*, Paris, Presses de Sciences Po, 2000.
Mayer, N. and Perrineau, P., *Les comportements politiques*, Paris, Armand Colin, 1992.
Michelat, G. and Simon, M., *Classe, religion, et comportement politique*, Paris, Presses de la Fondation Nationale des Sciences Politiques, 1977.
Michelat, G. and Simon, M., *Les ouvriers et la politique: Permanence, ruptures, réalignements*, Paris, Presses de Sciences Po, 2004.
Mossuz-Lavau, J., *Les Français et la politique*, Paris, Odile Jacob, 1994.
Penniman, H. (ed.), *France at the Polls: The Presidential Election of 1974*, Washington, DC, American Enterprise Institute, 1978.
Penniman, H. (ed.), *The French National Assembly Elections of 1978*, Washington, DC, American Enterprise Institute, 1980.

Perrineau, P. (ed.), *L'engagement politique: déclin ou mutation?*, Paris, Presses de la Fondation Nationale des Sciences Politiques, 1994.

Perrineau, P. and Ysmal, C. (eds), *Le vote de crise: l'élection présidentielle de 1995*, Paris, Presses de Sciences Po, 1995.

Perrineau, P. and Ysmal, C. (eds), *Le vote surprise: les élections législatives des 25 mai et 1er juin 1997*, Paris, Presses de Sciences Po, 1998.

Perrineau, P. and Ysmal, C. (eds), *Le vote de tous les refus: les élections présidentielle et législatives de 2002*, Paris, Presses de Sciences Po, 2003.

Pharr, S. and Putnam, R. (eds), *Disaffected Democracies: What's Troubling the Trilateral Countries?*, Princeton, NJ, Princeton University Press, 2000.

Salmon, Frédéric, *Atlas électoral de la France, 1848–2001*, Paris, Seuil, 2001.

Sartori, G., *Parties and Party Systems: A Framework for Analysis*, Cambridge, Cambridge University Press, 1976.

Williams, P., *Crisis and Compromise: Politics in the Fourth Republic*, London, Longmans, 1964.

Websites of polling institutes

BVA	http://www.bva.fr/new/index.asp
CSA	http://www.tmo.fr
IFOP	http://www.ifop.com/europe/index.asp
IPSOS	http://www.ipsos.fr
SOFRES	http://www.tns-sofres.com/archives_pol.htm

10 The administration

Foundations, myth and changing reality

The prime target of Jacques Chirac's 1995 presidential campaign was what he called a 'technostructure', which had 'confiscated power' in France and 'co-opted its members onto the shifting frontiers of the civil service, ministerial *cabinets*, and major public and private firms'. Behaving 'like a fashionable club, out of touch with reality', it paralysed France with a 'single mindset' (*la pensée unique*) favouring orthodoxy over creativity, safety over enterprise, budgetary balances over jobs. This was both a barely veiled attack on his arch-rival Édouard Balladur and an echo of his own political mentor Georges Pompidou, who a generation earlier had added his voice to a chorus of protest against the 'arrogant and inhuman dictatorship' of the administration.

On the face of it, Chirac seemed to be tapping into widely felt resentments. A SOFRES survey in September 1999, for example, found that only 20 per cent of respondents considered that the state 'acted in the general interest'; just 8 per cent considered the state 'effective'; 12 per cent thought it 'just'. The share of GDP spent by the state in France (including the social security system and local authorities) averaged 53.3 per cent from 1987 to 2003. The figure for 2003 (54.5 per cent) was financed by borrowing (4.1 per cent of GDP), non-tax receipts (4.4 per cent), but above all by taxes (46 per cent of GDP, up from 35 per cent in 1970). Within the EU15, such figures are only exceeded in Belgium, Austria and Scandinavia; even such relatively high-spending countries as Germany, Italy or the Netherlands are some 2–3 points below the French level; the UK is lower by 7–8 points. And over 40 per cent of public spending is accounted for by the wages and salaries of France's public servants. Their number amounted to some 6 million in 2003, or a nearly a quarter of all employment in France (compared with 14 per cent in the UK): 2.5 million for central government (up from 1.75 million in 1975), 1.4 million for local and regional authorities, 860,000 for France's public hospitals and other health services, and a further 1.2 million in quasi-public services with public-employee status such as energy (Électricité de France–Gaz de France), rail (SNCF) or telecoms. It has been estimated that 57 per cent of the French either work for the state, broadly construed, or are the spouse, child, or parent of someone who does.

Not only do France's civil servants (aside from a significant minority on short-term contracts) enjoy near-total job security, much envied at a time of high unemployment; at the very highest levels they have also enjoyed a unique range of opportunities to colonise the worlds of both business and politics (Chirac himself being a prime example of the latter). Yet there is no consensus for 'rolling back the state'. The same September 1999 poll found clear majorities of respondents claiming that the state 'did not intervene enough' in a wide variety of sectors, including the economy (53 per cent), employment (80 per cent), education (65 per cent) and agriculture (55 per cent). Surveys in 1995 showed that a general view (73 per cent) of 'the state' as remote did not prevent a positive appreciation (63 per cent) of the notion of 'public services' in general, or clear majority satisfaction with the performance of key services such as health and education, the post or the rail network. Agreement or dissent with the view that 'the number of civil servants should be reduced' was one of the clearest separators of left-wing and right-wing voters in April 2002, but a substantial minority (roughly 40 per cent) of right-wing supporters still disagreed with the proposition. When Chirac's first finance minister, the free-market-minded Alain Madelin, dared to suggest that there was 'surplus fat' to be cut away from France's administration and public services, he was soon sacked; his presidential bid in 2002, built on a neo-liberal platform, was rewarded with 1.1 million votes – under 4 per cent. There is a striking contrast between public reactions to Britain's public-sector strikes of early 1979, which helped ensure both Margaret Thatcher's election victory of May that year and widespread support for her subsequent attacks on trade unions and on the public sector generally, and the French experience of late 1995, when striking public-sector workers retained the sympathy of a majority of the population. If there is a consensus about the French state, it is neither favourable nor hostile, but schizophrenic.

These ambiguous relations of the French with their state, their administration and their public services have been shaped by two main elements. The first has been the persistent tension between the state's mythical status as the impartial embodiment of the nation through successive régimes, as the guarantor of the equality dear to republican values, and, more recently, as an agent of national regeneration during the *trente glorieuses* (issues discussed in Chapter 1), and the messy reality, daily encountered, of an unwieldy bureaucracy that appears neither impartial nor particularly rational. Secondly, the challenges posed to the French model both from without (Europeanisation and globalisation) and from within (budgetary constraints) have raised the stakes, prompting attempts to safeguard the 'French exception' at all costs, or to reform and adapt, or to accelerate liberalisation. It should be added, finally, that 'the administration' in France, even more than elsewhere, consists of two radically different universes: on the one hand, the vast majority of lower-level public employees, rule-bound, geographically and professionally rather immobile, and often provincial; on the other, the small policy-making and policy-influencing minority of perhaps 8,000 women and (mostly) men at the peak of the civil service, largely Parisian (but with increasingly European and international horizons), enjoying considerable freedom to move between the administration proper, ministerial *cabinets*, business and politics.

The foundations and myth of administrative power

The French administration has its roots in the institutions of the pre-1789 *ancien régime*. But it was systematised by Napoleon I, as Consul (1799–1804) and Emperor

(1804–14). The Napoleonic administration was intended as the embodiment of state power and of the general interest in a divided nation: disinterested, dispassionate, distant and depoliticised. Its top officials were France's best and brightest, attracted by generous pay, splendid residences, grand titles and elaborate uniforms. Technicians among them were trained in one of the specialised schools created under the *ancien régime* (the École Nationale des Ponts et Chaussées) or the Revolution (the École Polytechnique). Generalists received training within the *grands corps de l'État*: the prefectoral corps, the Cour des Comptes (Court of Accounts), the Conseil d'État (Council of state); all of them Napoleonic creations, but with roots in the *ancien régime*. The Napoleonic administration was hierarchical and highly centralised, both within each Parisian ministry and territorially: the prefects, the senior representatives of the state in each of France's ninety *départements*, were powerful in their localities but movable by, and subject to orders from, the interior minister in Paris. It was uniform, with a single organisational model for all public services and identical powers for each subnational authority, whatever its size. It was, finally, subject to stringent internal regulation, through a fierce disciplinary code, legal verifications from the Conseil d'État and audits by the Cour des Comptes; but immune from all other controls (in particular from the judiciary).

In principle, then, the Napoleonic model resembled a classic Weberian bureaucracy: hierarchical, impartial, rational, predictable, self-contained. It proved highly influential, not only in France but also in those European countries over which Napoleon cast his imperial shadow. But the practice never matched the model. To begin with, the administration was never separated from politics. From the start, it had to play at least two highly political roles: repressing the enemies of successive régimes (a role undertaken, with admittedly limited success, by the Justice, Defence and Interior ministries) and integrating outlying, and not very French, provinces such as Brittany, Savoy and Corsica. The most senior civil servants were always vulnerable to political replacement. In the nineteenth-century merry-go-round of French régimes, successive rulers sought politically reliable servants at the top: no fervent Catholics, for example, for the resolutely secular early Third Republic. Indeed, under the Third Republic political replacements in the most sensitive posts began to occur with each major change of government – though at the same time pressures within the civil service led to a spread of impersonal recruitment procedures in the other ranks. Moreover, civil servants themselves, especially under the Restoration and the Orleanist monarchies (1814–48), openly sought and won political office as parliamentarians; only in the Third Republic were rules of incompatibility introduced. This simultaneous politicisation of the civil service and bureaucratisation of politics belong to a French tradition with a long pedigree, though of variable intensity.

Uniformity was no more respected than political neutrality. Tocqueville's famous dictum that 'the rule is rigid, the practice flexible' summed up the behaviour of countless French officials bending rules to the diversity of local situations. Moreover, the growth of 'big government' – the extension of state and local authority activities to new fields such as education, labour legislation or the first urban utilities, and then the vast expansion, following the two world wars, into economic intervention, social welfare and the direct ownership and management of financial and industrial activities – strained the Napoleonic ideal further, in three ways. First, the unity of purpose inherent in the Napoleonic model became ever more impossible to achieve, as the bureaucracy expanded into a huge Balkan empire, its squabbling components each intent on establishing its own internal rules, grades, career structures, relations with client groups in society, and legitimacy, at the expense both of competitors within the administration and of any central direction. The development of co-ordinating structures merely displaced the problems and eroded the pyramidal organisation on which the model was based. Second, the civil servants began to act as an interest group within the state, unionising and winning an overarching statute in 1946. Third, the clear, sharp divide between the public and the private sectors became blurred as administrations (such as the Agriculture Ministry) developed symbiotic relationships with client groups, as specific activities (such as transport or water distribution) were conceded to the private sector, as 'mixed' public–private companies were created, as joint ventures were concocted between publicly owned and private firms, and as senior civil servants discovered the joys of *pantouflage*, temporary or permanent departures from the administration to manage nationalised or even private businesses.

The French post-war administration was thus both less and more than the Napoleonic model. It had lost – indeed, had never fully possessed – the clarity of structure and unity of purpose envisaged under the First Empire. But it had gained enormously in substance. In addition to its traditional missions as defender of the nation's boundaries, dispenser of justice and guarantor of public order, it had become a manager and moderniser of the economy, an owner of banks, utilities and industries, a guarantor of its social welfare. In little more than a century, the number of state employees (including teachers, who have civil service status in France, but not local government officials, hospital staff or employees of nationalised industries) had more than decupled, from 140,000 in 1839 to 1,500,000 in 1950. Moreover, the administration had, if anything, gained in legitimacy. In part this was for reasons common to most Western democracies, where the extension of the state was widely accepted by the post-war generation and brought a measure of economic citizenship to previously marginalised groups. In part, too, it was for reasons specific to France. Economic intervention, including large-scale nationalisations, appeared to work, bringing – or coinciding with – unprecedented growth. And the contrast between the unstable governments of the Fourth Republic and the permanent and predictable activities of the administration appeared to confirm the latter's role as guardian of the national interest beyond political contingencies. This legitimacy was to reach its peak in the early years of the Fifth Republic, a regime initially dedicated to reinforcing the role of the administration.

The French state at high tide: the Fifth Republic to 1986

La République des fonctionnaires – the 'civil servants' Republic' – was a term assigned, with no great benevolence, to the Fifth Republic almost from its creation. On some criteria it suited France better in 2005 than at any previous moment: never had the state's share of national income or the number of state employees been higher. But by that time the state had already been selling off its enterprises and shedding its powers to control the economy for some twenty years. Different aspects of the so-called *République des fonctionnaires*, therefore, have applied more or less well at different times. In most respects, the high tide came in the first generation of the Fifth Republic. The administration was ubiquitous, widely believed in and powerful – but within limits resulting both from the politicians' resolve to keep it under control and from its own internal weaknesses.

The bases of administrative power

Three main arguments supported the view that Fifth Republic France had become an 'administrative state': the powerful economic role played by the state; the backing given by the régime's founders to the extension of the administration's activities; and the capacity of civil servants to colonise powerful positions well outside the administration *sensu stricto*.

The state's economic role

The economic role of the state is encapsulated in the term *dirigisme*, which has been discussed in some detail in Chapter 1. It rested on seven foundations: ownership of firms, credit control, price controls, planning, loans and research grants, state purchasing policy and sectoral investment policies. In the first place, France had one of the biggest public sectors in the Western world after the nationalisations of 1981–82, and the one that was most directed to industrial activities of a purely competitive nature. Governments regularly used nationalised firms to pursue their own objectives, whether to ward off recession through increased investments, as in 1974, or to limit regional unemployment by keeping particular industries (such as steelworks or mines) running. Second, with an ownership of the banking and insurance sectors that was predominant by 1946 and almost total by 1982, it was relatively easy for governments to practise *encadrement du crédit* – the direct control of the money supply through limits on increases in loan volume. Third, price controls, which de Gaulle installed by decree during the wartime penury of late 1944, were still in force four decades later, only partially and temporarily reduced under the Barre governments of 1976–81 (though ineffective as a control on inflation, they still demanded much time and paperwork from firms seeking price adjustments). Fourth, 'indicative' planning, instituted under the leadership of Jean Monnet (head of the new Commissariat au Plan from 1946 until 1952, when he left to run the European Coal and Steel Community), was widely credited, inside and outside France, with post-war economic success. It worked best in the early years, when the Commissariat was a small group of youngish, talented civil servants, and there was basic reconstruction work to be undertaken, with the help of Marshall aid, in a context of post-war shortages. By the 1960s, though de Gaulle referred to the Plan as an 'ardent obligation', it was past its peak: the Commissariat, now somewhat bureaucratised, was unable, in a more complex context of growth, to make reliable forecasts of economic trends, still less of political events such as the Algerian war which had serious budgetary and economic consequences. Fifth, loans and investment or research grants were made available to private industry through public bodies such as the Crédit National, the Caisse des Dépôts and the Crédit Agricole. Sixth, state purchasing orders became large enough to protect specific industries for years if needed. The French tended to preach liberalisation of purchasing policies in Brussels but to practise the protection of home firms from Paris. Finally, economic development in every sector and every region was promoted by a dense network of institutions (cf. Chapter 1), including the Commissariat au Plan; DATAR (the Délégation à l'Aménagement du Territoire et à l'Action Régionale), the regional development agency set up in 1962; certain key divisions of the Finance Ministry (notably the Budget and Forecasting); innumerable specialised funds and agencies; and several interministerial committees such as the CIASI (the committee for industrial restructuring) whose notional purpose was to give the system some degree of co-ordination.

The extension of the administration's activities

This was the corollary of the limitation of the powers of parliament discussed in Chapter 6. Articles 34 and 38 of the constitution, by limiting the domain of law-making, in which parliament has at least a notional role, correspondingly extended that of decrees, in which the administration's role is critical. Many important laws became so-called *lois d'orientation* – broad-brush legislation which left the administration to fill in the details. Civil servants suffered less harassment from prying Deputies (pursuing constituency or pressure-group interests); their projects became more likely to survive unscathed. More than ever, the administration found it could exercise its influence *before* a piece of legislation was presented, through its role in drafting, *during* its presentation, through advice to ministers on the desirability of concessions to parliament, and *after* the passage of legislation, through its role in implementation. The frequent delays between the passage of legislation and the publication of the *décrets d'application* necessary to its coming into force reflected the administration's powers of obstruction. The Agricultural Act of December 1968 which still awaited full implementation nine years later, was just one example. After 1981, some of the difficulties of implementing the Left's programme were ascribed to the administration, with more than one Socialist Deputy demanding a purge of the 'wreckers' in the civil service.

The founders of the régime sought not only to extend the administration's activities and powers, but also to increase its efficiency. Michel Debré, de Gaulle's first prime minister and his constitutional *alter ego*, was one of the rare politicians to understand the importance of the administration: it was he who created, in 1945, the École Nationale d'Administration (ÉNA), the elite civil service school whose annual output of 50–100 graduates (known as *énarques*) has steadily filled many of the elite posts within, and indeed beyond, the French administration. In his book *La mort de l'État républicain*, published in 1947, Debré insisted on the need to 'rationalise' and 'depoliticise' the administration, to halt the incrementalism and the concessions to special interests characteristic of the Third and Fourth Republics – to return, as it were, to the Napoleonic ideal. Since 1958, the efficiency of the administration has been the object of countless and constant reforms. A Ministry for Administrative Reforms was created in 1962, to complement (the critics said duplicate) the work of older bodies; though dropped in 1968, it has been regularly revived ever since. One innovation of the Fifth Republic was the multiplication of 'missionary' administrations – small groups of high-fliers brought together either to address a structural issue neglected or blocked because of interministerial rivalries, or to resolve a specific problem, if necessary by bypassing the traditional administrative structures. The prototype for this type of team was the Commissariat au Plan itself. Its regional equivalent, DATAR, was headed by one of de Gaulle's closest lieutenants, Olivier Guichard. Paul Delouvrier, meanwhile, headed a team entrusted with the administrative restructuring of the Paris area. The economic development of specific regions was also confided to horizontally organised missions, those of Aquitaine and Languedoc-Roussillon being the best known, and the tackling of specific problems, such as the growing threat to the Côte d'Azur from pollution and property speculation, or the encouragement of a solar energy programme, was confided to other missions which were to cut through the entanglements of the traditional administrative jungle. Another example was the Mission de la Mer founded in 1978 to remedy the administrative deficiencies revealed after the *Amoco Cadiz* disaster had caused widespread coastal oil pollution (the pollution caused twenty-one years later by the wreck of the *Erika* suggested that not all of the lessons had been learnt). At government level, the régime's obsession with administrative co-ordination and efficiency explains the founding of new ministries, the periodic creation of super-ministries (such as the Ministry for Regional Planning, Public Works, Housing and Tourism (MATELT) headed by Guichard in 1972), the internal reform of almost all ministries, the increase in the number of interministerial committees and the introduction of 'rationalised' budgeting procedures in the 1960s. Some of these reforms added confusion to an already complex administration, and ensured that problems that had hitherto merely been difficult became insoluble. And the newest, most advanced agencies often had a hand in some of the early Fifth Republic's most spectacular administrative blunders – the commercial disaster of Concorde, the ecologically and economically catastrophic petrochemical complex at Fos-sur-Mer, the utter failure of the Plan Calcul to create an independent French computer industry, the ultra-modern meat marketing complex at La Villette which was torn apart and converted into a museum without ever serving its original purpose. What is certain, on the other hand, is that these innovations testified to a faith, even at the highest political level, in the usefulness of administrative change and the leading role of the administration in the task of national regeneration and modernisation.

The colonisation by the civil service of areas beyond the confines of mere administration

The Fifth Republic's founders, largely insensible to liberal notions of a clear separation between politics and administration, encouraged and accelerated the administration's tendency to move into new sectors and reinforce its hold on existing domains. This was true of the Élysée staff and of ministerial *cabinets*, which the civil service dominated as never before, accounting for over 90 per cent of their members between 1958 and 1972. And it was the civil servants in the *cabinets* who were the most frequent participants in the *réunions interministérielles* that constitute the daily round of executive decision-making in France. Civil servants also staffed the growing number of ad hoc and permanent specialised bodies – 500 councils, 1,200 committees, 300 commissions by the mid-1960s – created to link the organs of the state with the major pressure groups.

Little of the above is very remote from the habitual tasks of the civil servant in any developed state. More remarkable, however, was the move of civil servants into business and politics. As a consequence of *pantouflage*, virtually every nationalised industry – and there were many – was headed by a civil servant; most large private firms also had ex-civil servants on their boards. By 1970, 12 per cent of all *énarques* held jobs in business (a proportion that had risen to 17 per cent twenty years later). Viewed from the opposite perspective, the figures are even more striking. In 1984, 37 per cent of the heads of France's 200 largest firms were graduates of ÉNA or the École Polytechnique – schools created to train civil servants; 28 per cent were members of the *grands corps*. In few other countries is a civil service background seen as particularly suitable for senior positions in the automobile industry; in France it became practically a requirement for Renault, the state-owned firm (headed by men such as Pierre Dreyfus and Raymond Lévy, and, in its semi-privatised form, Louis Schweitzer), and common even outside the nationalised sector (Jacques Calvet, head for some years of Peugeot-Citröen, was an *énarque*, a member of the Cour des Comptes, and the former head of Giscard's *cabinet* at the Finance Ministry). These practices established a widespread network of complicities, vastly tighter than Oxbridge or the Ivy League, within which instructions and wishes can be transmitted from government to business on a purely informal basis.

Equally striking was the move of civil servants not just into politically sensitive posts on staffs but also into politics proper – parliamentary or ministerial office and positions in local and regional government. This is facilitated by the liberal rules under which civil servants may leave their administrative (or teaching) posts on a temporary basis, and return to them later, if they wish, without any loss of seniority (the contrast with Britain, where a civil servant must resign his or her post before even standing for parliament, could not be greater). At the last pre-war election, in 1936, 17.3 per cent of Deputies were civil servants or teachers. Over the post-war generation, their number reached about a quarter: 23.5 per cent in 1946, 20 per cent in 1951, 22 per cent in 1956, 19.5 per cent in 1958, 22.7 per cent in 1967, 29 per cent in 1968, 26 per cent in 1973. Thereafter, the proportion rose steeply: 33 per cent in 1973, 38.8 per cent in 1978, 50 per cent in 1981, 42 per cent in 1986, 41.4 per cent in 1988 – figures that look more like a throwback to the July monarchy than a characteristic of a modern democratic state. Since the vast majority of national politicians are also local politicians, it is hardly surprising that civil servants also figure prominently among France's city mayors, and among the presidents of the twenty-two regional councils and of the councils of the ninety-six *départements*. In government the concentration of civil servants is still higher. Over half the ministers who served de Gaulle and Pompidou were recruited directly from the civil service (see Table 5.1), or had been civil servants. Under Giscard and Mitterrand, the proportion approached two-thirds. Six ministers in Mauroy's left-wing government of June 1981 were *énarques*; so were thirteen members of Chirac's 1986 government – a third of the total. The most senior posts were particularly affected. Between 1959 and 1988, 80 per cent of foreign ministers and defence ministers, 75 per cent of finance ministers and 70 per cent of education ministers hailed from the civil service. And *all* Fifth Republic prime ministers until 1991 had spent part of their careers in the civil service: Debré, Pompidou and Fabius had been members of the Conseil d'État; Chaban-Delmas, Couve de Murville and Rocard started their careers in the Inspection des Finances (the most prestigious of the *grands corps*, despite having been founded more recently than the others, in the nineteenth century); Messmer is a former colonial administrator, Chirac is a member of the Cour des Comptes, Barre had been a university professor before becoming one of France's European Commissioners, and Mauroy left the teaching profession to become a full-time politician. It became hard, under the Fifth Republic, to know where the civil service ended and the government began.

The growing power and spread of this ubiquitous civil service caused widespread disquiet. The title of a popular book, *L'administration au pouvoir*, contained a warning, confirmed a popular prejudice and purported to state a fact. And there is no doubt that certain parts of the civil service and certain civil servants exercised a discretion bordering on the autonomous exercise of power (for their critics, in other words, they became a law unto themselves). Such individuals would include, for example, Jérôme Monod, head of DATAR from 1968 to 1975 (and thereafter secretary-general of the Gaullist party, and head of one of France's two biggest water companies, the Lyonnaise des Eaux, before becoming an Élysée adviser from 2000 to 2005); Pierre Massé, the planning commissioner from 1959 to 1966; François Bloch-Lainé, head of the Caisse des Dépôts from 1952 to 1967; or Gérard Théry and Jean-Pierre Souviron, directors-general respectively of communications and industry during Giscard's presidency. The power of certain *corps*, whether 'generalist' like the Inspection des Finances or technical like the mining engineers or the highway engineers (the Corps des Ponts et Chaussées), is well known and well founded. Well-documented studies showed that some civil servants retarded and distorted the 1960s reforms to regions and *départements*, while others, on the contrary, furthered the development of the electro-nuclear programme. The *train à grande vitesse* (TGV) was a typical product of the state railway engineers – a technical triumph, achieved at a cost that saddled France's rail network with unsustainable debts (covered, eventually, by the taxpayer), and starved smaller lines and other sectors (such as rail freight) of investment. The independent behaviour of heads of nationalised firms also exasperated their political 'masters': the clashes between Albin Chalandon, Gaullist ex-minister and head of Elf-Aquitaine, and his 'supervising' minister, André Giraud at Industry, more than once provoked Giscard's presidential intervention; the Socialist Finance Minister Jacques Delors attacked the heads of France's nationalised banks (for having the impertinence to act like private bankers) on the same day that Prime Minister Mauroy was claiming that the nationalisation of the remaining private banks would strengthen the state's grip over credit.

The interpenetration of France's political, administrative and corporate elites also attracted attention, not all of it favourable. The American observer Ezra Suleiman noted that a single summer garden party at the prime minister's Matignon residence sufficed to bring together almost everyone who counted in France – a far cry from the greater geographical and social fragmentation of elites in the United States. A more sinister interpretation of the same phenomenon was that the blurring of frontiers between politics and administration, local and national politics, and business and administration, had perpetuated the absence in France of a notion of conflict of interest – as Yves Mény argued in a book significantly entitled *La corruption de la République*. It did not help that some commonly accepted top civil service practices, such as the payment of *cabinet* members via envelopes of banknotes, rather obviously flouted the normal standards expected of ordinary citizens, and appeared to symbolise a tendency, observed by Jonah Levy, to bypass normal political channels, and to capture state resources and privileges through old boy networks and covert dealings.

An omnipotent administration?

That the administration, especially at its high tide, was powerful, few doubted; that links between the nation's elites were unhealthily close, many conceded; but the omnipotence implied in such expressions as *L'administration au pouvoir* or *La République des fonctionnaires* was (and is) open to question. It was so for four reasons: the propensity of civil servants to leave the administration proper; the determination of the founders of the Fifth Republic to subordinate the administration to politics; the deep internal divisions within the administration; and the administration's apparent inability to perform some of its most basic tasks.

The propensity of civil servants to leave the administration

The corollary of their colonisation of the worlds of business and politics is that civil servants readily desert their jobs as civil servants. In 1968, for example, a young *inspecteur des finances* would stay an average of sixteen years in the administration proper (the period halved in the ensuing generation: it is now not unusual to leave at 30). This eagerness to depart, among the cream of France's administrative elites, denotes either a habit of collective self-abnegation without parallel in French history or a realisation that greater rewards, more power, or both, may be found outside. The switch to business is easily comprehensible on financial grounds. Politics, on the other hand, offered no such material advantages: its attractiveness suggests that civil servants saw it as offering opportunities for the exercise of power that the administration lacked. For such individuals, a return to the administration was rarely an upward move: it was more likely to result from a political setback, and to precede either a further move outside, or retirement.

The determination of the founders of the Fifth Republic to subordinate the administration to politics

This, paradoxically, was the corollary of their wish to reinforce the administration. The Gaullists subscribed to the (half-true) legend that the real government of the Fourth Republic had been, not the changing, immobile and pusillanimous ministers, but the omnipresent and omnipotent administration. They were resolved to end the 'administrative state within the state' and to secure the loyalty and subordination of civil servants to a strengthened *political* executive: the government 'has at its disposal the administration', as Article 20 of the constitution puts it. Their determination was reflected in the 1959 revisions to the civil service charter of 1946; in the 1964 decree regulating relations between the state and the French radio and television network personnel; in (fairly slight) limitations on the right of state employees to strike; and in tightened control over nationalised industries, the police and the prefects – quite aside from the measures needed to bring the army into line in the aftermath of the Algerian war. Conflict was inevitable between civil servants who believed they were defending an impartial view of the national interest against politicians prey to the demands of parties, pressure groups or voters, and politicians who saw themselves as the embodiment of democratic legitimacy against antediluvian, lethargic, obstructive civil servants whose attachment to the status quo was equalled only by their appetite for new privileges for themselves. There were some epic struggles under the Fifth Republic between civil servants and politicians; between Debré (as defence minister from 1969 to 1972) and the defence chiefs; between the Education Ministry under Giscard and two successive higher education ministers (one of whom used methods described as those of a 'Gauleiter in occupied territory'); between Jacques Delors and the leaders of the nationalised banks; between Mitterrand's Interior Minister Gaston Defferre (and above all, his liberal Justice Minister Robert Badinter) and the police. The civil servants did not invariably get the better of such scraps.

Moreover, their political vulnerability was enhanced. Fifth Republic governments became increasingly willing to use constitutional powers of patronage to replace political foes with friends in the most sensitive posts. This did not entail an American-style spoils system. Posts circulate within a pool of eminently qualified civil servants; the happy appointees always had more than merely political qualifications; the victims of political change suffered no worse fate than confinement in a 'golden closet' – a fake job in an obscure corner of the administration. But jobs began to change hands, and in quite large numbers. Members of the Élysée staff and of the *cabinets* of the prime minister and ministers (between 450 and 650 individuals, 'unofficial' appointments aside) almost all change with their political masters. In addition, about 500 senior civil service posts are also liable to be filled, and forcibly vacated, for political reasons: most frequently in certain especially exposed ministries like Finance, Education, the Interior, Foreign Affairs and Justice. In the end, the senior officials in every ministry – notably the 220 or so *directeurs d'administration centrale* – are all vulnerable. So are key posts in the field services, especially the prefects and the *recteurs* of the Education Ministry's regions, over three-quarters of whom can expect to be moved within two years of a change of government. So are those at the top of a whole series of para-state organisations ranging from radio and television to nationalised firms to utilities to urban development organisations. The practice of political appointments, never wholly absent, was certainly intensified under the Gaullists: the result was soon termed the *État-UDR*, after the then name of the Gaullist party. The *État-Giscard* soon followed, as the Fifth Republic's third president sought to replace loyal Gaullists with his own men (a practice that became a major bone of contention within the pre-1981 Right). After 1981 it gave way to the *État Socialiste* managed by the *elite rose*: the Socialists changed two-thirds of *directeurs d'administration centrale*. Then the Right replaced over 80 per cent of them in 1986 – and so on, with each incoming government proclaiming its intention to halt or limit such political appointments before succumbing to the temptation more or less extensively. This politicisation of the civil service is the mirror image of the bureaucratisation of politics. Keenly felt, and sometimes resented, by the civil servants whose jobs became more exposed as alternation in power became more frequent, it suggested quite the opposite of an all-powerful administration.

Relations between civil servants and ministers are not always conflictual, though. In the first place, they may share the same views: the financially orthodox Giscard d'Estaing ruled for a total of nine years over a Finance Ministry inclined to financial orthodoxy. One of his successors, Michel Sapin, observed with some exaggeration that 'Bercy [the shorthand for the Finance Ministry since its move away from the rue de Rivoli in 1988] is never so powerful as when it is led, never so happy as when it obeys'. Second, civil servants may be passive, weak or largely managerial: the Quai d'Orsay, for example, seems to have done little to resist the foreign policy changes of the early Fifth Republic despite reservations about Gaullist positions within the ranks of the diplomatic corps. Third, a strong minister may be appreciated by his civil servants, whatever their political differences, simply for his or her effectiveness in representing the ministry's interests within the government. Fourth, a skilful and determined minister can usually (though not always) get the better of recalcitrant civil servants: such was the case of Edgar Faure, who got his mildly liberal educational reforms past an administration which considered them positively Maoist, and of Gaston Defferre, who imposed his decentralisation reform upon an equally sceptical Interior Ministry. Finally, many examples of administrative 'obstructiveness' turn out to have arisen in cases where the political executive has itself been divided and indecisive. The reform of subnational government in the 1960s, for example, was plagued by the government's inability to decide whether it wanted to render the administration at territorial level more efficient, more subordinate or more democratic. Debré, the first prime minister, anathematised any proposals as threatening the centralised state on which, in his view, the nation's existence depended; Pompidou cast a prudent electoral eye on the reaction of established local *notables*; but Jeanneney, the left-wing Gaullist responsible for preparing the 1969 referendum on Senate and regional reforms, believed he had a brief to increase public participation in decisions. The result was an unhappy series of compromises, and the first lost referendum of the Fifth Republic. And without a consistent political will among ministers, no amount of administrative tinkering will produce a consistent result. The assignment of responsibility for industrial decentralisation to the newly created DATAR in the 1960s, for example, quite failed to prevent the piecemeal interventions of staffs and officials from the Élysée, the prime minister's office, and the ministries of Finance, Interior, and Housing and Public Works. Under these conditions, DATAR turned into just one more interested party, complicating the problem it was intended to solve.

The administration's internal divisions

Internal divisions have also rendered the administration considerably less than omnipotent. Robert Elgie's account of the economic U-turn of March 1983, for example, shows the administration behaving not as a bloc but as a divided set of actors, putting forward different policies, with the president taking the final decision. There may, sometimes, be a Finance Ministry view or an Industry Ministry view; there is never an 'administration view'. Most of the evidence points to the administration's diverse and fragmentary nature (well expressed in the title of François Dupuy and Jean-Claude Thoenig's book *L'administration en miettes* – 'The administration in smithereens'). The interplay of the resulting divergent interests is often open, unlike in Britain, where differences are masked behind a screen of courteous yet apprehensive anonymity. Moreover, fragmentation is increased by the multiple and overlapping divisions within the administration. These divisions fall into five main areas.

First, the apparent uniformity of outlook of top civil servants is belied by the fierce group loyalties generated during and just after their education. The uniformity of *background* is certainly striking. Members of the civil service elite come mostly, and increasingly, from comfortable upper middle-class families (often including several generations of senior civil servants). They are still, overwhelmingly, men: as recently as 1998, women represented 44.6 per cent of the active population, 56.9 per cent of public servants, 13.2 per cent of the senior civil service, and just 7.7 per cent of *directeurs d'administration centrale*. They are frequently products of the top Parisian *lycées*, and almost all of one or another of the *grandes écoles* – the highly selective higher education institutions that channel the ablest students away from France's democratic and underfunded university system. The background, it is often argued, produces a common, and technocratic, language, and a certain uniformity of approach based on values of pragmatism, scientific rationalism, efficiency and apoliticism, and on a shared belief in the virtues of state interventionism. At the same time, however, the education process produces diversity and is rooted in merciless competition. Those of a scientific bent take a highly competitive examination to enter the École Polytechnique, and another one to leave it; they then progress to a specialist school such as the École des Ponts et Chaussées (for highway engineers), the École des Mines (for mining engineers) or the École de Génie (for military engineers). Generalists, meanwhile, pass an examination to go to the Institut d'Études Politiques, another, more competitive one, to enter ÉNA, and a third to win a place in ÉNA's passing-out order. New entrants to the civil service join a *corps*, according to their educational background and their success in examinations. In the early 1990s there were no fewer than 1,790 *corps*, 190 of which had stopped recruiting and were destined for extinction. The elite *corps* for generalists are the Inspection des Finances (with a total of just 237 members in 1990), the Conseil d'État (296 members) and the Cour des Comptes (359 members); their specialist counterparts include Ponts et Chaussées and Mines. Each has its own peculiar rites, norms and prejudices. The process of education and civil service entry may therefore produce both a number of common attitudes *and* many more particular loyalties, networks and rivalries generated by different *grandes écoles* and *corps*. It should be emphasised, furthermore, that *corps* cut across ministerial divisions. This may assist co-ordination between, for example, members of the same *corps* in a ministry, the prime minister's *cabinet* and a state-owned firm. But it may also be a source of division as rival *corps* seek to build empires by colonising particular posts: frontier disputes between the Mines and the Ponts et Chaussées over jobs in or linked to the Industry Ministry, for example, have been many and bitter. When Jean-Yves Haberer was called before the inquiry into the disastrously expensive collapse of the Crédit Lyonnais (for which, as the bank's chief, he was in great measure responsible), he found it quite natural to question the competence of his successor, Jean-Philippe Peyrelevade, on the grounds that he was not an *inspecteur des finances*, not even an *énarque*, but a mere *polytechnicien*, and so obviously unsuitable. Such animosity helps to explain why the French bureaucracy suffers from a reluctance to share information, with many projects viewed as a zero-sum game between administrations, not a positive-sum game for the public good.

Second, the outlook of individual civil servants may be affected by factors largely independent of education or *corps*. The fact that governments of both Right and Left are able to find politically sympathetic civil servants to fill key posts indicates the existence of varying political views, of at least a semi-public nature, within the administration. That has led some governments to accuse sections of the administration of political bias. The Conseil d'État, for example, incurred the lasting hostility of Gaullists by opposing two of de Gaulle's referendums on (well-founded) grounds of unconstitutionality – and doing so, moreover, by leaking its comments to the press. It was therefore hailed by the Left as a 'bastion of republican defence' – until, with a Left-wing government in office, it insisted on changes in several government bills. In fact, within the administration political views, more or less strongly held, combine in varying degrees with independence, institutional loyalty, commitment to apolitical service and opportunism. Quite different factors may also affect outlook and even behaviour. For example, some observers have noted the presence within the civil service of a gay network – rarely active in policy formulation, but ready to mobilise over issues of direct concern (Interior Minister Charles Pasqua's attempt to ban the leading homosexual magazine *Gai pied* was nipped in the bud).

Third, Ezra Suleiman has shown that one determining factor in differentiating the views and behaviour of civil servants is the function or role they perform. One such difference of perspective may occur between the permanent staff of a ministry and the minister's *cabinet*. The *cabinet* members have the minister's backing (usually) and the task of co-ordinating the ministry's activities. In doing so they may make impossible or conflicting demands on the permanent staff, or demand innovations which the latter see as impossible, or as damaging to the ministry's long-term interests. But the permanent staff have well-tried techniques of obstruction at their disposal, notably the manipulation of information and the reliance on rigid procedures. If the *cabinet* is dominated by mobile high-fliers from the generalist *grand corps* or the major technical *corps*, and the permanent staff by senior civil administrators and middle-ranking bureaucrats who spend a lifetime in the same division of the same ministry, this will not assist mutual comprehension. Ministries also dislike the administration's internal controls that are periodically visited upon them: the unannounced swoops of the Inspection des Finances, the legal supervision of the Conseil d'État, the audits of the Cour des Comptes. The so-called 'missionary' administrations are resented by the more established ministries, which resent the loss of some of their more interesting and prestigious tasks. The Finance Ministry, for example, waged unremitting war on the work of the Commissariat au Plan, whose policies it regarded as financially dubious and intrinsically inflationary, and created its own forecasting service to second-guess the planners' work (the ministry's final victory over its enemy was sealed by the post-1983 economic climate). Many of these enmities are entrenched and last for decades. But it is also noticeable that changes of function among members of the mobile elite *corps* may lead to changes of attitude. A member of a *grand corps* who takes up a position in a ministry frequently adopts the norms and prejudices of his or her new home (professional success may require it); prefects who are promoted to the Conseil d'État are often zealous and knowledgeable critics of the administrative malpractices of their erstwhile colleagues; a member of the litigation (*contentieux*) section of the Conseil d'État who joins a ministerial *cabinet* may become usefully inventive in circumventing the Conseil's tiresome and legalistic supervision of his or her minister's activities (often having been recruited to the *cabinet* to do just that).

The fourth source of fragmentation, conflicts between ministries, is common to all developed systems of government. Between Finance (more particularly the Budget division, the watchdog of the nation's wallet) and the spending ministries there is continuous struggle. The Interior Ministry has clashed with the Justice Ministry over the rights of immigrants, and with the Health Ministry over the treatment of drug addicts. The Environment Ministry has regularly opposed both Industry and Agriculture over issues relating to pollution (and has often, as a fairly young and small ministry, come off worse). Culture, a small but prestigious ministry, has fought running battles with Public Works over the preservation of historic monuments (and had great difficulty in shifting Finance from its long-held wing of the Louvre to its new, purpose-built, but less central premises at Bercy).

Conflicts within ministries, finally, are no less frequent, for most are large and compartmentalised federations of fiercely independent divisions. This is true, for example, of Education and Industry, while Finance in 1978 had 170,000 employees and 102 divisions, scattered between the Louvre and no fewer than thirty-four annexes: according to one observer, it is easier to turn a soldier into a sailor than it is to transfer from one of the Finance Ministry's divisions to another. Problems are compounded by the fact that no ministry, except for Foreign Affairs, Defence and (since 2000 only) Finance, has a single administrative head on the model of the British permanent secretaries: such figures are redolent, in the French political tradition, of the anti-democratic institutions of the Vichy régime. Conflicts also occur between the ministries in Paris and their field services in the provinces, responsible in many areas for implementation of laws and decrees on the ground: the field services often resent the central divisions' lack of contact with the grass roots, while the Parisians mistrust what they see as their provincial colleagues' tendency to 'go native' (though they may defend them stoutly against attacks from other ministries). Too often, as Olivier Duhamel remarks, civil servants 'attack each other, not the problem in hand'.

The administration's inability to perform some of its most basic tasks

This weakness resulted in great part from the vast area and depth of administrative intervention and made itself felt both at elite level and in the front-line delivery of services. Thus the economic intervention service of the Finance Ministry, at the very centre of French economic decision-making in the 1970s, was too overburdened with work to deal in any depth with the mass of matters that clamoured for its attention; the administration's apparently wide discretionary powers are often reduced to nothing by the constant effort to keep a minimum of administrative order in the face of an endless stream of laws, decrees, directives, circulars and instructions; parts of the labour code were rarely implemented because of the lack of inspectors, while illicit price-rings in industry flourished because of inadequate supervision. For, contrary to popular mythology, important parts of the administration were undermanned. That in turn added to the difficulty of effective administrative reforms on the ground: in the absence of adequate staffing, the unionised rank and file of the French administration proved deeply suspicious of any reorganisations likely to increase their own already excessive workload.

The myth of the French administration's omnipotence at high tide is fairly easy to understand. It attracted the ablest men (and a few – too few – women) of their generation. It contributed to France's impressive and (relatively) painless post-war mutation from a predominantly agricultural and rural to a largely urban and industrial society. It spread outwards to the worlds of business and politics, constituting the centre of a remarkable network or, rather, a series of interlocking networks. In some respects, though, it was a giant with feet of clay. It was constrained by politicians, on whose initiative the civil servants usually depended. It was divided, uncoordinated, deeply attached to precedent and at times staggeringly inefficient in delivering services. In the cases of several individual ministries, it was dominated and colonised by strategically placed interest groups. It could obstruct, but rarely initiated. It was perhaps the gulf between the administration's *potential* and *alleged* power and its *effective* power that contributed to a malaise in its ranks that was clearly apparent by the 1970s. The economic changes that followed widened the gulf, presented the administration with unaccustomed challenges and deepened the malaise.

The administration transformed?

Like other West European countries, France faced a number of unfamiliar pressures from the mid-1970s and even more from the 1980s: globalisation, faster European integration, slow growth and budgetary tightening, and an ideological shift away from the post-war consensus favourable to state intervention (cf. Chapter 1). By 2000, these pressures had transformed the shape of the French state in a number of ways. Changes to the French administration, on the other hand, were considerably less radical.

New pressures

Georges Pompidou was one of the earliest political leaders to grasp the potential impact of globalisation: in 1969 he told a business audience that 'when you have chosen international liberalism, you must also opt for internal liberalism', that 'the state must therefore diminish its hold over the economy instead of perpetually seeking to direct and control it', and that the state's control over foreign exchange and credit was a 'transient necessity'. The internationalisation of markets, combined with technological change and pressures from international organisations such as the General Agreement on Tariffs and Trade (since 1993, the World Trade Organisation), would make it hard to sustain France's post-war edifice of autarchic public sectors, protected national champions and restrictions on capital movements. But both Pompidou himself and Giscard's second prime minister Raymond Barre (who had voiced similar views) were restrained by a cautious electoralism from translating their free-market discourse into more than fairly limited measures (Barre's deregulation of bread prices produced a furore). The large-scale liberalisation of the French economy had to wait until after the economic U-turn of March 1983.

The acceleration of European integration, and in particular the Single European Act of 1986 and the Maastricht Treaty of 1992, also furthered liberalisation. The development of an activist competition policy led the European Commission to cast a newly critical eye on subsidies lavished by French governments on national industrial champions or on electorally sensitive lame ducks. It also threatened monopolies in public services such as telecommunications, gas and electricity, or rail transport. Indeed, the very notion of public service, and the exceptions to competition policy that it might entail, went unacknowledged in Europe's founding treaties – though the 1997 Amsterdam Treaty went a little way (partly as a result of French pressure) towards remedying this. In addition, the integration process affected France in ways that were not purely economic. The primacy of European law over the law of member states, asserted in a series of rulings by the European Court of Justice, was finally acknowledged in a series of decisions by the Conseil d'État between 1989 and 1992. That, and the widening range of European legislation, required a closer attention to the harmonisation of French law with the directives, decisions and rulings emanating from Brussels. In 1992, as Hayward and Wright observe, 22,445 EU regulations were directly applicable in member states and 1,675 directives had to be translated into states' law. This task of implementation fell onto the civil service. Meanwhile, employment in France's public services, long restricted to nationals, was opened (in principle) to other European citizens in 1991. Finally, integration began to erode the structure of relations between the French administration and its client interest groups; institutional changes, and especially the qualified majority voting that the Single Act of 1986 established as a reality, led growing numbers of such groups to lobby in Brussels as well as in national capitals.

The dramatic slow-down of economic growth from the mid-1970s also entailed new pressures, especially on the comfortable incrementalist assumptions of the *trente glorieuses*: no longer could ministries expect steadily rising budgets. These pressures were largely eluded during the Giscard presidency, when the public sector grew much faster than the economy and tax revenues as a share of gross domestic product rose by 6 per cent, to 42 per cent. The Left, on coming to power in 1981, both extended the frontiers of the state's intervention with its nationalisation programme and recruited

100,000 new state employees. Here again, the major turning point came after 1983 – and in particular, when Mitterrand insisted in 1984 that total taxation should not exceed 43 per cent of GDP in the following year's budget. Budget restrictions meant competition between and within ministries for stagnant or diminishing resources; they also made governments more reluctant to spend heavily to save ailing industries.

The ideological shift away from state interventionism in France had in common with the 'Anglo-Saxon' countries both a growing mistrust of the state's capacity to manage firms and a new interest in delivering public services, not through the procedure-oriented structures of old bureaucracies, but by the methods of private business. Like the 'Anglo-Saxons', France had its free-market ideologues. As early as 1979, Gérard Longuet, who had come to Giscard's party from the extreme Right, proposed hiving off 1,600,000 central state employees to autonomous agencies, leaving a core of just 400,000. Four years later, in more measured tones, Juppé argued that France should turn away, not only from the post-1981 left-wing 'experiment', but from the whole post-war interventionist consensus. Longuet's *alter ego* Alain Madelin, on being appointed industry minister in 1986, said he would prefer to rename his ministry the 'Grenelle consulting group' and maintain a staff of about twenty. Another argument used by the Right in France as elsewhere in the mid-1980s was that the state had spread itself too thin, and should concentrate more on its traditional, 'regalian' domains, especially law and order. In the longer term, though, the ideological shift went beyond the confines of the Right. Even the Left of the 1970s, attached as it was to an extension of the public sector, had reservations about *central* government: out of national office for a generation, but managers of growing numbers of local authorities, Communists and Socialists became steadily more committed to decentralisation. In addition, a significant current within the PS, initially associated with Michel Rocard, questioned the Jacobin assumptions of the post-war generation that the state could and should act as an enlightened agent of progress, if necessary against what was regarded as a conservative and narrow-minded civil society; for this *deuxième gauche*, to ignore civil society was to condemn the state, sooner or later, to impotence and sclerosis.

The relationship between the state, the public services and French society also changed in many ways. Where ministries had formerly been able to rely for successful implementation of policy either on their own democratic legitimacy or (more frequently) on a long-standing relationship with a very limited number of client groups, they now found themselves facing a greater variety of demands from a growing number of actors within society. The aftermath of May 1968 saw a spread of left-wing and ecological protest movements of all kinds, some of them taking as targets such tangible manifestations of the state's heavy hand as the extension of the Larzac military camp or the construction of the Creys-Malville nuclear plant. From the 1970s on, the multiplication of associations of all kinds (not all of them extreme or even left-wing), combined with the decline in such traditionally stable groups as trade unions, required ministries to take on a wider range of interlocutors. At the same time not only groups but also politicians placed new demands on public services, despite budgetary constraints. The SNCF was required not only to transport passengers and goods, but to contribute to regional development and environmental policy. Teachers were asked not merely to teach but to provide 'safe havens' in violent neighbourhoods or to compensate for the growing inequalities in the society around them. For the state's rank-and-file servants, the resulting strains were compounded by changes in public attitudes to them as their performance was judged more critically (especially, perhaps, in the case of the teaching profession) while their job security became the object of desire and envy among the growing proportion of the French who feared for their own employment.

A shrinking state

Within a decade or so of its Gaullist apogee, in short, the French state was undermined, from within by the conduct of some of its own servants and from without by a bizarre combination of global corporations, intergovernmental organisations, Eurocrats, right-wing zealots, left-wing mayors, Socialist intellectuals, eco-activists and others. Its contours changed as a result, in six ways.

• *Many of the tools of macroeconomic intervention established during the post-war generation were abandoned.* Foreign exchange controls, briefly tightened in 1982–83, were progressively lifted between 1984 and 1988. With them went the *encadrement du crédit*, since firms could now raise money on international capital markets (and many French credit institutions were soon privatised). Controls on prices, which had in any case become less and less effective, were ended in 1986. The automatic linking of wages to the price index had been ended two years earlier. The Plan, de Gaulle's 'ardent obligation' of the 1960s, became not merely unreliable but even irrelevant in an unpredictable global environment. The Commissariat au Plan was increasingly invited to produce, not five-year plans for the whole French economy, but long-term briefs about the future of labour markets or pensions policy. The de Villepin government finally abolished it in October 2005, promising to replace it with an umbrella organisation linking other strategic analysis groups set up in previous years.
• *France carried through a vast privatisation programme, and liberalised the management of the remaining state-owned firms.* Despite its *dirigiste* tradition, France was second only to Britain, and ahead of the rest of continental Europe, in the speed and scope of its privatisation programme. The total value of firms and stock sold between 1986 and 1997, largely by right-wing governments, was some $40 billion. After 1997 the Left raised a more than equivalent value, though with less fanfare.

The privatisations were, it is true, marked by the *dirigiste* tradition. Initially they involved industrial and commercial concerns only, and not services and utilities (except for water, which had never been a public monopoly: indeed France's world-class private water companies were enthusiastic buyers into privatised British firms). Initially, too, privatisation made rather little difference to the management structure of the firms, which were still run by the same caste of *énarques*, while the *noyaux durs* or golden shares of privatised firms preserved the interlocking share-holdings characteristic of what the Communist Party used to call state monopoly capitalism. Moreover, governments had other motives than revenue-raising in mind as they planned the sales. The Gaullist RPR was regularly accused, especially in the first wave of privatisations between 1986 and 1987, of selecting its own supporters to head privatised firms. No fewer than four ulterior motives have been discerned in Jospin's sell-offs after 1997: encouraging international alliances while retaining a controlling share for the state; establishing cross-shareholdings between leading French firms (such as Bouygues, Vivendi/Générale des Eaux and Alcatel); offering shares to the workforce on attractive terms; and, especially in financial services, reinforcing France's mutual sector.

It remained the case, though, that by the late 1990s almost no state-owned companies remained in what used to be considered as the competitive sector of the economy, except for one or two defence firms like Snecma or GIAT. Even Crédit Lyonnais was brought to market in 1999. Almost all the privatised firms were seeking international links (such as Renault's effective takeover of Nissan) and facing at least the possibility that this global integration would generate 'Anglo-Saxon' concerns about management performance among shareholders. The few remaining publicly owned firms were being run on a private-sector logic. The once popular habit of cross-subsidies has been ended (the fate of Air Inter, absorbed by Air France in 1996, illustrated the dangers of such practices); the near-military structure of the SNCF has been reformed. Even public-sector utilities were beginning to feel the pressure, as the notion of a 'natural monopoly' began to disappear; the reform to the status of EDF-GDF, the electricity and gas monopoly, was undertaken in 2004 with a view to its partial privatisation the following year. At the local level, the concession of key public services to private or mixed public/private firms, widespread before 1939, enjoyed a significant return to favour.

- *European integration had dramatically curtailed some of the most characteristic habits of French* dirigisme *by the century's end.* The *grands projets* like Concorde, so characteristic of the Gaullist era, were fewer and more likely to be undertaken at the European, rather than the national, level: examples include Airbus, the Ariane missile and, less successfully, high-tech projects such as Euram, Race, Eureka, or Jessi. Bail-outs of ailing firms, whose multiplication in the 1970s led the economist Élie Cohen to refer to the 'stretcher-bearer state', were increasingly limited by the combination of European competition rules and budgetary constraints (though Air France and Crédit Lyonnais in the 1990s, as well as Alstom in 2003, constituted striking exceptions). Competition rules also led to steps, more or less fiercely resisted, to deregulate former public-service monopolies. Some fifty firms now sell telephone services in France; air transport has been very grudgingly deregulated; rail (especially freight services) is also under pressure to open markets; the European energy charter has forced competition even in gas and electricity production, and thus change to EDF-GDF. Similar treatment for the postal service, on the other hand, has been fiercely resisted in Brussels by national governments, including the French. Competition regulations had also made some inroads into France's traditionally protectionist public-sector purchasing policies: in late 1999 it was even announced that some French police officers were to drive Fords.

The years following the Single European Act were also a period in which almost the whole of the French administration began to take European issues seriously. Previously such concern had been confined to ministries most obviously concerned with the earliest European policies, such as Agriculture. Now almost every ministry, indeed most divisions of every ministry, had a European 'cell'. The SGCI or Secrétariat Général du Comité Interministériel pour les questions de coopération économique européenne (renamed Secrétariat Général des Affaires Européennes (SGAE) in October 2005), an organisation set up in 1948 to ensure the co-ordination of France's European policy under the responsibility of the prime minister, grew significantly in importance in the 1980s: Élisabeth Guigou, its head from 1985 to 1990, was a close personal adviser to President Mitterrand, and both *grands corps* and ministerial divisions increasingly sought to have 'their' representatives on it.

- *The administration was subjected to an increasing range of controls.* The Napoleonic model provides for internal controls on the administration by such bodies as the Cour des Comptes or the Conseil d'État. Though the Cour des Comptes is unable to impose penalties directly, its annual report, an illuminating survey of the year's administrative malpractices and blunders, has received growing publicity in recent years. Some attempts have also been made to create forms of outside control. These include the Mediator, a complaints authority accessible to citizens via parliamentarians, created in 1973 and analogous to the British or Swedish ombudsman. The growth of the Mediator's caseload, from 2,000 to 43,500 cases between 1974 and 1996, indicates the strength of demand for his services, and he now heads a nationwide network of delegates who have often been able to resolve disputes at the local level. The public's rights vis-à-vis the administration were also reinforced by a law of 1978, which provided a limited right of access to administrative documents and limited the purposes for which files on individuals could legally be used. The Commission d'Accès aux Documents Administratifs was set up to implement this legislation, while another independent commission set up the previous year, the Commission Nationale de l'Informatique et des Libertés (CNIL), aims to prevent abuse of computer data by administrative or other authorities. Planning procedures now include a wider range of consultation procedures and impact studies, and where decisions (for example in planning issues) go against individual citizens, the administration is also required to provide reasons to the losing party. Finally, the various parliamentary evaluation offices set up in the 1990s (the Office d'évaluation des politiques publiques and the Office d'évaluation de la législation, as well as the Mission d'évaluation et de contrôle) clearly aimed at restoring some of the power to control the administration that parliament had lost since 1958.
- *Governments have created a growing number of autonomous agencies*, seeking to ensure that the performance of certain tasks is not entrapped in the meshes of the administration. A few such agencies are relatively old: the Commission de Contrôle des Banques dates from 1941, the Commission des Opérations en Bourse (COB), which supervises the Stock Exchange, from 1967 (it was merged with the Conseil des Marchés Financiers into the Autorité des Marchés Financiers in 2003). Most, though, have been created since the late 1970s. Two, the Commission d'Accès aux Documents Administratifs and the CNIL, have already been mentioned. Others include the Conseil de la Concurrence (1986), which monitors, not always very effectively, monopolies, illicit cartels, price-fixing and other restrictive practices; the Conseil Supérieur de l'Audiovisuel which supervises the political minefield of radio and television broadcasting; the Commission des Sondages (1977), which investigates complaints about opinion polls; the Commission des Infractions Fiscales (1977), the Commission de la Sécurité des Consommateurs (1983), the Commission de la Privatisation (1986), the Commission de Contrôle des Assurances (1989) and the Commission Nationale de Contrôle des Campagnes Électorales, whose titles clearly define their role. These bodies often handle questions of great political sensitivity, and exercise a discretionary power outside the control of the administration. For example, it was the food safety agency created in 1999, the Agence Française de Sécurité Sanitaire des Aliments (AFSSA), which led the Jospin government to maintain, against its political inclination, the ban on British beef. Another development has been the increasing resort to committees of *sages* (wise men and women) and independent experts, especially in the most politically

controversial areas such as the reform of the nationality laws, the financing of the social security system, the future of pensions and the freedom of the media. These two developments represent a further balkanisation and autonomisation of public policy-making and reduce the power of the traditional administration.

- *A large-scale decentralisation programme was undertaken* under President Mitterrand from 1982, and relaunched, with some difficulty, under the Raffarin government twenty years later. Its details are discussed in Chapter 12. Its impact on the state administration has been variable: some ministries were affected not at all (Defence, Foreign Affairs), some very little (Labour and the Interior), some slightly (Housing and Public Works transferred about 7–8 per cent of its personnel to local authorities) and one (Health and Social Security, which saw many of its tasks become the responsibility of *départements*) quite considerably.

The administration and the limits to change

The environment within which the French administration operates has therefore changed in important ways. The French state is smaller, thanks to privatisations; it is less able to intervene at will; it is more fragmented, both territorially (thanks to decentralisation) and functionally (thanks to independent agencies); it is more subject to controls, both national (slightly) and European (considerably). The transformation was less radical, on the other hand, within the administration itself, whether within the elite or at rank-and-file level.

The elite

The decision of the Chirac government in 1986 to cut the following year's intake to ÉNA by half, to about fifty, appeared to signal a long-term reduction in the size, if not the role, of the top-level administration. But the change was reversed after 1988. The Cresson government's attempt to move ÉNA physically from Paris to Strasbourg was fiercely resisted, with the result that the school was split between the two cities – a messy and expensive compromise that lasted some fifteen years before the final move to Strasbourg was made. More radical proposals, for example to cut the automatic links between ÉNA, Polytechnique and senior administrative posts, have not been adopted. Nor are they very likely to be, given the strength of the two schools' networks. The French administrative elite remains highly resilient: though it has faced significant challenges, its members have also sought to adapt by conquering positions in new domains.

The classic *cursus honorum* of a high-flying *énarque* in the early Fifth Republic – a ministerial *cabinet* followed by entry into politics or private business – still exists but is less typical than formerly. Ministerial *cabinets* have opened up somewhat to the rest of society: since 1984 only 80 per cent of their members have been from the public sector in its widest sense, compared with over 90 per cent between 1958 and 1972, and over 85 per cent under earlier republics. The proportion of *cabinets* occupied by members of the *grands corps* has declined more sharply, from 34 per cent between 1958 and 1972 to 16 per cent between 1984 and 1996 (though they still supplied nearly half of all *directeurs de cabinet*). The prefectoral corps and the Inspection des finances have been particularly inclined to disengage, though the phenomenon has extended to the Conseil d'État and the Cour des Comptes. The difficulty experienced by Laurent Fabius in recruiting a suitable 'dircab' on his appointment as finance minister in March 2000 testifies to the relative loss of attractiveness of these positions. In the National Assembly, while the public sector generally is still over-represented (at 46 per cent of Deputies in 1997, and 35 per cent in 2002), roughly half their number consisted of teachers. Only 6.4 per cent of the 1997 Assembly, and 5.9 per cent in 2002, were *énarques*, only 4 per cent from the *grands corps* – a figure that had fallen steadily from 14 per cent in 1978, 11 per cent in 1981, 13 per cent in 1986, 10 per cent in 1988 and 8.6 per cent in 1993. By way of comparison, some 45 per cent of 1997 Deputies had a background in industry, banking or the liberal professions. Only the administration's colonisation of the government appeared undiminished. The three prime ministers who governed from 1993 to 2002 were all *énarques*: Balladur a *conseiller d'État*, Juppé an *inspecteur des finances*, Jospin a member of the diplomatic corps. Raffarin, it is true, has a business education and worked as as marketing executive for Cafés Jacques Vabre; but he compensated for this by appointing nearly a third of his ministers from a civil service background, including *énarques* such as Renaud Dutreil, Dominique Perben, Hervé Gaymard, Henri Plagnol, Pierre-André Wiltzer and Jean-François Copé, as well as Dominique de Villepin. The appointment of Villepin, another *énarque* and diplomat, to succeed Raffarin in 2005 was a return to the dominant tradition.

At the same time the stability of senior jobs within the ministries diminished with the increasing regularity of *alternances*: 83 per cent of *directeurs d'administration centrale* changed in 1986–87, 46 per cent in 1988–89, 56 per cent in 1993–94, 43 per cent in 1995–96. As the requirements of the administration became more politicised, some senior civil servants sought to diversify their activities. A good example of this is the European Union, which members of the *grands corps* have seen as an opportunity and a challenge as much as a constraint since the mid-1980s. The challenge may be seen as one of gaining as much control as possible over the definition of France's policies in Europe; over the elaboration of European policies in Brussels; and over the implementation of European decisions and directives in France. It entails the representation of the *corps* not only on the SGAE, within France, but also within the European administration. Hence the contributions of *inspecteurs des finances* to European decisions on banking and single currency issues, as well as to European audit processes; of *ingénieurs des ponts et chaussées* to transport policies, of *ingénieurs des mines* to environmental policy, of prefects to 'Schengen' regulations on immigration and frontiers, of *conseillers d'État* to the work of the European Court of Justice. Luc Rouban observes that the French administration has acquired a European reach; that it has understood the potential importance for French industry of the definition of European product norms; and that these activities have placed it in a strategic relationship with French firms, many of which have been only dimly aware of the significance for their activities of decisions taken in Brussels.

A further avenue is business, which has become, if anything, more attractive to senior civil servants since the first wave of privatisations. Four phenomena encouraged this. First, private-sector pay outstripped that of the civil service by increasingly spectacular margins from the 1980s (indeed, according to one estimate, senior civil servants' purchasing power *dropped* 14 per cent in the fifteen years after 1982). Second, the content of ÉNA courses was increasingly oriented towards private business, leading experts like Michel Bauer to ask if ÉNA had not simply become a business school. Third, once privatised, firms were less likely to 'parachute' civil servants without business experience into their very top management positions; there was an incentive to acquire that experience at somewhat lower levels. Fourth, this incentive to leave from lower levels was reinforced, from 1995, by new restrictions placed on more senior civil servants moving to private business in cases where conflicts of interest might result. In 1980, the proportion of *énarques* of any given year who had worked in a firm was between 15 and 20 per cent; ten years later, the proportion was between 25 and 35 per cent. Whereas a young *inspecteur des finances* in 1968 could expect to stay sixteen years on average in his or her administration, this period had dropped to seven years by 1994.

The visibility of senior civil servants at the head of publicly owned, soon-to-be-privatised, or privatised businesses has become more pronounced since the 1980s because of the number of individuals involved; because the firms involved, even when they are still in the public sector, can no longer be viewed as extensions of the state; because their integration into the world economy gives their heads an international profile; and because some have been involved in spectacular crashes, with more than a scent, in some cases, of corruption.

Of the boards of major French groups in 2000, 45 per cent (rising to 71 per cent for Société Générale, 80 per cent for Elf and 100 per cent for Vivendi), were *polytechniciens* or *énarques*; of the 290 *inspecteurs des finances* in 2002, 122 had senior positions in the private sector. Some of these have performed respectably: Michel Pébereau (BNP-Paribas), Daniel Bouton (Société Générale), Louis Schweitzer (Renault), Henri de Castries (Axa insurance), Jean-Marc Espalioux (Accor hotels), or Marc Tessier (France-Télévisions) have turned in honourable results for their firms, and sometimes better (though it is noticeable that no French banks are among the world's top ten).

Others, especially *inspecteurs des finances*, did spectacularly less well. François Heilbronner lost 6 billion euros for the GAN insurance group between 1986 and 1994, Chirac's school friend Jacques Friedmann a more modest 300 million euros at UAP from 1993 to 1997 (UAP was then taken over by Axa). Georges Bonin lost 1.7 billion euros as the head of the Crédit Foncier de France (the bank was a casualty of the liberalisation of the economy, since over decades it had lived from commissions on state aids distributed, but Bonin had done little to end the extreme archaism of its management). These losses were dwarfed, in the mid-1990s, by the crash of Haberer's still-nationalised Crédit Lyonnais, which only survived thanks to three salvage plans and contributions from the taxpayer totalling 16 billion euros. Michel Bon resigned from France-Télécom in November 2002 leaving a deficit of 20.7 billion euros (the equivalent of the total state budget for housing, infrastructure and transport), a total debt of 70 billion euros and a share value which had fallen from 27.7 euros at the firm's partial flotation in 1997 to 6 euros in September 2002. The same autumn saw the departure of Jean-Marie Messier, an *inspecteur des finances* who had discovered the virtues of capitalism when handling privatisations in Balladur's *cabinet* in the 1980s, from the water-to-media group Vivendi Universal, leaving 60 billion euros of debt and shares which had also lost three-quarters of their value. Six months later, Pierre Bilger left the heavy engineering firm Alstom; its shares, valued at 31.25 euros when floated in 1988, were selling at 1.5 euros in March 2003.

This succession of failures not only demonstrated that *inspecteurs des finances* were not always very good at business (significantly, almost no non-French firms hire them), but also raised questions about collusion within the French elite. Thus Jean-Yves Haberer and the officials in the Bank of France and the Treasury division of the Finance Ministry who should have monitored his activities at Crédit Lyonnais more closely were all *inspecteurs des finances* who had previously worked closely together at the Trésor division of the Finance Ministry. Thus, too, the Commission des Opérations en Bourse (an *inspection* preserve since 1984) failed to observe that Messier was illegally using money earmarked for investments in public water concessions to cover losses on property deals. Such episodes occasionally led to the courts: in 2002, one *inspecteur des finances* in eight was involved in a judicial investigation of some sort. These events, however, are in some ways of secondary importance next to what was perhaps the most disturbing of all French scandals of the 1990s, involving the (formerly) state-owned oil company Elf and a complex web of corruption, money-laundering and political fixing that drew in Elf managers, senior civil servants, French politicians of both Right and Left, and African heads of state. Elf's unfinished business was still dragging through the French courts in 2005. Both this and the Crédit Lyonnais episode went some way to delegitimising the interlocking elites formerly identified with the successes of the post-war interventionist model; by 1995, 40 per cent of respondents to one SOFRES survey considered that France's elites were 'totally bankrupt'.

The adventures in the private sector of senior civil servants, especially the elite of the elite, should not obscure the fact that most – 81 per cent of the 5,000 or so *énarques* active in 1999 – continued to serve the state. But if part, at least, of the administrative elite was increasingly seduced by the charms of managing the private sector, it proved comparatively immune to the attractions of management within the administration itself; indeed, management per se is not a skill imparted at ÉNA. Luc Rouban's research into the attitudes of civil servants towards the adoption, within the administration, of skills imported from the private sector has shown that members of the *grands corps* were the most likely to be indifferent or even hostile to such changes and to see them as irrelevant to administrative skills and norms built up over decades or centuries. That lack of interest at the top goes some way to explain the slow pace of change, despite a rapidly changing context, in the ranks of the administration.

The rank and file: reform

Every developed state has faced the challenge, since the 1980s, of making its public services more cost-effective and more responsive to the complex and unpredictable demands emanating from civil society. The palette of measures from which most have selected their responses bears the label New Public Management. NPM may include management by objectives, contracts and targets (and the use of audits to verify their achievement); the formulation of performance charters and service standards, with the possibility of redress for users in the event of failure to achieve them; the use of information technology to strip out middle-management jobs and improve inter-service co-ordination; the deconcentration of executive tasks into independent agencies run on private-sector lines; the market testing of divisions and agencies, and its potential corollary, public–private partnerships or even the concession of core public services to private firms under more or less rigorous public supervision. Two essential principles underlie NPM: first, that as in the private sector, the cost and effectiveness of any given activity could and should be evaluated; second, that benefits, in particular greater flexibility in service delivery, will accrue if the state manages to be more of a regulator or facilitator and less of a doer.

French governments have not been oblivious to such ideas. As early as 1969, Chaban-Delmas proposed a type of management by objectives in the form of 'progress contracts' with public-sector firms and public services (he deeply shocked traditional

Gaullists, who took the view that such contracts placed the state on an equal footing with its own employees, and thus on a sure road to decadence). After the Left's heavy recruiting, under a Communist minister for public services, between 1981 and 1983, the Socialists committed themselves, from 1984, to public-sector 'modernisation', in particular by experimenting with contracts in relations between central government and the local and regional authorities, recently granted new powers under decentralisation. Between 1986 and 1988 the right-wing ministers Camille Cabana and Hervé de Charette concocted ambitious neo-liberal reforms, though these were prudently shelved. But between 1988 and 1991 the Rocard government engaged in perhaps the most ambitious programme of public-sector reform yet attempted under the Fifth Republic. Promising the renewal of public services via a transition 'from a procedural administration to a responsible administration', Rocard required modernisation programmes from each minister, and sought to devolve administrative and budgetary responsibility, to buy in management and professional training from the private sector and to place customer service at the centre of reforms. The Rocard programme did achieve successes in some areas: the postal and telecommunications sectors were thoroughly restructured, while observers like Luc Rouban or Lionel Chaty found that branches of the core administration responded positively to unfamiliar notions like responsibility centres and quality circles. Although it fell victim to Rocard's fall and to the financial constraints of the early 1990s, the programme began a dynamic. After Rocard, reform might be slow, discontinuous, messy and punctuated by confrontation between political actors and interest groups within the administration (which the interest groups often won), but it never fell off the agenda. Broad initiatives in the 1990s included the Citizen's Charter *à la française* drawn up by Rocard's successor Édith Cresson shortly before her enforced resignation in 1992, and Balladur's plans to 'reform the state', based on the highly ambitious Picq report, a shopping-list of measures (better training in customer reception, planned training periods, shorter administrative response times), but which lacked overall vision and the means of implementation.

Some of the more innovative developments have taken place in the articulation between central and local government. Under the *contrats de ville*, for example, ministries and local authorities define a global plan for an urban area, taking in such domains as urban development, education and training, employment, health and culture. The Education Ministry, the biggest employer in France (1.3 million of France's public servants, a million of them in the schools system and the rest in the tertiary sector) has also been targeted for reform, notably by Jospin's Education Minister Claude Allègre. Allègre sought to give the ministry's field services across France (the *académies*) greater financial autonomy, with globalised budgets; to decentralise the complex procedures for moving staff between schools; and to demolish some of the more rigid barriers within the ministry (for example, between divisions dealing with primary and secondary schooling). It is now common practice for contracts to set out objectives agreed mutually between the ministry in Paris and its field services, and at a lower level between the *académies* and schools, and for each school to have to develop its own project, in liaison with local authorities as well as the *académie*.

More generally, the dynamic of reform is likely to be maintained by three factors: budgetary constraints which no government will escape; the window of opportunity afforded as large numbers of public servants retire between 2005 and 2015; and the major reforms to budget procedures introduced from 2005 (see Chapter 6, p. 163), which should afford Deputies and Senators a clearer idea of the real cost of public-sector programmes.

The rank and file: rigidities

If the process of reform has changed the working lives of many of France's public servants, the *fonction publique* as a whole remains recognisably the same entity, with many of the same rigidities, as in the 1970s. State employees with the status of *fonction-naires* still enjoy, *de facto* if not *de jure*, a lifetime guarantee of employment, aside from a few cases annually of professional misconduct. The number of *fonctionnaires* continued to rise under Jospin, by about 120,000, and even under Raffarin, though by a much more modest 4,500 in 2003; they are expected to drop by some 17,500 in 2005 thanks to the non-replacement of departing staff. Recruitment procedures remain based on general competitive examinations rather than aptitude tests for specific jobs; appraisal and reward structures favour rigorous equality of treatment between personnel at the same grade, and promotion on seniority, regardless of performance. Behind the façade of a unified public service, divisions between *corps* remain, among the rank and file as much as at the top. The 25,000 employees of France's prison service are divided into fifteen *corps*, the 18,000 staff of the Culture Ministry into forty, and France's 5,000 university librarians into seven. Different training, qualifications and career structures of the various *corps* hinder mobility within and between ministries, as do the different bonus systems, vital complements to what are often low basic wages. The drawbacks and rigidities of centralisation, in other words, are not compensated by any very notable responsiveness to the centre.

These rigidities are important because they make it hard to transfer limited resources where they are most needed. The needs in some areas are enormous. The Labour Inspectorate, for example, has a staff of 900 to cover the health and safety of some 14 million private-sector workers. France is the only country in Europe where the annual cost of a university student (6,590 euros) is less than that of a high-school pupil (7,880 euros). Some of the old 'regalian' functions of the state have been relentlessly squeezed: the judicial system is clogged, the diplomatic service subjected to cuts which hamper the ambition of successive governments for France to play a world role (France's diplomats even went on strike for a day in 2004). As a result, at least in part, of underfunding, the *politique de la ville* has so far met with limited success in its attempt to salvage France's worst suburban housing estates from crime, poverty, drugs and (most recently) Muslim extremism. The research staff who demonstrated early in 2004 were fighting low pay and staffing cuts in what government officially considers a key area for France's future.

By contrast, surpluses may at least be surmised in the Agriculture Ministry, where employment rose by 17 per cent, from 28,000 to 32,850, between 1970 and 1998, a period when two-thirds of farm jobs were lost; or in the Industry Ministry, which grew by a quarter as a fifth of industrial jobs disappeared. The Finance Ministry, privileged through its direct control of revenue and spending, has become a byword for arcane and often expensive practices concocted without reference to either its political masters or its administrative controlling bodies. Ghislaine Ottenheimer has observed that in 1999, the Bank of France employed a total staff of 15,918, compared with 2,700 at the Bank of England. With the switch to the euro that year, the Bank of France's mission might be considered to have ended; it was therefore given the task – for which it was not obviously suited – of assessing requests for assistance from over-indebted households. Meanwhile the Bank's Monetary Policy Committee went on meeting regularly, with generous allowances for its members but nothing to decide, well into 2002. The assessment and collection of taxes is divided (except for large firms, whose political clout has secured them a one-stop service) between the 90,000 employees of the Tax Directorate (which calculates all taxes, and collects VAT and wealth tax) and the 55,000 staff of the Public Accounts Directorate (which collects income tax and corporation tax – as well as local taxes, which are then redistributed to local authorities); the computer systems of the two are not integrated. Not even the Ministry's impressive communications service (680 staff) can quite hide the fact that this is one of Europe's most costly tax systems to administer. Finance Minister Sautter's attempt to reform it in 2000 provoked a strike which saw managers locked in their offices and files thrown out of windows, before Sautter resigned and his successor Fabius abandoned the project. Even Francis Mer, who came to his post as Raffarin's first finance minister (of four in the three years after his appointment) imbued with the private-sector practices of the Sacilor steel firm (and the irreverance for finance of a *polytechnicien*) stayed away from this explosive area, though he did undertake a number of less spectacular but useful reforms, including clear targets for services to taxpayers.

The fate of the Sautter reforms is far from unique. His colleague Claude Allègre also lost his job in the spring of 2000 as a result of union opposition to his plans for changes to teaching methods and school governance and plans to decentralise the employment of technical staff. Five years earlier, Juppé's attempt to reform public-sector pensions had led to the strike wave of late 1995 and the terminal discredit of his government. Raffarin sought to draw the lessons of these experiences in his own government's reform projects, which included modifications to the 35-hour week (for all wage-earners), the raising to forty years of the pensions contribution requirement for public-sector workers and restrictions on the right of patients to consult medical specialists without the intermediary of a general practitioner. In each case he proceeded with limited objectives, went through the motions of consulting unions (as Juppé did not) and kept concessions in reserve to buy off or split opposition. On the other hand, he kept away from the most explosive areas, like his minister Mer: the special pension systems for groups such as rail drivers, for example, have been left untouched ever since Juppé's setbacks. Possibly Raffarin's patient and cautious approach is the only one possible, but his critics claim that its scope is not of a measure with the size and urgency of problems such as France's pensions overhang or the widening deficit of public health insurance. And Raffarin still managed to provoke a wave of discontent among public-sector workers that spread to other groups in the spring of 2005 and set a climate that favoured the no vote at the referendum of 29 May.

The failure, near-failure, or half-success of so many relatively mild attempts at reform contrasts sharply with the implementation of considerably more brutal programmes in Britain and the United States, and suggests structural rather than merely circumstantial causes. Seven can be cited. The first is the industrial power of a workforce that is all but impossible to sack, with a level of unionisation, at nearly 20 per cent, that is four to five times higher than in France's private sector, and willing to strike to defend established pay and working conditions: in six out of the seven years from 1995 to 2001, over 55 per cent of working days lost through strike action were in the *fonction publique*. The second is cultural. It is not just that France's public services continue to enjoy a high level of legitimacy, despite criticisms levelled at one or another of them. It is that this legitimacy extends to a certain *model* of public service, including uniformity of provision and thus a central role for the state, and the unrestricted right to strike. Even the suggestion that some public-service workers might be required by law to provide a 'minimum service' in case of strikes has received lukewarm support in the polls. This capital of sympathy for 'French-style public services' was shown dramatically in the high levels of approval for the 1995 strikes, and for a succession of actions since then involving railwaymen, teachers, hospital workers, public research staff. Third, the legitimacy of the public services is backed by law, in the form of a protective civil service statute. Radical reform of France's public services would therefore require the political battle entailed by primary legislation. Fourth, under these conditions no government has been inclined to take the political risk of a radical reform – or even of pressing a moderate reform to its full extent. The Left always risks its own core electorate (public-sector employees have been consistently more left-leaning than their private-sector counterparts). The Right in government was never, from 1981 till 2002, more than two years away from an election – with the exception of the hapless Juppé. Fifth, the political reluctance of national governments is often reinforced by that of local politicians (who may also be national ones) when faced with threats to local public services. Sixth, it is extraordinarily hard to get agreements that will satisfy all parties. This is not only because public-service unions are attached to their own entrenched positions within ministries, but also because they are divided: thus one Finance Ministry union could claim, in March 2000, that its rival union in the tax division 'has our destruction as its main aim, and is ready to accept any structural change in order to achieve that aim'. Finally, reforms have rarely had the full and enthusiastic backing of the public-service elite, many of whom have shown little interest in public-service management. All too often the *énarques* imposed changes in working practices on subordinates without applying them in their own *cabinets*.

For the public this means that the most hard-pressed services – often in poorer areas that need them most – remain underfunded. For the public servants themselves, it means that posts offering working conditions of bucolic languor (in some of the quieter rural tax offices) coexist with others requiring superhuman resistance to stress (school-teachers in the rougher Paris suburbs, nurses in many Parisian hospitals), with little if any pay differential. Staff shortages have been palliated by recruitment of personnel on temporary contracts without *fonctionnaire* status (their numbers exceeded a million in 2000, of whom 700,000 were direct state employees); and low pay by bonuses awarded on the basis of arcane and often spurious criteria (and amounting to over half the total remuneration of some Finance Ministry officials). Both expedients may be useful short-term correctives, but risk damaging both quality of service and transparency over time.

Concluding remarks

Élie Cohen has argued that France's industrial decline from the mid-1970s on derived partly from the fact that economic tools that had served the nation well during the *trente glorieuses – grands projets, dirigisme*, a permanent tax on savings through inflation, periodic devaluations – became useless, indeed positive handicaps, in a changed economic environment. A comparable argument could be attempted for the administration and the public services. As France, with its long history of political instability and conflict, underwent a period of unprecedented social transformation during the *trente glorieuses*, their contribution to the nation's cohesion was remarkable. Education offered upward social mobility for many (some of whom would realise that mobility within the public sector itself). A formerly rural population was housed in towns (with some delay) and given access to an unprecedented array of public services. Growing private affluence was matched, on the whole, with rising standards in such areas as public transport or health or cultural facilities. A technocratic elite enjoyed undeniable social prestige and significant political power thanks both to traditions stretching back to the *ancien régime* and Napoleon and to a more recent record of success.

The mission of national cohesion has been less obviously well performed in the more difficult times since the mid-1970s. Three failures stand out. First, neither the education system – despite its expansion – nor the administration provide the same opportunities for social mobility: at the outset of the twenty-first century, adult illiteracy stood at 12 per cent, 160,000 unqualified men and women were entering the labour market every year, youth unemployment stood at 26 per cent and poverty among young people at 17 per cent. An underfunded university system continues to fail half its annual intake at the end of their first year of studies – and even after such a ferocious weed-out, still produces graduates whom employers do not rush to hire. The administration itself recruits overqualified staff, who block the opportunities available to those of more modest educational achievement. Second, the desperate state of many of France's suburban public housing estates, where many public services operate with extreme difficulty or not at all, bear witness both to the longer-term costs of quick remedies to the post-war housing crisis and to the failure of public action to remedy the equally striking failures of the market. Third, both elite and rank-and-file public servants have suffered a more or less severe crisis of identity. For the elite, this has been linked to politicisation and the effects of alternation in power; to the very much more uncertain role of a *grand commis de l'État* in an open liberal economy and an integrated Europe; and to the corrosive effects of scandals in which senior public servants have appeared as self-interested, cliquish, incompetent and immune to sanction. The rank and file, accustomed to the simple delivery of services in conditions defined either unilaterally by the state or in liaison with a single client group, faced a new range of demands relating to quality of service, relations with user groups and efficiency – and in a context of budgetary uncertainty. The periodic calls from (mostly but not exclusively right-wing) experts and politicians for a reduction in the number of public servants may appear as positively insulting to the hard-pressed suburban schoolteacher, the nurse in a Parisian casualty ward, or the employee of a rail network which has lost two-thirds of its staff in fifty years. In this context, the defence of *avantages acquis* – the particular terms of employment that make life more tolerable for specific groups of public servants – may acquire the status of a struggle to protect public services generally, or even the Republic itself. That link was made particularly strongly during the campaign for the 2005 referendum on the European constitutional treaty, considered by its opponents to represent a direct threat to the French public-service tradition.

Not that the 'output' of France's administration and public services is particularly poor. In many ways and in many contexts they prevent public squalor from coexisting with private affluence. They often offer standards of medical care and public transport that can make their English counterparts appear barely civilised. The French remain attached to the public services they encounter from day to day, even when they consider that abstractions such as 'the state' or 'the administration' do not always operate in their interests. France still provides one of Europe's ablest groups of top civil servants. But France's public sector is capable of slipping. The death of fully 15,000 old people, many of them in the care of public retirement homes, in the summer heatwave of 2003 cast a shadow over the reputation of France's health system (as well as triggering a dive in the Raffarin government's ratings from which it never recovered). And it is increasingly expensive: one report by the Commissariat au Plan in 1999 claimed that by 2015 an extra 26 billion euros would have to be found annually simply to cover future pensions plus the long-term costs of the Crédit Lyonnais and SNCF debts. This limits the room both for tax cuts (promised but massively underdelivered by Chirac after 2002) and for improvements in funding for priority areas such as research.

Private-sector methods are not invariably appropriate for public services. But it is clear that the size and structure of France's administration and public services are and will remain a pressing policy issue. Large-scale and productive (and accepted) public-sector reform appears, however, to demand an unusual window of opportunity: an election-free political outlook; strong economic growth to release the extra funding necessary to ease any transition; widespread public agreement on the necessity of reforms; as well as the co-operation both of the civil service elite and of the rank-and-file unions. This seems an unlikely prospect. But the early twenty-first century appears to offer as good a chance for renewal as any – not least because nearly half of all the state's employees are due to retire by 2015. Whether this opportunity can be used productively will be a major stake both of Chirac's presidency and of his successor's. No domestic issue is likely to be more important for French governments of the early twenty-first century; and none will be more pregnant with political dangers.

Further reading

Armstrong, J., *The European Administrative Elite*, Princeton, NJ, Princeton University Press, 1973.
Birnbaum, P., *Les sommets de l'État: essai sur l'elite du pouvoir en France*, Paris, Seuil, 1977.
Bodiguel, J.-L. and Rouban, L., *Le fonctionnaire détrôné?*, Paris, Presses de la Fondation Nationale des Sciences Politiques, 1991.
Bourdieu, P., *La noblesse d'État: grandes écoles et esprit de corps*, Paris, Éditions de Minuit, 1987.
Brachet, P., *Du commandement au management: l'administration française entre souveraineté et service public*, Paris, Publisud, 1995.
Chagnollaud, D., *Le premier des ordres. Les hauts fonctionnaires, XVIIIe–XXe siècles*, Paris, Fayard, 1991.
Chaty, L., *L'administration face au management: projets de service et centres de responsabilité dans l'administration française*, Paris, L'Harmattan, 1997.
Cohen, E., *L'état brancardier: politiques du déclin industriel (1974–1984)*, Paris, Calmann-Lévy, 1989.
Cole, A., 'The *Service Public* under stress', *West European Politics*, 22(4), October 1999, pp. 166–84.
Cour des Comptes, *La fonction publique de l'État: Rapport public particulier*, Paris, Les éditions des Journaux officiels, 1999.
de Baecque, F. and Quermonne, J.-L. (eds), *Administration et politique sous la Cinquième République*, Paris, Presses de la Fondation Nationale des Sciences Politiques, 1981.
Duhamel, O., 'Les Français et l'État', in SOFRES, *L'état de l'opinion 2000*, Paris, Seuil, 2000, pp. 137–44.
Dupuy, F. and Thoenig, J.-C., *L'administration en miettes*, Paris, Fayard, 1995.
Esprit, no. 236, October 1997, 'Les elites de la République sur la sellette'.
Fauroux, R. and Spitz, B. (eds), *Notre État*, Paris, Robert Laffont, 2001.
Fauroux, R. and Spitz, B. (eds), *État d'Urgence*, Paris, Robert Laffont, 2004.
Gohin, O., *Institutions administratives*, 3rd edition, Paris, Librairie Générale du Droit et de la Jurisprudence, 1998.
Julliard, J., *La faute aux elites*, Paris, Gallimard, 1997.

Kessler, M.-C., *Les grands corps de l'État*, Paris, Presses de la Fondation Nationale des Sciences Politiques, 1986.

Olivennes, D., 'Les Français et l'État', in SOFRES, *L'état de l'opinion 1997*, Paris, Seuil, 1997, pp. 149–59.

Ottenheimer, G., *Les intouchables: grandeur et décadence d'une caste: l'Inspection des finances*, Paris, Albin Michel, 2004.

Pfister, T., *La république des fonctionnaires*, Paris, Seuil, 1990.

Pouvoirs, no. 40, 1987, 'Des fonctionnaires politisés?'; no. 53, 1990, 'Le ministère des Finances'.

Rainaud, J.-M., *La crise du service public français*, Paris, Presses Universitaires de France, 1999.

Rey, H., *La peur des banlieues*, Paris, Presses de Sciences Po, 1996.

Rouban, L., *Le pouvoir anonyme: les mutations de l'État à la française*, Paris, Presses de la Fondation Nationale des Sciences Politiques, 1994.

Rouban, L., 'Les énarques en cabinets, 1984–1996', *Cahiers du CEVIPOF*, 17, Paris, 1997.

Rouban, L., *La fin des technocrates?*, Paris, Presses de Sciences Po, 1997.

Rouban, L., *The French Civil Service*, Paris, La Documentation Française, 1998.

Rouban, L., 'La politisation des fonctionnaires en France: Obstacle ou nécessité?', *Revue française d'administration publique*, no. 86, April–June 1998, pp. 167–82.

Sadran, P., *Le système administratif français*, Paris, Montchrestien, 1992.

Schifres, M., *La désertion des énarques: du pantouflage en République*, Paris, Stock, 1999.

Schrameck, O., *Les cabinets ministériels*, Paris, Dalloz, 1995.

Suleiman, E., *Politics, Power and Bureaucracy in France: The Administrative Elite*, Princeton, NJ, Princeton University Press, 1974.

Suleiman, E., *Elites in French Society: The Politics of Survival*, Princeton, NJ, Princeton University Press, 1978.

Suleiman, E., *Les ressorts cachés de la réussite française*, Paris, Seuil, 1995.

Suleiman, E. and Mendras, H. (eds), *Le recrutement des elites en Europe*, Paris, La Découverte, 1995.

Thomas, Y., *Histoire de l'administration*, Paris, La Découverte, 1995.

11 The state and the pressure groups

The political culture of Jacobinism, as inherited from the French Revolution, has even less use for interest groups than for parties. Jacobins opposed the narrow, 'particular' (and inevitably selfish) interests represented by the groups to the 'general interest' which only the state could incarnate. The Le Chapelier Law of 1791, whose effective ban on such organisations as trade unions was confirmed in 1810 by Napoleon's penal code, was the legislative expression of the Jacobin view (Napoleon's code also helpfully banned gatherings of over twenty people). It was a view that contrasted with those of the more liberal 'Anglo-Saxons', less ready to attribute god-like qualities to the state and more inclined to limit its role to holding the ring between competing private interests whose social role was viewed as broadly beneficial. Even the much more liberal laws of 1884 and 1901, which conceded the principle of freedom of association, placed groups firmly within a framework defined by the state. The smallest *club de pétanque* still refers to itself as an *Association loi 1901*, while larger groups may apply to the Conseil d'État for the privileges associated with being recognised as *d'utilité publique*.

Not that government in France has remained impervious to the blandishments of well-organised interests. Under the Fourth Republic, for example, the home distillers' association was blamed for its energetic (and successful) defence of its members' right to destroy the livers of thousands of alcoholic French people each year, while the powerful colonial lobby was certainly guilty of encouraging the régime's more viciously inept policies and of obstructing the more enlightened ones in Indo-China and North Africa. In the light of these experiences, it was logical that as De Gaulle and Debré set out to 'restore the state' after 1958, they should make a point of affirming the Fifth Republic's independence from the 'feudal forces' which, in Debré's view, had colonised the Fourth: a law to phase out home distilling was passed as early as 1959. De Gaulle rejected any claim of groups to *determine* policy, on the ground that even the most representative of them 'is nevertheless, from the legal point of view, bereft of authority and political responsibility' – unlike the state, which is 'an instrument of decision, action, ambition, expressing and serving only the national interest'. At the same time, as numerous events showed (notably his reinforcement of the the Fourth Republic's Conseil Économique as the Conseil Économique et Social, and his ill-fated attempt to incorporate this body into a reformed upper chamber of parliament in the 1969 referendum), he readily conceded the right of groups to be *consulted*.

In doing so, de Gaulle was acknowledging that some form of exchange between groups and the state is essential to the working of a modern democracy. Groups look to government to provide a variety of goods: direct material benefits (subsidies for farmers or miners, pay rises for teachers, or protection or tax breaks for business); non-material policy benefits which may have substantial material consequences (such as rights at the workplace for unions, or tighter or looser regulation of health and safety, or competition, or environmental practices); or (what is normally a precondition for the other two) simple recognition as a valid interlocutor. Successful groups also, however, offer something in exchange. Businesses seeking an economic environment favourable to themselves claim that this contributes to job creation and general prosperity. Groups may also argue that only they, and not civil servants or ministerial *cabinets*, command the expertise necessary to ensure the technical viability of a particular complex policy, or the grass-roots political knowledge to assess the extent of opposition to a proposal. They may thus claim that the government needs their co-operation for the successful implementation of its policies. Groups able to cause disruption, notably in the transport sector, suggest that their own contentment is a condition of 'social peace'. All groups may offer political support to governments, and money to parties (which may or may not be legal) and to individual politicians (which is almost invariably not). Above all, perhaps, governments in modern democracies have looked to groups to help legitimate their policies within civil society.

In any democracy, therefore, dialogue between government and at least some groups is intense and continuous. Its forms vary: informal contacts between group leaders and politicians (who may themselves be former group representatives, from business, farming or trade unions), or between group leaders and civil servants (a frequent form of dialogue for established groups); formal negotiations through official consultative committees; or, for 'outsider' groups with no access to government, street demonstrations, strikes or other forms of direct action. Which patterns of exchange are most common varies between political systems. The nature of these relations can reveal much, not only about the degree of integration of groups within a given system but also about the location of power within the state's institutions.

Analysing the relationship (or rather, relationships) between the state and the groups is, however, fraught with difficulty. There is, first of all, the problem of where groups stop and parties start. The Greens have evolved since the 1970s from a pressure group into a party. More surprisingly, the shooting lobby has been fighting both European and regional elections as Chasse, Pêche, Nature, Traditions (CPNT) since 1989. Second, pressure on government may be exerted not just by groups or associations, but also by individual firms. Renault, for example, with 44,500 employees, eight assembly plants and ten components plants in France, as well as 5,000 suppliers depending on its orders, hardly needs to belong to an association to talk to ministers or civil servants; nor does Serge Dassault, head not only of the aircraft firm that bears his father's name but also of Socpresse, which owns *L'Express* and *Le Figaro* among other titles. Third, networks such as the Freemasons have been seen by parts of the French press as more influential than duly constituted groups. To some extent this is the stuff of conspiracy theory. But the Masons *were* quite openly influential under the Third Republic: 155 Masonic lodges participated in their own right in the first Radical Party Congress in 1901. Under the Fifth Republic they have been active in the PS (including men as close to Mitterrand as Roland Dumas and Charles Hernu, plus as many as 100 Socialist Deputies in 1986) as well as the RPR, and, in too many cases, as participants in the Elf scandal. Other networks remain an important, if ill-defined, part of group activity. Chapter 10 has outlined the significance of those linked to the *grandes écoles* and *grands corps*. Research has also indicated the existence of networks as varied as those of former *résistants*, former activists of the far Left or far Right, Left Catholics and *proctériens* (former Procter & Gamble (France) managers).

Fourth, the shifting boundaries between the state and the private sector since 1981, and the interpenetration between the two, have posed particular problems. When Ambroise Roux, former head of the Compagnie Générale d'Électricité, created the Association Française des Entreprises Privées (AFEP) in 1982, he underlined the fact that most of the big firms represented in the main employers' organisation, the Conseil National du Patronat Français (CNPF), were now nationalised, and thus in a sense part of the state. But a frequent pattern under the Fifth Republic has been a complex pattern of cross-shareholdings between public and private business, whether resulting from the acquisition of shares in private firms before 1981 or, more recently, from partial privatisations (France Télécom or Air France, for example) under the Jospin government. The fifth problem in analysing state–group relations follows from the fourth: pressure groups are also constituted by parts of the state machine, which defend their own corporate interests in competition or rivalry with other parts. The French nuclear energy programme of the 1970s was strongly backed by the nationalised electricity industry (EDF), the Commissariat à l'Énergie Atomique, the privately owned Creusot-Loire company, and the Communist-dominated trade union, the CGT. It was opposed, unsuccessfully, by the nationalised coal industry, the newly created state agency responsible for solar energy and the Socialist-leaning trade union, the CFDT. Public-sector banks and petroleum companies were also, in practice, powerful actors enjoying great autonomy and a capacity to pressure the state they were supposed to serve. The financial scandal of Crédit Lyonnais and the institutionalised corruption of Elf suggest that they were also resistant to the most elementary control by their main shareholder.

The sixth problem in studying state–group relations concerns the Europeanisation and internationalisation of the French economy. In many decisions, neither the French state nor the groups may be the ultimate arbiter. Farm policies are fixed in Brussels by the EU, or in Geneva by the World Trade Organisation. Employment prospects in the Alpine town of Annecy depend to a large degree on Gillette, a foreign multinational. In these circumstances a complex triangular relationship replaces the traditional dual one: the state is both a pressure group and a pressured group.

A final difficulty concerns the general approach to the subject of government–group relations. There has been, in France, an important Marxist school which produced valuable empirical research in areas relating to urban development and to the internationalisation of the French industrial and capital markets. Its theoretical underpinnings, however, have tended to the simplistic. Stressing the role of the state in preserving the long-term interests of the bourgeoisie and ensuring the optimal social conditions for the development of capitalism, the Marxists left little clue as to the behaviour of individual political actors, the diversity of groups within the bourgeois and working-class camps or the variations in policy outcomes within France. Similar shortcomings hamper the functionalist approach, in which the actions of the state and its agents are interpreted as a series of responses to needs – generally the needs to balance and to integrate divergent interests in the name of social harmony or consensus. The functionalists resemble the Marxists in that their overarching theory largely fails to apprehend the awesome complexity of many political situations.

Within the literature on state–group relations in the Fifth Republic (which is still somewhat sparse, despite work by American scholars such as Wilson, Keeler, Ambler and Schmidt, or French ones such as Barthélemy, Mouriaux, Offerlé or Weber), four general models of state–group relations in France deserve closer attention. For the sake of convenience they may be called the domination-crisis model, the endemic conflict model, the corporatist model and the pluralist model. Each has supporters who root their analyses in aspects of French political behaviour as well as in a general theoretical approach; each has some justification; but each is, ultimately, partial and inadequate in its explanations. Taken together, though, their analyses help to portray some of the complex reality and to answer some of the problems raised above.

The domination-crisis model

This model is largely associated with Michel Crozier and Stanley Hoffmann, who together, though from somewhat different viewpoints, reformulated in a more systematic fashion the views and prejudices of a long line of observers stretching back, at the least, to the great nineteenth-century political observer Alexis de Tocqueville. Those views are anchored in an analysis of French attitudes to authority and change, and may be briefly summarised as follows.

- The French fear face-to-face relations, and very readily have recourse to impersonal, highly formalised, distant and hierarchical rules imposed from above to govern social intercourse: only such rules are likely to prevent arbitrariness. Hence a powerful and centralised bureaucracy exists to enforce the rules.
- French political culture is characterised by both 'limited authoritarianism' and 'potential insurrection against authority', and the French oscillate between a normal servility towards authority and sporadic rebellions against it. Closely associated with this idea is the Tocquevillian view, echoed by Michel Poniatowski and many others, that 'France is a profoundly conservative country which dreams of revolution but rejects reform'.
- In a highly individualistic, atomised and anomic society, associative life is weak, for a French person fears the loss of liberty and individuality which results from belonging to groups. Those groups that do exist are fragmented, egotistical and generally anomic, and reject the principle of fruitful interdependence. In other countries, groups bargain and compromise with each other and with the state. Each French group, on the other hand, ferociously defends its rights against other groups, and resists any attempts by the state to impose change which might be prejudicial to its acquired interests: the term *droits acquis* is one of the most emotive in the French language, approximating either to fundamental and intangible rights or to illegitimate and exorbitant privileges depending on who is using it.
- Since the groups defend the status quo, change within society must be imposed by the bureaucracy: there is thus a gulf between a modernising administration and its highly conservative *administrés*.

- The state is viewed with mistrust by the ill-organised groups, since it threatens to impinge upon their *droits acquis*. Authority must, therefore, be resisted. This 'perpetual resistance' to authority found philosophical justification in the interwar writings of Alain – the pseudonym of Émile Chartier – who told his countrymen to build themselves 'barricades' against the encroachment of the state: the first rule in the handbook of government, he contended, was 'heroic idleness'. The result of the unremitting and obscurantist resistance is stalemate – *La société bloquée*, as the title of Michel Crozier's influential 1970 book had it.

- The state authorities view the groups as 'delinquent communities' (Jesse Pitts), as 'subservient clients' (Jack Hayward), which may be treated with authoritarianism (because of their normal servility) and with contempt (because of their obscurantism). Yet their *droits acquis* must be respected, because of their predilection for revolt.

- In this political culture, dominated by fear, suspicion and a 'perpetual resistance to the ruling elites', change can be brought about to break the stalemate not by peaceful means but only by more or less violent upheavals. But these 'functionally innovative crises' which introduce reforms are then followed by long periods in which the traditional rules of the game reassert themselves. In the domination-crisis model, the state dominates the groups and imposes its directives upon them in authoritarian fashion. But, fearful of insurrection, it is unable to impose radical reforms except during a crisis.

The domination-crisis model: evidence in favour

There is evidence in plenty to support the points outlined above. Groups are often weak and divided; the state has often intervened in an authoritarian manner; there are examples of the defence of *droits acquis* resulting in stalemate; and France has had more than its share of dramatic social crises.

Weak groups

The weakness of French groups is best illustrated by their low membership density – that is, their inability to recruit more than a small proportion of their total potential membership. The most obvious case in point is trade unions. Their membership density under the Fifth Republic peaked in 1975, at a mere 24 per cent of the workforce, compared with over 50 per cent at the time in the UK, and over 80 per cent in some Scandinavian countries. By the late 1990s the figure in France had slipped to about 8 per cent, or roughly 2.5 million, where it has since stagnated. Some 60–70 per cent of all union members are in the remaining public enterprises or in the public services; large swathes of the private sector, by contrast, are virtually union-free, with half of all wage-earners lacking any union representation at all within their firms. Trade unions are an extreme case, but a far from unique one.

Fragmented groups

The fragmentation of French groups, often on political lines, has been a constant of French social life ever since secularising republicans set up their own parallel networks of self-help organisations to break what had been the Church's monopoly on social welfare. Among trade unions (Table 11.1), the leading position of the venerable Con-fédération Générale du Travail (CGT), founded in 1895 and dominated by Communists since 1945, has been contested by the vigorously anti-Communist Force Ouvrière (FO), which split off from it at the start of the Cold War; by the anarcho-syndicalist Con-fédération Nationale du Travail (CNT), which split from it in 1946, was little more than a *groupuscule* for decades, but claimed 10,000 members in 2005; by the Confédération Française Démocratique du Travail (CFDT, of left-wing Catholic inspiration, which deconfessionalised in 1964, backed the vogue for workers' self-management in the wake of May 1968, and was more or less close to the Socialists until Mitterrand's victory of 1981, when they distanced themselves from the left-wing government); by the Catholic Confédération Française des Travailleurs Chrétiens (CFTC, the union of Catholics wishing to maintain a confessional identity); by the now defunct Confédération Fran-çaise du Travail (CFT, the creature of the pre–1981 right-wing majorities) and, among managerial staff, by the Confédération Générale des Cadres (CGC). Agriculture is an unusual sector where membership density has traditionally been high, and relatively concentrated. The dominant organisation, the conservative Fédération Nationale des Syndicats des Exploitants Agricoles (FNSEA), claims a membership of 600,000, or over half of all farmers (and won 52.4 per cent of votes in the 2001 elections to Chambers of Agriculture): a lower density than for the British National Farmers' Union, where the figure is nearer 90 per cent, but still high for France. But it has faced challenges not only from the Centre National des Jeunes Agriculteurs (CNJA, which the FNSEA absorbed in 1961), but also from groups on the Right and Left. The former have included the Fédération Française de l'Agriculture (FFA), founded in 1969, and, since the early 1990s, the Coordination Rurale, close in many respects to the far Right, which won 12.5 per cent of votes at the 2001 Chambers of Agriculture elections. On the Left, the Communist-affiliated Mouvement de Défense de l'Exploitation Familiale (MODEF), was joined in 1987 by the ecology-minded Confédération Paysanne; these two movements, which have co-operated locally, together won 31 per cent of the vote in 2001. Even employers' organisations have lacked the unity associated with their counter-parts elsewhere. The MEDEF (Mouvement des Entreprises de France, called the Conseil National du Patronat Français (CNPF) until 1998), itself a very decentralised body, has an often uneasy relationship with its affiliate the Confédération Générale des Petites et Moyennes Entreprises (CGPME), which many smaller business people prefer,

Table 11.1 The strength of major trade unions in France

Union confederation	Results at elections to industrial tribunals (councils of prud'hommes) (% of votes cast)						Total members claimed
	1979	*1982*	*1987*	*1992*	*1997*	*2002*	*2004*
CGT	42.4	36.8	36.3	33.3	33.1	32.1	650,000
FO	17.4	17.7	20.4	20.4	20.5	18.3	800,000
CFDT	23.1	23.5	23.1	23.8	25.3	25.2	865,528
CFTC	6.9	8.4	8.3	8.5	7.5	9.7	250,000
CGC	5.1	9.6	7.4	6.9	5.9	7.0	140,000
Others	4.6	3.7	4.3	6.9	7.5	7.7	n/a

Sources: *Le Monde* (elections) membership figures are those declared by the unions to the European Trade Union Confederation; while figures for most unions are fairly reliable, independent estimates put the true membership of Force Ouvrière at under 400,000.

and has faced competition both from the more militant Syndicat National des Petites et Moyennes Industries (SNPMI), from the more or less extreme CID-UNATI, and from Ambroise Roux's AFEP. Comparable divisions can be observed among the professional middle classes. For example, while most doctors belong to the Confédération des Syndicats Médicaux Français, this organisation is divided between an apolitical majority and a socialist minority; in addition, a few wealthy consultants who initially refused to enter the social security system are members of the Fédération des Médecins de France, and a few left-wing general practitioners have joined the Syndicat de la Médecine Générale. Lawyers are divided between the left-wing Syndicat de la Magistrature, the moderate right-wing Union Syndicale des Magistrats and the Association Professionnelle des Magistrats, sympathetic to the hard Right. Regionalist and nationalist movements, too, are similarly fragmented. Even a sector such as former deportees to Germany during the Occupation possesses several groups, prone to competition if not to unseemly squabbles.

Moreover, these groups are themselves divided. Both trade unions and employers' groups are federations of local and sectoral organisations, each more or less attached to its own traditions and autonomy. The CGT is divided between the Communist majority and the Socialist-leaning minority (and, now, between old-style and new-style Communists); FO between an anti-Communist majority and a Trotskyist minority; the CFDT between realists and those still attached to the ideals of May 1968. The FNSEA, once described as a 'battleground of feudal warlords', faces obvious difficulties reconciling the interests of large and small farmers, of different regions, and of different types of product – though it is better than most groups at uniting its forces, at least against an outside threat. The MEDEF's leadership has often been divided between factions representing smaller and larger firms, and between more and less ideological stances vis-à-vis governments. The election of Laurence Parisot to its presidency in 2005 was remarkable not only because Parisot is a woman at the head of a traditionally male-dominated organisation, but also because, as head of the IFOP polling institute, she represents the service sector rather than the mining and manufacturing interests long at the heart of the *patronat*.

Nor has time, or the end of conflicts linked to the Cold War, done much to heal these divisions; quite the contrary. For example, the Fédération de l'Éducation Nationale (FEN) was an umbrella organisation which united the major teachers' unions (the Syndicat National des Instituteurs (SNI) for primary schools; the Syndicat National de l'Enseignement Secondaire (SNES) for the secondary sector; and the Syndicat National de l'Enseignement Supérieur (SNESup) for universities) and the vast majority of unionised teachers, independently of the CGT and the other big confederations, for nearly half a century after the Liberation. But the FEN split in 1992 between a majority that supported the Socialists and a Communist-leaning minority who left to form the Fédération Syndicale Unitaire (FSU) – which soon overtook the truncated FEN in support. Among mainstream unions, although the CGT has distanced itself from the Communists (Bernard Thibault, its secretary-general since 1997, is the first CGT chief since 1945 not to have any official position in the PCF) and FO has dropped its earlier links with right-wing parties, the rapprochement was limited to common action at largely symbolic events such as May Day rallies. And when the CFDT moved to a 'realist' line of negotiations with employers in the late 1980s, its militant minority departed to create a new union, SUD (Solidaires, Unitaires et Démocratiques); SUD members, often close to Trotskyist parties, are strong in key public-sector branches such as the railways and postal services. Another case of recent divisions is the anti-racist movement, which grew in the 1980s thanks to the challenge of the far Right and the coming of age of a class of second-generation immigrants. It remains divided between the old Ligue des Droits de l'Homme, founded at the time of the Dreyfus Affair; the Communist-linked Mouvement contre le Racisme et pour l'Amitié entre les Peuples (MRAP); SOS–Racisme, set up in 1984 with verbal and financial backing from President Mitterrand and still close to the Socialists; and the Trotskyist-led Ras l'Front – as well as smaller organisations connected to Socialist personalities or anarchist groups.

Such divisions not only reflect a lack of social cohesion; they also perpetuate it, and ensure that almost no group is able to aggregate the whole range of demands within its sector. Moreover, fragmentation often leads to increased verbal militancy, since several groups are competing for the same clientele. The gulf between the expectations raised by such militancy and the results delivered then engenders disillusion and a further weakening of the groups. For governments, the obvious consequences of such fragmentation are the absence, in most sectors, of a single, stable, representative negotiating partner, and the near-impossibility of reaching agreement on any given subject with the whole range of possible partners. Faced with this situation, ministers may resort to one of four strategies: to pick one sympathetic group as an 'official' partner and ignore the rest – which will almost certainly leave at least a substantial minority of groups in the cold; to play upon the divisions between groups in order to impose government measures – which may demobilise opposition, but is unlikely to win much positive support; to attempt to build a consensus, which is time-consuming and may not work; or to ignore groups altogether. Each of these strategies involves the risk that discontent will be turned into extra-institutional channels. May 1968 can be explained partly in terms of the choices of partners made by the Pompidou governments: not the Communist-leaning Union Nationale des Étudiants de France (UNEF), but a students' union, the Fédération Nationale des Étudiants de France (FNEF), that they had practically created themselves; not the CGT, but solidly pro-capitalist CFT, one-twentieth the size.

The authoritarian state

A more or less authoritarian policy-making style on the state's part has been noted by countless observers. Jack Hayward, and Vivien Schmidt after him, have referred to a 'heroic' style of policy-making, in which the state is an actor and initiator, and consultation with groups is limited or non-existent. 'Heroic' policy-making has a pedigree going back to Louis XIV's chief minister Colbert. In some areas, it was even possible under the Fourth Republic because the parliament conceded some of its financial powers to the planners. But the possibilities were greatly increased with the reinforcement of the executive after 1958. Most of de Gaulle's and Pompidou's industrial policy initiatives could be placed in the 'heroic' category. So could Barre's 1976 anti-inflation plan, a characteristic example of the iron fist in the mailed glove. So could the Socialists' 1982 nationalisations or, more recently, Juppé's 1995 social security plan, or the Jospin government's 35-hour week.

Société bloquée

The *société bloquée* in which groups frustrate change in the name of their own *droits acquis* is a convincing interpretation of at least some aspects of state–group relations in

France. The teaching unions' defeat of Education Minister Claude Allègre in the spring of 2000 is merely the most recent case in point (though to be fair to the teachers, they believed Allègre's reforms to be damaging to education as well as to themselves). The deeply hostile relations between most trade unions and much of business in France since 1945 were another facet of the same problem, and contrasted with the more co-operative behaviour prevalent across the Rhine.

Social crises

Dramatic social crises have marked France more than once under the Fifth Republic. The prime example is May 1968, which led directly to greater trade union rights and educational reforms (and was followed by a period of stifling and routine-ridden conservatism, as the reforms were whittled away by the employers and the academic establishment respectively). The runner-up is probably constituted by the December 1995 strikes (though these did serve to *block* reforms – Juppé's social security changes – which were obviously against the interests of the strikers, rather than furthering or facilitating any social advances). It is notable that neither of these crises was in any sense engineered by the trade unions. Rather, the strikes broke out more or less spontaneously, and often not even through the actions of union members, and the unions were then constrained to follow the movements, and to regain control of them as best they could – if more militant, grass-roots 'co-ordinations' had not got there first. For France is the land *par excellence* of the unforeseen and often unforeseeable mobilisation, not only of the usual suspects (students and farmers being regularly effervescent in their own different ways), but also of previously tranquil groups such as nurses in 1991 and the unemployed in 1998.

The domination-crisis model: objections

There is enough in the above to lend continued persuasiveness to the domination-crisis model, even more than a generation after its formulation. Yet it provides an incomplete, and at times misleading, view of the behaviour of the French, of the groups, of the state and of social crises in France.

The spread of associations

France's vibrant associative culture belies generalisations about the French 'fear of face-to-face contact'. American observers in the 1950s noted disapprovingly that the French were not 'joiners'; this is no longer the case. France at the start of the twenty-first century had between 800,000 and 1 million associations, with some 62,000 new ones being registered each year – three times the level of 1960. Total membership of associations in France – roughly 20 million, or 49 per cent of men and 40 per cent of women – is comparable to the European average. They mobilise as many as 12 million volunteers (for example, the 43,000 helpers who distributed some 66 million meals to the destitute for the Restos du Cœur charity in the winter of 2004–5) and have 1.5 million full-time or part-time employees. Certainly, membership of parties, trade unions and professional organisations accounted for a rather small proportion of the total, about a fifth (sporting clubs had perhaps twice as many members). Nevertheless, the flourishing of environmental movements, free radio stations, cultural associations of all kinds, and groups supporting the rights of immigrants, the unemployed, the homeless, women, AIDS victims and any number of humanitarian causes (Médecins sans Frontières being a notable example) suggests that French society is no longer as pathologically individualistic as the domination-crisis model claims.

Associations and innovation

The existence of progressive and innovative associations demonstrates that the state has no monopoly on modernisation and reform. The CNJA, for example, led by the charismatic Michel Debatisse, played a crucial role in the modernisation of French farming in the 1950s and 1960s. More recently, the MEDEF launched an aggressive campaign in 2000 to renegotiate the whole basis of France's social security system. This was a highly controversial undertaking, opposed by all the major trade unions except the CFDT and viewed with deep misgivings by the Socialist government. In many ways it resembled the programme of a political opposition more than of an interest group. But it could not be characterised either as a simple defence of *droits acquis* or as a demagogic call to arms in the name of impossible goals or ideological slogans. It is also the case, as has been shown in Chapter 10, that the French bureaucracy is not invariably an engine of bold reforms, even when ministers would like it to be: civil servants are as attached to their own *droits acquis* as anyone, and more effective than most at safeguarding them.

State–group consultation

The widespread, regular and unspectacular consultation between the state and groups that does go on is overlooked or undervalued by the domination-crisis model. As Schmidt observes, the French may often be Jacobins at the formulation stage of policy-making, but when it comes to implementation, they are Girondins, ever ready to find accommodations to spare the interests or sensibilities of important groups. The principle of the 35-hour week, for example, was imposed by law, with very little discussion, on employers and unions – but the latter were consulted extensively on the detail. Similarly, the domination-crisis model tends to ignore the dense network of committees and joint negotiating bodies, from the Conseil Économique et Social down, which exist for the precise purpose of consultation between the administration and the groups.

Peaceful reform

The reality of peaceful reform also has little place in the domination-crisis model. The argument that crises breed reforms in France is borne out by the great transformations of the Liberation era, to a lesser extent by the change of régime in 1958, and arguably by May 1968 as well. But the claim that reforms *require* crises ignores the persistent and pragmatic changes undertaken since 1945 without such extreme pressures. The social and political reforms introduced by Giscard d'Estaing, which profoundly affected both the individual and the family, emerged, not from a revolutionary spasm, but from the normal and healthy electoral fears of a narrowly elected president. The Socialist reform programme introduced after 1981 may have corresponded to a 'heroic' model of policy-making, but it was occasioned by a presidential election: a perfectly normal political event, not a 'functionally innovative crisis'. The steady deregulation of the economy that has taken place since the mid-1980s has certainly responded to external events, but not to anything more dramatic than the normal range of pressures in a globalising economy. Raffarin's programme of reforms to France's pensions and welfare systems, which achieved some limited but undeniable successes, is predicated on the view that governments can engineer change on a step-by-step, unspectacular basis, and seek to carry at least some of the relevant groups with them. And the notion that France is a *société bloquée* appears steadily more questionable as one measures the immense changes, for the most part peacefully elaborated and equally peacefully implemented, which have taken place in France since 1945.

The permeable state–groups barrier

The complexity of interactions between the state and society is also largely ignored by the domination-crisis model. The rather strict separation between state and society that it assumes underestimates both the presence and intensity of divisions within the bureaucracy, and the existence, via *pantouflage* and all manner of old boy networks, of close lines of complicity that cross the state–groups barrier. Similarly, the separation between the state and groups overlooks the fact that a number of the biggest conflicts of recent years, especially under the Juppé and Raffarin governments, took place between the state's political masters and its rank-and-file servants.

The domination-crisis model, in short, provides useful insights, especially into the way many associations behave, but is not a convincing total explanation. Like most models, it raises more questions than it answers, and it is too neat and too selective in its choice of facts to convey the full complexity of the situation.

The endemic and open conflict model

This model is linked with, but distinct from, the previous school of thought. It shares assumptions about the authoritarian nature of the state, the fragmented nature of the groups and the impact of revolutionary crisis as a creative and reforming force. But it differs from the domination-crisis model in that its assumptions rest less on a view of the innate characteristics of French society than on an argument about the functioning of the political institutions of the Fifth Republic. It is maintained that with the decline of parliament, the natural safety valve of the Third and Fourth Republics, and the growth of a disciplined pro-governmental party coalition, the political leverage of the groups has been severely limited. Decreasing influence has led to increasing frustration. And frustration has led to mounting pressure of an extra-institutional and often violent nature. Such pressure has become endemic and has taken the form of open conflict, and this pressure has been instrumental in wresting concessions from governments. According to this school, the groups in their relations with the state are less quiescent clients than belligerent defenders of their interests.

The endemic and open conflict model: evidence in favour

Supporters of this thesis can point to the extra-institutional pressures of all kinds to which Fifth Republic governments of every stripe have been subjected. Such pressures may be considered under four headings: strikes, demonstrations, illegal obstruction and violent confrontation.

Strikes

Whereas in an average year Blair's Britain saw fewer than half a million working days lost to strikes (the figure of 900,000 for 2004 was exceptional), the comparable total for a typical year in France is anything from two to four times as high (Tables 11.2 and 11.3). They have involved not only blue-collar workers, but also groups as diverse as air traffic controllers, airline pilots, university and *lycée* students, doctors, lawyers and architects (in many cases, middle-class groups resorting to a proletarian weapon to stave off what they see as their own impending proletarianisation). The near-general strike of May 1968, with nearly 150 million working days lost, is the outstanding case. The strikes of 1995, though nowhere near as extensive (fewer than 6 million days lost), were still remarkable in a European context in which labour disputes had become much

Table 11.2 Working days lost through strikes in France, 1963–81 (000s: excluding *Fonction publique de l'État*)

1963	5,991	1970	1,700	1977	3,665
1964	2,497	1971	4,400	1978	2,200
1965	973	1972	3,800	1979	3,656
1966	2,502	1973	3,914	1980	1,674
1967	4,203	1974	3,380	1981	1,495
1968	150,000	1975	3,869		
1969	2,200	1976	5,010		

Source: Ministère des Affaires Sociales.

Table 11.3 Working days lost through strikes in France, 1982–2001 (000s)

	Fonction publique de l'État	*Private and nationalised firms*	*Total*	Fonction publique de l'État *as %* *of total*
1982	126	2,327	2,453	5.1
1983	333	1,484	1,817	18.3
1984	975	1,357	2,332	41.8
1985	341	885	1,226	27.8
1986	853	1,042	1,895	45.0
1987	785	969	1,754	44.8
1988	686	1,242	1,928	35.6
1989	2,322	904	3,226	72.0
1990	574	694	1,268	45.3
1991	239	666	905	26.4
1992	218	491	709	30.7
1993	389	533	922	42.2
1994	227	521	748	30.3
1995	3,763	2,121	5,883	64.0
1996	686	448	1,134	60.5
1997	383	455	838	45.7
1998	684	353	1,037	66.0
1999	752	574	1,325	56.8
2000	1,650	810	2,460	67.1
2001	1,115	692	1,807	61.7

Source: Ministère des Affaires Sociales.

rarer. The Raffarin reforms to the public-sector pensions system and to the status of auxiliaries in schools caused a further, if smaller, wave of strikes in the second quarter of 2003, with ten 'days of action' (strikes and demonstrations) in the spring and early summer. The big one-day strike of 10 March 2005, in which unions from both public and private sectors joined in an across-the-board fight for pay, is credited with helping to create the climate for the no victory at the May referendum.

Demonstrations

Mass demonstrations have been frequent under the Fifth Republic in virtually all economic or political climates. In 1975, not a particularly troubled year, there were 612 demonstrations in Paris, of which 312 necessitated the mobilisation of the police. Sarah Waters puts the annual number of demonstrations in the early twenty-first century at 10,000, of which about 1,000 take place in Paris. Under the early Fifth Republic, the Algerian war triggered off massive demonstrations in favour of peace, two of which were repressed with murderous ferocity by the police. May 1968 was, in this as in other respects, in a class of its own, with left-wing students in Paris, Bordeaux, Nantes, Strasbourg and other big university towns mounting enormous *carnavalesque* processions – and finally giving way, in Paris on 30 May, to a gigantic tricolour-waving pro-Gaullist rally. For demonstrations are not confined to left-wing groups. Even more picturesque than May 1968 was the farmers' *tour de force* in September 1991, when the Champs-Élysées was transformed into a wheatfield for a weekend. Demonstrations have brought out doctors, nurses, professors in gowns and, once in 1993, employers from the textile industry, complete with blazer-clad stewards specially hired for the day. Probably the largest demonstration held in Paris since the Liberation, on 24 June 1984, gathered 1.3 million defenders of Church schools against the Socialist government's reform projects; just under a decade later, some 600,000 supporters of secular education came out against the Balladur government's plans to raise subsidies to Catholic schooling. Numbers in excess of 100,000 have also rallied in Paris around causes as varied as the future of French farming (almost every year from 1982 to 1991), the social security system (at the CGT's behest, in 1987 and 1990), anti-racism (in 1990, after an attack on the Jewish cemetery at Carpentras by a group of skinheads close to the FN), health issues (in 1991), the education budget (in 1990), the Raffarin pension reforms (in May 2003, when the organisers claimed two million demonstrators across France and the police conceded half that number), the defence of the 35-hour week (in January 2005) and Alain Devaquet's plans to allow universities to select students and charge fees (in late 1986). Unlike most of the others, the anti-Devaquet demonstrations did not pass off peacefully, due to troublemakers among the demonstrators and poorly commanded and ultimately violent riot police, who beat one demonstrator to death.

What is most remarkable about the continuing predilection among the French for strikes and demonstrations is the amount of public support they generally enjoy. The CSA polling institute has shown that of fifty nationwide conflicts involving strikes, demonstrations, or both between 1995 and 2005, and taking in an impressive roll-call of groups as varied as truckers, hospital staff, the police, farmers, factory workers, researchers, teachers, university and high school students, doctors, actors, tobacconists and the unemployed, fully forty-five enjoyed the support or at least sympathy of over half of all respondents, while twenty-five were supported by two-thirds of respondents.

The conflicts concerned included disruptive strikes by teachers and railway workers (though strikes by railway workers alone, as well as Air France pilots in 1998, were among the minority without public approval). Similarly, the 'minimum service' on public transport in the event of a strike, though considered attractive as an idea by three-quarters of poll respondents, is rejected by the same proportion as a proposition to be enforced by law; hence, no doubt, the refusal of successive right-wing governments, despite the calls from their own exasperated Deputies, to use legislation to achieve this. This relative solidarity on the part of the public distinguishes the French case from, for example, Britain in the late 1970s, where endemic strike action played into the hands of a deeply anti-union Conservative Party.

Direct action

Illegal activity – usually undertaken by groups staring ruin in the face, or believing they are – has taken various forms. Steel workers during the crisis of the late 1970s disrupted the Tour de France, burnt down public buildings and held managers hostage; lorry drivers have blocked motorways, or driven along them very very slowly (a practice known as *opérations escargot*); farmers have regularly tipped unsold artichokes, tomatoes, peaches and apples, or (far worse) liquid manure onto the streets – slowing down even French drivers. The ecologically minded also have blocked the sites of proposed motorways, closed down ports to protest against oil pollution (when they were not closed by truckers or by fishermen protesting against high prices for diesel or low ones for fish) and, in Brittany, have invaded proposed atomic energy stations. In 1993 Act Up, the militant gay rights group, placed a giant condom on the obelisk in the Place de la Concorde. A favourite target of direct action is the local prefecture or subprefecture, still the physical representation of state authority in the provinces. The *cause célèbre* of the century's end was the August 1999 attack on a McDonald's restaurant (its perpetrators called it a 'dismantling') in the provincial town of Millau by a group of Confédération Paysanne activists. Led by the charismatic José Bové, they were protesting against punitive American duties on Roquefort cheese and, more generally, against the globalisation of the food industry. Bové's trial the following July brought some 50,000 supporters back to Millau.

Violence

Violence, whether premeditated or simply as an escalation of more peaceful forms of protest, has been a frequent feature of the politics of the Fifth Republic. According to official figures, there were about a hundred *attentats* a year in the 1960s and early 1970s, rising to 480 in 1976, 555 in 1977 and over 600 in 1978. Some *attentats*, such as the bombs in the rue de Rennes in September 1986, which killed six, or in the regional metro in July 1995, which left four dead, have been the work of North African or Middle Eastern terrorists. But there has been plenty of home-grown violence too, with origins in political extremism, national separatism or sectoral desperation.

Political extremism on the Left found its most violent expression in Action Directe, whose tiny handful of members carried out several killings in the late 1970s and 1980s. They were finally arrested in February 1987, some three months after having murdered Georges Besse, the head of Renault. More extensive, however, is the record of the far Right, starting with the Organisation Armée Secrète (OAS), the paramilitary wing of the supporters of French Algeria. Over a mere four months in the summer of 1961, the Interior Ministry recorded 726 *attentats* in France, almost all of OAS origin; this figure does not include either the countless terrorist outrages committed by the OAS in Algeria, or the dozen or so attempts to assassinate de Gaulle. Later groups on the far Right have been responsible for attacks on the homes of left-wingers and on Jewish offices and synagogues; and the Front National has regularly attracted individuals for whom casual murder is a logical extension of their racist beliefs.

Violence of a nationalist nature has taken place in Savoy and in the Basque country (the Basque separatist group Iparetarak committed some sixty *attentats* between 1973 and 1986, when it was officially dissolved), but more especially in Brittany and Corsica. In both of these places, moderate autonomous groups have been flanked by more extreme and more unruly paramilitary factions. Thus in Brittany, the legal Union Démocratique Bretonne, which has fought elections and won seats on local councils since 1964, had to compete against the Front de Libération Bretonne–Armée Républic-aine Bretonne, which specialised in armed attacks on state property in the late 1970s. Since then, the Breton nationalist cause has taken largely peaceful channels, thanks in part to a relatively enlightened policy of cultural concessions from successive govern-ments; it is significant that a violent attack on a McDonald's restaurant, which killed a waitress in April 2000, was roundly condemned by all established Breton nationalist groups. Corsica, on the other hand, has all the ingredients of an insoluble territorial problem: an underdeveloped and isolated peripheral region; resentment of property development and other incursions by the mainland French; a clan-ridden local political class which has used corrupt electoral practices for generations; a 'law of silence' (*omertà*) deeply rooted in local traditions; and a nationalist movement that is violent, able to command widespread passive sympathy or silence, closely linked to organised crime and thus well-funded, but also highly fragmented. Legal movements here, such as the Union du Peuple Corse or Corsica Nazione, are likely to be fronts for, rather than competitors against, the illegal ones, of which the most important has been the Front de Libération Nationale Corse (FLNC), banned in 1983. The FLNC split in 1989 into a *canal habituel* and a *canal historique*, groups which in turn have been prone to splits. None of this has halted the violence; there were an estimated 3,366 political *attentats* attributed to Corsican groups between 1975 and 1995, including forty-seven murders; early twenty-first century observers put the figures at 300 *attentats* and about thirty political murders a year (though these include the considerable number of crimes com-mitted by Corsican groups against one another). The Corsican question was put most firmly on the agenda when nationalists assassinated the regional prefect Claude Érignac in February 1998 (the prime suspect was able to hide for five years on the island before being arrested in 2003). Government policy has vacillated between neglect (in effect turning a blind eye to a corrupt local system), reform (the new local government system for the island brought in by Interior Minister Joxe in 1991), covert negotiation covered with apparently culpable laxity (the Juppé government's readiness to allow armed and hooded terrorists to give a press conference announcing a so-called truce) and ill-planned repression (after the Érignac murder). The Jospin initiative of early 2000, involving negotiations in Matignon with all the political forces on the island, had the merit of being open and direct, but it still failed after being attacked for the recognition it appeared to give to political organisations supporting terrorism. So did the Sarkozy plan to unify Corsican political representation into a single authority, narrowly defeated in the referendum on the island in July 2003.

Of a rather different nature is the violence that results from mass demonstrations or illegal protests which run out of control. Here, damage to property (such as the destruction by fire of the MEDEF offices in La Rochelle during the 2003 pensions reform protests) may be deliberate, but is not always planned, and very rarely executed with bombs or the other tools of the terrorist; loss of life may occur (whether on the side of the police or of the protesters) but is not intended. Like the illegal activities of which it is an extension, it usually involves groups facing marginalisation or ruin: small farmers or fishermen crippled by debts (a characteristic feature of the modernisation of these industries) which falling prices make it impossible to pay. For Breton fishermen in 1994, the historic fourteenth-century *parlement* building in Rennes was an obvious target: they burnt it down. The FNSEA has always tolerated its members' 'commando'-type actions against 'unfair' foreign imports, such as Italian wine or British sheep (some lorryloads of which they burnt alive in 1997). FNSEA members have also attacked individuals of whom they disapprove, especially women. In 1982 Agriculture Minister Édith Cresson was forced to flee a crowd of angry peasants by helicopter; in 1999 they sacked the offices of their favourite *bête noire*, Environment Minister Dominique Voynet. Another group of disgruntled rustics, the bird-shooters of CPNT, have also put a minister to flight (in 1999), and regularly issue implicit threats to turn their guns on the authorities if the shortening of the shooting season is enforced. The small businessmen of Gérard Nicoud's CID-UNATI were active in the intimidation of tax inspectors and destruction of tax files in the 1970s. The steel workers of Longwy and Denain, whose jobs were directly threatened by the restructuring of their industry from the late 1970s, regularly brought catapults and ball-bearings to demonstrations (the police, of course, responded with baton charges and tear gas). More recently, workers in a private firm scheduled for closure tried to enlist the support of the Labour Ministry by threatening to dump toxic chemicals in a nearby river. The early years of the ecology movement were also marked by violence on the part of its extremists, who blew up part of a nuclear power station at Fessenheim in Alsace in 1975, and the atomic energy authority offices in Tours the following year. Confrontation with the police at the site of the proposed nuclear power station at Creys-Malville in August 1977 ended in tragic deaths; the Larzac plateau, which was being turned into a vast military camp, and Plogoff in Brittany, site of another planned nuclear power station, were the two great (and sometimes violent) rallying points for Greens in the 1970s.

The newest form of open defiance to the authority of the state, however, has come not from interest groups at all. This is the rise in urban violence, typically but not exclusively concentrated in modern working-class suburbs and caused by young unemployed men, frequently of North African or sub-Saharan African origin: vandalism, the theft and burning of cars, and crimes against the person. This endemic unrest has been played out against a background of urban deprivation, the chronic neglect of ill-designed and ill-serviced estates, educational underachievement, widespread drug trafficking, and a perception that for young men with the wrong name, or skin colour, or religion, the opportunities of France's supposedly egalitarian Republic are closed. In 1997 it was estimated that fifteen young people had been killed and nearly 2,000 wounded as a result of this type of violence; official figures showed that some 28,000 cars were torched in the first ten months of 2005. That the state is challenged is shown by the difficulty the police have had in intervening against crime: many such suburbs became places where the police appeared either *en masse* or not at all. They have also been places where central and local government, even with the necessary funds to improve matters, have often had difficulty finding widely recognised local groups to talk to. Hence, in part, the nationwide rioting that followed the accidental deaths of two teenagers, apparently fleeing what they took to be pursuing policemen, in November 2005. This was France's worst outbreak of civil unrest since May 1968; it affected the outskirts of almost every major city in France, causing the destruction of some 10,000 cars, as well as numerous public buildings, in the space of two weeks; and provoked the de Villepin government into a characteristic mix of concessions (measures in favour of the suburbs that should have been taken without the encouragement of riots) and repression (the revival of a law dating from the period of the Algerian war allowing mayors to impose selective curfews in their towns).

Supporters of the endemic and open conflict thesis not only assert, with Alain Peyrefitte, that 'rioting is the national sport'; they also claim that direct action works – that it is an essential, if not the characteristic, form of group representation. Group representatives themselves appear to believe in the efficacy of direct action: 60 per cent of Frank Wilson's (admittedly quite small) sample considered that it could influence policy-making – though most also preferred other methods. Evidence that extreme activity can pay may be garnered from every period of the Fifth Republic. Strikes by miners in 1963, by wholesale fruit and vegetable suppliers in 1973, by doctors in 1983 and by train drivers in 1986–87, all forced an apparently resolute government to make major concessions. The big student demonstrations of 1986 led the Chirac government not only to withdraw its university reforms but also its planned (restrictive) reform of the nationality laws. The *lycéens'* movement of 1990 won an extra 4.5 billion francs for the Education budget – a week after the budget had been officially voted, and on the direct orders of Mitterrand, who had received the *lycéens'* leaders at the Élysée. The 1982 and 1991 reforms to the government of Corsica would not have occurred without the actions of a violent minority. The antics of farmers have regularly been met not only with indulgence (FNSEA membership virtually guaranteeing immunity from prosecution) but with concessions from government, such as the temporary bans on Italian wine imports imposed in the 1970s in flagrant breach of EC regulations. Direct action by fishermen won 45 million francs in subsidies in 1993. Supporters of Catholic schools in 1984 and of secular ones in 1994 helped ensure, by demonstrating, that the status quo was maintained against the reforming ambitions of governments of Left and Right. Truckers in September 2000 won 35 centimes a litre off the price of diesel fuel – and a host of European emulators. Demonstrations by the unemployed succeeded in reversing planned cuts in benefits early in 2004. And, as we have seen, the rioters of November 2005 obtained a package of measures in favour of their rundown suburbs – though it is far from clear that this was what they were asking for.

The endemic and open conflict model: objections

The endemic and open conflict model, while usefully underlining an important aspect of state–group relations, suffers on five main counts.

- Extra-institutional means have often been wholly ineffective in forcing concessions. The OAS, for example, only succeeded in accelerating Algerian independence. The assassins of Action Directe are behind bars. The truckers' strike of October 1997, or the *mouvement des sans-papiers*, calling for the granting of residence permits to several hundred thousand immigrants who had lost their right to residence in France after restrictive reforms to immigration legislation by right-wing governments, or protests by the unemployed in winter 1997–98, produced limited concessions. The short-term victories of farmers, fishermen, steel workers and small traders have done little or nothing to halt the longer-term decline of all these groups: in less than half a century, for example, the agricultural sector shrank from a quarter of the working population to a twentieth.

- The tradition of direct action is much older than the Fifth Republic. In the half-century before 1958, the years 1908, 1920, 1934, 1936, 1944, 1947 and 1953 stand out as especially conflict-ridden and/or violent. And such bucolic pursuits as the tarring and feathering of tax collectors who had the effrontery to demand tax payment stopped, not started, with the Fifth Republic.

- Political violence is far from unique to France. The FLNC and its offshoots are minor players compared to ETA in Spain or to the IRA in the UK; the forty-seven Corsican murders over a twenty-year period hardly bear comparison with the 2,000 or so deaths in Northern Ireland over the same years. Similarly, Action Directe had nothing like the impact, whether in terms of the body count or of the social malaise caused, of the Italian Red Brigades or even of the West German Red Army Faction. The fact that Spain, Britain, Germany and Italy all have rather different régimes from France also suggests that the link between direct action and the institutions of the Fifth Republic is tenuous or non-existent.

- The endemic and open conflict model, like the domination-crisis model, understates the amount of peaceful and fruitful dialogue that does occur between groups and the state.

- Finally, the model misinterprets the real nature of extra-institutional activities. Demonstrations are not always all-out confrontations with the state (indeed, their organisers usually negotiate the route with the *renseignements généraux*, France's equivalent of the Special Branch). They often attract mainstream (usually opposition) politicians who aspire to wield state power themselves through due electoral process; the big Gaullist demonstration of May 1968 was led by former Prime Minister Debré and Culture Minister André Malraux; the anti-racist demonstration after the 1990 Carpentras outrage included the president himself. French strikes rarely last long because they lack the organisation and funding that only strong unions can provide. In 1983, for instance, only 6 per cent of industrial strikes lasted longer than fourteen days, and only 2 per cent more than a month. With some notable exceptions (such as the conflicts of 1995, or the strike by security guards in May 2000 which left France's cashpoints without banknotes for a fortnight), they tend to be brief, ritualised affairs, often lasting no longer than a day or even a few hours. Such pressures may be simply part of an overall strategy of pressure which also includes highly institutionalised forms of bargaining. The deliberate dramatisation of a negotiation may enable a group not only to extract concessions from the sponsor ministry; it may also be exploited by both the group and the ministry in bringing pressure to bear on the government as a whole. Occasionally such dramatisation may help the government to persuade taxpayers that concessions are vital or, in the case of the farmers, to convince its European partners that without concessions revolution would be imminent.

The corporatist and concerted politics models

If the two previous models of state–group relations lay stress upon the conflictual nature of those relations and emphasise the generally authoritarian and insensitive nature of the organs of the state, the corporatist and concerted politics models describe the relationship as one of partnership, constant, permanent and mutually beneficial. Concerted politics, writes Jack Hayward,

> stresses the interdependence of the government and the interest groups, and the interpenetration of 'public' and 'private' decision-making characteristic of a mixed economy in which an increasing measure of state intervention has to be reconciled with an increasing measure of interest group intervention in all spheres of social activity.

The concerted politics model is both descriptive and prescriptive: it sees the state–group partnership as both desirable and inevitable. Indeed, for many proponents of this model, which was fashionable in the 1950s and 1960s, relations between the state and the groups were to take place 'within the framework of social justice', provided by the planning of the French economy.

Underlying the attempt to direct state–group intercourse into institutional channels was the search for consensus and for 'rational' decision-making. But the search proved illusory, for it was based on the myth that the alchemy of concertation could produce decisions acceptable to all interests. Concerted politics implicitly denied the primacy and inevitability of politics and the intrinsically conflictual nature of decision-making. One protagonist of concerted politics even proclaimed the need 'to depoliticise the major policy options of the nation'. In a country so ideologically divided this was a pious and foolish aspiration. The organs of concertation may have provided useful forums for airing grievances and occasionally played a useful educative role; but they were less the instruments of concertation than the institutionalised agents of muted conflict. This was gradually recognised, even by the economic planners: one of the later planning commissioners, Jean Ripert, discreetly abandoned the concept of *concertation* in favour of *consultation*.

If concerted politics was a fashion in some French governing circles in the 1950s and 1960s, corporatist politics became an academic mode of the 1970s and early 1980s. The two models are closely linked, since both emphasise the non-neutral nature of the state and the closeness and durability of the links between the state and the groups, and both insist upon the importance of consensus-building and conflict management as integral elements of the relationship. Finally, both point to the institutionalisation of the state–group dialogue. But there are differences between the two models: the corporatist model introduces notions such as hierarchy, integration, discrimination and privilege which are absent from the concerted politics model.

Philippe Schmitter has famously defined corporatism as

> a system of interest intermediation in which the constituent units are organized into a limited number of singular, compulsory, non-competitive, hierarchically ordered and functionally differentiated categories, recognized or licensed (if not created) by the state and granted a deliberate representational monopoly within

their respective categories in exchange for observing certain controls on their selection of leaders and articulation of demands and supports.

Very briefly, the corporatist model envisages the incorporation by the state of a few powerful monopolistic groups (normally peak organisations, each federating smaller groups in its own sector) into permanent institutionalised arrangements. Each group is expected to implement fully all agreements reached with the state, coercing and disciplining its members if necessary; in return, it enjoys an exclusive right to represent its sector's interests to the state, as well as other privileges which may strengthen it even further. Rival groups, if any, may be discriminated against, thus weakening them and rendering them less attractive – which is a source of further weakness.

Corporatism: evidence in favour

If the two previous models were developed to explain a specifically French pattern of relations, corporatism was initially used as a framework in quite other European countries: Austria, the Netherlands, Sweden and, to a lesser extent, Germany – all countries where, for example, three-way bargaining between government, unions and employers, leading to binding agreements, is common. In the light of some of the characteristics of French groups mentioned above – and notably their fragmentation and their frequent inability to control their members – France would seem to be a non-starter as a corporatist system. However, theorists of corporatism have cut their cloth to suit all comers, using the terms meso- or micro-corporatism to refer to instances where they consider patterns of corporatist policy-making to be present in particular sectors. The question, therefore, is not so much whether France is a full-blown corporatist system – it clearly is not – as whether the corporatist paradigm might help us to understand elements of state–group relations in France. Such elements might include the institutionalisation of state–group relationships; the privileges granted to officially recognised groups; the co-management by groups and the state of significant slices of public funds; the pattern of state–group relationships in particular sectors; and the relations between political leaders and groups at the local level.

- *The institutionalisation of state–group relationships* is at least 200 years old. Napoleon organised the major economic interests of his day into Chambers within each *département*: to this day, the Chambres de Commerce et d'Industrie, the Chambres d'Agriculture and the Chambres des Métiers command the compulsory membership of individuals and firms within their sectors, and have the power to tax them to finance local projects. Consultative organisations within the state have proliferated since the Liberation era. The 231 members of the Conseil Économique et Social, whose consultative role is conserved in the Fifth Republic Constitution, include delegates of trade unions, employers' associations family associations and mutual groups, as well as government appointees. Even in 1971, towards the apogee of the 'heroic' Gaullist state, some 500 councils, 1,200 commissions and 3,000 committees served as fora for state–group consultations. Current government estimates of the number of such bodies run to 20,000, including 645 national councils. In addition, important sectors of labour relations have been subject to arbitration in labour tribunals (*conseils des prud'hommes*) that bring officially elected representatives of capital and labour together under the state's aegis.

- *The privileges granted to officially recognised groups* entail obvious collusion between the state (or, at local level, regions, *départements* and municipalities) and these groups. Such privileges include the automatic right to representation on official consultative bodies; subsidies to train and pay for full-time officials; and in some cases the use of civil servants on secondment, and the right to co-manage certain social funds. These are open even to groups opposed to the government of the day. There are some indications, too, that official practices are paralleled by unofficial ones: for example, the very wealthy *comité d'entreprise* of EDF is a CGT stronghold that according to one account has siphoned off, chiefly through overbilled contracts, as much as 4 million euros annually for the union (and, indirectly, for the PCF), without being brought to book (hence, in part, the CGT's extreme reluctance to see EDF privatised). These privileges do not automatically guarantee full 'insider status' to their beneficiaries; the Coordination Rurale, for example, which won official recognition in June 2000 on the strength of having won 15 per cent in the last elections to the Chambers of Agriculture and having functioned for over five years in at least twenty-five *départements*, will never be on the same footing as the FNSEA in the foreseeable future. Nevertheless, recognised groups are always more 'incorporated' than rivals, having to rely simply on their ability to mobilise activists in order to win any kind of access. And representative status, once won, is rarely if ever lost, however steeply a group's real support may decline.

- *The co-management of public funds by groups and the state* applies most obviously to the enormous social security budget. This was administered for half a century by representatives of employers and unions without any parliamentary scrutiny at all. When parliament was given the right to vote on the social security budget in 1996, it was only after over a decade in which the taxpayer had had to cover the deficit without exercising control. The negotiations launched by MEDEF early in 2000 show how important the role of the 'social partners' in this sector still remains; they actually produced results over the next four years, in terms of a new agreement on vocational training and a new jobseeker's package that raised unemployment pay in return for evidence that the recipient was actively seeking work and would accept reasonable job offers. Other co-managed areas include in-service professional training (the preparation of the two major laws on training, passed in 1971 and 1991, was virtually subcontracted to the joint employer–union body responsible) and family allowances, where the Union Nationale des Associations Familiales has played a significant role since its creation just after the Liberation.

- *The pattern of state–group relationships in particular sectors* comes close to the corporatist paradigm. In agriculture, the FNSEA, with the CNJA, now its own young farmers' branch, dominates most Chambers of Agriculture and stretches into every French village and hamlet, not only through its 32,000 local unions and forty product-specialised associations (for cereals, wheat, beets and so on), but also via its hold on the Crédit Agricole, on farmers' social insurance schemes, and on a range of advice centres, mutual organisations and *lycées agricoles*, managed on behalf of the state. These ensure that farmers have every interest in keeping up their FNSEA membership, reinforcing the FNSEA's dominant position. At the summit, agriculture ministers throughout the Fifth Republic have had a regular Tuesday meeting with representatives of the FNSEA, CNJA and Chambers of Agriculture; in 1986, indeed, the FNSEA leader, François Guillaume, moved directly into the job of minister. The FNSEA was strong enough both to prevent the Socialists from diversifying their range of partners in the sector after 1981, and to force Édith Cresson's departure (she was replaced in 1983 by the more conciliatory Michel Rocard). French farming as a whole came under unaccustomed pressure in the early 1990s as the Uruguay Round of international trade negotiations demanded freer trade in farm products. But although the Uruguay Round did lead to an agreement (which the FNSEA leader Raymond Lacombe would have preferred to prevent altogether), the reductions to farm subsidies and protection were very much less, as well as considerably later, than had been hoped at the beginning: a testimony, in part, to the FNSEA's continuing influence, even in a fast-shrinking industry.

The other sector where analysts have observed corporatism at work has been that of education. Here, too, the main union (the FEN, before its split) established a symbiotic relationship with the ministry, which was if anything reinforced by attacks from outside (such as the battle with the Catholic school lobby in 1984). Thus the management of promotions and transfers within France's highly central-ised teaching profession is largely handled, for the ministry, by union officials. The power of the teachers' unions to block education reforms altogether, or to erode their impact during the implementation phase, is all the greater as it is exercised from within: teachers on the ground are managed by teachers in their unions and in the educational administration, who may themselves count on the support of teachers in the National Assembly. They are still capable of undermining and even destroying ministers who seek to bypass them, as the fall of Claude Allègre in March 2000 illustrates.

- *The local level*, finally, may also present a form of corporatist behaviour. Here, it is frequent for local authorities, and especially mayors, to enter a collusive relationship with local associations; subsidies and buildings, but also responsibility for the man-agement of specific local services, may be conceded to such associations by mayors and councils, in return for involvement in local policy-making and electoral support.

Corporatism: objections

Agriculture and education, however, are very much the exceptions. The extreme div-ision of groups alone would make corporatism appear quite inadequate as a *general* model of state–group relations in France. To this general point may be added four more specific objections to the model.

- The division of groups is often compounded by their inability to command the long-term loyalty of their members – a vital feature of corporatism because such loyalty is what ensures that deals reached at the summit will be accepted at the grass roots. In trade unions in particular, but also to some extent in farm groups and business organisations, there is a growing gap between full-time officials, often living off state subsidies, and the rank-and-file membership: hence, in part, the spread of more or less ad hoc 'co-ordinations', better trusted by ordinary members than regular unions at times of strong mobilisation.
- Many of the consultative organisations mentioned above are routine bodies which have little substantial effect on policy-making. Recent research on Chambers of Commerce, for example, has indicated a decline in influence over recent decades, with leadership positions in such bodies often taken by the least dynamic members of business communities.

- Whereas in fully corporatist systems (in Scandinavia or Austria), the relationship between groups and state practically excludes street protest, in France the one complements the other. Farmers are *both* France's most corporatist lobby *and* the one most prone to direct action. Such action is at the same time a means for farmers to exert additional pressure and a safety valve which the FNSEA tolerates and even encourages to prevent defections of militant peasants to competing unions. Similarly, teachers, despite their unions' solid positions in the rue de Grenelle ministry, are readier than almost any group (except for farmers – and students) to protest on the streets.

- The corporatist model, with its stress on consensual policy-making between the state and at least the 'insider' groups, does not acknowledge the possibility that the state – politicians and civil servants – may, at certain points, cut groups right out of policy-making. This, however, has often happened in France. Thus France's negotiating position in the closing stages of the Uruguay Round was fixed by Prime Minister Balladur and a small group of ministers (Foreign Affairs, Agriculture, Industry and the Budget) and officials from the SGCI, without bringing in the FNSEA; this was a reform that the FNSEA did not want, but more than merely agricultural interests were at stake. By 1999, indeed, the FNSEA had lost its status as the Agriculture Ministry's exclusive partner, even if it continued to enjoy a privileged position. Other examples include the crucial days in March 1983 when Mitterrand consulted advisers and ministers, but not interest group representatives, before deciding on his historic change of economic policy; Juppé's social security plan of 1995; and the Jospin government's decision to use legislation rather than negotiation to move to the 35-hour week. Jean-Pierre Raffarin and the minister, François Fillon, who at Education and Social Affairs was responsible for his most unpopular reforms, both praised the virtues of consultation with groups, and undertook consultation before proceeding to legislate; this did not, however, prevent the groups from complaining that the consultation had been purely formal. The 'autonomy of the state', in other words, is as much of an obstacle as the fragmentation of groups to the application of the corporatist model to the French case.

The pluralist model

The pluralist model, like corporatism, was developed for systems other than the French. The classical theorists of pluralism – A. F. Bentley, David Truman and Robert Dahl – were Americans describing their own country. Such theorists stressed the right of groups to organise as an essential democratic freedom. That right was the basis for free competition between groups, analogous to the free competition between political parties – or between businesses. Pluralism, they argued, helps to optimise political outcomes, because whenever one group wins excessive influence, it becomes open to criticism and attack, provoking the creation of other groups, ending its dominance, and thus ultimately ensuring responsiveness of government to citizens. Against the backdrop of interests in constant and inevitable conflict, the state's role is rather passive. Far from seeking to dominate the groups, it aims to ensure fair competition and dialogue by providing an institutional framework for the struggle. Decision-making is seldom 'heroic', and only rarely results from the imposition of rationally calculated policies; it involves rather the negotiation of small, incremental adjustments to the status quo.

Pluralism necessarily precludes major shifts in policy: they could be offensive to certain groups and could jeopardise the harmony of social institutions. In short, governments buy peace in the search for social harmony. Political elites are mediators or arbitrators in a vast and endless bargaining process in which coalition-building has to take place between groups with incomplete and overlapping memberships.

Pluralism: evidence in favour

Three sets of arguments can be cited to support the pluralist thesis. The first, already mentioned above, is the existence in France of a dense and varied network of associations. The avant-garde of the general tendency for the French to 'join' more than in the past has consisted of so-called new social movements (NSMs), many of them mobilising on a range of issues thrown up for the first time in the upheaval of May 1968. Although initially rather slow to form in France (for a variety of reasons, including the strong mobilisation around political change in the 1970s) NSMs have gathered momentum over the past two decades. Observers such as Andrew Appleton and Sarah Waters have identified over half a dozen major areas of NSM interest, all somewhat distinct from the concerns of older French groups.

- *The antiracist movements*, however divided, have pursued and harrassed Le Pen and the FN over two decades; their nationwide protests in the spring of 2002 probably helped limit Le Pen's second-ballot presidential vote. They were also instrumental in bringing the *sans-papiers* issue to the attention of governments, with partial success.
- *Women's movements* have been active both in promoting parity legislation and in attacking the 'Mediterranean' sexism which they see as still endemic in French society.
- *The anti-globalisation movement* (its activists prefer the more internationalist term *alter*-globalisation) is centred on Attac, France's association of supporters of the Tobin tax on capital movements. It has supplied the biggest European delegation to the World Social Forums at Porto Allegre, organised a European Social Forum (welcomed by Raffarin) in Paris in 2003, caught France's imagination with José Bové's anti-Macdonald's protests and attracted the endorsement, more or less sincere, of 100 French parliamentarians as well as Chirac. Attac supplied some of the most effective grass-roots activists for the campaign against the European constitutional treaty in 2005.
- *France's gay rights movement* has promoted the Pacte Civil de Solidarité (PACS) and organised the highly successful Gay Pride parades in Paris (to which party politicians have begun, prudently, to associate themselves).
- *'Solidarity' movements* have championed the swollen ranks of the socially excluded in France both through fierce criticism, from associations such as Droit au Logement, of government policy, and also via organised practical solidarity through groups such as the Restos du Cœur.
- *The unemployed movement* has marked up significant successes, notably in 2004, for a traditionally very difficult social group to mobilise.
- *Environmental activists*, where they have not turned to political activity via Les Verts, have penetrated local and regional government, raising environmental awareness and focusing on practical, grass-roots measures.

Although these movements are often divided, sometimes politicised (with Trotskyists and former Communists being especially active), and periodically maximalist, their reluctance (usually) to lose their independence to parties or to the state, their readiness to press achievable demands and their ability to undertake concrete activities within civil society sets them somewhat outside either the domination-crisis or the corporatist models. Hence Waters's claim that they articulate a new form of (post-Jacobin) citizenship.

Secondly, the ideological position of governments has become steadily more sympathetic to groups and more distant from the Jacobin standpoint outlined at the start of this chapter. The position set out in a circular issued by Chirac during his first premiership in 1975, stating that 'the state and the public authorities do not have the monopoly of the public good' and that groups should be encouraged and, where possible, assigned appropriate tasks by the state, has been reiterated by most governments since. The performance of the Juppé government in 1995, in drafting a large-scale reform not only without consultation, but in conditions of extreme secrecy, and then justifying it in terms of the government's exclusive democratic legitimacy, was in this respect the exception that proved the rule; given Juppé's fate, it is unlikely that any future government would attempt reforms in quite the same manner.

Third, and more generally, groups constantly affect policy-making in non-crisis situations, through normal, legitimate bargaining, without the benefit of either mass demonstrations or corporatist collusion. The 1980 bill on workers' participation in industry, for example, was substantially modified under pressure from employers. Group pressure in 1982 led the Socialist government to decide against allowing advertising on the newly legalised local radios. The *revenu minimum d'insertion*, brought in by the Rocard government in 1988 to assist the growing numbers of unemployed deprived of any income at all under the existing benefits system, was the product of years of consultation between government and local authority officials, associations active in the field of urban poverty and the Conseil Économique et Social. The Jospin government's provision that firms with under twenty employees could wait until 2002 before adopting the 35-hour week was a clear concession to employers. The withdrawal of plans to reform public-sector pensions in March 2000 followed a clear refusal from the major unions; the delicate question of the revision of legal conditions for police interrogation, including the presence of lawyers and recording of interviews, was handled in close consultation with police and magistrates' associations. Under Raffarin, plans to ease legal restrictions on employers' right to sack staff to safeguard the competitiveness of their firm were watered down in October 2004 after protests from unions and the Left. Moreover, the mere listing of such well-documented episodes certainly underestimates the routine involvement of groups in policy-making. Not all consultation prior to the publication of a bill is visible. The implementation phase of policy-making, as Schmidt points out, is particularly fertile in arrangements with groups – which may distort or even subvert the initial spirit of the law. Moreover, the implicit exercise of group influence may suffice to define the area in which a government feels free or able to act. Any government knows that there are political no-go areas: limits that cannot be transgressed, conventions that cannot be violated and rights that cannot be trampled upon, and that those limits, conventions and rights are established and protected, often unconsciously, by the groups.

Pluralism: objections

Like the other three models considered above, pluralism offers important insights into state–group relations in France; and, like them, it presents serious shortcomings as an explanatory model.

- Some objections, far from being unique to France, were formulated in criticism of pluralist theory generally. The perfect competition between groups of classical pluralist theory is no more a reality than the perfect market beloved of classical economists. Some groups are strong, rich and well-organised – enjoying, in a few cases, hegemonic or even monopolistic positions. Others are none of these things: the unemployed movement, which achieved quite a small proportion of its goals in 1997–98 but scored at least a defensive success in 2004, was the *first* serious attempt at organisation of this group in a generation of joblessness that directly concerned between 1 and 3 million people. The *unequal* power of different groups to influence policy is as fundamental to state–group relations in France as it is elsewhere.
- More specifically French objections may be guessed from earlier sections of this chapter. In the first place, the state in France does not, or does not often, conform to the rather modest role allotted to it in the pluralist paradigm. Indeed, for Frank Wilson, 'the most important difference between French politics and the pluralist model is the activist role of the state'. Several examples have been noted above of a 'heroic' style of policy-making, in which governments have practically ignored group representations, at least in the policy formulation stage. Governments may also impose their will on groups by exploiting their (often numerous) divisions. Even when they do not ignore groups or divide and rule, governments have some freedom to choose which groups to listen to and which to exclude. The Pompidou government had cut itself off from the mainstream union movement so thoroughly by the time the May 1968 crisis broke that when the junior social affairs minister (Jacques Chirac) arranged a first, tentative contact with the CGT, he went to the appointment armed. On the other hand, groups traditionally supportive of the Right – business and farmers – felt unwontedly neglected in the early years after the Socialists' victory in 1981. Not surprisingly, executive dominance after 1958 reinforced this (partial) independence of the state. It is easier to exclude certain groups when government and administration are dominated by a more or less homogeneous majority than in the unstable parliament-centred system of the Fourth Republic.
- A final objection is the frequency with which the interplay between the different groups, or between groups and the state, has failed to conform to the rather orderly and civilised pattern assumed by the pluralist model. In some cases, especially before 1981, groups such as the CGT and the government simply did not see eye to eye on the basic rules of the game. Even within a single sector, contact between groups and each other, or between groups and the government, could be non-existent. Moreover, as we have seen, extra-institutional forms of pressure, for which the pluralist model concedes at best an exceptional role, are commonplace in France.

An untidy reality

Each of the four models outlined above raises serious objections when applied to the French case; there is no overall pattern. The state may, on occasion, ignore groups more or less completely; it may have more or less exclusive, corporatist relationships with particular groups; or it may allow more pluralist patterns of representation to develop. It may react to direct or even violent action by repression, or it may choose to ignore it, or even cave in to it altogether. Groups tend, in general, to be fragmented and, frequently, to be internally divided as well – apart from the (rare) cases, such as the notaries, that are monopolistic and cohesive. Groups may seek cosy, collusive relationships with government, but even after achieving this may still resort to street protest. This pattern is untidy, despite the simplicity that the centralisation of the French state might be supposed to impart; as Ezra Suleiman has noted, 'centralisation mainly concentrates jurisdictions. It does not concentrate effective power.' Two sets of remarks, however, may serve to render appearances somewhat less chaotic. They concern models of state–group relations that accommodate more diversity than those discussed above, and the range of factors that affect the capacity of groups to influence policy-making.

Mixed models

Vivien Schmidt's account of relations between business and government in France since the 1970s contrasts two styles of policy-making under the Fifth Republic. The 'heroic' style, she argues, has typically been used by governments making economic and industrial policy: with a long tradition of *dirigisme* behind them to justify their interventions, and a determination to achieve quite radical goals – modernisation under de Gaulle and Pompidou, reinforced state control in the early Mitterrand years – governments formulated policy with minimal input from interest groups. Groups were eventually allowed their say, but only at the implementation stage. In other policy areas, on the other hand (Schmidt mentions education, centre–periphery relations and agriculture), a more 'everyday' style prevails. Groups (teachers' unions, local elected officials, farmers' unions) are involved in the formulation as well as the implementation of policy. Their blocking power may make certain reforms impossible. Schmidt's dichotomy should not be taken rigidly; policy-making has not always been 'heroic' in economic and industrial affairs, nor always 'everyday' in other areas. It should, on the other hand, be valued for two insights. First, although policy formulation without groups may be possible on occasion in France, policy implementation is not. Second, while French governments may have a capacity for 'heroic' action – and thus a greater independence than suggested by the pluralist model – the French state cannot be 'heroic' in everything all of the time; it must decide in which areas (if any) this mode is most appropriate, because it can never ignore *all* groups. To these may be added a third point: the state's diminished capacity for heroics after it remodelled itself in the 1980s and after, in what Schmidt characterised (in reference to privatisations and deregulation) as the 'heroic dismantling of heroic capability'.

A second, complementary, mixed model may be derived from the literature on policy networks which has become an important and growing feature of the study of state–group relations since the 1980s. The policy networks approach typically takes a policy sector, rather than a national pattern of state–group relations, as its main field of study: that is, it is concerned with the whole range of participants in a particular area of policy-making, the relationships between them, and between them and the outside world, and the way in which those relationships affect policy outcomes. A typical policy network will include, for example, civil servants, representatives of producer interests, experts involved in a particular sector and key legislators. Beyond that, though, networks may vary a great deal. In particular, they may be rather open to a wide and shifting range of participants (in which case they are often known as issue networks); or, on the contrary, they may be limited to a few participants who are able to exclude unwelcome intruders (a pattern referred to as the policy community). The range, openness and predictability of policy outputs is likely to vary with the number of policy-makers involved. The policy networks approach is not without its shortcomings. It is often better at describing configurations of policy-making in a given sector than at explaining why they came to be open or closed, or precisely how the set of relationships involved affected policy outcomes. It is also better at explaining stability in policy-making within a sector than at accounting for the radical changes that do occur. But its attractions remain considerable for the French case. In particular, it can accommodate several quite different configurations of state–group relations within a single national system. The coexistence of a close-knit, exclusive policy community in, say, the farm sector, with a very much looser set of relationships (and therefore less predictable policies) in the area of women's rights, poses no difficulties for the policy networks approach. Moreover, under certain circumstances actors within the state may seek to reconfigure policy networks within their sector to further the acceptance of a reform programme, as was clearly the case with agriculture in the 1990s. Finally, policy networks may form in localities or regions too – and reflect different alignments from those prevalent at the national level. In Le Havre, to take one example, the Communists and the CGT co-operated with a coalition led by the right-wing mayor that aimed to improve the port infrastructure in order to reinforce Le Havre's competitive position against rival ports like Antwerp, thus creating or safeguarding jobs; in this they were opposed by the local Greens and by groups within the local Socialist Party. The policy networks approach certainly does not provide a simple model of state–group relations in France; but it does make a minimum of sense out of the apparent chaos.

Determinants of group influence

Another way to make sense of the extremely diverse patterns of state–group relations in France is to ask what makes individual groups influential with governments, or what makes governments listen to some groups and not others. Nine answers can be suggested. They have the merit of highlighting both the unequal power of groups and the variations over time in their influence.

Access

Access to decision-makers is both a consequence and a cause of a group's power. This may be seen as a continuum, moving from the most marginal groups that lack any form of official recognition and rely entirely on their own resources; to groups that have won such recognition and the right to sit on official (but possibly powerless) consultative committees that goes with it; to the groups of all kinds that have built up strong and institutionalised links with the legislature (whether thanks to political links, such as those of the CGT with Communist parliamentarians, or to a more all-party appeal, via the many *amicales parlementaires* covering a wide variety of sectors); to those groups that enjoy regular official and unofficial access to the executive. Access to the executive will always be assisted by informal networks. Chirac's excellent relationship with the Dassault aircraft firm goes back to the days when his father had been Marcel Dassault's banker. *Polytechniciens, énarques* or other graduates of *grandes écoles* may be attractive employees for firms (including the French branches of foreign multinationals) not just for their qualifications or their intellects but for the doors they can open. There is also every reason to suppose that in France as elsewhere, help with campaign finance can improve access to decision-makers at central or local level. It is notable that many of the building, public works and utilities firms that generously (and, for once, legally) supported candidates in the 1993 parliamentary elections hedged their bets by spreading their money between candidates of all parties. The best forms of access, finally, are multiple because they allow their beneficiaries to exploit the many divisions within the state apparatus: this is borne out, for example, in Cohen and Bauer's analysis of relationships between the state and the major firms in the early 1980s.

Strategic importance

The perceived strategic importance of a group in the social and economic life of the nation inevitably affects its leverage (or lack of it) with the authorities. This is the foundation of the power of the FNSEA in the post-war period: it not only represented France's premier industry (in terms of workers if nothing else), but also determined the nation's ability to feed itself – a critical argument when food shortages were fresh in every memory. For similarly obvious reasons, neither business in general nor very large individual firms can be ignored for very long; their bargaining power has, if anything, been reinforced by Europeanisation and globalisation. The case of Renault was cited at the beginning of this chapter. Other world-class firms like Bouygues (building and public works), the arms-to-publishing group Matra-Hachette, Dassault, which dominated France's military aviation industry for the half-century after 1945, Alstom (heavy engineering), or the two water firms, Générale des Eaux (now Vivendi) and Lyonnaise des Eaux (now Suez-Lyonnaise) could be added. If Crédit Lyonnais was able to attract over 100 billion francs of taxpayers' money, it was because the bankruptcy of a major (and nationalised) bank would have had effects too catastrophic for the politicians to contemplate. Other groups may also command attention due to their strategic positioning: railway and metro drivers, air traffic controllers, water plant workers or truckers wield more leverage in this respect than the relatively powerless university teachers.

Such strategic importance may ensure a hearing, but in no way guarantees government compliance with a group's wishes. The steel employers of the Chambre Syndicale de la Sidérurgie Française, for example, were very successful at extracting financial and other concessions in the 1970s, in an expanding market and at a time when it was a government axiom that 'France needs a steel industry'. But in 1978 the government brought the loss-making industry under effective state control; in 1981 the Socialists nationalised it; and later in the 1980s the flow of cash stopped. More generally, even if its strategic position ensures the influence of 'business' in general, governments may still have to make choices between different businesses. The uncertain path that led to the privatisation of Thomson defence electronics, for example, saw the Juppé government choose Matra as Thomson's future partner, then drop the privatisation plan altogether; when the sell-off was finally effected, the Jospin government chose Alstom instead.

Electoral clout

Electoral importance also lends a group influence. The fact that women represent over half the total electorate was clearly one factor in the decision of the Jospin government (and, more surprisingly, the right-wing majority in the Senate) to back a constitutional revision and legislation in favour of parity in political offices between men and women. But electoral importance is not the same as sheer size. The number of farmers, for example, has fallen sharply under the Fifth Republic; their electoral importance has diminished, but less rapidly. It is protected by rural over-representation in the councils of the *départements*, in the National Assembly and, above all, in the Senate; by the key social position farmers still occupy, even though they are a minority in most rural communities; and by the increasingly competitive character of national politics, making rural constituencies vital for the Right to win. Farm policy was considerably more cautious in the 1970s than in the 1960s, although there were fewer farmers. The bird-shooters of CPNT terrorised numerous Deputies – and even more Senators – from sensitive *départements* like the Gironde or the Somme into voting against the law shortening the season in 2000, although the law merely implemented a European directive. Another recent example concerns the homosexual vote – not large, and above all not homogeneous in national terms, but important enough in some marginal constituencies, notably in Paris, to be courted by the Socialists in 1997. That contributed to the legal recognition given to same-sex relationships by the PACS in 1999.

Public support

The backing of public opinion, though not essential, may be useful to a group. Groups with wide public support have forced right-wing governments into humiliating climbdowns about once a decade: miners in 1963, students in 1986, public-service workers in 1995 (in the latter case, although public support was far from unanimous, it was in a majority, and government-inspired efforts to engineer citizen indignation at the paralysed transport network got nowhere). The counter-example is that of Air France staff, whose threat (quickly withdrawn in the face of public disgust) to strike as France prepared to host the 1998 World Cup was a memorable public relations disaster. Certainly all groups consider public opinion important enough to court it. Pharmacists defend their exclusive right to sell non-prescription medical and paramedical products at extortionate prices on the grounds of a high-minded insistence that users of such products should have access to the best possible advice. Schoolteachers are always motivated by their touching concern for the interests of children, of education and of equality of opportunity. The FNSEA identifies the narrow interests of its members with those of the broader community by claiming that 'il n'y a pas de pays sans paysans'.

The social, economic and political context

Social, economic and political circumstances can also enhance or damage a group's influence. The general point about unemployment weakening the unions has already been made. More specific developments also diminished the power of working-class groups. In 1996, for example, the chill winds of European competition led dockers, a once feared group, to accept with little protest the end of the privileged contractual status which they had enjoyed since the Liberation and which had led to chronic over-manning. To do anything else would have forced several French ports to close altogether and handed the business to European rivals. The economic and European environments also changed what business could hope to gain from government. Bail-outs of loss-making firms had been commonplace in the 1970s, and the Socialists made large capital injections into the firms they nationalised after 1981. But from 1983, such help to 'lame ducks' was increasingly seen as expensive and ineffectual; governments became more concerned to control inflation and the budget than to save jobs. European competition rules also made such capital injections more difficult: they became, if not impossible (the Crédit Lyonnais and Air France bail-outs in the early 1990s, and that of Alstom in 2003, testify to that), at least rarer. At the same time, however, business was more successful, in the new environment, at lobbying for better general conditions of operation: thus corporate taxation was steadily reduced from 50 to 33 per cent between 1985 and 1993, under governments of both Left and Right. A final example concerns farmers, where the inclusion of agriculture in the Uruguay Round transformed the political environment of the CAP, and ensured that henceforth the interests of the FNSEA, while not ignored, would be weighed more rigorously against those of other economic groups.

The political context also affects the fortunes of groups. The régime change of 1958 transformed both the structure of the state and the relationship of groups with it – although the close relationship established between large firms and the civil servants who ran the Plan changed little. Ten years later, May 1968 convinced right-wing governments of the need to keep lines of communication open to the union movement. The Socialists elected in 1981 listened to trade unions, including the CGT (notably over the Auroux laws on workers' representation in the workplace), as well as to the left-wing farmers' unions, more than their right-wing predecessors had; and to the CNPF, the FNSEA and the representatives of Catholic schools they listened less. The Right's victory in March 1986 opened the way for the application of proposals developed by the CNPF for the four previous years. The Left's victory in 1997 clearly furthered the causes of gay rights and the shorter working week, despite opposition from Catholics and from the CNPF, who usually find readier listeners on the Right. The contrast, though, is very far from total. Before 1981, for example, the Barre government, while maintaining close relations with the CNPF on an institutional and a personal level, still increased the social charges of firms; after 1983–84, even left-wing governments felt obliged to heed those partners they had hitherto shunned – while little of the economic policy of the 1980s was to the liking of unions. From 2002 till his retirement in 2005, the MEDEF's president Ernest-Antoine Seillière seemed to do little but complain of the Raffarin government's failure to attend sufficiently to the needs of business.

Government policy

Policy changes decided by the government may propel hitherto ignored groups into the limelight. After the damaging electricians' strike of 1969, and against the background of May 1968, the Chaban-Delmas government introduced a *politique contractuelle* designed to put industrial relations on a more coherent and peaceful footing. The *politique contractuelle* was based on agreements binding for a specified period, on guarantees of real wage rises and on close collaborative relations with unions (much to the shock of traditional Gaullists – even though the CGT chose not to participate). A more recent, though in the end unsuccessful, example concerns Jospin's decision, late in 1999, to take the Corsican problem in hand and negotiate directly with all parties, including for the first time Corsica Nazione, the political wing of an armed nationalist movement, in the process that led to the (doomed) Matignon agreements of 2000.

The ministerial view

The attitude of individual ministers may help to legitimise certain groups – and to shut others out. As the education minister responsible for a controversial university reform in the wake of May 1968, the politically shrewd Edgar Faure multiplied his contacts with a wide range of university groups so as to prevent hostility from within the sector fuelling the very real opposition to reform within the Gaullist majority. Thirty years later, on the other hand, another education minister, Claude Allègre, openly boasted of his success in facing down the teachers' unions and in breaking what he saw as their stranglehold on France's centralised education system. After the unions had forced Allègre's resignation in March 2000, his successor, Jack Lang, moved to rebuild bridges with them, and particularly with the FSU, the strongest union in the secondary sector – even at the price of scaling down several of Allègre's planned reforms.

Countervailing forces

The power of countervailing forces also affects the influence of groups over policy-making. For example, the Union Nationale des Associations des Parents d'Élèves de l'Enseignement Libre (UNAPEL), the vigilant defender of Catholic private schools, is a powerful, well-organised group in its own terms, but is unable, even under right-wing governments, to achieve all of its aims because the Comité National d'Action Laïque and the Ligue Française de l'Enseignement are just as well organised and equally fierce in their defence of secular education. The result, as the events of 1984 and 1994 show, tends to be a stand-off. Environmental groups, while enjoying widespread general sympathy, have provoked fierce and often effective reactions from farmers, bird-shooters and the roads lobby. If the small shopkeepers of CID-UNATI failed to halt the decline in their numbers and support (0.72 per cent in the employers' college at the *prud'hommes* elections of 2002), it was partly because of opposition from the more discreet but no less effective Fédération Nationale des Entreprises à Commerces Multiples, which looks after the interests of the supermarkets; the commissions set up in the 1970s, under pressure from CID-UNATI, to vet applications for new hypermarkets, regularly agreed to the proposals, often under the influence of thinly disguised bribes. A counter-example concerns the issue of parity in political representation between men and women: the organised support for the reform was relatively weak, and public opinion favourable but not overwhelmingly so – but the organised opposition was non-existent.

The group's own resources

A group's own resources, finally, may have a crucial effect on its capacity to influence policy. These resources include representativeness, internal cohesion, technical expertise, money and the ability to mobilise their members. Trade unions are weak on most of these counts: unrepresentative of the working population, both individually and collectively; internally divided; lacking, despite their full-time employees, both in any particular technical expertise and in anything resembling a serious strike fund; frequently unable to mobilise members for more than symbolic 'days of action', yet intermittently taken unawares by sudden outbreaks of militancy, as in 1968 or 1995. The CNPF/MEDEF has often appeared little different, prone as it is to feuds within its own elite, the object of competition from other groups, and only episodically able to control or mobilise more than a handful of the 800,000 firms it claims as its membership. The FNSEA is stronger: about half of the farming community are members; its internal divisions are more or less controlled; its specialised branches command significant technical expertise; it is well financed (including, as it does, the wealthiest farmers in the land as well as poor peasants, and enjoying a symbiotic relationship with such bodies as the Chambers of Agriculture and the Crédit Agricole); it has repeatedly demonstrated its ability to mobilise members for a wide range of activities, legal and (less frequently) illegal. The most enviable situations, however, are those of groups enjoying monopolies in their sector. The infamously antediluvian and reactionary Ordre des Médecins, created by the Vichy régime in 1940 and granted a monopoly by de Gaulle in 1945 as the doctors' professional association, is still able to insist on membership as an absolute condition of practising the medical profession. Other closed-shop middle-class professions, able when necessary to defend the indefensible to government, have included architects, auctioneers and notaries (the subject of a characteristically perceptive study by Ezra Suleiman). The CGT's affiliated unions among printers and dockers have enjoyed similarly enviable positions – though even these, as we have observed in the case of dockers, have not protected them indefinitely against competition from outside France.

Three final remarks should be made about these internal resources of groups. First, they vary over time. Thus fears provoked by the Socialist victory of 1981 allowed the CNPF to mobilise its troops with a facility not seen before or since, holding a mass meeting of 20,000 heads of firms in 1982. Second, groups tend to overcome their divisions most readily in opposition to plans from government: hence the criticism that many groups are reactive not proactive, able to oppose but not propose. Third, strong internal resources are no guarantee of success. For example, the immensely wealthy Union Nationale de la Propriété Immobilière and Fédération Nationale des Agents Immobiliers, representing the building industry and estate agents, were unable to prevent a new Tenants' Rights Act in 1982 which they viewed as an 'intolerable revolution'. The highly restricted circle of French stockbrokers were forced to surrender their monopoly position by the liberalisation of the stock market initiated under the Socialist Finance Minister Bérégovoy in 1984, and continued by his right-wing successors. Even the most entrenched French groups have been forced to make concessions to the forces of European integration and competition. To the case of the dockers, already mentioned, may be added, for example, that of the auctioneers, now facing unaccustomed rivals from outside France (notably from Britain).

No single one of the nine factors listed above ensures a group's capacity to influence policy-making to its advantage. Groups that enjoy good access to government, are strategically placed in the economy and society, wield electoral leverage and enjoy support from the public and at least one minister, have priorities compatible with the broad thrust of government policy, are threatened by no strong opponents, and are representative of their sector, cohesive and prosperous, enjoy influence. Those that lack any of these assets are unlikely to – aside, that is, from those cases in which private interests thrive on public incompetence, as has been true of firms trading on the weak enforcement of government competition legislation to develop informal cartels.

Between the two extremes, however, is the great majority of groups that possess some but not all of the advantages outlined, and whose influence is therefore variable and unpredictable. The picture is, of course, equally varied from the government's point of view. Some groups are largely domesticated and function practically as agents of the administration; others, on the contrary, colonise their sponsor ministry or division within the ministry which they transform into something close to 'institutionalised pressure groups' (Henry Ehrmann). Both the FNSEA and the major teaching unions display a fine mixture of public disgruntlement and private collusion, engaging in militant action on occasion while still participating in the running of – and even the making of policy within – their sponsor ministries. The violence of FNSEA farmers has usually been tolerated more readily than that of militant trade unionists – or that of the FNSEA's rivals from the Confédération Paysanne. So has the impunity with which the activities of the pig-farming community have polluted two-thirds of France's water tables with slurry. That illustrates the attitude of apprehensive and embarrassed tolerance taken by governments towards the activities of certain groups – turning a blind eye, for example, to tax evasion by small businessmen, shopkeepers and hoteliers as well as farmers. In other situations the state may favour some groups within a sector and maintain minimal links, or none at all, with their rivals. Between domination of the groups by the state and its opposite, in other words, there is a wide variety of situations.

Concluding remarks

At the beginning of this chapter, it was shown that the founders of the Fifth Republic sought to restore the state's dominance over the groups after the weakness of the previous régime. To a degree they succeeded in this: Wilson, for example, considers the régime change of 1958 to have had a radical impact on group behaviour in France. The downgrading of parliament dried up formerly fruitful avenues of co-operation between groups and important Deputies or Senators. Because groups like to 'shoot where the ducks are', many turned their attentions to the newly powerful executive – which colluded with some while shutting out others. But change in the structure of the French state did not stop in 1958; on the contrary, it has accelerated since the 1980s, and has been paralleled in the configuration of French groups.

On the state side of the balance, political changes have been threefold: the surrender of parcels of sovereignty to Europe; the emergence of a more independent judiciary; and decentralisation. All are considered more fully in other chapters. All, on the principle of shooting where the ducks are, have encouraged groups to mobilise in new areas – Brussels, the courts, local and regional authorities – without, however, abandoning Paris. Europe, moreover, threatened the potential break-up of entrenched policy communities if their basis was purely national, especially as competition policy began to bite; and it introduced an alien culture of implementation, less tolerant of the Tocquevillian tendency to bend rules to specific cases. All of these developments weakened the Jacobin state of de Gaulle's day. So did the retreat from *dirigisme*, which meant it could no longer steer the French economy as it had still been able to in the de Gaulle and Pompidou presidencies. So did slower growth and higher unemployment, which meant greater social demands on the state and (relatively) less money to address them. So did the wider disenchantment with France's economic, administrative and business elites by the 1990s, all of them more or less tainted with scandal and economic failure. The Juppé episode in 1995 showed how unreceptive the French had become towards heroic leadership. Governments came to need groups more – to legitimate policy – but because of their straitened circumstances had less to offer them in exchange.

The state's loss of power vis-à-vis the groups did not automatically entail the groups' gain. Indeed, traditional mass groups, unions in particular, were affected as much as the state and political parties were by declining public trust in almost any big established organisation. A survey in 1989, for example, showed that only 29 per cent of respondents trusted an established union to defend their interests at work. The collapse of communism also had an impact on unions. In particular, it deprived the CGT of a central mobilising myth, and damaged it as the PCF tried – to the annoyance of members and increasingly of leaders too – to use it as an organisational prop. In the longer term it also meant that Wilson's view, formulated in the early 1980s, about the absence of basic consensus among groups about the rules of the game (especially the legitimacy of capitalism) became somewhat less true, although revolutionary aspirations have not wholly disappeared from France's interest groups. In addition and rather obviously, rising unemployment weakened the bargaining power of unions in the private sector (though not in the job-secure *fonction publique*) – and increased that of private business, the necessary provider of the jobs on which the election prospects of any government since the 1980s have come to depend.

It would be quite false, however, to conclude on the basis of the above that an enfeebled state is matched by anaemic groups. We have observed, in particular, how vigorously associations in France have expanded and proliferated, and how new social movements have mobilised, especially since the 1980s, on a variety of new fronts and with some success. Other studies have elucidated some of the nature of this mobilisation. It has, in many cases, taken the place of support for and membership of political parties, which have declined continuously for some twenty-five years; political activism, especially among the young, is undiminished but finds different outlets. And as researchers like Jacques Ion have shown, in a more individualistic society, styles of activism have changed. Group membership is not a lifetime commitment. Rank-and-file group members demand more consultation from leaders, and tend to mobilise for shorter periods on more specific and concrete causes, the importance of which has been clearly demonstrated to them.

Typical traits of all four models outlined above may be discerned in France, but in different proportions in different sectors. Like the rest of government, the relationship between the fragmented state and the no less fragmented groups during the Fifth Republic is complex, intrinsically untidy and constantly changing. At the same time there are signs that developments since the 1980s have tilted the balance of state–group relations in France in the direction of pluralism. It is pluralism with a difference, or rather several. First, as in other societies, it is an asymmetrical pluralism in which business and its organisations, without getting all they want, still wield disproportionate strength. Second, it is unusual in the (partial, but still significant) blocking power held by public-sector unions, seen repeatedly over the decade beginning in 1995. Third, all parties may still bring much older habits to the pluralist table. The distinctive traits so persuasively noted by Tocqueville, though never amounting to the whole picture, have had a way of reappearing across generations in very different environments. The state authorities can still be high-handed and oblivious to group demands to the point where they are accused of 'autism'. Groups, new and old, can still be maximalist, fragmented and ideological. The assumption that any successful negotiation must be preceded by a large-scale, often disruptive, show of strength remains deeply ingrained among the groups and widely supported among the population as a whole. Groups that seek, like the CFDT, to acknowledge real but unpalatable difficulties (such as the existence of a potential pensions crisis) and to negotiate on that basis, will always find rivals ready to outbid them. Thus while the supposed weakness of civil society in France, central to Tocquevillian models, is at least questionable, the capacity for positive engagement between civil society and the state remains very uneven. Groups, for that reason, are hampered in their capacity to build effective links between the French public and their government (and indeed may not aspire to do so). These tendencies pose rather obvious problems for French public policy. As Ezra Suleiman remarked in 1995 and as the polls cited at the beginning of Chapter 10 show, the French state has never been so condemned by its citizens, or so much in demand. Without the effective support of at least some bodies within civil society, whether among groups or parties, it is doomed to disappoint.

Further reading

Adam, G., *Le pouvoir syndical*, 2nd edition, Paris, Dunod, 1983.

Adam, G., *Les relations sociales année zéro*, Paris, Bayard, 2000.

Appleton, A., 'The New Social Movement phenomenon', in R. Elgie (ed.), *The Changing French Political System*, London, Frank Cass, 2000.

Archambault, E., *Le secteur sans but lucratif: associations et fondations en France*, Paris, Economica, 1996.

Aubert, V., Bergounioux, A., Martin, J. and Mouriaux, R., *La forteresse enseignante: la Fédération de l'Éducation Nationale*, Paris, Fayard, 1985.

Bard, C., Baudelot, C. and Mossuz-Lavau, J. (eds), *Quand les femmes s'en mêlent*, Paris, La Martinière, 2004.

Barthélemy, M., *Associations: un nouvel âge de la participation?*, Paris, Presses de Sciences Po, 2000.

Bauer, M. and Cohen, E., *Les grandes manœuvres industrielles*, Paris, Belfond, 1988.

Berger, S., *Peasants against Politics: Rural Organizations in Brittany*, Cambridge, MA, Harvard University Press, 1967.

Capdevielle, J. and Mouriaux, R., *Les syndicats ouvriers en France*, Paris, Armand Colin, 1973.

Cerny, P., *Social Movements and Protest in France*, London, Frances Pinter, 1982.

Cerny, P. and Schain, M. (eds), *French Politics and Public Policy*, London, Methuen, 1980.

Cerny, P. and Schain, M. (eds), *Socialism, the State, and Public Policy in France*, London, Methuen, 1985.

Cohen, E., *L'État brancardier: stratégies du déclin industriel*, Paris, Calmann-Lévy, 1989.

Colas, D. (ed.), *L'État et les corporatismes*, Paris, Presses Universitaires de France, 1988.

Coulomb, P., Delorme, H., Hervieu, B., Jollivet, M. and Lacombe, P., *Les agriculteurs et la politique*, Paris, Presses de la Fondation Nationale des Sciences Politiques, 1990.

Crettiez, X., *La question corse*, Brussels, Complexe, 1999.

Crettiez, X. and Sommier, I. (eds), *La France rebelle: tous les foyers, mouvements et acteurs de la contestation*, Paris, Michalon, 2002.

Duhamel, O. and Méchet, P., 'Une grève d'opinion', SOFRES, *L'état de l'opinion 1996*, Paris, Seuil, 1996, pp. 33–48.

Duyvendak, J.-W., *The Power of Politics: New Social Movements in France*, Boulder, CO, Westview Press, 1995.

Ehrmann, H., *Organized Business in France*, Princeton, NJ, Princeton University Press, 1957.

Favre, P. (ed.), *La manifestation*, Paris, Presses de la Fondation Nationale des Sciences Politiques, 1990.

Geay, B., *Le syndicalisme enseignant*, Paris, La Découverte, 1997.

Giuliani, J.-D., *Marchands d'influence. Les lobbies en France*, Paris, Seuil, 1991.

Hayward, J., *The State and the Market Economy*, New York, Harvester Wheatsheaf, 1986.

Ion, J., *La fin des militants?*, Paris, l'Atelier, 1997.

Jobert, B. and Muller, P., *L'état en action: politiques publiques et corporatismes*, Paris, L'Harmattan, 1987.

Keeler, J., *The Politics of Neocorporatism in France: Farmers, the State, and Agricultural Policy-Making in the Fifth Republic*, Oxford, Oxford University Press, 1987.

Kesselman, M. and Groux, G. (eds), *Le mouvement ouvrier français: crise économique et changement politique*, Paris, Editions Ouvrières, 1984.

Labbé, D., *Syndicats et syndiqués en France depuis 1945*, Paris, L'Harmattan, 1997.

Lamarque, G., *Le lobbying*, Paris, Presses Universitaires de France, 1994.

Levy, J., *Tocqueville's Revenge: State, Society, and Economy in Contemporary France*, Cambridge, Mass., Harvard University Press, 1999.

Marie, J.-L., *Agriculteurs et politique*, Paris, Montchrestien, 1994.

Mouriaux, R., *Les syndicats dans la société française*, Paris, Presses de la Fondation Nationale des Sciences Politiques, 1983.

Mouriaux, R., *Les syndicats face à la crise*, Paris, 1986.

Mouriaux, R., *Le syndicalisme en France depuis 1945*, Paris, La Découverte, 1994.

Mouriaux, R., *Histoire de la CGT*, Brussels, Complexe, 1995.

Mouriaux, R., *Le syndicalisme en France*, Paris, Presses Universitaires de France, 1997.

Mouriaux, R., *Crises du syndicalisme français*, Paris, Montchrestien, 1998.

Nelkin, D. and Pollack, M., *The Atom Besieged: Extra-parliamentary Dissent in France and Germany*, Cambridge, MA, 1982.

Neveu, E., *Sociologie des mouvements sociaux*, Paris, La Découverte, 1996.

Offerlé, M., *Sociologie des groupes d'intérêt*, Paris, Montchrestien, 1994.

Ottenheimer, G. and Lecadre, R., *Les Frères invisibles*, Paris, Albin Michel, 2001.

Rand-Smith, W., *Organizing Class Struggle in France: Grassroots Unionism in the CGT and the CFDT*, London, Macmillan, 1986.

Rand-Smith, W., *Crisis in the French Labour Movement*, London, Palgrave Macmillan, 1987.

Reece, J., *The Bretons against France: Ethnic Minority Nationalism in Twentieth-Century Brittany*, Chapel Hill, NC, University of North Carolina Press, 1977.

Schmidt, V., *From State to Market? The Transformation of French Business and Government*, Cambridge, Cambridge University Press, 1996.

Schmitter, P., 'Still the century of corporatism?', *Review of Politics*, 36 (1974), pp. 88–102.

Segrestin, D., *Le phénomène corporatiste: essai sur l'avenir des systèmes professionnels fermés en France*, Paris, Fayard, 1985.

Shackleton, M., *The Politics of Fishing in Britain and France*, Aldershot, Gower, 1986.

Suleiman, E., *Les notaires: les pouvoirs d'une corporation*, Paris, Seuil, 1987.

Waters, S., *Social Movements in France: Towards a New Citizenship*, Basingstoke, Palgrave Macmillan, 2003.

Weber, H., *Le parti des patrons. Le CNPF, 1946–1990*, 2nd edition, Paris, Seuil, 1991.

Wilson, F. L., *Interest-Group Politics in France*, Cambridge, Cambridge University Press, 1987.

12 Paris and the provinces
The post-Jacobin state

Relations between France's capital city and the provinces have often varied between uneasy coexistence and open warfare. Traditionally, Paris was depicted as the malevolent centre of revolution which, in 1789, 1814–15, 1830, 1848 and 1871, disturbed the contented and peace-loving provincials. It was also portrayed as the diabolic purveyor of those modish doctrines and timeless temptations which undermined the austere virtues of provincial life, and as a harlot whose mindless frivolity had brought the country at least once (in 1870) to the brink of humiliating disaster. Paris was, in short, a politically turbulent Babylon, resented all the more because of its political, administrative, intellectual and cultural dominance over the rest of the country.

But the Jacobins who fashioned the First Republic and who bequeathed most of their institutions and many of their attitudes to later régimes did not view the capital in this lurid light. They saw it as an island of culture, a city of enlightenment, a torchbearer of progress assailed by oafish – and reactionary – rural clods, the ignorant troops of the Church and the chateau. Like the monarchs of the *ancien régime*, they imposed centralisation as their means of strengthening the régime against both internal opponents and external enemies. Napoleon perfected and future régimes consolidated the centralising work of the Jacobins. Each was uneasily aware not only of its own fragility but also of the very precariousness of the French national fabric. France is a country of great geographical and cultural diversity and was created by bringing together (with the persuasion of axe, sword and musket) peoples as distinct as the Basques and the Bretons, the Béarnais and the Burgundians, the Alsatians and the Auvergnats, the Normans and the Provençals. Parts of France such as Nice and Savoy are recent acquisitions (they were annexed in 1860), and Alsace was twice in the twentieth century (in 1918 and 1945) taken back from the Germans. Eugen Weber has estimated that as recently as the 1860s, only half the population of what is now France spoke French as their mother tongue (though universal primary schooling, military service and railways were to change that after the advent of the Third Republic in 1870). Autonomous sentiments have always been regarded with obsessive suspicion and crass insensitivity because it was felt that they could lead to the temptation of secession if allowed to flourish. Centralisation was also the instinctive reaction of governments to the invasions and military occupations entailed by successive wars, in 1814–15, 1870–71, 1914–18 and 1940–45.

Centralising tendencies were accentuated during the first three-quarters of the twentieth century, for four reasons. First, industrial development, hitherto dispersed in the provinces, came to Paris and its suburbs. The tertiary sector followed, especially with the modernising of France's industrial and financial structures, and the revolution in communications and the media, after 1945. The capital's economic, demographic and cultural dominance was thereby enhanced. By 1975, the Paris region (Île-de-France), which covers just 2.2 per cent of the territory of mainland France, housed a fifth of the nation's population, 35 per cent of its business headquarters and 60 per cent of its research scientists (as well as almost all of its actors and its few decent musicians). Second, the brief experience of rule from outside Paris – in 1940–44, when the German occupiers shifted the seat of France's residual government to the little spa town of Vichy – provoked a reaction in favour of the capital among the framers of the Fourth Republic's Constitution, for whom Vichy innovations like regions smacked of collaboration with the enemy. Third, the post-war rise of big government led the French state both to grow at the centre and, partly out of respect for the egalitarian aspirations of France's political culture, to impose minimum standards in politically sensitive areas such as education, housing and health on the localities responsible in various ways for administering them. Fourth, the Gaullists who shaped the Fifth Republic were at least as Jacobin in their instincts as the Socialists and Christian Democrats who had founded the Fourth. For President de Gaulle's first prime minister, Michel Debré, centralised state authority was essential to combat not only powerful 'professional feudalities', those major groups which threatened the 'general interest' by the pursuit of their selfish, particular goals, but also provincial threats to the 'one and indivisible Republic'.

Yet even at its Gaullist High Noon, French centralism met with resistance, in four forms. The first of these was the local political system itself, increasingly stable, well rooted and largely impervious for a century or so to the convulsions that periodically seized France's national polity. The second was the vogue for self-management (*autogestion*), and the corresponding disillusion with central state planning, that were part of the fallout of May 1968. The third was the regionalist movements in such areas as Brittany and 'Occitania' (roughly, south-western France), which turned leftwards at the same period after flirting with Fascism and collaboration a generation earlier. The fourth was the left-wing parties. The Communists and Socialists, out of office nationally for a generation after 1958, but increasingly powerful at local level, unsurprisingly discovered the virtues of local and regional autonomy in relation to an invasive Parisian bureaucracy. Perhaps slightly more remarkable was that François Mitterrand, having led his Socialists into office in May 1981, placed these concerns at the heart of his first-term plans. Decentralisation was not only proclaimed as *la grande affaire du septennat*; as early as March 1982, what became known as the Defferre Act opened a cascade of measures which gave it far-reaching, concrete, legislative form.

Decentralisation remains Mitterrand's major institutional legacy. However, the pre-1982 system was rather less centralised than was often claimed, and his decentral-isation reforms did not set free the localities quite as much as is often supposed. Hence the widespread assumption that there remained unfinished business, and the announcement by Prime Minister Raffarin of 'Decentralisation Act II', beginning with a constitutional amendment in 2003. The debate about decentralisation and local government in France is not, however, merely about institutional tinkering, or the ancestral mistrust (however lively) between Paris and the provinces. It touches on some of the most critical issues confronting contemporary French policy-makers: how to attract international investment and to encourage small and medium firms to grow and innovate; how to improve education and training within a knowledge economy; how to reclaim rundown and lawless suburbs for the local and national community; how to breathe new life into France's emptying countryside; how, finally, to place regional development within a European context. Before considering these points in more detail, it is worth looking briefly at the main institutions and the actors at local and regional level.

The institutions and the actors

Local government in France presents a particularly rich and varied tapestry. It is organ-ised, unusually for a unitary state (and in common with only four other EU25 members), at no fewer than three levels: regions, *départements* and communes or muni-cipalities. The number of units is very large: France has 38 per cent of the EU25's subnational authorities for 13 per cent of the population. In metropolitan France (the mainland plus Corsica) there are 22 regions, 96 *départements* (divided into 320 adminis-trative *arrondissements* and 3,872 electoral districts or *cantons*) and 36,564 communes (each with its own mayor and municipal council). The far-flung Départements et Territoires d'Outre-Mer (DOM-TOM), which will not be discussed in detail here, include another 214 communes, 4 *départements*, 4 regions, 4 territories and 2 'collect-ivities of special status', spread out across the globe from Guadeloupe and Martinique to New Caledonia, from Réunion to St-Pierre et Miquelon. In 2001 metropolitan France had over half a million elected local officials, 514,519 of them municipal councillors.

The communes date from 1789 but are based on the parishes of the *ancien régime*; the *départements*, created in 1790, resemble the old dioceses. The regions, on the other hand, are a creation of the Fifth Republic (they were envisaged by an *ordonnance* of January 1959, created in June 1960 and given their present shape in March 1964, July 1972 and March 1982). The size of the various territorial units varies widely. In 1999, 15.5 per cent (9,038,000) of France's metropolitan population lived in the 36 communes with over 100,000 inhabitants, and half (29,529,000) in the 874 communes with more than 10,000 inhabitants, while 26 per cent (15,142,000) lived in the 31,927 communes with fewer than 2,000 inhabitants and 12 per cent (6,833,000) in the 24,720 communes with a population of below 700. Also in 1999, 25 *départements* had a larger population than the whole Limousin region, while 15 regions had a smaller population than the single *département* of the Nord. Inevitably, there is a wide diversity of resources between the various types of territorial unit and within each type. In 1994 Paris (admit-tedly a unique case, as it has the double status of *département* and commune) had a budget of 33.5 billion francs and over 35,000 employees, whereas the vast majority of communes had minuscule budgets and personnel to match – often one part-time secretary. The budgets of the *départements* and the regions also vary enormously. Yet despite this extreme diversity, each type of territorial unit – region, *département* and commune – has, with rare exceptions such as Paris and Corsica, the same internal structure and the same legal powers.

In law, the relationship between the three types of local authority is not a hierarchical one (a principle shared only by the Danes among EU nations). That, plus the overlapping jurisdictions inevitable in all policy-making, has led to duplication, competition and rivalry. Councils of *départements* and municipalities are often deeply suspicious (like their counterparts in Italy or Spain) of attempts by the regions to co-ordinate their activities. Of the three types of local authority, the most important in terms of resources is the commune, and the weakest the region. This is reflected in terms both of personnel (of the 1,665,737 local authority employees in 2001, 1,076,809 were employed by the communes) and of budget size (Table 12.1). It is worth noting, however, where the fastest growth took place between 1984 and 2001: whereas the budgets of communes and *départements* approximately doubled in real terms, those of regions, and of the various forms of groups of communes, such as urban communities, which increasingly manage a range of municipal functions, have approximately quadrupled.

Decision-making takes place at all three of these levels, as well as in the groups of communes. Local decision-makers belong essentially to four categories of institution: the representative assemblies and their executives; the prefectoral administration; the provincial field services of the Paris ministries; and non-institutional actors such as local pressure groups, professional associations and major private firms.

Table 12.1 Local budgets, 1984 and 2001 (in billions of euros, constant at 2001 levels)

	Communes (1)		Départements (2)		Regions (3)		Groups of Communes (4)		Total (1, 2, 3, 4)	
	1984	2001	1984	2001	1984	2001	1984	2001	1984	2001
Income										
Taxes	20.9	38.7	11.5	21.7	2.0	7.4	2.5	10.4	36.9	78.1
Loans	6.8	7.3	2.6	3.5	0.6	1.8	2.4	3.1	12.5	15.7
Grants	18.6	22.0	11.0	12.6	0.8	4.1	5.1	10.4	35.5	49.1
Other	6.4	9.0	0.8	1.2	0.1	0.4	3.4	7.3	10.6	17.9
Total	52.7	77.0	25.9	39.0	3.5	13.7	13.4	31.2	95.4	160.8
Spending										
Current	35.0	51.5	18.6	24.3	1.3	6.2	6.4	18.6	61.3	100.5
(including interest on loans)	4.1	2.9	1.3	0.8	0.2	0.4	1.9	1.0	7.4	5.1
Investment	16.1	25.6	6.2	14.9	2.0	7.6	6.5	12.7	30.8	60.7
(including capital repayments)	2.7	7.8	1.1	6.0	0.1	2.0	0.8	3.3	4.7	19.1
Total	51.1	77.0	24.8	39.2	3.3	13.7	12.9	31.3	92.1	161.3

Source: Calculated from Ministère de l'Intérieur, *Les collectivités locales en chiffres*, 1987 and 2004.

Map 12.1 France: *départements* and regions.

Representative assemblies and their executives

Representative assemblies exist at all three levels of local government. At the regional level there are two assemblies. The more important of them, the regional council, ranges in size from 43 to 209 members, and has been directly elected, since 1986, on a modified proportional representation system based on the *départements*. Alongside it, and playing a consultative role, is the regional economic and social council (known as a committee till 1992), composed of representatives of businesses, trade unions and other pressure groups within the region. The powers of both assemblies are defined in acts of 1972, 1982, 1992 and 2003–4, and in the implementing decrees that followed. Since

1986, the region's chief executive has been the president of the regional council, chosen by the councillors after each regional election.

The council of the *département* (*conseil général*) varies in size from 25 (for Lozère, the smallest *département*, with 73,500 inhabitants) to 163 (for Paris, with 2.1 million). Like members of the regional councils, the *conseillers généraux* are directly elected for a six-year term. They differ in that only half are renewed at a time, every three years; and they are elected on a two-ballot majority system in single-member districts (the cantons). The functions of the *conseils généraux*, essentially as servicing agencies for the state, were outlined in an act of 1884. They were considerably expanded, however, by the Defferre Act of March 1982, which enshrined the president of the *conseil général*, chosen by the councillors after each partial renewal, as the chief executive of the *département*, and extended the powers of the *département* in such areas as social assistance and education, as well as in the provision of subsidies and technical assistance to small, rural communes.

In each of the 36,564 French communes, there is a municipal council, directly elected every six years. It elects a mayor, and exercises powers defined in acts of 1871, 1884 and 1982. Like the *département*, the commune is both a servicing agency of the state, incurring obligatory expenses, and a local authority able to intervene in other areas not specifically forbidden by law. Like the *départements* too, the communes saw their powers substantially extended in 1982 – notably in the areas of economic intervention and town planning. By 'communes', however, one can often understand 'mayors': for it is no very great exaggeration to claim that in most cases, the task of the 514,519 municipal councillors is to elect the 36,564 mayors and to ratify their decisions. The mayor has two main official roles. First, as the *representative of the state in the commune*. As such, he or she promulgates and ensures the implementation of laws, regulations, circulars and instructions emanating from Paris. The mayor is also the official registrar of births, deaths and marriages, and is responsible for drawing up the electoral list and for compiling official statistics (such as census figures) for the state. Second, the mayor is the *executive officer of the municipal council* and represents the commune in judicial proceedings, is the head of all communal staff, implements the decisions of the council, supervises its accounting and manages its revenues. The mayor has official responsibility for the commune's order, safety, security and sanitation. Just as important as these official tasks is the mayor's political role, taken in the widest sense of the term: for in marked contrast to his or her British counterpart, the French mayor is an important, influential personality. Almost all mayors remain in office for at least one full six-year term: most are re-elected for at least one further term. The French know who their mayors are (to a far greater extent than they can identify their Deputies, for example), and despite a spate of municipal scandals since the early 1990s, still tend to trust them; since the 1970s, a succession of polls has shown levels of confidence in mayors running at 75 per cent, compared with roughly 50 per cent for Deputies – and well under 30 per cent for 'politicians in general' or 'parties in general'.

The prefectoral authorities

The prefectoral corps is composed of regional prefects, prefects of the *départements*, and subprefects (one in each *arrondissement*).

* *The regional prefect* is a recent creation, dating only from 1959. His headquarters is

in the principal town of the region's main *département*, and he remains the prefect of that *département*. His powers were defined in measures enacted in June 1960, March 1964, July 1972, March 1982 and February 1992. His main task is to give cohesion to administrative planning, particularly in the area of economic planning. To that end, he must co-ordinate and direct the work of the prefects in each *département*. He is helped by a regional mission, a group of young civil servants who advise him and execute his decisions, and a regional administrative conference which brings together, about every month, the prefects of each of the region's *départements*, the regional representative of the Finance Ministry, and appropriate members of the field services of the Paris ministries. Although he lost his role as the region's chief executive to the president of the regional council in 1986, he may address the regional council with the agreement of its president or at the request of the prime minister.

In principle, the regional prefect, together with elected officials, has lent a regional coherence and rationality to local investment policies. The Joxe Act of February 1992, for example, required him to co-ordinate government policy across the region in the areas of culture, the environment, rural development and urban policy. In practice, he has often become one of the main agents for articulating the grievances of the *départements* and for transmitting to Paris economic packages bearing the marks of traditional incrementalism – though repeated legislation has gone some way to enhancing his authority over notional subordinates.

• A *prefect* is appointed for each of France's ninety-six metropolitan *départements*, and a subprefect for each *arrondissement*. Though the prefect can trace his ancestry to the *intendant* of the *ancien régime*, he is essentially a creation of the Napoleonic era, and his official roles have not changed dramatically since then. They may be considered under four headings.

First, the prefect is the representative of the state in the *département*, the personification of state authority, the living embodiment of the one and indivisible Republic. He has an official uniform, a sumptuous official residence (the *hôtel de la préfecture*) in the main town of the *département*, an official car and sometimes princely living expenses (a partial compensation for a salary which prefects consider meagre by private-sector standards). He is assisted by a *cabinet* and by a prefecture staff numbering anything from 100 to 800, depending on the size of *département*. He receives all visiting dignitaries and presides over all major ceremonies, and represents the state in its dealings with the local authorities.

Second, he is the representative of the government in the *département*, with the task of supervising and co-ordinating the work of the field services of the Paris ministries (with the exception of some parts of the work of Defence, Justice, Finance, Education and Labour, which escape his official jurisdiction) and he ensures that law and governmental directives are implemented. His role as the 'overlord' of the field services in the *département* was laid down in unambiguous terms in acts of March 1964, March 1982 and February 1992.

Third, he is the main agent of the Interior Ministry in the *département*, and, as such, is responsible for taking action against local authorities guilty of illegality or financial abuses. He also directly supervises those field services of the Interior Ministry responsible for the maintenance of law and order. He has the right to ban a film, a demonstration or a procession if he feels it is likely to be prejudicial to public order. Finally, the prefect organises elections. He was formerly seen as the main electoral agent of the minister of the interior in particular and the governing majority in general, and although there is no doubt that this aspect of his work has declined, his post remains politically charged. Like an ambassador, the prefect is expected to write regular reports on the political situation in his posting. He may also give advice, information and warnings to pro-governmental candidates. And the regular game of prefectoral musical chairs (with some prefects, inevitably, ending up unseated) that has followed the major changes of government since 1981 testifies to the political sensitivity of the post: as many as fifty prefects were moved on within a year of the Right's return to power in 2002. But the overt intervention in election campaigns typical of earlier years is now recognised as personally imprudent and politically counterproductive.

Until March 1982, the prefect was also the chief executive officer of the *conseil général* of the *département*, a role he has now lost to the president of the council. But the prefect retains a key position in the local political and administrative systems, at the intersections between centre and periphery, between national and local politics, between politics and administration, and between different territorial branches of the state services. This makes his co-operation essential for the plans of the *conseil général* and its president to be furthered. It is also revealing that several local authorities have recruited members of the prefectoral corps to head their administrative services.

The local field services

The state's authority in the *département* rests not only on the prefect but also on the field services of the several ministries. The five most powerful state officials outside the prefecture in most regions or *départements* are the Treasurer and Paymaster General (TPG, the main agent of the Finance Ministry), the Director of Infrastructure (*directeur de l'Équipement*), the Director of Labour, the Director of Health and Social Affairs (*directeur des Affaires Sanitaires et Sociales*) and the Director of Agriculture. The Defence Ministry is represented by a general in each region and *département* (responsible for the local gendarmerie among other things), the Ministry of Education by a rector, the Ministry of Justice by a state prosecutor. One of the major effects of the March 1982 act was the transfer of many state officials to the *départements*, and to a lesser extent to the regions. The field services, and their heads, have remained, albeit in often diminished form; while some of the officials, especially those belonging to highly prestigious technical corps with their own national networks of influence, remained powerful figures in their own right even when in the employ of the region or *département* rather than the state.

One state service, finally, was created by the Defferre Act of March 1982. This set up a court of accounts (*chambre régionale des comptes*) in each region, staffed by irremovable magistrates, who may be (and indeed must be, in the case of the president of each regional court) directly recruited from the prestigious Court of Accounts (Cour des Comptes) in Paris. The role of the regional court is to make regular assessments of the accounts of all the local authorities (or dependent bodies) within its area of jurisdiction, and it plays a crucial part in the more flexible financial control exercised by the prefects over the local authorities since 1982. It may also comment on the financial prudence (or lack thereof) with which local authorities run their affairs.

Other local bodies

Other influential local decision-makers include a wide range of bodies more or less closely related to the private sector. Official bodies such as the Chambers of Commerce and Industry, of Agriculture, and of Crafts (*métiers*) play a greater role than their British equivalents (if a lesser one than their counterparts in Germany). All firms, for example, must belong to a Chamber of Commerce and Industry. Each Chamber elects its own leadership group and has the power to tax members and to use this revenue for a variety of purposes, including building roads and bridges (both of the major bridges over the Seine estuary, for example, were Chamber of Commerce projects). Major players in the areas of housing and urban planning and regional economic development, and in the management of major social and cultural facilities, are the *sociétés d'économie mixte* (SEMs), para-public bodies grouping public and private capital and often wielding rights of compulsory purchase conceded to them by local authorities for specific projects; the number of local SEMs exceeded 1,400 by the mid-1990s. In many areas, individual private firms have played a major role, whether as major employers or, increasingly, as purveyors of a widening range of privatised urban services. Most of the major national pressure groups have local branches, although some groups, notably in the areas of culture and city planning, are exclusively local in character. Other, public, bodies may also play an important local role; the investment plans of the port authority, for example, may well be crucial to the development of towns like Le Havre or Marseille.

Mayors and other elected officials are obliged to establish a working relationship with at least some of these groups. In Bordeaux, for example, Jacques Chaban-Delmas built up a complex power network linking the Chamber of Commerce, old Protestant families who ran much of the wine trade and rugby clubs (in the late 1940s he was both mayor and a rugby international himself). In Le Havre, the class loyalties of the Communists who ran the city for a generation did not prevent them from cultivating good relations with the port authority and the Chamber of Commerce. In Lyon, the internecine conflict within the local right-wing parties may be seen at least partly as a struggle for influence between rival pharmaceutical laboratories. More generally, no right-wing list at election time can consider itself safe if it does not include a representative of the local Chamber of Commerce. It is also clear that in many rural *départements* both the biggest agricultural pressure group, the Fédération Nationale des Syndicats d'Exploitants Agricoles (FNSEA), and the Chamber of Agriculture enjoy easy access to, and influence with, local officials – as well as the means, if necessary, to bypass them and use direct access to Paris or Brussels. Most prefects, finally, still chair numerous consultative committees involving such groups; indeed, this role as a broker for a wide variety of local interests increased as the prefects' traditional legitimacy as the state's representatives was dented by decentralisation.

Jacobinism and its limits: France before decentralisation

If 1982 appears as a turning point in central–local relations in France it is because they really were transformed, in legal terms, by the flurry of decentralising legislation that opened within months of the Socialists' winning power. The political picture, however, is more complex, and presents important elements of continuity as well as the impact of forces quite outside the centralisation/decentralisation dichotomy. This section seeks to assess the bases of centralisation under the pre-1982 régime, and the sources of local autonomy which were already undermining it.

The bases of central power

The political bases of central power before 1982 were, it was argued, fivefold.

- *The statutory weakness of the local authorities was complemented by an obsessive control exercised by Paris and its provincial agents, the prefects and the technical field services.* The prefects' role as chief executives of regions and *départements* reinforced such controls at these two levels, for the prefects both prepared all the essential deliberations of the assemblies and managed the administrations that were to implement them, leaving the elected officials (who were not even directly elected, in the case of the pre-1986 regions) with few real resources to act as a counterweight. The acts of municipalities, where the mayor rather than a state-appointed official was the chief executive, still required a priori prefectoral approval – that is, the prefect's signature was necessary before they came into force. If any local authority wished to beg or borrow, add a new tax or change the basis of an existing one, build a new school or even name a street after someone, the state authorities could, and often did, intervene. Parisian control was all the more effective because the central government agents were omnipresent in the provinces, busily executing tasks that in Britain were left to local authority staff.
- *The archaic nature of local government structures rendered local government especially powerless.* France has retained, largely intact, the local government structures of a rural age in which social and economic expectations were non-existent. Perhaps nine out of ten communes were too small to meet the new demands placed upon them in an era of big government (though it is true that a hundred or so very small communes cleverly circumvented the problem by having no inhabitants at all). France's vast municipal mosaic reflects no contemporary demographic, occupational or economic realities. Incentives to merge communes (notably under the 1971 Marcellin Act) abolished fewer than 3 per cent of the total number – and some of these returned after de-mergers. The Guichard Report of October 1976, which envisaged consolidation of most functions into 'only' 4,350 local authorities, was shelved after fierce opposition from rural mayors. The mosaic remains.
- *The profoundly conservative nature of local elites deprived them of legitimacy in their dealings with state officials.* The chronic rural over-representation characteristic of France's fragmented local government system ensured that local government elites were profoundly unrepresentative: the big battalions of mayors and *conseillers généraux* came from the ranks of farmers, small business or the liberal professions; few, on the other hand, were managers or blue- or white-collar workers. Four-fifths of mayors and *conseillers généraux* (by the mid-1970s) were over 50; over 97 per cent were men. Such individuals were often unsympathetic to the moods and needs of a more modern France, and technically ill-equipped to meet its challenges. This reinforced their dependence on the expertise and the initiatives of the state services.
- *The financial dependence of the local authorities was virtually complete.* Local government finance, as Mrs Thatcher discovered in 1990, has always been a politically explosive issue, chiefly because of the difficulty of matching resources to needs in each locality. Such inequities were reinforced by the combination of extreme

local authority fragmentation with the rapid urban and industrial growth of the *trente glorieuses*. Many local authorities faced ever greater calls on financial resources that remained limited, despite tax rises running steadily ahead of inflation. For new investment projects, most local authorities had to turn to the state for subsidies and to state-run credit institutions for loans – which in turn entailed extensive technical, financial and legal controls by the various field services, sanctioned in the fullness of time by the signature (or non-signature) of the prefect. Procedures for allocating such loans and subsidies were in any case of a byzantine complexity. A senatorial report of 1973 enumerated no fewer than 150 kinds of subsidy available to local authorities, channelled through seventeen different agencies (after simplification, a mere 50 remained). Mastery of such complex procedures combined with the competing needs of local authorities afforded the state great financial leverage. This it readily used, whether as an instrument of macro- and microeconomic policy, by regulating local investment levels or directing local authorities' budgetary choices; as a means of promoting the reorganisation of local government; or as a way to reward the politically sympathetic and buttress their electoral chances.

- *The centralisation of most political, economic and financial actors complemented that of the state*. The federalism of states like the USA or Germany has always been underpinned by a territorial diversity of activity, and particularly by the separation of political from financial and industrial centres. Italy, too, is marked by the contrast between the political weight of Rome and the north's economic importance. Even the United Kingdom includes, in Scotland, a territory with a distinct legal identity and a cohesive, largely home-grown elite. France, however, appeared as comprehensively centralised: *Paris et le désert français*, the evocative title of a book written in the 1940s by Jean-François Gravier, was still, despite efforts by Gaullist governments to decongest the capital by creating new towns and to divert activities towards provincial centres, a dominant image thirty years later. Economic realities simply mirrored the constitutional and administrative facts that made Paris, as the seat of executive, legislative and judicial authority, the 'natural' centre of administration. French elections were increasingly conducted as national competitions, whether they were national, local or, from 1979, European. And the political culture of France was steeped in the 'central value system', to use Shils's term, of Jacobinism, which structured mentalities, expectations and actions as relations between the state and local authorities were played out. Small wonder, then, that major local politicians had to spend much of their time in Paris.

The pre-1982 picture thus appears a sombre one, with innocent and virginal provinces assailed and violated by a brutal and insensitive capital. In truth, however, the situation was much less melodramatic, and infinitely more complex.

Local influences in the one and indivisible Republic

Even before 1982, the rigours of centralisation were tempered by factors which ensured that local decision-makers were not the inactive spectators of their own collective fate. There were eight such factors.

The state's de facto *dependence on the localities*

The state depended on the localities in several important respects. Even before March 1982, the local authorities employed 850,000 people, raised nearly a fifth of the total taxes, accounted for some 60 per cent of non-military public investment projects, acted as a vital servicing agency for the centre, and played a direct and initiatory role in areas such as primary schools, crèches, housing, transport, culture, urban planning, local roads, traffic control, sanitation and sports facilities. The investment and employment policies of local authorities could therefore have an enormous impact on the financial and economic policies of the central government. The successful implementation of such policies required the co-operation of local authorities, as anyone tempted to bypass the periphery soon discovered. Local state officials, far from being the agents of enlightened national economic rationalism, often acted as spokespeople for local interests. Even DATAR (Délégation à l'Aménagement du Territoire et à l'Action Régionale), the regional planning unit set up in the prime minister's office in 1963, carried out its job of industrial decentralisation with one eye on economic imperatives and the other on the polling booths; it was therefore obliged to seek the co-operation of local elected officials, even at the price of concessions that detracted from the goals of 'rational' planning.

The fragmentation of the central administration

Provincial elites were able to exploit differences in the central government bureaucracy. 'The state' is no more a homogeneous entity in its relations with the provinces than it is in Paris; it is merely a convenient shorthand term (even if the French like to invest it with a quasi-mystical quality) embracing a vast variety of political, administrative, public and semi-public agents. And between these decision-makers, conflict was (and is) endemic and sometimes bitter. All was not sweetness and light between, for example, the ministries of the Interior and Finance, between the Ministry of Infrastructure and DATAR, or between the Ministry of Finance and the Caisse des Dépôts. Astute local *notables* could frequently exploit such endemic feuds. Rivalries also existed between the various field services, which tended to avoid conflict by avoiding each other, thereby minimising co-ordination; between the locally entrenched field services and their superiors in Paris, who played what Jean-Claude Thoenig has called 'an elaborate game of hide and seek', in which a local elected official was often the only link; and between the field services and the prefects, whose attempts to play their legal role as co-ordinators were liable to run into the sand without outside help.

The symbiosis between state officials and localities

State officials were often sensitive to local requirements. Unlike their British counterparts, top civil servants in France are allowed to stand for local (as well as national) office, and many do so, often under well-defined political labels. Many Paris officials have family roots in the provinces and wish to retain and even strengthen them by serving their local community. No *conseil général* is complete without at least one top civil servant based in Paris, and the ranks of French mayors also include members of the Paris administrations, of ministerial *cabinets* and of the *grands corps*. Such individuals could speak on equal terms with the prefect, bring pressure to bear upon him through Paris or even bypass him completely, thereby winning patronage for their own communes or cantons.

State officials in the field services were also susceptible to local influences, to the point, after a certain time lapse, of 'going native'. Enjoying some discretion in interpreting directives from Paris, they would often display great inventiveness in ignoring, modifying or violating them. The length of time that such officials stayed in given localities and were exposed to their pressures (generally much longer than prefects) goes some way to accounting for such behaviour. Another reason was money. Three-fifths of the work of the state field services was for the local authorities, which requested and paid for their help in the initial preparation of projects, and later in their implementation. Since the field services were also involved in verifying the legality of such projects and their compliance with technical norms, they were thereby placed in a dubious moral position. But moral convictions tended to disappear under the deadening weight of established practice and the anaesthetising effect of the percentage paid for work. The practice underlines the mutual dependence of elected and non-elected officials: the technical dependence of the former created and then sustained the financial dependence of the latter.

The power of the notables

The position of locally elected *notables* was much more powerful than the texts suggested. This observation, according to historians, was true as early as the July monarchy (1830–48). The position of local *notables* was reinforced by their justifiable claim that unlike the prefects and many other officials, their local roots were deep and strong: almost to a man, they lived in the localities they represented, and had usually been born there. Second, most elected *notables* showed great institutional longevity. A handful of mayors have served half a century: Édouard Herriot, mayor of Lyon from 1905 till 1957, and Jacques Chaban-Delmas, mayor of Bordeaux from 1947 to 1995, are two illustrious examples. Others have handed on local office from father to son like a family heirloom. Very many more have served, as mayors of villages or cities, or as *conseillers généraux*, for two to three decades. The *notables* thus had ample evidence for their claim to know local people and problems better than the prefects, who typically lasted just two or three years in any single post before disappearing from the *département* with the inevitability of Puccini heroines.

The third factor which strengthened many local *notables* in their relations with state officials was the phenomenon of the *cumul des mandats*, multiple office-holding. These offices may be purely local: many mayors are also *conseillers généraux*, and chair a number of local bodies, whether public housing authorities, hospital boards, *sociétés d'économie mixte* or associations. But offices may also be national in character. The extent of the *cumul* in the National Assembly over two decades is shown in Table 12.2. At any given time, and with great consistency, about half of the Deputies also held office as mayors, about half as *conseillers généraux*, and about a quarter as both. Multiple office-holding among Senators was, if anything, more widespread, since the members of the upper house were themselves elected by local elected officials. Looked at from the local angle, over half of the presidents of councils for the *départements* and regions have regularly been members of parliament. The dominant political figures of the Fifth Republic who have held or hold local office have included presidents Giscard d'Estaing, Mitterrand and Chirac: all of the prime ministers appointed by Pompidou

Table 12.2 Notables in the National Assembly, 1978, 1988 and 2002 (metropolitan France only)

Offices held at election	1978		1988		2002	
	no.	%	no.	%	no.	%
Mayor	235	50	262	47	280	50
Mayor: commune of over 20,000 inhabitants	98	21	96	17	103	19
Assistant-mayor (*adjoint*)	21	4	63	11	65	12
Conseiller général	256	54	279	50	189	34
Mayor + *conseiller général*	145	31	147	26	131	24
Regional councillor	n/a	–	141	25	83	19
Mayor + *conseiller général* + regional councillor	n/a	–	24	4	13	2
Any two local offices	164	35	298	54	271	49
Any one local office	363	77	490	88	490	85
Incumbent Deputy	292	62	380	68	284	51
Total in any of above categories	424	89	537	97	523	94
Total Deputies in National Assembly	**474**	*100*	**555**	*100*	**555**	*100*

Source: National Assembly.

and his three presidential successors were or later became local elected officials. The two Socialist mayors, Mauroy of Lille and Defferre of Marseille, who coined the term 'le régime des préfets', were themselves known to their critics as the Count of Flanders and the Duke of Provence. As (respectively) prime minister and interior minister after 1981, they would work to give institutional expression to the very great quasi-official powers that they and their like had accumulated (to the extent, indeed, that Defferre gave his name to the first wave of decentralisation reforms).

For there is no doubt that such *grands notables* were very powerful men indeed. Their standing might be enhanced by governmental office. Under Pompidou's presidency, for example, the most influential individual in the *département* of the Morbihan was not the prefect but Raymond Marcellin, president of the *conseil général* – and minister of the interior (the prefect's hierarchical head). But *grands notables* could just as easily be opposition politicians; no prefect could overlook the fact that Mauroy was the political boss of the Nord *département*, Defferre of Bouches-du-Rhône, or François Mitterrand of the Nièvre. Their power rested to a great extent on the *cumul*, and on the resulting opportunities to intervene at all levels of the administration, from the commune through *départements* and regions right up to Paris. This allowed the *grand notables* not only to attract resources to their own town or canton, but also to build networks of clients who would also benefit from their interventions. Such clients might be local elected officials of their own party, but might also be mayors or councillors from other parties, or even members of the administration. This meant that, if the support of a *grand notable* did not guarantee the success of an undertaking, his hostility almost invariably spelt its failure.

The limitations on prefectoral power

The power of the prefects was exaggerated and its nature misunderstood. Before 1982, a prefect exercised, in theory, regulatory and discretionary powers which enabled him to supervise the activities of local authorities closely. In practice, however, his power was always circumscribed in several important ways. First, his freedom of initiative and discretion were increasingly limited by a network of rules and regulations devised in Paris and by a body of administrative law, evolved under the guardianship of the Conseil d'État. Second, most prefects had neither the time, the technical expertise, the qualified staff nor the inclination to supervise the work of the field services. The March 1964 reforms, designed to assert the prefect's authority as 'overlord' of the administration in *départements*, therefore proved largely ineffective. Third, the prefect had little control over many pressure groups or big industrial concerns which had their headquarters in Paris and negotiated with the bureaucracy there. Fourth, rapid prefectoral turnover, fuelled by political rivalries in Paris (for example, by Giscard's wish to weed out Gaullist sympathisers) but also by the prefects' own ambitions to move on to more lucrative and prestigious postings, meant that a typical prefect was perpetually caught in a revolving door, with little time to become acquainted with local people and problems. Fifth, all of these factors diminished the prefects' authority in dealing with locally entrenched *notables*. Local patronage had long since been expropriated by the *notables*, particularly those who also sat in parliament. In the absence of a strong party system, governments in Paris bought parliamentary favour by granting individual Deputies and Senators the right to distribute local manna to their constituents. The *notables* were also consulted over the appointment, promotion and dismissal of prefects in their constituencies – a fact that few prefects were allowed to forget. In relation to such individuals, the array of formal controls exercised by prefects, for example over local budgets, remained all but unusable.

The relative financial autonomy of local authorities

The financial dependence of the local authorities, though real, should not be over-estimated. Financial control exercised by the centre over the provinces in the allocation of grants of various types was unquestionably strong, but its extent should not be exaggerated. French local budgets, though smaller than those in Sweden, Denmark, Germany or Great Britain as a proportion of total public spending, also had to pay for significantly fewer compulsory services. If real disposable income is the criterion, French local authorities enjoyed a degree of financial autonomy close to that of their European counterparts. And the central government funds on which the local authorities were dependent did at least enable poorer areas to develop services or implement projects the cost of which was beyond their limited resources; indeed, from this point of view, complete financial independence for local authorities would be a disaster, ensuring wide and growing inequalities of resources between authorities. Moreover, the strings attached to central government grants, as well as to the loans that were tied to them, tended to become fewer during the 1970s, as reforms in 1972 and 1979 began to move money from project-specific to block grants. That was combined, under Giscard's last interior minister, Bonnet, with the allocation of new rights for communes to determine the rate of the four main local taxes, allowing them, within limits, not only to fix the amount of the total tax take but also to place heavier or lighter burdens on businesses, landlords, owner-occupiers, or tenants as they saw fit.

The rise of urban France

There was an increase in the number, the size and the autonomy of big towns. In 1975, 68.8 per cent of the French population was defined as urban – the same percentage that was represented by the rural population in 1872. Of particular significance for local government was the increase in the number and size of big towns. By March 1977 there were 221 communes with over 30,000 inhabitants, compared with 193 in 1971, 159 in 1965 – and 47 at the beginning of the Third Republic, when the act which largely defined the powers of local authorities was passed. Among these large communes, the 1982 census identified 39 with a population of over 100,000 and 107 with over 50,000.

There has always been a tradition of jealous autonomy in certain cities such as Toulouse, Lyon and Marseille: facilitated by distance, their independence was often fed by political enmity. Here and in many other large towns, independence had increasingly solid material underpinnings: substantial tax bases that lessened their financial dependence on the state; strong bureaucracies, with technical services to rival those of the state, led by a secretary-general who was often an official of great ability and experience; growing experience, and scope for initiative, in important areas such as town planning (by the judicious use of building permits and land pre-emption and expropriation), housing and public transport, the creation of industrial zones, and social and cultural matters. Moreover, such towns often enjoyed the dynamic leadership of powerful, long-serving, paid, professional and full-time (as far as the *cumul des mandats* permitted) mayors. Defferre in Marseille, Chaban-Delmas in Bordeaux, Crépeau in La Rochelle, Dubedout in Grenoble, Pradel in Lyon, Pflimlin in Strasbourg, Fréville in Rennes, Médecin in Nice, Mauroy in Lille, Lecanuet in Rouen and Duroméa in Le Havre were among the many important mayors who determined the programmes and shaped the priorities of their towns, often giving them a particular image. Bordeaux, Strasbourg and Grenoble opened breaches in the reputation of provincial France as a cultural desert. La Rochelle offered its inhabitants the free use of bicycles to limit city-centre congestion. Pradel covered Lyon in concrete (a generation later, his Socialist successor Gérard Collomb would emulate La Rochelle's bicycle experiment). Such mayors made full and large-scale use of the status of elected local autocrats which a generous reading of the legal texts afforded them. A special case was that of the city of Paris itself, transferred, in 1977, from rule by a prefecture to a status comparable to that of other communes (with the added quirk of being simultaneously a *département* in its own right). That the capital's first mayor in over a century was Jacques Chirac ensured a high profile for the change. His enterprising, dynamic style of leadership, and his systematic use of the patronage opportunities afforded by a town hall machine, were crucial in preserving and furthering his national political career in often difficult circumstances.

The rise of local authority co-operation

The fragmentation of French local government was attenuated by increasing co-operation between local authorities. Few communes were persuaded to merge; a significant number, though, used a growing range of opportunities available for intercommunal co-operation. The simplest of these were voluntary syndicates allowing communes to co-operate on one or more tasks specified by themselves and run for the purposes of these tasks by a *bureau* composed of the main elected officials. By 1977 there were 1,893 SIVOMs (*syndicats intercommunal à vocation multiple*) involving 18,437 communes, and covering anything from technical services like water distribution or rubbish collection to strategic questions like town planning. Urban areas were offered more ambitious forms of co-operation: urban districts (provided for, like the SIVOMs, in an *ordonnance* of 1959) and urban communities (set up by a law of December 1966) controlled a wide range of services, including housing, fire-fighting, school construction and maintenance, water, rubbish disposal, cemeteries, public transport, town planning and public works, and disposing of a significant independent budget as well as a council composed of representatives of the councils of the constituent communes. By 1982 there were 154 districts, grouping 1,348 communes with a population of 5,580,000, and 9 urban communities, grouping 252 communes with over 4 million inhabitants. The only element of compulsion in the co-operation process was the creation of the first four urban communities (in Lyon, Strasbourg, Lille and Bordeaux). The voluntary character of this co-operation, and the resistance of local authorities to anything resembling mergers, contrasts with the record in Britain and other European states, where local authorities were reorganised, regrouped and in many cases abolished, by central government fiat in the 1960s and 1970s.

The structure of central–local relations before 1982 was a complex one, with much scope for variation on the ground between different local authorities according to relations between individual *notables*, state technical services, prefects and Parisian ministries; the size of the communes, *départements* and regions concerned; the quality of the technical services under the control of each player; and the electoral stakes of individual issues. The legalistic view, characterised by a dominant central state and subordinate localities, was challenged from the 1960s by observers like Jean-Pierre Worms, who analysed the relationship between the prefect and 'his' *notables* as one of mutual interdependence. If the mayor needed his prefect's co-operation to further his projects, the prefect also needed that of the mayor to help avoid local unrest and ensure a successful tour of duty and thus subsequent promotion. The two often shared defensive roles, especially in their relations with the field services, the pressure groups and the Paris bureaucracies. And each might need the other as a scapegoat to explain lack of success. Scholars like Jean-Claude Thoenig then extended the analysis beyond the mayor–prefect duo, and depicted the various actors as linked in a 'honeycomb structure', characterised by mutual interdependence and 'conflictual complicity', with no player holding all the cards, and each being obliged to seek conciliation and compromise to fulfil his aims. Since there were also incentives to seek intervention and arbitration at a higher level, the system was underpinned by a centralist logic. While this model captures the subtlety of the system as it developed, its tendency to stress immobility and *blocages* passes by three of the more attractive features of the French local system. The first of these was the relatively healthy state of local democracy, to judge by voter turnout – at least 74 per cent for every municipal election from 1945 to 1977, and 65 per cent or more for cantonal elections. Second, even at its most 'centralist', the system offered both unrivalled opportunities for participation in local government (roughly one French adult in eighty is a local councillor) and a visible, accessible, channel for the transmission of grievances, in the person of the mayor. Third, the notion of *blocages* was belied by the dynamism and energy displayed by members of France's local elites in the 1970s – who not only complained about excessive centralisation, but also intelligently circumvented the phenomena they denounced.

The decentralisation reforms reflected their criticisms, and swept aside texts that had, at least on paper, enshrined local subordination. But the reforms also bore the marks of the practices the *notables* had developed before 1982. In that sense, they also showed important elements of continuity with the past.

Decentralisation: the measures

The reform of relations between the state and local and regional authorities has proceeded in three phases under the Fifth Republic: an ambitious package of institutional reforms at the outset of the Mitterrand presidency, a series of complementary measures between 1986 and 2002, and a further large (and so far unfinished) package under the Raffarin premiership.

The Defferre reforms

Although 1982 is the best date to attach to decentralisation, the act of 2 March of that year was merely the start of a legislative avalanche: Jacques Baguenard has calculated that over fifty acts and over 350 decrees were devoted to central–local relations over the following decade. Many of the most important of the reforms have been alluded to above. They can be summarised under ten headings.

- Executive responsibility in *départements* and regions was transferred, respectively, from the prefect to the president of the *conseil général* (from 1982), and from the regional prefect to the president of the regional council (from 1986). Thus work such as convening the councils, preparing budgets and agendas, and supervising the implementation of decisions – and the real substance of executive power in each case – passed from an appointed state official to a chief executive chosen by an elected assembly.

- Regional councils were to be directly elected every six years instead of being drawn, as they had been since 1972, from Deputies, mayors and *conseillers généraux*. The first direct regional elections were held on 16 March 1986.

- The prefects' a priori control over the activities of communes was ended. Local authority acts, including budgets, came into force within two weeks of their being received by the prefecture. Building permits may be freely signed by mayors where an approved land use plan exists, without the scrutiny of the *direction départementale de l'équipement* or the prefecture. Prefectoral control over budgets and other acts is now a posteriori: that is, a prefect may refer his objections to regional courts of accounts (just as he may refer objections to other local authority acts to the local administrative courts). Such referrals, though sometimes successful, are very few: between 0.2 and 0.4 per cent of all local authority acts, depending on the year.

- An act of January 1983 explicitly shared out the respective responsibilities of communes, *départements* and regions as distinct *blocs de compétences*, and gave new responsibilities to each level. Town planning and housing were identified as tasks for communes, which also won the explicit right to intervene in local economic affairs; the *départements* had important new responsibilities in the area of social affairs; and the regions were to play a major role in regional planning (*aménagement du territoire*) including regional economic development and regional transport networks, in the preservation of the regional environment, especially parks, and in apprenticeships and vocational training, and in research funding. Each level was also given responsibility for a different set of school buildings: nursery and primary for the communes (as hitherto), middle schools (*collèges*) for the *départements*, and high schools (*lycées*) for the regions.

- The financial freedom of local authorities was enhanced by an accelerated move away from project-specific state grants and towards block grants, with annual allocations for current and investment budgets (the *dotation globale de fonctionnement*, the *dotation globale d'équipement* and the *dotation générale de décentralisation*, as well as the reimbursement to local authorities of their very substantial VAT receipts). In addition, the fiscal resources of local authorities were modestly enhanced, with taxes on vehicle licences and on electricity going to the *départements*, a tax on driving licences being allocated to the regions, and taxes on property transactions being shared between the two.

- The acts of 1984 and 1987 upgraded the career structure and status of the territorial civil service, creating the grade of *administrateur territorial* at a comparable level to that of many senior civil servants of central government. Servants of the state were also seconded to local authorities, particularly the regions, or transferred as (more or less) whole services to the control of the *départements*. The most striking example of this was the social services: most of the substance of the *directions départementales de l'action sanitaire et sociale* was transferred to the control of the *départements*. But other services, notably the *directions départementales de l'équipement* (infrastructure) were also affected.

- Decentralisation was complemented by administrative deconcentration, as certain tasks previously carried out in Paris were transferred to the state's field services. The 1982 act also declared the prefect's pre-eminence as 'overlord' of these services. Both of these points were reaffirmed by the Joxe Law of 1992.

- City councils were modestly democratised. The municipal elections of 1965, 1971 and 1977 in communes of over 30,000 inhabitants had been run on a two-ballot majority list system: all lists of candidates had to be formed before the first ballot; no lists could merge between ballots; and the winning list took all the council seats. The electoral law of November 1982, which applied to all towns of over 3,500 inhabitants, preserved the majority principle but allowed a chance for minority representation. The list that emerged victorious (whether by winning an absolute majority of votes at the first ballot or simply the most votes at the second) would gain 50 per cent of the seats, while the remainder would be shared out proportionally between all the lists, including the winning one. This system was designed to allow the municipal opposition a platform, while ensuring the election of a coherent majority on the council.

- The *cumul des mandats* was limited by an act of December 1985. Henceforth, elected officials would have to choose just two of the major offices: Deputy, Senator, Member of the European Parliament, regional councillor, *conseiller général*, mayor of a commune of over 20,000 inhabitants, assistant mayor (*adjoint*) of a commune of over 100,000 inhabitants.

- A number of measures, finally, made provision for special cases. These included the regions of Île-de-France, which was given particular responsibilities (and resources) for transport planning in the Paris region. The towns of Paris, Lyon and Marseille were given elected councils in each of their *arrondissements* by a law of 1982, initially aimed (unsuccessfully) at undermining Chirac's dominance in the capital.

The Socialists showed great determination and not a little courage in their decentralisation programme, which was pursued despite pressing priorities elsewhere and a busy parliamentary agenda. Moreover, local election results ensured that the Right would benefit first from decentralisation: the RPR–UDF alliance won 31 towns of over 30,000 inhabitants from the Left in 1983, and 14 presidencies of *conseils généraux* (bringing their total to 69 out of 96) over the two cantonal elections of 1982 and 1985. Aside from the short-term damage to the Socialists, however, these results had a longer-term advantage: decentralisation, which the Right had fought in the parliamentary debates of 1981, rapidly became the object of a cross-party consensus, at least on the general principles. It also reinforced the local and regional authorities as lobbies. If the Association of French Mayors is a venerable and widely respected institution, it was now flanked by associations for city mayors, rural mayors, and the presidents of councils for the *départements* and regions. Such associations did not always see eye to eye with one another. In particular, there has been a continuing debate between traditionalists, anxious to reinforce the established authorities of communes and *départements*, with the state at the peak, and modernists, whose attention is more concentrated on regions and on intercommunal structures, with a livelier attention to the opportunities offered by neighbouring states and by Europe. But the associations had two things in common. One was excellent links, thanks to the *cumul des mandats*, with parliament and government. The other was a general view that decentralisation was unfinished business, in need of further adjustment if not of new wide-ranging reforms.

Defferre to Jospin

The further reforms undertaken between the Left's victories in 1986 and its defeats in 2002 clearly fall into the category of adjustment rather than wide-ranging reform. In at least one case, however, the effects have been far-reaching.

- One series of initiatives can be viewed as going against the spirit of decentralisation, especially in the areas of finance and urban planning, and posed the dilemma of the intrinsic value of local autonomy in the face of what are viewed as important national objectives. The national priority in question was the desperate situation of France's deprived urban areas, with a sometimes explosive combination of unemployment, rundown housing, racial tension, drug-dealing and other crime, which was seen both as having an intrinsic national dimension (threatening the disintegration of France's social fabric) and as being beyond the power of the communes concerned, often dormitory suburbs with exiguous tax bases, to tackle. With scarce resources to underwrite what was known as the *politique de la ville* (but was in fact more directed to rundown suburbs), the Socialist governments of the early 1990s introduced measures to redistribute resources between richer and poorer municipalities (a reform accepted with ill grace by mayors who saw their communes' wealth as a sign of their own fiscal virtue). In addition, the 1991 *Loi d'orientation sur la ville* provided for 400 priority action zones: these were selected in Paris, and the task of setting up multidisciplinary action teams there was given to subprefects. But significant parts of the 1991 law remained without implementation decrees. Similar urban policy concerns therefore also prompted the Jospin government, in 2000, to pass a *Loi sur la Solidarité et la rénovation urbaine*, which obliged all communes to ensure that at least 20 per cent of housing units on their territory were HLMs (subsidised low-cost units). It also built in financial penalties for communes that failed to have a plan to achieve this goal ready within three years, and even allowed prefects to curtail the rights of those that had not co-operated to exercise their right of pre-emption on local land. Again, what was viewed as a national problem – the housing shortage in many major cities – was seen as justifying the curtailment of the freedom of mayors to plan a housing mix as they saw fit.

- One of the major lacunae of the Defferre laws, in the view of some (though quite rarely of mayors) was the lack of provision to enhance direct public participation in local government. A very partial remedy to this was attempted in a law of 1992, which allowed local authorities to hold referenda on a purely consultative basis. On the whole this was an embarrassment: of the few that were held, several concerned the presence of immigrant populations or the construction of mosques. A further, if partial, reinforcement of local democracy came with a law passed three months before Jospin's defeat in 2002 that *required* all communes of over 80,000 inhabitants to set up a network of neighbourhood councils and a public services users' committee, both of them consultative.

- There were also repeated attempts to handle the intractable Corsican problem. A law of 1991 transformed the island from an ordinary region into a 'territorial collectivity of special status' with somewhat broader powers. The July 2000 agreement on the island's future, which attracted a broad consensus of support in the Corsican assembly, allowed some limited rights, on an experimental basis till 2004 (after which they would be confirmed by a constitutional amendment), for the assembly to adapt national legislation to the island's 'specificities'. The agreement also provided for the teaching of Corsican in the island's primary and secondary schools, as well as for generous subsidies and tax concessions to compensate for what is claimed to be Corsica's backwardness in transport and other infrastructure. Widely criticised outside the island as representing concessions to the terrorists who had assassinated the regional prefect of Corsica as recently as 1998, and as a threat to the French language and to the unity of the Republic, the Matignon agreements also fell foul of the continuing violence on the island and then of the Left's defeat. Raffarin's first interior minister Nicolas Sarkozy attempted another line of reform that would have simplified the top level of Corsican government into a single assembly. This project also failed, after a narrow no result in the referendum of 2003. With its 260,000 inhabitants, Corsica therefore retains its territorial assembly and two *départements*, as well as 960 communes.

- The Jospin government also enacted a further limitation to the *cumul des mandats*, on the principle first that with decentralisation, local and regional leaders did not need to be parliamentarians as well to make their views felt, and secondly that above a certain level, a single elective office amounts to a full-time job. Opposition from the Senate prevented measures as wide-ranging as the government would have wished, but the law of 2000 bans Deputies and Senators from being MEPs at the same time; from holding more than one executive office (as president of a region or a *département* or as mayor); nor can they hold more than one post as a councillor (for a region or a *département* or a commune of over 3,500 inhabitants).

- Probably the most important legislation to come out of this intermediate period, however, was the encouragement given to intercommunal co-operation by laws in 1992 and 1999. They instituted a permanent committee on intercommunal co-operation in each *département*, and, more importantly, created new and more ambitious intercommunal structures. By the early twenty-first century, the fastest-growing forms of grouping were those with the broadest delegation of powers and a common business tax: the *communauté urbaine* for large urban areas (there were 14 by 2003, 9 of them in conurbations of over 100,000 inhabitants); the *communauté d'agglomération* for medium-sized towns (of which 143, grouping 2,441 communes, were set up in the four years after legislation created this type of grouping in July 1999); and the rural *communauté de communes*, of which 2,195, taking in 26,907 communes, existed at the beginning of 2003. By this stage, some 29,754 communes, with a total of nearly 49 million inhabitants – 84 per cent of the population of France – had joined one of these types of intercommunal grouping. These were more constraining than the old syndicates formerly favoured by most communes. To join a *communauté d'agglomération*, for example, contracting communes had to exercise powers jointly in economic development, planning and transport, housing and social policy, as well as in at least three of a further basket of policy areas including roads and parks, water, rubbish disposal, culture and sport, and the environment. The spread of intercommunality was partly due to the financial incentives offered by the state: from 27 euros per inhabitant for a *communauté de communes* to 72 euros for a *communauté urbaine*, or additional funding in excess of 15 per cent. It was also seen by local actors as a pragmatic answer to problems of local government fragmentation. Most remarkably, perhaps, the new groupings involve joint taxation. In 934 of them, representing 35.4 million inhabitants at the start of 2003, the *taxe professionnelle* was pegged at an identical level across the contracting communes within each community. This had the obvious advantage of preventing mayors from engaging (as they had in the past) in beggar-my-neighbour policies, offering unduly low local corporate taxes to attract all-important businesses.

Intercommunal co-operation has been a practical answer to some of the difficulties entailed by excessive local authority fragmentation. Within that general perspective, as Hervé Michel remarks, different actors have tried to use it for a variety of strategic purposes: to extend and control territory (for large central towns); to acquire financial security (for hard-pressed dormitory suburbs); to seek security in numbers under the leadership of the *conseil général* (for rural communes). Interestingly, a small number of mayors, like Alain Lamassoure of Anglet or Martin Malvy of Figeac, have chosen to resign from their mayoral office in order to commit themselves to the presidency of their *communautés* – a clear sign of where they felt the substance of municipal power to be gravitating.

These more or less piecemeal reforms did not alter the widespread view that decentralisation remained incomplete. It was in this context that the Jospin government commissioned one of the architects of the 1982 laws, the mayor of Lille (and former prime minister) Pierre Mauroy, to suggest possible future measures. Mauroy's report, from which the right-wing minority on his commission dissented, covered four main areas: the direct election of the councils that run intercommunal groupings; the possible consolidation of France's regions into ten or a dozen larger units; the replacement of the two main local taxes, the *taxe d'habitation* on households and the *taxe profession-nelle* on firms, by sources of revenue that were fairer than the former and less punitive to business than the latter; the clarification of the respective competences of France's three levels of subnational government, with a view to avoiding the confusion of responsibilities that had prevailed since 1982. This would probably have been the agenda for a Jospin presidency. Chirac and Raffarin had somewhat different priorities, but were equally committed to a broad new decentralisation initiative.

Decentralisation under Raffarin

Raffarin was unusual in coming to the premiership with more of a regional than a national reputation. A Senator and a former junior minister, the fact that he was best known as president, not only of the Poitou-Charentes region, but of the Association of Presidents of French Regional Councils, testifies to a certain continuity with the earlier handling of decentralisation by the *grands notables* Mauroy and Defferre.

The Raffarin reforms are remarkable for the contrast between the grand manner in which they were initiated – a constitutional amendment – and the relatively technical character of their substance: nothing in them is as spectacular as the creation of new directly elected assemblies, or the clipping of the prefects' wings, in the Defferre legislation.

The constitutional amendment of March 2003 both set out an agenda and ensured that further legislation would be less vulnerable to censure by the Constitutional Council. More specifically, it specified that the organisation of the (still 'indivisible') French Republic was 'decentralised'; gave constitutional status to the regions for the first time; constitutionalised a form of subsidiarity principle (under Article 72, 'terri-torial units may take decisions in all matters that are within powers that can best be exercised at their level'); allowed, across the whole of France, the sort of experimental derogation from national legislation which had earlier been so controversial in the case of Corsica; and extended provisions for local referenda, both by allowing them to be held by popular initiative rather than mayoral decision and by allowing them, under certain circumstances, to be decisive rather than merely consultative. The constitutional amendment also contained financial provisions: it promised both that local taxes and other own resources would represent a 'decisive share' of the income of local and regional authorities, and that responsibilities transferred from central to local or regional government would carry with them an adequate transfer of resources.

Over the next eighteen months, a series of laws put flesh on the bones of these amendments. All subnational authorities were allowed to run new services and/or develop new structures on an experimental, and temporary, basis; and all were allowed to hold referenda on issues relating to their areas of competence. Above all, legislation set out a transfer of competences: *départements* were given extended responsibilities for roads (and more kilometres to look after), rubbish disposal, healthcare and (already one of their major areas of concern) social assistance; regions saw their role reinforced in the areas of economic development (including grants to firms), vocational training and infrastructure. To go with them, they received – in the government's view – appropriate new resources, in terms of finance and personnel (150,000 employees, chiefly in the areas of health and social services, were transferred).

Full implementation of these provisions will not take place until 2006. But the Raffarin reforms shared one contextual characteristic with Defferre's: they preceded a big defeat at local level for the government majority, leaving much of the implementation to be done by local elected officials of the national opposition. The Left's victory at the 2004 regional elections was greatly amplified by a change of electoral system (pushed through by the government with the use of Article 49–3 of the constitution, against opposition from all sides) designed to favour the emergence of clear majorities on regional councils (and prevent the FN from holding the balance of power). This aim was so well achieved that Socialist presidents were elected in twenty out of the twenty-two metropolitan regions (all except Alsace and Corsica); the Left also did well in the traditionally conservative *départements*, controlling about half. Predictable squabbles about the transfer of resources broke out as the regions increased taxes for their 2005 budgets, claiming they had no choice, and the government and the UMP accused them of profligacy. Beyond the political point-scoring, there were real anxieties among elected officials of the Right as well as the Left about the budgetary implications of decentralisation. Before we turn to these, however, and to a more general assessment of the decentralisation laws, it is important to examine two other contextual elements, European integration and economic change.

Europe and the regions

European integration presented France's local authorities, and particularly the regions, with both new constraints and new opportunities. The constraints arose in part from the effects of economic integration, which penalised some (mostly peripheral) regions and rewarded others. They also came from the new corpus of law associated with the Single European Act (SEA) of 1987 which established the single market. European public procurement directives, for example, which came into force in 1989 and 1990, required formal advertising of public supply and maintenance contracts worth 130,000 euros and public works contracts worth 5 million euros, and outlawed discrimination against non-national firms. These thresholds were well within the range of local authority spending. Similarly, like any public- or private-sector organisation, French local authorities were bound by new labour and environmental standards, technical norms and health and safety requirements. Moreover, European competition rules increasingly handicapped traditional state-led regional policies, and required such policies to be integrated in a European framework: as Sonia Mazey notes, in the late 1980s the French government was forced by the European Commission to withdraw development grants from twenty *départements* which did not meet EU guidelines for regional assistance.

That framework was provided, in part, by the development of the European Regional Development Fund, transformed in 1988 from a channel of European finance to individual infrastructure projects into an instrument of the EU's commitment to economic and social cohesion. The most obvious opportunities offered by Europe to local authorities, therefore, are financial. Between 1989 and 1993, European regional development funds doubled in money terms, and rose from 19 per cent to 25 per cent of the EU budget. The use of the funds, however, had to be transparent, and matched (at least) by funds from the member states and regions that benefited. In this sense, Europe has actually encouraged and provoked European regional reform, since these conditions are most likely to be met by well-organised, dynamic regional authorities

(even when the regions themselves are poor). In France, the pluriannual planning contracts signed between the state and the regions (the *contrats de plan État–région*) include
European money. Of 33.5 billion euros earmarked for the contracts for 1994–99,
12 billion euros came from the state, 14 billion euros from the regions and other local
authorities, and nearly 9 billion euros from European funds; for the 2000–6 plans,
Europe was expected to supply 7 billion euros, the state 16 billion euros – leaving
18 billion (three years' worth of new investments) for regions. This largess, however, had
some strings attached. Regional aid was increasingly tied to European objectives, which
might be linked to specific regions (such as assistance to industrial restructuring in
declining industrial regions, or to promote development of the most backward rural
areas) or 'transversal' (such as fighting long-term unemployment). Regions were
required to draw up regional plans as a framework for their applications for EU subsidies. And since only central government can present formal applications for EU regional
funds, the potential remained for central government to impose its priorities on the
process: the *contrats de plan État–région* have been negotiated at the regional level
under the authority of the regional prefect and finalised nationally in a body called the
Conseil National pour l'Aménagement du Territoire, chaired by a minister and including representatives from DATAR as well as regional and local elected officials. At the
same time, however, the *contrats de plan* have triggered a process of institutional learning comparable to that provoked within France by decentralisation. Only 5 out of the
22 regions succeeded in preparing their own detailed strategic plans for the first round
of *contrats*, running from 1984 to 1988; the figure had risen to 14 for 1989–93; by the
2000–6 round, all the regions had done so. The process has favoured close partnership
with the state, other local authorities, European representatives, and other local bodies
such as chambers of commerce (the process appears to have varied from sweetness and
light in Brittany to acrimony in Rhône-Alpes); and it promoted a culture of regular
evaluation, obliging subnational authorities, and particularly regions, to lend at least an
apparent coherence and conviction to projects which might otherwise have lacked both.

By the end of the third round of contracts, however, there were signs of disenchantment among regions. Part of this related to the behaviour of state authorities, seen as
too ready (for example, in the case of the Infrastructure Ministry) to push their own
agenda and ask the regions to pick up the bill, and too slow to pay their share. A Senate
report complained in 2003 that only 70 per cent of credits for the third (1994–99) round
of contracts promised by the state had actually been paid, that the level for the 2000–6
round could be as little as 60 per cent, and that 'the realisation of the *contrats de plan*
therefore appears more and more virtual'. Finally, regional authorities are aware that
with the 2004 eastern enlargement, less EU regional development money will come to
France. The likelihood, therefore, is that while the contracts have brought valuable
infrastructure (as well as habits of partnership and evaluation) in the past, they will
hold a less central place in future policy-making. The generally disappointing record of
the EU's Committee of the Regions, a consultative body set up by the Maastricht
Treaty largely at the insistence of the German *Länder*, would appear to confirm this.

The EU has also, by instituting competition for funding of various types, encouraged
regional lobbying. By the early 1990s, seventeen out of the twenty-two regions of
metropolitan France were represented, either directly or through a grouping, in
Brussels. The more adventurous *départements* and cities were also following the same
path – as much to be close to sources of information and to spot possible funding
opportunities early as to engage in direct lobbying with European officials for a specific

local interest. The SEA also offered encouragement to the cross-border interregional associations which had been explicitly recognised by the 1982 Defferre Act five years earlier. Such associations include the Association of European Frontier Regions (dating from 1971), the Conference of EC Maritime Regions (1973), the Conférence des Régions de Tradition Industrielle; SAARLORLUX (Saar–Lorraine–Luxembourg) and the neighbouring grouping of Alsace with Baden-Württemberg, Rhein-Pfalz and the cantons of Basle; the Kent–Nord–Pas de Calais grouping formed to take advantage of opportunities offered by the Channel Tunnel; and the 'four motors' association of Rhône-Alpes, Catalonia, Lombardy and Baden-Württemberg. This too has provoked imitation by other local authorities: in August 2000 the mayor of Nantes and former minister Edmond Hervé inaugurated a Conference of Atlantic Arc Cities, including Porto, Cork and Glasgow as well as Nantes, Rennes and Bordeaux.

The development of a European regional policy has not realised the hopes of enthusiasts for a 'Europe of the regions', who imagined subnational authorities co-operating directly with one another and negotiating with Brussels without needing to refer to an increasingly irrelevant nation state. Europe has not emancipated France's local and regional authorities from the state's tutelage. It has, however, made available new sources of funding in ways that favour somewhat less hierarchical forms of co-operation than have been usual in the French politico-administrative system. And it has established that cross-frontier co-operation (and competition) is no longer solely a regalian function of a sovereign state, but may be a legitimate concern of subnational authorities as well.

Local authorities and private business

In opposition in the 1970s, the Socialists presented decentralisation as 'one of the most powerful levers for the break away from the capitalist system'. The irony of the Left's arrival in power in 1981 preceding a large-scale paradigm shift (described in Chapter 1) in favour of the liberal economy was as heavy at the local level as it was nationally: freed from (some of) the constraints of central government, local authorities were left increasingly unprotected from the rigours of the global market, and became more dependent for their prosperity on the investment decisions of large firms. The post-war expansion of French local government had taken place in a context of fast growth when the central problem was to deliver the infrastructure, housing, schools and other facilities to underpin rapid industrialisation. The jobs came more or less by themselves, so long as an industrial zone with a rudimentary level of utilities was provided. Left-wing municipalities disliked the idea of giving 'presents' to capitalists; right-wing ones, influenced by established local firms, were often disinclined to go looking for more companies that might compete for still scarce labour. But little of this applied by the late 1970s, and major towns began to seek ways – at the margins of the law – of intervening to ensure the survival of major local firms.

Decentralisation legalised such interventions: henceforth not only towns, but also *départements* and regions, made it their top priority to attract or retain firms. One way of doing this was direct aid to firms in difficulty, but this practice had largely disappeared at local level by the late 1980s, as it had (more or less) nationally (and for the same reasons of cost-effectiveness and competition legislation). Instead, local authorities increasingly aimed at creating a broad package, including local, national and international transport links by road, rail and air; financial concessions, including local tax holidays or loan guarantees; a range of services for firms including security surveillance, vocational training for workers and access to research institutes; proximity to local small and medium firms in the relevant sector; and an environment considered attractive for company managers (hence, in part, the rise in cultural spending by many authorities, as well as the burgeoning verdure of municipal golf courses in some of the most unlikely localities). The old industrial zones were replaced by new technology parks (*technopoles*), such as Grenoble's Europole, or Lille's EuraLille, which aimed to offer some or all of these advantages. Local authorities also sought to sell themselves much more aggressively, through mushrooming 'communication' budgets and inter-mediary associations for economic promotion, often run jointly with Chambers of Commerce and Industry or local employers' groups such as the Centres des Jeunes Dirigeants. All of these things were done in a more or less orderly fashion by the whole range of local authorities, since the decentralisation laws allowed economic interven-tion, in one form or another, by communes, *départements* and regions, and since jobs were, understandably, the prime concern of French voters in the last quarter of the twentieth century. Sufficient co-ordination between local bodies (and a sufficiently attractive region to begin with) could ensure significant success: such was the case in Rhône-Alpes, which includes the cities of Lyon and Grenoble. On a broader canvas, however, as Jonah Levy has shown, the efforts of French local authorities have too often taken the form of a proliferation of initiatives that are underfunded and overlap-ping, rather than focused and co-operative (as between, for example, different local authorities, business associations, and the state). This is especially true when it comes, not to the attraction of international investors, but the encouragement of local small and medium enterprises. This is a field where well-organised action by local authorities should play a critical role; in fact, well-implanted central government bodies such as the Agence Nationale de la Valorisation de la Recherche (ANVAR) have made most of the running.

There is another respect in which local authorities have become dependent, to a degree, on large firms: they have had increasing recourse to the private sector to run their services. The private management of local services in France has a long history which, as Dominique Lorrain has pointed out, has meant that much of the heat gener-ated in British debates over the merits of privatisation has been absent in the French local context. Before 1982, it is true, right-wing local authorities tended to farm out services to private groups, and left-wing ones tended to manage them directly; but the numerous exceptions on either side indicated that most mayors and councillors took a pragmatic approach to the issue. Pragmatism appeared, however, to point in the direc-tion of private-sector solutions at least from the early 1980s to the early twenty-first century. Thus Lorrain has noted that municipal water services were privately managed in some 60 per cent of cases in 1983 but 75 per cent a decade later. Sewage and rubbish disposal, and public transport, are among the other basic services often conceded to private firms. Local authorities have also resorted increasingly to public–private partnerships in the form of *sociétés d'économie mixte*. Formerly used chiefly for large-scale building projects, SEMs are now commonly used to spread the risks inherent in managing major social and cultural facilities.

Many of the incentives to privatise are common to local authorities throughout the developed world, driven to reduce costs in order to control spending levels or to release money for other purposes. Few local authorities in France or elsewhere accumulate substantial savings available for investment (and the fact that, in France, such reserves must be deposited in the Treasury at zero interest is scarcely an incentive to build them up). It may be easier for the private sector than for a town, *département* or region to absorb high short-term investment costs: in cases where such costs are not incurred, a private firm seeking a water contract, for example, may be willing to pay the town concerned an initial lump sum, which can then be invested elsewhere. Productivity gains through recent technological advances in the area of urban services have strengthened the hand of large firms, which increasingly compete in a global market. Such firms have also constantly sought new customers, whether for very large-scale new projects such as the metro systems built by Matra and Alstom for Toulouse and Lille, or the more modest range of luminous display boards, bus shelters and public toilets supplied by Decaux to towns all over Europe.

Specifically French factors have also been at work. Achieving cost competitiveness with the private sector is especially difficult for France's fragmented local authorities. France's private firms in the urban sector, on the other hand, are often of world class, such as the Générale des Eaux (part of the ill-fated Vivendi group) or Suez-Lyonnaise des Eaux for water provision, or Bouygues, Spie-Batignolles and Eiffage for public works. The concentration of technical expertise and financial leverage wielded by such firms (several of which have now also diversified into sectors as remote as television and film) is greater than anything a city could aspire to. They are also increasingly related to one another: a subsidiary of the Générale des Eaux, for example, took over the major transport firm CGFTE in 1987. Finally, where before decentralisation, French local authorities were obliged to borrow from lending organisations linked, in one way or another, to the public-sector Caisse des Dépots et des Consignations, they have increasingly had access to the private banking sector (which has in any case grown owing to privatisations). This allows the local authorities greater flexibility in financial management, but also ensures that the banks keep a watchful eye on their accounts. However, there were some signs in the early twenty-first century that the love affair of at least some local authorities with private-sector service suppliers was cooling off; indeed, rising costs of contracts with private firms convinced a number of mayors to turn back to direct management of water services.

A third element in the relationship between French local authorities and private firms has been corruption, usually for the purpose of political funding. Some cases have been proven in spectacular trials. The mayor of Grenoble, Alain Carignon, for example, was convicted and imprisoned after receiving large sums (used to finance his election expenses and use of private jets) from subsidiaries of the Lyonnaise des Eaux in return for the contract to manage the city's water supply. Carignon's case, though spectacular, was far from unique; plenty of evidence suggests that the problem was structural and widespread. At the parliamentary elections of 1993, held during the brief period (1990–94) when business donations for purposes of political finance were legal, a quarter of all such donations came from four large groups (Bouygues, Lyonnaise des Eaux, Générale des Eaux and Eiffage) closely involved in the provision of urban services or public works. The inevitable suspicion (confirmed by anecdotal evidence from politicians and business executives) was that these legal donations were merely the continuation of a long-standing illegal practice, and that they were made in return for, or in the hope of, contracts. What is certain is that they did not stop when legal avenues for business donations to parties were closed down from 1995. In the four years from January 2000, seventy-nine local elected officials, mostly mayors, were convicted of corruption-related offences, many of them involving personal profit. A quarter of metropolitan France's ninety-five presidents of *conseils généraux* were under judicial investigation in January 2004. Scandals involving the city of Paris, and possibly Jacques Chirac, have already been mentioned (above, p. 227). Closely linked to them was a further investigation, involving commissions paid to all of the major political parties, into building projects (especially the renovation of *lycées*) in the surrounding Île-de-France region. That trial opened in March 2005.

Whatever the precise mix of expected managerial efficiency and political sleaze involved in the privatisation of urban services, the importance of private firms in the local policy process has undoubtedly grown since the early 1980s, to the extent that in some cases private firms may act not merely as the executors of policies decided by central or local government, but as policy-makers in their own right, both conceiving and implementing major urban projects. This raises the question of whether the diversity of local policy outputs promised by decentralisation has in fact been stifled as local authorities fall under the tutelage, no longer of the state, but of large private suppliers of services, for whom standardisation is the natural corollary of cost competitiveness. Such an interpretation seems exaggerated in the French case: as Patrick Le Galès points out, French towns display a wide range of relationships between public and private sectors, and private-sector actors are by no means invariably dominant or even very united.

Assessing decentralisation: *plus ça change?*

Paradoxically, decentralisation is the object both of a wide-ranging consensus, in that no party seeks to restore the *status quo ante*, and of a growing chorus of criticism. Commentators such as Albert Mabileau or Bruno Rémond argue that the manner in which decentralisation was undertaken introduced damaging incoherences into the system of central–local relations (which had never been short of incongruities in the first place). It did so because the pursuit of its major objectives was hindered by their own incoherence, by the incrementalism of many of the reforms and by a lingering centralism. The objectives can be grouped under three headings: subsidiarity (to borrow a term from the politics of the EU), rationalisation and democratisation.

Subsidiarity

Subsidiarity – the redistribution of decision-making to the lowest possible level of government, to ensure proximity of decisions to the people affected by them – was achieved partially and was vulnerable to legislative reversal. Indeed, observers such as Yves Mény have argued that for its main beneficiaries, the mayors of big cities, decentralisation did no more than give official blessing to the unofficial but widespread practices of the pre-1982 era (perhaps unsurprisingly, since the major architects of decentralisation, Gaston Defferre and Pierre Mauroy, were both city mayors). The mayors of small rural communes, on the other hand, lack the financial and technical resources to take advantage of their new freedoms; few communes of 800 inhabitants can run to more than four employees in total. Such communes often rely on state officials to prepare their budgets (indeed, the Trésorier-Payeur Général was given the duty in 1988 of vetting and passing the accounts of communes of under 2,000 inhabitants); they refer their acts to the prefecture in advance of publication to verify their legality, having no legal services to do this themselves; they rely on outside technicians (though these may now come from the *département*, rather than the state) to prepare investment projects, and on project-specific subsidies from state, *département* and region to implement them. When, as has happened, ministerial field services are shrunk in the name of decentralisation, the local authorities that depend on them are likely to suffer.

It has also been argued that what appears to be one of the most tangible signs of real decentralisation – the fact that local authorities control more money (see Table 12.1) – may be seen as no more than the acceleration of a tendency, dating from the 1960s, for France's central government to place additional financial burdens on local authorities. According to Interior Ministry figures, the transfer to *départements* of responsibility for social assistance and for the upkeep of middle schools (*collèges*) added some 87 billion francs (13.26 billion euros) to their annual burden of compulsory spending between 1984 and 1995; the regions' new role in building and maintaining *lycées* and managing vocational training had entailed the transfer of 29 billion francs' (4.42 billion euros') worth of expenses to them over the same period. In other words, an increased role in implementation did not necessarily mean greater autonomy. The implementation of the minimum social assistance benefit (*revenu minimum d'insertion*, or RMI) decided by the Rocard government in 1988, for example, entailed significant new spending commitments which many *départements* were reluctant to take on. Similarly, while the expense of maintaining and building schools has been transferred to the local authorities, critical aspects of education policy, such as curriculum and staffing, remain firmly in the hands of central government. Paris may close a rural school, but it is the *département* which must then organise and pay for school buses for the children concerned to be educated further from home. In the area of vocational training, the regions have had great difficulty in breaking into a policy community that remains dominated by Education Ministry officials. Most recently, local elected officials have been worried by announcements from Raffarin's social affairs minister Jean-Louis Borloo on the need to expand apprenticeship opportunities, fearing a rise in charges for what is explicitly marked as a regional responsibility. It might be added that higher spending levels after decentralisation, though certainly significant, still left France's regions quite lacking the financial muscle of their German or Italian counterparts: in 1994 Hesse, Germany's fifth largest *Land*, was spending the equivalent to 19 billion euros, over double the combined total for all French regions.

If the state still imposes new constraints on local authorities, it also preserves at least some of the means to ensure local implementation of priorities defined in Paris. The prefects, though dispossessed of crucial powers as chief executives of *départements* and regions, retain other sources of authority and influence. They may require *départements* to engage spending to further the objectives of the RMI, or to prepare plans for the sorting and recycling of household waste; they may, under the law of 2000, order recalcitrant communes to build low-cost housing units to meet the minimum requirement of 20 per cent. More importantly, perhaps, they remain the key point of articulation between regional planning and the state, with a crucial role in preparing the *contrats de plan État–région*. Their responsibilities in the area of local economic development increased as governments' concerns with unemployment grew – and as prefects themselves came to see this as a promising area in which to recover some of their lost influence. Regional prefects chair a Comité Régional de Restructuration Industrielle, and may recommend fiscal incentives to restructuring projects such as mergers; prefects of *départements* also chair a Comité Départemental d'Examen des Problèmes de

Financement des Entreprises; they must be consulted by TPGs if a heavy tax bill threatens to bankrupt a major local firm (and may suggest rescheduling of outstanding tax debts in consequence); they also dispose of (limited) discretionary funds to assist local associations for job creation. Subprefects in areas of high unemployment convene a Comité de Développement Industriel Local. Other state officials in the localities have also retained important roles. The transfer of ministerial field services has been one of the slowest aspects of decentralisation to be implemented; ministries that have remained relatively untouched include not only Finance and Defence (because of their regalian functions) but also Education and even Culture.

Rationalisation

Rationalisation of local and regional authorities and their competences has been left largely unachieved because of the incrementalism of the reforms. First, decentralisation in itself did not address the issue of the fragmentation of France's communes, and the resulting weakness of those suffering from depopulation in rural areas, or from the strains of a worsening urban crisis in many poorer suburbs. Mayors have proved as allergic as ever to the idea of mergers. The intercommunal solutions outlined above have certainly proved a useful palliative. But they also pose awkward questions as they stand. Should they not, to be more effective, control a greater share of their constituent communes' resources – whatever the worries of mayors who resent intercommunal encroachments on 'their' tax base? And if they are given, as is now the case, the power to tax, should they not be directly elected? And if they are directly elected, are the communes and councils that make up the grouping not superfluous, politically and administratively?

Second, the reforms have failed to choose between the *département* and the region; many commentators viewed the preservation of three tiers of local government as wasteful of time and resources, especially when a hierarchical relationship between them is specifically excluded (the 2003 constitutional amendment merely said that for specific projects, one type of authority may take a lead role on a case-by-case basis). One of the weaknesses of the Raffarin reforms is said to have arisen from the conflict (perpetuating the refusal to choose) between a regionalist prime minister and a *départementaliste* president. Nor was there any attempt to remodel boundaries of local authorities to fit economic or demographic realities: hence the anomalies noted earlier in the populations of regions and *départements*. The regions, though reinforced by the reforms, remained both weak compared with their counterparts elsewhere in Europe and vulnerable to pressures from big towns and powerful *départements* on their own territory. This weakness was compounded by the lack of stable majorities on many regional councils, owing to their election by proportional representation, giving FN councillors significant leverage over policy in a number of cases – though this was remedied (to the Left's short-term advantage) by the 2003 electoral law. Third, the clear distribution of responsibilities between different tiers of local government into distinct *blocs de compétences*, which was the main justification for the refusal to grant any one type of local authority hierarchical superiority over the others, has never materialised. The classic example was that of building and maintaining schools, where municipalities were supposed to be responsible for the primary level, *départements* for middle schools, regions for *lycées*, as well as for the long-term planning of middle schools, and the state for universities. In fact, the interrelated nature of educational decisions (and often buildings), certain refinements to the rules, and the inclination of all players to intervene as and when they saw fit, meant that the allocation of tasks was no clearer than before. Similar examples could be found in the areas of culture and, above all, of economic development, where communes, *départements* and regions are all engaged, thanks to a generous interpretation of the texts; the result, instead of the complementarity the reformers hoped for, is often an unseemly and competitive free-for-all. Fourth, decentralisation was not accompanied by any structural reform of France's notoriously archaic local taxation system, which manages to combine gross injustice (taxes on built and unbuilt land, and above all the *taxe d'habitation*) with economic masochism (the *taxe professionnelle*). Left-wing governments considered replacing the *taxe d'habitation* with something more equitable, or at least reassessing its basis, but did neither, partly from the knowledge that reform would create losers as well as winners. Raffarin has done rather more about the *taxe professionnelle*, phasing out its most objectionable, payroll component as a preliminary to getting rid of it altogether; local and regional authorities are worried that the receipts from petrol taxes that they have been promised as compensation will not be enough. Fifth, the major financial innovation of decentralisation (albeit one begun in the 1970s), the replacement of project-specific subsidies by block grants from the state to local authorities, was eroded after 1990 both by the reappearance of project subsidies and by the redistribution of funds between local authorities.

Some of the constraints placed on local authorities by central government since 1982 should be interpreted in the light of these failures to reform. The *politique de la ville* was necessitated in part by the continued fragmentation of local authorities, while the piecemeal redistribution of resources between communes and regions palliated the absence of any serious reform of local finances. These are, in other words, lacunae in the decentralisation process that invite more action by central, not local, government.

Democratisation

Democratisation, which was presented as an essential justification for the decentralisation project, has been a marginal element in its implementation. In the first place, local elites have changed rather slowly. Interior Ministry figures showed that over 60 per cent of mayors elected in 1989 were over 50 years old (and nearly a third were over 60); the thinning ranks of farmers (39.5 per cent in 1977, 18 per cent in 2001) were compensated by the growing numbers of the retired (15.3 to 29.7 per cent over the same period). Blue- and white-collar workers, over 31 per cent of the adult population, accounted for less than 9 per cent of mayors. The proportion of women – 10.7 per cent of mayors in 2001, and 10.4 per cent of *conseillers généraux* – remains derisory, although where parity legislation has forced it, there has been change in some areas, with 31.6 per cent of women on municipal councils and 47.6 per cent on those of the regions. A certain complement of new blood was, it is true, provided at the urban and regional level by councillors elected from the ranks of educated, salaried professionals, but while this was a change from France's traditional local elites, it would be hard to present it as diversification.

Second, an obstacle to the diversification of elites was the timid limitation placed on the *cumul des mandats* by the 1985 act. Table 12.2 testifies to the continued addiction of France's politicians to multiple office-holding. Moreover, major *notables* soon learnt to circumvent even the modest restrictions of the act by keeping mayoral and parliamentary positions themselves and ensuring that lesser offices were held by their own political dependents (including wives in several cases). And thanks to the Senate, the reform of 2000 left the core combination of parliamentarian and mayor largely intact.

Third, decentralisation did little to democratise the inner workings of local and regional authorities. Indeed, the new powers given to city mayors and to the presidents of regional councils and *conseils généraux* led several observers to note that the Fifth Republic's original sin – excessive executive dominance – was now reproduced at local level. The title of Jacques Rondin's book *Le sacre des notables* translated a view that decentralisation merely reinforced the power of those who already had it. The role of the mayor as the commune's chief executive, administrative head, majority leader and assembly president is hardly a recipe for municipal collegiality: it has now been reinforced by the removal of prefectoral controls, and reproduced at the level of *départements* and regions. Local and regional oppositions have been, with a few exceptions, ineffective to the point of marginality: none, with the partial exception of Les Verts in Paris and Île-de-France, has played a major role in uncovering the numerous scandals that have tainted the record of local government since 1982.

Fourth, decentralisation failed to engage at all promptly with the issue of direct or neighbourhood democracy that had inspired many urban social movements prior to the Left's victory in 1981. Local-level associations, while numerous and growing in number since 1982, have often suffered from the authorities' tendency (mirroring that of the central state) to divide them into two categories: the worthy and subsidised (but ultimately cannibalised by the local authority) and the untouchable – a practice that hinders, though has not prevented, the emergence of a vigorous local pluralism. It remains to be seen how much the two laws of 2002 and 2004 on local consultation will do to promote it, and the more open and freely debated style of decision-making that should, in principle, go with it.

Finally, the poor fit between local and regional authorities and their electoral bases was, if anything, reinforced by decentralisation. The election of *conseils généraux* by halves every three years, in cantons still marked by rural over-representation, has helped to perpetuate low turnout in cantonal elections. The electoral system for regions hindered the emergence both of stable regional majorities and of strong regional political identities, at least from 1986 to 2004. That in turn, coupled with the relative institutional weakness of regions, may help to explain why the major interest groups have been quite slow to build strong regional-level organisations.

Two symbols, finally, may serve to reinforce the sceptical view of at least the earlier years of decentralisation. One is the mess made of Édith Cresson's attempt to transplant the École Nationale d'Administration from Paris to Strasbourg, which was suspended after stout resistance from the association of *énarques*, with the school being split between the two cities at great expense for over a decade. The second is the architectural legacy of François Mitterrand, the main artisan of decentralisation: it consists of five monuments – the Louvre pyramid, the Bastille opera, the arch at La Défense, the François Mitterrand library, the La Villette music centre – all of which are in Paris.

Assessing decentralisation: the local system transformed

The sceptical view of decentralisation is a useful reminder of its limits. France has not turned into a federal state overnight, or even in the space of two decades.

The reforms, and the continuing behaviour of major actors (central government, but also local authorities in relation to associations), retain the stamp of a Jacobin past. Decentralisation has nevertheless had a profound impact on central–local relations in France. In some respects, for example the freedom of *départements* and regions to choose their own executives, this impact follows directly from the texts. Other changes, however, are less obvious.

Local finance

The financial position of local authorities has changed radically, despite the failure to reform local taxation, in three main ways. First, Table 12.1 testifies to the rapid real-terms growth of local and regional authority spending. This was considerably faster than that of the national budget. If local and regional *spending* rose notably but unspectacularly from 5 per cent of GDP in 1982 to nearly 7 per cent in 1995, the local and regional authorities' share of total non-military public *investments* in France – arguably more important in terms of their power to shape the future – grew from some 60 per cent in the late 1970s to 75 per cent twenty years later. The results, in terms of new administrative buildings, theatres, opera houses, cultural centres, festivals and orchestras, are visible (and audible) in every French city. Second, the (partial) move away from project-specific grants and, above all, the greater freedom to borrow from banks rather than state-run credit institutions have provided incentives for financial management of considerably greater sophistication in local authorities. The new freedom to borrow could have disastrous consequences: the Socialist mayor of Angoulême had run his city into virtual bankruptcy by 1991. More typical, though, are cases such as that of Chalon-sur-Saône, which reduced its working capital needs from the equivalent of three months' spending in 1983 to just twenty-four hours' worth in 1990 (a useful achievement given that local authorities' spare cash must be deposited in the Treasury at zero interest), or the thousands of other communes now enabled to renegotiate old loans or to shop around for the most favourable conditions for new ones. Third, local and regional authorities increasingly subsidised one another, with communes more often seeking subsidies from regions, *départements* and intercommunal groupings as well as from the state. Fourth, joint financing has often been set within a pluriannual, and global, contractual process, a *contrat de ville* or a *contrat de plan*, somewhat on the model of the *contrats de plan État–région*, involving mutual commitments to a linked series of projects.

Local authority staff

The staffing and expertise available to local authorities have substantially increased. The number of local authority employees grew from 21.7 per cent of the total *fonction publique* in France in 1976 to 29.5 per cent of the total *fonction publique* at the start of 2002. Again, the increase should be accounted for in part by the transfer of new responsibilities to local authorities; and in any case, four-fifths of the total consisted of routine administrative or manual staff. Nevertheless, local authority leaders have also used their new freedoms, and the reform of the status of their employees, to recruit high-level staff. Luc Rouban, for example, notes that by the end of 1993, sixty-nine members of the prefectoral corps were working for local authorities. More than ever, cities, *départements* and regions could command levels of expertise comparable to those of the state's services. Mayors and the presidents of *départements* and regions also constituted *cabinets* modelled on ministerial staffs. In town halls, this perturbed what had been a fairly strict demarcation between a political mayor and a largely depoliticised administration. Local administrations became more political as local authority leaders sought to surround themselves with politically sympathetic brains trusts; at the same time, however, elected officials became more administrative as mayors and presidents of *départements* and regions found themselves obliged to take an interest in the technicalities of policy. Moreover, the impossibility of a single elected official monopolising such technical competence has lent new prominence to second-ranking officials such as assistant mayors (*adjoints*), whose possession of such expertise may enable them to carve out their own quasi-independent policy sectors in close collaboration with senior local authority employees.

Local economic development

Local authorities at all levels have intervened to promote economic development. As outlined earlier, the inclusion of economic development among the responsibilities of local authorities under decentralisation coincided with a growing awareness of the efforts necessary to retain and develop local employment prospects. By 1992, local and regional authorities were spending (in roughly equal proportions for the three levels) over 2 billion euros on economic development, and had guaranteed 40 billion euros of loans. Levy's somewhat pessimistic view of the ineffectiveness of local authority interventions may simply reflect the early stages of a learning curve. It is clear, in particular, that intercommunal solutions are designed in part to palliate precisely the difficulties – unproductive competition between fragmented communes – that he identifies.

Local policy-making

There is, quite simply, almost no area of domestic policy in France that does not require, in one form or another, the mobilisation of local and regional authorities. Often this goes beyond what is planned by legislation. Universities, for example, were intended to remain under national control under the Defferre laws. In practice, regions and even towns became increasingly involved. This was partly because central government sought to expand the system without financing expansion fully (student numbers rose by four-fifths during the Mitterrand presidency), but also because local and regional authorities sought to attract higher education to their territory. The Universities 2000 programme, initiated by Jospin as education minister in 1991, involved local and regional authorities; the *contrats de plan* included universities. No initiatives on sustainable development, or agriculture, or training, or industrial policy, or tourism, or policing or even counter-terrorism can afford to ignore local and regional authorities.

New local actors

Decentralisation has encouraged the emergence of new local actors. The obvious cases are the presidents of the regions and *départements*, vastly more powerful than their pre-decentralisation predecessors. To these should be added the presidents of the various types of intercommunal grouping (who are not invariably the same as the mayors of the largest communes concerned); assistant mayors and vice-presidents of *conseils généraux* and regional councils with important sectoral responsibilities; and the heads of the profusion of *sociétés d'économie mixte* and the representatives of private firms, to which local and regional authorities have increasingly delegated their activities.

Networks and local authority entrepreneurship

Decentralisation has transformed the behaviour of local actors. Although the pre-1982 system was less centralised and hierarchical than it appeared on paper, it was still structured around a central armature of state power, from ministries and *cabinets* in Paris to prefectures and field services in the *départements*. Relationships within the 'local politico-administrative system' described by authors such as Worms, Grémion and Thoenig depended above all on access to and influence within the state and its services in the *départements*. Decentralisation ended this: prefects and *directions départementales* remained important players, but important among others. A complex and highly fluid network of competition and interdependence between local actors has been shaped by this partial retreat of the state and by a variety of other factors discussed above, including the arrival of new actors in the local system; the spread of intercommunal co-operation; the lack of clear separation between the competences of the different local and regional authorities; the growth of cross-subsidies between local and regional authorities; and the availability of European money. At the same time, the changing economic environment has required local actors to promote local economic development and to sell their localities in France and abroad with far more vigour than in the past. If the local *notable* of the pre-1982 mould was a discreet mediator, using his influence within the state apparatus to get rules bent or subsidies granted, his successor is more likely to be an aggressive political and economic entrepreneur. It would be wrong, however, to present such individuals as autocrats; for they face constant competition on their own territory from other actors, whether representatives of the state or other local elected officials. In this context, the *cumul des mandats* is as much of an asset as it was before 1982, albeit for rather different reasons; but the limitations placed on it since 1985 – partial and subject to circumvention though they are – have diminished the power of a single local boss to control a whole *département* or region. The most successful *notables* are therefore those who manage to establish networks of co-operation – forced or otherwise – with other local actors.

A coherent model of the post-decentralisation local system has proved extremely hard to produce, so much does it resemble a Hobbesian competition for the control of territory, with few landmarks or fixed rules. One helpful distinction is between different types of local system: the urban, centred on big municipalities, enjoying considerable autonomy thanks to their large budgets and numerous, technically competent and specialised staffs; the rural, centred on small communes lacking such resources and dependent on outside help; and possibly also an intermediate system, centred on medium towns, neither wholly dependent on outside partners nor wholly autonomous. Second, within each system will be found varying patterns of conflict and co-operation. Mayors of major cities, for example, may vie for regional supremacy with presidents of regional councils – but each side may depend on the other's co-operation to realise a major project. Small rural communes may solicit the co-operation of the state's field services to escape the technical tutelage of the *département*, or vice versa, or may seek the prefect's support against both, or the support of all three against the ambitions of city mayors. Rural communes may also be courted by leaders of regions anxious to extend their sphere of influence. In all of these cases, intercommunal co-operation arrangements and their leadership have been an increasingly important stake.

Third, the pattern of conflict and co-operation varies from region to region, depending on rivalries that may be traditional (as the centuries-old conflict between Le Havre and Rouen), economic, political (with *notables* of the same party typically being the worst enemies) or even personal. Fourth, no account of the local system that stops at these institutional actors is complete. Analyses of local and regional economic development have increasingly used the concept of governance: the local system, they argue, is not merely about elaborating and applying legal norms, but is rather a complex structure of vertical and horizontal sets of relations between a range of actors, including public institutions, associations and private firms, each of which possesses a different type of power (with the state and local authorities monopolising the force of legal obligation, while the private sector wields the strongest financial resources). This is not, of course, wholly new: local authorities maintained and developed relations with a wide range of actors, including private firms, well before 1982. But decentralisation and the increased salience of issues linked to economic development have enhanced the appropriateness of governance models to a wider range of authorities. Other accounts have focused on the growing segmentation of local and regional policies as decentralisation has enhanced the professionalisation and specialisation of local actors: local policy networks, again grouping a wide range of elected and non-elected actors from central and local government and from interest groups and experts within civil society, have, it is argued, been able to win significant autonomy from the control of any one institution within the local system. Finally, the local system is still characterised by great fluidity, the product of its own incoherences and contradictions, of the learning experiences of the actors, and of a process of institutional reform that is manifestly incomplete.

Concluding remarks: a continuing process

Any local or regional government system is a patchwork of compromises. How to reconcile the self-government of local communities with, for example, national standards of public service? Or the freedom of local authorities to tax and spend as they see fit with the inevitable need to share local tax revenue between poorer and wealthier communities, with greater and lesser needs, or to ensure that firms are not deterred from investing where they are most needed? There are no correct answers to such questions. Each state resolves them, on terms that may be more or less permanent, as a function of the political priorities of governments, but also of the weight of historically entrenched institutions and the political cultures that go with them. For France, part of the historical legacy is Jacobinism. But as we saw at the start of this chapter, even in the 1960s the image of the top-down, Jacobin state was about as good a reflection of the realities as that of the 'monolithic' French bureaucracy. It is not the least paradox of such a formally centralised state to have secreted a local system that has both encouraged a form of grass-roots democracy (ensured by the sheer number of local councillors) and allowed local elected officials to be seen by voters as accessible and trustworthy defenders of their interests. Part of the French problem in addressing decentralisation was inventing ways for central government to let go safely, and enough. Another, though, has been remedying the extreme fragmentation of local government without changing urban mayors simply into technocratic professionals, or transferring powers from smaller mayors to more remote intercommunal groupings, both of which, however administratively rational, would risk destroying a major institutional asset.

It was the virtue of Mitterrand, Mauroy and Defferre – and the outcome of deliberate political decision, rather than economic necessity – to turn from a period of prudent experiment with decentralisation to one of bold action. The Defferre reforms did not, of course, resolve every aspect of relations between the French state and the localities. They engendered much wasteful spending and not a little corruption. They were too inclined to superimpose new structures onto the old, rather than replacing anything. They were less than effective at checking, let alone resolving, some of the most pressing local problems, especially the decay of working-class suburbs and remote rural areas. But they still initiated a period of optimism and institutional learning as local elected officials engaged with new responsibilities, took on more, and developed more collaborative, less hierarchical habits of work. Few considered the decentralisation process complete. But the genie was seen as definitively out of the bottle.

That was the background to the Raffarin reforms. The decision to enshrine decentralisation in the constitution was a symbolic as well as a practical step, a sign that the process had come to maturity. Within months of that March 2003 amendment, however, decentralisation appeared to have lost part of its consensual appeal. A poll in 1997, for example, had shown 56 per cent of respondents agreeing that 'decentralisation should be developed further'. By November 2003, however, this figure had dropped to 34 per cent, while the proportion who thought it had gone far enough or too far rose from 32 per cent to 57 per cent – a near-reversal of the figures in the space of six years. This disaffection was also reflected, with a time lag, among mayors, among whom a poll in November 2004 found that the proportion considering that decentralisation 'was on course' had dropped from 61 per cent to 35 per cent in a single year, while those saying it 'was going in the wrong direction' had risen from 28 to 43 per cent. It was perhaps unsurprising that Raffarin received the chilliest of receptions at that month's congress of the Association of French Mayors.

Part of Raffarin's difficulty was party political: he retained the support of most right-wing mayors, lacked it among those of the Left and was the object of vilification by the new Socialist regional council presidents. But there were wider concerns too. One concerned the loss of rural public services. This was spectacularly highlighted in October 2004 when 263 local elected officials of the Creuse, a rural *département* with 125,000 inhabitants (against twice that in 1900), resigned their positions in protest against post office and other closures. Again, most of the elected officials were left-wing, and the far Left came out in force to a rally held to mark the occasion. But over half the mayors polled the following month said they had little or no confidence in the government's ability to safeguard such services (Raffarin was later constrained to announce a moratorium). A second concern was budgets and taxation. Despite the constitutional guarantee that transferred responsibilities would be matched by transferred resources, a growing number of local elected officials have expressed their disbelief in such promises: even if they were formally respected, they argued, the money would be insufficient to cover new needs, or else the central government would, without any formal transfer of competences, announce new policies with spending consequences for local and regional authorities, or cut funding in areas (such as subsidies to associations) where the victims would quickly turn to communes and regions. Similar disquiet prevailed over taxation: the phasing out of two of the four main local taxes (on land and businesses) announced by the government would surely lead to further rises in taxes falling on households. Underpinning these worries, on the Right as well as the Left, was the familiar concern that central government was merely dumping its own responsibilities onto local and regional authorities. And underlying those was the more widespread inclination among the French, in a difficult context, to seek the protection of the central state rather than risk the dangers of institutional innovation. It was the somewhat improbable figure of de Gaulle who said in 1969 that 'the centuries-long centralisation of the French state no longer has any *raison d'être*'. The lasting significance of an autumn of discontent across France's town halls and village *mairies* cannot be rapidly judged. But it would be ironic if the view of the 'Jacobin' de Gaulle should lose currency, a few years after its general acceptance, on the initiative of local notables who on the face of it had most to gain.

Further reading

Ashford, D., *British Dogmatism and French Pragmatism*, London, George Allen and Unwin, 1982.

Becquart-Leclercq, J., *Paradoxes du pouvoir local*, Paris, Presses de la Fondation Nationale des Sciences Politiques, 1976.

Bernard, P., *Le préfet de la République, le chêne et l'olivier*, Paris, Economica, 1992.

Blanc, J. and Rémond, B., *Les collectivités locales*, 3rd edition, Paris, Presses de la Fondation Nationale des Sciences Politiques, 1995.

Borraz, O. and Le Galès, P., 'France: the intermunicipal revolution', in B. Denters and L. Rose (eds), *Comparing Local Governance: Trends and Developments*, Basingstoke, Palgrave, 2004.

Castells, M., *The Urban Question*, London, Edward Arnold, 1977.

Castells, M., *City, Class, and Power*, London, Macmillan, 1978.

Cole, A. and John, P., *Local Governance in England and France*, London, Routledge, 2001.

CURAPP/CRAPS, *La démocratie locale: représentation, participation et espace public*, Paris, Presses Universitaires de France, 1999.

Dion, S., *La politisation des maires*, Paris, Economica, 1986.

Dolez, B. and Laurent, A., *Le vote des villes: les élections municipales des 11 et 18 mars 2001*, Paris, Presses de Sciences Po, 2002.

Dupoirier, E. (ed.), *Régions: la croisée des chemins*, Paris, Presses de Sciences Po, 1998.

Fontaine, J. and Le Bart, C. (eds), *Le métier d'élu local*, Paris, L'Harmattan, 1994.

Gaudin, J.-P. (ed.), *La négociation des politiques contractuelles*, Paris, L'Harmattan, 1996.

Gilbert, G. and Delcamp, A., *La décentralisation dix ans après*, Paris, LGDJ, 1993.

Gleizal, J.-J. (ed.), *Le retour des préfets?*, Grenoble, Presses Universitaires de Grenoble, 1995.

Godard, F. (ed.), *Le gouvernement des villes*, Paris, Descartes, 1997.

Grémion, P., *Le pouvoir périphérique*, Paris, Seuil, 1976.

Hardy, J., *Les collectivités locales*, Paris, La Découverte, 1998.

Institut de la décentralisation, *La décentralisation en France*, Paris, La Découverte, 1996.

John, P., *Local Governance in Western Europe*, London, Sage, 2001.

Kesselman, M., *The Ambiguous Consensus: A Study of Local Government in France*, New York, Alfred Knopf, 1967.

Lacorne, D., *Les notables rouges*, Paris, Presses de la Fondation Nationale des Sciences Politiques, 1980.

Lagroye, J., *Société et politique: Jacques Chaban-Delmas à Bordeaux*, Paris, Pedone, 1973.

Lagroye, J. and Wright, V. (eds), *Local Government in Britain and France*, London, George Allen and Unwin, 1979.

Le Galès, P. and Lequesne, C. (eds), *Regions in Europe*, London, Routledge, 1998.

Levy, J., *Tocqueville's Revenge: State, Society, and Economy in Contemporary France*, Cambridge, MA, Harvard University Press, 1999.

Mabileau, A. (ed.), *Les facteurs locaux dans la vie politique nationale*, Paris, Pedone, 1972.

Mabileau, A., *Le système local en France*, 2nd edition, Paris, Montchrestien, 1994.

Machin, H., *The Prefect in French Public Administration*, London, Croom Helm, 1977.

Meissel, R., *Décentralisation et aménagement du territoire*, Paris, Le Monde/Marabout, 1995.

Mény, Y., *Centralisation et décentralisation dans le débat politique français, 1945–1969*, Paris, LGDJ, 1974.

Ministère de l'Intérieur, Direction Générale des Collectivités Territoriales, *Les collectivités locales en chiffres*, Paris, La Documentation Française, 2004.

Ohnet, J.-M., *Histoire de la décentralisation française*, Paris, Librairie Générale Française (Le Livre de Poche), 1996.

Perrineau, P. (ed.), *Régions: la baptême des urnes*, Paris, Pedone, 1986.

Pouvoirs, no. 24, 1983, 'Le maire'; no. 60, 1992, 'La décentralisation'; no. 73, 1995, 'La démocratie municipale'.

Rémond, B., *La région*, 2nd edition, Paris, Montchrestien, 1995.

Rémond, B., *La fin de l'état jacobin?*, Paris, Librairie Générale de Droit et de Jurisprudence, 1998.

Rey, H., *La peur des banlieues*, Paris, Presses de Sciences Po, 1996.

Rhodes, M. (ed.), *The Regions and the New Europe*, Manchester, Manchester University Press, 1995.

Rondin, J., *Le sacre des notables*, Paris, Grasset, 1985.

Schain, M., *French Communism and Local Power*, London, Frances Pinter, 1985.

Schmidt, V., *Democratizing France: The Political and Administrative History of Decentralization*, Cambridge, Cambridge University Press, 1990.

Schrameck, O., *La fonction publique territoriale*, Paris, Dalloz, 1996.

Sharpe, L. J. (ed.), *The Rise of Meso-Government in Europe*, London, Sage, 1993.

Smith, A. and Sorbets, C. (eds), *Le leadership politique et le territoire*, Rennes, Presses Universitaires de Rennes, 2002.

Tarrow, S., *Between Centre and Periphery*, London, Yale University Press, 1977.

Thoenig, J.-C., *L'ère des technocrates: le cas des Ponts et Chaussées*, 2nd edition, Paris, L'Harmattan, 1987.

Tobin, I., *Le préfet dans la décentralisation*, Paris, L'Harmattan, 1997.

Vital-Durand, E., *Les collectivités territoriales*, Paris, Hachette, 1994.

13 French justice and the elusive *État de droit*[1]

Politics as a profession is adjacent to law: many politicians inside and outside demo-cratic systems have legal training, and most spend part of their time legislating. In France, the discipline of political science is entwined with that of law: political science departments are often outgrowths of the *facultés de droit*. Law plays a central role in political institutions. It is a framework of public and private action, a medium of conflict avoidance and resolution, a means of aggregating and channelling political preferences to render them operational and enforceable. Yet political scientists, even in France, were for long relatively uninterested in the relationship between the justice system, the legal profession and politics. That is now changing; the law has acquired the power to fascinate political scientists. One reason has been the growing judicialisation of institutions and public policy – a widespread phenomenon in Western Europe, but one felt particularly in France, where it threatens long-held traditions.

Judicialisation will be a central theme of this chapter. It has been driven by Eurocrats and intellectuals, by public-spirited legislators, by courageous judges and (unintention-ally) by corrupt politicians, as well as by the wider developments observed elsewhere in this book – the changing relationship between the state, civil society and the market. Because it upsets traditions, judicialisation has provoked a debate in France about the emergence of an *État de droit* – a state bound by, and respectful towards, the rule of law and due process. That debate has also highlighted the lack of confidence of the French in their justice system, and in particular in its impartiality; for the *État de droit* in France is more embryonic than is fully realised. However, before turning to these themes it is necessary both to consider the judicial tradition inherited by the Fifth

---

1 An earlier version of this chapter appeared in *West European Politics*, volume 22, no. 4, October 1999, and in book form in Robert Elgie (ed.), *The Changing French Political System*, London, 2000 (Courtesy of Frank Cass).

Republic (and now endangered by the *État de droit*), and to present the major judicial actors of today.

French judicial traditions: law in the service of the state

For Jacobins, a powerful judiciary, independent of the representatives of the sovereign people, was no more palatable than freely organised interest groups or strong local government. Jacobinism, however, was only one (albeit a very important one) of a number of traditions anchored in the French judicial system by the time of the proclamation of the Fifth Republic and drawn, with imperfect consistency, from Montesquieu, Rousseau and a host of lesser-known but influential legal thinkers and practitioners. The system incorporated features acquired from the *ancien régime*, from the Jacobin Revolution and from the régimes of the two Bonapartes (but more especially the first), as well as from the Third Republic – features distinct yet interconnected, jostling uncomfortably with one another. They may be summarised as follows.

- *The formal equality of citizens before the law*. With two exceptions, this fundamental principle has never been formally called into question since its establishment in 1789. The first exception was the Vichy régime, which established a special *Statut des Juifs* as early as October 1940. The second concerns the periodic creation of tribunals with exceptional powers, under the impact of traumatic political events. Such tribunals (whether of military or mixed judicial and military character) behaved (as they were meant to) with repressive zeal, disregarding the most basic rights of the defence.
- *The ubiquity of law*. In France as elsewhere in Europe, a growing number of sectors came to be regulated and bureaucratised by legal stipulations – a process characterised in Germany as 'legal pollution' (*Verrechtlichung*).
- *Law established and policed by an 'imperial state'*. This *Étatisation du droit* was one of the major legacies of the Revolution and of Napoleon. Pursued by all successive régimes, it was rooted in that deep mistrust of autonomous self-regulating institutions observed elsewhere as being characteristic of Jacobin traditions. Regulation and control should be a monopoly of the state, which alone represented the 'general interest' and was therefore legitimately invested with superior rights.
- *An ingrained disrespect for the constitution*. Despite the rhetoric of jurists and politicians, whichever constitution was in force was viewed (perhaps unsurprisingly, as none before 1958 lasted longer than two decades, with the single exception of the Third Republic) as a mere rule in the wider game of politics: a means of regulating conflict rather than the foundation of political order.
- *An instrumental view of law*. Anglo-Saxon, and especially American, traditions have seen law as a mechanism for managing a diverse and pluralistic society, applying to individuals, groups and public authorities alike. The notion of a 'general will' standing outside such pluralistic interests was neither admitted nor much considered. In France, on the other hand, law was seen precisely as the expression of such a 'general will', which arbitrated between the interests in contention. It was also viewed as a mobiliser and legitimiser of the socio-political system. Far from being neutral, it was instrumental and output-oriented, intimately involved in

social guidance and social engineering, a tool for ensuring, among other things, social integration (based on a legally constructed concept of citizenship), political centralisation and even economic *dirigisme*.

- *An inquisitorial system of justice.* These different notions of law had practical consequences in the courtroom. In Anglo-Saxon systems, justice and truth are served by the adversarial clash between prosecution and defence, with the judge as referee and, in serious cases, the jury as final arbiter of the outcome. If, on the other hand, law is seen as the expression of the 'general will', and the state authorities as the representatives of the sovereign people, as in France, then the state, manifested as the Justice Ministry, has both the right and the duty actively to seek out the truth of each case. Hence the more active role of French judges, employed by the Justice Ministry, both in bringing cases to the courts and in participating in the courtroom proceedings (for example, in questioning witnesses and the accused).

- *An enduring hostility, both ideologically and politically inspired, towards 'judge-made' law and judicial review.* The 1804 Civil Code (Article 5) specifically forbids judges from using their adjudication of individual conflicts to create jurisprudence – that is, to make decisions of a general character that would bind later courts. According to the Jacobin and imperial visions, legal sovereignty lay with those authorities (parliament or executive depending on the régime) invested through election or referendum as the legitimate embodiment of the popular will. As the expression of that will, law was seen as, by definition, neither perfectible nor contestable. A profound practical suspicion of the judiciary as political actors also inspired this implacable hostility to judicial review. Lawyers and magistrates had played a major role in undermining the *ancien régime*. After 1789, once they had won (for many revolutionaries came from the legal profession), they set out to demolish the wrecking potential of their own profession. Bonaparte agreed with the revolutionaries on this point; so did all subsequent rulers. The problem was compounded by France's chronic régime instability between 1789 and 1958 (see Chapter 1): two empires, two monarchies and four republics, each a target for anti-régime attacks. The rulers of each new régime, instinctively suspicious of the judiciary they inherited, both purged the magistrature and mistrusted those remaining judges whom they had spared. An early but lasting expression of this mistrust of the judiciary was given in the celebrated proclamation of August 1790, which insisted on the separation of judicial and administrative power.

- *A dual system of law separating administrative and ordinary jurisdictions.* Both the ideological factors noted above and the suspicion of judges that was its practical corollary militated against any possibility that judges of the ordinary courts might be allowed to perturb the activities of administrative bodies or to call such bodies to account. From 1790, indeed, for the ordinary courts to interfere in the administration was officially a criminal offence. Instead, an internal system of justice, headed by the Conseil d'État (Council of State: see under the next section) was set up to try alleged illegalities within the administration. Theoretically, under such a system the state is simultaneously the alleged offender, judge and jury: hence the revulsion felt towards the dual system of justice by freedom-loving French liberals, and by British constitutionalists like Dicey who believed in 'the equal subjection of all classes to the ordinary law of the land administered by the ordinary law courts'. In practical terms, however, the administrative law courts did slowly begin to generate rights against the abuses committed by state officials.

- *A subordinate and politicised judiciary*. In the practice of the separation of powers, the judiciary was considered, not as a power (*pouvoir*) on an equal footing with the executive and the legislature, but as a mere 'authority' (*autorité*) – a term clearly indicative of its lower ranking. Some practical expressions of this subordination were the hierarchical supremacy of the Justice Ministry over part of the judiciary; the requirement, common in the nineteenth century, that prosecuting magistrates (*procureurs*) become electoral agents for the régime and keep a close and punitive eye on its enemies; the inclusion of members of the judiciary in special tribunals established to try political 'crimes' (which included, in 1851, defending the constitution); the persistent political interference in judicial appointments; and the constant pressure on prosecuting magistrates to close the files on politically embarrassing cases.

- *Judicial self-restraint*. Judges might be active participants in the courtroom, but within their profession they were socialised into a role of discretion. Judicial creativity or activism, anything that smacked of an attempt to establish jurisprudence, or to question the doctrines of state supremacy and political sovereignty, was frowned upon.

It would be exaggerated but not wholly untrue to argue that the characteristics noted above – the state-based, instrumental and inquisitorial character of law, the widespread disregard for the constitution, the absence of judicial review, the dual civil and administrative legal systems, the mistrust, subordination and politicisation of the judiciary, and judicial restraint – flowed inexorably from a Jacobin conception of the role of the state and its relation to society. In practice, the system was more complex than that. The separation of powers was almost as frequently violated as it was invoked, for example, and practical political authority did not always lie where it was legally supposed to: thus parliamentary sovereignty in the late Third Republic was undermined by the executive's increasing use of *décrets-lois*. The fraught process of defining what was often an uncertain borderline between civil and administrative law led to regular disputes between ordinary and administrative judges, and ultimately to the creation of the Tribunal des Conflits in May 1872 to settle such disputes. More significantly, judges played a much more important role as policy-makers than official texts and doctrines suggested. The Conseil d'État was vital in this respect: it slowly transformed itself into a fairly impartial (if politically sensitive) administrative court, capable (in most circumstances) of protecting French citizens against the illegalities of state officials and its own members from dismissal. The late nineteenth and early twentieth centuries saw a steady narrowing of the area within which the Conseil d'État was prepared to treat executive acts as non-justiciable (or not subject to the law). During this period too, the two bases of administrative law, the *recours pour excès de pouvoir* and the *régime de la responsabilité administrative*, were established, refined and extended. They not only provided the citizen-plaintiff with the right to seek the annulment of an act or decision; they also enabled the Conseil d'État to fly in the face of Jacobin principles and create a substantial and important jurisprudence. The scope of this judge-made law covered almost all the law concerning the public administration and its officials: the rules, regulations, procedures and responsibilities of the administration, as well as the basic ideas of what constituted *service public*, a public agent and the public domain (concepts which were to become critical in the privatisation debates of the 1980s and after). The Conseil went further than that: well before 1958, it had begun to define a *general* set of constitutional principles – 'fundamental general principles of law' – that could be cited in court cases. These included conveniently elastic concepts (allowing judges a certain interpretative latitude) such as 'equality before the law', 'freedom of conscience', 'non-retroactivity' or 'individual freedom'. At the same time, the direct impact of this juris-prudence should not be exaggerated. In particular, the Conseil d'État specifically stated that it could not test the constitutionality of the law, which was the expression of the general will.

At the beginning of the Fifth Republic, then, the constitutional and political trad-ition of the country were permeated far more by an *Étatisation du droit* – law in the service of the state – than by an *État de droit*. And for those who favoured the latter, the Fifth Republic had unpromising beginnings. The constitution itself was scarcely reassuring: the Conseil d'État was not mentioned as an administrative judge (though its consultative role was strengthened); the newly created Constitutional Council was made up exclusively of political appointees, and its role defined as a policeman of the executive–legislative spheres of competence rather than as a judge; the guarantor of the independence of the judiciary was to be the president of the Republic, while the Conseil Supérieur de la Magistrature (Higher Council of the Judiciary) was allowed only to advise on appointments. Constitutional practice was hardly less alarming, for de Gaulle regularly infringed both the letter and the spirit of the constitution (see Chapter 4). Moreover, the early years of the régime saw a number of disturbing incidents that specifically concerned the judiciary. Several appointments to key posts were flagrantly political. The government and the Conseil d'État engaged in public rows: over the Conseil d'État's clearly expressed view that the 1962 referendum on the direct election of the president was unconstitutional; over the sacking (an extraordi-nary step) of one of the Council's own members, André Jacomet, who, as a senior official in Algeria, had openly opposed the government's policy of self-determination; and, most spectacularly, over the Canal affair in which the Council, in emergency session, saved the life of an individual who had been condemned for treasonable activities in Algeria by a special military court. Political pressure on the judiciary led to several highly dubious *affaires* being hushed up: the Ben Barka affair (involving the assassination of the leader of the Moroccan opposition, with the connivance of the French secret service, in December 1965 as he prepared for a personal meeting with de Gaulle); the mysterious murder of the Prince de Broglie, a politician of illustrious ancestry and grubby social contacts, in 1978; the no less curious discovery of Robert Boulin, labour minister and leading Gaullist, dead in 2 feet of water in 1979 (the verdict, contested by his family, was suicide); and the *Canard Enchaîné* affair, which concerned the bugging of France's leading satirical and (more importantly) investiga-tive weekly. Little of this could have inspired confidence in the reinforcement of a state ruled by law. Yet over the succeeding generation France took an unexpected number of steps towards an *État de droit*. This was thanks to a wide range of judicial actors, both French and European.

Main actors in the contemporary judicial system

The French legal establishment embraces a plurality of institutions each, in principle, functioning within an apparently well-defined sphere. The major institutions are as follows.

The European Court of Justice (ECJ)

The European Court of Justice in Luxembourg was created under the treaties that established the European Coal and Steel Community of 1952 and the European Economic Community of 1957. By the mid-1990s the Court's main principles of supremacy, direct applicability and, to a lesser extent, direct effect of European law had been firmly entrenched, and largely tolerated by French administrative and judicial elites, even if some politicians remained suspicious. The early decision of the ECJ that the European Community 'constitutes a new legal order . . . for the benefit of which the states have limited their sovereign rights, albeit in limited fields' initially provoked hostility and resistance in some French judicial quarters, notably in the Conseil d'État. Indeed, well after the Court of Cassation, the supreme civil court, had accepted the supremacy of European law (and the ECJ) in the landmark *Jacques Vabre* case of 24 May 1975, the Conseil d'État stubbornly continued to reject the doctrine. However, in a series of landmark decisions between 1985 and 1992, the Conseil d'État reversed its earlier hostility, accepted and then propagated the supremacy of European law, and extended its scope. The Constitutional Council, the supreme constitutional body in France, initially more reluctant than hostile to becoming involved in the issue of sovereignty, was eventually, in April 1992 (*arrêt* Maastricht I) to declare that France 'can enter – under the condition of reciprocity – international agreements in order to participate in the creation or development of permanent international organisations, possessing a judicial personality, and that in consequence France, as other states, accepts the transfer of competences'. Thus agreements reached at European Union level are now enforceable directly in France, and the Union, in conjunction with French courts, can strike down national legislation and policies which conflict with EU law. This position has now been constitutionalised by a ruling of the Constitutional Council. Under the Treaty of Rome, national courts were not envisaged as the principal enforcers of European law. But the ECJ, through its case law jurisprudence, has created a new role for national courts as critical mediators of the European legal system – and this role of national courts has helped legitimise European law at domestic level. The extent of 'judicial dialogue' between the ECJ and national courts may be seen both in the frequency of preliminary references to the ECJ from French national courts (486 between 1972 and 1994), and the frequent interaction between judges, lawyers and scholars in Luxembourg and France. Access to the courts is normally reserved to the member states and the Commission (acting on its own behalf or on that of an injured party) but it is also available, in some circumstances, to national courts and even individuals. Critically, under the transformed preliminary ruling procedure, individuals can raise cases based on EU law in national courts and may require the application of ECJ decisions. The ECJ tries cases relating to competition law, but, more generally, by its jurisprudence, it has tolerated or encouraged the slow expansion of the EU's competence: those EU powers not explicitly enumerated are given a generous interpretation; it has interpreted loosely the doctrine of implied powers, invoked under Article 235; and it has introduced a doctrine of pre-emption – a member state is precluded from introducing legislation once the Union has acted on that particular issue.

The European Court of Human Rights

The European Court of Human Rights, which is part of the structure of the Council of Europe not the European Union, has the mandate to interpret the European Convention on Human Rights and thus set normative human rights standards across Europe. It is the only court with the power to review national legislation concerning alleged violation of human rights in politically delicate areas such as immigration and asylum, and discrimination based on gender or sexual orientation. France ratified the European Convention by a law of 31 December 1973. By an additional protocol of 2 October 1981, the new Socialist government, which reformed several aspects of the judicial system, gave citizens direct access to the Court of Human Rights.

The Constitutional Council

The Constitutional Council was one of the most significant innovations of the Fifth Republic, even though its full significance was unintended and unsuspected, and in its early practice unpromising. Indeed, the intention of the framers of the constitution was to create not a real judge but a consultative body and a protector of the prerogatives of a reinforced executive against a seriously weakened parliament. It comprises nine members (and the ex-presidents of the Republic, of whom only Giscard has availed himself of the right), three each appointed by the president of the Republic (who also appoints the the Council's president), the president of the Senate, and the president of the National Assembly. Members of the Constitutional Council hold their posts for nine years on a non-renewable basis. The powers of the Constitutional Council are threefold. In the first place, it has certain formal competences: it must be consulted if the president of the Republic decides, under Article 16 of the constitution, to exercise emergency powers; in the event of the president of the Republic being incapable of carrying out his functions, the Constitutional Council declares the office vacant (Article 7). Second, the Constitutional Council oversees the regularity of referenda and of elections to the presidency, and to the two houses of parliament, and rules on contested cases arising out of parliamentary elections (Articles 58 to 60). Finally, the Constitutional Council is a constitutional referee. Thus, it polices the executive–legislative boundary, with the initial intention that the latter did not impinge upon the former: it delimits the areas within which parliament is entitled to legislate, leaving all other matters to be governed by administrative enactments. Furthermore, any proposed law of a constitutional character (*loi organique*) and any new parliamentary standing order require the assent of the Constitutional Council. Most importantly, the constitution (Article 61–2) provided that the conformity to the constitution of any treaty or government act may, before its promulgation, be tested before the Constitutional Council. Once petitioned, the Council possesses the power to invalidate, in part or in its entirety, any law on the grounds of unconstitutionality. A law, once referred, can be promulgated only after the Council has given its assent. Its decisions are not subject to appeal.

For the first ten years of the Fifth Republic, the Constitutional Council carried out its task as a self-effacing guard dog of the executive and its prerogatives. A number of reasons explain this situation. First, the intentions of the framers of the constitution were clear: the preamble of the 1958 constitution declares the solemn attachment of the people to the preamble of the 1946 constitution (which contains a set of rights), but the framers, fearful of government by judges and sensitive to the need to protect statutory sovereignty, insisted that neither preamble enjoyed constitutional status (i.e. the status of an enforceable supra-legislative body of norms). Second, access to the Council was limited to the president of the Republic, the prime minister, and the presidents of the Senate and of the National Assembly, and for most of the early years of the régime the first three belonged to the same Gaullist party, and the fourth was a moderate right-winger deeply attached to parliamentary sovereignty and equally deeply suspicious of the 'government of judges'. Third, the capacity for judicial review was limited by the constitutional provision that once a law was promulgated it was immune to judicial review – it was constitutionally pure – even if the Constitutional Council had not been asked for a ruling. Fourth, the judges themselves, political appointees to a man, displayed a less than assertive attitude in their judgements. The impact of this combination of factors was unsurprising: the Council was asked to rule on only seven cases, and on each occasion did so in favour of the executive, and it displayed great restraint when presented with an opportunity to expand its interpretative powers. On only one occasion was the Council specifically asked to rule against the executive – to invalidate President de Gaulle's attempt, in 1962, to amend the constitution (in order to introduce direct election of the president) by way of referendum – a procedure not provided for in the constitution. The Constitutional Council and the Conseil d'État, when consulted, were against de Gaulle's project, but in November 1962, after the referendum had endorsed de Gaulle's proposal, the Constitutional Council, ruling on a petition from the president of the Senate (a bitter opponent of de Gaulle) declared that it had no jurisdiction to control a law passed directly by the people. How the Constitutional Council came to expand its role and became a major actor in policy-making is examined later in this chapter.

The Cour de Justice de la République (Court of Justice of the Republic)

This court was created by the constitutional reform of 1993. Its duty is to judge members of the government accused of committing illegal acts in the exercise of their ministerial functions. It is composed of members elected by the National Assembly and the Senate, and of magistrates of the Court of Cassation (see below) elected by the court itself.

The ordinary courts

The ordinary courts, and the purely judicial magistrates (*juges judiciaires*) are organised in a network of Parisian and provincial courts and headed by the Court of Cassation (Cour de Cassation), which is the final court of appeal for civil and criminal justice. Magistrates (6,000 of them in 1997, of whom a quarter were women, and of whom the vast majority were graduates of the École Nationale de la Magistrature in Bordeaux) are divided into two groups. On the one hand, there are the sitting magistrates (*magistrats du siège*) who are independent, free from most political pressures and protected by a range of measures including irremovability. This group is further divided into presiding judges, as in Britain, and investigating or examining magistrates (*juges d'instruction*, of whom there were 728 in 1996). All magistrates in this group are appointed after the advice of the Conseil Supérieur de la Magistrature (Higher Council of the Judiciary). On the other hand, there are the prosecuting magistrates (*magistrature du parquet* or *magistrature debout*, since they stand in court while prosecuting) who form what is known as the *ministère public*. Comprising, in hierarchical order, general prosecutors (*procureurs généraux*), prosecutors and sub-prosecutors, the *magistrature debout* is under the hierarchical control of the minister of justice. These magistrates are appointed from a list provided by the minister of justice, who can remove them from a particular post (by transfer or promotion), and who can, and does, give instructions to them. They play a crucial role in the justice system, since they supervise the preliminary police investigations. The official investigating magistrate (*juge d'instruction*) cannot proceed with a case until it has been referred by the *parquet*, and cannot expand its scope to take account of new evidence unearthed without the *parquet*'s further authorisation.

The Conseil d'État (Council of State)

The Conseil d'État (Council of State) is the supreme French administrative body (it heads a network of regionally based administrative tribunals), and has a host of super-visory and judicial functions. It is also one of the most prestigious of the *grands corps* and a major nursery for the French public and private, political, administrative and industrial elite. The Conseil d'État is hierarchically structured: it is presided officially by the prime minister, but in practice by its own vice-president (a political appointee, but non-removable and drawn from the Conseil's more eminent members), and run by the presidents of the various sections of the Conseil (each shadowing two or three ministries) who are also political appointees though invariably chosen from among the *conseillers d'État*. The latter are mainly promoted on a seniority basis, from the ranks of the *maîtres de requêtes* (the next rank down) who, in turn, are recruited, on a seniority basis, from the lowest ranks of the Conseil d'État, the *auditeurs* who are all the products of the École Nationale d'Administration (ÉNA), seedbed of the administra-tive elite. The government has the right to appoint the vice-president, the presidents of the sections, and a number of *conseillers* and *maîtres de requêtes*. Although its origins may be traced to the *ancien régime*, the Conseil d'État was officially founded by Napoleon Bonaparte (Article 52 of the constitution of 13 December 1799) with the general remit of resolving problems arising from administrative affairs. From early on, it had two main tasks. The first was to judge the abuse and misuse of administrative action: Bonaparte, like the revolutionaries of 1789, mistrusted judges from the ordinary courts, and decided that judicial review of administrative acts should be left to adminis-trative judges, to be appointed by himself. The second function was legislative, and involved the scrutiny of all bills. Throughout its chequered history (it was dissolved or radically purged on several occasions) the Conseil d'État preserved its principal activity as administrative judge, even though its role as *conseiller du Prince* was greatly dimin-ished. It also slowly built itself a reputation for impartiality, created a set of safeguards for its own independence (in practice, if not in law, members of the Conseil d'État cannot normally be dismissed, though there were purges in 1879, 1940 and 1944, while the Canal episode noted earlier (p. 393) stands as an exception within the Fifth Republic), and established, in 1872, the important principle that it rendered *justice déléguée* (i.e. decided in its own right) and not *justice retenue* (decided in the name of the executive). It also, and most significantly, by a series of ingenious and sometimes audacious legal decisions, progressively extended the scope of judicial review of state administrative activities. During the Fifth Republic, the essential judicial role of the Conseil d'État has remained largely intact even though it has become even more a court of appeal: it takes decisions relating to very important issues, and acts as a court of appeal for contested decisions of the subordinate administrative courts. Initially, the latter were the thirty-three administrative tribunals (twenty-six in metropolitan France) which had been set up in 1953. However, the second Chirac government, in an attempt to relieve an overloaded Conseil, created, by the law of 31 December 1987, five provincial administrative courts to deal with appeals against the decisions of the thirty-three administrative tribunals.

The Conseil d'État has two principal jurisdictions. In the *pleine juridiction* it considers cases in which a complainant alleges the infringement of a right by an administrative body, and seeks compensation. In making a decision, the Conseil d'État applies its own case law (which is broadly in line with civil law). The second jurisdiction is *juridiction d'annulation*: on pain of annulment at the suit of anyone with a sufficient interest, the Conseil d'État insists that all administrative acts should conform not only to the enacted law or decree, but also to 'the general principles of law' which the Conseil, through its case law, has defined and which provide extensive protection for the individual against the abuse of administrative power. The consultative and advisory role of the Conseil d'État has been strengthened during the Fifth Republic. The constitution of 1958 defines the cases in which it must be consulted: all government bills (Article 39); all proposed *ordonnances* covered by Article 38 (which allows the government to seek parliamentary approval to take, on its own, measures normally requiring primary legislation and hence explicit parliamentary approval); all government decrees (which do not require parliamentary approval) which modify texts of a legislative nature (which do require such assent) adopted before the promulgation of the 1958 constitution. To this list has been added, since 1992, all European Union acts having a legislative character in France. In this consultative role, the Conseil d'État scrutinises proposals for their constitutionality, and for their consistency with existing statutes. It may also make recommendations to the government on the implications of its proposals. Although the Conseil d'État must be consulted in all three cases outlined above, its advice is not binding. The government may (there is no obligation) also ask it to give advice on particular issues: there are thirty or so such requests each year, although in 1993 the figure rose to fifty-eight. Finally, the Conseil d'État may undertake, at the request of the prime minister or of its own vice-president, a major study of a particular issue or problem. A new section within the Conseil was eventually established to carry out this function: between 1969 and 1991, sixty-three such studies were undertaken, several becoming the basis for subsequent legislation (see below).

The Cour des Comptes

The Cour des Comptes (Court of Accounts), established by Napoleon in an act of 16 September 1807, was given constitutional status in 1946. The essential task of the court is to help the government and parliament in controlling the legality of the use of public funds (including, since 1976, those of public enterprises). It is structured hierarchically and comprises some 200 members: the lowest rank of the hierarchy, the *auditeurs*, are all recruited from ÉNA, while the other ranks have been promoted internally on a seniority basis, or chosen from outside the court in the government. By the act of 2 March 1982, a court of accounts (*chambre régionale des comptes*) was established for each of the twenty-two regions and given the legal right to scrutinise the use of local authority funds (see Chapter 10). Their decisions are subject to appeal before the national Cour des Comptes. If the court decides that there has been a misuse of public funds, the relevant official may be declared personally responsible. The decisions (*arrêts*) of the court may be challenged in the Conseil d'État, which acts as the final court of appeal. Apart from this official role, the Cour des Comptes has a wider administrative role: in its annual report it draws public attention to waste, irregularities and abuses in the use of public money. Some of the more dubious (and hilarious) financial escapades of public officials are exposed in the popular press. Officials found guilty of personal financial impropriety or management incompetence leading to misuse of funds may be brought before the Cour de Discipline Budgétaire et Financière and heavily fined.

There are, therefore, courts of a European as well as national constitutional, administrative and civil character. There is also a vast range of courts and quasi-judicial bodies of a more specialised nature (children, commerce, social security) which regulate the activities of their members in specific sectors, or even on specific issues. Technically, the latter are not *juridictions*, although they exercise a quasi-judicial character, either because their decisions are often penal in nature or because their procedures are heavily juridified. Several other bodies create 'soft law' or what some legal scholars describe as 'officially sponsored indigenous law'. Others exercise a *magistrature morale*, defining the ethical limits of the bodies they control. They include the independent administrative agencies (IAAs), the first of which – the Commission de Contrôle des Banques – dates back to 1941. The number of IAAs has multiplied under the Fifth Republic; some of the more important of them are listed in Chapter 10, p. 300.

One of the most interesting of the IAAs is the *Médiateur*, an institution created by the act of 3 January 1973, and designed to ease relations between citizens and their parliament. The *Médiateur* is appointed for six years, non-renewable, and is totally independent. His task is to deal with complaints concerning the central administration, local government, any public establishment or any body carrying out a 'public service mission'. Since 1976, he has been able to make general recommendations to the incriminated body, even though such recommendations are always triggered by specific complaints. Members of parliament directly or indirectly on behalf of affected individuals have the sole right to raise a complaint with the *Médiateur* – and only after the incriminated body has been contacted and has refused to act upon the point at issue. The *Médiateur* has the right to put written questions, to summon an official for questioning, to ask for any document relating to the complaint, to carry out an inquiry or ask a state body to carry out such an inquiry. Some 45,000 complaints are currently addressed to the *Médiateur*, who is assisted by a central staff of thirty or so and a delegate in each *département*. The *Médiateur* also has the task of arbitrating in the dispute, and while over three-quarters of all cases are considered either inadmissible or answerable on a purely informative basis, a core of some 15 per cent of the total does nevertheless receive an effective ruling.

Soft law is also created by other kinds of regulatory bodies – the Agence Nationale des Fréquences (which deals with radio frequencies) and the Autorité de Régulation des Télécommunications, created in January 1997, charged with regulating the newly liberalised and shortly to be privatised telecommunications sector. Finally, there is a range of special tribunals, such as professional disciplinary bodies (e.g. for doctors or architects) whose decisions may be quashed, on appeal, by the Conseil d'État (executing a *juridiction de cassation*).

The judicialisation of public policy

The judicialisation of public policy has taken several forms, each distinct and triggered by a somewhat different mix of factors.

The spread of litigation

There has been a quantitative leap in litigation in all branches of law – constitutional, administrative, civil and criminal. The number of suits brought before the Courts of Appeal and the Court of Cassation, and before the administrative tribunals and the Conseil d'État, for example, approximately tripled between 1968 and the early 1990s. As the number of judges has not grown anything like as fast, an ever-longer backlog of cases has resulted, delaying (and thus in some degree denying) justice. This is by no means a uniquely French phenomenon; legal scholars have referred to the 'legal pollution' currently affecting Europe.

The reinforcement of judicial review

The process of judicial review has increasingly established the parameters of public policy as a result of challenges in the Conseil d'État, and, more significantly, in the Constitutional Council, to decisions of public authorities on the grounds of unconstitutionality. The Conseil d'État has, in its judicial capacity, continued to develop its jurisprudence in the light of 'general principles of law', framed by the wider context of republican legality. Crucial decisions by the Conseil d'État have established the supremacy of European Union law, have defined fundamental human rights (for example, the right of foreign citizens to bring their families to France, and the conditions surrounding the expulsion of illegal immigrants), and the rights of public officials (for example, the rights of pregnant women) and of their clients (such as hospital patients). The outcome of Conseil d'État litigation was officially recognised, in two important decisions of the Constitutional Council in 1980 and 1987, as having constitutional status (although it had already acquired this status in practice).

The reinforcement of the Constitutional Council's role as the setter of parameters in public policy has been even more striking – and controversial. The transformation of the Council from the quietist body of the early Fifth Republic to its current active self has two foundations. The first was the landmark Constitutional Council ruling of 16 July 1971. This struck down an act that would have required the prior approval of a prefect to register an association – a major break with the (relative) freedom of association enshrined in the law of 1901. In itself, the Council's majority verdict (obtained by a vote of six to three) was an unwonted act of defiance towards the executive. What gave the verdict its critical importance, however, was the grounds on which it was based. For the Council invoked 'fundamental principles recognised by the laws of the Republic', embedded in the Declaration of the Rights of Man of 1789 and the Preamble of the 1946 constitution. In effect, the Council was incorporating these two documents, which guaranteed a range of (not always consistent) citizens' rights, into the *bloc de constitutionnalité* against which all future legislation would be judged. The Council was, it is true, building on an established legal tradition, going back to a Conseil d'État decision of 1936 which invoked 'principles enjoying constitutional status'. But the 1971 ruling was nevertheless both historic and in direct contradiction to the intentions of the constitution's framers.

The second foundation of the Constitutional Council's greater activism was a constitutional reform. In 1974, the newly elected president of the Republic, Giscard d'Estaing, sensitive to the need to provide a limited counterweight to the executive's dominance of the régime (a sensitivity inspired in part by his own inside experiences of executive power – but also by the awareness of how narrow his own victory had been, and of how helpful safeguards might be against a future government of the Left), pushed through a constitutional amendment which allowed any sixty Deputies or sixty Senators to refer a bill to the Council. Left-wing opposition leaders, who had dismissed the change as a 'réformette' (François Mitterrand had earlier called the Council 'de Gaulle's errand-boy'), soon found it to be one of the most useful weapons in their fight against the governments of the Giscard presidency. The number of referrals in the seven years after the reform was five times greater than in the preceding fifteen years: 9 laws were referred between 1959 and 1974, but 47 (45 of them on the initiative of parliament) between 1974 and 1981. The rhythm was especially intense in the 1980s: 92 laws were referred during the first Mitterrand presidency and 49 of them were wholly or partly annulled (66 referrals and 34 annulments under the left-wing governments of 1981–86, 26 referrals and 15 annulments under the 1986–88 Chirac government). Not surprisingly, this was the period of some of the Constitutional Council's most controversial decisions, including the total annulment of the Socialists' 1981 nationalisation bill on grounds of insufficient compensation to shareholders (the government was forced to reintroduce the bill after arranging for a larger payment). Today, most legislation of a seriously controversial character (between a tenth and a fifth of the total) and sections of all annual budgets are referred to the Council. Not surprisingly, therefore, the content and implications of the Council's rulings have been wide-ranging. It has continued, as before 1974, to monitor the executive–legislative boundary (but in a more balanced way) as well as exercising its function as electoral referee. Its jurisprudence has provided a framework for other branches of law – administrative, electoral (including the specification of guidelines for redrawing constituency boundaries), penal, fiscal and budgetary. Some of the Council's most visible rulings have confirmed its role as a key actor in protecting public freedoms. It has limited police powers to search cars (12 January 1977) and to detain suspects (9 January 1980 and 3 September 1986) as well as protecting the freedom of association (16 July 1971), the inviolability of domicile against the tax authorities (29 December 1983), the freedom of education (23 November 1977), the independence of university professors (20 January 1984), the right to strike (25 July 1979), the independence of magistrates (9 July 1978) and the freedom of press and communications (29 July and 18 September 1986). Its key decisions on asylum and immigration issues have strengthened the rights of immigrants and have ensured that magistrates (and not just policemen) are involved in expulsion proceedings.

Some of the Council's decisions have provoked an instant political outcry: its ruling on abortion in January 1975; its generosity to the expropriated shareholders of the firms nationalised by the Socialists in January 1982; its hostility, in 1984, to the conditions surrounding the Socialists' attempt to dismantle the media empire of Robert Hersant (a press baron who might be described as France's Rupert Murdoch, but more right-wing and less scrupulous); its rejection, in 1986, of major provisions of a series of laws inspired by Charles Pasqua, the hard-line Gaullist interior minister, and designed to restrict the rights of the accused, to lengthen sentences for certain crimes, and to extend the discretionary powers of the police; its annulling, in January 1984, of several elements in the Savary Act on Higher Education; its renewed attack, in 1993, on the illiberalism of Pasqua, who during his second stint at the Interior Ministry tightened the rules on immigration and nationality (the decision caused a public row between the government and the president of the Constitutional Council); its insistence, in January 2003, that the government's revision of the electoral law for regional and European elections be modified. The Council has also made important rulings on the constitutionality of treaties: the 1976 treaty on direct elections to the European Parliament, the 1985 Convention on protecting fundamental rights and freedoms, the Maastricht Treaty, and the European Constitutional Treaty of 2004. In the case of Maastricht, the Council objected, in a decision of 9 April 1992, to the single currency, to common visa rules for non-EU citizens, and to the rights of citizens of other member states to vote and stand in French local elections. These objections led to constitutional amendments being introduced before parliament (which amended the bill further), passed by a joint sitting of the National Assembly and the Senate at Versailles, and finally submitted to the people at a referendum, in September 1992, which the yes vote won by a mere half-million majority. With the European constitutional treaty, the Council effectively set out, in February 2004, how the French constitution would have to be amended to bring it into line with the European document. The amendments were duly effected a year later – whereupon the French voters rejected the treaty itself.

This near-systematic character of referrals has affected the behaviour of the Council itself, of the parliament from which the vast majority of referrals now originate, and of the executive. The Council has taken on a quasi-legislative role: it is capable, not merely of striking down bills in whole or in part, but of specifying in its verdicts what changes would suffice to render the proposed legislation constitutional. In many cases, these passages have simply been copied word for word into the revised bill. The Council has also extended its range by verifying the constitutionality of acts (even those passed under earlier Republics and therefore outside its purview) where these are amended by new legislation. For parliamentarians, their right of referral signalled the beginning of a new assertiveness observed since the 1970s (cf. Chapter 6); the *motion d'irrecevabilité* (because of non-conformity to the constitution) tabled by opposition Deputies in major parliamentary debates is usually a warning that the bill in question will be referred. For the executive, the strong possibility of referral, and the obvious concern to avoid annulments wherever possible, led to self-restraint in the drafting of legislation. The 1986–88 Chirac government, for example, openly admitted that certain public-service monopolies would escape privatisation because of the likely reaction of the Constitutional Council, and the inevitable self-interest that attended its redrawing of France's constituency boundaries in 1986 was limited by the certainty of the Council's scrutiny.

The extension of judicial intervention

Intervention by courts and by judges has increased at the expense of politicians and administrators. This process has involved either the courts rendering policy issues justiciable (subject to the law) or the transfer to judges of decision-making power in new policy areas hitherto regulated by government, parliament or the administration. The late 1980s and early 1990s, for example, saw the juridification of competition law. This was driven both by the European Union (there have been some high-profile affairs dealing with supermarkets, book price-fixing and civil aviation liberalisation), and by the activism of the Conseil de la Concurrence, many of whose decisions have led to legal appeals (in 1996 it fined thirty-six firms for price-fixing and other anti-competitive practices in public-sector projects). Even the European Court of Human Rights, usually considered a weak body, has helped to bring administrative decisions under judicial control: France has been condemned by this Court several times, over issues as varied as irregular detention, slow procedures before an administrative court, telephone tapping, customs controls and discrimination against transsexuals.

The criminalisation of new areas

Activities previously outside the scope of the law have been criminalised. Within society at large, there has been a reinforcement of repression in areas such as juvenile delinquency and immigration policy, while financial market malpractices have been criminalised. Within the machinery of government, political and administrative officials have increasingly been held personally responsible, since the mid-1980s, for their acts, and subject to criminal proceedings in cases of negligence. Civil service anonymity and political responsibility for errors, the traditional defences of the negligent public servant, have become less and less respected (or respectable). Thus, when part of a Corsican football stadium collapsed, and when an ill-regulated camp site was swept away by a flash flood (along with many of the campers), the prefects in question were placed under formal judicial investigation and faced possible prison sentences (by the end of 1996, six prefects or subprefects were under investigation for negligence). Similarly, the Director General of the Health Ministry, who was implicated in the transfusion of HIV-contaminated blood to haemophiliacs, was tried and imprisoned. The Court of Justice of the Republic, established by constitutional reform in 1993, was quickly given three cases: the contaminated blood scandal (a deeply emotional affair which involved both the ex-health minister and the former prime minister Laurent Fabius); a sordid financial fraud allegedly perpetrated by the former junior minister for the handicapped; and the Noir–Botton affair, a complicated matter involving the mayor of Lyon, former minister Michel Noir, his son-in-law Pierre Botton and large-scale financial improprieties that drew in a number of media celebrities as well as politicians.

The internalisation of judicial constraints

Public officials have increasingly internalised judicial constraints. Governments are now sensitive, as a matter of course, to possible future rulings of the Constitutional Council. Within the administration, French civil servants who in the past might have ignored or circumvented judicial constraints, counting on the slowness and leniency of any actual penalties, or on the fact that responsibility for making amends lay with an anonymous state, have been given pause for thought by the growing personalisation of responsibility.

Judges as policy-makers

Judges have played an increasing role outside the judicial arena as public policy-makers. The British tradition of asking judges to chair ad hoc commissions on specific policy issues has spread to France. Marceau Long, a distinguished vice-president of the Conseil d'État, was a ubiquitous policy-maker, chairing several important commissions, including one established on the vexed question of citizenship rights (especially sensitive in relation to second-generation immigrants). The new independent administrative authorities also recruit members of the Conseil d'État as members – or, indeed, as chairpersons: in 1995, the Commission des Opérations en Bourse, the Commission Nationale d'Informatique et des Libertés, the Commission d'Accès aux Documents Administratifs and the Commission des Sondages were all chaired by members of the Conseil d'État. Another, Paul Legatte, held the post of *Médiateur* from 1986 to 1992. Administrative judges are also ubiquitous within the executive and legislative branches of government. Pompidou was a *conseiller d'État*, Chirac entered Pompidou's *cabinet* from the Cour des Comptes; among prime ministers, Michel Debré, Pompidou, Laurent Fabius and Édouard Balladur have all been *conseillers d'État*; members of the *grands corps* in general and of the Conseil d'État in particular have penetrated the Council of Ministers, the National Assembly, the Senate, the General Secretariat of the Government, and the ministerial *cabinets*, as well as major posts in public and private business. Members of the Conseil d'État have also chaired many of the disciplinary sections of the various professional self-regulating bodies.

The decline of special courts

Questions previously dealt with by exceptional bodies have been passed to judges: thus, in 1981 and 1982, Mitterrand and his Socialist government abolished a number of military tribunals, including the Court of State Security (Cour de Sûreté de l'État).

The spread of quasi-judicial procedures

Judicial methods have spread outside the judicial province proper. There are many examples of this process. The rights of the defence have been increased; the presence of a judicial authority has been required in cases of expulsion of allegedly illegal immigrants. The Constitutional Council has obliged independent administrative authorities to juridify their procedures, while their decisions are now subject to appeal before either the Conseil d'État or the Court of Cassation.

Judges as policy advisers

Judges have taken on a growing role as policy advisers. The constitutional requirement, strengthened under the Fifth Republic, for the Conseil d'État to be consulted on a range of legislative issues, has already been noted. Consultation has also been required, since 1992, on all European Union acts with a legislative character – no fewer than 946 bills or decrees in the first year alone. The Conseil d'État's advice, though not binding on the government, is almost always followed; an unfavourable and ignored opinion may easily be leaked to the press, exploited by hostile pressure groups, and used by opposition parliamentarians to justify a referral to the Constitutional Council. The Conseil d'État may also be consulted by a government in need of advice. The government has done this on some thirty occasions each year, on issues ranging from the price structure of tickets for the TGV (high-speed train) to the status of France Télécom employees when their enterprise was scheduled for partial privatisation, to the rights of asylum seekers or the right of young Muslim girls to wear a headscarf at school (a highly publicised issue that was left to schools and courts to manage from 1989 till the issue was made the object of legislation in 2004). Finally, the prime minister or the

Conseil d'État's own vice-president may request general studies from the Council. Such studies, generally two or three a year, are undertaken by the *section du rapport et des études*, and often serve as a framework for future legislation. They have covered a variety of administrative and judicial issues including the impact on France of European Union law, questions surrounding information technology, bioethics and urban planning.

The reinforcement of judicial independence

The judiciary has displayed a growing independence in its behaviour. The constitution of 1958 reasserted the independence of *magistrats du siège* (see p. 396): they cannot be dismissed, transferred or even promoted without their consent. The constitution also established the Conseil Supérieur de la Magistrature, whose nine members, all appointed by the president of the Republic, were charged with protecting the independence of the *magistrats du siège* and submitting proposals for appointments. The constitutional reform of 19 July 1993 changed both the composition and the remit of the Conseil Supérieur de la Magistrature. Appointments to it were henceforth to be shared by the presidents of the Republic and of the two houses of parliament, and by the judiciary itself; and its responsibilities were extended to allow some limited right to give opinions on appointments to *magistrats du parquet*. Several important laws and Constitutional Council rulings (notably the decision of 22 July 1980 and the law of 6 January 1986) have reaffirmed the independence of judges, and extended the status of judge to members of the Cour des Comptes, and to members of administrative courts and tribunals. The Constitutional Council has made it clear that neither the legislature nor the executive can censure the decisions of the courts, or attempt to shift the exercise of their competences to other bodies. Successive presidents of the Republic have expressed respect for judicial independence. President Chirac even intensified the debate over the links between the *parquet* and the Justice Ministry by setting up an independent commission to examine the question, with a view to weakening or cutting the umbilical cord between the two (though a constitutional reform to this effect was sabotaged in 2000 by Chirac's own party).

Judicial activism and corruption cases

Activist judges have been increasingly inclined fully to implement the law, despite (or sometimes because of) pressure from politicians, the media and pressure groups. Two aspects of this tendency may be highlighted. First, the implementation of new legal norms, whether recent EU directives or national laws and decrees, is more assiduously monitored (though implementation is certainly far from perfect). Thus one section of the Conseil d'État has the task of tracking implementation performance; the results are published in its annual report.

Second, not only is legal redress increasingly sought; the law is also increasingly active in punishing wrongdoers, in cases whose political sensitivity would formerly have led to a discreet closure of the file. One example of this, the prosecutions for negligence of officials (in the ordinary courts) and of ministers (by the Cour de Justice de la République), has already been mentioned. Another is the last set of prosecutions linked to France's war years. The trials of Paul Touvier, a zealous collaborator with the Gestapo in Lyon, pardoned by President Pompidou but tried for crimes against humanity in 1994, and of Maurice Papon, secretary-general of the Gironde prefecture under the Occupation, Paris Prefect of Police in the early 1960s, budget minister under Giscard, convicted in 1998 for sending Jews by rail on the first leg of their journey to the concentration camps, were exemplary in this respect (with the one exception that Papon benefited from early release on grounds of illness).

The largest group of cases of this type, however, concerns the corrupt activities of politicians and business executives, too often swept under a politicially negotiated carpet in the past but now brought under the full glare of publicity, and sometimes (not, it is true, always) heavily penalised. If political corruption has become one of the favourite themes of the French press (and of the far Right, which claims, not very credibly, to be clean in this respect), it is partly because of the prominence of the individuals concerned. The list of convicted politicians includes Bernard Tapie, a flamboyant self-made businessman and, briefly, a minister in the Socialist governments of 1992–93, whose misdeeds ranged from large-scale tax evasion to football fraud, and who characteristically agreed to play himself in a film on his release from prison; Michel Noir, mayor of Lyon from 1989 to 1995 and former RPR trade minister (who also discovered a brief thespian vocation after his disgrace); Michel Gillibert (ex-minister for the handicapped); Jean-Michel Boucheron (whose extravagances bankrupted the city of Angoulême, of which he was mayor before his precipitate flight to Argentina); Jacques Médecin (the right-wing former minister for tourism and mayor of Nice, who had to be extradited from Uruguay to face well-founded allegations of fraud and embezzlement of city funds); Jean Bousquet (the former mayor of Nîmes, sent to prison in December 1996 for using municipal funds to maintain his private chateau); Alain Carignon, mayor of Grenoble, whose case has been mentioned in Chapter 12; and Maurice Arreckx, president of the *conseil général* of the Var, who tried to justify his misappropriation of public funds by the need to provide financial security for his family.

These are the more colourful cases. More important, perhaps, is the fact that, at least before the laws of 1988 and 1990 which regulated political finance for the first time, all political parties and most candidates lived by corrupt means, and some have done so since then as well. The unhealthily close relationship between parties and firms in building, public works and the urban utility sector was illustrated during the brief period from 1990 to 1994 when business funding of parties and electoral campaigns was authorised and (relatively) transparent: it was estimated that some three-quarters of all business funding at the 1993 elections came from firms liable to bid for contracts with local authorities run by party politicians. In one (probably not unique) corruption case, that of the school renovation contracts signed by the Île-de-France region, it appears that kickbacks paid by the contractors were shared out between majority and opposition parties on the regional council. Its president, the influential Gaullist *notable* Michel Giraud, also used regional funds to pay his domestics at home. He and other defendants stood trial from early 2005 (over a decade after the original offences).

As a party, however, the Socialists were the first to be found out, partly because the Urba network, a nationwide front organisation they had set up to cover and channel the kickbacks paid by firms in return for contracts with the municipalities they controlled, was relatively easy to unravel. The Urba scandal was in part responsible for the Socialists' political disgrace in the early 1990s; and when Henri Emmanuelli, former president of the National Assembly, was convicted and temporarily removed from his parliamentary seat, he was atoning for the sins of the whole Socialist Party in his capacity as its treasurer. But the Socialists (whose troubles began again, in a modest way, in the late 1990s, with the revelation that their members had mismanaged the

Mutuelle Nationale des Étudiants Français, the insurance fund of the main students' union) have not been alone. In 1996 Robert Hue, the national secretary of the Communist Party, and his predecessor Georges Marchais (who died the following year) were placed under formal investigation as part of the inquiry into a consultancy firm, the Sicopar (a subsidiary of Gifco, an urban services group close to the party), and the Compagnie Générale des Eaux (now Vivendi), which had siphoned some 15 million francs into the coffers of Sicopar between 1984 and 1994. Charges against Hue were dropped for technical reasons. The UDF and its constituent parts, notably the CDS and the Parti Républicain, were altogether more complex matters, involving individual local elected officials (such as Pierre-Yves Tenaillon, president of the *conseil général* of the Yvelines *département* just outside Paris) and an intricate series of offshore accounts; but they too were under investigation in the 1990s. Investigations into the RPR, finally, increasingly centred on what was Jacques Chirac's former stronghold of Paris, by far France's biggest and wealthiest municipality. Chirac's successor as mayor, Jean Tiberi, and his former assistant mayor in charge of the city's finances, Alain Juppé, were found to be using the city's private housing stock to favour their families (a revelation which made Juppé's honeymoon period as prime minister in 1995 especially short). Cases of officials on the municipal payroll working full-time for the RPR (including senior members of Juppé's private office in his time as party secretary-general) have been well documented. The electoral register of the fifth *arrondissement* (where Tiberi is, and Chirac was, elected as a Paris councillor) have been found to have been tampered with at least since 1989, the year Chirac won his second 'grand slam' municipal election victory in all *arrondissements*. The management of the Paris HLM office, which controls over 100,000 low-cost housing units in the capital and its suburbs, has been found to be opaque both in its award of tenancies to candidates from a long waiting list and in its attribution of maintenance contracts (curiously, the head of the office, who resigned suddenly in 1995, was also the mayor of Meymac, a commune in Chirac's parliamentary constituency in Corrèze). The Paris investigations, finally, have ramifications that spread out into the whole Île-de-France region: thus Xavière Tiberi, Jean Tiberi's wife, was found to have been paid 200,000 francs for a worthless 36-page report by the *conseil général* of Essonne, whose RPR president Xavier Dugoin was sent to prison for corruption. As of 2005, Tiberi had faced a series of charges, none of them successful; Juppé's political career had been broken, or at least badly damaged, by his conviction for his role in paying party officials from the municipal payroll; and Chirac was protected – in theory, only as long as he remained in the Élysée – by presidential immunity.

Revelations of political corruption inevitably went hand in hand with investigations into corrupt business practices; it takes two to tango. The scale of corruption outdid even the most sensational predictions, and – especially at a time, in the mid-1990s, when the French were suffering rising unemployment and being treated to sermons on the need for budgetary rigour – fed public demands for exemplary punishments. From the late 1980s a growing list of captains of industry were placed under investigation in an unprecedented anti-corruption clampdown by the judiciary: by early 1997, the heads of nearly a quarter of the companies in the CAC 40 stock market index were being formally investigated for one or another infringement. They included such pillars of the business community as Martin Bouygues, head of France's biggest construction group, and Patrick Le Lay, head of TF1 (the privatised television station owned by Bouygues), whose use of corporate funds included false invoices and the channelling of money, via Swiss bank accounts, to Pierre Botton, son-in-law of Michel Noir; the chairman of

Matra-Hachette (Jean-Luc Lagardère, a personal friend of Chirac), of Saint-Gobain and of Alcatel-Alsthom (Pierre Suard, who was charged with using company funds to pay for 4 million francs' worth of building work in his Paris mansion and his country estate). The place of the oil company Elf-Aquitaine (merged in 1999 with Total-Fina) deserves particular attention. Its head in the early 1990s, Loïc Le Floch-Prigent (known as Pink Floch owing to his Socialist connections), was accused of using the company's credit card to buy some 500,000 francs' worth of personal items for himself and his wife and spending nearly 4 million francs on his private residence. These, however, were relatively minor items in the vast catalogue of corporate wrongdoing, including bribes paid to heads of several African states (notably Gabon) and to Germany (for the purchase of an East German refinery), with the knowledge and approval of President Mitterrand. A further aspect of the Elf affair was the company's role as an intermediary in persuading the Socialist government of the early 1990s to support the sale of frigates to Taiwan, a deal to which it had been opposed for political reasons. The *affaire des frégates* drew in the former foreign minister Roland Dumas, accused of accepting indirect bribes from Elf via his mistress, an Elf employee. Dumas was ultimately acquitted, but not before these accusations had led, in March 2000, to his resignation from the end-of-career post to which Mitterrand had appointed him five years earlier – as president of the Constitutional Council. The prosecution of eminent public officials in high-profile corruption cases was not the only aspect of judicialisation in French politics and policy – but it was certainly the most spectacular.

Explaining judicialisation

The growing judicialisation of French public policy may be explained by a range of factors, some specific to France and others common to several European countries. But there is a fundamental distinction to be made between elements that increase the scope of law, and elements that reinforce the role of judges in determining and interpreting law. Distinctions are also necessary between policy sectors: competition policy and the treatment of juvenile delinquents may both have been judicialised, but for quite different reasons. And there are different types of judicialisation: there is little direct relation between the causes of the judiciary's growing assertiveness and those of the extension of soft law and regulatory agencies. A final distinction should be made between the different types of law (constitutional and administrative, civil and criminal), and the different agents and motives that inspired their separate growth.

The quantitative growth of judicial activity is easily explained. Despite rhetoric to the contrary, government activity has grown; privatisation, liberalisation and even deregulation have tended to produce more, not less, regulation. Deregulating the labour market, for example, demands a sustained legislative and legal effort. And the political agenda of the 1980s and 1990s – law and order, immigration, environmental and consumer protection, and issues of gender and sexuality – has required the state, and the law, to move into new areas. Society has also become judicialised because it has become weaker: both traditional modes of social regulation – deference to 'betters', trust towards equals within a clearly identifiable community – and traditional institutions such as the family and the Church, have been seriously eroded, in France as in other Western societies.

A more complex task is to account for the growing role of judges and judicial processes within the overall increase in legal activity. This involves a wide variety of often complex factors, which are listed below.

- *The Europeanisation of French law*, though limited, has had four clear effects. First, it has furthered the judicialisation of certain policy areas such as immigration and competition policy. Second, it has allowed judges a degree of interpretative freedom as it is generally drafted in terms less specific than those of French law. Third, it has arguably accustomed judges to the idea that parliamentary statutes can be overridden by a higher judicial authority. Fourth, it has allowed individuals, firms and groups to invoke European law (and thus the higher judicial authority) in the national courts, offering pro-EU constituencies a new avenue through which to press for the promulgation and implementation of EU law.

- *Ideological changes* referred to in Chapter 1 have tended to replace a paradigm based on collective goods, the public interest and citizenship by one that stresses private goods, individual rights and consumerism. Rights-based political cultures entail a questioning of authority and thus tend to increase demands for arbitration of a legal character.

- *Economic change* has also fed judicialisation. One economic translation of the ideological shift noted above was the replacement of traditional *dirigisme* by privatisation and arm's-length regulation; but the latter necessitates a new judicial armoury. As elsewhere in Europe, areas such as telecommunications are to be regulated not by ministers but by a regulatory agency, generating a massive need for a quasi-legal sort of indirect regulation. At the same time, the social problems caused by long-term mass unemployment – family breakdown, rising crime rates, and racism and xenophobia – have all triggered demands for legislative, and thence ultimately judicial, action. Immigration, for example, has been the object of often wide-ranging government bills in every parliament since 1973, not least because it is often considered a cause of unemployment. Its increasing regulation has tended to criminalise offenders; an economic problem has become a social and political problem, and finally a legal one.

- *Managerialism*, also closely linked to the ideological paradigm shift, has several implications for judicialisation. The delegation of state power to autonomous agencies; the attempt to make public services more consumer-driven (and hence to give the 'users' of services enforceable rights); and the increasing use of private firms to deliver public goods (especially at local level, where much service delivery is done), entailing contractual relations between the authority responsible for the service and the company that provides it: all offer plenty of scope for litigation.

- *Cultural factors* have also contributed to the judicialisation of certain issues. As the capacity of the one and indivisible Republic to integrate all of its citizens through traditional methods – universal laws, a secular state education system used by all or nearly all, and military service – has diminished, so recognition of the growing diversity and multiculturalism of French society has grown. That entails problems which politicians long found it expedient to transfer to the courts. Is the headscarf worn by a Muslim girl at school, for example, an acceptable expression of cultural otherness, a symbol of women's subjection under Islam, or a badge of religious identity to be excluded from a secular school? As education minister in 1989, Lionel Jospin preferred to leave the answer to the Conseil d'État. Even when Chirac faced the question of legislating on the issue in 2003, he took care to appoint an all-party committee, chaired by the centrist Bernard Stasi, to give a formal report first.

- *Technological change* has generated judicial activity by raising urgent ethical issues related, for example, to the flow of pornography and racist material across national frontiers on the Internet, biotechnology, data protection and copyright.

- *Political initiatives* have, in some cases, deliberately sought to strengthen the role and the autonomy of the judiciary. Examples include Giscard's opening of access to the Constitutional Council to parliamentarians in 1974, mentioned above; the juridification of procedures in areas such as planning, the environment and immigration; the increasingly tight regulation of political funding; the reforms of the 1980s which strengthened the personal responsibility of public officials for their acts; and the replacement of the prefects' a priori control of local government acts by the a posteriori control undertaken by the regional courts of accounts. Most recently, a reform passed in 2000 protected the rights of the accused – not only of those in high-profile political cases but also of the 400,000 or so individuals arrested each year, 95 per cent of whose cases are never scrutinised with the (relative) neutrality of an examining magistrate but dealt with by the *parquet* and the police. To relatively minor reporting restrictions (such as a ban on publishing photographs of suspects in handcuffs) were added innovations such as the video recording of police interviews (initially only for minors) and the presence of a lawyer from the first hour of preventive detention: the beginnings of a judicial framework that countries more progressive in their treatment of accused and convicted prisoners had adopted years before. That said, this record was partly reversed, and the rights of the accused significantly reduced, by the Perben legislation passed after the 2002 elections in a climate highly favourable to law and order.
- *Democratic demands* have increasingly been channelled through the courts as well as by more traditional methods of political organisation or demonstration. Pressure groups may find satisfaction from the courts where they have failed to obtain it at the political level – especially when, as is the case in the Conseil d'État, pursuing a case is both cheap and surprisingly simple. Citizens have also used the justice system to seek to punish corruption: thus well-organised citizen groups were instrumental in pressuring the authorities into judicial activity against the mayors of Cannes, Angoulême and Grenoble, while the Green opposition in Paris has played a major role in promoting investigations into corruption in France's biggest town hall. Public opinion, moreover, generally backs greater judicial autonomy – and ferocity towards public officials. According to a 1997 survey, large majorities of the French considered that the French justice system was lenient with senior civil servants and politicians, as well as too expensive, too slow, too partial, too easily influenced by political authorities, too old-fashioned and lacking the material means to do its job properly. Despite (and because of) these criticisms, 71 per cent of the sample declared for greater independence of the justice system.
- *Media support* for the activities of the judiciary has grown, though it remains far from universal. The *Canard Enchaîné*, a venerable exposer of sleaze on the part of politicians, industrialists and public officials, has been joined by other newspapers, notably *Le Monde* and *Libération*, in the encouragement of investigative journalism. A more liberal broadcasting régime (France has, fortunately, moved on from the days of the de Gaulle presidency when the information minister used to give daily instructions to television chiefs on the content of their prime-time news programmes) has allowed television and radio to follow, or at least to publicise the findings of the print media. In one respect, indeed, the press has been an important ally of the judges. For examining magistrates, fearful of having their investigations

quietly sidelined by a *procureur* acting on instructions from the Justice Ministry, have repeatedly allowed their findings to be leaked in order to create a fait accompli that places an unacceptable political cost on any move to close the file. When a key witness in the electoral fraud case in Paris told a *juge d'instruction* that the mayor, Jean Tiberi, had personally supervised the cooking of electoral registers, details of his statement appeared in the *Canard* within forty-eight hours. It is also thanks to leaks that we know, from an initialled letter, that Jacques Chirac as mayor of Paris recommended the promotion of employees on the city's payroll whom he knew to be working full-time for his party, the RPR. The media's support for judicial activism is not, it is true, universal: the right-wing journalist Éric Zemmour expressed his opposition to the process in a polemical work entitled *Le coup d'État des juges*. But the development of judicial independence, particularly in corruption cases, would have been very much more difficult without media backing.

- *The judges' own collective demand for autonomy and independence* has grown. The Conseil Supérieur de la Magistrature has been openly critical, in recent reports, of the government's appointments policy. And during the 1997 election campaign, over a hundred senior magistrates (of all political persuasions) addressed a petition in favour of greater autonomy to President Chirac.

- *Organisational expansionism* has also, at times, favoured greater judicial independence. Like any organisations, courts, and especially relatively new institutions like the European Court of Justice, the Constitutional Council, or the independent administrative agencies, often seek to establish and then expand their areas of activity and influence. Both co-operation and competition between courts may further this. The ECJ, for example, both made allies of the national courts by providing them with a new capacity for judicial review, and reinforced its own authority as a court of final appeal owing to competition between higher and lower courts and between the civil and administrative supreme courts of member states. Individuals, too, can play important roles: Guy Braibant, a highly influential member of the Conseil d'État, Robert Badinter, the Socialist former justice minister whom President Mitterrand made president of the Constitutional Council in 1986, and who left a potent jurisprudential legacy, and Adolphe Touffait, a strongly pro-European member of the Court of Cassation, are all cases in point.

- *The spread of corruption* has also been a factor in the spread of juridification. This is hard to quantify: corruption was a commonplace under the Third, Fourth and early Fifth Republics, as several high-profile court cases confirmed. Nevertheless, it has been argued that several elements rendered it even more pervasive from the 1980s. These included the sharpening of political competition at all levels, as *alternance* succeeded *alternance* after 1981; the more capital-intensive nature of political campaigning, as opinion pollsters and image consultants and designers of all stripes sought to sell their wares to politicians and parties; and the greater freedoms afforded to local elected officials by decentralisation after 1982 to spend local budgets as they saw fit. Certainly the *perception* among France's elites (beginning, in 1987, with President Mitterrand and Prime Minister Chirac, who agreed to call a special parliamentary session to consider the matter) that corruption had got out of hand, and was threatening to discredit the whole political class, was instrumental in juridifying the previously unpoliced area of political finance, via the laws of 1988, 1990, 1993 and 1995. Among the public, too, the perception of corruption has given rise to demands for *judicial* retribution. Political sanctions for corruption, though potentially powerful (as witness the Socialists' post-1991 disgrace), are uncertain: parties hesitate to extract the maximum political benefit from their opponents' embarrassment as a result of corruption cases, because they know that it may be their turn soon.

•   *The courage of individual judges* (usually examining magistrates, like Thierry Jean-Pierre, Éric Halphen, Renaud van Ruymbeke, Patrick Desmure and Eva Joly) in pursuing particular cases of wrongdoing, resisting political pressure, bypassing their own hierarchy and appealing directly to public opinion, has raised the profile of the administration of justice as an issue, and helped render public the unacceptable and justiciable practices that had been concealed, connived at and practically immune from prosecution.

Numerous factors, therefore, running in parallel yet uncoupled, explain judicialisation. Some, such as political reforms, are direct, purposeful and top-down; others are indirect, unwitting and bottom-up. Judicialisation is a multi-pronged process. It combines imposition (the role of the ECJ), political will, spillover from new public management or new modes of regulation, internal dynamics of an individual and collective nature, and pressure from journalists, polls, judges and even street protest. But judicialisation is far from an all-conquering force. Although it has not found an immovable object in the Jacobin state, it has certainly encountered powerful resistance.

The *État de droit*: obstacles and resistance

Increasing judicialisation has undoubtedly been a major development in French politics since the 1980s. Courts have been drawn into highly contentious and politicised issues in areas such as race relations, asylum policy, environmental (or anti-environmental) projects, police powers, medical ethics and (within a very short space of time) both nationalisation and privatisation. Competition policy is just one of several policy areas, formerly immune from the attentions of judges, which have been brought within the purview of courts or of regulatory bodies. The 'legal state' has undoubtedly been reinforced. There is more law; the courts are playing a greater role in its creation, interpretation and even enforcement; decision-making procedures in many areas have become less arbitrary and more juridified; judges have been emboldened to assert their autonomy and independence. Such developments have had a multiple impact on policy-making. Specific laws or decisions have been struck down by judges. Policies or procedures underlying certain acts have been modified or reversed. New policy development has been constrained, both by explicit guidelines issued by judges and by the anticipation of judicial challenge on the part of policy-makers. And the moral and ideological parameters of public and private action have become increasingly bounded by general principles rooted in one or another form of constitutionalism.

All of this runs counter to the Jacobin and imperial concepts of the popular executive or parliamentary sovereignty outlined earlier in this chapter. Many recent developments have been anathema to such traditions: they include the acceptance of the supremacy of European law, the general (though not universal) support for 'government by constitution', with its inevitable corollary, the judicial review of political action; the growing role of courts as policy-makers; the spread of diverse sources of 'soft' law via independent regulatory agencies; and even the criminalisation of public officials for negligence or of politicians for corruption. It is less clear, however, that such changes have shaken the Jacobin edifice to the ground and replaced it with an *État de droit*, a state in which all the actors, including the political elite, respect and uphold the accepted normative order, the hierarchy of laws, and the independence and autonomy of the judiciary. There are five main reasons for scepticism about the existence of such an entity in contemporary France.

The first of these is constituted by the continuing restrictions on the power of the courts. The annual report of the Cour des Comptes, for example, almost invariably contains revelations, by turns depressing and hilarious, about the misdeeds and incompetence of public officials, but corrective action follows its findings far more rarely. Similarly, the Conseil d'État lacks the effective means to enforce its decisions, and, despite some recent tightening up, administrative miscreants are often extremely slow to take remedial action. Where the Conseil d'État can annul an abuse, it can only do so *ex post facto* – and, inevitably, after delay: which may be too late for individuals such as asylum seekers. And while the Conseil d'État has the right to be consulted on all government bills, its advice may be (and has been) ignored by governments; and it has no right to examine either amendments to bills on which it has already been consulted or private members' bills. The effective jurisdiction of the Constitutional Council is even more restricted. Laws once promulgated are off-limits: this category includes all legislation passed before the 1958 constitution came into force unless new legislation amends it, and all legislation which is not specifically referred to the Constitutional Council (including some highly sensitive texts, such as the acts authorising medical experimentation on handicapped persons (1988) or forbidding the public denial of the Holocaust (1990)). The principle of abstract, a priori control means that the Council has absolutely no powers to correct those defects of a law which may only appear in its concrete application to specific cases. And the Constitutional Council's procedures are rather less than transparent, unlike those of the Supreme Court of the United States, with no dissenting opinions being published in the (normal) case of a majority decision. It should be added that determined governments have at least the potential means to override or circumvent rulings by the Constitutional Council. They may be overridden by constitutional amendment, which requires the text to be voted in identical terms by both houses of parliament and then voted either by referendum or by three-fifths of a joint meeting of the two houses of parliament: serious hurdles, but not impossible ones, especially for a right-wing government with the usual right-wing majority in the Senate. It has so far happened only once, on 29 November 1993, when a Constitutional Council ruling against an immigration law was overturned by an amendment to Article 53–1 of the constitution. The Constitutional Council may also, in principle, be circumvented: it will not give a ruling in cases where the sovereign people has made its own direct decision on a law, by referendum. In theory, since the constitutional amendment of 31 July 1995 widening the scope of the referendum, a wide range of matters could be so treated, though the political risks attached to referenda are such as to make their use extremely sparing.

A second obstacle to the development of the *État de droit* has been the stout resistance in the legislature to its extension. Two failed constitutional amendments illustrate this. In 1989 Robert Badinter, the president of the Constitutional Council, proposed that individual citizens should have the right to refer existing laws to the Council – in effect, both greatly widening access and relaxing the ban on a posteriori control by allowing laws to be referred after their promulgation. He convinced both President Mitterrand and Prime Minister Rocard, and a reform proposal passed the National

Assembly; but the Senate, whose agreement is necessary to any constitutional reform, voted so many amendments to the proposal (including its limitation to laws passed before 1974) that the government preferred to withdraw the project altogether. Ten years later, the Justice Minister Élisabeth Guigou attempted to increase the role of the Conseil Supérieur de la Magistrature in the appointment and promotion of *magistrats du parquet*, and to prevent ministers giving instructions to these prosecuting magistrates. In this she was supported not only by the Socialist government of which she was a member, but also, initially by President Chirac, who had created a commission to study the question in 1996. But the proposals were too much for (right-wing) Jacobins in the National Assembly and above all in the Senate, for whom the political control of judges remained a guarantee of democracy and popular sovereignty. Quite possibly Chirac too changed his mind. At all events, the opposition, centred on the RPR (Chirac's party), mustered enough votes to block a constitutional amendment, and Chirac cancelled the parliamentary Congress that was to have voted it in January 2000.

The emergence of an *État de droit* has been limited, third, by the regular practices of some politicians, civil servants and even judges. The Conseil d'État's scrutiny of government bills, for example, is weakened by the government's tendency to submit them in a hurry, late in the parliamentary cycle, thus giving the Council (and, for that matter, the parliament) very little time to consider them properly: a point which has provoked repeated complaints from the vice-president of the Conseil d'État. At the local level, the activities of the Regional Courts of Accounts have been limited by the reluctance of many prefects to refer cases to them; the prefects often prefer pre-litigation negotiation (*négociation précontentieuse*) with the local authority concerned. In most years, fewer than 0.5 per cent of the acts of local authorities are referred to a court, a number that has diminished since 2000, and many of these cases are dropped before a decision is reached. Politicians have also regularly tried to halt potentially embarrassing judicial investigations. The efforts of Charles Pasqua's Interior Ministry to discredit judge Éric Halphen early in 1995 were worthy of the Keystone Cops; their comic potential, though, was exceeded a year later when the RPR justice minister Jacques Toubon tried to halt one of the many investigations into the city of Paris by chartering a helicopter to seek a countermanding signature from the Paris *procureur général*, who was on a mountaineering holiday in the Himalayas at the time. More surprising have been the periodic obstacles placed by judges in the way of the development of the *État de droit*. One example was the extraordinary decision of the Court of Cassation, on 6 February 1997, which overturned a previous ruling of 1992 and restricted the area in which firms can be taken to court (in effect ruling that bribes did not constitute a misuse of company funds if the company received something in return). Another was the decision of the Constitutional Council, on 22 January 1999, that the president of the Republic enjoys complete immunity during his term of office from all prosecutions, excluding only impeachment on charges of high treason before the Haute Cour de Justice, for which a special vote of parliament would be necessary: a ruling that went well beyond the president's immunity covering acts committed in office, specified in Article 68–1 of the constitution, to encompass (in Chirac's case) his whole period as mayor of Paris between 1977 and 1995. The Constitutional Council ruling has since been confirmed by a number of ordinary courts, which have claimed that for the president to be prosecuted would 'violate the principle of the separation of powers'. The one partial qualification to it was a ruling by the Court of Cassation that on the expiry of his term, the president would become liable to prosecution for all outstanding offences, however long ago they had been committed. A constitutional amendment designed to settle the question of presidential immunity was pending early in 2005 (and had been so for over a year). Meanwhile the more zealous UMP Deputies were proposing that former presidents should become members of the Senate – and thus immune to prosecution – for life.

Fourth, the growing independence of the judiciary has not freed it from its continued politicisation (itself an entrenched violation of the principle of the separation of powers). Part of this has perfectly formal, constitutional bases. The constitutional guarantor of the independence of the judiciary, the president of the Conseil Supérieur de la Magistrature, is the president of the Republic. In the Conseil d'État the government has the right to appoint all the presidents of the working sections, one third of the *conseillers d'État*, and a quarter of the lower-ranked *maîtres de requêtes* (some appointments to the Conseil in the early Mitterrand years provoked a mixture of incredulity and hilarity); discussions of the Conseil d'État's general assembly are open to ministers, who may vote on matters within their competence. All members of the Constitutional Council, too, are openly political appointees; the composition of the Council thus follows the vicissitudes of electoral politics, but (given the nine-year tenure of members) with a certain time lag, allowing a left-wing government to be confronted with a right-wing Council, and vice versa (Table 13.1). Important politicians or presidential advisers have been chosen on several occasions, though membership of the Constitutional Council has always been incompatible with ministerial or parliamentary office, and, since January 1995, with other elective offices as well. Presidents of the Republic, in choosing the president of the Constitutional Council, invariably select sympathisers of their own political camp: Léon Noël, a former Gaullist Deputy, in 1959; Gaston Palewski, former Gaullist Deputy and minister, in 1965; Roger Frey, former Gaullist Deputy, minister and Senator, in 1974; Daniel Mayer, president of the Ligue des Droits de l'Homme and lifelong left-wing sympathiser, in 1983; Robert Badinter, Mitterrand's justice minister, in February 1986 (a choice that was considered

Table 13.1 The political composition of the Constitutional Council

Date	Left	Right
1981	0	9
1983	2	7
1986	4	5
1987	3	6
1988	3	6
1989	5	4
1992	6	3
1993	6	3
1995	5	4
1996	4	5
1997	4	5
2000	3	6
2005	2	8*

Note
* Includes Valéry Giscard d'Estaing, who from 2004 exercised his right as an ex-president of the Republic to sit as an *ex officio* supernumerary member of the Council.

especially political, because it was precipitated by Mayer's premature departure, just weeks before parliamentary elections which the Right was expected to win, and because Badinter moved straight to his new post from the Justice Ministry); Roland Dumas, Mitterrand's former foreign minister and long-term personal friend and confidant, in 1995; Yves Guéna, former Gaullist Deputy, minister and Senator, in March 2000 after Dumas's resignation; Pierre Mazeaud, another former Gaullist Deputy and minister, in February 2004. Members of the Constitutional Council, it is true, often display considerable independence, thanks in part to their nine-year non-renewable term. Such is not always true, on the other hand, of the *magistrats du parquet*, the prosecuting magistrates who remain hierarchically attached to the minister of justice, who can move or promote or transfer prosecuting magistrates at will (and is also the vice-president of the Conseil Supérieur de la Magistrature). Jacques Toubon's appointment, in 1996, of his own former *directeur de cabinet* Alexandre Benmakhlouf to the key post of *procureur général* in Paris, just as investigations into the Paris city hall were gathering momentum, was an outstanding but not exceptional example of such a political nomination. Justice ministers still enjoy the right to issue formal and informal instructions to magistrates: with the exception of Élisabeth Guigou, Jospin's minister from 1997 to 2000, who publicly declared her intention to issue no such instructions, they have used this power in order to slow down or bury politically embarrassing cases. Indeed, Henri Nallet, justice minister when the Urba affair broke in 1990 (and also a key fundraiser for Mitterrand's 1988 campaign), was criticised by his ministerial colleagues in private for his inability to 'control his judges' – considered hitherto an essential part of a justice minister's job.

This kind of 'top-down' politicisation is compounded by the activities of many judges. For members of the Conseil d'État to stand for elective office, or accept a ministerial post, is to declare openly partisan convictions; to accept a post in a ministerial *cabinet* may, depending on its sensitivity, entail the same; yet on quitting their political, or quasi-political, posts, they invariably take up their judicial posts in the Conseil again, as the law permits. A change of parliamentary majority and government, therefore, sets up a sort of merry-go-round as some members of the Conseil d'État return from political postings while others more in sympathy with the new majority depart. Within the civil judiciary, politicisation takes the different, but equally clear, form of union membership: judges who join a professional trade union (and many do) have the choice between the left-wing Syndicat de la Magistrature, the moderate right-wing Union Syndicale des Magistrats and the Association Professionnelle des Magistrats, sympathetic to the more muscular Right. Governments appointing to sensitive judicial posts therefore find it relatively easy to recognise their political friends. In the case of Thierry Jean-Pierre, the examining magistrate whose enquiries first unravelled the Urba affair, his reputation for impartiality suffered a blow when he was elected as an MEP on the right-wing de Villiers list in 1994; the reputation of Éric Halphen was not enhanced when, in 2002, he left the judiciary and came out in support of Jean-Pierre Chevènement's presidential candidacy.

The fifth limitation to the *État de droit* in France is one that lies at the base of the other four: a continuing cultural aversion to the rule of law. This phenomenon affects many groups: the ordinary citizens who evade and avoid taxation or pull strings to get out of fines or threatened legal proceedings; the drivers responsible for France's ghastly toll of road deaths (which, for a comparable population and despite recent laudable steps to cut it, exceeds that in the UK by 130 per cent); the interest groups, whether farmers, lorry drivers or bird-shooters, who use illegal and sometimes violent tactics but are rarely brought to book for doing so; the businessmen who berated the examining magistrate Eva Joly for her obtuseness in failing to realise that 'the whole of French capitalism is built on insider dealing'; the state officials who manifest their contempt for the 'legal pedantry' of judges. The press denounces illegalities but treats suspects as guilty long before they are tried, giving extensive publicity not only to the charges brought but to selected pieces of evidence, in violation of the principle of the presumption of innocence. If their more important and influential targets usually have the means to answer back, the less well-known ones accused of everyday crimes on the inside pages of the regional press do not, and it is far from certain that the 2000 law on the presumption of innocence has done much to change this. At the same time, what would elsewhere be politically scandalous facts, such as President Mitterrand's use of a publicly owned apartment to house his mistress and their daughter gratis, may remain both concealed to the public for years and open secrets to reporters in the know, anxious not to compromise their access to the Élysée. Magistrates who leak confidential documents about *sub judice* cases to the media may be seeking to escape from, or reverse, political pressures on them to abandon their enquiries; but they are still violating the rule of law. Politicians, however, are among the worst offenders in this respect. The Left's protests against the Constitutional Council's striking down of clauses of the nationalisation law of 1981, and the Right's response to the Council's treatment of the privatisation law five years later, have an ironical symmetry to them; both were attacking the very legitimacy of rulings that went against them. The Right's outrage at the decision on the 1993 immigration laws verged on the hysterical. Various attempts were made by parliamentarians in the 1970s to limit the power of the courts, and especially of the ECJ and the Constitutional Council; as late as 1986, the justice minister proposed measures to limit what he called the Council's 'vast discretionary power'. Politicians have regularly hindered legal investigations by invoking considerations of national security (*secret défense*), or blocked judges' investigations by withholding police assistance. A remarkable instance of the latter was the refusal of Olivier Foll, head of the Paris judicial police, to assist the examining magistrate Éric Halphen who was seeking to search the apartment of Jean Tiberi, mayor of Paris. Foll was openly backed by the interior minister Jean-Louis Debré, who was publicly rebuked by the Court of Cassation – but supported by President Chirac, who as well as being the constitutional protector of the judiciary was Tiberi's predecessor as the capital's mayor. Chirac's attitude to the judiciary, though, was hardly more cavalier than that of his predecessor François Mitterrand, whose 'anti-terrorist' cell in the Élysée illegally tapped the telephones of some 150 people, including judges, politicians, lawyers and journalists, with the president's knowledge and approval – often with the purpose of keeping Mitterrand's many sexual peccadilloes from prying eyes and ears. The Péchiney affair of 1988–89 revealed the penchant for insider dealing of several of the president's friends, under Mitterrand's cynical eye. The *Rainbow Warrior* affair of 1985, in which a Greenpeace boat tracking French nuclear testing activity in the Pacific was blown up by French agents in Auckland harbour, causing one death, created much more stir abroad than in French political circles (the main worry of the right-wing opposition was that French prestige had been damaged because the agents had been found out). And executives of both Right and Left have tolerated the activities of the Renseignements Généraux (the police special branch), which is effectively exempt from normal judicial restraints such as search warrants and which has compiled secret files on politicians, business people, journalists, trade union officials and even (or perhaps especially) other police units. Equally remarkable, however, is the public's high threshold of tolerance. The widespread cynicism about politicians, considered to be 'generally corrupt' by a majority of the population, has the paradoxical result that *individual* politicians suspected or even convicted of being so are still regarded as fit for office because they are assumed to be no worse than the rest; hence Chirac's ability to head the poll in April 2002 despite the gravity of the accusations against him.

It may be added, finally, that judicial policy in Chirac's second term appeared intent on reversing some of the gains made over the previous decade in the independence of the judiciary and the safeguards in judicial procedure. First, two major laws on criminal procedure greatly reinforced, in the name of fighting organised crime, the powers of the police to hold suspects without charge (for up to four days) and to limit their access to legal representation, as well as the powers of the *parquet* to order telephone taps and invasive search procedures. Their passage through parliament was punctuated by demonstrations by lawyers in full robes in front of the Justice Ministry. Second, another major innovation of this legislation, the opportunity for a suspect to plead guilty and avoid a lengthy trial, rapidly ran into serious difficulties of implementation, largely because the secrecy of the new procedure was in direct contradiction with the principle of open and public trials. Third, the Conseil Supérieur de la Magistrature's advice on appointments to the *parquet*, some of it based on the competence of the candidates concerned, was repeatedly ignored. Fourth, Dominique Perben, the justice minister from 2002 to 2005 (and author of the new legislation), returned to an active policy of issuing instructions to prosecutors, which his Socialist predecessors had eschewed. Fifth, within this new context the Paris prosecution service, which handles most of the politically sensitive cases, took renewed care in keeping the activities of examining magistrates on a very tight rein. The cumulative effect of Perben's period in office was the return, at least partial, of a climate in which the subordination of the judiciary to the political executive, and of the individual to the powers of the police and the prosecuting service, were viewed as acceptable and even necessary.

Concluding remarks

In a context where the highest in the land regularly display indifference or contempt for the rule of law, it is perhaps unsurprising that the French lack confidence in their justice system. Among EU nations, indeed, only the Belgians, who have been treated to a series of grotesque judicial and political scandals since the mid-1990s, are more mistrustful of their judges (Table 13.2). Among French institutions, the justice system is regularly voted in surveys as among the least trustworthy – less so, for example, than parliament. Not only is the system considered to favour the wealthy; it is viewed as too much in the pocket of politicians in power. Hence the overwhelming public support for reinforcing the independence of the justice system.

As the previous sections show, France has certainly moved closer to being an *État de droit* than it was at the outset of the Fifth Republic. Despite the record of 2002–5 outlined above, some of these processes, such as the embedding of European law or the internalisation of legal constraints by policy-makers, are likely to continue.

But it would be wrong to see the *État de droit* as a point at which France is sure to arrive given time. Both material and cultural obstacles stand in its way. A critical difficulty is the chronic underfunding of the justice system. As Olivier Duhamel has

Table 13.2 Public confidence in the justice system in Europe, 1999

Country	No confidence	Confidence
Denmark	25	70
Austria	28	61
Finland	30	61
Luxembourg	28	59
Netherlands	35	59
Greece	42	55
Sweden	36	53
Germany	40	52
Ireland	37	49
UK	40	48
Portugal	45	42
Spain	52	40
Italy	53	36
France	56	35
Belgium	72	22

Source: Eurobarometer.

pointed out, when demonstrations by *lycée* students won an extra 4.5 billion francs for the education budget in 1990, they were obtaining a sum equivalent to 30 per cent of the *total* budget of the Justice Ministry. The consequences of this underfunding are all too predictable. The courts, in President Chirac's words, have reached the point of asphyxiation. A serious criminal case takes thirty-nine months on average (and often up to five years) to go through the courts. With 40 per cent of the 55,000 inmates of France's jails on remand awaiting trial, France has one of the highest levels of preventive detention in Europe; the Dickensian squalor in which such (technically innocent) inmates are kept is hardly compatible with the notion of an *État de droit*. The Service Central de Prévention de la Corruption created by the Justice Ministry in 1998 to investigate large-scale fraud, money-laundering, corruption and other financial crime was described by one of its members, Eva Joly, as 'window-dressing to give the impression that something is being done'. It employs just thirteen examining magistrates, each with some 40–80 cases; poor pay and a heavy workload make each of them all too susceptible to the temptations offered by large private firms who can turn their knowledge of financial legislation to corporate rather than public use and double or triple their salaries. The head of the service left for the private sector late in 1999; other examining magistrates, such as Joly and Halphen, have left the profession, worn down by years of fruitless labour punctuated by administrative bullying, hostile press campaigns and death threats. It has also been claimed that lack of resources prevented any major drugs case coming to trial in France between 1995 and 2000. To be capable of punishing large-scale corporate offenders as readily as it locks up suspected petty criminals, the justice system requires a massive injection of funds – and thus enough political will on the part of government to defend the allocation of such funds to Justice rather than to other ministries more likely to produce direct and tangible benefits to the taxpayer. In the most literal sense, a truly strong and independent justice system has a price tag; it is far from certain that the French are willing to pay it. There is also a more figurative cost to an *État de droit*, in terms of a cultural shift towards respect for the law, among both elites and ordinary French men and women. Such a shift would, for example, entail judges feeling sufficiently free from political intervention not to need to leak details of *sub judice* cases to the press – and the press being sufficiently respectful of due process and the presumption of innocence not to seek to print such details. This is still a long way off.

Nor is every increase in judicial power an unalloyed good. Some of the objections raised by the sceptics in the debate on the *État de droit* are highly pertinent. No democracy can be ruled by judges. Judges are unelected (in France at least), unaccountable either to the public or (if secure in their posts) to any political masters, and as affected by their own beliefs and prejudices as any other public figures. The record of the United States Supreme Court in the 1930s demonstrates the capacity of judges to sabotage the policies of a democratically elected government in the name of a tendentious interpretation of the constitution. One cost of a truly independent justice system is that the opinions of judges may be radically at odds with the views of the wider public. Even given an independent, impartial and value-free judiciary, an excess of judge-made law poses serious practical problems for public policy-making. Judges may be oblivious of the consequences of their decisions, whether in terms of public spending commitments, or of the delicate political bargains essential to public policy formation, or of the wider implications in distant but related policy areas, or of the real possibilities of implementation. Judicial proceedings, often lengthy, always reactive and unpredictable, perturb and therefore damage medium- to long-term policy planning – the more so as judges, and therefore courts, may and do disagree with one other. And (even more than politics) they tend to favour the well-off, the educated and the informed.

The costs and benefits of judicial independence should be situated in a wider set of trade-offs between market forces, social regulation and mobilisation, efficient processes of government and judicial review. To build a successful *État de droit* requires a recognition that judicialisation is a complex, diverse process, and that some elements, but not all, need strengthening. For while litigation serves an essential role in public policy, it can never be its only basis. One does not need to be a Jacobin, or to subscribe to a mystical concept of the general will or to inflated notions of 'parliamentary' (often, in practice, executive) sovereignty, to take the view that a coherent vision of the public interest is not always best served by jurisprudence resulting from courtroom confrontations between particular interests. Government in France would certainly benefit from the consolidation of those beginnings of an *État de droit* observed since 1958. But even competent and independent judges are no substitute for general laws that produce an authoritative and legitimate allocation of goods based on electoral assent and political accountability.

Further reading

Avril, P. and Gicquel, J., *Le Conseil constitutionnel*, 4th edition, Paris, Montchrestien, 1998.
Bell, J., *French Constitutional Law*, Oxford, Clarendon Press, 1992.
Bernard, C., *La justice entre soumission et émancipation*, Paris, Le Monde/Marabout, 1998.
Braibant, G. and Stirn, B., *Le droit administratif*, Paris, Presses de Sciences Po, 1997.
Brown, N. and Jacobs, F., *The Court of Justice of the European Communities*, London, Sweet and Maxwell, 1989.
Canard Enchaîné, Le, *L'horreur judiciaire*, Paris, Les Dossiers du Canard, 2005.
Charon, J.-M. and Furet, C., *Un secret si bien violé: la loi, le juge et le journaliste*, Paris, Seuil, 2000.
Chevallier, J., *L'État de droit*, Paris, Montchrestien, 1992.
Cohen-Tanugi, L., *Le droit sans l'État*, 3rd edition, Paris, Presses Universitaires de France, 1992.

Cohen-Tanugi, L., *La métamorphose de la démocratie Française: de l'État jacobin à l'État de droit*, 2nd edition, Paris, Gallimard, 1993.

Colas, D. (ed.), *L'État de droit: travaux de la mission sur la modernisation de l'État*, Paris, Presses Universitaires de France, 1987.

Colliard, C.-A. and Timsit, G., *Les autorités administratives indépendantes*, Paris, Presses Universitaires de France, 1988.

Costa, J.-P., *Le Conseil d'État dans la société contemporaine*, Paris, Économica, 1993.

Dehousse, R., *La Cour de justice des Communautés européennes*, Paris, Montchrestien, 1994.

Fanachi, P., *La justice administrative*, 4th edition, Paris, Presses Universitaires de France, 1995.

Favoreu, L., *La politique saisie par le droit*, Paris, Économica, 1988.

Favoreu, L., *Le Conseil constitutionnel*, Paris, Presses Universitaires de France, 1991.

Favoreu, L. and Philip, L., *Les grandes décisions du Conseil constitutionnel*, 6th edition, Paris, Sirey, 1991.

Garapon, A., *Le gardien des promesses: justice et démocratie*, Paris, Odile Jacob, 1996.

Garapon, A. and Salas, D., *La République pénalisée*, Paris, Hachette, 1996.

Gentot, M., *Les autorités administratives indépendantes*, Paris, Montchrestien, 1995.

Guédon, M.-J., *Les autorités administratives indépendantes*, Paris, LGDJ, 1991.

Haenel, H. and Frison-Roche, M.-A., *Le juge et le politique*, Paris, Presses Universitaires de France, 1998.

Halphen, E., *Sept ans de solitude*, Paris, Denöel, 2002.

Hamon, L., *Les juges de la loi: naissance et rôle du Conseil constitutionnel*, Paris, Fayard, 1987.

Joly, E., *Est-ce dans ce monde-là que nous voulons vivre?*, Paris, Éditions des Arènes, 2003.

Kessler, M.-C., *Le Conseil d'État*, Paris, Presses de la Fondation Nationale des Sciences Politiques, 1965.

Lochak, D., *La justice administrative*, 3rd edition, Paris, Montchrestien, 1998.

Massot, J. and Marimbert, J., *Le Conseil d'État*, Paris, La Documentation Française, 1988.

Mathieu, B., Renoux, T. and Roux, A., *La Cour de Justice de la République*, Paris, Presses Universitaires de France, 1995.

Minc, A., *Au nom de la loi*, Paris, Gallimard, 1998.

Pouille, A., *Le pouvoir judiciaire et les tribunaux*, Paris, Masson, 1985.

Pouvoirs, no. 92, 2000, 'La responsabilité des gouvernants'.

Rassat, M.-L., *La justice en France*, 5th edition, Paris, Presses Universitaires de France, 1996.

Robineau, Y. and Truchet, D., *Le Conseil d'État*, Paris, Presses Universitaires de France, 1994.

Roussillon, H., *Le Conseil constitutionnel*, Paris, Dalloz, 1994.

Soulez-Larivière, D., *L'avocature*, Paris, Seuil, 1995.

Soulez-Larivière, D., *Grand soir pour la justice*, Paris, Seuil, 1997.

Stirn, B., *Le Conseil d'État: son rôle, sa jurisprudence*, 2nd edition, Paris, Hachette, 1994.

Stone, A., *The Birth of Judicial Politics in France: The Constitutional Council in Comparative Perspective*, Oxford, Oxford University Press, 1992.

Stone Sweet, A., *Governing with Judges: Constitutional Politics in Europe*, Oxford, Oxford University Press, 2000.

Taisne, J.-J., *Institutions judiciaires*, 3rd edition, Paris, Dalloz, 1992.

van Ruymbeke, R., *Le juge d'instruction*, 3rd edition, Paris, Presses Universitaires de France, 1996.

Vernier, D., *La justice en France*, Paris, La Découverte, 1992.

14 France and European integration

Over more than half a century, France has been both an ardent promoter of European integration, and the fiercest of defenders, within European institutions, of national interest narrowly construed. Of course, all member states have sought in different ways to maximise the benefits of integration while minimising its constraints: to have their cake and eat it. In the French case, however, the tension has been especially acute. On the one hand, France's conception of Europe, as articulated by Christian Democrats, many Socialists and even some Gaullists, has been very ambitious, whether in political, social, or economic terms. On the other, there has been a reluctance, most readily expressed by Communists and some Socialists, Gaullists and the far Right, to accept the transfers of sovereignty that would give Europe the means of fulfilling such ambitions. The process of European integration can be divided into two periods, each corresponding to different resolutions of that basic conflict: a Europe of fairly limited scope, but with equally limited delegations of sovereignty from member states, until the mid-1980s; a Europe of wider ambitions and more substantial transfers of sovereignty since then. This second Europe, though not a little of France's making, has posed more serious dilemmas to French policy-makers than the first, threatening both a loss of French influence within European institutions and painful political and economic adjustments at home. That in turn has increased – though episodically more than continuously – the salience of European integration as a political issue within France, cross-cutting existing party divisions.

The integration process, vastly more complex than the diptych suggested above, is briefly narrated in the opening section of this chapter. Because the question of what drives the process – its own internal forces or the decisions of the member states – has both divided academics and informed most analysis of European affairs, the major interpretations of integration are also outlined. The second section deals with French approaches to Europe, and in particular the view of benefits and costs that France's policy-makers have applied to the integration process and how they have changed over time. An important element of any such view is France's special relationship with the Federal Republic of Germany, seen both as one of the benefits of integration and as a tool to help promote French interests within Europe. The second section also explores the dynamics of this relationship, as well as highlighting the distinctive approaches to integration of successive presidents. A third section discusses how France engages with the European policy process. Arrangements for policy co-ordination in Paris and for the promotion of French policy priorities in Brussels reflect a Jacobin desire that France should 'speak with one voice' in Europe, an approach which has drawbacks as well as advantages in terms of legislative or regulatory outcomes; the fact that some outcomes have not suited France is reflected in the reluctance, also covered in this section, with which France has implemented some European legislation.

The fourth section considers the substantive results, for France, of European policy developments in three areas: the Common Agricultural Policy, Economic and Monetary Union and the economic paradigm shift surrounding it, and the Common Foreign and Security Policy. Each, in different ways, reflects France's capacity to win lasting acceptance for its own policy priorities at the European level. For a long time a 'permissive consensus' among publics in France and other European states allowed governments to pursue their priorities without much reference to the voters. This is less and less the case. As the fifth section observes, French voters share many of their elites' ambiguous views about the costs and benefits of European integration, and have been increasingly divided over the really hard European questions, with at times disruptive effects on France's parties and party system. These divisions were most dramatically expressed in the May 2005 referendum on the European constitutional treaty.

European integration: process and interpretation

European integration has progressed in fits and starts, rather than the smooth process suggested by the term 'ever closer union between the peoples of Europe' enshrined in the Rome Treaty of 1957. The process has been simultaneously economic and political. It has been driven by the deliberate actions of Europe's nation states, but also by the dynamics of European institutions, and by the leaders of both. It has involved great leaps forward, barely perceptible shuffles, and even steps back; unexpected bargains and the incremental consolidation of institutional relationships. The account given below, though compressed, therefore remains complex; the academic interpretations of the process, outlined below it in simplified form, have been varied, subtle and hotly contested.

The narrative of integration

To a significant degree, as Table 14.1 and the following account show, the history of European integration is that of its big bargains – both successful and not.

- *The European Coal and Steel Community* (ECSC), proposed on 9 May 1950 by France's Foreign Minister Robert Schuman, signed by the six original member states (France and Germany in the first instance, joined by Italy, Belgium, Luxembourg and the Netherlands, with the blessing of the United States) at the Paris Treaty of April 1951, was operational by February 1953. The ECSC created a common market in coal and steel, but its institutions were more ambitious than anything

Table 14.1 A chronology of the EU, 1950–2005

1950 (May)	Robert Schuman proposes the European Coal and Steel Community (ECSC).
1951 (April)	The Six sign the Treaty of Paris, creating the ECSC.
1952 (May)	The Six sign a second Treaty of Paris, establishing the European Defence Community (EDC).
1953 (February)	The ECSC comes into force.
1954 (August)	French National Assembly rejects ratification of the EDC treaty: Gaullist and Communist opposition, reinforced by many Socialists and Radicals, overcomes Christian Democrat-led support for the treaty.
1955 (June)	Messina Conference between the Six: agreement in principle to create an Economic Community; a committee led by Paul-Henri Spaak is charged with drafting specific proposals.
1957 (March)	The Six sign the Treaties of Rome, establishing the European Economic Community (EEC) and Euratom.
1958 (January)	EEC and Euratom come into force.
1958 (June)	De Gaulle returns to power in France.
1958 (September)	De Gaulle–Adenauer meeting at Colombey-les-Deux-Églises.
1959 (January)	Common Market comes into force with first round of tariff reductions.
1961–62	Fouchet Plan for political co-operation proposed by de Gaulle, but ultimately rejected by France's partners.
1962 (January)	Agreement of the Six on key principles of Common Agricultural Policy.
1962 (May)	De Gaulle's 'Volapük' speech attacks European federalism.
1963 (January)	De Gaulle vetoes UK entry to EEC, but France and Germany sign the Élysée Treaty promising friendship and co-operation.
1965	The Merger Treaty, joining the institutions of the three communities from July 1967, is signed by the Six; France boycotts EC institutions in the Empty Chair crisis.
1966 (January)	The 'Luxembourg compromise' ends the Empty Chair crisis, and preserves effective unanimity on Council of Ministers.
1967 (November)	De Gaulle vetoes EEC enlargement a second time.
1968 (July)	The EEC's customs union fully operational with elimination of last tariffs.
1969 (December)	Summit at The Hague: agreement to 'complete, deepen, and enlarge' the EEC.
1970 (April)	'Own resources' for EEC budget, and greater oversight of it by the Parliament, established under Luxembourg Treaty.
1972 (April)	The 'Snake' established by the Six to limit exchange rate fluctuations between European currencies.
1972 (April)	France votes yes (by 68.3 per cent of votes, 36.4 per cent of registered electors) in a referendum on enlargement of European Communities.
1973 (January)	Denmark, Ireland and the UK enter the Communities.
1974 (December)	Regular summit meetings of EC heads of state and government – the future European Council – launched; agreement on direct elections to the European Parliament.
1979 (March)	Establishment of European Monetary System, successor to the Snake, agreed in 1978.
1979 (June)	First direct elections to the European Parliament (they are held at 5-yearly intervals, so in 1984, 1989, 1994, 1999, 2004 . . .).

1981 (January)	Greece joins the EC.
1984 (June)	Fontainebleau summit: resolution of the issue of British budget contribution clears the way for further development of the Community.
1985 (January)	Jacques Delors President of the European Commission.
1986 (January)	Spain and Portugal join the EC.
1986 (February)	Signature by the twelve member states of Single European Act (SEA), providing for the creation of a single market by 1 January 1993.
1988 (June)	European Council at Hanover committed to drafting proposals for Economic and Monetary Union (EMU) within one year.
1989 (November)	Fall of Berlin Wall signals the impending reunification of Germany and withdrawal of Central and East European states from Soviet bloc.
1989 (December)	European Council at Strasbourg agrees to intergovernmental conference to achieve EMU, and adopts plan for a European Social Charter.
1990 (June–July)	France, Germany and Benelux countries sign Schengen agreement to remove border controls. In July, liberalisation of capital movements within the Twelve.
1991 (June)	Mitterrand calls for a European Confederation, expecting a period of 'decades' before Central and East European states join EC.
1991 (December)	Maastricht summit on EMU, and on political union.
1992 (February)	Signature of Maastricht Treaty on European Union.
1992 (September)	French referendum on ratification of Maastricht Treaty passes by 51–49 per cent.
1993 (January)	Single Market comes into force.
1995 (January)	Austria, Finland and Sweden join the EU.
1997 (October)	Signature of Amsterdam Treaty.
1998 (June)	Agreement on the founding members of EMU.
1999 (January)	Exchange rates between EMU countries irrevocably fixed in preparation for transition to the euro (single currency).
1999 (March)	Resignation of the Commission after fierce criticism from Parliament over accounting practices, centred on French Commissioner Édith Cresson.
1999 (December)	Luxembourg summit recommends immediate opening of enlargement negotiations with Central and East European states, Malta and Cyprus. Turkey's official candidacy recognised.
2000 (December)	Signature of Nice Treaty.
2002 (January)	Euro banknotes and coins come into circulation.
2002 (February)	Creation of Convention on the Future of Europe, chaired by Valéry Giscard d'Estaing.
2003 (July)	Convention submits draft European constitutional treaty.
2004 (1 May)	Entry into EU of Cyprus, Czech Republic, Estonia, Hungary, Latvia, Lithuania, Malta, Poland, Slovakia, Slovenia.
2004 (18 June)	At Brussels summit, EU leaders adopt a modified version of the constitutional treaty.
2004 (14 July)	President Chirac promises referendum on the European constitutional treaty to be held in 2005.
2004 (December)	EU begins negotiations on Turkish entry.
2005 (29 May)	French electorate votes no by 54.7 to 45.3 per cent in referendum on European constitutional treaty.

required by a mere trade agreement. They included a supranational High Authority, headed from 1952 to 1954 by Jean Monnet, the French Planning Commissioner who had inspired the initial project; a Council of Ministers delegated by member states; a Court of Justice designed to ensure full and fair application of ECSC decisions; and a Common Consultative Assembly composed of delegates from national parliaments. The scope of these institutions, which would constitute the basis for the future European Union, reflected the double purpose of the ECSC: an economic organisation, it was also intended for a political purpose – to ensure that Germany's industrial recovery was put to peaceful use and to lay the foundations for long-term Franco-German reconciliation and European peace. Britain, at the time Europe's largest steel producer, stayed out of the project.

- *The project for a European Defence Community* (EDC) was a big bargain that never was. In effect an integrated West European army, and a framework for rearming Germany, with a European Political Community associated to it, EDC was proposed by French Prime Minister René Pleven in October 1950, signed by the Six in May 1952, but killed by a negative French ratification vote in August 1954.

- *The Rome Treaties*, signed by the Six in March 1957, created the European Atomic Energy Community (Euratom) and the much more important European Economic Community (EEC). Under the EEC treaty, the Six agreed to eliminate all customs barriers between them within twelve years from 1958, to apply a common external tariff to non-member states, to negotiate international trade agreements jointly, and to set up a Common Agricultural Policy (CAP): a package quickly known as the Common Market. The EEC was given very similar institutions to those of the ECSC (which which, indeed, they were merged in 1967): a Commission which took the role of the High Authority (enjoying the monopoly of legislative proposals, though with fewer independent decision-making powers), a Council of Ministers with the last word on all Community legislation, a Court of Justice and an Assembly of the European Communities (renamed the Parliament in 1980). On the other hand, the treaty's general aim of 'ever-closer union' was paralleled by other relatively vague commitments: no specific arrangements were made in the treaty to set up the CAP, or to implement a promised common transport policy, while the dates by which the Council of Ministers might abandon unanimous decision-making in favour of majority voting, or when the Assembly might be directly elected, were left deliberately uncertain.

- *The de Gaulle presidency* could be viewed as a phase of implementation of the previous big bargain, with the realisation of a Common Market (completed in 1968, eighteen months ahead of schedule) and the start of the CAP from 1967. It was also, in at least one way, a turning point where nothing turned. The so-called Fouchet Plan, de Gaulle's ambitious project for an intergovernmental European political confederation (by implication, under French leadership) was rejected by other member states, and particularly the Benelux countries, in 1962; its residue was the Élysée Treaty of January 1963, formalising processes of friendship and co-operation between France and Germany but failing to distance Germany from the American orbit as de Gaulle had hoped. In the so-called Empty Chair crisis of 1965–66, de Gaulle prevented the move towards majority voting in the Council of Ministers which had been anticipated in the Rome Treaty; the unanimity rule on the Council was effectively safeguarded by the so-called 'Luxembourg compromise' of January 1966. He also twice blocked attempts by other European states – Denmark,

Ireland and above all the UK – to join the EEC. The 1960s could thus be seen as an illustration of what the determined leader of one member state could do to shape – and, in many ways, to stall – Europe's development.

- *The agreements reached at The Hague in December 1969* by the heads of state and government of the Six – and above all by Pompidou, elected French president in June, and Willy Brandt, elected West German chancellor in October – served to 'relaunch' Europe after de Gaulle's departure. Though not a new treaty, the summit conclusions served both to 'complete' earlier undertakings, and to set an agenda for the EEC's 'deepening' and 'enlargement'. 'Completion' referred chiefly to the CAP, now set on a permanent footing and financed through its own resources – a share of receipts from VAT and from taxes on imports to Europe from outside the Six – rather than more politically vulnerable national contributions. 'Enlargement' meant the opening of the EEC to new member states, hitherto kept out by de Gaulle's veto. Denmark, Ireland and the UK joined the EEC in 1973 (and would be followed, after other negotiations, by Greece in 1981; Spain and Portugal in 1986; Austria, Sweden and Finland in 1995; and the Czech Republic, Slovakia, Hungary, Poland, Latvia, Lithuania, Estonia, Slovenia, Malta and Cyprus in 2004). 'Deepening' covered two initiatives: European Political Co-operation (EPC), or attempts to co-ordinate foreign policy, and the setting-up of a team chaired by Pierre Werner, prime minister of Luxembourg, to report into prospects for European Economic and Monetary Union (EMU). Each had more limited short-term effects than expected, but set a longer-term agenda. EPC proved quite insufficient, for example, to formulate a European response to the energy crisis of 1973–74, but laid the foundations for a future Common Foreign and Security Policy (CFSP). EMU took three decades to achieve, not one as initially hoped, but the Werner Report was the basis for the 'Snake' (1972–76) and the European Monetary System (EMS) of 1979–99 – both initiatives undertaken to achieve a measure of monetary stability in Europe during the turbulent period following the collapse of the Bretton Woods system of fixed exchange rates in August 1971.

- *The Giscard presidency*, though not a period of intense institutional activity, saw both the two steps towards monetary co-ordination noted above and two significant institutional developments. From December 1974, the EEC heads of government (or, in the French case, the president) agreed to meet at least thrice yearly, in summits which were to be known as the European Council, hosted by whichever country held the six-monthly rotating presidency of the Council of Ministers. And the first direct elections to the European Parliament were agreed in principle in 1974 and held in June 1979.

- *The Single European Act* (SEA), signed in 1986 and ratified in 1987, was a major treaty revision of both economic and institutional importance. Economically, it committed member states to eliminating non-tariff barriers to trade, and implementing on the ground the free movement of persons, goods, capital and services throughout the EEC by 1992. While barriers to trade were, first and foremost, variations in national norms and standards (some of which served clearly protectionist purposes for member states), the SEA also placed certain practices of governments – non-competitive tendering for contracts and subsidies to favoured firms – in the Commission's sights as obstacles to effective competition. The implementation of the Single Market therefore involved a much more complex and invasive reappraisal of national economic policies than the mere dismantling of customs duties provided for by the Rome Treaty. Meanwhile, the major institutional change, the adoption of Qualified Majority Voting (QMV) on the Council of Ministers, for Single Market questions, was adopted to remedy the obstacle represented by the *de facto* unanimity rule on the Council of Ministers to the achievement of a Single Market within a reasonable timescale. QMV gave each member state a number of votes on the Council of Ministers in (very) approximate proportion to its size, and fixed a minimum number of votes – typically about 70 per cent of the total – necessary for a proposal to be carried. The adoption of QMV for SEA matters meant the beginning of the end for unanimity on the Council of Ministers as preserved by the Luxembourg compromise. The SEA also provided for two lesser, but still important, institutional changes in the direction of supranationality. The European Parliament's role, hitherto almost entirely consultative, was reinforced for Single Market issues by the new co-operation procedure of legislation; and a Court of First Instance was created to lighten the burden of business in the Court of Justice – a significant acknowledgement of the growing importance (and caseload) of the European judiciary.

- *The Treaty on European Union* (TEU), signed at Maastricht in 1992 and ratified by all signatories by 1993, committed most member states to phased steps leading to Economic and Monetary Union – a single currency to complement the single market (the UK, and then Denmark, opted out of EMU). Exchange rates of participating member states were irrevocably fixed in 1999, after a period of economic convergence marked by strict financial discipline (or at least the appearance of it) on the part of governments and central banks; Europe's single currency – the euro – has circulated since January 2002. While EMU was the centrepiece of Maastricht, it was far from the only component. The single currency was to be flanked by the bases – at least minimal – of a common social policy, in the Social Protocol, linked to the Treaty but not, at British insistence, included in it. Institutional reforms within the EEC included a modest extension of QMV on the Council of Ministers to new areas; a further strengthening of the Parliament, now empowered to vet an incoming Commission as well as to censure an incumbent one, and, under the new co-decision procedure, to block legislation on certain issues; and the creation of a (consultative) Committee of the Regions, reflecting a greater recognition of Europe's regions that had also found expression in a doubling of regional aid since 1988. And the EEC itself was complemented by 'Political union', represented by two distinct areas of co-operation, for which the unanimity rule would apply to decisions in the Council of Ministers: the Common Foreign and Security Policy (CFSP) and Justice and Home Affairs (JHA). These three 'pillars' – the EEC, the CFSP and JHA – would together constitute the new European Union. At the same time, however, the principle of 'subsidiarity' – that Europe should handle only those tasks that were best addressed at the European level rather than at those of states or subnational authorities – was formally incorporated into the TEU.

- *The Amsterdam Treaty of 1997* was the first of three treaty changes designed to adapt the EU's institutions to new responsibilities and to the perspective of enlargement to a total of at least 25 member states following the end of the Cold War. The fact that this took three treaty modifications in seven years illustrates the difficulty of the task, and especially the reluctance of large member states to surrender their traditional leading role in a bigger EU. Amsterdam saw an extension and simplification of the co-decision procedure and a corresponding enhancement of the power of the European Parliament (significantly, the Parliament chose to flex its muscles in 1999 by provoking the collective resignation of the whole Commission over allegations of corruption and nepotism; five years later, it would reject Italy's nominee for the Commission on the grounds of his reactionary religious and social views, forcing a recasting of the whole Commission). It created a limited institutional opening for 'flexibility', or enhanced co-operation on specific issues between some but not all member states. It moved some provisions on immigration and asylum questions, linked to issues of the free movement of people between member states, from the EU's third (Justice and Home Affairs) pillar to the first, and thereby subjected these policies to QMV. Amsterdam also created a 'Monsieur PESC' – a High Representative for Europe's foreign policy, alongside (and not always in perfect harmony with) the Commissioner for External Affairs. It put the Maastricht convergence criteria for EMU on a permanent footing, with the new name of the Stability and Growth Pact. But many critical issues, in particular how to bring European institutions closer to Europe's peoples and how to adapt Europe's decision-making procedures, initially designed for the Six, to a much larger membership, were barely addressed. Even the cap of 700 on the membership of the Parliament was broken in 2004, when MEPs numbered 732. Indeed, the Commissioner who presented the Amsterdam Treaty to the public expressed his dissatisfaction by calling it 'an impenetrable and complex Treaty, timid in the most sensitive areas such as the common foreign and security policy and weak on the institutional aspects'.

- *The Nice Treaty of December 2000* appeared to achieve one, albeit limited, step towards rationalising Europe's decision-making by fixing the new voting strengths of each member state, and the new Qualified Majority, for a Council of Ministers in a future 27-member EU, as well as by limiting the number of future Commissioners appointed by each state to one from 2005, even for the five larger states hitherto accustomed to two. The Treaty also extended QMV on the Council into new (though mostly uncontentious) policy areas. In addition, the Nice summit approved a European declaration of fundamental human rights, though at Britain's insistence this was not given treaty status. By the time of its signature, however, the Nice Treaty already appeared inadequate and outdated, in the face of calls for a much more comprehensive constitutional settlement, emanating from European parliamentarians, government ministers such as German Foreign Minister Joschka Fischer and, much more guardedly, from Chirac.

- *The European constitutional treaty of June 2004* offered the promise of closing the cycle of enlargement-driven reforms. Pressures for a long-term constitutional settlement had led the Laeken EU summit of December 2001 to set up a Convention on the Future of Europe to be chaired by former French president Giscard d'Estaing. The Convention presented its draft constitution in July 2003. In some respects it simply consolidated earlier treaties and existing institutional tendencies: for example, the co-decision procedure (defining the respective roles of Parliament, Commission and Council of Ministers) and QMV (for voting in the Council of Ministers) were to become the norm for most EU legislation, with the Parliament achieving full status as a co-legislator with the Council of Ministers in most areas. The Charter of Fundamental Rights of the Union, joined as a simple declaration to the Nice Treaty, became an integral part of the constitutional treaty. Inevitably, the Convention produced uneasy compromises; it was, after all, attempting to streamline the EU's institutions, and especially its executive, without producing a fully federal project, which would be unacceptable to most member states, and certainly to Britain and France. Thus the question of a single executive head of the Union was avoided by proposing a dyarchy between the president of the Commission and a president of the European Council, now to be elected for two-and-a-half years, replacing the six-monthly rotation of the presidency between member states. The post of European foreign minister was created, to replace both the external relations commissioner and the newer 'Monsieur PESC'. The new official would have the office of a vice-president of the Commission but would be appointed (and revocable) by the European Council. Among the most controversial among the Convention's proposals, however, was the replacement of the complex Nice formulas for QMV with a much simpler rule: legislation would pass in the Council of Ministers if supported by at least half the member states representing at least three-fifths of the population. This readjustment, which reduced voting rights of some states (especially Spain and Poland) by comparison with Nice, wrecked Italian Prime Minister Silvio Berlusconi's plans for the constitution to be agreed in December 2003 in a second Rome Treaty. Only the election of a new government in Spain in March 2004 opened the way for the compromise including the raising of the thresholds to 55 per cent of member states and 65 per cent of the EU's population, which allowed a revised draft to be signed in Brussels in June 2004. It remained for member states to ratify the treaty, whether via national parliaments or, in a number of states including France, by referendum by the choice of President Chirac. On 29 May 2005, after a bitterly fought campaign, the French said a resounding no to the treaty by a margin of nearly 55 to 45 per cent of valid votes cast. Three days later the Dutch made the same choice by the even greater margin of 62 per cent to 38. At the Brussels summit the same June, Europe's leaders, under pressure from Britain, suspended the ratification process.

It should be stressed that even if it were ratified (an eventuality which appeared unthinkable by mid-2005), the term 'constitutional treaty' would not make the EU into anything approaching the superstate of Eurosceptical fantasy. The EU budget amounts to barely 1 per cent of GDP, compared to over 40 or even 50 per cent in most member states. Many key attributes of state sovereignty have escaped the EU, partly or wholly. The common stuff of politics in every member state – taxation, education, healthcare, social security, defence, policing and justice – remains overwhelmingly under national control. Despite the ambitions of federalists for a much stronger European defence force, or for tax harmonisation, this was not about to change. Hence the difficulty of analysing the EU: although it is more than an intergovernmental organisation and possesses some state-like qualities, its development is still very much shaped by complex deals between member states that retain the attributes of sovereignty.

Interpreting integration (1): realism, intergovernmentalism

The complexity and unevenness of the integration process has been reflected in the academic interpretations that have developed in parallel with it. To simplify greatly, these can be divided into two main camps: those that draw inspiration from international relations and see Europe as an arena of competing nation states, and those that view Europe as a polity in its own right, whose government and politics have their own internal dynamics which may be compared with those of any developed democracy. Within each of these, in turn, two main perspectives can be identifed.

International relations perspectives on European integration focus, perhaps unsurprisingly, on Europe's big bargains, on the decisive steps forward in integration – as well as on its failed opportunities, those turning points in recent European history at which nothing turned. These were the moments when the leaders of Europe's nation states took the most obviously decisive roles. On this view, therefore, the EU and its preceding bodies are best seen as rather elaborate international organisations, providing an arena within which the crucial actors, nation states, play out their rivalries, conflicts and alliances. 'Realist' approaches to integration, identified with such veteran Europe-watchers as Stanley Hoffmann, see nation states as unitary actors of unequal strength and more or less permanent geopolitical interests, competing for hegemony, or for a privileged relationship with a leading power, within a region and the wider world system. European integration is the product of inter-state bargaining, with a leading role cast for the two most powerful of the founding states, France and the Federal Republic of Germany. But the institutions it has created – the EEC or, more recently, the EU – have little autonomy; they are the precarious outcomes of a particular, and temporary, regional balance of forces.

A number of the strictures laid by realists against the Euro-optimists of the early 1960s ring true forty years later. The integration process has suffered from a lack of clarity (even among its advocates) about finalities and from a lack of citizen identification either with a strong European project or with Europe's institutions. Much of the negotiation of the big bargains outlined above has been marked less by a common sense of European purpose as by bad-tempered and drawn-out haggling among representatives of member governments, of which the meetings at Nice in 2000, at Rome in 2003, or Brussels in June 2005 are only the most recent examples. Whenever integration has moved from (relatively) painless areas such as the removal of tariff barriers towards core attributes of sovereignty – the currency, immigration, defence, or even taxation, for example – it has encountered opposition from member states and deep misgivings among their populations; in the case of EDC, this happened as early as 1954. The naked assertion of national interest in the European arena by de Gaulle (in the Empty Chair crisis, for example) or Thatcher (over the budget) has been paralleled by the more discreet pursuit of national objectives by every other member state. Despite this range of evidence to confirm their case, however, the realists face an obvious difficulty in accounting for the forward motion that has taken place: for surrenders of sovereignty under Mitterrand and Chirac that would have been unthinkable under de Gaulle, and even for the resilience of European institutions and their growth, over time, into something considerably more than those of an alliance or an intergovernmental organisation.

Liberal intergovernmentalists such as Andrew Moravcsik share many of the realists' perspectives, insofar as they approach Europe from an international relations perspective, and are sceptical of the importance and autonomy of supranational institutions. Like the realists, they focus on a Europe of big inter-state bargains. But they are less inclined to view states as unitary actors acting as a function of more or less permanent geopolitical interests. Rather, they see government preferences as more plastic, reflecting shifting balances of economic and political forces. They bring 'low politics' into the big bargains, placing significant emphasis on interest groups, and especially business groups, national but also transnational, in shaping the preferences of governments. In the EMU debate, for example, German policy-makers were continually pulled between the sound-money preferences of Germany's powerful central bank (and of public opinion, still marked by memories of the currency collapses that followed both world wars) and their industrialists' wish for a competitively valued currency to assist exports. And Moravcsik's account of de Gaulle's European policy pays at least as much attention to the General's relationship with the French farm lobby as to the grander and more frequently analysed geopolitical concerns. Liberal intergovernmentalists have the capacity to explain movement in the integration process both through the changing world economic context (for example, the currency instability caused by the American abandonment of Bretton Woods in 1971, or European worries about the slowing-down of international trade and member states' growth prior to the Single Act of 1986) and through changing balances of forces within member states. But European integration is not, for liberal intergovernmentalists, driven by its own momentum, structures, or leaders. Rather, they see European institutions – the Commission and the Court of Justice in 1957, the European Central Bank forty years later – as artifices devised to ensure that inter-state deals are respected once struck. The artifice may need to be permanent; but in the end, for liberal intergovernmentalists, the principals in the process remain states, while European actors are merely agents, created to do their bidding, whose freedom of action remains limited. Convincingly argued where the big (and very substantially intergovernmental) bargains are concerned, this case suffers from its relative neglect of the more humdrum activities of Europe, in which everyday patterns of co-operation are established, institutions bedded down, new needs discerned, apparently trivial but potentially far-reaching laws and regulations drafted, and significant bodies of case law built up by successive judgements of the European Court of Justice.

Interpreting integration (2): neo-functionalism, institutionalism

Neo-functionalists, by contrast, break with the international relations perspective to view the European Union as a nascent polity, an infant federal state. At times they have stressed the autonomy of the integration process to a degree that almost relegates the nation states to the background. The key concept of early neo-functionalists, such as Haas, was spillover. As European institutions are given new tasks, they argued, the need to perform the task well will draw them into seeking new, often unforeseen, areas of control, thus moving the integration process further along still. Among elites, moreover, the educative process of working together facilitates further extensions of European competence. Many events in the integration process may be considered typical of spillover. For example, following the completion of the Common Market in 1968, many states tried to protect powerful domestic lobbies by imposing non-tariff barriers on imports, a form of protectionism by stealth; that practice generated pressure for the Single Market, with its new array of common European norms designed to phase out non-tariff barriers, along with the new European institutional procedures that their elaboration entailed. The Single European Act, in turn, was viewed as incomplete without monetary union. Although partly autonomous, spillover is not automatic; it is helped along, in the neo-functionalists' view, by leadership from those European institutions with most to gain from the integration process. This is true in particular of the Commission, an institution that becomes increasingly powerful and entrepreneurial as integration progresses, of the European Parliament (EP), and of the European Court of Justice (ECJ). With Jacques Delors, Commission president from 1985 to 1994, the Commission reached its ideal neo-functionalist type, entrepreneurial and ready to use the many opportunities available to press its own federalist agenda. Perhaps the most obvious evidence in support of the neo-functionalist case for European integration as a steady, incremental process is the fact that the process has never been turned back: no treaty has significantly reversed any provision of previous treaties. The neo-functionalists' problem, however, is how to explain those periods, like most of de Gaulle's presidency, when European integration has been stalled; when the Commission has been powerless to bully or cajole any further concessions of sovereignty from the states; or, most recently, when the Commission has even lost much of its agenda-setting power.

Institutionalists, finally, share with neo-functionalists a focus on the internal forces driving the integration process. However, where neo-functionalists have tended to view Europe as a unique institutional experiment, institutionalists are readier to draw on perspectives of comparative politics, and to conclude that while the EU is not itself a state, the study of state systems, and particularly those of federal states, can shed valuable insights in to its functioning. At the very least, argue the institutionalists, the institutions of the EU 'matter', and the integration process cannot be adequately analysed without taking into account the path dependency arising from their existence: states are not free to conclude the bargains they wish. Indeed, European institutions, even if initially constructed on an inter-state basis, have acquired a life of their own which plays a crucial role in determining how Europe's business is done. For analysts like Hix, Europe is neither an artifice of inter-state bargains nor a process *sui generis*, but rather a polity which, while far from identical to a nation state, shares enough characteristics – legislative, executive and judicial functions, a party system of sorts, an intense and thriving arena of interest group activity, a complex and active bureaucracy – to be compared with one. A profusion of studies of European policy-making, in areas ranging from telecoms to transport to agriculture, have focused on the complex processes of interaction between national and European policy-making systems, and (often) on the newness and malleability of the networks established. Other users of comparative politics approaches, such as Marks, have focused on the idea of governance – the messy, complex, networked process of running a polity, contrasted with older models of government stressing hierarchy and command – and stress the 'multilevel' character of most European policy-making, ranging from the EU to national to regional to local levels. This, argue multilevel governance theorists, tends to weaken the nation state by transferring some of its responsibilities upwards to Europe and others downwards to local and regional authorities, leaving national authorities 'hollowed out' to a greater or lesser extent. The difficulty with institutionalism, on the other hand, is that its arguments about institutions shaping particular balances of power and patterns of path dependency can be turned two ways; it may just as well be argued that these are even truer of nation states, all of which are older than the EU, and that these should be (re-)placed at the centre of analyses of European policy-making.

None of these approaches offers an exhaustive account of the development of what has probably become the most complex polity in human history. To some degree, indeed, they – or at least the liberal intergovernmental and the institutional perspectives – are complementary. Liberal intergovernmentalism offers a stronger account of the big bargains, struck at summits or intergovernmental conferences, which have periodically accelerated the integration process – as of the stalemates which have almost as regularly blocked it. Here, national players, in the form of heads of government (or, in the French case, the president) are most directly responsible for the outcome. European institutions, and in particular the Commission, may play a role as agenda-setters, but take a secondary role in the negotiations themselves. By contrast, the more humdrum business of European governance may be much more profoundly affected than the big bargains by European institutional actors – not only the Commissioners who table proposals to the Council of Ministers and who oversee their implementation, but the Commission officials who draft proposals, the parliamentarians whose power to amend them has grown since the 1980s, the European justices who rule on compliance issues, as well as the ever-growing constellation of interest groups that find it worth their while to lobby at European rather than, or at least as well as, at national level. Moreover, it is at this level, in the detailed fleshing out of policies on agricultural markets, or competition, or environmental protection, that the pressures build that may generate demands that spill over towards further economic and political integration.

Such a division of labour – intergovernmentalist approaches for big bargains and neofunctionalism or institutionalism for the day-to-day workings of the EU – is, of course, an oversimplification. European actors, especially activist Commissioners and Commission presidents, have played major roles as agenda-setters for the major bargains. Governments, on the other hand, have a significant input at the day-to-day level, with their instructions flowing in a near-constant stream to the member states' permanent representations in Brussels, and working groups composed of national civil servants monitoring the activities of the Commission and forming a steadily more important underpinning of the Council of Ministers.

A final point about approaches to European integration is that they are not merely academic analyses. The 'Monnet method' of European integration – a paced succession of limited but practical steps, agreed between elites without excessive publicity, rather than a grander, more comprehensive, more public, but possibly unachievable programme – was practically predicated on spillover, and indeed on the creation of strong European institutions, explicitly with a federalist bias 'above' the concerns of nation states. Similarly, an intergovernmental Europe, with the role of European institutions downgraded to a merely technical and administrative one, leaving member states firmly in charge both of the integration process and of the day-to-day running of the Community, has been the strongly preferred goal of member states and politicians sceptical of the notion of supranationality. Such a member state, for much of the integration process, has been France.

France and the integration process

France's role in the integration process has been one of initiation (from the launch of the ECSC onwards), of acceleration (for example, of the customs union), of co-operation (notably with Germany) but also of obstruction (most obviously over institutional questions during the de Gaulle presidency, and most recently over the constitutional treaty) and of fairly consistent opposition to a fully federal project. The French have been Europeans, but of an intergovernmental stamp. The Janus face presented by France to the European project can be explained most simply in terms of a national view, fairly consistent over time, of benefits and costs; in other words, something close to a realist account. While such an account is not sufficient, for reasons that will be explained below, the consistencies in the French design on Europe remain important. That the French have been able to realise a substantial part of their goals was due, in part, to their special relationship with Germany. The dynamics of that partnership have changed since 1989, representing a corresponding challenge to France's role in Europe.

France and Europe: benefits and costs

France's often decisive support for European integration may be explained, in simplified terms, by four motives: two geopolitical and two economic.

Of the geopolitical considerations, none has been more important than France's relations with the Federal Republic of Germany. The European project sought to break, not only with France's brief post-war preference for the permanent dismemberment of Germany, but also with the diplomacy of the preceding half-century, when attempts to contain France's eastern neighbour via more or less adversarial alliances had failed, both in 1914 and in 1939. For Europe's founding fathers – for Robert Schuman, whose native Lorraine had been transferred from French rule to German and back again twice in a single war-torn lifetime – European integration, from the Coal and Steel Community on, served to render another Franco-German war materially impracticable. Their approach was new in that it was centred on practical rather than merely diplomatic reconciliation. Since then, the Franco-German couple, reinforced by the Élysée Treaty of January 1963, has been a crucial motor of integration, as well as, more occasionally, an obstacle to European reforms. But if Franco-German reconciliation has been an important leitmotif of European integration, French policy-makers have still been anxious to contain a Germany whose economic, diplomatic and even potential military strength have remained a source of concern. For German leaders, meanwhile, Europe in general and the alliance with France in particular have served as a means to engineer their country's slow reintegration into the (Western) international community after 1945, a framework within which to pursue national goals without national assertiveness. The relationship, which will be considered in more detail in a later section, has never lacked critics on both banks of the Rhine, and has never been immune from breakdowns; yet it has clearly survived – sometimes to the dismay of other member states – well into the third millennium.

The second geopolitical use of Europe for France has been as a diplomatic lever. France's past great power status had been based, first on its position as the largest state in Europe with the biggest population and army, and then on her possession of the world's second largest colonial empire. By the early 1960s both of those assets had been lost. If France remained a great power, it was due to the legacy of the past, materialised in a permanent seat on the UN security council, and to the possession of a very small quantity of atomic, and then nuclear, weapons. In that context, Europe offered France what de Gaulle called a 'lever of Archimedes'. With Britain turned, until the early 1960s, largely towards its Atlantic and Commonwealth relationships, Germany both divided and diplomatically disabled by the legacy of World War II, and Italy too disorganised and the Benelux countries too small to aspire seriously to a leading role, the diplomatic leadership of Europe was France's for the taking. If only the Economic Community could be transformed into a political alliance, argued de Gaulle privately to his minister Alain Peyrefitte in discussing the Fouchet Plan, France might hope to 'regain the status she lost at the battle of Waterloo, as the first among nations', at the head of an 'imposing confederation' that would be dominated neither by the Soviet Union nor (crucially) by the United States. The French ambition of a strong European diplomatic and military identity, friendly towards but independent from the United States and with France playing a – indeed *the* – leading role, has punctuated the development of Europe and won a new lease of life with the end of the Cold War.

But for France to have embraced European integration for geopolitical reasons would have made no sense without the incentive of economic gains. The most tangible of these has been the Common Agricultural Policy (CAP). As Europe's biggest agricultural producer, whose farmers had, thanks to productivity improvements since 1945, been producing more and more food even as their numbers diminished, France has been the CAP's principal beneficiary, and farm exports a significant part of French foreign trade. The CAP has been more and more the target of attacks on the grounds of its expense, its remoteness from market disciplines, its environmental costs, and the fact that it has benefited large farmers not small, producers not consumers, and the agricultural industry to the detriment of the environment. France remains, however, a vociferous defender of the CAP, with the generally consistent, if less and less enthusiastic, support of Germany. The details of France's addiction to the CAP, and the policy's partial transformation since 1990, will be covered later in this chapter.

Altogether more controversial within France has been the broader free-trade thrust that has been central to European integration from the ECSC onwards. This has entailed a progressive break with France's protectionist traditions. Successive French leaders since 1957 have used the economic liberalism at the heart of the European project as a lever for economic modernisation within France. De Gaulle's decision to implement the provisions of the Treaty of Rome, signed fifteen months before he returned to power in 1958 and ratified over the opposition of most Gaullist Deputies, was motivated in part by a simple equation: no great power status without a world-class economy; no world-class economy as long as French firms remained, as they had been since the 1890s and beyond, sheltered by tariff barriers. Pompidou, on the eve of his election in 1969, stressed that France, having opted to liberalise trading relations with Europe, had no choice but to liberalise the internal economy as well. For Giscard, the monetary disciplines of the EMS were a necessary backdrop to Prime Minister Barre's economic austerity programmes aimed at restoring France's budgetary and trade balances while safeguarding the franc's value against the deutschmark. For Mitterrand, Europe replaced socialism as the central presidential project after the economic U-turn of March 1983: as an accepted economic discipline, and as a justification for sacrifices imposed. The Single Market, and then the single currency, would offer a stable environment within which French business could thrive, and a framework for the construction of a European economic superpower to rival the United States. Nor was this merely a matter of government rhetoric: by the 1990s, 62 per cent of French exports went to EU countries, which also held 65 per cent of France's foreign direct investments. No member state has a more intense economic relationship with its EU partners.

Each of these benefits has been amply realised. Europe has given France a strong and predictable relationship with Germany, an enhanced role on the world stage, a subsidised market for farm exports, and a regulatory, monetary and ideological framework for economic modernisation. None, however, has come without a price tag.

The most obvious cost of Europe, from the French viewpoint, is the affront that it represents to a long-standing tradition of national sovereignty reinforced by great power status. In this France resembles the UK, another old-established state, another former first-rank power. The contrast could hardly be greater, on the other hand, with the case of Germany – a newer state, but above all one with a post-war tradition of limited sovereignty, defined by division, foreign occupation and federalism. For Germany, the integration process has coincided with the progressive recovery of much of the sovereign status lost in 1945. For France, on the contrary, it has proceeded at the price of sometimes painful surrenders of sovereignty, which French politicians – beginning with Mollet in the negotiations preceding the Rome Treaties – have sought to resist or limit.

European institutions are, moreover, quite alien in many ways to France's dominant state tradition. Jacobinism supposes a state that is unitary, hierarchical and powerful. There is little place in it for the checks and balances represented in other polities by an active judiciary, by a vibrant tradition of local and regional government with embedded constitutional rights, or by vigorous group representation within civil society. In the Jacobin scheme, as we have noted in earlier chapters, there is little place for judicial review; interest groups are regarded with suspicion; and clear chains of command reach from an all-powerful centre to citizens in the most remote periphery. Although the practice has been somewhat different, the power of the pervading myth should not be discounted, especially as Jacobinism reached its Gaullist apogee. Against this, Europe represents an impossibly (and increasingly) untidy picture: a conglomerate of interlocking and interdependent institutions, an exuberant hothouse of interest group activity, a world of messy compromises, package deals, side payments, activist and politically adept judges, and ad hoc coalitions.

These political challenges are compounded by an economic one: Europe's free-trade ethos has represented not only a spur to modernisation but also, by the same token, a powerful threat to the two French economic traditions, outlined in Chapter 1, of protectionism and *dirigisme*. The Common Market put an end to the one; the Single Market sounded the knell of the other. The losers (real, potential, or imagined) in each case, were not slow to draw attention to their plight: small businesses in the early 1970s, unemployed miners and steelworkers from the late 1970s, all manner of public-sector workers from the 1990s, and small farmers and fishermen throughout.

In France's European heaven, these costs would be minimised even as the benefits were reaped in full. France's farmers would export ever-growing amounts of food with the subsidies of (other, mostly German) European taxpayers. The opportunities of the Single Market would in no way threaten the protected status of France's public services or industrial national champions; indeed, French practices in these areas, as well as in social protection or taxation, would be uploaded to the European level. The single currency would ensure monetary stability and low interest rates, ending the old upsets of the franc–deutschmark fluctuations, but France's fiscal freedom would be unconstrained by the Stability and Growth Pact. The core attributes of sovereignty – defence, foreign policy, justice and home affairs – would remain under national control, but other member states would accept French leadership in forging a European identity clearly distinct from an American-led 'West' or an 'Atlantic community'. Infrequent big bargains would keep the integration process firmly under the control of heads of state and of government; the Council of Ministers would continue to run routine decision-making; spillover would be reined in; and Europe's characteristically supranational institutions – the Commission, the Parliament and the

Court – kept weak. In short, as observers such as Menon have argued, France typically seeks a strong Europe – in the sense of having ambitious policies, whether internally or in relation to the rest of the world – but with weak institutions: the central ambiguity of French approaches to Europe.

This is not, however, to say that French leaders have always made European policy in the same way. They have not, for three reasons. First, European policy-making is played out in a wider international context – one which has made the ambiguity harder to sustain since the 1980s. Second, they have been beholden to different domestic constraints and constituencies, increasingly critical of the European project in the name of French sovereignty. Third, however, they have not, as individuals, been the passive tools of circumstance. As we have seen, French presidents when not constrained by cohabitation enjoy greater margins of manoeuvre than almost any West European executives to place their own stamp on foreign, including European, policy.

Presidential perspectives

Alone among Fifth Republic presidents, de Gaulle viewed European integration, as defined in the Rome Treaty, as ultimately expendable. The phase of vigorous European activism of the first four years of his presidency achieved two significant goals – the first tariff reductions and above all agreement on the launch of the CAP. But having failed to secure clear French diplomatic leadership via the Fouchet Plan, he shifted his focus to the wider world stage, and his actions from 1963 served to slow both deepening (the Luxembourg compromise) and widening (the vetoes on UK entry). In private, he stressed his indifference to the future of the EEC, and would state in his memoirs that he had threatened to withdraw France and thus wreck the whole Community if a satisfactory arrangement on the CAP were not found. For Pompidou, such *hauteur* was an impossibility. As a presidential candidate in 1969, he had claimed to offer an 'opening' to Europe. In part this was for electoral reasons – he had to attract the support of pro-European centrists to win – but his reasoning was not merely tactical. As president, more sensitive than his predecessor to his country's internal and external vulnerability, he viewed Europe as a means to protect France's position in the world, as the necessary setting for the economic modernisation which, carried to a successful conclusion, could save France from a repetition of May 1968; UK entry as a means to counterbalance the growing economic power of West Germany; Economic and Monetary Union as a tool to protect the CAP from the impact of currency fluctuations. For Dyson and Featherstone, Pompidou was a 'European of the head', a prudent, reasoned supporter rather than an outright enthusiast for the European project. This did not prevent him from sharing much of the traditional Gaullist antipathy to supranational institutions (a view always encouraged by traditionalists within his own party) and refusing any strengthening of the Commission or the Parliament; nor from rowing back from monetary union as its more unpalatable institutional and economic consequences became clearer.

By contrast, Dyson and Featherstone view both Giscard and Mitterrand, unlike their Gaullist predecessors, as 'Europeans of the heart', supporters of the European project for its own sake. Giscard and most of the non-Gaullist moderate right-wing groups that he coralled into the UDF were always less prickly than the Gaullists about transfers of national sovereignty. As finance minister, Giscard had favoured moves to monetary union as early as the mid-1960s, and the EMS stands as one of the major integrationist moves of his presidency. His second prime minister, Raymond Barre, had been a

European Commissioner. Neither of the two institutional reforms of his presidency, direct elections to the European Parliament and the launch of the European Council, would have been possible under Pompidou. The former was blocked by the reluctance of Gaullists (including the president) to give a European institution the legitimacy of universal suffrage. The notion of regular summits suffered from suspicion from France's European partners towards anything resembling a big power directory or a revival of the Fouchet Plan – a suspicion that was much moderated once France had a non-Gaullist president. And Giscard's post-1981 record, especially his chairmanship of the Convention for the Future of Europe in 2002–3, testifies to his continuing European credentials. At the same time it would be quite false to present Giscard as an out-and-out federalist. With the exception of direct elections to the EP, the advances made in European integration during his presidency were either outside the scope of treaty institutions altogether, or of an intergovernmental stamp (the European Council, itself only recognised in a European treaty in the Single European Act, twelve years after its creation). The Giscard presidency saw neither a strengthening of the Commission nor any challenge to the Luxembourg compromise. Moreover, the president was operating under greater constraints than his predecessors. Giscard's main European partner, Helmut Schmidt, had little time for supranational European institutions; the wider political environment, in the aftermath of the first oil crisis, did not favour new European initiatives that would tie the hands of national governments; and the Gaullist partners in Giscard's right-wing coalition were quick to attack any perceived sell-out to Brussels. Even a fully federalist president, therefore, would have faced difficulties advancing the integrationist project much further.

François Mitterrand's support for European integration, though underplayed during his 1981 election campaign, represented one of the few consistencies of opinion in the course of his career. He had, for example, backed the EMS project in 1978. And it is hard to imagine a de Gaulle or a Pompidou saying, as Mitterrand did in 1986, 'France is our *patrie*, but Europe is our future'. Mitterrand's creativity in accepting a large-scale liberalisation of France's economy (and in doing so, following a conservative-liberal consensus which had been growing in the Finance Ministry since the late 1970s), but harnessing it to a European project that was given the stamp both of neo-Gaullism (Europe as an economic pole independent of the United States) and of social democracy (Europe as a model of the social market economy) transformed an economic constraint into a political opportunity. At the very least, it was an impressive sleight of hand; arguably it was the major achievement of his presidency. Mitterrand also had accomplices. Helmut Kohl, throughout a long chancellorship (1982–98), explicitly linked his ambitions for Germany to the development of Europe, and sought thereby to make them as non-threatening as possible. Jacques Delors had left his post as Mitterrand's finance minister to become the longest-serving president of the European Commission (1985–94). Determined to make Europe a model of economic growth and of social justice, Delors was also keen to use the opportunities offered by the European agenda – notably the Single Act and EMU – to reinforce the standing of the Commission generally and of his office in particular. Mitterrand did not share the quasi-federalist views of Delors, and in common with other European leaders was careful, in the Maastricht negotiations, *not* to link Europe's new areas of competence to big increases in the Commission's powers (hence the intergovernmental character of the second and third pillars of the new EU). But Delors was an important ally because of his ability to bend European rules in France's favour on occasion, his skill at reinforcing

French networks in the Commission, and the reassurance he offered the public that integration was a French project. Like Delors, Mitterrand was in no doubt of the historic importance of what he was attempting. Of detractors who criticised him for tying the hands of future generations, he answered 'They understand perfectly. That is exactly what we have tried to do; to arrange matters so that no-one will ever be able to turn the clock back.'

There is a sense in which the Chirac presidency, in relation to Europe, has been everything that Mitterrand's was not. The first president of Gaullist family since Pompidou, Chirac had distinguished himself during the first direct European election campaign, in 1978–79, by a histrionic attack on the Giscardians as agents of a foreign power (by implication, Germany). This did not mean that Chirac's European views were a throwback to those of the General; indeed, he fought the 1984 European elections in tandem with the same Giscardians he had denounced five years earlier, supported the Single European Act, and after much hesitation threw his weight behind a yes vote for the Maastricht Treaty (which, given the narrowness of the result, might be said to have saved the whole project). It would be more accurate to say that Chirac has approached Europe, like most political issues, as a tactician without excessive regard for consistency, but always with one eye firmly fixed on domestic politics, in sharp contrast to de Gaulle. In the 1995 presidential campaign, that meant setting himself apart from his orthodox rival Balladur by espousing a form of left-wing Euroscepticism, questioning France's obligations under the Maastricht Treaty and even calling for a further referendum before the final transition to the euro. No such referendum was held after Chirac's victory, and within six months he had effectively adopted the *balladurien* sound-money policies that he had attacked in the spring. With fewer fixed views, Chirac also lacked comparable partnerships to those of his predecessor. Kohl was politically weakened towards the end of his chancellorship, and would lose power in 1998 to a Social Democrat, Gerhard Schröder, for whom Europe was a lower priority. The replacement of Delors by Jacques Santer as Commission president, meanwhile, signalled the reining-in of the Commission as a leading actor, a tendency that would be confirmed when the Santer Commission resigned in 1999 after being investigated by the Parliament over corruption allegations.

There were many reasons why the treaty negotiations of the 1997–2004 period – Amsterdam, Nice and the constitutional treaty of 2004 – were more ill-tempered and nationally competitive than the SEA or Maastricht. They included the inherent difficulty of institutional reform to accommodate a much larger EU, France's long cohabitation of 1997–2002 and the rise of Euroscepticism among many European electorates in the post-Maastricht period; but to these should probably be added the absence of a mutually trusting and confident core group of integrationist European leaders. Chirac's priorities were often defensive: preserving France's (near) parity of representation with Germany on the Council of Ministers, despite Germany's greater population (he achieved this, at the cost of much ill feeling, at Nice, though not in the 2004 treaty); ensuring that a Frenchman, Jean-Claude Trichet, would be the second governor of the European Central Bank; resisting Schröder's attempts, in the framework of the Agenda 2000 initiative, to cut Germany's net budget contribution; safeguarding the CAP, at least for a few more years. The opening of the debate on a European constitution, in 2000, saw both Chirac and indeed his Socialist Prime Minister Jospin cut very cautious figures by comparison with the more radical Germans, especially Foreign Minister Joschka Fischer. The one area in which Chirac might be identified as an innovator was in the Common Foreign and Security Policy, where he seized the opportunity presented by the British acceptance of an EU-linked defence structure to promote the constitution of a 60,000-strong Rapid Reaction Force dedicated to peacekeeping and peacemaking tasks in Europe. The CFSP remained, however, on a strictly intergovernmental footing, and the experience of the 2003 Iraq war, while it found Chirac deeply in tune with most European publics in his opposition to war, was also a striking display of continuing foreign policy divisions between France and Britain, the two leading European powers in terms of defence capability. But Chirac will be remembered above all as the president who called the referendum of May 2005 on the European constitutional treaty, again largely for tactical reasons, and lost it owing to a combination of an unfavourable context (rising unemployment and an unpopular government), a vigorous no camp (given the unexpected reinforcement of Laurent Fabius and a large wing of the PS) and a poor yes campaign that alternated between silence and arrogant claims that the no supporters were irresponsible and anti-European.

French presidents vary in their commitment to European integration, but their freedom to translate such commitment into practice has also depended on context and on the backing of other member states. Even de Gaulle's refusal of supranationalism during the Empty Chair crisis won the tacit connivance of other governments, reluctant to see a too-powerful Commission. Presidents who have sought to further integration have always acted in partnership. Of the partners available, none has been more important than Germany. That relationship, though now less kind to France than in the past and less powerful itself in a larger EU, remains crucial to France's position in Europe.

The Franco-German partnership: reconciliation, collusion – and decline?

There are three reasons for the centrality of the Franco-German alliance to the process of European integration. The first arises, simply, from the size and population of the two countries: with over 60 per cent of the inhabitants of the Six, any Franco-German partnership was bound to be the dominant one in the original EEC. Even in 2004, France and (united) Germany still had a very substantial 31 per cent of the EU25's population. The second reason is that the partnership represents a union of opposites: compromises that satisfied these two states would usually (though not, as we shall see, always) be acceptable to most of the others too. Their oppositeness has had three dimensions. In terms of institutions, France's Jacobin tradition has tended to favour European policies that are intergovernmental and nationally minded, while the Germans' federalism at home, combined with the need, under the post-war Federal Republic, to share sovereignty in order to regain a parcel of it, has left them more comfortable with notions of federal government and divided or shared sovereignty at a European level. In terms of international relations, French governments have viewed Europe as an asset but also a possible constraint in their efforts to maintain France's rank in world affairs; for Germany, for most of the history of the EU, Europe has been a means to regain lost status. France sought to escape dependence on the United States during the Cold War; for Germany, geography made such dependence both inescapable and vital. Geography continued to differentiate perspectives in the two countries after 1989, with the Germans more obviously ready than the French to promote stability to the East by welcoming the countries of Central and Eastern Europe – Germany's historic backyard – as soon as possible, and the French more reticent. In economic terms, finally, French *dirigisme* contrasted with German 'ordo-liberalism': that is, a form of capitalism in which the state is expected to play a regulatory role, and firms to accept their social responsibilities, while employees expect to be involved and trusted, but where state ownership and planning *à la française* have little place. The German obsession with price stability, born of experiences of currency collapse after both world wars and reflected in the charter of the Bundesbank, guardian of the deutschmark, differed sharply from France's relatively high tolerance of inflation before the 1980s. German industry demanded not only European outlets but relatively free world markets, since non-EU countries absorbed nearly 60 per cent of German exports in 1993; French agriculture demanded protection and subsidy. Any compromise on these wide-ranging political and economic differences, therefore, would usually represent a broad enough tent to accommodate the preferences of most other member states.

The third reason for the importance of the Franco-German partnership was that despite their profound and wide-ranging differences, the two countries have established and nurtured a special, bilateral relationship within, but distinct from, the structures of Europe. The symbolic and emotional underpinning of that relationship – reconciliation – and the fact that each was indispensable to the other for a peaceful and prosperous Europe, were complemented by other, distinct purposes for each country. For France, the 'axis' meant not only harnessing Germany's economic power to promote French leadership of Europe, but also the 'containment' of its eastern neighbour, the assurance that Germany would neither return to its old expansionism (a remote prospect), nor try to carve out a new sphere of influence in Eastern Europe, nor drift into neutralism or an accommodation with the Soviet Union. On the German side, the alliance was the means to achieve a discreet return to the international arena, an avenue to make proposals without arousing the suspicions of other European partners, a balance to Germany's all too dependent relationship with the United States, an assurance that France would not engage a full-scale *rapprochement* with the Soviet Union (with which de Gaulle had signed a treaty of friendship in December 1944).

What Haig Simonian called the 'privileged partnership' was enshrined in the 1963 Élysée Treaty. This included provisions for consultation in foreign policy and defence, on the model of the Fouchet Plan: defence ministers were to meet every three months, military chiefs of staff every two months, and the president and the chancellor every six months at least. These institutional arrangements were complemented by the creation of the Franco-German Economic Council and Defence and Security Council in 1988; from 2003 the two countries even began holding joint full government meetings. The treaty also provided for reinforced cultural co-operation, from which tens of thousands of exchange students on both sides of the Rhine have benefited. In 2004, three Germans even graduated from ÉNA and joined the French civil service, while Chirac agreed with Schröder to reinforce the teaching of German in French secondary schools and vice versa in order to resist the growing popularity of English as an EU language.

The importance of the Élysée Treaty needs qualifying in five ways. First, the institutions have been less important in themselves (indeed, neither the two councils created in 1988 nor the joint programmes on specific policies supposedly linked to the joint government meetings have worked with the expected regularity) than as the basis for more informal relationships and networks, both at the civil service level and at the summit. Second, while this quite weakly institutionalised partnership has never been seriously endangered since 1963, its vitality has varied greatly according to both personalities and the international and economic contexts. The latent potential for Franco-German conflict, noted above, has surfaced most readily during the chillier relationships between the French president and the German chancellor – de Gaulle/ Erhard, Pompidou/Brandt, or Mitterrand/Schmidt, or to a lesser extent Chirac/ Schröder – and in times of economic difficulty. The failure of EDC in 1954 or of the Snake in 1976, or the setback of the Empty Chair crisis (with de Gaulle retrospectively accusing Commission President Hallstein of using his office to promote German interests) are all cases of such breakdowns. Third, it is also the case that determined opposition from other states may still block a Franco-German project: the Fouchet Plan was initiated by France, backed by Germany, and torpedoed by the Benelux countries. Fourth, it is even true that an excessive focus on the Franco-German tandem ignores the agenda-shaping capacities of other actors – smaller states (which made much of the running in early negotiations leading to the Treaty of Rome), or (in the case of the Single Act), business, transnational networks and even the Commission. Finally, within Europe, the Franco-German couple has no conventional, institutionalised power; it neither makes rules nor distributes money.

Despite these caveats, the most successful Franco-German partnerships at the top have been extremely creative in terms of policy achievement: the implementation of the customs union and launch of the CAP for de Gaulle and Adenauer (chancellor from 1949 to 1963); the launch of the European Council, directly elected parliament, and the EMS for Giscard and Schmidt (chancellor from 1974 to 1982); the Single Act and Maastricht for Mitterrand and Kohl, who met on an almost monthly basis from 1982. This string of successful joint initiatives testifies to the power of the couple, however informal, to shape Europe's agenda and institutions. Hence the (exaggerated) view that the partnership is an unstoppable motor of integration: that Franco-German initiatives always succeed. A more modest, and more realistic, version of the same view is that while the partnership cannot invariably dictate to Europe, it often can; and it also wields a veto power over major projects, such as large-scale reform of the Common Agricultural Policy. Either way, France's special relations with Germany have provided a formidable lever with which to exercise European leadership.

Relatively uncontentious for the first thirty years or so after the Treaty of Rome, this view of the Franco-German partnership has been open to challenge since, approximately, German unification. Three arguments may be suggested: that France's influence in the couple has declined; that the couple itself has diverged politically since 1989; and that the capacity of the couple (as well as of France) to promote its own agenda and to sideline unwelcome initiatives has therefore diminished.

The decline of French influence within the couple is hard to dispute, at least in principle. Before 1989, as we will see in a later section, France had already been forced to make adjustments towards a German low-inflation economic model. German unification and the end of the Cold War provoked a more radical shift, to France's disadvantage, in the balance of Franco-German interests noted at the start of this section. This was not just a matter of Germany's greater post-unification population, which would translate in due course into greater representation in the European Parliament and, under the draft constitution, the Council of Ministers. More important was that with sovereignty as well as unity recovered at the closure of the post-war European order (the last Russian troops left the East German *Länder* on 31 August 1994, and on 8 September the forces of the Western allies left Berlin), Germany had less use for

France as a partner for a return to the international community, and less of the pre-1989 republic's need to share sovereignty in order to regain it. In addition, France's nuclear weapons were of no very obvious relevance in the post-Cold War world, their possession therefore a trump card of dubious value, and French claims to European diplomatic leadership correspondingly less credible. Finally, it could be argued that the Germans, burdened as they were by the absorption of their own Eastern *Länder*, were no longer prepared to pay for the privilege of being led by bankrolling the EU budget and, in particular, by subsidising French farmers through the CAP. Each of these points, though, needs qualifying. If France was no longer the only political heavyweight in the duo, it remained Germany's main European partner, bound by decades of close co-operation and – still – by the fact that Germany can not behave quite as if it was simply Europe's most powerful member state. In the short term, German unification – despite Mitterrand's initial but short-lived public misgivings – provoked an accelerated convergence between the two countries that gave much of its shape to the Maastricht Treaty. Chancellor Kohl was persuaded by Mitterrand into a definite commitment to EMU as part of the price of winning European (and especially French) acceptance of unification. And Mitterrand himself was readier to accept the political union sought by Kohl as a means of securing Germany's links with Western Europe. A decade later, German attempts to shift the burden of CAP finance through the Agenda 2000 discussions in 1999 could still be outmanoeuvred by the French, with strong leadership from President Chirac. Even in 2000, France was still not *behaving* as a junior partner.

There are also, however, arguments – aside from the budgetary point made above – to suggest divergence between the two countries in many policy domains. In foreign policy, a newly assertive Germany was quick to recognise and then to back Croatia in the Yugoslavian wars of the early 1990s; France's lingering sympathies initially remained with Serbia. Germany, concerned to ensure stability beyond the new eastern border of the Oder–Neisse line, supported early eastward enlargement; France, alarmed at the budgetary implications, dragged its (or Europe's) feet, helping delay the start of serious negotiations with Central and Eastern Europe till 1999. French attempts to give greater substance to a 'social Europe', based on the Social Protocol signed at Maastricht, received limited backing from Germany in the 1990s. At Amsterdam, attempts by the newly elected Prime Minister Jospin (with rather little support from President Chirac) to build an 'economic government' into EU institutions to offset the power of the European Central Bank were all but rejected by Chancellor Kohl, aside from the face-saving device of a 'jobs summit' later in 1997. More generally, the half-baked character of the Amsterdam and Nice treaties testified to the failure of the two countries to reach a strong joint position in advance of the intergovernmental conferences. At Nice, Chirac let it appear too readily that his main objective in negotiating pre-enlargement adjustments to EU rules was to preserve French parity with Germany on the Council of Ministers; he succeeded, but at the cost of bullying Chancellor Schröder in ways that did much to discredit the Treaty and the French presidency that had led up to it. The Germans' *bête noir* of 2004 was French finance and industry minister Nicolas Sarkozy, described by Schröder as 'incredibly nationalist' for his refusal of a partnership between Siemens and the troubled French engineering firm Alstom, and for his support of a raid by the French firm Sanofi against the Franco-German pharmaceutical giant Aventis. Sarkozy, for his part, took to musing in public about 're-thinking the central core' of an enlarged EU, and stressing multilateral relations with other big European states, especially Britain, rather than the face-to-face dialogue with Germany.

The divergence argument, though, can also be exaggerated. The Franco-German couple is built, not on perfect harmony on all issues, but on the mutually beneficial transcendence of conflicts. From that point of view, the Sarkozy affair was no more than the usual stuff of trans-Rhenish dialogue (of which one variety is name-calling for the benefit of a domestic political audience). Contrasting diplomatic postures in the 1990s had been resolved with French acceptance of enlargement, military co-operation between the two countries in the Balkans (notably in Kosovo and Macedonia), and the common promotion of the CFSP. France and Germany were notably at one in their opposition to the Iraq war of 2003. The summoning of a constitutional convention in 2002 was preceded by a public dialogue, over the summer of 2000, between French and German leaders over the future 'final state' of Europe's institutions. Even the two countries' budgetary policy converged, in 2003, when they both recorded budget and public sector deficits of over 4 per cent of GDP, 1 per cent in excess of the limit set by the Stability and Growth Pact of 1997. Finally, the central institutional reforms of the draft constitution – the election of a Commission president by the European Parliament, the election of a European Council president for two-and-a-half years, the creation of a single post of European foreign minister – arose from a Franco-German proposal, itself a characteristic compromise between French intergovernmentalism and German federalism. Whatever the ultimate fate of the treaty, this is not the behaviour of two countries that are cutting their mutual ties.

Evidence can also be presented for the declining power of the couple. Their bid to include ambitious provisions for 'strengthened co-operation' (or, effectively, a multi-speed Europe) at Amsterdam was watered down by smaller member states, anxious to avoid a Franco-German directory in the EU. Six years later, the flagrant disregard of both Germans and French of their obligations under the Stability and Growth Pact in 2003 led to their censure, first by the Commission and then by the European Court of Justice. At almost the same moment, the provision in the Convention's initial draft constitution that a vote on the Council of Ministers would be carried by a double majority of 50 per cent of member states and 60 per cent of the EU's population, provoked fierce opposition from Poland and Spain, which claimed that the two 'big countries' were downgrading their effective voting rights against the Nice Treaty. After the failure of the Rome summit in December 2003, it took the election of a new government of Spain in March 2004, and the raising of the thresholds to 55 per cent of member states and 65 per cent of the EU's population, for the revised draft to be accepted in June 2004. Under this arrangement, the Franco-German couple would need, to carry a proposal on the Council of Ministers, to win the support of twelve more states representing a population of 154 million in addition to their own. Similarly, the veto power of the Franco-German couple should not be overstated; their joint support for the CAP, under strain in the 1990s, could not prevent its substantial (if belated) reform from 1999 on. More critically, perhaps, the EU's liberalising thrust, in the areas of both competition policy and regulatory policy, challenged both *dirigisme* and German ordo-liberalism, more than the leaders of either country could have expected when they signed the Single European Act and the Maastricht Treaty. From a neo-functionalist perspective, this is relatively easy to understand: the unanticipated energies released by the Single European Act, in particular, and channelled by successive competition commissioners in alliance with powerful transnational business groups, were too powerful even for the Franco-German couple to resist. With enlargement, the prospects of doing so will recede further because of the free-market public policy leanings of the post-Communist entrants of Central and Eastern Europe. Once again, though, this vision of a declining couple can be exaggerated. It is noticeable, for example, that the Commission's strictures on their infringement of the Growth and Stability Pact were only backed up by a minority of the ministers of the euro zone, and that the 'penalty' paid by France and Germany was not the fine threatened by the Amsterdam Treaty but the setting-up of a committee aimed at rendering the Pact more flexible. And the high content of Franco-German ideas in the draft Constitution hardly speaks of a couple in process of marginalisation.

Compared with the view of a near-omnipotent Franco-German 'motor', the current power of the tandem to shape the future of Europe is indeed limited. It is also the case that as Europe has enlarged, both France and Germany have engaged in dialogue with a wider range of partners (France with Britain over defence questions, for example, or Germany and the Eastern countries over trade). Given their diminished weight in the Council of Ministers, they could hardly do otherwise, and this greater promiscuity will complicate the Franco-German relationship. The centrality of that relationship is not about to disappear, but its continued resilience will depend more than ever on a strong joint leadership sometimes lacking in recent years. It will also need to rely on both partners' success in coalition-building, both at the summit and at the day-to-day administrative level. It is to the apparatus for the co-ordination and furtherance of French public policy in Europe that we now turn.

Europe, the French state and French public policy-making

It was, ironically, Chirac who, as Giscard's young prime minister in 1974, declared that 'European policy is no longer part of our foreign policy.' Even thirty years later, he was not quite right. European high politics remain – fully in 'normal' times, and to a significant extent even under cohabitation – part of the presidential *domaine réservé*, and the Quai d'Orsay, France's Foreign Ministry, still plays a leading role in much of France's European diplomacy under the watchful eyes of the Élysée. But France, like other EU member states, has faced a relentless process of adjustment to Europe: of creating the tools for adequate representation of the French position in European institutions and for the transposition of European directives into French law; of mobilising, not only the structures of central government, but also regional and local authorities and even interest groups to respond to and shape the widening spread of European interventions; of negotiating (and where possible limiting) the adjustments to French public policies required by European legislation. To some extent, this is a task of co-ordination, of ensuring that 'France speaks with one voice': not straightforward, but hardly new either to the *énarques* at the heart of the French executive. In other respects, however, effective policy advocacy in Brussels demands the honing of less familiar skills: not only the forceful expression of a coherent national viewpoint, but the construction of wide-ranging, often loose, coalitions straddling networks in the Council of Ministers, the Commission, the European Parliament, even the Court of Justice, as well as the ever-growing number of lobbyists and interest groups attracted to the European capital. This untidy process poses a challenge to officials steeped, still, in France's Jacobin tradition. The policy outcomes, moreover, now include directives that are less than enthusiastically received by policy-makers within

France; hence, in part, a record of European policy implementation among the slowest in Europe.

Speaking with one voice? France and European policy-making

Europe's institutions positively encourage fragmented, sectoralised policy-making. The Commission, though small compared with almost any national bureaucracy (about 25,000 civil servants), has regularly been described as a collection of baronies rather than a close-knit organisation; its directorates have often been inclined to deal, if they can, directly with the officials and interest groups that concern them directly in each member state. Moreover, while the Commission still enjoys (almost) exclusive rights to initiate legislation, the legislative role is shared by the Council of Ministers and, increasingly, the European Parliament, which is itself notably sectoralised. The lack of congruence in sectoral responsibilities as between the Commission, the Council of Ministers, the European Parliament and member states is a further problem.

France enjoys clear advantages in negotiating this quagmire. The Republic remains, despite decentralisation, one and indivisible; subnational authorities play a modest – though not negligible – role in European affairs compared to some of their European counterparts. Detailed parliamentary, or indeed press, scrutiny of the executive's foreign policy performance is very limited. Once the presidency has put its weight behind a policy proposal, no significant voices of dissent are likely to be heard within the governing majority, at least outside periods of cohabitation. Hence the French talent for grand European initiatives: they come more easily from Paris because the French president has greater freedom of action in this area than the prime ministers of most parliamentary democracies. It is true that France's core executive, like that of any member state, suffers from interministerial and intraministerial conflicts that are both structural and contingent, and that these are compounded in France by the twin-headed nature of the executive, by tensions between officials and *cabinets*, and by the often difficult relations between the ministers of Foreign Affairs and of European Affairs, especially when the latter has a direct line to the Élysée. On the other hand, the machinery of co-ordination at the summit of the executive, in both the Élysée and Matignon, is well-oiled and, as we have seen in Chapters 4 and 5, usually works. Even at times of cohabitation, whatever the adversarial relationships between staffs (especially in 1986–88), presidency and government found a *modus vivendi* that allowed presidents to attend European summits in tandem with their 'adversaries' from the government – prime minister or foreign minister – without betraying significant disagreements to their European partners, whether on the European Council or at the more important of the meetings of the Council of Ministers. The French ambition – to be at the avant-garde of integration, but on French terms – is underpinned at the highest levels by reasonably effective arrangements for policy co-ordination.

Much European policy, of course, is not decided at the summit. Europe's key legislative institution (though subject to competition, since the Maastricht Treaty, from the Parliament) remains the Council of Ministers. However, a mere 10–15 per cent of the business of the Council of Ministers is really transacted by ministers (and even this total does not exclude meetings of the Council of Ministers to which one or more member states, including France, send their most senior diplomat in Brussels, the Permanent Representative, instead of a minister). The rest is decided, either at meetings of Europe's Committee of Permanent Representatives (COREPER), whose meetings account for some 15–20 per cent of Council business, or at working groups within the COREPER structure (some 70 per cent of Council business). It follows that the quality of a member state's input into Europe will depend significantly on the quality of its permanent representation in Brussels, and on that of the instructions and briefs that the permanent representation receives from the member state.

Here, too, France possesses some of the technically strongest machinery of co-ordination in Europe. France's permanent representation in Brussels, at some 160 people including 60 Grade A administrators, is one of Europe's largest – equal to that of the United Kingdom, smaller only than Germany's, and staffed with high-level Quai officials interspersed with experts from each of the technical ministries and, since 1989, attachés for relations with business. The permanent representation receives most of its Parisian instructions and briefs from the SGAE (Secrétariat Général des Affaires Euro-péennes, formerly the SGCI). Established in 1948 with the initial purpose of organising co-operation with other European states receiving Marshall aid, the SGAE operates under the responsibility of the prime minister (although the minister for European affairs reports to the foreign minister) and is the central government organ of co-ordination of EU business at a day-to-day level. With some 180 staff in 2000, the SGAE deploys an impressive mix of senior officials from every ministry and *corps*, though usually led by diplomats from the Quai (turnover is high, but SGAE high-flyers usually move on to influential posts elsewhere in the civil service). Its primary task is to supply officials and ministers in Brussels with negotiating briefs. More precisely, it involves monitoring the opportunities and threats inherent in upcoming legislation; elaborating negotiating strategies; assessing possible trade-offs with other member states; ensuring that French positions are agreed in time for the Council or COREPER meetings con-cerned, and possibly arbitrating between different positions, with or without the prime minister's help, or that of his *cabinet*, depending on the importance of the issue; and foreseeing the national legal implications of Court of Justice proceedings. In 1992, according to Anand Menon, a daily average of five conflict-resolution meetings took place at the SGCI, preceded by lengthy telephone calls. The SGAE's divisions cover the whole gamut of European business (Economy and Finance, the Common Agricultural Policy, juridical and institutional issues), in addition to others such as documentation, energy, regional transport, social affairs, trade and relations with Mediterranean countries.

For the French, therefore, effective European policy-making depends to a great extent on the success of the SGAE at ensuring that French priorities are clearly formu-lated and uploaded as effectively as possible to the European level. The SGAE–permanent representation model for doing this is a centralised one – as are those of the British and Danes but not, for example, the much less co-ordinated Germans, or other states like Austria, Belgium, or the Netherlands where the lead ministry on each issue is responsible for delivering a national position. In France, co-ordination is at a premium, and most observers agree that the SGAE–permanent representation tandem does its job well, at least in a technical sense. French positions are, in general, clearly formulated and consistent across ministries. The permanent representation works to its briefs from the SGAE – and the SGAE takes account of views from the permanent representation in formulating them. French officials in the permanent representation have a reputation as tenacious negotiators, with a preferred tactic of stating and restating the French position until partners are worn down.

That said, there are eight respects in which the French system has been open to criticism. First, co-ordination is good but not perfect. The ministries with the best-established European roles – Agriculture, Finance, Transport, or Foreign Trade – also have the best informal Brussels networks in Commission, Council and Parliament, and deal directly with them (informal networks helped keep the system going during the first cohabitation, when the Chirac government sought to bypass the SGAE that Mitterrand had left in place, and above all its highly political chief, Élisabeth Guigou). Individual ministers are also prone to take initiatives without sufficient consultation within the government. That prime ministers from Debré to Juppé have felt it necessary to send circulars stressing the requirement that all official French contact with Brussels should pass through the SGAE indicates the extent to which this rule is honoured in the breach.

Second, co-ordination is less well underpinned than in the UK by a culture of information-sharing between and within ministries, meaning that early warnings of impending measures are sometimes missed. Third, although the SGAE works to the prime minister, it sometimes lacks the authority to produce a real synthesis between the positions of different Parisian players. Sometimes, indeed, it simply reproduces them in microcosm. Disagreements may be resolved by splitting the difference rather than thinking strategically, or by producing a fairly general brief rather than the more detailed instructions normally expected in the British representation.

A fourth difficulty is the downside of the French interest in speaking with one voice. Several observers have remarked that France's smooth and co-ordinated system of representation, though very focused on the issues at hand, may lead to inflexible positions, in which opportunities for coalition-building with other member states, and the linkage of different sectors to produce package deals, is lost. These practices have become increasingly important with the spread of QMV on the Council, and with enlargement; no longer can the Franco-German axis be counted upon to carry the day; a close knowledge of other states' negotiating positions, at least, is of great importance. Paradoxically, the open, flexible, pragmatic and consensus-seeking style of the Germans, Dutch, or Swedes, however poorly co-ordinated compared to that of the French, may work better when it comes to building winning coalitions. A series of events in the early 1990s, including the McSharry CAP reform of 1992, the de Havilland incident (when a Franco-Italian consortium was prevented, by the Commission and in the name of competition, from aquiring a competitor), the attempt to agree 'voluntary' quotas on Japanese imports in 1991, or the reform of the Common Fisheries Policy in 1993, all showed the weakness of the traditional French style of negotiation. Inflexibility, moreover, is mathematically more effective at obstructing (by constituting a blocking minority against a proposal) than at achieving (bringing together a qualified majority); it is therefore unsuited to a country seeking to carry a positive proposal, as France sometimes does.

Fifth, the French have been criticised as excessively reactive in their approach to European legislation. Instead of seeking to influence the (often relatively junior) officials who draft legislation in the first place, French officials in the past tended to engage with a legislative proposal only after it had taken official form, by which time it had been on the legislative agenda for weeks or months: too late to secure significant changes. The same is even truer of the implementation stage. The notion that 'a phone call to Jacques Delors can solve everything', common in the early 1990s among French officials and their business interlocutors, was probably unrealistic even during Delors's Commission presidency, and has certainly become so since.

The sixth area of concern lies in the apparent difficulty of the French in making strategic linkages. Neither the SGAE nor the European Affairs Ministry possesses a strategic planning group. The traditional division (especially marked during cohabitation) between routine affairs, channelled through the SGAE, and sensitive political questions treated by the Élysée, has meant the needless exclusion of the undoubted expertise of the SGAE in the highest-level negotiations, as well as a lack of sensitivity to cases where a multitude of low-level negotiations may point to a larger political issue. This is probably compounded by the lack of frequency – monthly not weekly – with which France's Permanent Representative in Brussels reports home to Paris. The low level of involvement of the SGAE in the Amsterdam inter-governmental conference, especially at the early stages, has been held up as an explanation for the uncertain French performance there.

Seventh, it is argued that although the French are good at winning high-level posts in international organisations generally, and the Commission in particular (a Frenchman, for example, has headed the Commission's Agriculture directorate since 1958), they have been less effective at securing influence in the lower levels of the Commission, to say nothing of other EU institutions like the Parliament, where other member states such as Britain and Germany have been considerably more active. There was also, for a long time, a lack of synergy between France's Commission officials and the administrative elite in Paris; indeed, it was only in 1990 that ÉNA began to give its future high-flyers a serious grounding in European affairs. This has changed somewhat in recent years: for example, France's permanent representation now has an official dedicated to the job of maintaining good relations with French staff working in the Commission (including via a newsletter) and, in liaison with Paris, of securing promotions for them at the right moment. But experience in Brussels is still less valued than experience in Paris for promotion purposes within the French administrative elite.

Finally, the French have been slow, not least because of a traditional Jacobin mistrust of 'partial', intermediate interests, to involve interest groups in their European negotiations This has had two drawbacks: the French negotiators bypass not only the expertise, but also the access to Europe-wide policy communities that the groups may have to offer; and the groups feel no sense of responsibility for any legislation on which they have not been consulted. Again, there are signs that this has changed, notably with Prime Minister Édith Cresson's creation of a *Cellule Entreprises et Communication* (CEC), and at the local level of *Groupes d'Études et de Mobilisation*, including senior civil servants, interest group representatives, and local elected officials, with the aim of improving France's poor record on mobilisation of interest groups concerned with business relations from the 1990s, but this is not as far as some other member states have gone.

In short, there is a case for arguing with Menon that France, having been highly effective at shaping the early European Community to its own requirements, has been much less successful in adapting to the more complex business of policy-making in the newer Europe. Here, systems centred on member states have been complemented – even swamped – by a plethora of new players, whether from the Parliament, the lower levels of the Commission, the bureaucracy that has developed around the Council of Ministers, and above all interest groups, which national governments have had to incorporate as best they can into shifting networks and alliances. In this Europe, to speak with one voice is no guarantee of a favourable outcome.

Implementation: the slow man of Europe?

If the French appear to have lost influence, or at least their former preponderance, in the day-to-day making of European policy, they have not distinguished themselves in its implementation at the national level either. This is despite France's system of government undergoing a process of 'Europeanisation' comparable to those of other member states. Until the late 1970s, Europe was the business of a handful of ministries only: Foreign Affairs, Foreign Trade, Finance, Agriculture. Since then, all French ministries (except for the ex-servicemen's ministry, which has no counterpart anywhere in the EU) have acquired European sections, whether as divisions in their own right within the ministry (Foreign Affairs has had a *Direction de la coopération européenne* since 1993, as well as a ranking *ministre délégué* since 1984), or as a spread of units within a range of existing divisions (Finance may send as many as eight different representatives to SGAE meetings). When the SGAE gives formal notification of upcoming European legislation to relevant ministries and (under legislation of 1990–94) to both houses of the French parliament, it opens a process of debate in which issues of transposition – the reformulation of general European directives into national legislation – are immediately raised and discussed, with a view to facilitating implementation once the European legislation is adopted. The SGAE now holds regular meetings with parliamentarians.

Despite these developments, France's record on the implementation of European policy is, to say the least, undistinguished. At the end of April 2004, France ranked fourteenth out of fifteen member states for notification (to the Commission) that national measures implementing European directives had been taken: only Greece had a poorer record, while Eurosceptical member states like the UK and Denmark were among the best implementers. This was, moreover, *after* French efforts to catch up: some twenty directives were quickly transposed into French law by decree in January 2004, after a package of fifty had received the same treatment under the Jospin government in 2000.

The significance of France's rank order in itself should not be exaggerated; the difference between an average level of notification of European directives of 98.43 per cent of the total and France's, at 97.57 per cent, is after all slight. But five other factors confirm an impression of French reluctance to implement European law. First, as we have seen in an earlier chapter, France's courts were slow to recognise the full import of the European treaties: it took the Cour de Cassation seventeen years to agree that European law had primacy over national law, in 1975 (in the *Cafés Jacques Vabre* case); the Conseil d'État waited until the *Nicolo* case of 1989 to come to broadly the same conclusion. Second, France's record has been consistently poor since the 1990s. Only Italy, over the five years from 1998 to 2002, received more formal notices of infringement of European directives from the Commission than France. No other member state, over the same period, was referred so often to the European Court of Justice for infringements: indeed, the total number of French referrals, at 138, stood at two-and-a-half times the EU average. Third, the French record of implementation has been poorest in core areas of EU activity: it is in the fields of competition policy and the Single Market, the environment (where France has hardly legislated at all without being told to by the EU, and then only late and unwillingly), and employment and social affairs, that France's record has been the furthest below the European average. Fourth, some at least of the failures to implement have been highly political. The 1979 European wildfowl directive remained without any satisfactory translation into French law for two decades because of pressure from the bird-shooters' lobby and its political wing, CPNT. There were also delays in liberalising the telecoms and energy markets, in both of which French public-sector monopolies had reigned supreme for half a century. The EU directive opening the market for electricity distribution was transposed into French law in February 2000, a year after the official deadline, and envisaged a fully competitive market for domestic users only in 2007. Even then, the French legislation cushioned the position of the national monopoly, EDF, by requiring firms operating in France to respect French public-sector salary and benefit rules. None of this prevented subsidiaries of EDF from competing for shares of the energy market in member states that had liberalised earlier: in 1998, 48 per cent of nuclear-produced electricity consumed in the EU was of French origin. Legislation on telecoms liberalisation was only put onto the French parliamentary timetable in February 2004, years after France Telecom had purchased the British mobile telephone operator Orange. Indeed, Maire McLean has argued that French firms have systematically benefited from late liberalisation, exploiting opportunities offered by early liberalisers abroad while resisting deregulation at home. Fifth, slowness to implement has been paralleled by an occasionally cavalier attitude to European commitments freely entered into by France, the most extreme example being the Stability and Growth Pact. In September 2003, as France crashed through the 3 per cent ceiling on public-sector deficits specified in the pact, Prime Minister Raffarin stated that 'My first duty is to French jobs, not to producing accounting equations or to solving mathematical problems in order to satisfy some office in some other country'. Four months later, the Commission referred France, along with Germany, to the Court of Justice for infringement of the pact.

France's leaders have regularly presented their country as being at the forefront of European integration. France disposes of one of Europe's most impressive (though by no means unproblematic) bureaucracies at the domestic level and at the domestic–European interface. French governments enjoy an enviable capacity to legislate at speed when they want to. Moreover, both politicians and senior officials in Paris have periodically seen Europe as a lever with which to impose modernisation on what they see as France's antiquated state structures – while being able to blame the costs for affected groups on Brussels. Despite this, France's record of engagement with the day-to-day realities of European policy-making often appears more characteristic of a weak state passively accepting, with ill grace, measures imposed from outside. One reason for this is that the liberalising thrust of much European legislation since the Single European Act directly challenges the *dirigisme* to which successive French governments, both of the Left and (less intensely, but with a weather eye to public-sector unions) the Right, as well as large sections of the voters, remain attached. Ideologically, the French notion of public service can be seen as an expression of Jacobin beliefs in equality through uniformity: the equality of citizens as users of public services is guaranteed, in principle, by the same services being available from a single provider across the national territory. Doubtless such ideological attachments would wear thin if France's public services were believed to have performed poorly. Such has not, however, been the case; polls in 2001 recorded satisfaction levels of 74 per cent or more for hospitals, postal services, and EDF and France Télécom. And the penetration of foreign markets by French public-service monopolies is more often a source of satisfaction than a subject for political debate in France. In this context, French governments have embraced some liberal legislation (in the case of the SEA) or accepted it from a minority position (in the case of some later competition legislation), but have rarely – with the exception of the Right in 1988 – presented it as a positive good. Nor have they – or French MEPs – been successful in creating a European rampart against further liberalisation by promoting *le service public à la française* as official European policy. Attempts to persuade either the Commission directly or the Parliament to adopt a standard European framework for public services that would allow competition to be limited and subsidies to be freely given have so far proved inconclusive, as have similar efforts to include precise notions of public service in the draft constitution.

Discernible in the implementation record, in short, is the impression of a European agenda escaping France. This impression is considered in more detail in the next section.

France and European policies

Controlling the European agenda is valuable for a member state because it offers the chance to upload national policies to Brussels – to transform national policy into a universal model for Europe. To achieve this, as Yves Mény argues, the successful state will need to be able to engage with the policy at the earliest moment of formulation; to sell a policy paradigm capable of widespread recognition to the point of dominance; and to demonstrate a competitive advantage in its own way of doing things. The main attraction of such uploading is that it is other states, and their companies, that bear the costs of adjusting to Europe in the policy area concerned. France has successfully uploaded in the past; it has had more difficulty since the mid-1980s.

This section considers France's ability to secure Europe-wide acceptance for a French agenda in three policy areas: agriculture, the complex series of changes involved in the Single European Act and Economic and Monetary Union, and the Common Foreign and Security Policy. It opens with the Common Agricultural Policy, a prime example of successful uploading for France. The CAP corresponded to the interests of France's strongest agricultural constituency, the larger farmers who controlled the FNSEA, and to a French policy model. By the 1990s, however, that model was challenged and then largely discredited both outside Europe and by many of France's partners. French success, with German help, in keeping the CAP alive in its old form beyond 2000 should not obscure the policy's longer-term vulnerability. France's relationship to the Single Act and Economic and Monetary Union was more complex: both were sought actively by Mitterrand and his governments, although both arguably opened up unanticipated and unwelcome consequences for France. The third case, the Common Foreign and Security Policy, is a case of a policy central to France's view of the proper (ambitious) role of Europe, but one in which the French have so far had great difficulty in imposing their views.

The Common Agricultural Policy

If anything could justify the German description of the EU as *ein Französicher Garten* (a French garden), it is surely the Common Agricultural Policy (CAP). The Rome Treaty of 1957 has sometimes been described as a bargain between Germany's industrial exporters and France's agricultural ones. That is partly true, though with the important rider that the CAP, and especially the subsidies central to it, were fixed at a high level in order to accommodate politically influential German farmers, whose efficiency was lower than that of many of their French counterparts. What is crucial, however, is that the Mollet government was determined to secure the inclusion of a common market in farm produce in any treaty (the CAP appears in articles 32–38), and that de Gaulle was equally resolved on the implementation of such a market. As the General argued in the memoirs of his presidency, France had enough farmland to feed twice its population and therefore needed export markets; but for farmers to export at world prices while simultaneously enjoying a decent standard of living would require subsidies that no French government could afford to pay alone. Hence the 'relentless efforts' deployed by France in the early years of the EEC – including threats to sabotage the whole EEC project – in order to secure acceptance by the Six of a common market in foodstuffs within which the burden of farm subsidies would be shared – in other words, a Community which maximised France's advantages as an agricultural producer while spreading the costs among all member states.

If France's success in achieving this owed much to de Gaulle's persistence, it was also due to the widespread recognition within Europe that agriculture was a unique type of economic activity, for four reasons. First, memories of wartime and post-war privations served as reminders of the unique importance of secure food supplies. Second, the rural world remained both central to the identity of most European states and politically over-represented in all of them. Third, the market in farm produce is intrinsically unstable because supply is dependent on the weather and demand is inelastic; this leads to extreme price fluctuations, with the attendant risks of ruin for farmers or penury for consumers, unless the market is regulated. Finally, the multitude of small producers typical of the farm sector cannot respond quickly to changes in demand, of which they might in any case be only barely aware. For all of these reasons there was a European consensus that agriculture required intervention to stabilise markets sufficiently for the necessary investments to be attractive to farmers. Added to that was a liberal argument that a European market for farm produce would both be more stable than national ones, and better guarantee improved productivity. This was a highly favourable context for French negotiators to press for a French-style subsidised and protected agriculture to be uploaded to the European level. They also found a strong ally in Belgian Foreign Minister Paul-Henri Spaak, who chaired the committee that drew up the initial Common Market proposals.

The declared aims of the CAP in the Rome Treaty were to increase agricultural productivity through technical progress, to ensure decent living standards for farmers and farm workers, to stabilise markets, to ensure secure food supplies for Europe and to bring food at reasonable prices to the tables of consumers. The mechanisms were underpinned by three principles: market unity (farm produce could circulate as freely within the Community as industrial goods), Community preference (or protectionism vis-à-vis non-EEC producers) and solidarity (the Guarantee Fund would be Europe-wide, not national). The last two principles were victories for France, which effectively required other member states to provide markets for French produce and to pay for the privilege. The essential mechanisms of the CAP were, first, a system of price-fixing for each product, centred on the notion of a target price (set sufficiently high for less efficient farmers to make a living) and an intervention price (a floor at which surplus produce would be bought up with money set aside for the purpose in a European Agricultural Guarantee Fund); secondly, a system of variable import levies, corresponding to the difference between the costs of imports and the intervention price, ensuring that imports could not compete on price; and third, subsidies that would allow EC producers to export at world prices (usually lower than European ones) while receiving the same income as if they had sold into Europe.

As it came into operation for cereals in 1967–68, and for a range of other products (rice, milk, butter, sugar beet, sunflower oil, beef, olive oil, wine) shortly after, the CAP had significant merits. Above all, it gave European farmers the incentives to modernise and raise productivity to such an extent that the Six were self-sufficient in most food products by the early 1970s. The objectives of improved productivity, stabilised markets and secure supplies were thus rapidly achieved. Moreover, the CAP was for a long time the only truly common European policy. As such it offered a source of hope for federalists frustrated at the progress of integration, an opportunity for European governments to collaborate on a day-to-day basis, albeit in one sector, and a paradigm for how joint European policies might look in other areas.

Yet the dysfunctions of the CAP became equally clear over the decade following its launch. In the first place, productivity improvements rapidly led to overproduction uncorrected by market mechanisms: the open-ended promise of the CAP meant that surplus production was simply bought up by the Guarantee Fund and stored, at the taxpayer's expense, in what became known as wine lakes and butter mountains. Secondly, consumers also subsidised farmers by paying prices above world rates for their food; in this sense, the CAP objective of bringing food to consumers at reasonable prices was not achieved. Third, the principle of the single market in farm produce was undermined by the impact of currency fluctuations and the measures taken to adjust for them. The notion of single Europe-wide prices for farm products was inevitably threatened by the devaluation of any member state's currency, beginning with that of the franc in August 1969. The corrective mechanisms adopted – 'green' currencies, with different values from those of the everyday currencies they shadowed, for the calculation of farm prices, and monetary compensatory amounts payable when goods passed between member states – hampered the free movement of goods, and vastly complicated the working of the CAP, raising its administrative costs and leaving the true volume and distribution of subsidies unclear to all but specialists. Fourth, the opacity of the policy's workings were an invitation to a series of grey practices or straightforward fraud under which Community produce was subsidised twice, or imports were disguised as European goods, in order to attract guarantee money.

The fifth problem lay in the sheer size of CAP funding, which ran at some three-quarters of the total EEC budget through the 1970s, with no clear indication as to how it would be controlled as long as subsidies were linked to production and production was limited neither by market mechanisms nor by regulation. As the budgetary constraints faced by member states grew in the 1970s, the open-ended nature of CAP finance attracted growing criticism. But the EEC's agricultural spending still doubled – and more – between 1975 and 1990, against a 48 per cent growth in member states' GDP. Sixth, the predominance of the CAP in the EEC budget enshrined a system of unequal financial returns from the EEC. Big agricultural producer countries, especially France, were net beneficiaries of the EEC budget. Industrial nations tended to be the biggest net contributors. Within the original Six, this meant West Germany first and foremost. For the Germans, this was long relatively uncontroversial, once the negotiations of the 1960s had been completed, because of the other benefits that the Federal Republic drew from the EEC. The British, by contrast, were less tolerant, and Margaret Thatcher sought a rebate on the UK net contribution within a year of coming to office in 1979, obtaining it on a lasting basis by 1984. Seventh, the distribution of CAP funds was as unequal between producers as it was between nations. As long as subsidies were directly linked to production, the CAP would favour the largest farmers: in the 1980s, the Commission estimated that about 20 per cent of Europe's farmers received some 80 per cent of subsidies under the CAP. Poverty among small farmers persisted, compromising the farm income objective of the CAP. While farm populations fell throughout the EEC, Commissioner Sicco Mansholt's proposal, made in 1970, to redirect subsidies away from production towards income support for farmers leaving the land was only minimally followed (just 7 per cent of the CAP budget was allocated to this 'guidance' fund in 1995). Indeed, critics of the CAP such as Wyn Grant have argued that the policy is of less benefit to most farmers than to those in ancillary occupations: to suppliers of farm goods (machinery, fertilisers and pesticides), to financiers of farm debts, to owners of food storage facilities, to food processors and last but not least to professional frauds. Eighth, the CAP increasingly distorted world trade in foodstuffs. Third World countries, backed by left-wing friends in Europe, attacked the destructive effects on their economies of agricultural dumping through export subsidies. Europe's developed rivals, especially the United States, complained of the CAP's combination of export subsidies and internal protectionism. At the opening of the Uruguay Round of world trade talks in 1985, the United States placed agriculture firmly on the agenda for tariff reductions, as it had not been in previous rounds of the General Agreement on Tariffs and Trade (GATT). European resistance to this demand risked wrecking a new round of reductions and depriving European industrial and service firms that stood to benefit from freer world trade. The final criticism of the CAP, of which consumers and green groups became increasingly aware in the 1980s, was of its environmental and health impact. The 'productivism' inherent in the CAP rewarded intensive, high-volume agriculture with large inputs of fertilisers and pesticides and the attendant ills of torn-up hedgerows, destruction of animal habitats and exhaustion or pollution (or both) of water supplies; payments to tobacco growers and vineyards subsidised lung cancer and alcoholism.

France has been a staunch defender of the old-style CAP. The broad economic reasons appear obvious. The CAP had enabled France to become the world's second exporter of farm produce, processed and not, with exports equivalent to some 75 per cent of those of the United States by the early 1990s, most of them in subsidised products such as wheat, meat, butter, or milk powder. It had encouraged the development of a world-class food processing industry in France, of which the dairy giant Danone was the emblem. And even in the 15-member Europe of 1995–2004, France attracted nearly a quarter of all guarantee revenues, for 15 per cent of the EU's population. But there were other, more political reasons as well. The quasi-corporatist relations between the FNSEA and French governments – unsuccessfully challenged by the Left between 1981 and 1984 – and the domination of the FNSEA by large producers, long ensured France's devotion to a productivist, high-input model of agriculture that rewarded large-scale units. Finally, Jacques Chirac's symbiotic relationship with the FNSEA, dating from his period as agriculture minister between 1972 and 1974, ensured that the leading farm union had a more or less unconditional advocate in one of France's two leading right-wing politicians.

France could not, of course, carry Europe alone in its commitment to the old CAP. The Germans, with their own marginal farmers, well-organised in a politically pivotal lobby, were the key partners, but Spain (the third major beneficiary after France and Germany), and even efficient and export-driven countries like Denmark and the Netherlands, also gave frequent support to French positions – or at least, were not consistent supporters of reform. Of course, the old CAP did not exclude modest adjustments under pressure. Thus the Fontainebleau summit of 1984 settled the most pressing concerns by setting up a long-term rebate on the UK budget contribution, and by limiting production for the first time through the introduction of dairy quotas. Four years later, a special European Council meeting in Brussels fixed future increases in agricultural funding at 74 per cent of the overall increase in the European budget, and greatly expanded non-agricultural regional spending, ensuring that the CAP's share of the total European budget would fall to 'only' half in the 1990s and roughly 40 per cent by 2005. Neither reform, however, changed the CAP's essential characteristics: in the late 1980s, Europe's farm policy still appeared locked into a pattern largely dictated by de Gaulle a generation earlier.

It was unlocked in 1992–93, largely under pressure from the Uruguay Round of world trade talks organised under the auspices of the General Agreement on Tariffs and Trade (GATT). At France's insistence, agriculture had been left out of all previous GATT rounds of tariff reductions. By the early 1990s, however, it had become clear that Europe's trading partners would make significant reductions in agricultural subsidies a condition of any new GATT agreement. That determined the 1992 reforms to the CAP, bearing the name of Agriculture Commissioner Ray MacSharry, which in turn allowed an eleventh-hour Uruguay Round agreement the following year, incorporating a reduction of 36 per cent in export subsidies over six years. The events of 1992–93 were a turning point for the CAP, less because of their short-term consequences for European farmers (indeed, the CAP budget rose and most French farmers enjoyed a significant rise in incomes up to the mid-1990s) than in two political breaches that were opened. In the first place, the MacSharry reforms uncoupled some farm subsidies from production for the first time, by establishing payments to farmers who set aside a proportion of their land from production. Such direct payments to farmers, it was argued, distorted trade much less than price subsidies. Necessary to a GATT agreement, this step created a dangerous precedent for the old CAP, for subsidies once dissociated from the price mechanism became more transparent and more vulnerable to political attack. Second, the GATT negotiations, despite the concessions won by the Europeans at French behest (the Americans drastically scaled down their demands for cuts in farm subsidies from 90 per cent to a third), ensured that European agriculture would no longer be the preserve of a small and largely autonomous agricultural policy community. Henceforth a wider group of stakeholders, including European heads of state and government and commissioners for trade and industry, were to consider agricultural policy as part of their legitimate concerns insofar as it affected their wider political objectives. Finally, the French agricultural policy community, if not precisely sidelined, was left fighting a rearguard action against reforms that it had neither wanted nor shaped nor even really prepared for. The MacSharry reforms, in other words, could be identified as the moment when the farm policy successfully uploaded by France to Brussels some thirty years earlier became officially open to challenge from all sides.

The mismatch between France's attachment to the old-style CAP and the changing priorities of France's European partners continued for much of the 1990s. Post-Uruguay Round Brussels began to consider a wider variety of approaches to agriculture, ranging from the liberalism of countries like the UK, chiefly preoccupied with cheap food for the consumer, to a range of more recent concerns such as food quality (a growing worry in the aftermath of a series of food crises of which BSE was by far the most serious), animal welfare and 'multifunctionality', a notion that embraced the social and environmental role of agriculture. Meanwhile the FNSEA, and to a significant extent French governments before 1997, remained attached to a traditional view of the CAP and above all to France's share of the guarantee budget, and sceptical of new objectives. The French ability to veto change in farm policy, however, was somewhat reduced, for three reasons. First, as institutional views of the EU would predict, what was possible for a single large state in a Europe of six, or even nine or ten, and unanimous voting became more difficult in a Europe of fifteen where a qualified majority could change the policy. Second, France's allies in defence of the CAP were less reliable, whether because of concerns to limit the policy's cost before the big eastern enlargement of the EU or, in the case of Germany, because of a wish to limit contributions to the EU budget, and an interest in the notion of 'renationalising' CAP payments to do so. Third, France's own FNSEA-led policy community became significantly weaker in the 1990s, both because there were fewer farmers (of the 1,017,000 French farms of 1988, only 664,000 survived in 2000, a drop of a third in twelve years) and because the FNSEA was weakened within the sector. Support for the alliance between the FNSEA and the CNJA (the young farmers' confederation) at elections to Chambers of Agriculture dropped from 62 per cent in 1989 to 56 per cent in 1995 and 52 per cent in 2001, while votes for the left-wing Confédération Paysanne, the farmers' union most critical of productivist agriculture, rose from 18 per cent in 1989 to 27 per cent twelve years later. At the same time the FNSEA also faced criticism from within its own ranks without precedent since the 1960s, and from a CNJA increasingly reluctant to play the role of the FNSEA's youth branch. Inside the FNSEA, the larger cereal and dairy producers, increasingly allied to the food-processing industry in a system of vertical integration, have seen their hegemony questioned by smaller farmers, ready to contemplate a greater emphasis on quality products with higher added value, and on environmental protection. These tensions have spilt over into the FNSEA's links with right-wing parties, now somewhat more distant than in the earlier days of the policy community.

This contributed to a period of remarkable fluidity both in Europe's agricultural policy and in France's relationship to it. At the European level, a series of reforms, undertaken in 1999 and 2003, and planned for 2005, have had a common thrust: to uncouple subsidies from production, thus rendering the CAP compatible with the world trade agreement expected to emerge from the Doha Round of talks begun in the new millennium; to align European prices progressively on world prices, maintaining only a (low) European floor price for each product; to compensate farmers for losses of sums received as price supports; but to replace these compensation payments progressively by payments to sustain projects such as rural development, conversion to organic farming, or the switch of agricultural land to forestation or permanent meadows; to make subsidies dependent on the fulfilment of environmental conditions; and to give member states more autonomy in the application of this new 'second CAP'.

The relationship of French governments to the new CAP divides partly, but only partly, on Left/Right lines. The Jospin government's 1999 *loi d'orientation agricole* embraced the multifunctional thrust of the new policy, seeking a speedy build-down of compensation payments and the conclusion with farmers of *contrats territoriaux d'exploitation* that would include socio-economic and agro-environmental objectives to be achieved over five years in return for subsidies. Jospin's agriculture ministers, Louis Le Pensec and Jean Glavany, also succeeded (where their left-wing predecessors of the early 1980s had failed) in ending the FNSEA's *de facto* monopoly on dialogue with the government and broadening access to include the Confédération Paysanne, consumer groups and even environmental campaigners; significantly, too, the *loi d'orientation* won the support of the CNJA, despite its former allegiance to the FNSEA and the Right. Even Raffarin's right-wing government, though it quickly suspended the *contrats territoriaux d'exploitation* in favour of a cheaper alternative, accepted a measure of environmental conditions for farm subsidies, and a transfer of some aid to rural development; nor has there been any return to the old FNSEA monopoly. At the same time Chirac, both during and after the 1997–2002 cohabitation, was capable of intervening in European agricultural policy, using traditional methods – deals with the German chancellor – to secure more traditional French aims. At the first of these meetings, in 1999, he both succeeded in limiting Chancellor Schröder's budget-cutting ambitions and reduced the scope in the revised CAP for the build-down of compensation payments (and also, therefore, the money available for 'multifunctional' priorities). At the second, in 2002, the Chirac–Schröder tandem agreed, much to the irritation of Prime Minister Blair, that the CAP should be perpetuated at current levels of finance until 2013 and that new member states should be admitted to a full share of its benefits only gradually.

From one point of view, France has maintained an impressive grip on agricultural policy. The CAP budget remains undiminished (even as the number of farmers, French and European, continues to fall); France's share of it remains at a quarter, with East European farmers being admitted gradually; the scope of innovative provisions for 'multifunctionality' has been limited, with the most prosperous farmers in France retaining the bulk of national income from subsidies even after the basis of those subsidies changed. Two things, on the other hand, have been lost, in ways that point to a longer-term transformation. One, at the European level, is the *automatic* character of the old CAP; its successor is open for renegotiation every five or six years, in fundamental aspects including its overall size and purpose, as well as mere details. At the national level, meanwhile, the policy community which underpinned the old CAP has been eroded, whether in terms of the numbers of farmers or the FNSEA's unity and hegemonic position. Despite Chirac's best efforts, therefore, the old elites of the FNSEA cannot be expected to dominate France's agricultural policy-making indefinitely, nor can France expect to do the same within Europe. France in future years will face choices over both alliances (the Franco-German tandem, or a more varied group of agricultural countries including new member states like Poland or Hungary), and the strategies deployed by such alliances (retaining as much as possible of the old CAP, or embracing the social and environmental goals of multifunctionality, or accepting the liberalisation sought by the OECD or the World Trade Organisation (WTO)). The nature of the choices made will not only determine the shape of French agriculture but, given that one half of France's farmers are due to retire by 2015 and may not be replaced, whether France will retain a significant agricultural population at all. The outcome will also reflect France's ability to maintain, under a new form, what was always the clearest reflection in Brussels of French economic priorities.

France, Europe and the neo-liberal paradigm change

A major external source of transformation of the CAP was the neo-liberal paradigm shift observed in all developed Western nations from the early 1980s onwards and outlined in Chapter 1. This change affected France's whole economy, not just its farmers. More unpredictably, it transformed France's relationship to Europe.

Under the first three presidencies of the Fifth Republic France succeeded to a significant degree in squaring the European circle. Although the Fouchet Plan had failed, France's diplomatic role in Europe, underpinned by the special relationship with Germany, was second to none, with European political co-operation an opportunity rather than a constraint. In institutional terms, the Europe of the 1960s and 1970s remained overwhelmingly intergovernmental. Walter Hallstein's activist Commission of the early 1960s had been successfully reined in by the Empty Chair episode. The Luxembourg compromise safeguarded unanimity on the Council of Ministers. Though Giscard was the 'most European' of the first three presidents, the development of the European Council during his presidency had given a further intergovernmental tilt to the institutional balance, only partially compensated by the direct election of the European Parliament. France's own institutions remained relatively unaffected by Europe. The EEC remained a division of foreign policy, and the primacy of European law over the law of member states was not yet fully recognised within France. For most of the French, this was a low-impact Europe. Over its first generation, Europe's direct effect was felt in few lives outside the thinning ranks of French farmers, in few ministries outside the Quai d'Orsay and Agriculture.

The EEC's economic record, too, conformed broadly to French objectives. The CAP, which suited France's governing elites very well, was the only truly European policy. More broadly, the disappearance of customs barriers had furthered the type of economic modernisation which the Gaullists would have sought anyway. What was important for de Gaulle, and above all for Pompidou both as prime minister and as president, was to marry France's *dirigisme* to the new European economy: to accelerate the construction, often through state-sponsored mergers, of 'national champion' firms that would compete at the highest level in a tariff-free Community and in the wider world.

By 2004, on the other hand, France had accepted or even actively promoted a series of transfers of political sovereignty and of economic autonomy that would have been unthinkable to the policy-makers of the Gaullist era. Europe's institutions had been given a significant supranational tilt by the general extension of QMV on the Council of Ministers, and of the co-decision procedure involving a greater role for the European Parliament; and France's long-standing parity of representation with Germany in the Council of Ministers had been signed away (subject to ratification) in the European Constitution of 2004. The core attributes of sovereignty into which France had accepted extensions of European intervention included immigration and asylum policy under the Maastricht and Amsterdam treaties; and the invasive competition policy of the Single European Act, pregnant as it was with dangers to France's public services and nationalised industries. EMU embodies the surrender of monetary sovereignty; a measure at least of budgetary autonomy was lost with the Stability and Growth Pact. France's supreme judicial bodies, the Cour de Cassation and the Conseil d'État, had both accepted the primacy of European over national law. The low-intensity, intergovernmental Europe of the first generation gave way to a Europe whose impact on the government machine was no longer limited to the ministries of Foreign Affairs, Finance, and Agriculture, but extended to every government department and to regional and local authorities as well; a Europe that engaged French interest groups, divided parties and even, on occasion, mobilised citizens, permanently upsetting the delicate equilibrium hitherto achieved. This qualitative leap in the integration process from the mid-1980s had multiple causes, including the neo-liberal paradigm shift; the end of the Cold War and the resulting transformation of France's diplomatic position, and especially of Franco-German relations, noted above; successive enlargements; and – for the constancy of French policies should not be overstated – the decisions of France's own leaders since the 1980s, all of whom have drawn inspiration from the Gaullist approach to Europe rather than following it in every detail.

But the process would be inconceivable without the fallout from the economic crises of the 1970s. These crises had two main origins: the release of inflationary pressures resulting (largely but not wholly) from the oil price rises of 1973–74 and 1979–80; and the break-up, in August 1971, of the Bretton Woods system of fixed exchange rates between the currencies of the developed capitalist world. These developments called into question France's *dirigiste* model, and brought in their train a switch to economic orthodoxy that found expression in the European initiatives of the 1980s.

Dirigisme had served France well for most of the post-war boom years of the *trente glorieuses*. French GDP growth regularly exceeded rates in the UK and the United States by 1 or even 2 per cent, the OECD average by a smaller one, and even (narrowly, at the end of the period) Germany's. But two characteristics of *dirigisme* made France especially vulnerable to the crisis. The first was what Élie Cohen has called the inflationary social compromise. France's growth in the *trente glorieuses* was, in a real sense, financed by inflation, as state-controlled banks paid negative real interest rates to savers and supplied cheap capital to firms whose debts then shrank from year to year in real terms. The loss of competitiveness resulting from inflation triggered periodic monetary adjustments within the Bretton Woods system: there were eight devaluations between 1944 and 1958, and while de Gaulle held the franc's value for a decade, the higher wage costs conceded in May 1968 forced him into desperate measures (including tough exchange controls) to hold its parity the following November before leading to a new devaluation under Pompidou in August 1969. Secondly, Cohen has characterised *dirigiste* France as 'capitalism without capitalists'. France's national champions, whether state-owned or not, were seriously under-capitalised by Anglo-Saxon standards. They prospered thanks to the efforts of the state, which paid for research in publicly owned laboratories, supplied low-interest loans (to favoured firms) through the big publicly owned banking sector, placed domestic orders with attractive advances (through state-owned firms such as Air France for Concorde, the SNCF for the high-speed train, or Électricité de France for the nuclear industry), prospected foreign markets through the Quai d'Orsay, guaranteed major export deals such as arms contracts or big civil engineering projects, and – in the crisis years after 1974 – stood ready with a bail-out for champions in trouble. Meanwhile, the tissue of small and medium-sized firms, increasingly important to the economies of Germany or Italy, had suffered underdevelopment under *dirigisme*. Officially viewed as backward and narrowly protectionist, they were increasingly marginalised from government policy-making and from its benefits (hence, in part, the attraction of militant small business groups like Gérard Nicoud's CID-UNATI); by the late 1970s, France's small and medium firms (with fewer than 500 employees) received a total of 3.5 per cent of state subsidies for research and development.

Third, as a country without significant natural energy resources of its own, France immediately suffered the consequences of oil price rises in terms of inflation (up to 15 per cent in 1974), the balance of external trade (a surplus of $773 million in 1973 became a deficit of $3.9 billion in 1974), and the demand for public spending (which rose from 35 per cent to 43 per cent of GDP in the Giscard presidency). Fourth, devaluation became a vastly riskier tool of economic adjustment to inflation, both because, in the post-Bretton Woods world, exchange rates were fixed by markets rather than by governments, and because any devaluation would further increase the cost of imported oil and gas, which was paid in dollars, with the risk of a self-perpetuating spiral if no effort was seen (by the markets) to be made to bring inflation under control. Fifth and finally, in the aftermath of May 1968, governments were highly reluctant to place additional burdens on wage-earners. The effect of May 1968 was compounded by Giscard's very narrow victory over the Left in 1974, and by the poor relationship between the two major parties of the Right – each keen to blame the other for unpopular measures – thereafter. Real wages continued to rise through the Giscard presidency, with the costs of adjustment being borne by business (employers' social security costs rose by the equivalent of 3.7 per cent of total French GDP), and by the unemployed.

An obvious life raft in this newly dangerous environment was improved monetary co-ordination with European partners, already planned in the 1971 Werner Report on monetary union. The attraction of the Snake and, later, of the EMS, was that by linking European currencies to one another, with modest room for fluctuation, they offered some of the security of Bretton Woods, albeit in a single region of the developed capitalist world. Their drawback, noted by Pompidou as early as 1971, was that they tied the French franc to Europe's strongest currency, the deutschmark, and thus to a monetary guardian, the Bundesbank, whose constitutionally defined anti-inflationary mission was at the polar opposite to France's post-war economic practices. The cost of (relative) exchange rate stability, therefore, would be the partial or total subordination of French economic and monetary policy to Bundesbank requirements: in other words, a concerted attempt to tackle inflation even at the price of high real interest rates, low or zero growth and rising unemployment with the political unpopularity that would result. The reluctance of France's governments to go down this road is illustrated by France's erratic record in the Snake, with the French franc in at the start in 1972, out in January 1974, back in in July 1975, and finally out in March 1976. France's record in the EMS was more consistent, but Barre's attempts to bring inflation down after 1978, although they brought him, and ultimately Giscard, unpopularity in plenty, were undermined by the political legacy of the inflationary social compromise.

The crisis of March 1983 was caused by the collision between the French tradition of inflation and devaluation – accelerated but not initiated by the Socialists' victories of 1981 – and the German-dominated anti-inflationary logic of the EMS. With the franc under intense pressure from the markets, despite two devaluations in 1981 and 1982, Mitterrand faced a stark alternative, to leave the EMS or to seek another monetary realignment within it. Each choice entailed much broader implications. Advocates of an exit from the EMS suggested a whole alternative economic strategy based on protectionism, for example by invoking the emergency clauses of the Rome Treaty that allowed temporary protectionist measures in the event of a balance-of-payments crisis. In the long term, this would barely have been compatible with continued EEC membership. The choice (which Mitterrand eventually favoured) to devalue but to remain within the EMS, on the other hand, effectively required convergence with West German economic and monetary policy. This was all the more the case when Mitterrand sought France's third monetary realignment in three years, as he aimed to achieve this by a small devaluation of the franc (limiting the franc's fall against the dollar, and thus the rise in imported energy prices) coupled to a revaluation of the deutschmark and other strong European currencies like the Dutch florin. The Kohl government's conditions for accepting such a realignment were that France should adopt effective measures on interest rates and public spending that would reduce inflation and limit the need for further devaluations. The outcome of the March 1983 crisis – reinforcing, it is true, a growing neo-liberal conviction among France's administrative elite, starting with the Trésor division of the Finance Ministry – was to develop a consensus, across parties and governments of Left and Right, in favour of low inflation and a strong franc. But cutting inflation removed one of the key motors of France's post-war economic system by depriving major French firms of their old sources of inflation-fuelled finance. Henceforth they would begin to seek capital on international markets – with the encouragement of governments, concerned to keep their own spending down. Reforms to the (formerly sluggish) Paris bourse were undertaken within a year of the March crisis to facilitate this; the privatisations undertaken by the 1986–88 Chirac government, though still effected within a highly controlled, statist framework, represented a big *rapprochement* between French firms and international capital markets.

The developments in France's European policies that followed from the 1983 crisis were both greater and slighter than might have been expected from the immediate turning point. They were greater because Mitterrand chose to embrace Europe, instead of socialism, as the centrepiece of his policy: no member state was more instrumental than France in accelerating the pace of integration in the decade after 1983. They were slighter because, although the anti-inflation policy removed one mainspring of *dirigisme*, no government attempted or wished to sweep the whole structure away. No member state was more concerned than France to preserve state-owned monopolies in public services, or to retain the power to bail out major firms in difficulty, or to head off moves towards a fully federal Europe.

French priorities in Europe under Mitterrand, in short, remained as ambiguous as those of earlier presidencies. But in the changed post-1983 context, the stakes of treaty modifications to achieve further integration were higher. Among possible projects, the Single Market was the idea for a relaunch of Europe that commanded the widest support among member states in the mid-1980s, certainly more than Delors's ideas about Social Europe. General European concerns about non-tariff barriers were complemented by more specifically French ones about German barriers squeezing out French goods, as well as by a belief that a unified European market would reinforce the position of European-based multinationals against American competition, and a wish to further free trade in financial and other services – this in the name both of French exports and of French access to capital markets. Remarkably, Mitterrand's government supported the goal of QMV on internal market matters, an acknowledgement of the slow progress made on the Single Market since it was first tabled in the EEC in 1968. In order to achieve these goals, however, the French had to accept encroachments on political and economic sovereignty. Institutionally, the most obvious change was the introduction of QMV, which itself set in train a significantly more supranational legislative process with a greater role for the European Parliament. Economically, the 280-plus Single Market directives adopted by the end of 1992 included restrictions on common, long-standing French practices – state-promoted mergers producing monopoly firms, government subsidies to national champions, anti-competitive public procurement policies. The SEA provisions did not, it is true, affect everything: telecommunications and energy, for example, were initially left out. And there was always room for exceptions; with the SEA in force for a decade, EU member states were still subsidising economic activities – industry, services, agriculture, transport and mining – to the tune of 49 billion euros for the year 2002. But this figure had dropped by 27 per cent in five years, as the Commission scrutinised aid projects and cut them, refused them, or subjected them to conditions. The agreement in 1995 to a French government subsidy to Air France was given on the understanding that there would be no more. The historically large Crédit Lyonnais bail-out package of 1996 was made conditional on the bank's privatisation. In 2004, partly in response to the government help given to the troubled engineering firm Alstom (in the shape of the purchase of 31.5 per cent of Alstom's shares by the state), the Commission fixed as a general rule that any major firm should pay half the cost of any restructuring package itself before government aid became acceptable. In the long run, then, the existence of a competition policy with teeth, the inevitable corollary of the Single Market, represented a direct challenge to *dirigisme*.

Maastricht was at the same time a logical extension of the Single Market, with monetary union supported from the late 1970s by a small but influential intellectual community; a more specifically French initiative aimed at softening some of the rigours of the EMS; and a German project intended to reassure European partners in the wake of unification, even at the sacrifice of the deutschmark. Like the SEA, it entailed substantial costs and adjustments for France. For post-1983 French governments, EMS membership had meant being tied to the anti-inflation mission of the Bundesbank (or Buba). The Buba translated its mission into policy with an eye, not to wider European conditions, but to events in Germany – which meant, after 1989, a fierce struggle to master the highly inflationary consequences of unification and of the Kohl government's political decision to accept East German marks at parity with the deutschmark. And where the Buba led, notably in the matter of interest rates, other, weaker, currencies of the EMS had to follow – with an added premium on the rate to ward off a new, and always unpredictable, attack from the markets. According to the leading French economist Jean-Paul Fitoussi, real French interest rates ran at 5–8 per cent for over a decade. This was a formidable constraint on investment, growth and employment. For eighteen years after 1983, joblessness never fell below 9 per cent of the French labour force. It was the voters' main worry and the single most important cause of their propensity to throw out governments whenever they had the chance. If only, reasoned Mitterrand and his Finance Minister Bérégovoy, French bankers could sit alongside German and other colleagues at the table where Europe's monetary policy was decided, the verdict would be given with at least some thought to conditions in France. But that could only be achieved by monetary union. And the Germans would not concede monetary union – the dilution of post-war Europe's most successful currency with others of distinctly less promising pedigree – without stringent conditions. The European central bank, like the Bundesbank, must be quite free from political control. And to adopt the single currency, member states would need to respect the Maastricht convergence criteria – ceilings on inflation, interest rates, public-sector borrowing (no more than 3 per cent of GDP in any one year) and public-sector debt (not more than 60 per cent of GDP in total) – and its perpetuation as the Stability and Growth Pact at Amsterdam in 1997.

From the French point of view, then, the two big European initiatives of the 1980s, the Single Market and EMU, were part of a wider process of adjusting to the new, liberal, political economy as it took shape in the world of the late 1970s and beyond.

For that reason it is hard to separate the specific effects of European policies from what might in any case have been undertaken at national level to respond to the constraints of a global marketplace. That process has not been the disaster predicted by its gloomiest opponents. Indeed, the remarkable improvements in French business competitiveness over the period since 1983, analysed in detail by observers such as McLean and Schmidt, is reflected in a number of economic indicators. Over the eleven years preceding the entry into force of the Single Market on 1 January 1993, France had run an average trade deficit equivalent to 0.93 per cent of GDP; the eleven years from 1993 to 2003, on the other hand, saw an average trade *surplus* of 1.79 per cent. If this does not prove a relationship of cause and effect (falling oil prices also helped), it at least indicates that France was capable of holding its own in a free-trade Europe. Similarly, France enjoyed three years of unusually strong growth – above 3 per cent – in the period immediately before and after the final fixation of European exchange rates in January 1999.

It is also clear that an element of flexibility was in practice built in both to many Single Market provisions and to the Stability and Growth Pact. We have already noted that the tendency of the Commission has been to bear down steadily on anticompetitive practices rather than to halt them at a stroke. Its rulings have certainly affected individual cases (though the Commission has never forced a major French firm into bankruptcy by refusing an aid package), but since French governments had themselves taken a much more restrictive attitude to bail-outs after 1983, it is uncertain that the Commission had a major impact on the policy *in general*. Competition policy has also, as noted above, had a limited effect on French public services, with France complying late but benefiting from open markets in other member states. Similar remarks can be made about the overall impact of the Maastricht convergence criteria and then the Stability and Growth Pact. In the eleven years from 1981 to 1992, France's publicsector debt grew from 21.8 per cent of GDP to 39.6 per cent; by 2004, it had reached 64.7 per cent of GDP. In the Maastricht negotiations, the French had ensured that any decision to fine a member state for infringement of the criteria would be politically determined; when (with Germany) they infringed the criteria (on both deficits and debt, in 2003), they duly escaped the fines. If Maastricht has acted as a straitjacket on government borrowing, it has been a rather loose one – probably not much tighter than basic financial prudence would have imposed.

Despite this record, there are three reasons why the SEA and Maastricht signalled a transition from a low-impact Europe to an EU which was seen to have a direct – and often negative – effect on the lives of all French citizens. The first is the economic climate in which the two measures bedded down as central components of French economic policy. Between 1990 and 1997, French growth rates averaged a mere 1.4 per cent, including negative growth (–0.9 per cent) in 1993. Over the same period, France lost half a million jobs; even after the good years 1998–2001, total employment growth over the thirteen years 1990–2003 was a modest 6.8 per cent. In industry, employment fell from 4.3 million in 1990 to 3.6 million in 2003, an almost continuous fall amounting to 16 per cent. This record had a variety of causes, including a world recession in the early 1990s, affecting Britain and the United States as well as the euro zone states, and the long-term tendency of developed Western states to shed industrial jobs and to replace them with employment in the tertiary sector. Nevertheless, France's economy suffered all the more because this transition towards the euro was marked by a paroxysm of the franc–deutschmark relationship, as the Bundesbank imposed high interest rates on Germany to damp down the inflationary consequences of unification and the other central banks of the future euro-zone had to follow, with a further premium, or risk devaluation and the destabilisation of the euro project. It was this setting of real interest rates, in the name of the *franc fort*, at levels without precedent since 1945, and the resulting low growth and high unemployment, that fixed the association between Europe and the gloom of the French economic climate in the early to mid-1990s.

The second reason for the wider impact of the SEA and Maastricht was political. The attacks on EMU of left-wing and right-wing Eurosceptics are resumed in a single phrase, Jean-Pierre Chevènement's claim that 'the choices of Maastricht are the choices of unemployment'. Chirac's announcement, in October 1995, that France required an austerity plan to cut deficits 'if only to be able to join the single currency, to which we are committed' was an equally striking example of the unenthusiastic endorsement of EMU by a notionally 'favourable' leader (who had, it is true, run a distinctly Eurosceptical presidential campaign six months earlier). In both cases, 'Brussels' was transformed into a foreign scapegoat for domestic austerity policies – as it was by Raffarin in 2003.

Third, the neo-liberal constraints of the SEA and Maastricht were never balanced to any commensurate degree by the 'social' Europe, or indeed the European industrial policy, sought by French governments, especially of the Left. This is not to say that neither has existed. EU regulations, especially under the European Social Charter, launched in 1989 and incorporated into the Treaty of Amsterdam in 1997, cover a range of employee concerns including health and safety, maternity benefits and parental leave, the organisation and limitation of working time, and the rights of temporary, disabled, and young employees. But the social policy has been very far from generalising the French provisions on the working week, the minimum wage, social protection, or redundancy provisions at the European level. Indeed, the European Council's special meeting on employment at Lisbon in March 2000 set out an agenda for raising employment levels in the EU that reflected neo-liberal (especially British) approaches in both form and content: not regulation but loose voluntary co-operation between member states, not ambitious programmes of European public works, a favourite theme of Delors, but the emphasis on training and labour market flexibility preferred by the Blair government. European industrial policy has suffered a similar fate. True, an array of European-level research projects has been set up with French backing – Eureka and Race (advanced telecommunications), Euram and Esprit (information technology), Brite (industrial technology). Airbus, the Toulouse-based aerospace giant, is a prime case of a 'European champion' firm able to confront its American rival Boeing on equal terms. But Airbus is a unique case: no other enterprise, nurtured (and subsidised) by the public authorities on the French model, has risen to carry the torch of national champions to a European level. The research programmes have failed to create or safeguard any future for a European electronics or computer industry. And European competition policy has on occasion infuriated the French by preventing (in the case of de Havilland, where a Franco-Italian aerospace consortium was prevented from making a further acquisition in 1991) or hindering the development of major European groups.

Like the earlier treaties, the SEA and Maastricht were agreements by European leaders to tie their hands. Both were new departures in the firmness of their commitments. Both were also, however, in close continuity with earlier policies. The SEA was a deepening of Common Market provisions in a changed context. The EMU project had been discussed since the 1960s and was a extension of France's attempts to escape from the worst constraints of linking the franc to the deutschmark. Both had consequences that were substantially unforeseen or at least underestimated at the moment of agreement: the competition policy for the SEA, and the combination of high German-led interest rates and a world recession with the implementation of the convergence criteria for Maastricht. Neither was flanked by the type of social or industrial policy that the Social Charter or the various research programmes had appeared to promise, despite the attempts to further them of successive French governments, especially of the Left. As the EU impinged on the lives of the French in the 1990s, therefore, it was in a highly restrictive role, as an entity that enforced competition policy or demanded government spending cuts or tax increases in the name of an abstract liberal orthodoxy that was easy for its opponents to attack and hard for its advocates to justify. Europe as the creator of new social rights or the motor of new world-class industries was far less visible, either on the ground or in political discourse. Nor did the EU offer a focus of loyalty for its ability to cut a distinctive European figure in the world; the early steps towards a European foreign policy remained deeply hesitant.

The Common Foreign and Security Policy

French governments have consistently aspired, certainly under the Fifth Republic and even, to a degree, under the Fourth, to a measure of strategic independence from the United States. This is most readily explained in terms of a desire never to repeat France's total dependence, during World War II, on American military power for the liberation of national territory: an experience that contrasts radically with the British experience of partnership with the United States, albeit on increasingly unequal terms, over the same period. The notion of a 'Euro-Atlantic world', common currency in Britain or Germany, has enjoyed only minority recognition in France. France's aspiration to independence found expression in the launch of an atomic bomb programme in 1954, and its amplification into the development of a full, if small, nuclear arsenal during the de Gaulle presidency; and in the progressive withdrawal from the NATO integrated command between 1959 and 1966.

The most potentially attractive framework for the furtherance of France's aspiration, however, was Europe. Even a nuclear-equipped France could never expect to rival the superpowers' military strength. But a European defence structure led by France might reasonably aim to stand up to Washington (and to Moscow). This was the sense of the Fouchet Plan of 1961–62: a European foreign and security policy, centred on and led from Paris, linked to the Atlantic alliance but with a stronger and more independent voice within it. The plans were rejected by France's partners for two (well-founded) reasons: they (and especially the Benelux countries) feared both a Franco-German directorate over the nascent EEC and (especially with the continued exclusion of the UK) a loosening of Western Europe's ties with NATO. Even the residual treaty with Germany, signed in 1963, was only ratified by the Bundestag with a rider (included after vigorous lobbying from the United States) that the treaty would in no way affect Germany's commitment to NATO; for the West Germans, placed in the front line of the Cold War, the United States would always be preferred to France as an insurance policy against a Soviet move West.

The setback over the Fouchet Plan meant, not that de Gaulle scaled down his aspiration to independence, but that Europe henceforth formed no part of it. As a nuclear power outside the NATO integrated command (though within the Atlantic Alliance, and maintaining basic working relations with NATO through the Ailleret-Lemnitzer agreements), with permanent membership of the United Nations Security Council, good relations with non-aligned states, and a sphere of influence in its former African colonies, France under de Gaulle and after was still able to play a unique world role: as frequent critic of American foreign policies as they affected the Third World, as occasional broker between East and West (the Vietnam peace talks opened in Paris in May 1968) and as robust supporter of the United States at moments of Cold War confrontation – over Berlin in 1961, over Cuba in 1963 and over Euromissiles in the early 1980s. To this world role, Europe was of secondary importance. This was true even after the foundations of European political co-operation (EPC) were laid at The Hague in 1969 (significantly, after de Gaulle's resignation). Tested in the Yom Kippur War and the 1973 oil crisis that followed, EPC was wholly unable to prevent European states from scrambling to secure their own oil supplies with whatever means lay to hand, and with little more than formal reference to a joint European policy. When President Giscard d'Estaing met the Soviet President Brezhnev in Warsaw in 1980 during the last downturn of the Cold War, he barely informed his own foreign minister, let alone his European partners.

The end of the Cold War changed this largely ornamental status of political co-operation. The events of 1989–91 presented Western Europe with a series of opportunities and threats that appeared to point, in many ways, to the type of European foreign and defence policy that France had long sought. In the first place, the end of the Soviet threat removed acute dependence on the United States of the West European countries, West Germany first among them, for their security; indeed, the ensuing decade would see the American troop presence in Europe drop from 300,000 at the height of the Cold War to 100,000. Europeans could henceforth envisage, in principle, an independent future for defence and foreign policy. There was even an organisation apparently ready to take on this role: the Western European Union (WEU), created in 1948 as an alliance between the UK, France and the Benelux countries, eclipsed by NATO the following year, briefly revived in 1955 as a vehicle to accommodate West German rearmament, but largely dormant from then till the mid-1980s. For some Europeans, the WEU appeared an altogether more attractive organisation for collective security than NATO, whose purpose might be seen to have ended with the Soviet threat; and it was altogether too easy, in the aftermath of 1989, to underestimate the extent to which the United States, victors of the Cold War and the only remaining superpower, was committed to the reinforcement and extension, rather than the liquidation, of NATO. Second, among Germany's European partners, especially the British and French, German reunification generated a (largely misplaced) alarm and a desire to tie Germany in to Western Europe to ensure a continuation of Germany's stable and non-assertive foreign policy. Chancellor Kohl was broadly willing to accept such demands as a means of winning acceptance for reunification, claiming that he wanted a 'European Germany, not a German Europe'. Third, the end of the Iron Curtain raised the question of the future of former Communist states and their relations with Western Europe. One aspect of this was the question of their future entry into the EU. However, the question of the EU's Eastern approaches was posed with the greatest urgency in 1991, when civil war broke out between the central Yugoslav authorities in Belgrade and the secessionist states of Croatia and Slovenia (and, later, Bosnia-Herzegovina) – the first war on Europe's mainland since 1945. Each of these elements highlighted the glaring absence of a common European approach: Helmut Kohl's rapid recognition of Croatia and Slovenia, for example, provoked Mitterrand's public disapproval.

This was the context for the inclusion (strongly supported by France) of the CFSP as the new, second pillar of the Maastricht Treaty. But the early CFSP was an extremely weak institution, little more than a codification of EPC, for two main reasons. First, there was a general consensus that it should be wholly intergovernmental rather than *communautaire*, with unanimous voting, no role for the Commission and almost none for the Parliament. This view was shared as much by the French, reserved about surrendering core attributes of sovereignty, as by the British, who rejected outright any Europeanisation of foreign or defence policy. Second, the Franco-German concept of a CFSP linked to a European defence framework constituted by the WEU was not realised; other member states, especially the Atlanticist British and Dutch, were alarmed by any prospect of a transformation of the EU into a defence organisation that might seek to rival NATO. The Maastricht Treaty merely suggested that the CFSP 'might in time lead to a common European defence'. In the meantime, however, the CFSP's role was limited to joint actions varying from humanitarian assistance to political or economic sanctions, election monitoring and the formulation of 'common positions' – unanimously decided – on zones of instability such as Sudan, Haiti, or Rwanda. The nucleus of a possible European defence force existed in the Franco-German brigade formed in 1987, and expanded into the Eurocorps – officially 50,000 strong from 1992, and including troops from Spain, Belgium and Luxembourg; but this had no treaty status.

The poor practical record of the early CFSP was most evident in the case of former Yugoslavia, where European actions proved uncoordinated and, aside from some humanitarian assistance, largely ineffective; only the military and diplomatic engagement of the United States (through NATO, for the military strikes) secured a peace settlement in Bosnia-Herzegovina in 1995. Against that, the successful EU monitoring of Russian elections was a relatively minor achievement. Nor were habits of consultation between member states noticeably improved by the CFSP; President Chirac's unpopular decision to resume French nuclear testing in May 1995 was taken without any consultation with European partners. In retrospect, however, a failure at least as great as the EU's inability to secure peace in the Balkans without American help was its incapacity to engage rapidly and closely with its Eastern neighbours. De Gaulle's rhetorical flourish about 'Europe from the Atlantic to the Urals' was belied by considerable French reluctance, once the opportunity was there, to welcome the countries of Central and Eastern Europe into the EU. President Mitterrand had set the tone in June 1991, when he had offered a rather ill-defined European Confederation to the countries of central and eastern Europe but insisted that their full incorporation into the EU would take 'decades and decades'. Europe's foot-dragging over enlargement, in which France (far more than Germany) played a leading role, contrasted sharply with the actions of NATO, of which Poland, the Czech Republic and Hungary became full members in 1999. The fact that the United States was quicker than the EU to organise the return of the countries of central and eastern Europe into the ranks of the developed Western nations was to have a lasting impact on the loyalties of these states even after EU enlargement finally took place.

The outcome of the Bosnian conflict effectively set the seal on this first phase of the CFSP by establishing that NATO would continue to be the central arbiter of European security and that any attempt to set up a rival European security organisation was doomed to failure. From the mid-1990s, therefore, the French aspiration to a stronger

European defence role became centred on the development of a 'European Security and Defence Identity' (ESDI) *within* NATO, not on the building up of a more or less independent WEU linked to the CFSP (indeed, the WEU was finally dissolved in 2000). That supposed a *rapprochement* between France and NATO, which was effectively engaged after the election of Chirac to the presidency in May 1995 (Chirac quickly announced, for example, that France was resuming its full place at meetings of NATO Defence Ministers whenever they were held). The high point of the early ESDI was the 1996 Berlin summit of NATO, at which the United States gave its blessing to Combined Joint Task Forces (CJTFs) in Europe – military forces that could operate in Europe under NATO auspices but without full NATO participation. But the Berlin summit was slow to produce concrete results, for three reasons. First, it was long on principles but short on ways and means of constituting the CJTFs. Secondly, Britain, with France the strongest military power in Western Europe, still refused to contemplate a serious defence role for the EU. Third, France's *rapprochement* with NATO was short-lived. Negotiations expected to lead to the return of Chirac's France to the integrated command were mishandled on both sides and ended in disagreement over whether a French officer should be given NATO's southern command. In this context, the creation, under the Amsterdam Treaty of 1997, of a 'Monsieur PESC', a high representative for the CFSP who would also be secretary-general of the EU's Council of Ministers, still appeared to be more about style than substance, even if the first appointee, Xavier Solana, was a former NATO secretary-general.

What gave the CFSP and the ESDI a minimum of consistency was a change of British policy after the Labour victory of 1997. Tony Blair's conversion to a defence role for the EU within a year of his election stemmed chiefly from his alarm at the lack of autonomous European resources to handle even a limited European crisis such as the one that developed in Kosovo late in 1998, as well as from the British defence industry's need for a viable partner outside the United States. It found expression, in a Franco-British summit at St-Malo in December 1998, in a joint declaration calling for 'a full and rapid implementation of the Amsterdam provisions on the CFSP' and stressing 'the responsibility of the European Council to decide on the framing of a common defense policy of CFSP' and the need for 'the Union [to] have the capacity for autonomous action, backed up by credible military forces and the means to decide to use them . . . to respond to international crises'. The St-Malo summit, endorsed by the whole European Council at Cologne the following June, also agreed that the EU should possess a Rapid Reaction Force, based on the Eurocorps, deployable within sixty days, and capable of undertaking a range of tasks including 'humanitarian and evacuation missions, missions for maintaining peace and missions using combat forces in crisis management, including missions for the establishment of peace'; the target level of the force was set at the Helsinki summit of December 1999 at 50,000–60,000 troops, 4,000 aircraft and 100 ships. The momentum was continued by the Nice Treaty of 2000, which established, within the Council of Ministers, new permanent political and military structures: a Political and Security Committee and a Military Committee, as well as a staff of military experts seconded by the member states to the Secretariat of the Council of Ministers. This institutional panoply and the existence of what looked like an embryonic European army might appear to lay the foundations of a more independent foreign and security policy for Europe.

Four problems, however, stand in the way of such a full-fledged policy being developed. The first concerns the military means available, especially by comparison with the world's leading military power, the United States. At the end of the Clinton presidency in 2000, the United States defence budget stood at nearly 300 billion dollars, or four times the combined budgets of France and the UK. The gap widened dramatically under George W. Bush; with European budgets already under strain from the burden of ageing populations, there is no realistic prospect of its being significantly narrowed. Moreover, the spending disparities underestimate the difference in military might: the Americans have the advantage of standardisation, a long experience of projecting military power across the globe, and a larger share of total military spend devoted to research and procurement (and less on men in uniform). Thus according to François Heisbourg, the Europeans in 2000 mustered less than one-fifth of the Americans' airlift capacity and less than one-tenth of their strength in strategic reconnaissance and in precision-guided air-delivered weapons. These differences have practical consequences. In the 1999 Kosovo war, American aircraft delivered 80 per cent of the weapons dropped. The credibility of any independent security policy must be limited as long as the Europeans lack the capacity to take on an adversary the size of Serbia without help. One might add that important items in France's military budget – a fifth of which (down from nearly a third in the 1990s) is still spent on the nuclear deterrent – appear redundant to most of the threats Europe is likely to face. Though Europeans are increasingly aware of many of these difficulties and are making progress in such areas as common defence procurement policies, Europe remains an underdeveloped military power.

Second, the relationship of European defence to NATO remained largely unclear. For Jospin's defence minister Alain Richard, the development of the ESDI opened the possibility of three types of European military operation: fully NATO-run, as in Kosovo; European-led but with NATO planning, logistical and other support; or fully European, without NATO support (and implicitly not requiring NATO approval). Quite aside from the question of means, however, France's enthusiasm for such a 'third option', and thus for a genuinely independent European defence capability, found limited echoes elsewhere in Europe. Again, the issue has practical consequences. Making a 'third option' workable would mean developing an independent European defence planning capability alongside that of NATO, a project that would be certain to generate tensions with the United States and which, for that reason, has been less than warmly welcomed by France's European allies.

The third difficulty in the way of a common foreign and security policy lies in the flagrant inability of the European powers to define a common position in relation to the 2003 Iraq war. The EU included both America's most acerbic opponent in the developed world in Chirac's France, supported by Belgium and, crucially, by Germany, and its staunchest ally in the UK, backed by Spain (until the 2004 elections), Italy and most of the Eastern accession countries. That difference, famously defined by Secretary of State Rumsfeld as 'old' versus 'new' Europe, reflected attitudes not only to the war but also to the United States of George W. Bush. To that extent they were likely both to last and to spill over into a wide range of foreign policy issues.

Finally, the structure of the CFSP lacks the institutional leadership necessary to overcome such divisions. Centred on the European Council (and thus depending on the six-monthly rotating presidency), requiring unanimity among member states, placing each member state on a footing of formal equality (and thus ruling out any possibility of a 'directory' of larger states), excluding the Commission as a force of proposition, dividing EU responsibilities between a Commissioner for foreign relations and the High

Representative, the structures of the CFSP are too cumbersome to permit anything like the swiftness of diplomatic decision-making in a member state. The draft EU Constitution, upgrading the post of High Representative to that of foreign minister (who would simultaneously be vice-president of the Commission), as well as stabilising the European presidency, would certainly address some of these issues. Whether they would suffice to overcome the formidable difficulties noted above and develop a CFSP that was more than rhetorical remains uncertain.

As Jacques Chirac cajoled and bullied Europe's leaders into accepting the voting rights on the Council of Ministers enshrined in the Nice Treaty, a German diplomat complained that 'Europe is the continuation of France by other means'. Recent developments in European policy do not, on the whole, bear this out. The CAP, the most thoroughly French-inspired of European programmes, has been slowly prised away from its former impregnable position, in particular with the progressive uncoupling of subsidy from production; Chirac's skilful defence of the policy's main past beneficiaries has every appearance of a rearguard action. The CFSP, a French aspiration for nearly half a century, has barely advanced beyond a rudimentary, rhetorical existence; Chirac's observation that the Eastern European countries supportive of United States policy in Iraq had 'missed a good opportunity to shut up' reflects a sense of frustration at this outcome. Comparable arguments could be advanced for other policy areas. The social charter has lacked the scope of Europe's competition policy and the strict deadlines and requirements of EMU. Demands, articulated especially by the Jospin government in 1997, for an 'economic government' to counterbalance the European Central Bank's role in managing the single currency, found expression in regular meetings of the euro-zone finance ministers, but left the ECB's independence intact.

And as we have seen, Europe's competition policy has been resisted by France, with some consistency, by means of delays in transposing directives into French law. Part of this reflects a liberal turn in European affairs which the French helped effect but for which they were not fully prepared; part, too, France's central EU dilemma: ambitious goals for a proactive Europe in social, industrial, economic or foreign affairs require, for their realisation, more supranationalism than France has traditionally been ready to accept. The ambiguity applies not only to politicians, but also to ordinary French voters.

Voters, parties and Europe

In many ways the behaviour of governments towards European issues reflects the views of the French electorate. In some ways these views are unremarkable. French public attitudes towards integration are situated close to the European average: the French are neither curmudgeonly Eurosceptics like the British or Danes, nor unconditional Euro-enthusiasts like the Italians or Spanish. In over two decades of *Eurobarometer* polls, French answers to the questions of whether their country's membership of Europe was a 'good thing' or a 'bad thing' never varied from the European average by over 10 percentage points; the variation has more frequently been 5 points or less (Table 14.2). The general movement of backing for integration has been comparable in France and across Europe: a steady rise in support during the 1980s, peaking in the second half of the decade (*Eurobarometer* recorded 74 per cent of the French taking a positive view of their country's EEC membership in 1987) before dropping sharply in the post-Maastricht period of the early 1990s. While the popularity of integration, in both

Table 14.2 Attitudes to European integration in France and Europe, 1980–2004 (answers to questions: 'Is your country's membership of the EEC/EU a good thing/bad thing?' and 'Has your country benefited from EEC/EU membership?')

	Good thing		Bad thing		Neither good nor bad	
	France	EEC/EU	France	EEC/EU	France	EEC/EU
1980–84	55	54	8	14	30	25
1985–89	69	63	5	10	23	22
1990–94	59	62	11	11	26	23
1995–99	50	52	15	14	31	27
2000–4	47	51	15	14	34	29
	Has benefited		Has not benefited		Don't know	
	France	EEC/EU	France	EEC/EU	France	EEC/EU
1986–89	58	54	22	29	20	18
1990–94	48	51	31	30	21	19
1995–99	46	46	34	34	21	21
2000–4	49	48	30	31	21	20

Source: Eurobarometer.

France and the rest of Europe, has varied somewhat with the economy, the brief recovery towards the turn of the millennium was short-lived, and never brought support back to the levels of the late 1980s. Thus while at least half of French respondents took a positive view of EEC/EU membership in every poll from 1981 to 1995, the figure reached 50 per cent in only one-third of polls between 1996 and 2004. Heroic leadership in Europe in the late 1980s corresponded to a degree of public optimism; for political leaders to attempt the same a decade later would be much more hazardous. At the same time, support for European integration varies, in France as in the rest of the EU, both with age and with levels of education and income (Euro-enthusiasts thus tend to be young and educated, or else elderly – having known the war years – and retired). Better-educated respondents are likely to be more informed about and more supportive towards the EU; they are also somewhat more likely to be better-placed on the employment market and less personally vulnerable to the risks of heightened competition entailed by integration.

But it is where French opinions diverge from European averages that the ambiguities of France's role, discernible among the political elite, are most clearly reflected among the public. Like their leaders, the French take a more ambitious view of Europe, in some respects, than other European citizens. This is notably true of questions of defence and foreign policy. As early as 1987, 20 per cent of French respondents, against an EEC average of 9 per cent, said they thought of the EEC's international role when they thought of Europe. In 2004, 52 per cent of French respondents, against 45 per cent across the 25-member EU, supported defence decisions being taken by the EU, and not national governments or NATO. On a wide range of measures linked to the CFSP, including the need to reach common foreign policy positions, to have a single European foreign minister, and even to move to a single European representative on the UN Security Council, French support for integration was higher than the European average. At the same time French respondents remained more worried than the European average by a whole series of concerns closely linked to the French economic and social model: job losses to cheap-labour East European countries, the downgrading of social benefits, or new difficulties for farmers (Table 14.3). These concerns helped make the French public more opposed than any in Europe to Eastern enlargement, and while these misgivings had moderated by the spring of 2004, they remained more intense than among most of France's partners.

On the face of it, therefore, it appears that there is a more or less perfect fit between voter attitudes and the behaviour of mainstream French politicians in relation to European integration – grandiloquently warm towards the principle, deeply cautious about the material implications. The impact of Europe on French politics is, however, less predictable than such an observation would suggest. Europe has affected French politics and even the French party system, but in largely indirect ways.

In the first place, the French, like other Europeans, are not actively engaged with Europe from day to day, and this inevitably affects their behaviour at European elections. Only 12 per cent of French poll respondents in 2004 took the view that the European parliament had a substantial effect on them personally, against 34 per cent for the French government and 28 per cent each for the National Assembly and their regional council. This fairly dismissive attitude to the EP again reflects that of French politicians, who tend to treat European elections as a beauty contest for political parties and personalities rather than as a process designed to give some 700 MEPs a democratic mandate to legislate. By 2004, thanks in part to their habit of multiple office-holding, French MEPs had a worse attendance record than those of any other EU country. Almost every senior French politician, including Chirac and Juppé, Hollande and Fabius, has won election at one time or another to the European parliament, in order to achieve a good personal or party score, only to resign a few weeks after the poll; with limitations on the *cumul des mandats* in force, a town hall and a National Assembly seat have almost invariably proved more vital assets than a seat in Strasbourg (Bernard Tapie, the exception that proved the rule, hung onto his Strasbourg seat so as to claim parliamentary immunity and stay out of prison). Rare, too, have been the mainstream parties that have campaigned on European rather than national issues. This is an invitation to voters, themselves uncommitted to the institution of the European parliament, to vote with their spleen or not at all. French turnout at European elections (Table 14.4) has followed a fairly steady downward path, usually at levels 2–4 per cent below the (similarly declining) European average.

Table 14.3 French fears of Europe, spring 2004 (% agreeing in each case)

	France	*EU15*
Fear loss of power of nation states	51	41
Fear increase in own country's budget contribution	68	57
Fear loss of social benefits	64	46
Fear European economic crisis	57	45
Fear job losses to cheap-labour countries in EU	83	69
Fear greater problems for farmers	73	58
Confident that EU can control effects of globalisation	21	27
Opposed to the 2004 enlargement	47	40

Source: Eurobarometer 61, 2004.

Table 14.4 Turnout at European elections in France and EEC/EU, 1979–2004, as % of registered voters

	1979	1984	1989	1994	1999	2004
France	60.7	56.8	48.8	52.7	46.8	42.8
EEC/EU	62.4	60.7	56.2	56.7	49.6	44.2

Secondly, as we have noted in Chapter 9, the behaviour of those of the French who do vote at European elections differs from that of French voters at most presidential or legislative elections; and proportional representation ensures that this is reflected in the results. Although the first European elections, in 1979, gave an outcome roughly within the framework of the bipolar quadrille (though with an unprecedented showing for an ecologist list, which won over 4 per cent of the vote), every vote since then has produced surprises. These have included:

- in 1984, the emergence of the FN at over 10 per cent of the national vote, and a big new fall in support for the PCF, on top of that of 1981;
- in 1989, a rebellion of younger politicians of the mainstream Right (the *rénovateurs*) during the campaign; the success of Antoine Waechter's Verts in winning over 10 per cent of the vote; and the first electoral outing of the *Chasseurs*;
- in 1994, the historically low score of the PS with a mere 14 per cent; the zenith of the Radicals under the mercurial leadership of Bernard Tapie; and the emergence, for once on European themes, of the Eurosceptical Left (under Chevènement, whose list achieved a mere 2.5 per cent) and the Eurosceptical Right (under Philippe de Villiers, who managed a more impressive 12.4 per cent);
- in 1999, the split and defeat of the mainstream Right, with the Eurosceptical Pasqua/de Villiers list winning 13.1 per cent against a mere 12.7 for the 'official' Sarkozy/Madelin list; the split and defeat of the Front National; strong performances for both the *Chasseurs* of CPNT and their enemies Les Verts; and the arrival of the Trotskyist far Left in the Strasbourg parliament;
- in 2004, under a more restrictive regionalised semi-proportional system, the defeat of the governing UMP, reduced to a mere 16.6 per cent of the vote and flanked by competitors of the Centre (the UDF) and the Eurosceptic Right.

More generally, European elections have tended to produce very fragmented results; in 1999, for example, twenty lists ran nationally, of which nine passed the 5 per cent threshold to win seats. To some extent these results should be treated as inconsequential, a 'rite of passage before serious business starts', as the UMP Deputy Pierre Lellouche described European elections. Or as Philippe Méchet observed in 2000, 'Every five years, France becomes Italy, but always returns straight afterwards to the specificities of its own system.' Yet the dispersal of votes that this type of election has encouraged has tended, with time, to spill over into electoral behaviour at national elections, most obviously to the presidency in 2002 (see above, p. 267).

The French electorate has also had the chance to affect Europe's future more directly, in the three referendums of 1972 (on enlargement), 1992 (on the Maastricht Treaty) and 2005 (on the European constitutional treaty). Each referendum has seen an unexpectedly good mobilisation of the Eurosceptical camp. In 1972 this led to a strong yes result but high abstention, largely due to the Socialists. In September 1992 the yes won by barely half a million votes – 51 per cent to 49 – despite having led the polls by 69 per cent to 31 the previous June. In May 2005 the yes camp, having led by the same margin six months earlier, was in a minority of barely 45 per cent on polling day.

One reason for these unexpected results is that the fuzzy pro-European sentiments of some voters have not withstood exposure to the more concrete stakes of Europe as presented in the referendum campaigns: as we have seen, Europe has become the focus of many French fears. Another reason has been that the presidents who initiated each referendum have done so, at least in part, for reasons of narrow and above all ill-calculated political advantage. Each was intended to place the president centre-stage and enhance his standing with a victory at the polls – in Pompidou's case in order to refocus attention on himself rather than his prime minister Chaban-Delmas, in Mitterrand's and Chirac's to recover from a period of deep unpopularity. In no case did they succeed in this. The yes vote at the referendum of 1972 was too lukewarm to help Pompidou, that of 1992 too close to reinforce Mitterrand, while Chirac saw his popularity plummet to new lows after his defeat in 2005. On the other hand, each referendum was also meant to split the opposition, and in this respect presidents have met with growing, but increasingly dangerous, success. In 1972, the Socialists and Communists agreed to differ (the Communists voted no, the Socialists abstained), and simply resumed their march towards the Common Programme after the poll. Twenty years later, the Gaullist RPR rebelled against Chirac's support for the Maastricht Treaty: Charles Pasqua and Philippe Séguin mobilised some two-thirds of RPR voters against it. But the right-wing opposition regrouped within a fortnight of the poll, going on to win a resounding victory in the March 1993 parliamentary elections. Similarly, when Chirac announced on 14 July 2004 that the European constitutional treaty would be submitted to a referendum he certainly aimed to divide the left-wing opposition, and especially the Socialists, who had scored impressive victories at elections in March (to regional councils) and June (to the Strasbourg parliament). In this he was probably more successful than he wished; it was the unexpected opposition to the treaty of clear majorities of Socialist and Green voters (Appendix 5) that handed victory to the no camp.

Underpinning these presidential strategies has been the fact that the positions of French voters, and indeed of French parties, over European issues cut right across habitual party divisions. Whereas some West European countries, like the UK since the late 1980s, have a broadly pro-European Left and a more Eurosceptical Right, and others, especially the Scandinavian countries, are more Eurosceptical on the Left than on the Right, the French graph of support for Europe against the Left–Right division is (like those of Belgium or Germany) an inverted parabola. The far Left opposes European integration because of a deep-seated suspicion of the economic liberalism central to the European project. The far Right opposes it for nationalist reasons, out of hostility to anything resembling a transfer of sovereignty. *Most* parties between centre-Left and centre-Right support integration, but, elements of them may be persuaded to join the Eurosceptical extremes depending on the context.

This pattern, and its variable nature, were clear from the parliamentary votes on ratification of the European treaties of the 1950s. Thus the ECSC, carried in 1951 by the mainstream parties of the Fourth Republic – Socialists, Christian Democrats, Radicals and most conservatives – was unsuccessfully opposed by Gaullists, Communists and a minority of conservatives. These usual Eurosceptical suspects were joined in the 1954 EDC vote by a further contingent of conservatives, the Jacobin left wing of the

Socialists, half the Radicals and even a handful of Christian Democrats, the most consistent pro-Europeans on the French political spectrum; a combination big enough to sink EDC for good. Forty years later this distribution was reproduced, approximately but by voters not Deputies, at the Maastricht referendum. The FN had replaced the Gaullists on the far Right of the spectrum, and the yes vote was skewed leftwards (and the no rightwards) because it was Mitterrand who had called the referendum. But the resemblances to the pattern of the early 1950s remained striking. The no won majorities among supporters of the PCF (84 per cent), the RPR (69 per cent), the FN (93 per cent) and those with no party preference (64 per cent); the yes vote was concentrated chiefly among supporters of the PS (76 per cent) and to a lesser extent among those of the two Green parties (57 per cent) and the UDF (59 per cent).

These figures pose the question of the emergence of a 'European cleavage' in French politics that durably structures the behaviour of parties and voters. The answer to such a question should probably be negative, for two reasons. First, voters' rejection of Europe has tended to go hand in hand with a wider opposition to the political establishment generally, and with a range of 'anti-universal' (ethnocentric and authoritarian) values: Euroscepticism (or for that matter Euro-enthusiasm) has proved hard to isolate from these other traits. Secondly, there is little evidence that a European cleavage is a powerful structuring agent in election after election, in the same way as the Left/ Right distinction clearly is. In March 1993, for example, when the French returned to the polls to elect their Deputies just six months after the Maastricht referendum, the Left/Right pattern fell back into place, with plenty of help from France's institutions: the RPR and the UDF, despite European differences, ran joint candidates in most seats and even Socialists and Communists cobbled together a second-ballot withdrawal agreement.

Nevertheless, even if the notion of a cleavage should be rejected, it is clear that European issues have affected the French party system. They have led to splits, albeit limited ones, within the PS and the UDF (both in the aftermath of Maastricht) and the RPR (after the Amsterdam Treaty). They also highlighted long-term fault lines even within the surviving big parties. Within the PS, for example, there had always been tensions between the statist, Jacobin wing of the party and the more Girondin, reformist wing, long led by Rocard and more inclined to delegate state power to Europe, regions and civil society. A similar division operated on the moderate Right, coinciding partly but not perfectly with the division between the UDF (with its big contingent of Christian Democrats) and the neo-Gaullist RPR. While the Eurosceptic parties that emerged from these splits tended to be small or ephemeral, they were not negligible either: Chevènement's presidential candidacy, for example, could certainly be said to have cost Jospin, if not the presidency itself, then at least his place at the run-off in 2002. Moreover, if Europe did not establish a new and distinctive cleavage pattern, it still demonstrated a capacity to modify electoral behaviour durably. This is indicated most tellingly, perhaps, by the loss of PS support, after the Maastricht referendum, among those social groups – the less educated, and blue- and white-collar workers – which had constituted significant electoral reserves for the PS but which were among the most reluctant to vote for the treaty signed by Mitterrand. The PS voter of the 1990s and after had an increasingly bourgeois aspect, embarrassingly for a party that aimed to redress inequalities in society.

This was the context of the campaign for the 2005 referendum. Both history and circumstance made it wholly predictable that the treaty would be opposed by the FN

(Le Pen had campaigned for France to leave the EU in 2002), by the 'sovereignist' wing of the moderate Right (de Villiers, but also a fraction of the UMP led, since Pasqua's and Séguin's effective withdrawal from politics, by Nicolas Dupont-Aignan), by the PCF (whose leader, Marie-Georges Buffet, saw an opportunity to regain some of the radical credentials her party had lost in government before 2002), by the far Left and by the much reduced Chevènement forces. What was crucial, though, was the capacity of the no camp to attract personalities and voters from the parties of the centre. This was assisted, first, by the nature of the treaty itself. Though much simplified by comparison with the European treaties it was intended to replace, the document distributed to the voters was, at 448 articles and over 80 close-packed pages (plus as much again in annexes and additional protocols) distinctly longer, more technical and more obscure than the constitution of, say, the Fifth Republic. Easy to pick at and criticise, it was much harder to present as offering an attractive vision for Europe's future.

On the Right, objections to the document itself focused chiefly on the end of the Maastrichtian distinction between the economic 'pillar' of the EU, governed by quali-fied majority voting on the Council of Ministers, and the other two pillars, covering the regalian branches of state activity (justice, home affairs, foreign policy, defence) and still requiring unanimity for legislation to be adopted. If the treaty came into force, justice and home affairs would now, with few exceptions, fall under the qualified major-ity régime, and a range of policies on asylum, immigration and citizenship would be decided at European rather than national level. At least as important as this, however, was the way in which the debate on the treaty itself was paralleled – or polluted – by another, on the admission of Turkey. This was premature. Although Turkey began formal negotiations for entry to the EU in December 2004, the European Commission had made it clear that Turkey would enter, if at all, only after a decade and more of negotiations and convergence – a long delay for a country that had been an associated state of the EEC from 1959, and an official entry candidate since 1987. And the adop-tion, or not, of the constitutional treaty would not affect the Turkish issue one way or the other. But Chirac, conscious of public misgivings, had promised that once Bulgaria and Rumania (due to join in 2006) had entered, France's acceptance of any further EU members (meaning Turkey among others) would be conditional on a yes result in a referendum. This provoked an immediate debate in the National Assembly in October 2004, and a rash of opinion polls. The political debate blurred not only traditional party boundaries but also France's normal divisions over Europe. As early as 1963, de Gaulle, no enthusiast for enlargement in general, had spoken of Turkey's 'European vocation' (in a rather more welcoming tone than he used for Britain in the same year); forty years later, his successor Chirac was one of Turkey's foremost advocates. By contrast, the UDF, the most 'European' party but also the most attached to Europe's Christian legacy, was largely opposed; while the Communists, outright opponents of Maastricht in 1992 and of the Constitution in 2004, still favoured Turkish entry on grounds, officially, of internationalist solidarity. Whatever the party divisions, however, the French voters were full of misgivings, with between two-thirds and three-quarters of poll respondents ready to vote no at a (distant) referendum on Turkish entry. That reflected a widespread view that Turkey was too big, too poor, too Asian and too Muslim to be a comfortable European partner; it was a favoured theme of de Villiers, whose campaign linked it clearly, and misleadingly, to the constitutional treaty.

But it was from (some of) the ranks of the Left that the loudest objections were raised in the months after the European Council adopted the Constitution in June 2004.

These objections were far from unanimous: for some, including François Hollande, Lionel Jospin, Michel Rocard, Élisabeth Guigou or Martine Aubry, the EU offered the world's best chance to resist an unrestricted 'Anglo-Saxon' capitalism, and the constitution, whatever its faults, offered an indispensable reinforcement for Europe's institutions. For others even within the PS, for left-wingers like Henri Emmanuelli and Jean-Luc Mélenchon but also for former ministers like Paul Quilès, Pierre Joxe and above all Laurent Fabius, the constitution was 'incompatible with socialism'. Its long series of articles (III-130 to III-166) systematising long-standing European bans on most imaginable obstacles to free trade and fair competition, contrasted with a much shorter sequence (III-167 and III-168) setting out possible exceptions (such as public subsidies for disaster areas, underdeveloped regions, or major joint European projects). Meanwhile, the industrial relations and worker protection policy set out in the constitution was defined in general terms, and explicitly excluded minimum wage levels, or the rights of association, the right to strike, or the right to lock workers out – making any 'levelling up' of worker protection impossible, according to the constitution's left-wing critics, and encouraging a 'race to the bottom' between European states from which French wage-earners would suffer. The notion of public services, with their indispensable guarantee of equal access to all, received only brief and general mention in the text. As Olivier Duhamel (a Socialist member of the Convention, and a vigorous supporter of the constitution) wrote, getting public service into the text at all was a struggle, won at the price of abandoning any reference to what services should be covered or what principles should govern them.

For Duhamel, Hollande, or Jospin, this was better than nothing and certainly no worse than the status quo of the existing treaties, from which most of Part III had in any case been drawn, at the insistence of the governments of member states. But a key argument among Socialist opponents of the draft constitution was that by supporting a text that contained so few of the guarantees of jobs, public services and social protection that they had sought, the PS would cut itself off permanently from those groups – the blue and white-collar working class, especially in the public sector – which were central to its identity as a left-wing party. By refusing a constitutional treaty proposed by Chirac on the basis of a draft submitted by a convention chaired by Giscard, on the other hand, the PS would be putting clear water between itself and a right-wing, and highly unpopular, president and government, and sending a clear message to workers that their support mattered.

Among PS members, the yes camp won the argument, by a margin of 56 to 44 per cent, at the internal party referendum on the treaty held in December 2004. This, assumed most observers from Chirac down, would guarantee the solidity of the pro-treaty forces at the centre – PS, UMP and UDF – and thus a successful referendum. Three elements proved them wrong. First, the leaders of the no camp in the PS took no account of their party's vote and went on campaigning against the treaty, some (like Mélenchon) in open and effective partnership with the PCF and the far Left. Their party leader Hollande, no doubt wishing to hold the PS together, did nothing to stop them. Second, the no camp made the most of a wave of industrial unrest, linked to pay demands and to government measures to introduce 'flexibility' in the application of the 35-hour week, that affected France during the first quarter of 2005. Third, the so-called Bolkestein directive (known after the Dutch commissioner responsible for it) on the single market in services added further grist to the no camp's mill, as it suggested that suppliers of services across the EU could work under the labour laws of their country of origin, not of the state where the services were supplied. This allowed the treaty's opponents to conjure up a mythical image of the 'Polish plumber', who would take advantage of the directive (and of the treaty) to undercut his French competitors on their home ground. Chirac's sudden message to the Commission that the directive was 'unacceptable in its present form' (he had signed it without misgivings in 2002) was too late and too tactical; the damage was done. The second week of March 2005 saw both a big demonstration on pay and the 35-hour week and the peak of the controversy over the Bolkestein directive. Within days the yes camp's lead in the polls had evaporated. Its fate was sealed by the ineptitude and disorganisation of the yes campaign, which alternated between quietism, arrogance (the claim that it was impossible for pro-Europeans to vote no) and incomprehension (a disastrous television broadcast in which Chirac faced the hostile questions of a group of young people); and by the attempts of the Raffarin government to suppress a public holiday, Whit Monday, just a fortnight before polling day.

The salience of these concerns about social protection, and the fact that it was a right-wing president who had called the referendum in the first place, gave the no vote a leftward skew. The extremes – 95 per cent of PCF voters and 96 per cent of FN supporters – were solidly, and symmetrically, against the treaty. The moderate Right was kinder to it than it had been to Maastricht: both UMP and UDF supporters voted yes by a margin of three to one. More remarkable, however, was the rejection of the treaty by a clear majority of the moderate Left – 64 per cent of Green voters and 59 per cent of Socialists. Most striking of all was that class, an increasingly poor predictor of voting on the Left–Right spectrum, became a rather good one for the referendum. The no camp attracted 81 per cent of the blue-collar workers who voted, 60 per cent of the white-collar workers, 55 per cent of the small business vote, and 54 per cent of technicians and lower management; managers and professionals, voters with a university education and the retired were the only groups that showed a majority in support of the treaty (Appendix 5). Compared with Maastricht, all categories moved towards the no camp (except for small business owners, who remained stable); the strongest shifts were among the old blue-collar working class, and among public-sector wage-earners – favourable to Maastricht, and believing their jobs secure, in 1992, but hostile to the constitutional treaty, which they viewed as a threat to their livelihoods, in 2005.

The previous no majority at a French referendum had signalled the end of an era; de Gaulle was gone within less than 24 hours of the result, true to his belief that office without the voters' support was not worth keeping. Chirac, for his part, merely sacked his prime minister. This did not prevent the president, as well as Raffarin, from being a casualty of the referendum; his poll ratings dropped to a record low in the following weeks. He could take some consolation from the damage done to the PS and in particular to its leader François Hollande, whose successful record in 2004 was wholly eclipsed by the referendum result; but not from the reinforcement of Sarkozy, who had remained discreet in the referendum campaign and who was now invited to combine party and government office. Beyond France, the no vote produced few of the results its supporters had hoped for. In particular, the chances of a renegotiation of the treaty to include more of the social provisions dear to the French left, held out by the no campaign as a real possibility, appeared more remote than ever a month after the referendum. France's role in Europe was damaged, temporarily at least; at the Brussels summit that followed the debacle Chirac was not even, quite, able to rally twenty-three more states against the British budget rebate. The EU, meanwhile, though not thrown into crisis – the Nice, Amsterdam and Maastricht treaties remain its framework of governance – suffered a lowering of horizons, comparable to that of the later de Gaulle period: able to continue on a day-to-day basis, but hardly to progress, still less to lead.

Concluding remarks

Having influence in Europe matters. It matters partly for geopolitical reasons, as a multiplier of national influence on the world stage, but above all, as Anand Menon has observed, for the economic advantages of being able to upload national policy to the level of Europe, with its market of 400 million.

Yet if Europe, as Mitterrand said, is France's future, it appears to be a future of declining French influence. We have already noted several signs of this. The CAP has been dethroned from its pre-eminent place among EU policies. The CFSP has not so far furthered a European foreign policy, still less a substantial defence capability, enjoying any great degree of independence from the United States: the French stance on Iraq, though shared by several governments (notably the German and Belgian) and by a majority of European citizens, was still not a European policy, rather to Chirac's frustration, and the chances of reinforcing France's political identity in world affairs were badly damaged by the defeat of the constitutional treaty. The French tradition of public services is threatened by competition policy, France's predilection for deficits by the Stability and Growth Pact. Disputes with the Commission over subsidies and mergers, and over the size of the French deficit, as well as France's slowness to transpose European legislation into national law, testify to a difficulty, or reluctance, to adjust even to EU measures consented by France. Three other signs, of a more trivial kind, can be mentioned.

- *The achievements of France's European presidencies.* France's presidencies of the European Council in 1984 and 1989 were both sumptuous (the latter especially, coinciding with the celebrations for the bicentenary of the 1789 Revolution) and successful. The 1984 presidency achieved a settlement to long-running budget disputes, opening the way to the relaunch of Europe in the mid-1980s. That of 1989, in many ways the high point of *mitterrandien* European leadership, agreed the Social Charter and the convening of an intergovernmental conference on EMU for the following year (both decisions, significantly, reached against British dissent). By contrast, the 1995 presidency, cut in half by the French presidential election, accomplished little, and that of 2000 achieved the widely derided Treaty of Nice, besides giving the French on both sides of *cohabitation*, and especially European Affairs Minister Pierre Moscovici and Chirac himself, a reputation for amateurism, arrogance and bullying.
- *France's Commissioners.* Although Commissioners take an oath to shed national loyalties and represent only European interests once in office, the capture of important positions on the College remains a focus for intense competition, linked to prestige, among member states. France has boasted some of Europe's most illustrious Commissioners, including two presidents (François-Xavier Ortoli, and above all Delors) as well as leading figures such as Pascal Lamy, Delors's former chief of staff and Foreign Trade Commissioner from 1999 to 2004. The appointment to the rather lowly Transport portfolio in the 2004 Barroso Commission of Jacques Barrot, a Christian Democrat of solid national rather than European

reputation, was widely seen in France as a setback – the price of Chirac's refusal to re-appoint Lamy – especially as 2004 saw large countries limited to just one Commissioner for the first time.

• *Language.* For its first fifteen years, the EEC was above all a French-speaking organisation. The entry of two anglophone member states – Britain and Ireland – signalled the end of that predominance. By 2002, 29 per cent of documents produced by the Commission were drafted in French, against 57 per cent in English. In the Council of Ministers, a mere 18 per cent of documents originated in French in 2002, against 42 per cent in English as recently as 1997. The Commission's economic studies are *only* published in English, while in the European Parliament English has acquired the status of a lingua franca. Only the minutes of Commission meetings and the decisions of the Court of Justice remain as strongholds of French expression; but not necessarily for long.

While France remains one of the leading players, as a founder state and one of the four largest countries, it has indubitably lost the pre-eminent position it enjoyed until the early 1990s. One obvious interpretation of this decline is that all member states taken individually, France among them, have seen their influence diminish with the reinforcement of the EU. As the EU has taken on a more constraining and state-like role, adopting QMV in more areas, strengthening the role of the Parliament, and reinforcing a legal order headed by the Court of Justice so all national sovereignties have been eroded, as they were meant to be. And as the EU has accepted successive enlargements, its early clubbish style has given way to altogether more rule-bound and bureaucratic operating procedures; the Permanent Representatives' lunch, for example, traditionally an excellent informal setting for settling differences between member states, has now succumbed, as it was bound to beyond a certain size, to the usual paraphernalia of interpreters and microphones. The difficulty with this view, however, is that other states, notably the UK, appear, on the contrary, to have gained European leverage as the EU has enlarged. The explanations of France's decline lie rather in the change in the balance of power and policy preference within the new EU, and the manner in which different member states have reacted to them.

Three external constraints, all dating from the early 1990s, go some way to accounting for France's changed position. The first is the changing balance of Franco-German relations after 1989. The enhanced position on the European and world stages that France drew from the 'privileged partnership' always depended on Germany's acceptance of a politically subordinate status that was at variance with growing German economic strength. A consequence of the defeat of 1945 and of the Soviet threat, and thus inevitably temporary, this political subordination was (largely) thrown off, with unexpected speed, after unification and the break-up of the Soviet Union.

The second external development that worked to France's disadvantage was spread of the neo-liberal world economic order which has taken shape in parallel with European integration. Not only has trade liberalisation been central both to the EEC and to the EU; both have constantly interacted with global trade liberalising measures ever since the Commission negotiated in the name of all the member states in the Kennedy Round of tariff reductions undertaken within the framework of the GATT in the mid-1960s. What has changed since 1989 has been the acceleration of this process, as outlined in Chapter 1, with the disappearance of a Communist bloc and the consequent arrival of new countries within the global trading system and the WTO, the diminution of technical obstacles to free trade, and the extension of the range of economic activities within the WTO's purview. This had inevitable consequences for the EU: most directly, the increased pressures on the CAP. More broadly, given the impossibility of opting out of the world trading system (unthinkable for France after the decisions of 1983, let alone for the UK, Holland, or Germany), it required the EU countries to adapt to a vastly more competitive environment. For France, as a country with a long-standing preference for *dirigisme* and protectionism, ready to liberalise but at a measured pace, this posed particular problems of adjustment.

The third and most recent development has been the eastward shift of the EU's centre of gravity with the admission of the states of the former Eastern bloc in 2004. This is likely to prove more than a mere geographical shift. Most of the new members were vigorously Atlanticist and supported the 2003 Iraq war, much to Chirac's irritation; most were also strong supporters of Thatcherite neo-liberalism; and most were historically part of an Austro-German sphere of economic influence to which they returned after 1989. The position in the EU of countries like France, which sought independence from the United States abroad and safeguards for social protection at home, was correspondingly weaker.

France's loss of influence, however, has also arisen from national difficulties in rising to these challenges. Two in particular are worth highlighting. One is that France's traditional approaches to interacting with partners have been much less effective in the 'new' Europe of the 1990s and after than they were in the old one. An American observer, Charles Cogan, has argued that French negotiators tend to value the forceful exposition of their own position, and the wearing-down of the opposition, rather than systematic attempts to understand and test the opposition's viewpoint and to work towards compromises from an early stage. Effective in a small European Community in which unanimous voting was still the norm, it becomes a much less helpful approach, even to the single member state practising it, in a larger EU where all action requires the patient building of coalitions and where the national veto is the exception not the rule. Similarly, the *petits arrangements*, the gentle rule-bending with which the French have regularly softened the sharper edges of the Jacobin state at home, and which Delors applied to European policy during his Commission presidency, have been harder to secure in the larger and more rule-bound Europe of the 1990s and beyond.

A second French difficulty, noted at the start of this chapter, lies in the long-standing ambiguity at the heart of French preferences for a strong Europe with weak institutions. This contrasts with, for example, the readiness of German governments to accept greater concessions to supranationality for the sake of an activist Europe, or the British reluctance to see either a reinforcement of European institutions or an extension of Europe's spheres of activity.

Yet it can be argued that the art of French presidential leadership in Europe – a leadership less politically constrained, at least outside cohabitation, than that of any other European head of government – has consisted, precisely, in finding a point of balance on the ambiguous French continuum, and in articulating it clearly. This was done rather restrictively by de Gaulle, more pragmatically by Pompidou and in altogether more ambitious terms by Mitterrand until 1993. Chirac has so far been unable to achieve such a balance. To do so would not have been easy. The president was more or less shackled for five years by cohabitation, and has faced an electorate prone, since the Maastricht referendum, to accesses of euro-pessimism and unwilling, as the strikes of 1995 demonstrated, to accept sacrifices in the name of the convergence criteria or the Stability and Growth Pact. Some of Chirac's difficulties, though, arise from his own long-term tendency to see European issues through the same tactical prism with which he views domestic politics, and thereby to lose sight of longer-term goals. He followed his referendum defeat of 2005 with a vigorous attack on the British budget rebate combined with an equally fierce defence of the CAP: these were old and tried values for the president's home voters, but hardly an exercise in European leadership.

Further reading

Alter, K. J., 'The European Court's Political Power', *West European Politics*, 19(3), July 1996, pp. 458–87.

Association Georges Pompidou, *Georges Pompidou et l'Europe*, Brussels, Complexe, 1995.

Axtmann, R., *Globalization and Europe*, London, Cassell, 1996.

Bitsch, M.-T., *Histoire de la construction européenne*, Brussels, Complexe, 1996

Boniface, P., *La France est-elle encore une grande puissance?*, Paris, Presses de Sciences Po, 1998.

Boussard, I., *Les Agriculteurs et la République*, Paris, Économica, 1990.

Cerny, P., *The Politics of Grandeur*, Cambridge, Cambridge University Press, 1980.

Chafer, T. and Jenkins, B. (eds), *France: From the Cold War to the New World Order*, Basingstoke, Macmillan, 1996.

Cogan, C., *The Third Option: The Emancipation of European Defense, 1989–2000*, Westport, CT, Praeger, 2001.

Cogan, C., *French Negotiating Behaviour: Dealing with La Grande Nation*, Washington, DC, United States Institute of Peace Press, 2003.

Cohen, S. and Smouts, M.-C. (eds) *La politique extérieure de Valéry Giscard d'Estaing*, Paris, Presses de la Fondation Nationale des Sciences Politiques, 1985.

Cole, A., 'The *Service Public* under stress', *West European Politics*, 22(4), October 1999, pp. 166–84.

Cole, A., 'National and partisan contexts of Europeanisation', *Journal of Common Market Studies*, 39(1), 2001.

Cole, A., *Franco-German Relations*, Harlow, Longman, 2001.

Cole, A. and Drake, H., 'The Europeanisation of the French polity: continuity, change, and adaptation', *Journal of European Public Policy*, 7(1), March 2001, pp. 26–43.

Coleman, W. and Chiasson, C., 'State power, transformative capacity and adapting to globalization: an analysis of French agricultural policy, 1960–2000', *Journal of European Public Policy*, 9(2), April 2002, pp. 168–85.

Criddle, B., 'The French referendum and the Maastricht Treaty, September 1992', *Parliamentary Affairs*, 46(2), April 1993.

d'Arcy, F. and Rouban, L., (eds), *De la Ve République à l'Europe*, Paris, Presses de Sciences Po, 1996.

de Gaulle, C., *Memoirs of Hope*, London, Weidenfeld and Nicolson, 1971.

Delorme, H. (ed.), *La Politique Agricole Commune*, Paris, Presses de Sciences Po, 2004.

Dinan, D., *Ever Closer Union: An Introduction to European Integration*, 2nd edition, Basingstoke, Palgrave Macmillan, 2005.

Drake, H. and Milner, S., 'Change and resistance to change: the political management of Europeanisation in France', *Modern and Contemporary France*, 7(2), 1999, pp. 165–78.

Duhamel, A., *Une Ambition française*, Paris, Plon, 1999.

Duhamel, O., *Pour l'Europe*, 2nd edition, Paris, Seuil, 2005.

Dyson, K. and Featherstone, K., *The Road to Maastricht*, Oxford, Oxford University Press, 1999.

Elgie, R. (ed.), *Electing the French President*, London, Macmillan, 1996.

Evans, J. (ed.), *The French Party System*, Manchester, Manchester University Press, 2003

Ferry, J.-M., 'La référence républicaine au défi de l'Europe', *Pouvoirs*, 100, December 2001, pp. 137–52.

Flynn, G. (ed.) *Remaking the Hexagon: The New France in the New Europe*, Oxford, Westview Press, 1995.

Frears, J., *France in the Giscard Presidency*, London, Allen and Unwin, 1981.

Gaffney, J. (ed.), *Political Parties and the European Union*, London, Routledge, 1996.

Grant, W., *The Common Agricultural Policy*, Basingstoke, Macmillan, 1997.

Grosser, A., *Affaires extérieures, La politique de la France, 1944–1984*, Paris, Flammarion, 1984.

Guyomarch, A., 'The European dynamics of evolving party competition in France', *Parliamentary Affairs*, 48(1), January 1995.

Guyomarch, A., Machin, H., Hall, P. and Hayward, J. (eds), *Developments in French Politics 2*, Basingstoke, Palgrave Macmillan, 2001.

Guyomarch, A., Machin, H. and Searls, E., *France in the EU*, Basingstoke, Macmillan, 1998.

Hancké, B., *Large Firms and Institutional Change: Industrial Renewal and Economic Restructuring in France*, Oxford, Oxford University Press, 2002.

Hanley, D., 'French political parties, globalisation and Europe', *Modern and Contemporary France*, 9(3), August 2001, pp. 301–12.

Hennis, M. 'Europeanization and globalization: the missing link', *Journal of Common Market Studies*, 39(5), December 2001, pp. 829–50.

Hix, S. and Lord, C., *Political Parties in the European Union*, Basingstoke, Macmillan, 1997.

Howarth, D., 'The European policy of the Jospin government', *Modern and Contemporary France*, 10(3), August 2002, pp. 353–69.

Howarth, D., 'The French state in the euro-zone: "modernization" and legitimizing *dirigisme*', in K. Dyson (ed.), *European States and the Euro: Europeanization, Variance, and Convergence*, Oxford, Oxford University Press, 2002, pp. 145–72.

Howorth, J., 'Foreign and defence policy in a post-Cold War world', in A. Guyomarch *et al.*, *Developments in French Politics 2*, Basingstoke, Palgrave Macmillan, 2001, ch. 8.

Howorth, J. S. and Keeler, J. T. S. (eds), *Defending Europe: The EU, NATO, and the Quest for European Autonomy*, New York, Palgrave Macmillan, 2003.

Keeler, J. S., *The Politics of Neocorporatism in France*, Oxford, Oxford University Press, 1987.

Kessler, M.-C., *La Politique Étrangère de la France*, Paris, Presses de Sciences Po, 1998.

Laborde, F. and Mano, J.-L., *Les Mammouths et les Jeunes Lions*, Paris, Belfond, 1990.

Lequesne, C., *Paris-Bruxelles: Comment se fait la politique européenne de la France*, Paris, Presses de la Fondation Nationale des Sciences Politiques, 1993.

McKay, D., *Rush to Union: Understanding the European Federal Bargain*, Oxford, Oxford University Press, 1996.

Maclean, M., *Economic Management and French Business: From de Gaulle to Chirac*, Basingstoke, Palgrave Macmillan, 2002.

Maillard, P., *De Gaulle et l'Europe*, Paris, Tallandier, 1995.

Menon, A. and Wright, V. (eds), *From the Nation State to Europe? Essays in Honour of Jack Hayward*, Oxford, Oxford University Press, 2001.

Mény, Y., Muller, P. and Quermonne, J.-L. (eds), *Adjusting to Europe*, London, Routledge, 1996.

Moravcsik, A., *The Choice for Europe: Social Purpose and State Power from Messina to Maastricht*, London, UCL Press, 1999.

Muller, P., 'Entre le local et l'Europe: la crise du modèle français de la politique publique', *Revue Française de Science Politique*, 42(2), 1992.

Nelsen, B. and Stubb, A., *The European Union: Readings on the Theory and Practice of European Integration*, 3rd edition, Basingstoke, Palgrave Macmillan, 2003.

Nugent, N., *The Government and Politics of the European Union*, 5th edition, Basingstoke, Macmillan, 2002.

Perrineau, P. and Ysmal, C. (eds), *Le vote des douze: les élections européennes de juin 1994*, Paris, Presses de Sciences Po, 1994.

Perrineau, P. and Ysmal, C. (eds), *Le vote des quinze: les élections européennes de juin 1999*, Paris, Presses de Sciences Po, 1999.

Perrineau, P. and Ysmal, C. (eds), *Le Vote des Européens 2004–2005: de l'élargissement au référendum français*, Paris, Presses de Sciences Po, 2005.

Peyrefitte, A., *C'était de Gaulle*, Vol II, Paris, Gallimard, 1998.

Prate, A., *La France en Europe*, Paris, Economica, 1995.

Richardson, J. (ed.), *European Union: Power and Policymaking*, 2nd edition, London, Routledge, 2001.

Ross, G., *Jacques Delors and European Integration*, Oxford, Polity Press, 1995.

Schmidt, V., *From State to Market? The Transformation of French Business and Government*, Cambridge, Cambridge University Press, 1996.

Schwok, R., 'La France et l'intégration européenne: une évaluation du "paradigme identitariste" ', *French Politics and Society*, 17(1), Winter 1999, pp. 56–66.

Séguin, P., 1993, 'Les Français et l'Europe, regard d'un anti-Maastricht', SOFRES, *L'état de l'opinion 1993*, Paris, Seuil, pp. 93–104.

Simonian, H., *The Privileged Partnership: Franco-German Relations in the European Community, 1969–1984*, Oxford, Clarendon Press, 1985.

Smith, A., 'La Commission européenne et les fonds structurels: vers un nouveau modèle d'action', *Revue Française de Science Politique*, 46(3), June 1996, pp. 474–95.

SOFRES, *L'état de l'opinion*, Paris, Seuil, 1993, 1997, 1999 and 2000 (Europe chapters in each of these years' issues).

Teasdale, A., 'The politics of majority voting in Europe', *Political Quarterly*, 67(2), 1996, pp. 101–15.

Trouille, J.-M., 'Franco-German relations, Europe and globalisation', *Modern and Contemporary France*, 9(3), August 2001, pp. 339–54.

Vaïsse, M., *La Grandeur*, Paris, Fayard, 1998.

Wallace, H. and Wallace, W., *Policy-Making in the EU*, 3rd edition, Oxford, Oxford University Press, 1996.

Webber, D., *The Hard Core: The Franco-German Relationship and Agricultural Crisis Politics*, Badiana di Fiesole (Italy), European University Institute, 1998.

15 Conclusion

The political aims of the founders of the Fifth Republic were clearly stated: to destroy the weak and despised régime of the Fourth Republic, which had been undermined by a defective constitution, by unstable and short-lived governments, by a parliament which was omnipotent in theory but impotent in practice, by divided and undisciplined parties, by a ubiquitous and powerful administration, by a resentful and disobedient army and by overactive pressure groups. The new Republic was to be both strong and respected, underpinned by a constitution which strengthened the powers of the executive and ensured the president's pre-eminence in all matters affecting the nation's long-term future; parliament, the parties, the administration and the pressure groups – as well as the army, the immediate cause of the Fourth Republic's downfall – were to be relegated to their proper, and subordinate, place.

The founders achieved many of these goals. In dramatic contrast to its predecessors, the new régime quickly won a degree of consensual support, or at least acceptance, among elites and people alike. The powers of parliament were effectively curbed. The antics of small and undisciplined parties no longer dominated the political scene. Voters were offered a new clarity of electoral choice within a bipolarised party system. Prime ministers enjoyed longer periods in office, and governments the appearance of stability.

The change of régime had a salutary effect, too, on policy outcomes. Difficult policy decisions were taken, and stuck despite opposition from large and sometimes powerful minorities of the electorate: the spending cuts of 1959, the generalisation of subsidies to Catholic schools, the opening of the French economy to European competition and above all the withdrawal from Algeria. The army, the 'State within the State' during the previous régime, was reduced to silent obedience to the civil authorities. Diplomatically, France quickly ceased to be the object of international derision that it had been before 1958. In the newly stable political environment, with the disruption of ruinous colonial wars removed and the opportunities afforded by European integration added, an extra point was added to France's economic growth, which averaged 4.5 per cent from 1950 to 1960 but 5.5 per cent from 1960 to 1973. And growth was no longer disturbed, as it had been under the Fourth Republic, by periodic crises involving inflation, the trade balance, government finances, or all three at once.

Perhaps the most important, and certainly the most striking, political change in the years after 1958 was the emergence of the presidency as the major focus of political decision-making in France. The reasons for the growth of presidential power in the early Fifth Republic have been analysed at length in this book: the desire of successive presidents to extend the scope of their powers; their use and abuse of the 1958 constitution; the strengthening of their electoral legitimacy by the reform of October 1962; the reinforcement of the Élysée staff; the transformation of ministers into political servants; the largely unexpected emergence of the *fait majoritaire*, giving presidents the backing in parliament of a sympathetic and disciplined party coalition; the weakness and divisions of the political opposition in the early period when the régime was taking shape; and the exploitation of propitious political circumstances. Personal, constitutional and political factors combined, therefore, to ensure presidential supremacy. Before March 1986, that supremacy was demonstrated on innumerable occasions. For instance, de Gaulle's unilateral decision not to devalue the franc in the autumn of 1968 was matched by Giscard's personal decision to halt the extension of the Paris left-bank motorway in the summer of 1974, and Mitterrand's personal decision to withdraw the Savary education bill in 1984. Moreover, the general guidelines of important policy areas bear the unmistakable personal imprint of successive presidents. France's foreign, European and defence policies were shaped by de Gaulle; industrial policy bore the Pompidou hallmark; the liberalising measures in the social field taken between 1974 and 1976 owed much to the personal determination of President Giscard d'Estaing; the spate of reforms of the 1981–83 period, whether ephemeral (nationalisations) or more lasting (territorial decentralisation and political liberalisation), were very much inspired by the preferences and priorities of Mitterrand. In some respects, therefore, it is not totally misleading to describe the French political system as 'presidential'. Certainly, the presidency was *perceived* as the major focus of decision-making by the general public, by the political and administrative elite, and by the pressure groups. Abroad, the combination of security of tenure (*à l'américaine*, but with seven years not four, until the reform of 2000 reduced the French figure to five) and an *apparent* ability to control parliament (*à l'anglaise*) made the French president appear the most powerful head of the political executive in any Western democracy.

The newly salient presidency of the Fifth Republic had its ideological opponents, Mitterrand among others at first. They attacked it as too personal, too far removed from the parliamentary traditions of the French Republic, too Caesarist. More practical critics also focused on the personalisation of power. Would the Republic survive its founder? or the Gaullist ascendancy in French politics? or a full *alternance*? In fact, the Fifth Republic proved robust enough, and flexible enough, to do all three, and more. De Gaulle's resignation was followed, not by chaos or régime change, but by a straight-forward presidential election. So was Pompidou's death. The Gaullists' loss of the presidency to Giscard precipitated no 'return to the Fourth Republic'. Alternation in power, long despaired of by the Left, was peacefully achieved in 1981. The election of a parliamentary majority opposed to the president, while it certainly entailed a radical change to the location of political power within the Fifth Republic, produced, not the expected constitutional crisis, but the equipoise of cohabitation – delicate but still workable.

This régime's adaptability extended beyond mere survival. It could also be discerned, arguably, in the transformation of the local government system, described in Chapter 12, and in the dialectical relationship to Europe, at once shaping and being shaped by the construction of the EU. Above all, perhaps, it could be seen in the responses – however delayed – to the more difficult economic environment of the late twentieth century. France under Mitterrand resolved to squeeze inflation out of France's economy, even at the cost of low growth and unpopularity. Nationalised industries were first allowed to behave like private businesses (and thus to lay off workers) before being sold off in what was for long Western Europe's biggest privatisation programme, engaged by the Right but followed, albeit with rather less enthusiasm, by the Left. Exchange controls were removed. France's Stock Exchange, once one of the sleepiest in Europe, was revolutionised. This 'heroic dismantling of heroic capability', in Vivian Schmidt's words, pursued by Right and Left alike, made of France, once the land of state-owned national champions (some more accurately described as lame ducks), home to some of the world's largest international businesses. The Forbes list of the world's 2,000 biggest companies featured 61 French-based firms in 2005, more than for any other country except for the United States, the UK, Japan and (narrowly) Germany. The top 50 included Axa, the world's largest insurer by sales; Total, the world's fourth oil company; and two French banks (BNP Paribas and Société Générale). Renault, recently a national producer as prone to losses as its cars were to rust, became the main shareholder of Nissan in 1999, able to impose both a managing director and a ferocious cost-cutting programme on the Japanese firm; the Renault-Nissan group is the world's fourth car producer, with plants in over thirty countries (and France, unlike Britain, has preserved a home-based motor industry). France's water companies have moved successfully into the UK and other markets. France's Carrefour retailing group achieved sales equivalent to those of Britain's Tesco and Sainsbury's combined. French household names in the Forbes list also include Danone in dairy products, Bouygues or Lafarge in the construction industry, Michelin in tyres, or L'Oréal, Dior and LVMH in the more traditional luxury goods sector.

France was also one of the world's most attractive locations for foreign direct investment, ranking fourth among OECD countries across the four years 2000–3. This was due in part to size and geographical location, but also to the ability of successive governments to preserve some of the best features of the Jacobin state at it had developed over the post-war generation: a level of infrastructure (motorways, urban transport systems, the high-speed train) and public services (notably health) that were second to none. France has at least limited that combination of private affluence and public squalor which J. K. Galbraith identified half a century ago as a characteristic feature of modern liberal capitalism. And the resources of the Jacobin state have been mobilised to ensure that the cost of the late twentieth century's economic upheavals does not fall solely on their victims.

Yet this benign view of France's régime and of its successes in policy terms, while not false, represents splashes of sunlight in what has become, in other respects, a more sombre picture. The weaknesses both of France's domestic policy record and of its political structures suggest the need for a more radical transformation than any undertaken since 1958.

Slow growth, unemployment, public spending

France's policy record by the early twenty-first century displayed three rather obvious weaknesses, alluded to in earlier chapters. The first, common to much but not all of the euro area, was slow growth. Over the ten years from 1994 to 2003, annual growth in

France averaged 1.7 per cent – higher than reunited Germany and (marginally) than Italy, but lower than every other country in the EU15. The second was mass unemployment, lasting (so far) across a whole generation. Since 1981, joblessness has fluctuated between 8.9 and 12.6 per cent; after a brief drop between 1997 and 2001, it resumed its upward trend and again exceeded 10 per cent by March 2005 – with the total reaching over a quarter among the 18–25-year-old age group.

Low growth and high unemployment are of course closely linked. Left-wing employment policies have tended to focus on sharing out what was believed to be a limited overall amount of work available, most obviously through provision for earlier retirement and longer holidays (after 1981) and a shorter working week (after 1997). The apparent success of the 35-hour week in promoting job creation between 1998 and 2001 seemed to confirm this view. But the costs in government subsidies to the scheme of various types were high, and France's economy did not weather the world downturn of the early twenty-first century better than others. Though less active in the promotion of work-sharing policies, the Right long did little to question the underlying assumption – and its corollary, that when the baby-boom generation began to retire, from about 2005, unemployment would fall as the labour force shrank. By the early twenty-first century France had one of the lowest levels of labour market participation in the developed world. French workers, though among the world's most productive, entered the labour force late (at over 20 on average, and often at 25, after completing higher education), left it early (at 57 on average) and worked fewer hours during their active years. Only from 2002 did a right-wing government move simultaneously (and cautiously) to lengthen the working week and the working lifetime. It was given intellectual backing in 2004 in a report from a committee chaired by the former International Monetary Fund head Michel Camdessus, which argued that France's unusually low labour market participation held back growth rather than stimulating it.

A third area of weakness concerned public finance. Public spending in France – by central government, local authorities and the social security system – now runs at some 54.5 per cent of GDP, a level only exceeded in Scandinavia. High public spending does not necessarily entail economic weakness, as the contrast between strong Scandinavian growth rates and Japanese lethargy from the early 1990s indicates. The difficulty arises from the sources of spending and the uses to which it is put. In France it has proved unsustainably sourced, economically ineffective (in part) and socially unjust.

French public expenditure has exceeded receipts in every year since 1981 – by 4 per cent of GDP in 2003, and nearly that much in 2004. Public-sector debt as a proportion of GDP has more than tripled, from 20 to over 64 per cent, since 1981. Both deficit and debt exceed European Stability and Growth Pact limits. Annual interest payments are equivalent to 14 per cent of the state budget, or, in 2005, roughly the totality of France's (admittedly quite low) income tax receipts. The burden on tomorrow's taxpayers will be heavier.

Economically unproductive expenditures coexist with colossal unfulfilled needs in other areas. In the former category could be placed, in addition to the interest payments noted above, the cost of the 35-hour week (estimated at 1.2 per cent of GDP); or the cost of tax collection; or the *revenu minimum d'insertion*, a dole which keeps its recipients just short of destitution but which has not so far been complemented by serious measures to assist them to return to work; or the usual run of abortive public projects skewered annually in the reports of the Cour des Comptes. Against such items, by contrast, should be set the chronic underfunding of France's university system (French university students are less well funded than those in secondary school; half fail their second-year examinations at the first attempt), and to a lesser extent of vocational training, and the underinvestment of the public sector in research, especially in new technologies. If left uncorrected, according to the Camdessus report, the combination of low labour force participation and low research spending risk dragging France's growth potential permanently below 1.8 per cent from 2015.

French public spending is also rather ineffective at achieving the social cohesion that the French rightly value. Perhaps the best symbol of this are the big rundown public housing estates on the outskirts of most major French cities, with their concentrations of crime and unemployment and the absence or degradation of public services. France's social spending is comparable to Sweden's (at 28.5 per cent of GDP to Sweden's 28.9 and the OECD average of 20.3) but French child poverty is twice as high (at 7.3 per cent of the population under 18, against Sweden's 3.6 and an OECD average of 12.1). Moreover, as analysts such as Timothy Smith have argued, French social spending favours older white men against younger people, especially if they are women or first- or second-generation immigrants, and protects workers in permanent jobs to the detriment of the three million on short-term contracts or in part-time work, or the 2.5 million unemployed. The juxtaposition in the same society of large numbers of comfortable pensioners with unemployed or underemployed young people is not an obvious recipe either for social cohesion or economic success in the long term. It is all the more dangerous when combined with the racial tensions arising from France's failure to integrate a large proportion of second-generation immigrants: in that light, the riots of November 2005 could be viewed as a sign of worse to come.

If this (very summary) diagnosis is founded, it follows that – even without cutting tax revenues from their current level of 46.5 per cent of GDP – there is an urgent need both to reduce public spending (to remedy France's structural deficit) and to redirect part of it towards areas that do more to promote future prosperity and to reinforce social cohesion. Such action has taken place, but to a limited degree; successive governments have failed to bring public finances under long-term control. This failure suggests that nearly half a century after its foundation, the features most readily valued in the Fifth Republic – its decisiveness and authority – have weakened, while those most frequently criticised – its tendency to authoritarianism and its difficulty in engaging with civil society – have persisted. The problem is less that France's governments operate under constraints (all governments do, as the next section outlines) as that they have become less effective at operating within them.

The politics of constraint

Any government faces constraints of at least half a dozen types. Perhaps the most obvious, discussed above, is budgetary. Another is external, especially in the economic and monetary domains. This has a long pedigree. It was a monetary crisis that signalled the downfall of both the Cartel des Gauches, in 1925, and Léon Blum's Popular Front government, in 1937. But we have argued at length in Chapter 1 that external constraints intensified from the 1970s, in ways that have taken the umbrella name of globalisation. To this may be added, as we have suggested in Chapter 14, the EU, which binds its member states even if they themselves tie the knots. A third set of constraints arises from the configuration of voter and party support on which the government rests, from the power and mobilisation of parties and factions within the ruling coalition, from the proximity of elections, and from the government's popularity with voters. A fourth lies in the machinery of government itself. Governments need bureaucracies to function. Bureaucracies generate every type of irrationality, from budget-maximising competition to turf disputes to the capture of parts or the whole by forces or groups in civil society. Attempts to co-ordinate bureaucracies may themselves create problems of co-ordination, especially in a large, complex and centralised state like France. The journey from political decision to results on the ground is often, therefore, long and hazardous. A fifth type of constraint arises from civil society, from those (usually organised) groups whose active co-operation or passive acceptance governments require for the successful conception and implementation of policy. Sixth, constitutions are an obvious constraint on governments – even if that of France is comparatively easy to amend, and even if it has been violated with impunity on a small number of occasions, chiefly by de Gaulle. The seventh type of constraint is constituted by the range of political and institutional norms and prejudices usually labelled as political culture. Political culture, however slippery a notion, is what best explains why a dissolution of parliament to suit the government's political convenience, though acceptable in Britain, is viewed as suspicious or downright dishonest in France (hence, in part, the Right's defeat in 1997).

The final constraint, common to all states but unique to each, is the past. Yesterday's commitments are today's enforced priorities; yesterday's mistakes are today's pre-occupations. The Fifth Republic, in spite of claims to the contrary by its apologists, inherited a great deal from its predecessor. After May 1958 the upper part of the political superstructure may have been modified, but there was no upheaval in the social, economic and political substructure. Nor did basic cultural traits disappear with the waving of a Gaullist wand. The same social forces remained intact, the same economic interests continued to strive for superiority, the same administrative machine still functioned, and no one dismantled the vast and complex web of committees, commissions and councils which had proliferated since the end of World War II. The Fourth Republic bequeathed much to its successor: a booming economy and a rapidly changing occupational structure; a vague yet pervasive ideology rooted in a not always consistent series of traditions such as the primacy of universal suffrage, 'republican legality', the (relative) independence of the judiciary, the legitimacy of governmental interventionism within the framework of a mixed economy, and respect for free speech and association; its basic institutional framework; most of its political and administrative elite (the departure from politics of the last two Fourth Republic ministers, Mitterrand and Chaban-Delmas, had to wait till 1995); a jumble of political norms and conventions (such as the usefulness of the *cumul des mandats* described in Chapter 12) that could be transgressed only with the utmost caution; a wide-ranging series of domestic, diplomatic and defence commitments (for example, to an extensive system of social welfare, to the North Atlantic Alliance, to the European Economic Community); a tangle of social and economic expectations (full employment and rising living standards were taken for granted, practically for the first time in French history); a welter of established rights and privileges involving many powerfully placed groups; a number of seemingly intractable problems such as the Algerian war, which dominated and poisoned the politics of the early Fifth Republic. In many policy areas, such as housing, health, education and energy, the advent of the Fifth Republic was not a watershed, but a largely irrelevant political event.

The configuration of constraints never presents itself in identical form to different governments. To take an obvious example, growth and tax receipts may be dramatically raised or lowered by international events over which governments have no control. The power of groups within and outside the state apparatus may be by turns stable, structured, apparently invulnerable and durable, or else fluid and variable. Such power is sometimes personal, sometimes institutional. It may be manifested sporadically or exercised persistently. Certainly the power configuration in any modern state, and France is no exception, is multifaceted, complex and evanescent.

Successful government could be characterised as the successful management of constraint. Constraint can be managed in three ways: by acceptance of the unmovable, accompanied by an effort of pedagogy towards voters; by using the available assets of governments – electoral legitimacy, the referendum, or simply money – to overcome or at least to modify those constraints that are not set in stone; or by transforming constraint in one domain into a tool to act on those in other areas. An example of the first could be observed in de Gaulle's acceptance of the need to devalue the franc in 1959 – and his accompaniment of this by the monetary reform launching the new franc. The second is well represented by de Gaulle's decision to face down the army and the French settlers in Algeria who had brought him to power; the third by the tendency of successive governments to use the European 'constraint' as a lever for the modernisation of France's economy. From this perspective, too, an unsuccessful government may be seen as characterised by its failure to follow any of these courses; and by its tendency to submit to constraints without either mobilising against them or explicitly acknowledging their presence.

A weak régime?

The preceding chapters have highlighted the extent to which the strengths which set the early Fifth Republic apart from its predecessor have either diminished with half a century's use or have been bought at the price of weakness in other areas. This is true, first and foremost, of the presidency, which suffers from being unaccountable and overpersonalised while at the same time curiously hampered in other respects.

Outside periods of cohabitation, the president may dictate policy to the government, in the assurance that parliament will do little to oppose him, and without any constitutional obligation to defend his actions to any official body. Such actions may involve anything from the reinforcement or downgrading of France's nuclear deterrent to the choice of architect for the new national library. Constitutionally unable even to set foot in parliament while in office, the president defends his actions only to the media, before journalists and at times of his own choosing, and with no equivalent right of reply for the opposition. The Chirac years, moreover, have established that the president is immune from prosecution for anything less than high treason. Such privileges are unusual among chiefs of democratic executives. An American president may see his legislative programme wrecked by Congress; a European prime minister appears regularly before parliament. Neither applies to the president of France – who is also the only head of a democratic executive able to dissolve the legislature without placing his own job at stake. If accountability in a democracy is a virtue, France suffers from a shortage of it at the very top.

A second dysfunction of the Fifth Republic presidency has been the personalisation of political power. This has not led to the tyranny feared by the régime's early critics. Nor is it unique to France; the rise of television has encouraged personalisation even in parliamentary democracies. What makes France an extreme case, however, is the combination of a powerful, directly elected presidency with traditionally weak political parties. De Gaulle's vision of a president above parties quickly proved a chimera, but one that cast a long symbolic shadow. The result has been an ambiguous, and therefore unhealthy, relationship between the president and his own party: all Fifth Republic presidents have followed de Gaulle's example and eschewed overt partisanship, while constantly intervening, forcefully if indirectly and above all covertly, in their own party's affairs. Parties, on the other hand, suffer from an almost permanent state of competition between *présidentiables*, in which policies serve more as ammunition than as means of promoting the public good.

Unaccountable and overpersonalised, the presidency is nevertheless far from omnipotent. Though considerable, his powers are limited both by constitutional and political restrictions (the two are closely intertwined) and by the difficulty encountered by any single individual in managing a complex political system. Every president has limited time at his disposal. The time-consuming business of political management is common to the head of any political executive; but on top of that, in the French case, come the ceremony and travel required of an official head of state. The time left for policy-making is therefore limited, and a president who assumes an over-interventionist role may find it physically crushing. Moreover, whereas in other democratic systems, heads of state or of government – the obvious case being the president of the United States – are assisted by large staffs, the Élysée team, though expanded and strengthened since 1958, is still small compared to the *gros village* which works for the prime minister. In some ways this is an advantage; large staffs present their own problems of administration and co-ordination. But the size of the Élysée staff obliges the French president to be selective. For this reason, he has to delegate many of his powers, and practically all control over policy implementation, to his prime minister and other ministers, who, in turn, are obliged to devolve authority onto *cabinets* and an army of civil servants.

There are also limitations to the president's powers in which the personal is closely linked to the political. A president who becomes too absorbed in the minutiae of legislation may disqualify himself from his wider role as the impartial arbiter and judge of the wider political implications of government action. And too intimate an involvement in making policy, some of which is bound to be politically controversial, may damage his image as the statesman above the political battle, the embodiment of the unity of the nation, the guide to its future action and the guardian of its basic interests. Opinion polls clearly reveal that the more active the president becomes in policy questions, the more his popularity declines; hence the frequent popularity of presidents during periods of cohabitation, whose policy-making role is much reduced. In addition, the over-concentration of political power in the hands of the president may lead to public identification of the president with the régime itself – an identification assiduously fostered by de Gaulle in his dire warnings to the voters of *moi ou le chaos*, but which was not without its dangers. Under these circumstances, episodes of presidential weakness may be magnified into periods of wider national dislocation. That was true when de Gaulle was absent or indecisive during the May 1968 crisis, when certain members of the government and the top civil service displayed the sense of purpose and direction of freshly decapitated chickens; in the later months of Pompidou's debilitating, and finally fatal, illness; in the summer of 1976, when inflation was high and rising, the franc low and falling, and the president abroad and hunting big game; or March

1983, when Mitterrand's vacillations over macroeconomic policy encouraged squabbles within the government and created that uncertainty which business so much dislikes. The same may prove to be the case of the weakened Chirac presidency following the 2005 referendum defeat.

If the Fifth Republic presidency of 'normal' times has not fulfilled the worst fears of the régime's opponents, therefore, it is very far from achieving the hopes of its founders. De Gaulle sought to be a leader above parties; the presidency has become the chief focus of inter-party and intra-party political competition. De Gaulle wanted the president to rise above day-to-day government and give his full attention to France's long-term interests; real presidents, both by inclination and by force of circumstance, have stepped into the front line of governing – and faced the practical limitations noted above.

This, of course, excludes the case of cohabitation. The election of a politically hostile National Assembly majority in 1986, 1993 and 1997 meant that many of the constitutional provisions which limited presidential power and which fell into abeyance after 1959 were revived: no longer, for example, could the president feel free to hire and fire ministers, including the first among them, at will. More important, perhaps, is that while cohabitation has not precipitated a major constitutional crisis, and can therefore be said to have 'worked', it has done so at considerable cost: France's Tweedledum and Tweedledee representation on the international stage, the sheer waste of time resulting from the state of permanent cold war within the executive, and the perception – all too clear in April 2002 – of complicity between the mainstream Left and Right are all illustrations of this. Cohabitation may have proved the régime's flexibility, but the political contorsions it entailed may also be viewed as a sign of its intrinsic perversity: as an alternative to constitutionally unchecked and unaccountable presidential power, it offers checks and balances, not so much between different branches of government as within the executive itself. Though cohabitation was rendered less likely by the shortening of the presidential term from 2002, it remains a possibility. Voters could split their tickets as their American counterparts have done and elect a president and a parliamentary majority of opposed political camps within a few weeks of each other, while presidential deaths, resignations and dissolutions all hold the potential to de-synchronise the elections.

The presidency is the Fifth Republic's defining feature; hence the prolonged attention we have given it. But it is not the régime's only flawed institution. The French parliament has, it is true, recovered partly from the largely supine state to which de Gaulle reduced it – a recovery that may be reinforced as the budgetary reform of 2001 is implemented. Yet it continues to suffer from the characteristic weaknesses of most contemporary democratic legislatures: with the civil service writing laws and drawing up budgets, the media holding the executive to account, and party discipline placing (most) legislators in straitjackets, parliaments and parliamentarians have lost much of their former centrality to the political process. In France this is compounded by the constitution's specific restrictions, set out in Chapter 6; by the separation of the presidency from the legislature, and the fact that (cohabitation aside) the government proceeds from the president's more or less free choice, reducing the role of parliament as a legitimiser of governments; and by the *cumul des mandats* and the absenteeism it encourages. As a forum for the expression and confrontation of competing forces within civil society it remains profoundly inadequate.

France's administration and public services have been credited with giving France, at first largely unaided by the politicians, the growth and prosperity of the *trente glorieuses* – and also vilified as idle and unproductive: it was Clemenceau who observed that a characteristic of any French administrative building was that you could see late-arriving employees passing those leaving early on the stairs. There is some justification in both views. France's administrative elites include exceptionally able men and women who retain a high-minded commitment to *le service public* – as well as others, less scrupulous, who use the civil service and the security of tenure it affords as a spring-board for careers in business or politics for which they are not necessarily best fitted. Lower in the hierarchy, hard-pressed teachers and healthcare workers coexist with the understretched and the bloody-minded. But assigning praise or blame to individuals or groups is beside the point. France's administration contrives to achieve many of the drawbacks of centralisation – insensitivity and slowness of response to specific or local needs – while failing to benefit from the supposed advantages of a chain of command: responsiveness to central direction too readily falls victim to deep fragmentation between ministries, directorates, services and *corps*, with even the core of the executive frequently resembling a huge Byzantine court riddled with feuding factions. The aspir-ation of policy-makers after 1958, that greater governmental powers, stability and authority would make decision-making and resource allocation more 'efficient' and more 'rational' than during the Fourth Republic has all too frequently given way to a fitful and supine incrementalism. And the difficulty of moving resources to match the changing needs of society inevitably detracts from the Jacobin ideal of equal access for all to public services of uniform quality. That reforming France's public services to allow greater flexibility should face resistance from public service workers is unsurpris-ing. So is their discourse of 'defending public services'. What is more remarkable is the regular support such resistance receives from the public, requiring any attempt at reform to be undertaken with infinite precaution if at all.

This explains, in part, the dilemma of recent French governments in relation to decentralisation. The chief beneficiaries of the Mitterrand decentralisation reforms, in the first instance, were those who had already been accumulating local power over the previous decades: city mayors above all, and presidents of the *conseils généraux* (figures who, in the view of observers such as Yves Mény, reproduce at local level the personal-isation of power assured nationally by the presidency). Perhaps inevitably, the reforms avoided some of the more difficult choices, and left much unfinished business. A gener-ation later, governments are still left with two intermediate territorial units, the region and the *département*, where one would probably do; with the ancient mosaic of muni-cipalities, partly compensated for by a system of intercommunal co-operation which increasingly places responsibility in the hands of indirectly elected councils; with an outdated, regressive and unjust system of local taxation; and with a range of public services – most obviously in education – that remain highly centralised. The Raffarin government's 'second wave' of decentralisation, though sanctioned by a constitutional amendment, encountered resistance as soon as it began to tinker with these issues: first from the Socialists who had pushed through the reforms of 1982, and then from a much wider range of local elected officials who feared, at a time of budgetary constraint, the transfer of responsibilities to local and regional government without the resources to discharge them adequately.

A particularly under-resourced arm of the state is France's judicial system. This, as we saw in Chapter 13, is the branch of the public services for which the French have the least respect – with a level of confidence unusually low even by European standards. It is seen not only as slow (an issue of resource), but also as ineffective (in its supposed leniency towards petty criminals) and above all as unfair. This is more than a matter of mere inconsistency, of an inability to strike the right balance between the rights of the accused, the aspiration to rehabilitate criminals and the popular demand for punishment. The view that the well-connected, and especially corrupt politicians and business executives, benefit from special treatment from the justice system while ordinary citizens face the full rigours of the law is deeply anchored among the French. And as we have seen, the opinion that politicians are 'generally corrupt' (entertained by 62 per cent of poll respondents in November 2003) has had an especially corrosive effect on French politics. For politicians of the mainstream parties there is no obvious escape from this. To attack their opponents as corrupt (even when they are) is to risk a bout of mutual mud-slinging which will merely reinforce the public's dim view of politicians 'in general'; to keep off the subject is to court accusations of complicity between parties of government. In the wider world, meanwhile, France figured in twenty-second place in Transparency International's index of perceptions of corruption in 2004, behind all of the EU15 states except for Spain, Portugal, Italy and Greece as well as a range of non-European countries including Hong Kong, Chile, Barbados and the United States.

Corruption is one feature of the French public's disenchantment with political parties, and especially with the mainstream parties of government. So is the sense of distance from the world of politics: 81 per cent of poll respondents in 1997 believed that 'politicians don't care what people like me think'; 70 per cent of poll respondents considered that they were 'not well represented' by a political party (and 74 per cent by a political leader) in 2000. So is the economic underperformance outlined above, and the resulting sense of failure in government, above all for households affected directly or remotely by unemployment. So is the perception of complicity between the mainstream parties, particularly lively during periods of cohabitation. Two months before the 1995 presidential election, 64 per cent of poll respondents agreed that 'whether the Right or the Left is in power, it adds up to the same thing'; two weeks before that of 2002 only 37 per cent discerned a significant difference between Chirac's and Jospin's programmes, compared with 57 per cent who did not. A decreasing proportion of the French are party members; a generally falling proportion, too, turn out to vote (unless, as in May 2005, they are given the opportunity to say a resounding no). The campaign of April 2002 was marked by each of these traits. They were aggravated by poll forecasts that at the run-off, the voters would have to choose between Chirac and Jospin; and by the availability of thirteen other candidates of Left and Right, each determined to measure his or her party's electoral strength by the first-round result even at the expense of their putative political allies. The widespread mobilisation against Le Pen underlined the continuing commitment of the great majority of the French to democratic values, but not to mainstream politicians. Chirac's re-election at the second ballot by 82 per cent of voters (and 62 per cent of registered electors) resulted above all from a wish to avoid the worst. He had, after all, been the first choice of under 20 per cent of voters (and only 13.75 per cent of the registered electorate), and as subsequent events showed, it gave him no unusual moral authority among the French to govern.

Disenchantment, even disgust, with parties and politicians has not meant either detachment from democratic values (at least in opinion polls, the public's commitment to these has strengthened rather than the reverse) or depoliticisation. For over a decade, observers have noted political mobilisation in France taking other forms, most obviously that of single-issue groups. The French were traditionally viewed as a nation of non-joiners; associations now attract as many members as in other Western democracies – some of them, such as Emmaüs, Médecins sans Frontières, or Attac acquiring an international dimension. In the aftermath of May 1968, France was partly left out of the wave of new social movements that crossed Europe; now a whole panoply of such movements mobilises French activists, from the various anti-racist groups to the unemployed movement, from the resurgent feminists of the late 1990s to one of Europe's most successful gay rights movements. Many of these per-form important functions, aside from the pursuit of short-term goals, of political agenda-setting, wielding what might be termed an *innovatory* or *pedagogical* power. Equally, however, it is the case that a wholesale shift of citizen mobilisation away from parties, which at least in principle aim to aggregate and reconcile diverse social demands into something resembling a programme of government, and towards single-issue groups, is unlikely to make governments more legitimate or their task any easier – especially in a country where the tradition of protest or insurrection is as lively as in France. At times, indeed, group mobilisation has appeared as a sort of extravagant alternative to normal political processes; the anti-Le Pen mobilisation between ballots in 2002 almost certainly helped keep the far Right-wing vote down at the run-off, but Le Pen could more economically have been eliminated altogether by a handful more votes for Jospin. Other groups, moreover, have exercised a more *intimi-datory* power; if they become sufficiently well known for turbulent or even violent activities, and if these are tolerated by apprehensive governments anxious to 'defuse the situation', then the most oblique and implicit of threats may achieve a result. Such groups join others, equally numerous, able to exert a more discreet form of *inhibitory* power. Public-sector unions may have achieved notable successes – for example, against the planned Juppé reforms in 1995 – by street mobilisation and well-supported strikes; the judges of France's commercial tribunals were just as effective, through more discreet channels, in preventing the Jospin government's attempts to reform entrenched practices that had been denounced by a parliamentary inquiry as a national scandal.

Taken individually, few if any of the political problems outlined above are unique to France. Most democratic countries complain of an overbearing executive and a weak-ened parliament, of a machinery of government which is overloaded, defective and inefficient. It is of the nature of local government to be an untidy patchwork, and of local taxes to be unfair. Most justice systems are overloaded, and pulled alternately between the development of a rights culture and popular (or populist) demands for tough sentencing. Virtually every established democracy has seen growing public dis-enchantment with government and political parties, often (though not always) fuelled by corruption. All have veto groups of one sort or another, and most have seen single-issue groups develop at the expense of parties. But two things distinguish France from most other democracies. The first is that France has experienced practically all of these difficulties, together, in a more or less acute form: a particularly unaccountable execu-tive, an unusually weakened parliament, an especially unwieldy bureaucracy governing (if that is the word) peculiarly centralised public services, an exceptionally fragmented local government system, courts held in rare contempt, a near-continuous rumble of corruption cases over fifteen years, and an uncommon range of veto groups. The sec-ond is a curious combination of hostility and high expectations: disgust with what is seen as the bias and favouritism of the public authorities coexists with a continuing regard for the public services and above all for the state – to the point where France's state-centred model is still seen as something that less enlightened systems would do well to emulate.

What readily results is a vicious circle. Poor economic performance, and above all rising unemployment, limit the freedom of manoeuvre of governments, financially but also politically – the more so as they may already have been destabilised by corruption scandals. Attempts to reform in order to improve economic performance, or to restore the public finances, rapidly encounter resistance, centred on interest groups that stand to lose out but often supported by much of the public and by opposition parties, whether moderate or extreme; the proposals are duly modified or withdrawn. Economic performance stays poor, losing popularity for the government and encouraging protest parties, but also leading growing numbers of voters to look to the state for protection (and to value the existence of the protected employment it offers). This reinforces resistance to reform, limiting the government's freedom of manoeuvre and perpetuating unstable finances and poor economic performance.

If this somewhat pessimistic account is accurate, it matters well beyond the confines of France. In the most general terms, first, the prosperity and political stability of the world's fifth largest economy are of interest to its partners and neighbours. More specifically, France's problems, though perhaps concentrated, extend to other countries at the heart of the euro-zone, Germany and Italy in particular. Finally, France's political difficulties have spilt over in dramatic form into the European arena. The defeat of the European constitutional treaty at the referendum of May 2005 will affect the future of the continent more profoundly than France's failure to ratify the Paris Treaty creating the European Defence Community half a century earlier.

At one level, the no vote reflected the dynamic of political alienation outlined above. It was a vote of protest both against an unpopular government (reflecting the poor poll ratings of both president and prime minister) and, more generally, against established mainstream parties and elites. At another level, the vote reflected the central ambiguities at the heart of France's relations with Europe: the preference for a strong Europe with weak institutions; the reluctance of an old nation state to surrender sovereignty to a supranational body of which it was nevertheless a founding member; and the aspiration to resolve both of these contradictions by making Europe in France's image. The debate on the constitution, even more than that on the Maastricht Treaty in 1992, laid bare these ambiguities. France's voters were invited to agree to a palpable strengthening of European institutions at the expense of national governments; an economic and social settlement within which, even if the free market was not engraved in stone as the treaty's left-wing opponents claimed, the notions of public services and social protection had no very privileged place. As in 1992, the no vote attracted right-wing nationalists, left-wing Jacobins and anti-capitalists. What was new was the wider circle of voters, especially those working in the public services, whose diffuse pro-European sentiments were counteracted, for the first time, by a sense of personal risk in the face of a Europe increasingly seen as a vector of globalisation and neo-liberal economics.

The irony of a no result is likely to be that it achieves the opposite result to that intended by its supporters. Some distinctive features of this old, complex, self-conscious and (still) highly political society may thereby be better safeguarded, within the confines of France, at least in the short term. But France will be in a weaker position to promote a French vision of the continent within the institutions of the EU. And the EU, without a constitution, will have less authority to further a distinctively European project in the wider world. Whatever his preoccupations with French sovereignty, it is unlikely that the founder of the Fifth Republic would have welcomed such an outcome.

Further reading

Baverez, N., *La France qui tombe*, Paris, Perrin, 2003.

Camdessus, M. (ed.), *Le sursaut: vers une nouvelle croissance pour la France*, Paris, La Documentation Française, 2004 (also on website http://www.lesrapports.ladocumentationfrancaise/BRP/044000498/0000.pdf).

Forbes data (leading companies) on http://www.forbes.com/lists/

Marseille, J., *La guerre des deux France*, Paris, Plon, 2004.

OECD, social statistics on France on http://www.oecd.org/dataoecd/35/22/34555346.xls

Smith, T., *France in Crisis: Welfare, Inequality and Globalization since 1980*, Cambridge, Cambridge University Press, 2004.

Transparency International, 2004 report on perceptions of corruption, on http://www.transparency.prg/cpi/2004/cpi2004.en.html

Appendix 1: Chronological table

Main events from the Revolution to the collapse of the Fourth Republic

1789	July	Fall of the Bastille.
	August	Abolition of all feudal rights.
1792	August	Fall of the monarchy.
	September	Establishment of the First Republic.
1793	January	Execution of Louis XVI.
1799	November	Bonaparte becomes First Consul.
1804	May	Establishment of First Empire.
1814	April	First abdication of Napoleon I and restoration of Louis XVIII.
1815	June	Battle of Waterloo, second abdication of Napoleon and second monarchical restoration.
1824	September	Charles X succeeds Louis XVIII.
1830	July	Revolution in Paris, abdication of Charles X, accession of Louis-Philippe.
1848	February	July monarchy overthrown, Second Republic proclaimed.
	December	Election of Louis Napoleon to the presidency of the Republic.
1851	December	*Coup d'État* by Louis Napoleon.
1852	December	Proclamation of the Second Empire, Napoleon III proclaimed emperor.
1870	July	Outbreak of the Franco-Prussian War.
	September	Battle of Sedan, collapse of the Second Empire and proclamation of the Third Republic.
1871	January	Armistice.
	March–May	Revolutionary Commune in Paris.
1875	January–December	Constitutional laws voted in parliament.
1877	May–June	Dissolution of the republican-dominated Chamber of Deputies by President MacMahon.
	October–December	Victory of the republicans in the elections.
1879	January	Resignation of the president of the Republic, republican victory in the senatorial elections, foundation of the 'Republican Republic'.
1887	November–December	Wilson scandal, leading to resignation of President Grévy.
1887–89		Republic threatened by General Boulanger and his supporters.
1892–93		Panama scandal.
1894	June	President Carnot assassinated.
1897		Beginning of the Dreyfus Affair, which drags on for seven years.
1903–5		Anti-clerical legislation culminating in the separation of Church and state.

1914	July	Assassination of Jaurès, socialist leader.
	August	Outbreak of World War I.
1918	November	Armistice.
1919	June	Versailles Treaty signed.
1920	December	Tours Congress, foundation of the French Communist Party.
1923	January	French occupation of the Ruhr (until 1930).
1934	February	Violent right-wing demonstrations in Paris.
1936	March	German re-militarisation of the Rhineland.
	April–May	Victory of the left-wing Popular Front in the elections.
	June	Popular Front government under Léon Blum.
	October	Spanish Civil War begins.
1937	June	Collapse of the Popular Front government.
1938	September	Munich Agreement.
1939	March	Germany occupies Czechoslovakia.
	September	Outbreak of World War II.
1940	May–June	France invaded, Pétain becomes head of government, de Gaulle to London, armistice. Half of France occupied.
1941	June	Germany invades Russia.
1942	November	Allied invasion of North Africa, the whole of France occupied.
1944	June	Allies land in Normandy.
	August	Paris liberated.
	September	General de Gaulle sets up government.
1945	May	End of World War II in Europe.
	October	French vote by referendum to end the Third Republic.
1946	January	General de Gaulle withdraws from the government.
	May	France votes against first proposed constitution.
	November	Constitution of the Fourth Republic accepted by referendum, and outbreak of the war in Indo-China.
1947	January	Election of Auriol as president of the Republic.
	April	Foundation of the first mass Gaullist movement – the RPF.
	May	Communists leave the government.
	June	Marshall speech on financial aid to Europe.
	November–December	Wave of political strikes.
1949	April	North Atlantic Treaty signed.
1951	April	Coal and steel agreement between France, Germany, Italy and the Benelux countries.
	June	General election.
1952	March–December	Pinay prime minister.
1953	January	Official end of the RPF.
	August	Sultan of Morocco deposed.
	December	Coty elected president of the Republic.
1954	May–July	Dien-Bien-Phu, end of war in Indo-China negotiated by Premier Mendès-France.
	November	Outbreak of the Algerian war.
1956	January	General elections in France, Poujadists fare well.
	February	Demonstrations in Algiers against Premier Mollet.
	March	Independence of Tunisia and Morocco.
	October	Anglo-French intervention in Suez.
1957	March	Treaty of Rome establishing European Economic Community.
1958	May	Revolt by French settlers in Algiers.
	June	General de Gaulle becomes head of government.
	September	Referendum on the Constitution of the Fifth Republic resoundingly passed.

Appendix 2: Chronological table

Main events from the foundation of the Fifth Republic until 2005

1958	September	Referendum on the Constitution of the Fifth Republic; 79.25 per cent vote in favour.
	October–November	Creation of the Gaullist UNR, general elections. Big Gaullist gains.
	December	General de Gaulle elected president by 78.5 per cent of the votes of the electoral college.
1959	January	De Gaulle proclaimed president of the Republic, Michel Debré appointed prime minister.
1960	January	Uprising in Algeria.
	April	Creation of the PSU.
1961	January	Referendum ratifying de Gaulle's policy of self-determination in Algeria: 75.26 per cent vote in favour.
	April	Army coup in Algeria against French government.
1962	March	Évian agreements on Algeria.
	April	Referendum ratifying Évian peace settlement with Algeria: 90.7 per cent of voters in favour. Pompidou becomes prime minister.
	August	Unsuccessful attempt on de Gaulle's life at Le Petit Clamart.
	October	Motion of censure passed against Pompidou government, parliament dissolved. Referendum for direct election of president of the Republic: 61.75 per cent in favour.
	October–November	General elections. Big gains for government.
1963	March–April	Miners' strike, government obliged to climb down.
1965	September	Creation of the FGDS (Fédération de la Gauche Démocrate et Socialiste) of Socialists, Radicals and left-wing clubs.
	December	De Gaulle re-elected president of the Republic at the second ballot against Mitterrand.
1966	February	France withdraws from NATO.
1967	March	General elections: narrow victory for the government.
	November	Creation of the Gaullist UDVe.
1968	May	The 'events' – student revolt and general strike, National Assembly dissolved.
	June	Big victory of the government in the general elections.
	July	Couve de Murville replaces Pompidou as prime minister.
	November–December	Collapse of the FGDS, Mitterrand withdraws temporarily from political life.
1969	April	Referendum on the Senate and on regional reforms: de Gaulle resigns after 52.4 per cent voted against.

1969	June	Pompidou elected president of the Republic at the second ballot against Poher. Chaban-Delmas appointed prime minister.
	July	Creation of the CDP and of a new Socialist Party under the leadership of Alain Savary.
1970	November	Death of General de Gaulle.
1971	June	Creation of the new Socialist Party: Mitterrand becomes first secretary.
1972	April	Referendum ratifying enlargement of the Common Market to include Great Britain, Ireland and Denmark: 67.7 per cent in favour, but abstentions, spoilt and blank votes total 46.75 per cent.
	June	Joint Programme of Government signed between the Socialists and the Communists.
	July	Messmer replaces Chaban-Delmas as prime minister.
1973	March	General elections: victory for the government, but with much reduced majority.
1974	April	Death of President Pompidou.
	May	Election of Giscard d'Estaing to the presidency at the second ballot against Mitterrand. Jacques Chirac becomes prime minister.
	October	Many leaders of the PSU join the Socialist Party.
1976	February	Twenty-second Congress of the PCF.
	March	Departmental elections: big gains for the Left.
	August	Chirac replaced as prime minister by Raymond Barre.
	December	Creation of the RPR headed by Chirac.
1977	March	Local elections: sweeping victory for the Left.
	May	Creation of the Republican Party (ex-Independent Republicans).
	September	Breakdown of negotiations between the Communists and the Socialists.
1978	February	Creation of the *Union pour la Démocratie Française* (UDF), electoral alliance grouping non-Gaullist parties of conservative presidential coalition.
	March	General elections: victory for the government by comfortable majority.
1979	March	Violent demonstrations in north and east to protest against government's economic policies.
	March	Departmental elections: left-wing gains.
	June	European elections.
1980	September	Senatorial elections: Socialist gains.
	November	Mitterrand announces candidacy for presidency.
	December	Law and order bill, 'Sécurité et Liberté' adopted.
1981	April	First ballot of presidential election.
	May	Election of Mitterrand to the presidency. Resignation of Prime Minister Barre who is replaced by Mauroy. National Assembly dissolved.
	June	Historic victory of Socialists in legislative elections. Mauroy forms second government which includes four Communists.
	October	Devaluation of the franc.
	November	Unemployment reaches 2 million.
	December	Nationalisation Law voted.
1982	January	Constitutional Council rejects several articles of the Nationalisation Law.
	February	New Nationalisation Law voted.

	March	Defferre Act on decentralisation voted. Elections to departmental councils: right-wing successes.
	June	New devaluation of the franc and austerity programme.
	November	Reform of electoral system for town councils.
1983	January	FLNC dissolved.
	March	Elections for municipal councils: Left loses 31 towns of more than 30,000 inhabitants. Mauroy forms his third government. Second austerity programme and new devaluation of the franc.
	April	Violent farmers' demonstration in Brittany.
	May	Doctors' strike.
	June	Demonstrations by police.
	August	French intervention in Chad.
	September	By-election at Dreux: extreme Right does well. Senatorial elections: gains for right-wing opposition.
1984	January	Several Communist attacks on government policies.
	February	Lorry-drivers block motorways.
	March	Demonstration by Catholics against Savary Bill on Church schools. PCF denounces restructuring of the steel industry.
	April	Demonstration by Lorraine steel workers in Paris: leaders of Communist Party participate.
	June	Elections to European Parliament: defeat of Left; extreme Right wins 11 per cent of poll. More than 1 million demonstrate in Paris against Savary Bill.
	July	Mitterrand withdraws Savary Bill. Mauroy resigns as prime minister; replaced by Laurent Fabius. Communists refuse to enter government.
	September	Press law voted.
	October	Unemployment reaches 2.5 million.
	November	Mitterrand meets Col. Kadhafi in Crete.
1985	February	Twenty-fifth Congress of PCF.
	March	Elections to departmental councils: new gains for Right.
	April	Michel Rocard resigns from the government.
	May	Central Committee of PCF critical of government.
	June	Rocard announces candidacy for 1988 presidential elections. Electoral system for legislative elections changed.
	August	*Rainbow Warrior* affair.
	September	Charles Hernu, defence minister, resigns as result of *Rainbow Warrior* affair.
	October	PS Congress at Toulouse: Rocard faction wins 28.5 per cent of votes.
1986	February	Three terrorist explosions in Paris. New French intervention in Chad.
	March	Legislative elections: Left defeated; small majority for moderate Right: Front National wins 31 seats; further decline of PCF. Regional elections: Right wins 20 of 22 councils. Chirac appointed prime minister. Series of bomb explosions in Paris.
	April	Right-wing programme presented to National Assembly: included wide-ranging privatisation and changes in nationality laws. CERES abandons Marxism and changes title to Socialisme et République.
	June	Mitterrand criticises government's proposals on reform of nationality laws.
	July	Mitterrand refuses to sign *ordonnance* on privatisation.

1986	September	Senate elections. Left loses ground.
	October	Mitterrand refuses to sign *ordonnance* on electoral constituencies. Electoral law for legislative elections: pre-1986 system re-introduced.
	November	Mitterrand again expresses disagreement with government over reform of nationality laws. Mitterrand publicly disapproves of bill destined to privatise part of prison service.
	December	Student demonstrations in Paris: Higher Education Bill withdrawn. Public-sector strikes.
1987	January	Mitterrand receives delegation of railway workers. Mitterrand expresses his disapproval of government policies in New Caledonia.
	March	Demonstration by 30,000 against proposed changes in nationality laws. Demonstration by 200,000 in Paris to defend social security system.
	April	Lille Congress of PS. Extreme Right organises demonstrations in Marseille against immigrants.
	May	André Lajoinie selected by PCF as candidate for 1988 presidential election.
	October	Pierre Juquin, dissident Communist, announces presidential candidacy.
1988	January	Jacques Chirac announces candidacy for presidential election.
	February	Raymond Barre officially announces candidacy for presidential election.
	March	Mitterrand officially announces candidacy for presidential elections.
	April	First ballot of presidential elections: Mitterrand and Chirac go through to the next round; Le Pen wins 14 per cent of votes. Lajoinie does badly.
	May	Re-election of Mitterrand as president. Michel Rocard appointed prime minister. National Assembly dissolved.
	June	Election to National Assembly: PS biggest party but no overall majority. Rocard reappointed prime minister.
	October–November	Wave of public-sector strikes.
	November	Referendum on the future of New Caledonia: the yes vote wins 80 per cent of votes cast, but abstentions, at 63 per cent, reach a record level. The Rocard government establishes the *revenu minimum d'insertion* (RMI), and the *impôt de solidarité sur la fortune* (ISF), to help pay for it.
1989	February	Roger-Patrice Pelat, a close friend of President Mitterrand, is charged with insider dealing during the purchase of American Can by the nationalised French firm Péchiney. Pelat dies of a heart attack the following month.
	March	Municipal elections. Socialists make up some of the ground lost in 1983, but Chirac wins every *arrondissement* in Paris. Green and Front National councillors elected in many towns.
	April–May	Abortive 'renovators' movement in RPR and UDF.
	June	Arrest of Paul Touvier, former leading member of the Vichy *milice*. European elections. Joint RPR–UDF list led by Giscard d'Estaing leads the poll, 5 points ahead of Fabius's Socialist list. Greens win 10.6 per cent of the vote and their first seats in the Strasbourg parliament.

	July	Celebration of bicentenary of the French Revolution.
	November	'Islamic scarf' affair. Education Minister Jospin seeks opinion of Conseil d'État to resolve the issue of whether Muslim girls should be allowed to wear a headscarf at school.
	December	Front National candidates win a parliamentary by-election at Dreux and a cantonal by-election at Salon-de-Provence. Complete end to exchange controls.
1990	January	Law on party finance increases state aid to parties, allows business funding and includes an amnesty for past offences.
	February	RPR congress. An unprecedented internal opposition motion tabled by Charles Pasqua and Philippe Séguin is defeated by a 2–1 vote.
	March	Chirac confirms refusal of any electoral agreement with the Front National. Socialist Congress. Confrontation over leadership posts between supporters of Laurent Fabius and Michel Rocard.
	April	Magistrates criticise the law on political finance after the amnesty of former minister Christian Nucci, tried for his involvement in the *Carrefour du développement* affair.
	May	Profanation of a Jewish cemetery at Carpentras provokes unanimous condemnation from all political parties except the Front National, and massive silent demonstrations.
	June	Fiftieth anniversary of de Gaulle's first London broadcast marks climax of the 'de Gaulle year', confirming the near-unanimous national veneration for de Gaulle. Creation of Union pour la France, an RPR–UDF confederation intended to co-ordinate policy and choose a common candidate for the presidential election in 1995.
	November	Demonstrations by *lycée* students force financial concessions on education budget from government. Government creates a new tax, the *contribution sociale généralisée*, to cover the widening social security deficit.
	December	Twenty-seventh Congress of PCF marked by relatively open debates.
1991	January	Beginning of Gulf war, with French participation alongside British, American and Arab forces. Jean-Pierre Chevènement resigns as defence minister in opposition to French policy.
	March	End of Gulf war.
	May	Mitterrand sacks Rocard as prime minister and replaces him with Édith Cresson.
	June	National Assembly ratifies Schengen agreements on abolition of European border controls. Chirac's speech on 'noise and smells' of immigrant families.
	September	200,000 farmers demonstrate in Paris.
	October	Beginning of contaminated blood scandal, as three Health Ministry officials are charged with failing to prevent the use of HIV-contaminated blood for transfusion to haemophiliacs. Poll shows 32 per cent of French 'agree with Le Pen's ideas'.

1991	November	Mitterrand announces plans for referendum on large-scale institutional reforms, including an element of proportional representation, for the second half of 1992.
	December	Mitterrand's popularity reaches record low as a result of scandals, rising unemployment and Cresson's poor performance as prime minister.
1992	January	Pierre Mauroy resigns as first secretary of PS, and is replaced by Laurent Fabius. Examining magistrate Renaud Van Ruymbeke searches PS headquarters in the course of investigations on the Urba affair.
	February	Signature of Maastricht Treaty on European Union.
	March	Regional and cantonal elections. Rout of Socialists, who keep one regional presidency out of 22. Strong showing of ecology groupings: a Green president of Nord–Pas-de-Calais.
	April	Mitterrand replaces Édith Cresson as prime minister with former finance minister Pierre Bérégovoy.
	June	Parliament adopts constitutional reform necessary to ratification of the Maastricht Treaty.
	September	France ratifies the Maastricht Treaty by a 51 per cent vote at referendum. Mitterrand is diagnosed as suffering from prostate cancer.
	December	Three Socialist former ministers, including Laurent Fabius, charged with offences relating to the contaminated blood scandal.
1993	February	Michel Rocard suggests left-wing alliance between Socialists, Greens, centrists and dissident Communists.
	March	Legislative elections. Right-wing landslide: RPR wins 257 seats, and UDF 215, against 57 for Socialists. Édouard Balladur appointed prime minister.
	April	Michel Rocard takes over Socialist Party after collective resignation of leadership.
	May	Suicide of former prime minister Pierre Bérégovoy.
	July	New privatisation law promulgated. Constitutional Council strikes down several parts of new immigration and nationality law.
	August	Wave of speculation against the franc leads to widening of fluctuation bands within the European Monetary System.
	October	Rocard becomes Socialist first secretary.
1994	January	Major demonstrations in support of secular schooling after failure of government attempts to increase state aid to Catholic schools. Twenty-eighth Congress of PCF. Official end to 'democratic centralism'. Georges Marchais, PCF secretary-general since 1972, hands over the leadership to Robert Hue.
	February	Unemployment reaches record level of 3,300,100, over 10 per cent up in a single year.
	April	Paul Touvier sentenced to prison for life for crimes against humanity.
	June	European elections. Michel Rocard resigns party leadership after Socialists' worst result since 1971 (14.5 per cent). Philippe de Villiers's Eurosceptical right-wing list wins 12.4 per cent. Adoption of Toubon Law on defence of French language.

	July	Pierre Suard, head of Alcatel Alsthom, is arrested and charged with corruption. Resignation of Communication Minister Alain Carignon, also later charged with corruption-related offences.
	September	Unemployment at 3,322,800, or 12.6 per cent of labour force. Revelations on Mitterrand's wartime past cause shock among Socialists.
	October	Alain Carignon, former minister and mayor of Grenoble, placed in custody awaiting trial for corruption-related offences.
	November	*Paris-Match* publishes photos of Mazarine, Mitterrand's natural daughter, whose existence had previously been concealed from the public. Jacques Médecin, former mayor of Nice, charged with corruption offences and imprisoned after extradition from Uruguay. Jacques Chirac announces his presidential candidacy.
	December	Liévin congress commits Socialists to a strongly left-wing line. Jacques Delors, outgoing European Commission president and a favoured figure in opinion polls, announces that he will not be a presidential candidate.
1995	January	Socialist Party members choose Lionel Jospin as presidential candidate after a one-member, one-vote selection process.
	February	Mitterrand appoints Roland Dumas to presidency of Constitutional Council. Balladur announces presidential candidacy, and promptly loses what had been a commanding poll lead.
	April	First ballot of presidential election. Jospin leads with 23.3 per cent to Chirac's 20.8 and Balladur's 18.6, but a total right-wing vote of over 59 per cent makes Chirac's future victory almost certain. Le Pen wins 15 per cent.
	May	Second ballot of presidential election. Chirac elected president with 52.6 per cent of votes. He resigns as mayor of Paris, leaving the succession to Jean Tiberi. Alain Juppé becomes prime minister. Bernard Tapie, businessman and former minister in Socialist governments, sentenced to a year in prison for corruption offences. Henri Emmanuelli, Socialist first secretary, given a suspended prison sentence of one year for offences related to corrupt party funding. Jacques Médecin, former mayor of Nice, sentenced to two years.
	June	*Le Canard Enchaîné* reveals that apartments belonging to the city of Paris have been rented out to senior elected officials of the city and their families at below-market rents. Municipal elections. Left-wing parties show strong resistance, and win several *arrondissements* in Paris. Front National wins Toulon, Marignane and Orange. After a four-year moratorium, Chirac announces resumption of French nuclear tests in Mururoa atoll.
	July	Seven die after Algerian Islamic militants plant a bomb in Saint-Michel metro station. Constitutional revision extends area of application of referendum.
	August	Resignation of free-market Finance Minister Alain Madelin.

1995	August–September	Chirac's and Juppé's popularity falls after tax rises and revelations on Juppé's son's use of an apartment belonging to the city of Paris.
	October	Chirac goes on television to reaffirm France's commitment to Maastricht convergence criteria, at expense of his presidential programme.
	November	Reshuffle removes most of the women appointed to the government in May. Juppé announces reforms to social security system and to public-sector pensions.
	December	A wave of demonstrations and strikes forces Juppé to withdraw parts of his reform plans, and leaves him, the government and Chirac deeply unpopular.
1996	January	Death of François Mitterrand.
	February	France's last nuclear test at Mururoa before switch to simulated testing.
	June	Juppé announces plans for an austerity budget to meet Maastricht convergence criteria.
	August	After some signs of recovery since 1994, unemployment rises again, to 12.5 per cent.
1997	February	Front National candidate Catherine Mégret wins municipal by-election at Vitrolles. Left-wing parties mobilise against reform of nationality laws.
	March	Jean Tiberi, mayor of Paris, charged with corruption offences. Front National's Strasbourg congress provokes large anti-Fascist demonstrations, and sets the scene for confrontation within FN between Le Pen and Bruno Mégret.
	April	Chirac announces dissolution of National Assembly, ten months before the end of its term in March 1998.
	May	First round of legislative elections. Left–Green alliance wins 42.5 per cent of votes cast, against 36 per cent for mainstream right-wing coalition and 15.1 per cent for the far Right.
	June	Left–Green alliance wins a majority of seats at second round of legislative elections. Juppé resigns and is replaced as prime minister by Lionel Jospin, who forms a government with Socialist, Communist and Green ministers. Juppé also leaves leadership of RPR, where he is replaced by Philippe Séguin.
	June	Signature of Amsterdam Treaty, effecting limited reforms to EU, notably in common immigration policy.
1998	January	Wave of occupations of benefit offices by unemployed workers is ended by police interventions and limited government concessions.
	February	Claude Érignac, prefect of Corsica, murdered.
	March	Regional and cantonal elections. Right loses six regional presidencies to Left. Four right-wing presidents stay in office thanks to alliances with the Front National, provoking damaging controversy within mainstream Right.
	April	Maurice Papon, secretary-general of the Gironde prefecture during the Occupation, convicted of crimes against humanity for his role in deportation of Jews. Roland Dumas, president of the Constitutional Council, charged with corruption offences related to the sale of French-built frigates to Taiwan.

	May	Launch of 'The Alliance' grouping RPR and UDF. Alain Madelin withdraws Démocratie Libérale from UDF.
	July	France's World Cup victory confirms climate of renewed national optimism, with renewed growth and falling unemployment.
	December	Split of Front National as Bruno Mégret leaves with a significant number of the party's cadres. Government adopts bill on the 35-hour week.
1999	January	The euro becomes Europe's currency in commerce and on money markets, though not yet in the pockets of individuals.
	March	Start of Kosovo war between Western allies, including France, and Serbia.
	April	Séguin resigns as president of RPR, and is temporarily replaced by Nicolas Sarkozy.
	June	End of Kosovo war. European elections. Defeat and division of both mainstream Right (divided between three lists) and of far Right. Pasqua and de Villiers create a new Eurosceptic right-wing party, the Rassemblement pour la France. Strong showing of Green list led by Daniel Cohn-Bendit (9.7 per cent), and of CPNT list, which wins over 6 per cent and seats in Strasbourg parliament. Start of parliamentary debates on reform of the justice system. Constitutional amendment encourages parity of political representation between men and women.
	November	Resignation of Finance Minister Dominique Strauss-Kahn, suspected of having received payment for non-existent consultancy work with France's main student insurance firm.
	December	Michèle Alliot-Marie elected president of the RPR, the first woman to become leader of a major French party.
2000	January	Chirac abandons plans for constitutional reform to the justice system in the face of opposition from right-wingers in National Assembly and Senate.
	February	Parity law voted, implementing the 1999 constitutional amendment.
	March	Laurent Fabius and Jack Lang enter government in reshuffle. Roland Dumas resigns as president of Constitutional Council. He is replaced by a Gaullist, Yves Guéna.
	May	Unemployment falls below 10 per cent. Former president Giscard d'Estaing announces intention to put down a private member's bill reducing the presidential term to five years.
	June	Chirac approves the shortening of the presidential term, which is voted by parliament.
	September	Referendum on five-year presidential term. Abstentions exceed 70 per cent, and blank and spoilt ballots over 4.5 per cent of votes cast. But the reform is passed by 73 per cent of valid votes. A testimony by Jean-Claude Méry, formerly an RPR fundraiser, recorded on video and released posthumously, gives details of the illegal finance of the RPR and accuses Chirac of direct involvement.
	December	French presidency of EU ends with Nice Treaty.

2001	March	Municipal elections. Left wins in Paris, Lyon and Dijon, but right-wing victories in provinces and several large towns.
	March	Unemployment below 9 per cent.
	May	Publication of memoirs of General Aussaresses relaunches debate on torture in Algerian war.
	June	Revelations on Chirac's purchase, in 1992–93, of air tickets for over 2 million francs paid in cash again raises the question of the relationship between politics and justice.
	11 September	Attacks on New York. France quickly moves to help defeat Taliban in Afghanistan.
2002	1 January	Euro banknotes and coins replace francs in France.
	21 April	First round of presidential election. Elimination of the Socialist Prime Minister Lionel Jospin by Le Pen. Almost all parties call for Chirac vote.
	5 May	Jacques Chirac re-elected with 82 per cent of vote.
	6 May	Jospin resigns and is replaced by Jean-Pierre Raffarin.
	9 and 16 June	Legislative elections. Big majority for new right-wing party, the UMP.
	20 November	UMP formally launched at congress.
2003	12 February	Government uses Article 49–3 of the Constitution to pass reforms to electoral law for regional and European elections. The reform is censured by the Constitutional Council.
	17 March	Constitutional amendment specifies 'decentralised' nature of Republic.
	19 March	Beginning of second Iraq war, opposed by Chirac.
	20 March	Start of Elf trial.
	May–June	Strikes to protest against government pensions reform.
	13 June	Convention for the Future of Europe releases draft constitutional treaty.
	August	Heatwave kills estimated 15,000 elderly people, damaging popularity of Raffarin government.
	3 September	Raffarin announces continuation of tax cuts despite risk of France exceeding Europe's 3 per cent deficit target.
	December	Intergovernmental conference in Rome fails to agree on constitutional treaty.
2004	30 January	Alain Juppé, former prime minister and the president of Chirac's party, the UMP, receives a suspended 18 months' prison sentence plus a ten-year ban on holding elective office for his role in city hall corruption.
	March	Law banning visible religious signs (such as the Muslim scarf or veil) from schools is passed, after December 2003 report from Stasi Commission.
	21 and 28 March	Regional elections. Big gains for the Left, which wins over 50 per cent of votes for first time since 1988. FN stagnates with 13 per cent, moderate Right drops to 37 per cent. Chirac seeks a more 'social' dimension to his government. The defeat for the Right is followed by a government reshuffle, in which Sarkozy is moved from the Interior to Finance.
	1 May	Ten new member states (Latvia, Lithuania, Estonia, Cyprus, Malta, Poland, the Czech Republic, Slovakia, Slovenia, Hungary) enter the EU.

	1 June	Noël Mamère, mayor (Vert) of Bègles (outside Bordeaux) celebrates France's first gay marriage, but is censured for it in the courts.
	6 June	Sixtieth anniversary of D-Day landings. For the first time a German chancellor and the Russian president take part in the celebrations.
	13 June	European elections. Record abstention (over 57 per cent of electorate). Victory for former *gauche plurielle* with 43 per cent of vote (29 per cent for PS, 7.4 per cent for Greens, 5.25 per cent for PCF). Extreme Left and Right stagnate with 2.6 per cent and 9.8 per cent respectively. The UMP wins only 16.6 per cent of vote, and the UDF 11.9 per cent.
	18 June	European Council signs the European constitutional treaty.
	14 July	Chirac announces referendum on the European constitutional treaty.
	September	Within PS, Laurent Fabius declares opposition to European constitutional treaty.
	November	Juppé resigns from UMP leadership, and is succeeded by Nicolas Sarkozy. Sarkozy resigns position as finance minister.
	December	PS members vote in favour of the European constitutional treaty at an internal party referendum.
2005	February	Finance Minister Gaymard resigns after minor property scandal.
	February	Reforms incorporate a Charter of the Environment to the French Constitution and adapt the text to the European constitutional treaty.
	March	Big demonstrations over the 35-hour week and wages are followed by the first no majority in the polls on the referendum on the European constitutional treaty.
	29 May	European constitutional treaty defeated at referendum by nearly 55 per cent of voters.
	31 May	Raffarin resigns, to be replaced as prime minister by Dominique de Villepin. Sarkozy re-enters government as interior minister, but keeps his post as party leader.
	1 June	Dutch referendum rejects the European Constitution.
	16–17 June	European summit. Deadlock on the issues of the British budget contribution and the future of the Common Agricultural Policy.

Appendix 3: Voting behaviour, presidential election, first ballot, 21 April 2002: penetration of each social group by candidate

(Source: SOFRES, *L'état de l'opinion 2003* (Paris, Seuil, 2003), pp. 91–2)

	Far Left (3 candidates)	Hue (PCF)	Jospin (PS)	Other moderate Left (2 candidates)	Mamère (Verts)	Chirac (RPR)	Other moderate Right (4 candidates)	St-Josse (CPNT)	Le Pen (FN)	Mégret (MNR)
Total	10.4	3.4	16.2	7.7	5.2	19.9	13.8	4.3	16.9	2.3
Men	8	4	13	8	6	17	11	7	23	3
Women	12	3	18	7	5	22	15	2	12	2
Age range										
18–24	19	2	10	8	13	12	15	2	16	1
25–34	12	0	17	13	7	15	14	6	17	1
35–49	12	3	14	7	6	14	15	6	20	3
50–64	9	6	16	8	3	18	12	5	21	2
65 and over	5	5	20	4	2	36	13	2	10	3
Employment group										
Self-employed	8	0	8	5	4	18	31	9	17	0
Public-sector employee	14	3	17	16	8	11	12	4	14	1
Private-sector employee	13	2	16	6	5	14	12	6	23	3
Unemployed	17	3	14	7	11	17	5	2	20	4
Not economically active	8	5	17	6	4	26	15	3	14	2

Occupation of head of household

Shopkeeper, artisan, small business	4	2	5	7	2	23	29	5	20	3
Professions, managers	8	2	11	17	10	15	27	1	8	1
Intermediate groups	13	2	14	18	7	12	11	4	18	1
White-collar worker	20	3	10	13	6	16	10	3	18	1
Blue-collar worker	15	3	4	15	5	12	7	7	27	5
Retired	8	5	6	18	3	28	12	3	15	2

Educational qualifications

None	10	3	0	21	2	28	9	5	16	6
Primary	9	6	4	17	2	29	13	3	16	1
Secondary (baccalauréat)	10	4	5	14	4	17	12	7	23	4
Secondary (technical)	14	3	10	16	5	15	14	4	18	1
University or equivalent	11	2	12	16	10	17	18	2	11	1

Religion

Regularly practising Catholic	4	0	5	12	2	37	27	1	10	2
Occasionally practising Catholic	7	1	7	14	2	24	23	5	17	2
Non practising Catholic	12	3	7	15	6	18	10	6	21	2
Other religion	4	1	6	29	7	22	16	4	6	5
No religion	18	8	9	18	8	8	9	3	16	3

Appendix 4: Voting behaviour, legislative elections, second ballot, 9 June 2002, in constituencies where one left-wing and one right-wing candidate present: penetration of each social group by Left and Right

(Source: IPSOS poll on http://www.ipsos.fr/CanalIpsos/poll/7573.asp)

	Left	*Right*
Total	47	53
Men	49	51
Women	45	55
Age range		
18–24	53	47
25–34	54	46
35–44	54	46
45–59	48	52
60–69	23	77
70 and over	39	61
Employment group		
Self-employed	21	79
Public-sector employee	56	44
Private-sector employee	50	50
Retired, not economically active	35	65
Occupation of interviewee		
Shopkeeper, artisan, small business	26	74
Professions, managers	54	46
Intermediate groups	58	42
White-collar worker	49	51
Blue-collar worker	56	44
Educational qualifications		
Primary or technical	40	60
Secondary (baccalauréat)	56	44
University or equivalent	49	51
Income level		
Low	49	51
Average	46	54
High	48	52

Appendix 5: Voting behaviour in two referendums on Europe, 20 September 1992 and 29 May 2005

(Source for 1992: SOFRES, *L'état de l'opinion 1993* (Paris, Seuil, 1993), p. 86; source for 2005: exit poll on tns-sofres.com/études/pol/290505_referendum_r.htm)

	Maastricht referendum, 20 September 1992		Referendum on European constitutional treaty, 29 May 2005	
	Yes	*No*	*Yes*	*No*
Total	51	49	45.5	54.5
Men	49	51	44	56
Women	53	47	46	54
Age range				
18–24	52	48	41	59
25–34	51	49	41	59
35–49	49	51	35	65
50–64	47	53	45	55
65 and over	57	43	63	37
Occupation of head of household				
Farmer	29	71	—	—
Shopkeeper, artisan, small business	44	56	45	55
Professions, managers	70	30	62	38
Intermediate groups	57	43	46	54
White-collar worker	44	56	40	60
Blue-collar worker	42	58	19	81
Educational qualifications				
None	43	57	40	60
Primary	46	54	32	68
Secondary (technical)	40	60		
Secondary (baccalauréat)	61	39	41	59
University or equivalent	71	29	57	43
Party preference				
PCF	16	84	5	95
PS	76	24	41	59
Les Verts	57	43	36	64
UDF	59	41	76	24
RPR (1992), UMP (2005)	31	69	76	24
FN	7	93	4	96
None	36	64	37	63

Appendix 6: Abbreviations for French parties

1 The Right

1.1 Alliances

UNM	Union pour la Nouvelle Majorité (1981)
URC	Union du Rassemblement et du Centre (1988)
UPF	Union pour la France (1990)

1.2 Gaullists and neo-Gaullists

RPF	Rassemblement du Peuple Français (1947–53)
UNR	Union pour la Nouvelle République (1958–67)
UDVᵉ	Union des Démocrates pour la Ve République (1967–68)
UDR	Union des Démocrates pour la République (1968–76)
RPR	Rassemblement pour la République (1976)
RPF, again	Rassemblement pour la France (Gaullist Eurosceptics: 1999)
UMP	Union pour une Majorité Présidentielle (April–November 2002); Union pour un Mouvement Populaire (since November 2002); party formed of former RPR and most of former UDF (below)

1.3 'Giscardians', or non-Gaullist moderate Right (NGMR)

RI	Républicains Indépendants (1962–77)
PR	Parti Républicain (1977: successor to RI)
DL	Démocratie Libérale (1997: successor to PR)
UDF	Union pour la Démocratie Française (1978 : Giscardian confederation, including (1) PR, (2) right-wing Radicals, and (3) CDS – see below – plus smaller groupings); PR (now DL) withdrew in 1998; a single party since 2002 when most members and cadres joined the UMP (above)
PPDF	Parti Populaire pour la Démocratie Française

1.4 Other Right

CNIP	Centre National des Indépendants et des Paysans
CPNT	Chasse, Pêche, Nature, Traditions

2 The extreme Right

FN	Front National (1972)
MNR	Mouvement National Républicain (1999)

3 The Centre

MRP	Mouvement Républicain Populaire (IV Republic)
PDM	Progrès et Démocratie Moderne (late 1960s–early 1970s)
CD	Centre Démocrate (late 1960s–early 1970s)
CDS	Centre des Démocrates Sociaux (1976–96)
UDC	Union du Centre (1988–93)
FD	Force Démocrate (1995–98: successor to CDS; fully merged into UDF from 1998)
CDP	Centre Démocratie et Progrès
PSD	Parti Social-Démocrate

4 The Socialists and close allies

SFIO	Section Française de l'Internationale Ouvrière (1905–71)
FGDS	Fédération de la Gauche Démocrate et Socialiste
CIR	Convention des Institutions Républicaines
PSU	Parti Socialiste Unifié (1960–90)
PS	Parti Socialiste
MRG	Mouvement des Radicaux de Gauche (allies of PS, 1972–96)
PRS	Parti Radical Socialiste (MRG's name since 1996–98)
PRG	Parti Radical de Gauche (from 1998)
RCV	Radicaux-Citoyens-Verts
MRC	Mouvement Républicain et Citoyen
MDC	Mouvement des Citoyens
CERES	Centre d'Études, de Recherches et d'Éducation Socialistes

5 The Communists

PCF	Parti Communiste Français (since 1920)

6 The extreme Left

LCR	Ligue Communiste Révolutionnaire
LO	Lutte Ouvrière
OCI	Organisation Communiste Internationaliste
PCI	Parti Communiste Internationaliste
MPPT	Mouvement pour un Parti des Travailleurs

Appendix 7: Other abbreviations

AFEP	Association Française des Entreprises Privées
AFSSA	Agence Française de Sécurité Sanitaire des Aliments
ANVAR	Agence Nationale de la Valorisation de la Recherche
BNP	Banque Nationale de Paris
CAP	Common Agricultural Policy
CFDT	Confédération Française Démocratique du Travail
CFSP	Common Foreign and Security Policy
CFT	Confédération Française du Travail
CFTC	Confédération Française des Travailleurs Chrétiens
CGC	Confédération Générale des Cadres
CGPME	Confédération Générale des Petites et Moyennes Entreprises
CGT	Confédération Générale du Travail
CIASI	Comité Interministériel pour l'Aménagement des Structures Industrielles
CID-UNATI	Comité Interprofessionnelle de Défense–Union Nationale des Artisans et des Travailleurs Indépendants
CNIL	Commission Nationale de l'Informatique et des Libertés
CNJA	Centre National des Jeunes Agriculteurs
CNPF	Conseil National du Patronat Français
CNT	Confédération Nationale de Travail
COB	Commission des Opérations en Bourse
COREPER	Committee of Permanent Representatives (Europe)
DATAR	Délégation à l'Aménagement du Territoire et à l'Action Régionale
DOM-TOM	Départements et Territoires d'Outre-Mer
ECB	European Central Bank
ECJ	European Court of Justice
ECSC	European Coal and Steel Community
EDC	European Defence Community
EDF-GDF	Électricité de France–Gaz de France
EEC	European Economic Community
EMS	European Monetary System
EMU	Economic and Monetary Union
ÉNA	École Nationale d'Administration
EP	European Parliament
EPC	European Political Co-operation
ESDI	European Security and Defence Identity
EU	European Union
Euratom	European Atomic Energy Community
FEN	Fédération de l'Éducation Nationale
FFA	Fédération Française de l'Agriculture
FLN	Front de Libération Nationale (Algeria)
FLNC	Front de Libération Nationale Corse
FNEF	Fédération Nationale des Étudiants de France

FNSEA	Fédération Nationale des Syndicats des Exploitants Agricoles
FO	Force Ouvrière
FSU	Fédération Syndicale Unitaire
GATT	General Agreement on Trade and Tariffs
GDP	gross domestic product
HLM	Habitation à Loyer Modéré
IAA	Independent Administrative Agency
ISF	Impôt de solidarité sur la fortune
JHA	Justice and Home Affairs
MEDEF	Mouvement des Entreprises de France
MEP	Member of the European Parliament
MNEF	Mutuelle Nationale des Étudiants Français
MODEF	Mouvement de Défense de l'Exploitation Familiale
MP	Member of Parliament (UK)
MRAP	Mouvement contre le Racisme et pour l'Amitié entre les Peuples
NATO	North Atlantic Treaty Organisation
NPM	New Public Management
NSM	new social movements
OAS	Organisation Armée Secrète
OECD	Organisation for Economic Co-operation and Development
PACS	Pacte Civil de Solidarité
PEEP	Parents d'élèves de l'enseignement public
QMV	Qualified Majority Voting
RMI	Revenu Minimum d'Insertion
SEA	Single European Act
SEM	Société d'Économie Mixte
SG	Société Générale
SGAE	Secrétariat Général des Affaires Européennes (new name for SGCI from October 2005)
SGCI	Secrétariat Général du Comité Interministériel pour les questions de coopération économique européenne
SIVOM	Syndicat Intercommunal à Vocation Multiple
SNCF	Société Nationale des Chemins de Fer Français
SNES	Syndicat National de l'Enseignement Secondaire
SNESup	Syndicat National de l'Enseignement Supérieur
SNI	Syndicat National des Instituteurs
SNPMI	Syndicat National des Petites et Moyennes Industries
SUD	Solidaires, Unitaires et Démocratiques
TEU	Treaty on European Union
TGV	Train à Grande Vitesse
TPG	Trésorier-Payeur Général
UNAPEL	Union Nationale des Associations des Parents d'Élèves de l'Enseignement Libre
UNEF	Union Nationale des Étudiants de France
VAT	value added tax
WEU	Western European Union
WTO	World Trade Organisation

Index